Articles and Insights

The Washington Post
Feature Writing Companion

John W. English
University of Georgia
and
The Washington Post Writers Group

Allyn and Bacon
Boston • London • Toronto • Sydney • Tokyo • Singapore

Editorial Director: Bill Barke
Senior Editor: Steve Hull
Editorial Assistant: Brenda Conaway
Cover Administrator: Linda Dickinson
Manufacturing Buyer: Louise Richardson
Cover Designer: Suzanne Harbison

ISBN 0-205-14040-8

This book is printed on recycled, acid-free paper.

Printed in the United States of America

10 9 8 7 6 5 4 3 2 1   97 96 95 94 93 92

Contents

Preface

During the last two decades, the *Post's* Style section has become recognized as a pioneer model of magazine-style feature writing. (A sample of early work was published under the title "Writing in Style" in 1975.) The *Post* has continued to refine the form, while virtually spawning a whole new generation of writers adept at it. As the number of different bylines in this volume attest, the *Post* has clearly assembled a talented staff of feature writers.

Using models from the *Post* for this anthology made sense because the paper has both journalistic quality and diversity of topics, a combination in a single medium that's extraordinary in this era of ever-more-specialized publishing. The journalistic standards of the *Post* are commendable, ones that other media would do well to emulate.

The magazine-style features chosen here are all products of daily journalism, with all the limitations of time and budget that the trade entails. They may not be perfect, but they are typical of the high quality journalism being turned out by working professionals at the *Washington Post* these days. They set a high standard for other newspapers and magazines.

This collection of articles fulfills a number of functions. Stories were selected to represent a spectrum of interests and points of view, but the dictates of editing made some choices difficult. I intentionally sought articles that I believed students in magazine article and feature writing classes would find engaging. I attempted to blend what I thought they would want and what I believed they needed. Other constructs included topic and treatment, and it was not always possible to find the perfect combinations of each. Whatever shortcomings readers may find in the selections reflect my pedagogical objectives more than preferences of the *Post's* writers and editors.

I also wanted the collection to be fresh, so every piece here was published in the 1990s. All topics had to be current and have popular appeal. Some stories deal with issues and debates in the public sphere of life; others explore private experiences such as sexuality. The book's chapters represent clusters of journalistic writing, offering diverse examples of fine writing in a number of fields. While this assemblage is lively, it surely is not comprehensive or exhaustive.

By design, stories of varying lengths were selected. There are a few featurettes or department-length stories, in the 1,500-word range, and there are several long features, more than 3,500 words. The longest article here is more than 8,000 words, a piece from the *Post's* Sunday magazine. Most articles fall in the standard range for magazine articles, between 2,000 and 3,000 words.

My editing methodology was relatively simple. Assisted by my companion, Karen, a psychologist, avid reader, and sometime writer, I skimmed through every issue of the *Post* for 1990 and 1991 using the microfilm facilities in the dank basement of my home institution, The University of Georgia in Athens. From that initial search, I picked every article that showed any promise. We made a long list of first-round choices, some 430 stories in all, and faxed that list to Bob Lyford, one of the *Post's* librarians. He printed out each story from the company's computer system and then shipped them to me by overnight carrier. So it was possible for me to read hard copy instead of microfilm when making my final selections. In addition to the convenience and comfort advantage, the process also eliminated all headline, photo and graphic elements of the original story presentation, so I could focus entirely on the text, which is exactly what writers and editors do.

The first thorough reading narrowed our list from 430 to 150 relatively easily, but the final winnowing was full of tough choices. Finally, a number of excellent stories had to be dropped, not because of quality but for length and pedagogical criteria. The *Post's* writers themselves would probably not agree with some of my choices. In fact, when I told Tom Shales which pieces of his I was using, he wanted me to consider others he thought better. I appreciated his pride in his work and his enthusiasm for the project, but politely demurred.

My role proved to be as much fun as work. In many instances, I found myself laughing out loud at some great line in a story. Real emotional responses were also part of my litmus test for story selection.

This project was not my first effort in such editing projects. Earlier I edited outdoor journalism articles from a now-defunct regional magazine called *Brown's Guide to Georgia* into a collection of biking-, hiking- and canoeing-trip articles. And, I assembled a collection of superb pieces about the State of Georgia from the *Atlanta Weekly,* the late Sunday magazine of the *Atlanta Journal and Constitution.* That anthology is titled "Slices of the Peach."

My thanks go to Bill Dickinson of the *Post's* Writers Group, who helped pave the way, and to series editor Steve Hull for his guidance, patience and encouragement. Obviously I am most in debt, however, to the remarkable features staff at the *Washington Post,* which continues to publish one of the most lively and literate newspapers in the world.

Plan of the Book

This book was originally going to be organized by story type instead of subject, but that idea was scrapped because feature writers generally use a mixture of treatments in each story and so it proved quite tricky to figure out which type of treatment was predominant. More worrisome was my concern that readers would not recognize the primary type. So we opted to cluster stories by their subject matter. As the range of the Table of Contents illustrates, feature stories cover every topic imaginable.

Let's hope you enjoy reading this collection as much as we enjoyed putting it together.

J. W. E.

Introduction 1

In these days of instantaneous and simultaneous communications in which people get much of their information by looking at and listening to high-tech media, writing may seem like an unlikely or even anachronistic activity. Yet writers are still driven to sit in front of computers, stare at cursors and think about what they want to say to distant, abstracted readers. One wonders what animates people in their pursuit of such work.

Why do writers write? Personal motivations usually dominate their responses: to explore interests with expert others, to discover new ideas and different ways of looking at the same thing, to live passionately in the self-absorbed world of ideas, to make thoughts completely clear with no misunderstandings, to gain attention and share a quirky sensibility, to persuade others of held views so they might share a common vision, to sort out what one knows and thinks about a subject and to explain it to oneself, to provide an outlet for self-expression. Other motivations may reflect a tinge of altruism: to probe and comprehend a subject so thoroughly it could be clearly explained to a sixth grader, to interpret a phenomenon and see how this new thing compares with the old, to assign value by shedding light on some things and ignoring others, to impose order on a chaotic world, to take up the challenge of discovering the unknown or unstated, to entertain and tell amusing stories.

It's questionable whether professional writers have a stronger desire to read than enthusiastic readers have to write. Clearly, the bond between skilled writers and devoted readers is interactive and grows out of a basic, shared love of language. It also involves learning, a synthesis of accumulated experience, knowledge and, on occasion, wisdom. Some writers and readers prefer highly specialized information, while others have catholic interests. In either case, the factors that make any article compelling generally have more to do with the quality of the writer's mind than the intrinsic merit of the subject involved. Riveting reading and quality writing are inexorably linked. While some critics might still consider journalism to be more craft than art, others, such as Matthew Arnold, would insist that the best journalism "is literature in a hurry."

While readers may be more interested in the writer's finished product, writers revel in the creative process—the intrigue of research, the dialogue of the interview, the struggle to organize vast amounts of material, to think clearly about a subject and to say something sublimely well. In short, the act of writing is a frantic pursuit of perfection.

1

That simple act of connecting the minds of the writer and the reader is more powerful today than it's ever been. It's also easier than ever. The proliferation of new media forms have actually enhanced, rather than replaced, old ones. Readers now have more print media to choose from than ever before—daily newspapers and specialized weeklies, some 15,000 magazines ranging from general-interest consumer types to specialized business, industry and trade publications, thousands of journals and newsletters and some 50,000 book titles published annually. In short, print is not disappearing, as some doomsayers earlier predicted. The amount and range of reading material has never been more plentiful. And, the better educated members of society continue to be avid readers, albeit much of their reading is work-related. Reading for pleasure, surveys indicate, occupies about 10 percent of our leisure time. Given the inherent advantages of print—permanency, portability, relatively low cost and a format which can dissect complicated issues in clear and logical ways—the need for print has actually increased as society has become more complex and faster paced.

Definition of Feature Writing

Feature stories are a hybrid form in which reporters cannot manipulate the facts or truth to improve their work, but have considerable latitude to shape story structure, utilize a wide range of storytelling techniques and even contribute their personal style. A curious blend of journalistic and literary approaches, feature stories have all the rigors and strictures of reporting and truth-telling and all the creative freedom of short story writing. Literary license gives feature writers more freedom than writers of other forms of journalism enjoy. Feature writers rarely have to justify whether a story is timely or newsworthy; they only have to worry about making their article irresistible reading.

The primary difference between the best contemporary journalism and modern literature as an art form is no longer excellent writing, but subject matter: fiction deals with fabrication and journalism focuses on truth. The fundamental difference between the two forms, then, rests on journalists' reliance on depth reporting.

There are surely no restrictions on subject matter. Anything that interests a writer presumably will interest readers. The writer's challenge is to make every story compelling. Articles on esoteric topics, such as rain, Barcaloungers, sweat, patents, crayons and daily life in a city park can be just as engaging as profiles on pop celebrities.

It has never been possible to differentiate news stories from features on the basis of topic, since feature writers have routinely produced stories in almost every beat, from history to the arts, from sports to business, from politics to psychology. Veteran newspaperpeople long ago perjoratively tagged traditional features "soft news" in contrast to the "hard news" of politics, the economy, crime, war or natural disasters. Several examples in this anthology prove that the "soft" label clearly does not fit. Hard-nosed reporting is the basis for David Streitfeld's debate on public health and safety involving electromagnetic fields in "The Consummate Consumer" and for Joel Achenbach's examination of the Gainesville, Florida, murders, "Serial Killers: Shattering the Myth."

Feature writers have extraordinary journalistic freedom when it comes to form. Simply stated, there is no formula for a feature story. The inverted-pyramid structure used in conventional news stories does not apply to features. The form a writer devises for a feature is imposed on the topic and springs from the material gathered to tell it. Structure and story are entwined, as readers will notice in David Finkel's "Coming of Age in Room 223," Roxanne Roberts's "The Bachelors," and Henry Allen's "Our Artist, Right or Wrong."

Feature articles in both newspapers and magazines are clearly more similar than different these days. The most apparent similarity is story length. Magazine editors have long recognized that specialized readers need longer stories in order to comprehend a complex topic. But it was a major shift in policy for newspaper editors to permit writers to produce expanded features of more than 750 words.

Feature writers aren't restricted to that truncated and turgid news-speak style of news articles. They have the journalistic equivalent of luxury—editorial space. If the topic of a feature is worth more than five hundred or a thousand words and the writer can sustain reader interest in his story, editors now have little hesitation in commiting space to it. While most articles are in the 2,000-word range, some included in this anthology are less than half that standard ("The Day the Ants Lost Their Head") and one article is more than four times that length ("The Least Exclusive Club in the World").

The difference in the time perspective between newspaper and magazine articles is narrowing. Because magazine-style features tend to focus on causes, trends and interpretation of phenomena, they necessarily take a long-range view. In contrast to breaking news stories, magazine-style features may cover a current event, but do it more thoroughly and in a longer time frame so that the article could be published anytime within, say, several weeks to six months and still be current. For example, in "Whatever Happened to the Hero?" Elizabeth Kastor considers changing societal attitudes toward role models, including the ascendancy of South African leader Nelson Mandela and the downfall of baseball star Pete Rose. Her interpretive stance takes a long-range time perspective to these events.

Feature writers also enjoy expansive rhetorical freedom in writing style. They are expected to use colorful and descriptive prose. (Sportswriters are the only other journalists with such privileged free expression.) Writers assume readers share their love affair with words, so they strive to select a vocabulary that perfectly conveys their thoughts about a topic, rather than settle for the common-denominator syntax of a typical news story. An excerpt from James L. Morgan's piece, "Frisky Business," illustrates both the freedom and precision of language use:

> *For years, Hugh Hefner has thought that the sexiest word in the English language is nude. He's wrong. The word is panties.   Roll those two*

words on your tongue and let them pique your senses. Nude: What image does that invoke? The picture isn't altogether unpleasant, but unless you're an adolescent male who still believes the destination is different from the journey, there's a certain fait accompli quality about it. Even the word itself is abrupt, like rude or thud. Now consider panties, a dainty, silken, infinitely unfolding word: You men, notice how the diminutive -ies makes you feel big and strong? Sense the tactile pleasure of silk between thumb and forefinger? Feel your mind wandering to forbidden bureaus fragrant with sachet? From my male point of view, it's obvious: If God hadn't wanted us to take pleasure in presents, She wouldn't have invented gift wrap. All of which is why Victoria's Secret catalogue, and not Mr. Hefner's magazine, is widely considered by men to be the sexiest publication in America today.

Like essayists, but unlike news reporters, feature writers are also free to express a point of view. Although they are not allowed to editorialize, crusade for a cause, or vent a prejudice in a feature story, they make no pretense of objectivity. Subjective writing doesn't necessarily mean that the writer will have a singular view. It also doesn't mean the writer won't be fair in presenting the views of others. A feature story may clearly reflect a writer's point of view, but it also may represent the views of those cited in the story, which may differ from the writer's perspective. Peter Carlson's "The Least Exclusive Club in the World," has a strong viewpoint, which pokes fun at the Congress and yet offers a fair account of its members: "In the last few months alone, members of the House of Representatives have compared themselves to thieves, zombies, dope fiends, Donald Duck and babies in need of toilet training. We wouldn't dream of disagreeing—but hey, they still put on the best show in town."

Functions of the Feature Story

An analysis of print media content quickly differentiates material by intent: stories that inform, persuade or guide, interpret and entertain. News stories clearly set out to tell what happened—the who, what, when, where of significant events. Editorials and op-ed columns and essays stress advocacy, urging a particular line of thinking or action. Feature stories explain why and how something occurred, interpreting the story behind the story. They serve the double role of informing and entertaining. The story, "Building the Feel Good Car" by Warren Brown, explains how Japanese autobuilders use "feel engineering" to produce cars that consumers perceive as high quality while implying that the American industry is remiss. Henry Allen's description of a cultural trend, "Young Fogies," is amusing and yet offers a societal insight at the same time.

Feature writers take their collective impulse from literature, the short-story form. Yet they are also reporters and, as such, must strive for the same level of accuracy and credibility as any professional journalist. They convey details and insights, using hard facts and a panoply of emotions to enhance understanding.

Feature writers must be clear thinkers, relentlessly probing for the truth of any story within its own context, whether it's puzzling out a person (in "Jack Nicholson, Unleashed" and "Oliver Sacks, Hero of the Hopeless"), a place (in "Charlottesville's Web" and "New York: The Reel Thing"), an event (in "Pee Wee's Nightmare" and "'Phantom's' Moveable Feats") or a trend (in "The Acid Kids" and "To Be PC or Not to Be"). Sure, any writer draws on his or her personal experiences, perceptions, conscience and emotional makeup, but he or she must also be scrupulously fair both to sources and to readers. Personal agendas and ideological fervor remain the province of editorial pages.

Types of Feature Writing

The type of story treatment or format is an important factor in determining which combination of research techniques and elements writers will use. Many magazine-style features employ more than one type of approach and commonly combine a variety of types. This list of common formats should help beginning writers recognize that longer stories are rarely one type exclusively, but more likely combinations of treatments. The typology was devised to help categorize stories by readership appeal. There are numerous varieties within each type, many distinct enough to represent another type; but to simplify our analytical approach here, a dozen types of treatment and some examples are described below:

1. Informational. Such stories are largely descriptive in nature and occasionally include service journalism material. News-related features, sometimes called color stories or sidebars, often have a timely news "peg" or link to a current news item. An overview, round-up or perspective story simply recaps developments and expands its context. One such example is "The Patent Truth of a Bygone Age" in which Henry Allen examines how America is losing its edge in patenting new inventions.
2. Exposé or investigative. These stories not only get behind the scenes, but often uncover and bring some unethical or illegal practice to the public attention. New threats to privacy emerge in Daniel Mendel-Black's and Evelyn Richards' feature, "Peering Into Private Lives," which reveals that computer databases are being compiled on consumers' personal habits.
3. Interpretive. These stories attempt to explain why a phenomenon is the way it is, taking into account a range of possible interpretations, especially from academic experts. Two quite different interpretive features are Richard Harrington's look at the rock band Red Hot Chili Peppers in "The Medium is the Mayhem" and Henry Allen's exploration of the national depression sparked by recession in "Red, White and Truly Blue."

4. Profile/Interview. These biographical stories range from personality sketches of people in the news to interviews with celebrities on promotional tours. Some profiles have a narrow focus or angle and others examine a subject from a number of perspectives. Interview stories use lots of direct quotations from the primary source. Some even reduce the role of the reporter to questioner by publishing the dialogue in an unedited question-and-answer format. Among the profile examples in this book are "The Writer and the Joys of Paranoia," Elizabeth Kastor's study of Ishmael Reed, and a look at photographer Annie Liebovitz in "Artist of the Portrait" by Judith Weinraub.

5. Sociological. Slice-of-life stories take a sociological approach in which a reporter may position himself in a particular location to keep tabs on what occurs there. Stories describe typical events, not extraordinary ones and, thus, are low-key rather than dramatic. Depending on the complexity of the story, the reporter may identify and detail one or several case studies to illustrate the point of the story rather than tell it in explicit terms. In "The Grass Menagerie: Views From the Park Bench," feature writer Phil McCombs reports on everyday activities in public parks, while Martha Sherrill's "Charlottesville's Web" discovers "shabby chic" in the Virginia university town.

6. Reconstruction of an event. Here the reporter tries to recreate an event from interviews with those who were there, official records and other information. Narrative treatment uses third-person voice and sometimes is a dramatic re-enactment of others' accounts of a story. It assumes an omniscient viewpoint, as if the writer were there but not part of the story. In a light vein, Marsha Sherrill reports on a cat show in "Major Meows and Kitty Glitter."

7. Trend. In these features, a writer observes a trend over time, beginning with the present and utilizing the past to explain how we got to this point and then speculating where this direction will lead in the future. It's a simple treatment that describes the trend, explains and interprets it. Phil McCombs' feature, "Men's Movement Stalks the Wild Side," examines the ways modern men are seeking identity and happiness. In "Armchair Activism" Dan Oldenburg ponders some easy ways for couch potatoes to participate in the movement to protect the environment.

8. Personal experience. There are several variations of this type of feature, including witness reporting in which the reporter is virtually a participant in history and writes his version of the account in first person. Reporters may also be introspective about a topic with which they have some experience and share these observations in varying modes: reflections and ruminations, memories and even confessions. Marjorie Williams's own engagement to be married prompted her feature "The Ecstasy and the

Agony" on wedding rituals. Another example is John F. Cullicott's account of a hike along the Appalachian Trail in "American Ways."

9. Essay. This treatment also has a number of variations, including think pieces that argue a particular line, criticism that weighs in with an assessment and protest articles that address a current controversy. These articles are characterized by clear and strong points of view and are identified as such. A pair of essays on weather illustrate this type: "Let It Rain" by Henry Allen and "The Befuddled Autumn" by Joel Achenbach.

10. Inspirational. Such stories are heart-warming and uplifting, often told poignantly with case studies that illustrate the point. Jim Naughton's profile, "The Slam-Jam Joy of Michael Jordan," is subtitled "The Transcendence of the Ballplayer" in case sports fans miss its point.

11. How-to. Usually these stories work best in departments, in which the reporter is trying to provide specific information that people need and want. Reporters often rely on experts to assist them. Consumer stories on how to buy the best product or how to cope with a particular problem are common examples. These stories often take a step-by-step story line and include all costs, tools and materials involved. The feature, "When Your Kids Go Punk" by Marcela Kogan, offers advice to parents whose teenage children are taking the experimental route.

12. Humor/Satire. Most stories have a light side and can use a little levity to keep the reader engaged and amused. While sarcasm rarely works, satire can be an effective way to make a point. Two of Henry Allen's features are serious fun: "Ugly, Ugly, Ugly, Ugly, Ugly" and "Omens: You Know You Are In Trouble When...."

Evolution of Feature Writing

Feature writing has long been an established form of newspaper journalism, but the old formula for traditional feature stories was predictable enough to be boring for both writer and reader. Since conventional features were generally short (in the 500-word range), they took less time, industry and imagination on the part of the writer. All that was called for was a lead capable of grabbing the reader's attention, a couple of anecdotes, liberal use of direct quotations from an interview with a single primary source and an ending with a kicker. Most stories were put together from telephone research and a blitz writing effort under deadline pressure. Features focused mainly on local events and trivial matters, usually had a timely "news peg" and adhered to other news conventions, such as relying on official sources and writing with detached perspective.

During the 1970s and 1980s, feature writing evolved into a highly refined art. Newspaper features changed radically, virtually becoming like magazine articles. The "magazining of newspapers," as author Bill Rivers of Stanford University calls it, evolved in response to the competition of television. Print writers took advantage of their ability to offer what television counterparts couldn't: in-depth coverage of a variety of topics in a range of story formats available when and where readers were ready to read them.

Newspapers shifted their emphasis to features and thoughtful, analytical articles in an attempt to counter TV's immediacy, wrote the *Washington Post's* editor Ben Bradlee in 1979. Such features were "in-depth stories about people," which dared to tell what subjects were really like. Katherine Graham, the *Post's* Chairman of the Board, further noted that "It's no accident that long (feature articles) on big subjects in the daily press are called 'magazine pieces' because they have more lead-time and perspective than the daily press, more permanence than broadcasting, more immediacy and wider readership than most books."

Ms. Graham's point is well taken. It is no longer possible to identify a magazine-style feature on the basis of where it's published. Among the major newspapers that regularly run magazine-style features are the *Washington Post,* the *Wall Street Journal* with its front-page leader articles, the *Los Angeles Times's* Calendar section and, of course, the *New York Times's* Sunday Magazine. In leading metro dailies, innumerable magazines and other publications, then, the traditional distinctions between magazine articles and newspaper features, which used to be blatant, have become blurred.

As newspaper feature sections virtually became daily magazines, they were at first enlarged and then were spun off into separate units with as distinct a character as sports or business sections. For example, when the *Washington Post's* feisty editor Ben Bradlee created the Style section in 1968, he stamped his complex personality into its editorial style. Just as magazines have traditionally been products of editors with strong personalities, the *Post's* Style section earned a reputation for being at once irreverent and witty, uninhibited and fastidious, profane and prudish, outrageous and relentlessly professional, all dichotomies with irresistible appeal to a wide range of readers. Bradlee quietly infused the *Post* with an original brand of New Journalism, which allowed writers unprecedented opportunities to practice their craft with precision and creativity and which served readers with compelling story ideas, well-researched and informative content and stylish writing in inventive non-fiction forms. It was pure rapture for writers and readers.

The widespread adoption of New Journalism techniques forever altered the craft of feature writing. Fresh story ideas cropped up like mushrooms after a spring rain. Articles emphasized the human interest elements within conventional topics. A merry band of New York journalists, among them Gay Talese, Tom Wolfe, Jimmy Breslin and Michael Herr, challenged "snore-mongering" colleagues and traditionalist editors to produce appealing and readable non-fiction writing with incisive reporting and honed literary skills. Their lively reportage and old-fashioned story-telling first appeared in the Sunday magazine of the now-defunct *New York Herald-Tribune* (later *New York* magazine) and at national magazines such as *Esquire* and *Harpers',* and then spread elsewhere throughout the media landscape. Wolfe claimed that New Journalists had taken over the lofty role that novelists held in earlier eras and had become the principle chroniclers of the morals and manners of the times.

Among the techniques attributed to the New Journalism style were:

- Saturation reporting or depth research, total immersion into the culture or lifestyle of the subject.

- Scene-by-scene construction of stories, which makes reading almost cinematic in nature.

- Presentation of scenes through one pair of eyes, which gives a story a subjective point of view.

- Writing from the conviction of truth, instead of remaining objective and inconclusive about a subject.

- Using dialogue to capture the interaction within a scene, instead of just quoting a series of individuals interviewed.

- Notation of status details within a milieu, if they make a symbolic point about the subject.

- Playful and inventive use of language, especially popular idioms.

Some crusty observers stirred up debates in journalistic circles over the early excesses of the form: more flash than substance, egocentric writers whose center-stage presence in stories detracted from the subject, sloppy, superficial research, verbal pyrotechnics, advocacy journalism and the questionable ethics of constructing composite characters.

The author's own estimation of the importance of New Journalism was first published in a 1975 anthology edited by Marshall Fishwick:

> *What interests most readers (and writers and editors) about the form is its power of attraction. This commercial asset is based on the popular culture subject matter New Journalists tackle rather than its style, though no one has said reading couldn't be fun and full of surprises, too.*

What distinguishes New Journalists is the mark of any good writer: a contemporary way of seeing a complex world with an emphasis on showing (an emotional approach) rather than telling (an intellectual process) so that readers can feel a story as well as know about it; and a devotion to utilizing every attention-getting device used to communicate: italics, dialogue, interior monologue, symbolism and using scenes or anecdotes as metaphors, interjections, new work creations such as "mysterioso" and "tricknology," onomatopoeia and high-energy enthusiasm.

Using subject reality as a guideline for investigating and selecting facts—that is working on a story until you know it from the inside and can write it from the center—these New Journalists have been illuminating areas of human experience heretofore dealt with in official, surface and dull ways: backroom campaign politics, pop religion, cultural celebrities, the Mafia, astronauts, interracial dating, ad infinitum.

Sure, New Journalists have excesses, but their bylines sell magazines and newspapers and they also offer readers zing, life, humanized prose and a new depth of reality and truth that is both intellectually and emotionally exciting. What more could anyone ask?

Despite initial skepticism about New Journalism, feature writers and editors at newspapers responded to the demand for a high quality editorial product. Impressively well-crafted magazine-style features became the standard. Feature readers were rewarded with insights and revelations as significant as those found in any genre of journalism.

Elements of a Feature Story

The traditional style of feature writing was virtually transformed after the New Journalists launched a bold assault on stagnant editorial practices. Today the only restraints to free journalistic expression are the limits of imagination and talent. Curiously, a writer is most effective when his literary devices and techniques are least apparent to readers, so style must never draw attention to itself or detract from the subject.

In the articles presented here, writers have made a series of stylistic choices as they have woven together all of the components they have assembled—facts, direct quotations, anecdotes, observations—to make a story read as if it were seamless. The dexterous combination of elements is what makes an article flow. The net effect is similar to the blending of the instruments of an orchestra in an engaging and memorable symphonic piece, much more impressive than the playing of a composer's individual notes. One is generally more aware of the whole than its specific parts, unless there's a clinker in the mix.

1. Themes. These could be the capital Roman numerals in an outline of a story, the major points being made about this topic. Most stories dwell on only two or three major themes, with a number of contributing subpoints. These themes shape the "slant" of an article but may never actually be written in the text.

2. Structure. Readers should be almost unaware of the story's structure, because it virtually becomes transparent. But a writer knows what the skeleton of his story is and sets up the sequencing of themes.

3. Voice, Tone and Vocabulary. The writer's point of view dictates his voice. Point of view stems from a writer's deductive perceptions of the truth about his topic. As you know from personal conversation, no one always speaks in the same boring monotone. When you want something, you increase your chances of getting it by asking in a soft voice that al-

most purrs. When you're angry, your voice expresses that stridency. A writer's voice is determined by the story being told. Tom Shale's appreciation of the contributions of Muppeteer Jim Henson is a poignant tribute:

"It's not as if this is a world into which happiness is easily brought. Bringing even a little can be a major undertaking. Jim Henson brought a lot. The precise amount is immeasurable.

"A visionary, a magician, a comedian and a technician—part Hans Christian Andersen and part Thomas Edison—Jim Henson revolutionized puppetry and helped reinvent children's television. He did it through craftsmanship and showmanship and even salesmanship, but he also did it by keeping alive within himself the child he once had been."

Voice affects a story's tone, which also varies from story to story. Many stories are straightforward, some express curiosity, suspense and outrage, others amazement, incredulity, sarcasm. Some are satirical and humorous. The tone is generally consistent throughout, otherwise the reader may become confused. The writer's building blocks for stories are words. Vocabulary is a powerful asset to create nuances in tone. The shades of meaning that are delineated by the carefully chosen word contribute significantly to the impact and meaning of a story. Henry Allen's incisive commentary, "Our Artist: Right or Wrong" establishes the tone of the controversy right at the outset through precise verbal distinctions:

"We prefer our artists to be disturbed but not disturbing, messianic but not pugnacious, confessional but not vulgar. Hence our distaste for Thomas Hart Benton, who was cranky but not neurotic, egotistical but not martyred, lurid but not decadent."

4. Quotations. Direct quotations are essential because they introduce interpretation, opinion and emotion into features. These quotations generally come from primary sources, mainly interviews or public utterances; but they can also come from secondary sources, if used minimally and with clear attribution to their origin. While direct quotations help humanize a story, they are largely used as supporting evidence for an assertion the writer makes about the topic.

5. Anecdotes and Cases. Anecdotes are actual vignettes that make a clear and specific point about the topic. Anecdotes are generally effective because they show how something happened rather than just tell about it. They are always true stories that illustrate something the writer wants the reader to know. Anecdotes provide specific evidence to support

generalizations. Writers also often cite cases as concrete examples that illustrate and affirm their point. A reminiscence feature, "When You Were Hot, You Were Hot," relates a series of anecdotal memories about life before air-conditioning. Don Gasbarro's feature on off-beat hobbies, "Diversions: A Congregation of Collectors," details a series of cases of people who have compiled unusual collections.

6. Facts and statistics. Statistics describe aggregate behavior numerically and help establish a context or overview for the story. Many times the "facts" of a story are disputable because there are several different versions of the "truth." (Rarely are there only two sides to an issue.) So a writer attempts to construct a consensual version of the truth by finding two or three sources that will corroborate each contentious point. The truth, then, becomes the mutually agreed upon version. David Streitfeld's feature, "Safety in a Can," examines the controversy surrounding self-defense sprays. In "Ads, They're Everywhere," Paula Span delves into the increasing intrusiveness of advertising into people's lives.

7. Descriptive detail. Generally, details give a story presence and help the reader fabricate a clear picture of the scene in his head. These details are often the observations a writer gathers in the process of reporting, not only telling what happened or what someone said, but how it unfolded and in what kind of atmosphere. Details are an important element because they help the reader visualize specific images, thus enhancing story credibility. Martha Sherrill's feature, "Summertime, and the Poolman is Busy..." captures the sights encountered on the job:

"It's another day of empty pools—lots of water but not people. This one's an indoor pool, a pale-blue rectangle sitting in Bethesda under a retractable skylight. There's also a terra cotta-tile deck. Ten plastic plants. A sauna. Stereo speakers. Silver inflatable rafts and boats. The sliding door has been left open for him. He's Paul Wahler. Poolman."

8. Topic sentences, transitions and flow. Writers employ topic sentences to propel the story along in their voice. Transitions link paragraphs and ideas, so the reader has the sensation that the story is seamless and keeps reading. If a writer omits transitions, the story becomes disjointed and the reader may become disoriented. A smooth flowing text is created from the logical sequencing of ideas and its sure movement from point to point to point.

9. Leads and Endings. Ways to begin and end stories are equally important. Writers (and editors) usually invest more energy into hooking a reader into a story with a clever lead, but then will let the story trail off, rather than conclude decisively. Feature stories should emphasize closings as

well as openings. Anecdotal (see above) leads and endings are a common type. In the lead of "Hard Knocks 101," Elizabeth Kastor empathizes with readers about a shared teen ritual:

"It is the thing your parents make you do. It is the place where you first fall in love. It is the way you learn the disturbing truth that many people's work is tedious. It is what you will be nostalgic about—but not for many, many years. It is the last time you have to know how to make a lanyard.

"It is the Summer Job, that moderately distorted Introduction to Adulthood—accurate to the extent that it introduces you to paychecks, taxes and getting up early, false to the extent that come Labor Day it is over."

The ending of Henry Allen's ode, "Sweat," asks readers to tolerate the human condition:

"If you don't like to sweat, imagine what life would be like if you couldn't. Imagine those high-tension occasions when you dread sweating, and think of the alternatives—giving a speech, say, and having to periodically pick up the pitcher of ice water and pour it over your head, like an elephant. Or doing a job interview while slavering like a Saint Bernard.

"Better to sweat."

10. Mechanics of Expression. Editors expect writers to have fully mastered the language, correct grammatical usage, punctuation and spelling. These skills are basic to being an effective writer.

Techniques of Feature Writing

Educated readers have high standards for quality journalism. They want stories to anticipate and answer their questions about the subject. They seek the involvement that's offered in behind-the-scenes views. They long for writers to confide in them and to create articles that are fascinating to read and as full of surprises as a lively conversation.

The best writing actually advances our knowledge of a topic, offering more than a retracing of what's already known. Reporters must be disciplined researchers who ferret out original material, so each story offers readers something new about a topic. Some of the motivation for and pleasure derived from writing stems from pursuing, identifying and sharing that new element.

Reporting is central to effective non-fiction writing, and depth reporting is a requisite for magazine-style features. Reporters have to get behind the scenes, be skeptical of public images and look beyond the stereotypes. Intrepid reporting is required to chronicle social change. Reporters are expected to be more than stenographers who carefully take down what others say and later regurgitate it. They offer counterpoints and contradictions to reveal a person's character. They must be obsessed with facts and accuracy. Writers have a professional obligation to assure that readers are served with stories representing the best of what is currently known about a subject.

Magazine-style features now demand numerous interviews with a range of sources plus some unobtrusive reporting techniques, such as participant observation and role-playing. Reporters are expected to synthesize a large body of information from both primary and secondary sources and then distill the salient elements into a pithy but powerful article.

It's axiomatic that the media embrace controversy. Magazine-style features should illuminate these conflicts, rather than shrink from or gloss over them. Yet writers should still allow readers to make up their own minds and form their own judgments. While writers are ethically bound to represent all sides fairly, they also have to be candid with readers. Features become a mirror in which people and events are depicted truthfully. The ideal is to have all the principals in a story read the published version and acknowledge its honesty and accuracy, whether they agree with its tone or their image or not.

Foremost among the writing techniques made acceptable by the New Journalists is the adoption of a clear point of view. This technique allows readers to "see" a story through the writer's eyes and offers the same kind of subjective "vision" a cinematographer applies in filming a movie scene. Recognizing the writer's subjective perspective marks a clear departure from the traditional objective news stance. Personal journalism allows writers to put their imprint on their work and to include their perceptions about their own lives and experiences, but it still doesn't permit them to advocate personal opinions or causes.

That line between point of view and advocacy may seem blurry to a beginner, but to practitioners, it's clear. Feature writers no longer remain detached and on the fringe of a story; they dive into its center, so they will be able to write it from the "inside." They know better than to take on assignments in which they have (or even appear to have) too strong a self-interest or, worse, a conflict of interest. Such purity and independence allow writers to conduct their research with the moral objectivity of a judge and jury in a court of law. However, once all of the material has been gathered, they examine it and adopt a vantage point from which to tell the story. Reaching that perspective is different from coming to a "verdict" and declaring "right" and "wrong." That's advocacy again. Adopting a point of view requires careful consideration of all the "evidence" compiled as well as concentrated, clear thinking about the subject. Weighing all the facts, ideas and opinions requires an open mind and common sense. To win readers' trust, writers have to exhibit fairness and resist bias and prejudice.

The process of saturation reporting requires feature writers to dig for abundant details which they'll use to emphasize description and to enhance reader involvement. To anchor stories in time and place, writers must offer precise description of scenes. To catch the mood of a story, features should contain information about the sights, sounds, smells and activity of the setting. The expected role of eyewitness reporters, then, is to capture the sensations of the experience. Such reporting details let readers into stories in the same way that television cameras help establish a sense of place. Details make people and events appear vivid and give clarity to a story's visual dimension. Even though the advantages of reporting details may seem obvious, news stories still often lack any sense of presence (despite a dateline).

Detailed descriptions of people also include status symbols, because these items offer clues about value systems. Non-essential items generally linked to status are reliable indicators of a person's self-perception. Such details are not superfluous because they may provide a key to understanding a person better. A reporter's inclusion of status symbols in the story is sure to intrigue readers who are looking for insights about the person's world. Consider Rita Kempley's observations about Jack Nicholson's shoes in her profile: "His loafers, appaloosa-hide and dandified, are a made-for-strutting fashion statement. Rivaling Imelda Marcos when it comes to footwear, he purportedly owns 74 more pairs, as well as 25 pairs of sunglasses."

Reverse-snob appeal helps form an impression of Far Side cartoonist Gary Larson in James Kindall's profile:

> *"In person, his manner is the jeans and T-shirt persona of relaxed antic-*
> *ipation. Wire-rim glasses and thinning, collar-length hair grant him grad*
> *student chic. Shy and soft-spoken (he rarely gives interviews), he seems*
> *flustered by the confines of speech as well as befuddled by the*
> *practicalities of life. He seems the kind of guy who might discover cold*
> *fusion and, when you pointed out that he had altered the course of his-*
> *tory, would reply, 'Hum, guess so.' "*

Expansive reporting also utilizes dialogue, which can serve either as an alternative or supplement to direct quotations. Since it's sometimes natural to talk with sources in group configurations, that dialogue (or a selected portion) more accurately reflects how the reporter gathered those ideas and opinions. And the group context often doesn't let a source get by with saying things that he may attempt in one-on-one conversation. A reporter may be a participant in those discussions at times and not at others. Note the frequent use of dialogue in Peter Carlson's feature on skateboarding, "Ragin' on the Ramp."

Writers are now allowed to reflect a sense of humor in their work. Readers are savvy enough to know that there are often funny twists to otherwise serious stories. Acknowledging such ironies in a story allows a writer to entertain and inform. Roxanne Roberts' feature on "The Bachelors" begins with the most eligible man in Washington:

*"He's a bookworm who looks like Pat Paulsen. His idea of excitement is
a long hike in the woods. He does impressions, for God's sake. He wears
extremely bad ties.*
"David Souter is not your standard hunka hunka burning love."

The Future of Feature Writing

New Journalism may have begun as an "experiment," but it eventually revolutionized feature writing and created a new elevated standard. For both newspapers and
magazines, that standard is the magazine-style feature. In the process, feature writers won new freedom to explore a broad range of topics and to write in their own
voices, privileges earlier reserved only for novelists, humorists and columnists.
That freedom appears likely to mature as long as editorial credibility remains a
paramount concern. As any visit to a newstand or bookstore will attest, contemporary readers have developed an affinity for quality non-fiction writing and the supply meets the demand.

Patterns of Passage 2

While traditional news values favor the unusual and off-beat to the everyday and mundane, it's more challenging for writers to find intriguing stories in commonplace activities. Education beat reporters routinely emphasize school budget crises, parent-teacher political flaps, administrative scandals, crime, conflict or technological changes, yet often ignore what goes on in classrooms. To focus on the heart of the matter, how learning takes place, a magazine-style feature writer has to penetrate superficial elements. In "Coming of Age in Room 223," writer David Finkel captures the sense of a typical high school by reporting the details of students' lives—their schedules, diets, relations with parents and absurdist humor. He also observes young people confronting and coming to terms with failure, old age, suicide and tragedy through the vehicle of the play. As the students act out the play, they also learn important lessons in life, so it becomes clear to readers why other facets of school regimen such as tests may seem quite boring to them.

In-depth reporting recreates the presence of a story and builds reader involvement in it. A realistic account of the experience is enhanced by detailed observations and the writer's interpretation of their significance. Reporters don't avoid issues inherent in any story, they try to sort them out and illustrate how some values always conflict. In Paul Taylor's look beyond commencement exercises, he defines a jittery generation struggling with idealistic human concerns and harsh economic prospects.

To report on subtle societal changes, writers have to adopt a macrocosmic perspective, at times applying the insights of a sociologist and at others assuming the role of an anthropologist. Developmental stories dwell on universal human growth, struggle and change. Every generation has its rites and Laura Blumenfeld's story on "The Acid Kids" takes a clear look at how teenagers of the 1990s party. Her intrepid witness reporting is both a slice of life and an exposé of what young people really do when their parents aren't around.

In "Young Fogies," Henry Allen accumulates evidence to illuminate the habits of those young adults in their twenties who act fiftyish. His perceptions are piercing, persuasive and hilarious.

Coming of Age in Room 223

DAVID FINKEL

The play is an American classic, filled with timeless insights about life. For a long time, Lee J. Cobb starred in it; later came Dustin Hoffman. Now, 41 years after its premiere, it has made its way to Phoebe Stevens's fifth period English literature class at Richard Montgomery High School in Rockville.

" 'Death of a Salesman,' " Mrs. Stevens announces, holding up a copy of the play. It is a dogeared thing, 139 pages long. Stacked on a table are two dozen other copies, all stamped "Property of Montgomery County Public Schools." In two weeks, the play will be the subject of a test. Until then, it will be read during class, a process that begins with Mrs. Stevens passing out the copies to her students. All of the students are juniors. Most of them are 16. Most of them think they are in the midst of the most important year of their lives.

She gives a copy to a girl who is having problems with her 23-year-old boyfriend and is carrying around a book called *You're My best Friend, Lord.*

She gives another copy to a varsity football player who went out cruising a few months ago, ended up at a pizza place and beat up some people he decided were gay.

She gives copies to a boy with a pack of cigarettes tucked in his pocket, a girl in a black leather jacket and black pants and black boots whose favorite music group is Nuclear Assault, a boy whose dream is to play first horn for the National Symphony Orchestra, a boy who wants to play major league baseball, a girl whose friends have been calling her a "wussy" because she is afraid to talk to a certain boy, a boy who says he began drinking when he was 11, another who says sex began at 13. The play they get tells of what can happen when children become adults, of mistakes and disintegration and death. "Kids think they're infallible" is Mrs. Stevens' explanation for choosing such a play. "They don't have the perception of tragedy."

Most of the students take a moment to glance at the cover, which shows Dustin Hoffman as Willy Loman, an old man who seems beaten down and frightened. Some look out the window instead. There is a magnolia tree out there and a sky that is cloudless and blue. There is a breeze too, and when it comes in the window, it causes the Venetian blinds to momentarily rattle, a lazy, distracting sound.

"Okay," Mrs. Stevens says. "Who wants to be Willy Loman?"

Willy Loman, of course, is anything but 16. He is a salesman who can no longer sell. He has bills he can no longer pay. His sons are failures, his wife is wearing down, his dreams are all but exhausted. He is about as far from 16 as you can get, especially 16 the way people like to remember.

That age—after the fact, at least—can seem like one of the best ages of all. It was the time when everything was possible, when nothing was hard. For some people, it's the year they've used as a measure for everything since, even after they've married, had children, had 50 years of successes and joys. Maybe their honeymoon was wonderful and their marriage is happy, but it's a clumsy night in the grass with someone long vanished that stands in the memory most vividly. Maybe their new Mercedes can be regarded as a gauge of success, but it's their first car, ragged and dirt-cheap, that seems the most special of all. "I remember 16," says Mary Hopkins, a security officer at Richard Montgomery High, smiling at the thought. "It was the year I had more fun than any other year in my life."

She remembers 16 even though it happened back in the 1950s, which was when Tom Quelet, the school's principal, spent his 16th year at the Mighty Mo drive-in in Baltimore "in a '53 Chevy," which was when Tony Deliberti, the school's community service organizer, spent his 16th year in Brooklyn going to church, eating pizza and, every now and then, drinking a beer. "A beer," he emphasizes.

And so goes 16 in retrospect: memories that bring smiles. For those living it now, a lot of it is the same. But not all of it. Their concerns may be the same—parents who don't understand, the futility of school, self-doubt, the meaning of love—but the context for their lives isn't what it was even 10 years ago. I'm 26. I can remember 10 years back. I can remember I was not so easily swayed by peer pressure," says Liz Hamernick, the school's home economics teacher. Now, she says, "the peer pressure is incredible."

"I have kids who are anorexic, bulimic, a couple of drug addicts, kids whose family is in such disarray that they don't have anyone to turn to," says Watson Prather, a guidance counselor at the school. "We have conferences here where the parents are at each other's throats, and the kid is sitting there in the middle. And that's got to be tough. People outside can hear the screaming, and then you have to walk outside and face your friends . . ."

"I was in the hallway earlier," says Mary Hopkins, "standing next to a boy who was watching girls go past, and he said, 'Damn, she was good last night.' I said, 'What?' He said, 'You heard what I said.' I said, 'You're lying.' Another one walked past. 'Her too.' These are girls who look like they're babies. I said, 'You've got to be kidding.' He said, 'No, I'm not, either.' He said, 'Miss Mary, I could go on and on.' "

Maybe the boy was lying, maybe not. If studies of teenagers can be believed, half of the girls and most of the boys will have had sex by the time they are 17. Most of them will also have smoked cigarettes and perhaps half will have tried a drug other than alcohol. As for alcohol: According to one recent study, 9 out of 10 students tried it sometime during high school; according to the students themselves, a lot are getting falling-down drunk from cheap beer and wine coolers.

All of which makes 16, for those just reaching it, an amazing and anxious time. One day they're 15, a kid, and the next day, just like that, they can drive, quit school, go to work. Their parents, they are realizing more and more, aren't necessarily heroes. Above all, the pressures on them are building. The inclination is to keep goofing off, which is how a lot of them have gotten by for 15 years, but they are suddenly being told by parents, by teachers, by guidance counselors that the time for goofing off is over, that they have to get good grades, so they can go to a good college, so they can get a good job, so they can retire financially secure, so they'll never be failures, so they can always pay their bills. Which, in the myopia of 16, can make life seem like nothing more than a long march down a narrowing tunnel.

"I see it as you're born, you go to school, you get a job, you die," says Judy Swope, one of Mrs. Stevens' students.

"I feel personally like sometimes I want to scream," says another student, Lauren Funkhouser.

"I remember," says Mrs. Stevens, thinking back to the days when she was 16, "that it was the first time I heard kids use cuss words." Of her students now, she says, "I look at them all the time. I look at them and think, 'Boy oh boy.' "

Michael Hal volunteers to be Willy Loman. He is one of Mrs. Stevens's best students, the one who one day wants to play in the National Symphony, who brings to school lunches of Fritos and pudding and meatloaf croissants. During the time it takes to read the play, he will turn 16 and get a car. "I can drive now," he will say of how it feels to be rid of 15. "I guess it doesn't seem like there's a whole lot of time left before college."

Tonya Palmer volunteers to be Willy's wife, Linda. In the course of the play, she will break up with her 23-year-old boyfriend, whom she had been dating for more than a year. "Boys have me stressed out," she will say afterward. She will also watch a film in another class where, in the dark, the student next to her will whisper something about drugs, roll up her sleeve and say, "You want to see the needle marks?" Tonya won't look but will whisper back, "You can die from that stuff." "But you're gonna die anyway," the girl will nonchalantly say.

Act 1.

"Willy," Tonya says, reading the first line of the play. The stage directions tell her that her voice is to show trepidation, but it comes out pretty much flat.

"It's all right," Michael Hall says, reading Willy's reponse. His voice is pretty flat too.

In this manner, the play stumbles along, quickly losing something In the translation. Mrs. Stevens is an enthusiastic teacher, but she can do only so much. Climaxes become dirges, cues are ignored, fingers are chewed on, feet tap, yawns are deep. Constantly, eyes shift around, but in Room 223, as typical a high school classroom as can be found, there isn't much to see. The blinds are about the same milky color as the walls, as the acoustical ceiling, as the tile floor, as the face of the broken clock whose hands haven't moved in a month. The door is open, but even the hallway is empty. In a few minutes, when the bell rings, that will change. Precisely when is a mystery because of the clock, but it will ring, and then it will be time for lunch. Some students will go to McDonald's, one will go out back for a quick smoke because "it calms my nerves," some will go to Little Caesar's, and John Ferguson, who had three bowls of cereal for breakfast, will probably just have Twinkies. "I eat Twinkies all the time," he says.

"You eat Twinkies?" a girl who has overheard this asks.

"I eat Twinkies all the time," he repeats.

"They're nasty. They're gross. You could bury Twinkies in the ground, and they'd be there, like, forever."

"I love Twinkies," John Ferguson declares.

Some students won't eat at all. Instead, they'll simply hang around hallways that once seemed unnavigable and now are as comfortable as their own homes. Between classes, those hallways are jammed with 1,200 students, from freshmen who are pitifully small to seniors who look like they're approaching 30. It is a typical mix in a typical suburban school, and for five minutes lockers are flung open, boys kiss girls who lean against walls, girls duck in to bathrooms where they write messages of love in lipstick on the mirrors, boys throw out wrappers from foods like Lance Giant Size Spicy Beef Snack. Until the bell, though, the halls are deserted, and the only sounds at all are the ones coming from different classrooms.

In Room 203 one day, a 16mm film is working its way through a projector with a single, tinny speaker. "We Americans are a proud people," the narrator is saying.

Another day, in cooking class, the focus is on Chinese food. "This is duck sauce," Liz Hamernick is saying to her students. "What do you think the main ingredients are?"

"Duck," comes the first answer.

"Duck bladder."

"Duck rain."

"Daffy Duck."

Meanwhile, back in Room 223, Tonya Palmer and Michael Hall are working their way through Act 1.

"Willy, dear, I got a new kind of American-type cheese today," says Tonya.

"Why do you get American when I like Swiss?" says Michael.

"I just thought you'd like a change," says Tonya.

"I don't want a change! I want Swiss cheese. Why am I always being contradicted?" says Michael. There are several such exchanges between Willy and Linda Loman as their lives fall apart, and during one of them Mrs. Stevens asks a question.

"Does any of this sound familiar"

Some of the students nod their heads. Some laugh. "Yes."

Act 2.

Willy's deterioration continues. His life is closing in on him. "The woods are burning," he says. He is hallucinating, answering to ghosts, dwelling on the day when his older son, Biff, his bright light, failed an exam in math. "That son of a bitch," Willy says of Biff's teacher.

"That son of a bitch," whispers Lauren Funkhouser. And smiles.

Lauren Funkhouser, a bright, giggly girl who epitomizes the sweetness of 16, has been awake since 6:15. It is when she awakens every weekday. She showers, dresses in clothes she selected the night before, dries her hair, curls it, sprays it, puts on foundation, blush, eye shadow, mascara, lipstick and perfume, and is out the front door by 7. She doesn't worry about breakfast because she'll make up for it during the day. The day before, for instance, she had a meatball sub, pizza, turkey slices, peanut M&Ms, two Fruit Roll-Ups, macaroni and cheese, a salad and a Coke. So breakfast can be missed. It's more important to get to school, get through the first four periods and come to Mrs. Stevens's class, where she sits three rows away from a boy named Tom Farrell.

"I'm in love," Lauren told Mrs. Stevens during the second week of school.

It was the first time in her life she had said such a thing. Until this year, she had attended private Catholic schools. In elementary school, the boys were like brothers; in grades 9 and 10 there were no boys at all. This year, she transferred to Richard Montgomery because "I was just so sick of Catholic school." It was her choice to switch, but she didn't know quite what to expect. "She thought she'd be mugged in the halls," says Watson Prather, her guidance counselor. Instead, she discovered that in public schools, there are young men who aren't like brothers at all. "I know everything about him," she says of Tom. "I know where he lives. I've got his number memorized. I know he has an older sister. I know he's not anything, any religion, and that's really weird for me. I know he's got great blue eyes. I like his eyes. I like his smile. He has a great smile. He has straight teeth."

The only thing she doesn't know about Tom, it seems, is how to get to know him. "All my friends call me a wussy because I cannot go up and talk to him," she goes on. " 'Wussy, wussy, wussy.' Oh my God."

Lauren has no idea if Tom knows she likes him. He does know, of course, because Mrs. Stevens, among others, told him. But, so far, he hasn't been inclined to do anything about it, perhaps because he realizes how different he and Lauren are. In his freshman year, for instance, he dated a senior. He has been to big parties. He has been around. Lauren is emerging. Tom has emerged. Definitely, they are different. Lauren's bedroom is decorated with frilly curtains and ecru bedsheets; Tom's has posters of cars, posters of girls and some road signs. Lauren talks to her mother about everything; Tom says he hardly talks to his parents at all. "A couple of years ago, you needed them for a lot more stuff," he says. Now, "You need them for a roof over your head, stuff like that. I don't really tell them about problems."

Instead, he goes home after school, eats whatever he can find in the refrigerator, watches TV, plays Nintendo. Late in the afternoon, his parents come home. Sometimes they seem happy, he says, sometimes they argue. "About anything," he says. "I don't really pay attention. I usually leave the room. Either that, or I turn the TV up, or I ask them to leave the room. Sometimes they quit, sometimes they get mad at me." Usually, after dinner, he goes out with his friends. Often by the time he gets home, the house is dark. He goes to his room, watches TV, does his homework. Sometimes he just thinks. He thinks about life, about "how we're out in the middle of nowhere, in the middle of the stars." He thinks about how he loves his parents but doesn't really want a life like theirs. He thinks about how things might be, and how they are now. "You're basically told not to, not to."

By the time he gets to sleep, it is often past 1 a.m., an hour of the night that Lauren rarely sees.

In the reading of "Death of a Salesman," Tom has none of the parts. Lauren does. She is The Woman, who is in a hotel room with Willy, dressed in nothing but a slip, when Biff shows up unexpectedly to tell his father he has failed his exam in math.

"All right. Where is Willy now?" Mrs. Stevens asks as the scene begins to unfold through another of Willy's hallucinations.

"In bed," says Lauren.

"In Boston," says Tom.

That's right, Mrs. Stevens says, looking at Tom. "In Boston. Where in Boston?"

"In bed," says Lauren.

"In the hotel room," says Tom.

"That's right," Mrs. Stevens says, this time looking at Lauren. The hotel room."

The bell rings. Lauren gathers her books. Tom leaves. Lauren follows.

"Hormones," Mrs. Stevens says with a laugh.

"When that team came out—he was the tallest, remember?" Willy says. He is having another flashback about Biff, this one back to a day when Biff still adored him, before he discovered that his father was a flawed and ordinary man. "Oh, yes," Linda says. "And in gold."

"Like a young god, Willy says. Hercules—something like that. And the sun, the sun all around him. Remember how he waved to me? Right up from the field, with the representatives of three colleges standing by? And the buyers I brought, and the cheers when he came out—Loman, Loman, Loman! God Almighty, he'll be great yet."

It is a Friday night, a varsity football game, and John Ferguson is on the field, lying still in the grass. He had been running, and out of the blue came someone else, running even harder. John kept going, the other boy leaped at him, and now John is on his back, blinking back the pain and waiting for help from the team's paramedic, a man who was on Richard Montgomery's championship football team a generation before, his dad.

"What happened?" Jack Ferguson says, bending over the kid in a helmet, seeing the number on the shirt, realizing it is his son.

"My knee," John says.

Now there is a crowd around. The knee is looked at, touched. Now John is being lifted by his father, two players and a coach. Now he is being carried off the field to an ovation, with his father cradling the bad leg.

And now, five days later, with a brace around his bruised knee, John is in Mrs. Stevens's class, reading the part of Willy Loman's other son, Happy. It is uncanny. Happy is the son who wants to become his father. John is too.

"My dad is cool," he says, "Other dads act like 'Brady Bunch' dads. My dad, he acts my age. I don't know what I'd do without my dad."

Look at John's face, big and friendly, and you see his father. Look at the way he carries himself, big and unafraid, and that is his father as well. "I keep close to him," Jack Ferguson says of his son. "I always have." He has coached John in football and baseball, and he has brought him to work at the Rockville Fire Department so many times that John is thinking of becoming a firefighter. When John was little, his father would take him to burned-down houses and tell him that's what happens when kids play with matches. Now that John is older, they have ridden together to fires, to car crashes, to worse.

"He's seen a guy hit by a Metro train," John's closest friend, Phil Hannum, says one night. "My dad's got the video. My mom can't stand watching it," John says. "One time, we went to a Red Lobster because there was an electrocution," Phil continues. "The floor was wet, and the guy was plugging something in . . ."

They are eating as they say this, shoveling in potato skins and fried cheese at the Bennigan's on Rockville Pike. Outside of John's father, Phil Hannum is John's closest friend. Phil is quieter than John, less confident, more complicated. He also has one of the best cars in school, a 1987 Cougar with a V-8 engine, wide tires, power windows and seat warmers.

"Nice car," says John, who has yet to get his license. "I love it." When they go out, Phil drives while John hangs out the passenger window, yelling and waving at girls.

They do this most Saturday nights. They start after dinner and go up and down Rockville Pike. They cruise through the parking lot of a shopping center called Congressional Plaza. They go to McDonald's and Bennigan's and back to Congressional Plaza. They head north to the high school and south toward the restaurants, and sometimes they keep heading south until they're in Washington.

"Sometimes we just drive back and forth to see what's going on," John says.

"Just to see how lucky we are," Phil says. "A lot of those kids just hang out on the street, not doing much. The houses are small. The neighborhoods aren't places I'd wanna live." "You hear about these killings," John says. "I wanna see one. Not the killings, but the police cars and the police line."

"Yeah," Phil says. He starts to say something else, changes his mind, takes a drink of his soda. John looks at him, and Phil mumbles something about the time at the pizza place. John shrugs. So Phil tells how they stopped at a restaurant one night, and John began making fun of a few people who seemed gay and then got in a fight with them.

"I kicked their ass all over the parking lot," John says. He is proud of this, not at all ashamed. "I hate gays," he explains. "They pissed me off."

He and Phil keep eating. After a while, he says, "I do some really immature things sometimes." He laughs.

Phil laughs too. "He does things, like he'll go up to nerds and stuff and say, 'Down, boy,' and push them around."

"Just playing around," John says. "Being intimidating. Like my dad."

"John," Phil says, "is one of the most popular kids in school."

Which is true. A week after John was injured in the football game, there is another game. He is in the stands for this one, still using a crutch to get around. He is surrounded by friends and is with a new girlfriend. At one point, he is standing with his girl, leaning on his crutch, when his father comes over with a hot dog. John takes a bite, and his father, in a gesture of kindness, tries to wipe off some mustard that John has gotten on his chin.

"Dad! Stop!" John says. He pretends to take a swing at him.

"He could beat you up real fast," the girl says to John's dad.

"Yeah?" Jack Ferguson says. And with that, lightning fast, he kicks John's crutch out from under him. And then smiles at his son.

Who smiles back. "Would you like a drink or something?"

Matt Derrick, who is 17, says this to Lillian Lehrer, who is old enough to be his grandmother. They are in the cafeteria of the high school, attending a "Senior Senior Prom" that the school's community service club is putting on for senior citizens. In Mrs. Stevens's class, Matt has been reading the part of Biff. "That boy is going to be magnificent," Willy says of Biff, and he might as well be talking about Matt. The band has just finished playing "Stardust," and Matt and Lillian have just finished a dance in which Matt held Lillian's shoulders while she swayed back and forth on legs that no longer easily move.

Now Lillian is looking at Matt, saying nothing, just smiling and seeming as if she might cry. He brings her some punch. He is a young man with a constant smile, good grades, plans for college, dreams of playing major league baseball and a girlfriend who is president of the community service club. "I see him getting less self-confident because of the pressures of school," his mother, Linda Whitcomb, worries, but on this afternoon, he seems completely at ease. He kisses Lillian on the cheek and goes off to dance with someone else.

It is something to see, this prom. Several hundred students have shown up, and so have several hundred senior citizens. They have come by bus and van from apartment complexes and nursing homes throughout Montgomery County. Some of the men are in ties, some are in hats, a few are wearing slippers. Most of the women are in dresses, some are draped in shawls, some are wearing diamond rings that they were given a long time ago, when their lives were uncertain and still filled with options. Now they are widows and widowers who know how things can work out. One woman, in a pink dress with a lace collar, can't seem to stop crying when she sees what the students have done.

"They're so cute," one student says, watching the old people dance.

"They're look happy," says her friend.

"Like there's no tomorrow," the first girl says.

Matt is wearing a tie and white shirt that his mother ironed for the occasion. He dances with Neva Goldthorpe, who has 14 great-grandchildren. "There wasn't smoking, there wasn't drinking, there wasn't drugs," she says, thinking back to her prom. "We danced cheek-to-cheek."

He dances with Dorothy Allen, who has seen two of her children die and has been a widow for 21 years. "They've got big surprises coming up," she says of the students. "Lots of surprises."

He dances again with Lillian Lehrer, who was married for 50 years. He takes her shoulders, and she begins to sway.

"Sixteen," she says, thinking back. "That's when you're so young."

The climax approaches. Biff is in the hotel room now, his childhood dropping away by the second as he stares at a stammering man who has suddenly become contemptible. "She's nothing to me, Biff. I was lonely," Willy pleads. "Liar!" Biff screams. "You fake! You phony little fake! You fake!" At that moment, his childhood falls away completely and he cries his first tears as a man. And Mrs. Stevens shouts, "Epiphany!"

Her students look at her. "Epiphany!" she repeats. "It's a realization. A sudden realization."

A few students write this down. Judy Swope, who just turned 17, doesn't. She is the girl in the black leather jacket. She doesn't write anything down, and she hardly ever talks. But more than anyone else in Mrs. Stevens's class, she knows what an epiphany is. Last year she was falling apart, and this year she isn't.

No one knows this, though. She is a shadow around school, rarely laughing, always quiet. She doesn't go to football games. She doesn't go to any after-school activities. She likes heavy-metal music, nothing else, dark clothes, nothing else. Every day at the end of fifth period, when the bell rings and her classes end for the day, she heads off to Rockville Pike, smokes a cigarette, climbs on a bus and disappears to an after-school job at a pet shop. "She's real different than anybody else," Phil Hannum says of her. "It's like she's trying to get people to dislike her."

Actually, it's more that she's not sure if she and the other students have very much in common. "I am different," she agrees. She has a mother who she says is insistent on her children's success, a father who she sometimes thinks has given up on her, and a legacy of failures from seventh grade on. In ninth grade, when other students seemed so busy trying to fit in, she was already on the fringe, getting grades that were mostly D's and E's. In 10th grade, when she got all E's on one report card, she laughed about it and thought about suicide. Her life outside of school, meanwhile, was characterized by an overwhelming feeling of disconnection.

There was a time when her grandfather, whom she had never met, fell gravely ill. Her father insisted she visit him, so they drove to West Virginia. "It was like 9 or 10 hours," she says, describing her memories of the trip, "and then he didn't even die. It was such a waste."

Then another relative did die, a great-grandmother. About that, she remembers going to the funeral, looking at the body and, instead of feeling sadness, thinking how nicely the dead woman's hair had been prepared. She wondered if they had used hair spray, if they would actually put hair spray on a dead person, so she leaned close, as if to say goodbye, and blew, and blew again, and decided they must have because her hair hardly moved at all.

And that was how Judy Swope's mind was working. She was thinking about everything, silly and not so silly, sifting, wondering. She tried to imagine the face of God. She tried to envision the entire universe, how it couldn't go on forever, how it had to end somewhere, with some kind of a wall, but what would be on the other side? She would think of these things, wanting to know the answers, and then she would go to school, get bored, cut class, bring home report cards that caused nothing but sighs and silence.

Then, last school year, a few things happened.

Her grandfather did die. Back they went to West Virginia, but this time it was different. "It was more immediate," she says. "It was my father seeing his father dead, and someday I'm going to see my father dead. And then, at the end, my father wasn't close to him, and he went over and hugged him, hugged a dead body, and said, 'I love you. I'm sorry I didn't tell you when you were alive,' And then he started crying, which is really rare for my dad, and I did too."

She also was put in a math class taught by a teacher named Judy Green, who looked at the new student, her dark clothes, her clouded face, and didn't immediately write her off. "She just spent a lot of time with me," Judy Swope says of Ms. Green. "She was the first teacher that actually, like, cared." By the end of the year she still had enough failures to cause her to spend part of this year repeating 11th grade. But in math she got an A, and when she brought home her report card, her mother hugged her and took her out to dinner to celebrate.

Now, so far this year, her grades have been A's and B's. She is not sure what the turning point was—maybe it was the A, maybe it was simply having someone take an interest in her, no questions asked—but the difference is there. Outwardly, she is still content to dress like a shadow, but inwardly, where all of her questions about herself had been turning over and over, she says, "I feel a lot better. I feel a lot different. I feel a lot happier."

Her epiphany, she says, was this: "I realized I wasn't stupid. I guess somewhere in the back of my head, I thought I was."

The time has come for Willy Loman to die. The illusions have won. The only way for Willy to save his family, he has decided, is to kill himself. It is nighttime. His family is upstairs. He gets in his car, hits the gas, drives off. He will leave behind a wife who is sagging from years of accommodation, two troubled sons and an undistinguished life that didn't go according to plan.

"Willy?" says Tonya Palmer, reading the part of Linda.

"Pop!" says Matt Derrick, who is reading the part of Biff.

"Screeeeeech," says someone in the back of the room, embellishing the moment by imitating the sound of squealing brakes. "Kapow!!!"

And so ends the life of Willy Loman as he lived it in Room 223.

Time for lunch.

There is a test, of course, to see what the students have learned. "Do not write on this paper," it begins and goes from there.

"According to Willy," it asks, "what kind of man gets ahead in the business world?"

"In a well-written essay, using three examples, prove that Biff is actually the central character of the play."

"Charley" is: "A. Willy's neighbor; B. Biff asked him for a job . . ."

In other words, the test is designed to see if during the last two weeks the students have been paying attention. Nowhere are there questions about the deeper lessons of the play, whether the students have learned anything about themselves.

Maybe they have too. Maybe the rantings of an old man have somehow touched them. Maybe Tonya Palmer has discovered something new to say to a classmate who boasts of needle marks, and John Ferguson has absorbed something about compassion. More generally, as Mrs. Stevens had hoped, maybe something has been learned about tragedy, and fallibility, and the fine line between an illusion and a dream.

And then again, maybe not. When you're 16, after all—no matter how much things have changed over the years—you're still that. Sixteen.

The day after the test, Mrs. Stevens shows her students the video of "Death of a Salesman." It is the version starring Dustin Hoffman, whose first big film, "The Graduate," came out seven years before most of Mrs. Stevens's students were born. Now, in "Death of a Salesman," he is gray-haired and bewildered and a day away from death. At one point, as he stumbles around outside, his wife tries to defend what he has become.

"I don't say he's a great man," she begins.

John Ferguson is stretching his leg as she says this; Phil Hannum is rubbing his neck.

"Willy Loman never made a lot of money," she continues.

Lauren Funkhouser is staring at Tom Farrell, who is resting his head on his desk.

"His name was never in the paper."

Around the room, fingers drum, feet tap, eyes shift from the TV to the broken clock.

"He's not the finest character that ever lived."

Any minute now, the bell is going to ring.

"But he's a human being, and a terrible thing is happening to him."
Here comes the bell . . .
"So attention must be paid."
Maybe it does. But not here. Not now. Not yet.

November 25, 1990

Class Of '91 Jubilation & Jitters

For the Children of the Post-Boomer Bust, the Commencement of a Shaky Future

PAUL TAYLOR

Applause and apologies, please, for the high school graduating class of 1991—the creatures from the bottom of the baby bust.

They were born in 1973, when fertility in America hit its low mark of the second half of the 20th century. Small generations are supposed to have it good—there's less jostling for the nursery school teacher's time, the college recruiter's eye. But these poor busters have had it . . . baaaaddd! Families that fell apart on them. School test scores that sank like a stone. Heroes who disappointed (or whom they never had). Nasty Little epidemics like AIDS and crack.

And now adulthood looms, like a cookie jar that somebody else already picked clean. Will the busters ever be able to match their parents' standard of living? The cost of starting out in life—college and a first house—has been racing ahead of inflation and wages ever since they were born. Meantime, adults have rung up nearly $3 trillion in national debt in the busters' brief lifetimes, virtually all of it on consumption for themselves. The busters will get stuck with the tab.

"The world is gearing up to punish them for sins they didn't commit," said Neil Howe, who with William Strauss has written "Generations," an ingenious new book about the relationships among generations through American history. "And they know it."

"Somebody screwed up," said Dan Markey, 18, his matter-of-fact voice conveying neither rancor nor complaint. "No names, but somebody must have made some major mistakes, because it seems like we have a lot of things that were just kind of neglected, and now they are cropping up as major problems.

Markey, who graduated yesterday from Walter Johnson High in Bethesda, is among the best and brightest of his generation. he was ranked third in his class of 330, played fullback on the varsity soccer team, had a major role in the school production of "Cabaret" and went seven-for-seven this spring in acceptance letters from prestigious colleges. No Bart Simpson, he.

He has had a childhood of upper-middle-class privilege—certainly when compared with others of his generation. The year after Markey was born, children in America surpassed the elderly as the nation's poorest age group; today, children are nearly twice as likely to be poor as adults. Markey knows he is one of the lucky ones. I can't imagine an easier time for someone like me to be a kid, he said.

So who messed up his corner of the world?

Markey finds it perplexing that even in affluent Montgomery County, school budgets are being cut. He's daunted by the size of the federal debt. He's worried about the environment. And even in his own short, fortunate life, he's felt the pinch of an inhospitable economy.

This fall, he won't be attending either of his two top choices of colleges—Haverford or Princeton—because he bumped into an increasingly familiar situation for busters: They wanted him, but he couldn't afford them. He'll enroll this fall instead at Johns Hopkins University (no slouch of a school, to be sure), where he won an academic scholarship worth 60 percent of annual tuition, room and board.

"My parents (both chemists at the National Institutes of health) left the choice to me, but they made it clear that if I went to one of the schools where they were going to have to pay full cost, I'd have to earn money during college to help pay for it, he said. "I didn't want to have to worry that much about making money."

Turning down the Ivy League was once virtually unheard of; now the sticker shock of $100,000 BA degrees sets off conversations like that in middle-class families all over the country. Even the top colleges have had to resort to more aggressive recruiting and to draw deeper into their waiting lists to offset the dual effects of the baby bust and the financial crunch. "I think there are some students who are getting into schools that wouldn't have taken them in other years, said Sharon Dick, a career and college counselor at Walter Johnson. The colleges need the paying customers."

The cost-consciousness cuts both ways. "You hear stories about college kids who go up to a professor after a dull lecture and say, 'Hey, that wasn't worth the money,' " said Markey. "Another thing about going to these expensive schools is that once you're out, it really affects your career choice. I mean, it's very hard for someone to say that I'm going to leave a college that I spent $23,000 a year to be in, and then become a schoolteacher—which is something that may be very rewarding but, you know, the starting salary, you just kind of laugh."

Markey's generation has a worst-of-all-worlds relationship with money. They were egged on by the culture of the 1980s to think of it as life's report card; they're nervous at the dawn of the 1990s that it's a test they can't possibly pass.

There's ample reason for their concern. Householders under the age of 25 were the only age group to lose income during the boom years of the 1980s (about 10 percent, in inflation-adjusted dollars), and home ownership rates among people under 30 have fallen more than 10 percent since 1970. Even before the current economic downturn, college graduates had been routinely boomeranging back to their parents' homes, unable to afford to strike out on their own. Now a recession has added insult to injury; busters with high-priced diplomas are waiting tables or tending bar.

In addition, the busters' small generation size bodes ill for them over the longer haul. There will be fewer workers per retiree during their tenure in the labor force, meaning the burden of paying out Social Security obligations to the massive baby boom generation will take a disproportionate bite out of the paycheck of each buster. Ditto for paying interest on the $3 trillion federal debt.

Meanwhile, the consumerist values (in everything from designer sneakers to designer jeeps) of the busters have earned them the enduring scorn of the baby boomers, who continue to wallow in the righteous aestheticism of their youth, even as they reap the material rewards of an economy that was far richer in opportunity for them when they were 18 than it is for busters now.

Markey said he thinks his generation is slowly adjusting to the prospect of hard times by scaling back its collective appetite. "Five or 10 years ago everybody was saying, yeah, we're going to make lots of money. Now it's a very unpopular thing to say. It makes you sound like a real loser. I mean, don't you have anything else? Don't you have any standards?"

A national survey of entering college freshmen done each year by UCLA Prof. Alexander Astin confirms the apparent start of a value shift. The percentage of students who said that one of their major goals in life was to be well off financially nearly doubled from 1969 (39.1 percent) to 1987 (75.6 percent), but has since receded a few points. So has interest in business majors and business careers.

At Walter Johnson, there's been a revival of social conscience. Amnesty International has a large chapter at the school. Activist students volunteer at soup kitchens for the homeless, recycle trash and have been fighting a proposed incinerator in Montgomery County that they fear will be an environmental hazard.

But it's still a long way from the wild and crazy '60s, a decade that leaves these pragmatic busters cold. "I personally don't think I would have wanted to live through that—that complete state of confusion," said Walter Johnson senior Ilana Preuss.

Student protests nowadays are more efficient. When the Montgomery County Board of Education considered funding cuts for schools this fall, 50 Walter Johnson students showed up at a meeting to protest, but, said Principal Frank J. Masci, "it was all very orderly, all within channels."

And sometimes the students surprise their elders by forgoing protest altogether. Given the political liberalism of the Bethesda community that Walter Johnson serves, Masci recalled that when the Persian Gulf War broke out, "I thought to myself, 'Oh, God, I'm going to have anti-war protests.' Instead, I had kids wanting to play 'The Star-Spangled Banner' over the PA system during morning announcements."

Whatever their politics, these seniors lack the expressive abandon of earlier generations of youth. Teachers at Walter Johnson say it's because their lives have been shaped, in large ways and small, by a sense of economic constriction.

The emblematic event of the year they were born, 1973, was the first oil embargo, the dawn of the age of limits. The busters are too young to remember the long lines at gas stations, but they've grown up in a nation that has been shaken ever since about its perch in the international economic marketplace.

All the appliances in their homes are made in Japan, said Elaine Parker, a history teacher at Walter Johnson. That simple fact has shaped a lot of their view of the world. It is not an optimistic time, and they are not an optimistic group. . . . When I was their age, I was like a rolling stone. What did I know? You never worried about the future, because the future seemed so abundant.

These kids have grown up in a pressure cooker," she continlued. They see the lifestyles their parents have been able to achieve, and they're haunted by the notion that they may not be able to match it. Whenever I tease my classes by saying, 'Future yuppies, please pay attention,' everyone groans. They hate that word."

As a teacher, you have to spend a lot of time pumping confidence into them," said Greg Dunston, who teaches math and coaches swimming. "They say, 'I'm not going to be able to do this, I'm not going to be able to qet into that.' "

It's not just money that seems problematic to the busters. It's also balancing career and family—a feat they don't think their elders have managed especially well. Today's 18-year-olds are the children of the divorce revolution; nearly half have spent some or most of their youth in single-parent homes. They say they're determined to be more doting parents, but they can already sense the conflicts.

Ina Rhee, the valedictorian of the Walter Johnson class of 1991, will be heading off to arvard this fall. Her father is a scientist, and her career inclinations lead her in that direction too. But she has trepidation, some of which she gets from him.

"My father keeps telling me that I should find something else I like," Rhee said. "He says he hates to say it, but if I'm going to have a family it's not in my interest to pursue a career where you have to spend 12 hours a day in the lab. he says he's seen a lot of women go through his lab and get divorced. That's the big thing I worry about, being able to find something which I like doing but which I can balance with having a family."

Busters of both genders worry about that balance. The age of first marriage has been rising steadily ever since they were born—partly because the economics are unfavorable, partly because today's young are more wary of making commitments. At Walter Johnson, group socializing is more common than traditional dating; students float in and out of being friends and being boyfriend-girlfriend with an ease that elders find mystifying.

Maybe it's because the commitments they do make have so often proved unreliable. When a half-dozen graduating seniors were asked recently to name their heroes, the question drew give-me-a-break eye rolls all around.

"They always have something wrong with them," said Markey. "I put up a poster of {Diego} Maradona {the Argentinian soccer star} and then I found out he's arrested for cocaine. So I had to rip it down. It's really depressing. You worship Sugar Ray Leonard and you find out he takes drugs. And he beats his wife. You can't trust these guys. I mean, now when I see one of these athletes who seems too good to be true, I always expect there's got to be something wrong with them. And there always is."

Caleb Mason, 18, said his hero would be an honest politician. He added: "I haven't found one."

Disillusioned before their time, saddled with low expectations, bad reputations and harsh economic prospects—is there any hope for children of the bust?

As a matter of fact, yes, say Strauss and Howe. The busters' bum luck and bad timing will turn them into tough, savvy, streetwise adults, the authors predict, with a "seasoned talent for getting the most out of a bad hand . . .

"They will make near-perfect 50-year-olds. On the one hand, they'll be nobody's fools. If you really need something done, and you don't especially mind how it's done, these will be the guys to hire. On the other hand, they'll be nice to be around. More experienced than their elders in the stark reality of pleasure and pain, {they'll} have that Twainlike twinkle in their eye, the Trumanesque capacity to distinguish between mistakes that matter and mistakes that don't."

Maybe so. But age 50 is far away. Right now, when Markey thinks of adulthood, he thinks of stories his grandfather told of sweeping floors during the Depression: I'm not saying it's going to be as bad as that, but it's kind of like, when you get out of school, there might not be anything automatically waiting for you.

As soon as he served up the analogy, three friends jumped all over him. "You're going to have the world at your feet, Markey," they said, almost in unison.

"Because I'm one of the lucky ones," he shot back.

June 11, 1991

The Acid Kids

If You Think LSD is History, What Happens at This Suburban Teenage Party May Blow Your Mind

LAURA BLUMENFELD

About This Story

A *Washington Post* reporter was allowed to attend the LSD party described in this story on the condition that the identities of the participants would not be disclosed. Accordingly, the students are identified only by their first initials.

They are golden children, lying in the grass, bathing in the midsummer sunset. The orange light repaints the large white house, gilds its windows, sends shadows into a neighbor's yard where a suburban Everyman pushes a lawn mower. The sky is periwinkle. The lawn mower is buzzing. The cicadas are buzzing. The 17-year-olds are buzzing.

"I saw God," J brags, rolling up onto his knees.

"What's He look like?" asks V. She puts down her copy of "Walden Two."

"I saw Him in the woods," he says. "He's like a tree spirit; He's like the Earth."

They laugh. A car pulls up. A mother is driving.

A chorus of sweet voices greet the mother. She sees strong arms, soft eyes, clean brows.

What mother would suspect they had just taken LSD?

R sheepishly gets out of the car. He settles next to a group of friends in the grass.

It is suburban Maryland. It is another summer vacation twilight for the group of student leaders, A and B students, sports team heroes. They wear thick cotton T-shirts and stone-washed cutoff jeans, the uniform of comfortable youth. They are handsome, "apple pie kids," as one of them puts it, headed for their senior year at a Montgomery County high school. It is V's party. She is willful, bold. She has a Botticelli face and light brown hair that ripples down her back. Her father, a doctor, her mother, a mother, are away on vacation.

"Bye, kids!" R's mother says cheerfully and disappears into the evening.

J resumes his account of the day he saw God. It was the end of 11th grade. He was tripping on LSD.

"I dropped two around lunch, he says, and by the time I got to English—the teacher was wearing this black and yellow outfit—I thought she was a bumblebee!" His gray-green eyes search his audience. They aren't impressed. Some of them say they have taken as many as five hits of acid at once. And the ones who haven't dosed before don't believe him.

The light is nearly gone from the sky. It's been almost an hour since they popped onto their tongues the small white squares of paper printed with blue stars. The drug dissolved; the stars melted like grape candy, staining their pink tongues purple.

The night is lit by a half moon. Before tonight is over, the teenagers will say they see faces in rocks, skeletons in hedges. Rose bushes will dance and blossom on command. Flowers will dig for corn. Light bulbs will balloon, turn green. Lamps will chase them up stairs. Before the 12-hour acid trip is over, they will wander the streets of their parents' middle-class subdivision, picking up cigarette wrappers and broken glass. They will believe that the scraps are rare treasures.

Lysergic acid diethylamide. The kids rattle it off like the name of a new rock group.

"It takes your brain cells, throws them up, and when your mind comes down it's in little pieces," explains G, a lanky 17-year-old with a Keanu Reeves haircut but John Lennon sunglasses.

These kids are '90s-'60s hybrids. The sneakers are Reebok but the ankle bracelets are beaded. The T-shirts are Champion but the accessories are rainbow macrame.

G proudly reveals that he has done 50 hits of acid in the past three years. "I heard that after seven hits, you're legally insane," he says. He isn't worried.

Neither are his friends. They haven't been scared by the bogus horror stories that circulated in the '60s: that acid would scramble your chromosomes, deform your children. That acid made you stare into the sun until you went blind. But they also haven't been scared by the real perils of the drug: that it's unpredictable, that the strength of cheaply manufactured doses varies drastically, that adverse reactions can include panic attacks, terrifying hallucinations, flashbacks; that LSD can accentuate mental illness, violent tendencies and, if taken in large doses, trigger convulsions.

G believes acid is benign. He explains its pharmacology: "It's like turning up the power source in your mind, like turning up the volume in your head."

Montgomery County authorities say there is no significant LSD problem in local schools." It's infinitesimal. It's not something the kids are doing; it was never something high school kids did," says Ed Masood, director of the Board of Education's division of health and physical education. "There's no LSD use by any kids in any school."

What about an acid party?

"That would seriously surprise me," said Lt. Thomas Evans, commander of the drug enforcement section of the Montgomery County police. "We hear nothing about kids using LSD."

Maybe they're just not listening. Nationally, the Drug Enforcement Administration reports that LSD-related "emergency room episodes"—nationwide admissions for psychotic reactions, self-mutilation, unconsciousness—have increased 100 percent since 1985. Most victims are white and under 20. More than a quarter of those are 17 or under.

Peter Luango, director of the Montgomery County Division of Addiction and Youth Treatment Services: "There has been an increase in {LSD use} in the past 18 months although I don't see it as an overwhelming drug of choice. We have no new strategies to combat it. The police, he said, "haven't started" focusing on it.

At the high school that V and G and the others attend, LSD usage has increased alarmingly, said one teacher, especially among the wealthier white students.

V, the party hostess, tries to explain: People her age, she says, have no identity. They had no defining war, no Watergate; they were born the year Gerald Ford took office. Searching for cultural touchstones, they have adopted the icons of the 1960s, she says.

"Tripping has a natural kind of '60s image and that's really in today," she says. V has embroidery on her jeans. She has a 3.5 grade point average. She calls herself "Miss Activities." She has tried acid twice so far. She says the kids who experiment with LSD are frustrated with a world that defies understanding.

"We always have conversations about society," she says. "It makes no sense. The government makes no sense. School makes no sense. Why don't people have enough to eat? Why do we have to stress ourselves out and kill ourselves in jobs?"

The kids who don't try acid, she says, are sheep.

"They're like, 'Mommy says no. Society says no.' They don't have the guts to question authority," she says.

Socio-philosophical explanations aside, she also offers the most common reason given for flirtation with LSD: "It was something new to do that sounded neat."

The New Rules

J is sweating. He is panting. His face is flushed, his pupils gigantic. The dark hair that frames off on his 30th trip, he says.

"Oh wow! I'm starting to feel it," J says, pulling off his T-shirt.

The party moves inside the big white house. There are about 20 partyers now. They rollick over hardwood floors, Persian rugs, through bedrooms, past book-lined, framed-art walls. They are still in reality," they say. No hallucinating yet. One guy heads for the bathroom in the hall. He leaves the door open, his proud yellow arc for all to see.

On the wall near the bathroom door is taped a red and white sign in rounded teenage girl writing.

RULES:

1. No smoking in the house.

2. Put all trash in cans.

3. Must share all beer, alcohol and drugs with occupants of the house.

4. Must not drop/drink/smoke and drive.

Someone had taken a black felt pen and crossed out "not."

Before V's parents left for vacation, they lectured her: No smoking, no beer, no boys. V has a great relationship with her folks, she says. It's just that they are a little strict.

"No one allowed to take more than three doses at my house!" she commands as her friends scatter.

"I'm taking four!" J yells.

"I'm taking six!" his friend outbids him.

It is a birthday party. One of the girls is turning 17. Pink streamers and tie-dyed purple ballons decorate the dining room. An orange construction paper "HAPPY BIRTHDAY" is taped to the den door. The block letter loops are filled with peace signs.

"This is my birthday present," the birthday girl says, in a voice that sounds younger than 17. "It is my first time tripping."

She has light blond hair that coils like her friend's. She has light blond skin and middle-of-the-ocean eyes. She wears a teddy bear T-shirt and a rainbow anklet. She gets A's ("and one B"). She is a virgin. She is pretty. Popular. Part of the right clique.

In the den, kids are taking turns on the telephone. They shut out screaming friends and blaring MTV, and dial their parents to check in. First to the phone is a barefoot girl with polished pink toenails.

"Dad? Hi, Get Mom." Pause.

"We're going out to dinner."

While Dad finds Mom, she squeezes her friend's hand—her friend is drinking a beer—and mimics her father's voice, a singsong rebuke: "You're just running around, you're out of control."

"Hi, Mom! We're leaving now. I'll call you tomorrow morning. I'll be ready to go home."

"Bye."

She hangs up the receiver and says to her friend, "That woman is crazy." The girls run out back and land on white patio furniture. The boys follow. The acid makes them hot, they say. Some have sweated through two T-shirts already. They need air.

The birthday girl, stretches out on a white lounge: "Oh, whoa, I'm disoriented."

The boom box is pumping out "Groove Is in the Heart" by Deee-Lite, a '90s group with '60s packaging. Kids are yelling, drinking orange juice ("Vitamin C enhances the trip"), smoking cigarettes, laughing. J is dancing in the middle of the toss of bodies.

"This tripping is {expletive} awesome! My body feels like a rubber band!" J says, and his shirtless, lithe body does look elastic.

He calls himself an acid baby; his parents took LSD in the 1960s.

A guy scoops up some birthday cake and then pie-faces the birthday girl. She squeals. A chocolate icing smear-fight breaks out.

"This is out of control," V laughs, surveying the mayhem on her deck.

"OUT . . . OF . . . CONTROL!" echo the delirious partyers.

V is opening and closing her hand in front of her nose, transfixed by the "trails," the afterimages she says her fingers are leaving in the air. "I feel like I'm not here," she says dreamily. "My face is tingling."

"It's not fair; I think I'm immune to it," another girl whines.

R is sulking. His mother dropped him off too late. He missed out on taking acid. I want to trip my {expletive} off, he says.

"I'm starting to feel shaky," the birthday girl says. Her voice betrays alarm.

"I want to totally lose it," R says, tuning her out. He has a shy smile and an earnest dirty-blond crew cut. He's wearing white shorts, white sneakers and a gray Champion T-shirt. He is skinny. He is reminiscing about the thrill of taking acid and driving.

"The lights come at you real fast, he says. His father is a lawyer. "He'd kill me if he found out."

R's prayers have been answered. A car just pulled up around front with a fresh supply of acid. G and a bunch of other guys have gone off to buy some for the latecomers.

"Acid car!" Everyone runs to greet the returning heroes.

"I'm taking four!" someone cries.

High Tide G and his cohorts are sitting around V's kitchen table. They are popping Pepperidge Farm goldfish, breaking the "No smoking in the house" rule, recounting how they scored. The boys cruised for a while. They found a Deadhead, a guy with curly blond hair and a nose ring. He took their $60 and promised to return with 20 hits of acid. The dude never came back.

So they found another dealer. Easy.

"Right now it's high tide," one boy says.

These days, acid is easier to buy than pot, he says. Partly because the Grateful Dead and its trip-happy fans were in D.C. in June, and partly because acid is "in," he says. Get this, the kid says: He went out earlier to buy some beer and discovered that the store manager also sells acid.

G usually buys LSD from a 21-year-old friend. The dealer has an arrangement with a phony video company in California, G says. Mails them $3,000. Gets back

100 sheets of acid-soaked blotter paper, 100 hits per sheet. Sends out high school kids to sell the stuff at $5 a hit. Bags $50,000 cash.

G doesn't deal anymore. But he is considering selling a couple of sheets of acid to make extra money for school. He says he used to spend $50 for a 100-hit sheet at a Grateful Dead concert. He would sell the stock at $5 a hit, making $500 in sales.

"That's 1,000 percent profit," he calculates. "My job at the mall—I make $4.50 an hour—that's kind of lame."

Selling LSD is a felony, but the prospect of jail doesn't scare him.

"Nothing is illegal unless you get caught," G says, then immediately looks sorry that he said it. "I guess that sounds criminal. I guess it is criminal." He pauses. He thinks. His 17-year-old confidence is faltering. Finally: "I don't like any kind of authority. And besides, I don't see any reason society should inhibit the use of any part of our minds."

The prospect of blowing someone's mind with too much acid doesn't worry him either.

"I'd sell it first to a guy I didn't like and let him test it," he teases. "Maybe I'd give it to my dog."

Entrepreneurial

G's friend, M, also says he was involved in LSD distribution. He says he financed two 11th-graders from Bethesda who manufacture the drug in their basement. M has tried acid twice (it's good for exploring) but he says he generally is against drug use. He backed the teen drug dealers for strictly financial reasons.

"And I wanted to make my father proud," M adds.

He is serious.

M turned 17 this month. He is a 140-pound demi-adult with Superman sheets on his bed and a taste for Nietzsche and Schopenhauer. He tells his story freely:

His father, who like his mother has a PhD, owns a small, successful business. M wanted to be an entrepreneur like his dad. He had been working for him every summer since he was 12, loading boxes.

"I was sick of working with my hands," he explains. "I wanted to be a white-collar worker."

So when he got to be friendly with two guys at a Montgomery County community center and they pitched the LSD financing scheme, he agreed. Last November, he withdrew $120 from his savings account. He put the money in an envelope and hand-delivered it to Bethesda. The envelope was printed with his father's business logo.

A week later, the guys gave him $240, doubling his investment.

"I was like a cartoon character with dollar signs popping in my eyes," M says. It became a routine. He would invest $200. A few weeks later he'd get back $400. Over a six-month period, he made $1,000.

"It didn't really seem illegal," he says. (It is. Knowingly financing a drug deal is a felony.) "I didn't think about the legal aspects." And if he were caught, he reasoned, it was his first offense and he was still underage.

"I thought, who are the cops going to trust, a preppie dude like me or some acid freak, Deadhead deadbeat?" he says. "I'm a good boy."

M bought himself a tie at Banana Republic. He bought his mother flowers. He felt independent. He decided it might be time to buy his first razor.

"There was no guilt factor here. I thought if I'm not doing it, someone else will capitalize on it," he says.

One April afternoon, he decided it was time to show his father what a good businessboy he had become. His father was sitting in the living room reading the paper when M walked up to him and spilled it. His father looked as if he'd been punched. He sent M to his room and hardly talked to him for weeks. The connection with the dealers was terminated immediately.

"My dad called me a hoodlum and a drug dealer," the boy says. "He used the word 'disappointed' with me, and that's the worst word."

He still keeps the envelope with his father's business logo on his desk.

In the Blood

J, the "acid baby," also told a parent about his involvement with LSD. His mother, who took acid several times during the late '60s, says she doesn't approve of his use but sees no way to stop it.

Besides, she says, there are advantages: She and her son are "more on the same wavelength" since he tried the drug, she told *The Post*.

It changed his perspective, opened up his mind, she says.

But she worries. She has friends who have fried their brains on acid.

Today's children, she says, "see it glamorized. There's a kind of a hero worship when they realize, 'Oh, my parents were at Woodstock, I want to experience some of the things they did.'

"They think they're immortal—drinking, driving fast, swimming in deep water—kids do all kinds of stupid things."

She says she hopes J stops "before he loses his faculties." In the meantime, she says, he needs a guardian angel. "When you're a parent you say a whole lot of prayers."

The Argument

The smell of cinnamon fills V's kitchen. The breeze from an open window circulates the sweet flavor. The kids are chewing Wrigley's Big Red gum. They put the freshly purchased squares of blotter acid on the cinnamon gum and pop the sticks in their mouths. The new blotter pieces are imprinted with pictures of tiny blue unicorns.

R finally is taking his coveted dose. He retrieves the pink wad of gum from his mouth and examines it, worried that somehow he "lost" the acid. J contravenes V's three-hit limit and takes three more hits of LSD.

The hostess and the birthday girl, forever twins, split a hit.

V instantly regrets it.

"I have a feeling something bad is going to happen at my house," she says.

They wait for the new doses to kick in. They paint each other's faces with fluorescent markers. They make statues out of multicolored clay. They play board games. They watch music videos. They stare at a painting of a girl and argue about what they see in it:

"A mermaid grabbing trees."

"A panther."

"A dove. No, a dragon."

"It's a pink and purple and orange planet."

"I see a lady strangling her cat."

"There's a baby with an evil screaming face."

The phone rings. V takes the call and then announces: "The maid's coming tomorrow, you guys!" Her voice is hoarse from all the yelling. "So if you wake up tomorrow and there's a black lady standing over you, don't be freaked out!"

R, the latecomer, is a little freaked out already. His stomach hurts. ("From the strychnine—that's rat poison, it makes the acid stick to the paper.") His chest feels tense. He is crushing an empty container of Minute Maid. He can't let go of the plastic jug. He hears the blood rushing through his brain, he says.

"Can't handle it, he's a pussy boy," taunts a classmate.

J glimpses himself in the hall mirror. He sees a wolf. He flashes elongated canines and growls. V checks herself next.

"I look like a dead woman," she says. "I'm the Devil."

The birthday girl is leaning against the staircase railing. She has been gripping a paper palm tree in her left hand for the past hour.

It's on fire! She suddenly exclaims and scampers outside. Her friends follow. She is standing on the deck, fanning the paper palm tree. Pink Floyd's album "The Wall" is playing. The birthday girl and her palm tree start to dance.

"My birthday is freedom, mad, wild," she announces. "I want to fly forever."

By now, about 30 teenagers are wandering around V's house. Many aren't tripping. None of the handful of black guests has taken the drug. The "reality dudes," as they call the ones who aren't on LSD, are getting drunk on Budweiser. The trippers say that being with people in reality makes them nervous. A boozed-up boy starts lecturing them on the evil nature of drugs. A guy who's had four hits of acid, and is twice his size, socks the drunk kid in the jaw. Everyone is screaming. Girls start to cry.

"I'm going to go insane!" V shrieks, her cheeks crimson. "All people who aren't tripping, get the {expletive} out of my house!"

She rants. She begs. Finally, the non-tripping teenagers leave.

It's close to their parents' bedtime. A couple of kids go inside and shut the den door, silencing Pink Floyd. They call their moms and dads to say good night.

The Sky, the Stars, the Deck

R has settled in a deck chair. He is examining his hand with binoculars. V is standing in the grass, whirling her cigarette against the dark sky, hypnotized by the orange trails of fire she says she sees. J is on his knees, staring at the knots and knurls and bumps on the wooden deck.

"Oh my God, there's a lady in the floor," he says. A bunch of kids join him to inspect the wood. Her face. Her breasts. Look at all those people trapped in the wood. "I'm stepping on the souls of every person that ever lived," J says.

Up next for scrutiny is the sky: The sky is contracting. The stars are swirling. The stars are melting. They see red, white, blue flashes of light.

"It's the Fourth of July up there," the birthday girl sums it up.

A boy comes running around from the front yard. He is frantic, flailing his arms. He has bad news. He saw Little J. Little J is here!

"I saw him on a truck! He's drunk!"

No. He must be hallucinating. Little J couldn't possibly be at V's house! They drift around front to check.

A large van, with a boy lying on the roof, cruises by the driveway. The crowd is stunned. Scared.

"I'm never doing this again," V says, stricken.

"I want to go home," says J.

The van loops around and rolls by a second time. Little J is on his back, propped up by his elbows on top of the van. He isn't wearing a shirt. His straight brown hair is flying. He averts his eyes from the gathering on V's lawn.

Death's Visitor

Two weeks ago, Little J nearly died tripping, his friends say. No one could forgive him for losing at their new game.

It was going to be a blast. C's parents were out of town and that meant: party! Little J took a hit of acid before he left his summer job.

He is a slight boy, 17 but much smaller than his buddies. More studious. They call him a worrier. But that night he was feeling bold.

Nine guys took LSD at C's house. (The blotter sheet had a "Star Trek" theme: A man in a spacesuit. An energy field. And across the bottom, the message "Beam me up, Scottie. There is no intelligent life down here.") Some of the guys were dosing for the first time, some for the 30th. They played guitar. They sat in the yard, watching hallucinatory lightning streak the sky, feeling imaginary tremors in the rocks beneath them. The guys drifted inside.

"I was upstairs talking to someone and then all of a sudden I just lost it," Little J remembers. "Something freaked me out."

He started worrying about making it to work the next day. How much longer would the trip last? He wanted a watch. He wanted to shower. He wanted his car. He wanted his mother. He wanted to leave. He was afraid to leave.

J, ever the audacious one, had tape-recorded his LSD trips before. He persuaded the rest of the guys to set up a tape deck in the den to record their experience. It turned out to be a record of a nightmare:

"I don't know where I am," Little J can be heard saying, stumbling around the den while the other guys relax on the couches, chatting. "I don't want to do this anymore." He approaches each guy, addressing each, surreally, by first and last name, asking: "How many hits of acid have I taken?"

They tell him he's had two. They tell him he is fine. They throw snap firecrackers at his feet. They tell him to shut up.

He rambles on. He can't understand them. He can't see straight. There are translucent squares floating through the dimly lit room. The ceiling looks like bedsheets undulating on a clothesline. A glaze covers the lamp, the chairs, his friends' faces.

"Get these pieces of acid off of me," he cries, scraping his arms to remove invisible scraps of LSD paper. "Don't give me any more acid."

The guys laugh. Little J is getting desperate. It's hard to stand up. "I think I'm going to die," he says.

C, the host, suggests dialing a drug crisis hot line. Little J staggers out the front door. C grabs him.

"Call 911," Little J implores.

"You have a scrambled brain," J says. "Why don't we handcuff him?"

Remember N? The guys remember. He had a weird trip on prom night and flipped out. They're getting nervous. They are trying to deal with a terrifying crisis, but they are 17 years old, and they are tripping on acid.

"Call 911 on the phone," Little J persists.

"No way are we going to prison!" someone says.

"I'm going to die," Little J is pleading.

"So what, man."

"I feel bad for him," says a guy who's on his 10th trip. "He got the bad side of the drug. We got the good." The guy says he wants to stop the tape recorder. It will be too weird to play it back.

"People write books about this. . . . Ever hear of the book 'Kool-Aid Acid Test'?" asks J.

Another boy, an A student, says soon he'll be making his own acid. He's going to study chemistry in college.

Little J is yelling now: "Find me my MOM! I think I'm DEAD!"

Acid has seeped into his clothes, he believes. He pulls off his Nike Air shirt. Down go his pants. Off with his underwear. His naked body is drenched in sweat.

His friends consider the alternatives: Knock him out. Rick him out. Send him to the hospital.

If they take him to the hospital, they'll put him in a straitjacket for the rest of his life, argues one kid. He saw it happen in a movie at school. C suggests they make their own straitjacket.

"I'll strangle the mother {expletive}," someone says.

"Jesus, are we going to be arrested? That's all I have to say," says a guy who has, in fact, not spoken up before.

"Let me GO!" Little J is thrashing around. "I'm totally INSANE! Find me my MAMA!" He is running around the room. "I'm STONE COLD DEAD!"

His friends try to dress him. He's wailing. He's spitting. He has six hours of the acid trip left to go.

"I KNOW WHERE I AM! I'M DYING!" he screams. "DIAL 911!"

Most of the partyers have moved outside, away from the bad trip scene.

Little J runs into the hall. He backs into a wall and falls over. He can't feel anything. He is banging his head on the yellow tile floor.

"My God! My God!" gasps C.

Little J is lying face down, his body convulsing.

They drag Little J into the living room. Spasms contort his body. They watch his skin turn a dark, frightening color. He goes rigid.

"Our friend's gonna die on us," says the boy who was worried about getting arrested.

C is cradling Little J. "I can hear him breathing," he says. Someone knows CPR. They lay him on his side. Keep his tongue out of his trachea.

Somebody mentions 911 again.

"He had too many worries, man," J diagnoses. "Too much mental stress. . . . It took over his body."

Somebody checks for a heartbeat. They cover him with a blanket. Guys drift out of the room.

Little J comes to 15 minutes later, looking drained. Three hours later, at 3:30 a.m., he tells his friends: It's okay, I've come down. They go into the kitchen and nuke a pizza.

By morning, he was overwhelmed by embarrassment about his fit. He was exhausted. His back ached ("because acid drains your spinal fluid and it doesn't exactly go back"). He vowed to never again drop acid, smoke pot or even drink beer. The only reason he had dropped acid in the first place was that he was bored, he said.

"We needed a new form of entertainment. You can only see so many movies," he said.

He was thankful his friends ignored his plea to be hospitalized. The doctors would have strapped him down, he said.

"I remember saying 'call 911' 'cause I thought I was going to die, but the hospital wouldn't have helped me anyway," he said. "And they would've called my parents."

A Disappearance

On this night, no one is feeling sorry for the frail, shirtless boy on the van. The kids in V's driveway want the Kid Who Almost Died to go away. They want the bad trip to disappear.

The van leaves. The trippers immediately distance themselves from his terrifying experience.

"He has a feeble mind, that's why it happened," J says.

"He made himself have a bad trip. The drug doesn't do it to you," adds V.

G's adage about bad trips: Fear causes hesitation and hesitation causes your worst fears to come true.

The group returns somberly to the back yard. They head for the reassuring flicker of lightning bugs in the grass. But nearly everyone who has used LSD before has an almost bad trip story: From a tree branch, the Grim Reaper summoned one boy. A giant black spider chased another guy. R once was pinned to his car, paralyzed. Snakes wrapped themselves around G's ankles.

J says he saw his best friend die; the room went dark with blood.

"My fingernail is alive, all my energy is in my nail," says the birthday girl. She is running her thumb over the pink nail polish on her index finger. "I can't stop feeling it. I want to cut off my nail and kill it," she says to V.

V is quiet. She is far away. She is thinking. Peering into a vast, black pool of thoughts. Everything dark and unknown to her is floating at the bottom of the pool. She doesn't want to look. She can't help herself from looking. She feels utterly alone.

The kids are quiet now. They gather by a weeping willow. They are silver children, lying in the grass, bathing in the midsummer starlight.

They plan another party for late August.

August 18, 1991

Young Fogies

The City's Twentysomethings, Up Close and Impersonal

HENRY ALLEN

They are the Young Fogies, and Washington is full of them nowadays. You see them all over downtown, the Hill, the agencies, the law firms—baby fat in horn-rim glasses, white bread in black wingtip shoes, 24-year-old staff assistants whose conversations resonate with words like "escrow" and "breakfront," 29-year-old lawyers doing the Burberry Shuffle down K Street, their raincoats belted right under their armpits as they move along with a kind of anxious bustle, as if their snap-front boxer shorts were riding up.

"The ones with the suspenders and the Mont Blanc pens?" asks Dan Buck, who is administrative assistant to Rep. Pat Schroeder. "The ones who never had a real job in life, for example delivering pizzas? They're the ones down at the White House who have never been anywhere or done anything, who think they're in charge."

"I think you're talking about the interns, or the Schedule C's from the '88 Bush campaign," says Chase Untermeyer, director of presidential personnel at the White House. "You'll find a lot of them over at Commerce."

You see them at night in restaurants, both sexes checking their watches when the waiter asks if they want coffee. You see them at deadline in newsrooms, frowning with bewilderment at jokes about the latest massacre or bus plunge story. You see them eating yogurt lunches in law firms and looking forward to careers in trusts and estates—"they're most comfortable working with the dead," says James M. Spears, general counsel at the Federal Trade Commission.

What is the meaning of all this?

There is very little meaning.

You won't see a "Young Fogies" cover on Time magazine, which has already come up with the name "twentysomethings" for the generation to which the Young Fogies are a footnote, a codicil. They are not trend-setters, culture heroes, role models, neo-liberals, proto-fascists, preppies or yuppies—a yuppie, for instance, knows within five seconds where you bought your shoes, while a Young Fogy is more apt to know what you got on your SATs. They are just a collection of impressions you get from passing enough of them on the sidewalk, an eddy in the slow-moving stream of consciousness that is life in Washington.

There's nothing new about them. (The name was used almost a decade ago to describe the editors at the *Spectator* in London.) They've always been around, setting their sights on joining the White House press corps or showing up to work in campaign headquarters, particularly Republican ones—though they are not to be confused with what used to be known at the National Review as "the doddering young men of the hard right."

It's just that there seem to be so many of them around right now. Or is it that there are so few young people having any fun?

In any case, we should be grateful. The Young Fogies may be the younger generation we need. In the Washington of Reagan's irredeemable national debt, of Congress's stagnation, of media that fewer and fewer people pay attention to, they are not so much architects of the future as its caretakers, sort of the cruise control for the aging four-door sedan of state.

We know so little about them, and that's just the way they want it. They discovered long ago that invisibility is the key to success, that quiet resentment can be a way of life.

But you know whom we're talking about here. You've probably been noticing them for a while now, in your office, at the Kennedy Center, in upscale furniture stores. There's a primness, an odd way of being wary and presumptuous at the same time. They were the children who identified with the coyote in the Road Runner cartoons, who asked for combination-lock briefcases for graduation presents, who decided to devote their lives to the public good after seeing Margaret Tutwiler hold a State Department press conference on TV.

The women are proud of having a certain mousiness. They borrow cocktail dresses and Kenneth J. Lane door-knocker earrings from their mothers. They'll buy garden party hats, but they're afraid to wear them, though sometimes you'll see them on house tours, carrying them at their sides. The men get their shirts boxed at the cleaners instead of putting them on hangers. They cultivate a fussy domesticity, and may own a pair of gardening kneepads from Brookstone.

They tend to be short, with uncertain handshakes. They have that odd quality of looking much older than you even when they're younger, sort of like your parents in their high school yearbook pictures. This observation would not trouble them. Young Fogies love hanging out with their parents, their grandparents, their parents-in-law and their friends' parents, with whom they go to brunches and restaurants—their idea of a great restaurant is the kind their parents used to take them to, with popovers and a little waterfall out back. Among the Young Fogies, parents are a favorite subject of conversation, along with the foibles of cleaning women. They tell each other: "Your parents are such neat people."

Young Fogies need a lot of reassuring. They want to know they're doing things right.

"These people are so passive," says Tony White, a manager at Olsson's Books and Records at Dupont Circle. "They'll ask us if something is good even while they're listening to it."

They like things packaged, listed, tidy—classic rock, prix fixe dinners, season symphony tickets, Pentagon press briefings, summit meetings.

"They're the reporters you see on campaign planes balancing their checkbooks," says Julia Reed, a writer and editor at *Vogue.*

They buy a lot of life insurance. They buy picture frames and then find pictures to fit—botanical prints are popular, with the Latin inscriptions, Narcissus major flore multiplice. They buy extended warranties.

"Okay, we'll buy it," says the Fogy husband to the Fogy wife as they study a wingback chair. "But promise me—we're not going to sit in it till we've Scotchgarded it."

They like antique hunting, which they call " 'tiquing." They would like to collect something but can never decide what, though they have collected huge quantities of umbrellas—at home, in the car, the briefcase, the office, in case they ever lose one, which they never do. They read lots of memoirs and biographies, preferably of Winston Churchill, of whom they do imitations at their dinner parties. "We will nevah surrendah."

They like giving dinner parties so they can worry about the seating arrangements and use their silver. They like filling out expense accounts. They love taking standardized tests—College Boards, bar exams, Graduate Record Exams, medical boards.

They shop by catalogue whenever possible—the women buy bathing suits from Lands' End, for instance. They have a blackboard next to the kitchen phone, and they leave messages in color-coded chalk. They keep a Christmas card list. They take it with them when they go to Europe and use it for sending postcards that begin "Hi Guys" in their tiny handwriting.

Who better to usher America into the new world order, into "the end of history" we were talking about a year or two ago?

They take a custodial position toward all of reality. They are strong environmentalists—they like the orderliness of the recycling ritual. They see soul mates in Al and Tipper Gore—Mr. Green and Mrs. Clean. They read the *New Yorker,* and enjoy the memoirs of childhoods in other countries. They are apt to own their own videotapes of "The Big Chill" and "Brideshead Revisited"—they feel nostalgic for other people's pasts, never having had childhoods of their own. They liked "Ghost," which told them they could be dead and still live in a good neighborhood. They went to the early show.

They watch a lot of television and say they feel guilty about it, though they don't really. They tried watching "Twin Peaks," but the next day they wandered around the office asking people to explain it to them. They don't understand "The Simpsons" either. They think Bart is "going nowhere fast."

They say they like almost anything on public television—"Mystery," "Masterpiece Theatre," the Fred Astaire movies. Their secret vice, the thing they stay up past 10 o'clock for, is the fund-raisers. The people doing the talking on screen, touting the umbrellas and tote bags, are cult figures to the Young Fogies, who hope someday to have their friends see them on the fund-raiser phone bank, taking viewers' calls.

They like almost anything on National Public Radio, with the exception of "Car Talk"—they disapprove of the way the Tappet Brothers laugh at their own jokes, and, deep down, they don't really like cars.

They have a hard time with parallel parking, for one thing, and they will never learn how to drive standard shift. They drive like people who didn't learn how until they were 23, which they often didn't, they were so busy with SAT prep courses, internships, fellowships and networking. They may drive Volvos or Toyotas, but their favorite car is the old Buick Electra their grandparents gave them after the move to Florida. If it gets dented, the Young Fogies say, "Grampa would be heartbroken."

They buy houses in Old Town Alexandria, Falls Church, Cleveland Park, Chevy Chase. They spend a lot of time decorating the guest bedroom. They like working fireplaces, except they have a hard time making them work. This causes arguments that have a sudden, inexplicable and ferocious quality, sort of like their sex lives.

"Did you open the flue?"

"Yes, I opened the goddam flue, do you think I'm a complete idiot?"

"I was just . . ."

"Do you? Do you? I want an answer."

It is not true that they are sexless. Eros entered their lives in college, usually—the men recognized it as a sort of required course, and the women may have had flings with a professor or two. Now passion gets renewed with the arrival of the Victoria's Secret catalogue or a new canopy bed. They plan to have children—they picture having sons who look like miniature versions of George Will.

They can be wicked too. They take terrific relish in cutting their friends to pieces after they go home—one of the reasons they get married is to have someone to gossip with.

They don't exercise with much gusto. Sometimes a Young Fogy couple goes out and buys a badminton set. They play in the back yard, all by themselves.

Both their parents and their grandparents are secretly disappointed in them, of course. "I just wish they were having more fun," say the parents. "Do you think it's normal for people that age to go to Bermuda on vacation?"

The Young Fogies may be anxious and resentful, but they are not disappointed. They are resigned to the fact that their tickets are punched but their train is rusted to the rails. They don't expect much, which is why they work so hard to take care of what they've got. They aren't leaving anytime soon. If we threw them out, where would they go? Wilmington? Hartford? They're not quite living fossils, not quite an endangered species, but Washington is their habitat.

August 16, 1991

Study Questions

Chapter Two

1. Writer David Finkel captures the essence of high school life by describing students' diets, schedules, relations with parents and so on. What reporting elements would you suggest to describe the world of a retired person?
2. Play campus sociologist and identify subcultures present in college life. Clubs. Ethnic groups. Leaders. Rivalries.
3. Sometimes witness reporting is the only effective way to gather information for a story, as Laura Blumenfeld illustrates in "The Acid Kids." Think of an activity that's likely to interest readers and that you could report on by just being where the action is. Could you obtain entry? What difficulties might you expect?
4. Reporters don't avoid values in their writing, they report them, expose conflicts and often adopt a point of view in their own text. Review the value-laden issues in the stories contained in the chapter.
5. Developmental stories make readers aware of subtle changes in life, such as growth experiences. Identify some pivotal points in adolescence stemming from your own observations.

3 *Looking for Love*

In journalism, stories about human relations have long been the exclusive province of feature departments because news editors simply refuse to connect news value to them. Such features, which used to appear on women's pages, are standard fare in family or lifestyle sections.

For some stories, such as the Miss America Pageant, feature treatment is the only plausible way to handle coverage. In his article on the annual spectacle, Joel Achenbach interviews and quotes anthropologists, event organizers and contestants, plus contributes his own observations. Achenbach muses about the American ideal of beauty, while at the same time pointing out the paradox of dwelling on physical perfection in beauty contests in the wake of feminism. It's substantive writing that no longer takes an American institution for granted.

Phil McComb's examination of the emerging men's movement shows a keen reporter's eye for social change. Curious readers are not yet likely to know much about mythopoetics, so it's incumbent on the writer to share the ideas and attitudes emanating from its seminars and authors.

The article on Washington bachelors is as much about political power and status as what passes for social life in the nation's capitol. The list that writer Roxanne Roberts constructs establishes a hierarchy of "Eligibles" in the city and also becomes the story's structure. While its tone is light and fun, the piece also makes some serious points about workaholism and the party circuit, political combat and gossip, social climbing and games, professional and personal lives and even flaunting it vs. privacy. Including each bachelor's office phone number at the end of the story is pure editorial cheek.

Whether summer romances ever amount to more than seasonal flings is a topic rarely written about. While Ron Gassbarro's story attempts to explore some psychological dimensions of such trysts, quoting an author and a psychologist, it mainly recognizes the commonness of the experience.

Powerful memories are an asset to reporters who utilize their own recollections of the subject in their stories. Marjorie Williams writes about her thoughts leading up to her own wedding as she also investigates the rituals, customs and rationale of marriage rites. It's easy to identify with Williams' confessional voice in her essay as she ponders the cultural imperatives and choices available to her.

The complicated relationships of sisters are illustrated with carefully selected examples in Barbara Mathias' article. Her work describes five cases of different family patterns and blends interviews with introspection, adding a service component at the end.

Don Oldenburg's story, "Higher Love," looks beyond clinical sexuality to a collective yearning for spirituality. Oldenburg takes an enlightened, yet off-beat and possibly controversial tack on a topic in which most readers may be curious, but will also believe they already have expertise from their own experience. The writer utilizes a variety of sources, from workshop leaders to book authors, professors and religious leaders. He frames sexuality in a more holistic manner than the media, especially advertising, does.

Straight talk about a sensationalized news event involving a celebrity's illegal social behavior often is in short supply in the media. Joel Achenbach views Pee Wee Herman's arrest for public masturbation as an aberration that's more pathetic than a serious crime.

The Miss America Paradox

If They're So Smart and Talented, What Are They Doing in Those Swimsuits?

JOEL ACHENBACH

And now it comes to this: A Washington lawyer puts on a swimsuit, jacks up on high heels and parades down a runway under bright lights. If she makes the final 10 in tonight's Miss America Pageant, she'll take that same unnatural stroll, shakeless and sexless in the pageant tradition, in front of 50 million people.

Her name is Carolyn Ladd, she's Miss Oregon, and she's the ultimate example of what has happened to the Super Bowl of Womanhood. She's a lawyer for the National Labor Relations Board and a graduate student in labor law at Georgetown University. Just because she's resume-heavy, though, doesn't excuse her from her cheesecake duties.

"I just wanted to walk fast and get off the stage and change into my next outfit," she said after Wednesday night's preliminary competition. Is the swimsuit romp an anachronism? She answered, " I believe that in the future it will be phased out. . . I hope it is."

In 1991, Miss America is a troubled, internally conflicted icon. She is stuck between the past and the future, her mind liberated but her body still loyal to the beauty cult. She goes to college but still plays girlish dress-up games. She's a crusader for causes, fighting against AIDS prejudice, perhaps, or against domestic violence, and yet she still engages in something called the "evening gown competition."

The typical Miss America hopeful has been tweezed, teased, primped, tucked, taped, lacquered, burnished, adhered, oiled, lubed, and filtered to a state of visual perfection—she is, in essence, an engineering marvel, designed in accordance with the jutting-clavicle school of architecture—and yet she will say, without irony, that her secret to enjoying life is "to just be myself."

Years ago there was no pretense that this was anything other than a beauty contest. The new apotheosis of womanhood was crowned in a bathing suit until 1947. If she could talk, so much better. Today, it's supposed to be called a "scholarship pageant," and one is supposed to ignore, if possible, the fact that most scholarship programs don't require mannequin-smooth thighs. One is supposed to take the whole thing terribly seriously even though at the trade show next door you can buy feels-real silicon gel falsies for $140 or $180 a pair, depending on cup size.

Much is made of the decreased importance of the swimsuit competition, which now makes up only 15 percent of a contestant's score. But the contestants still have to parade around like airhead beach bunnies, a fact that no doubt pleases someone like Miss Utah, Elizabeth Anne Johnson, whose six-foot Amazon frame swept away the honors in Thursday's preliminary swimsuit contest,

"The swimsuit competition has always been and may always be our Achilles' heel," says Leonard Horn, the South Jersey lawyer who runs the pageant with a mephitic cigar as a baton. "Personally I find it difficult to rationalize putting young intelligent college women in a swimsuit and high-heel shoes."

So how does he rationalize it? He denies it's because of the TV ratings. He says it's important that the pageant emphasizes "fitness." Apparently, a component of physical fitness is an ample bosom.

"If you're looking for a role model, you can't have somebody who is not physically fit," he says, and then adds, for some reason that isn't quite clear, "Margaret Mead was a good role model, but she may not have looked good in a swimsuit."

Margaret Mead in a swimsuit! Let's meditate on that for a spell. Certainly she would have loved the anthropological mystery of the Miss America pageant. What is this dress-up culture all about? Why do people in the 1990s behave this way? There is, of course, a scientific perspective on all this.

"Woman are competing with each other for males, and males are competing with each other for females, and the currency of female competition tends to be physical appearance, because that's what men value," says Donald Symons, anthropologist at the University of California at Santa Barbara. The "male value" of a woman, Symons argues, is closely tied in with her youth. Men, he says, are valued more for their demonstrated prowess and status. That's why the "ideal male age" is, he says, is at least 10 years older than the ideal female age. (The pageant, meanwhile, is changing the rules in 1993. No longer can a Miss America be up to 26 years old. The new age bracket is 17 to 24. The official explanation is that 25- and 26-year olds don't need the scholarship money.)

It is a visual culture, and that's really depressing, when you stop to think about it," says Miss Illinois, Cheryl Lynn Majercik. "That's the cruelty of the world. People are very visually oriented toward symmetry. That's what shows up in tests. Symmetry is beautiful to the beholder. Anything quirky or protuberant is abhorrent to the connoisseur of beauty. No wonder so many contestants look the same: They have generic pretty faces, manufactured by Mattel.

A University of Louisville study five years ago showed that the percieved ideal female face has eyeballs one-four-teenth the height of the face, chin length one-fifth that same height, and a nose that covers only 5 percent of the area of the face. And so on. There may also be a hidden truth in Horn's statement that the judges are looking for a woman who is the best "composite" of all the right attributes of womanhood: According to studies by Judith Langlois at the University of Texas, a beautiful face is one that is one that most resembles the average face of a given society. No wonder Miss Rhode Island who comes back every year to watch, says, "I always get all the blonds mixed up."

The golden age of the ditsy bottle-blond is long over, though. Not that there aren't some daffy contestants this year—and every other one is a blonde—but someone who says her main interest in life is "sincerity" won't be able to compete against the total package Superwoman. One strong contender is Majercik, Miss Illinois, who is a professional opera singer and has won a pageant Quality of Life Award for her work on behalf of an AIDS clinic. Another good bet, and also a professional opera singer, is Miss New York, Marisol Montalvo. Other strong contenders include Miss Texas, Rhonda Rene Morrison, who sings well and has the kind of looks and charm that would make traditionalists happy; and Miss Iowa, Lisa Somodi, who won a talent contest with a frenetic piano performance.

What the pageant is, ultimately, is a sport. It's horse racing, a contest of creatures with great teeth. As in all sports, the competition gets stiffer over the years. "Preparing for the Miss America pageant is directly correlated to training for the Olympics," said Miss Oklahoma, Gina-Lynne Smith. "Our hair has to look nice, our nails have to look nice, we have to be the total package, the woman of the 90s."

Not to insinuate that it's a hair-and-nails contest. These young women train their minds too. The contestants are almost obsessively poised. For them, every night is Poise Night Out. They look you in the eye so intently during interviews it's as though they see retina damage. It's a gaze meant to suggest intelligence. Smith says: "I subscribe to 13 new magazines. I watch CNN every day. I watch 'Good Morning America' and I tape the 'Today' show. I have voice lessons three times a week. I go to the gym five days a week at 6 in the morning. I lift weights for an hour and then I do aerobic activity for an hour."

She weighs 110 pounds, stretched across 5 feet 7 inches. "My director sent me here with five bags of candy corn in fear that I would lose weight," she said.

Many of the contestants look as if they don't eat actual solid food. The combined rear endage of, say Miss Oklahoma and Miss Colorado would equal the mass of a single normal human buttocks.

Miss Tennessee, Jill Horn, fainted in the shower Sunday and had to be hospitalized. She blamed a stomach virus that affected many other contestants, and denied a published report that a crash diet had caused her spell. "In no way have I starved myself," she said. Every day she works out for at least an hour, she added. "I get a day off a week to rest, which is Sunday, which I always look forward to." She is 5-6 and weighs 112 pounds.

Miss Maryland, Debra Renea Fries, who put on a heroic baton-twirling show Thursday to win a talent preliminary, says she used to anorexic and bulimic.

"I thought to be liked I had to be a very thin individual," she said.

She's still very thin, but it's a "healthy thin," she says. She adds, "Society needs to redefine what healthy is, what thin means, what diet means."

Meanwhile, in the contestants' galley, they were handling out free copies of the premiere issue of *Slim-Fast* magazine.

It will be interesting to see what happens if Montalvo, Miss New York, wins tonight. She is a dark-complexioned Puerto Rican. The last two Miss Americas have been black. Told this week that Montalvo won a preliminary talent competition, Leonard Horn, said to a USA Today reporter, "Are you telling me I could have another minority Miss America?"

Horn insisted that would be great with him, but his unguarded remark points to a not-so-simmering tension within the larger pageant community. Pageants are huge in the South, where beauty queens haven't been expected in recent years to hold doctorates in philosophy. When Marjorie Vincent, a Duke law student and daughter of Haitian immigrants, won last year, there were plenty of nasty comments from some of the pageant traditionalists. There will not be a third consecutive black Miss America. There are no black contestants.

September 14, 1991

Men's Movement Stalks the Wild Side

Lessons in Primitivism for the Modern Male

PHIL MCCOMBS

What is it with men these days, anyway?

Why are so many men unhappy and unfulfilled?

Why can't they speak from their hearts to their friends, to the women in their lives, to their children and to their parents—especially their fathers?

Why do so many men feel isolated and alone?

And why are 1,500 of them paying $75 each to beat drums, share intimate self revelations and listen to a poet and a mythological storyteller hash out answers to thosequestions in "A Day for Men" beginning at 9:30 this morning in Lisner Auditorium?

"An affirmation and strength comes from a bonding between men that's impossible to put into words," says Ed Honnold, the mild-mannered federal lawyer and founder of the Men's Council of Greater Washington, one of six such local groups salving men's deep inner pain through communal rituals of dancing and roaring, hugging and weeping. "This experience was known to men in the past, but has been forgotten. American men face a desperate situation and don't even know it. There are large numbers of men wandering lost in some personal wasteland of jobs with little meaning, personal lives with little passion, and massive confusion about the reasons why."

He pauses thoughtfully and adds "There's a lot of hurtin' cowboys out there."

The truth, says Robert Bly, who will lead today's gathering with storyteller Michael Meade, is that a man's life is a shocking descent into grief, and not the upwardly mobile American dreamscape of high-flying success that so many want. Bly, the big poet with the multicolored vest and wild white hair, author of the new bestseller "Iron John: A Book About Men" and head guru of the so-called Mythopoetic Men's Movement, says flatly that "the door to men's feeling is grief, and to be able to make that turn downward, break the upward spiral, and start thinking about what actually went on in your family" is a key to what people in the movement like to call "mature masculine."

American men never learned to be men, Bly theorizes, because after the Industrial Revolution their fathers weren't around to teach them. They were raised by woman who, no matter how wonderful, didn't know how to convey "the distinctive male mode of feeling." Thus, the theory goes instead of mature or "kingly"

58

men, what we tend to have these days are mama's boys, filled with intense "father hunger," which feel uncomfortable in the company of men but who certainly can't stand up to a woman either.

Gruff and grandfatherly at 63, Bly thinks an answer can be found in ancient stories and myths that all male retreats into the woods—or into Lisner—for male "soul talk," rituals and initiation ceremonies can help men "nurture" one another toward growing up. "Men have lived together in heart unions and soul connections for hundreds of thousands of years," he writes in his book. "Contemporary business life allows competitive relationships only, in which tha major emotions are anxiety, tension, loneliness, rivalry, and fear. ... Having no soul union with other man can be tha most damaging wound of all."

When men get together seriously, he thinks, they can help one another touch their grief. "Everybody tells men they should cheer up and be the strong one in the family," he says over a big breakfast: of bacon and eqgs during an earlier book promotion tour in Washington, "but when they go to a men's group thay're allowed to weep over their fathers and they're not considered weak. In fact, the other men consider it tremendous to be able to weep either over the remoteness of your father or the sufferings that your father went through."

The other thing is to get in touch with your "Wild Man."

In "Iron John," Bly spins a mesmerizing mix of modern psychological and ancient mythological speculation around the Grimms' fairy tale of a hairy Wild Man (the essential masculine) pulled from the depths of a lake (the male psyche) and locked in a cage in the castle (the constraints of civilization). The king's son steals (significant: He doesn't ask) the key from under his mother's pillow (very significant: break with mother), unlocks the cage and rides into the forest on the shoulders of the Wild Man, who teaches him about Life. In the end, drawing upon these lessons taught by Iron John, he claims his full manhood through suffering and courage, and wins the hand of a princess.

"That Wild Man's job," Bly writes, "is to teach the young man how abundant, various, and many-sided his manhood is. ... To receive initiation truly means to expand sideways into the glory of of mountains, glaciers, horses, lions, grasses, waterfalls, deer. A man needs wilderness and extravagance. Whatever shuts a man away from the waterfall and the tiger will kill him."

Working through his bacon and eggs, he discourses extravagantly, occasionally roaring like a giant and screeching like a witch as he recounts mythological literature that he's translated. He takes delight in the thought that practices of other cultures might be applied to our own. The "old initiators" in Africa and New Guinea, he says, "take a boy off into the woods, make a vagina 20 feet long out of twigs old brush, send the boy in one end and greet him at the other, and they say, 'Now you're born a second time, you're born for men this time.' They give him a new name, and cover his face with ashes to indicate that the son of the mother is dead."

He guffaws. Then changing mood tells of a poem he wrote about sorrow as "the storehouse of wheat, barley, corn and tears. ... and I say to myself, 'Will you have sorrow at last? Go on, be cheerful, be stoic, calm. Yeah. Or, in the valley of sorrows, spread your wings.'"

He stops munching.

Says, somewhat matter-of-factly: "A man doesn't get wings until he comes into his own grief. Before that, he's like a chicken hopplng around on the ground."

The Explosion

The new men's movement has grown explosively since January 1990, when a Bill Moyers special on Bly, "A Gathering of Men," appeared on PBS. Transcripts and videocassettes of the show became bestsellers, as did tapes by Meade and other national movement leaders. "Iron John," in its seventh printing with more than 200,000 hardcover copies sold, according to a spokesman for the publisher, Addison-Wesley, is No. 1 today on both the *Washington Post* and *New York Times* bestseller lists. David Russell, associate editor of *American Bookseller* magazine, says men's books are now "one of the fastest growing segments of the new age or psychology book trade." Courses on men and masculinity have sprung up in hundreds of universities.

"I really think the '90s will be the decade of men, just as the '60s and '70s were the decades of women," says Chris Harding, editor of *Wingspan: Journal of the Male Spirit,* a quarterly tabloid whose circulation shot from 15,000 to 125,000 last year largely through the pro-bono efforts of an Arlington fund-raising consultant, Forrest Craver. "There's clearly bean a feminization of American culture as a result of the women's movement," says Craver. "Our wives and children often don't see our innate humanity, our beauty, our essence as men."

The last issue of Wingspan lists dozens of publications and events for men around the country, including a "New Warrior Training Adventure Weekend" in Wisconsin, "Drumming and Dancing for Men" in Massachusetts, "Brother to Brother' in New York, "Healing the Father Wound" in California and "Afro-American Males at Risk" in New Jersey. A recent "Grandfather Ceremony" at the Fairfax Unitarian Men's Council featured drumming on a "5 1/2-foot Thunderheart" drum. In this area, there are three large councils in Virginia, one in Gaithersburg and another in Baltimore. The Men's Council of Greater Washington, which Honnold started in June of 1988 witn 50 men, is the largest, with 2,000 members and 50 newcomers arriving for each monthly meeting.

Late one night in January, at the council's meeting in the Washington Ethical Society auditorium on upper 16th Street NW, Honnold sheds his Clark Kent image as he leads 500 men who are pounding drums and chanting. The sweating windows shake with rhythmic thunder that reverberates up and down the street as they raise Honnold—gyrating and clapping—high overhead and parade him about the room. Then group leaders circulate with large feathers and clay pots, wafting the smoke of burning sage into waiting face in what is termed a Native American ritual, designed to put you in touch with generations of male ancestors.

It's easy to make fun of this sort of thing, and many news reports have been highly skeptical. As a man never having experienced it before, you feel distinctly uncomfortable at first. Perhaps it's the arm-over-arm ouhmmm, ouhmmm, ouhmmm stuff they do, or the unexpected whiff of real paganism so jarring to the Judeo-Christian sensability, or just the group mentality with its slight suggestion of coercion. On the other hand, there's a kind of charming innocence here too, harking back to clubhouses and hiqh school locker rooms, and suddenly you remember the slap of wrestlers on the mats, the shouts of drill sergeants in the smoky pre-dawn chill down at Fort Jackson, or the way your bare feet toughened to the road gravel over the long summers when you were a kid running on it with your friends.

There are no women in the meeting, and reporters aren't allowed to take notes or names. On this particular night, two of the movement's national leaders, Robert Moore and Douglas Gillette, authors of another new bestseller, "King Warrior Magician Lover: Rediscovering the Archetypes of the Mature Masculine" (Harper San Francisco), are on hand to explicate their work. Moore is a Jungian analyst and professor of psychology and religion at Chicago Theological Seminary, and Gillette a "mythologist" and co-founder of something called the Institute for World Spirituality.

Moore lays out his theory of how these four archetypes are contained in what he calls "the hard-wiring of the masculine psyche," and Gillette backs him up with a cross-cultural slide show demonstrating how they have been historically present in men in many societies. They're enthusiastic about another new book; by State University of New York anthropology Prof. David D. Gilmore, "Manhood in the Making: Cultural Concepts of Masculinity" (Yale University Press), a scholarly overview suggesting that "manhood" in the form of toughness, aggression and stoicism is nearly universal,

The Jungian approach—with it's emphasis on archetypes, myths, spirituality and collective unconscious—is critical to the new men's movement, laying a basis for the assertions not only that men and women are different, but that men are a certain way and no other. Bly, for example, attacks what he calls "soft males," the "Woody Allen-types" who came of age alongside the feminist movement and who Bly thinks have left behind the necessarily "fierce" aspect of manliness. "Many of these men are not happy," he writes. "You quickly notice the lack of energy in them. They are life-preserving but not exactly life-giving."

Yet the new mythopoetic leaders, in rediscovering this ancient male "gender ground," as it's called, claim they're rejecting the John Wayne image as well. They're seeking something new, dusting off the old ferocious, enthusiastic energy of men and seeking to govern it with high moral purpose toward ends other than the control of women, the despoliation of the earth and the slaughter of populations. Moore and Gillette believe, as their book jacket puts it, that "mature masculinity is not abusive, domineering, or grandiose, but generative, creative and empowering of the self and others."

Thus Bly and Meade plan to lead a candlelight "grief march" at the Vietnam Veterans Memorial tonight to mourn the loss of life in the Middle East war. The Washington council, whose membership is divided on the war, is taking no offical position.

James Hillman, another movement leader who is a former director of studies at the C.G. Jung Institute in Zurich, thinks men are spending too much time turned inward, and in a meeting in San Francisco last March yelled at the audience of men that he's "outraged at you being outraged at your father, or your mother, and not being outraged about what else is happening in the world!" Craver, who has raised funds for the National Organization for Women, thinks "it's fine to stand for poetry, for increased mythological awarenes, {but} we must respond to the urgent challenges of our moment in history. Mature masculinity is defined in terms of stewardship of the earth, compassion, care for younger men."

Nevertheless, the mythopoetic movement seems more than anything a highly intellectualized personal enricchment program for upper-middle-class whites, who are seeking to solve their problems through mythology and poetry just as they might otherwise do in a psychiatrist's office or a 12-step program. While readers say that blue-collar men are involved, that wasn't evident in visits to council meetings here or in interviews with dozens of observers nationwide. The Moore-Gillette evening, leaving aside the smoke and drums, seemed like a graduate seminar at Harvard, only with many of the participants middle-aged and bearded.

One man, after the lecture, quizzed Moore closely on the intrinsic opposition between the male personality traits of Warrior ("the energy of self-disciplined, aggressive action" in the Moore-Gillette formulation) and Lover ("the energy that connects men to others and the world"). Then the man turned and explained enthusiastically to a reporter that he had improved since his Lover days, when he "had 14 relationships going. Now I've sent my Warrior down to set boundaries, and I'm happier. Of course, I'm not getting laid as much."

What About Black Men?

Only a few black men attended recent meetings of the Washington council, and Bly and other leaders are so concerned about the absence of blacks in the movement generally that they've started a "scholarship fund," setting aside a portion of the often considerable proceeds of meetings (today's gate may be in the $100,000 range) for this purpose. Craver has teamed wlth the Rev. Calvin Morris, professor of pastoral theology at Howard University School of Divinity, to put on a "Weaving the Male Soul" weekend here in March, which is expected to be attended by both blacks and whites.

And in May, a week-long retreat is being planned for the Washington area in which half of the teachers and participants are supposed to be black and half white. Bly, Meade and Hillman will teach, "but we haven't got the black teachers yet," admits Neil Froemming, an Arlington computer specialist who has branched out into mythopoetic drumming and storytelling in his spare time.

There are several ironies at work in all this. One, as Froemming points out, is that "black men are ahead of whites in mentoring youths in schools." Another is that African drumming and stories have become key parts of a white movement. Froemming himself just returned from a visit to West Africa to study these traditions, and in a recent meeting of the Washington council accompanied himself on the drum as he recounted a powerful Bantu legend about murderous soul-fighting between a young man and his father. Honnold learned to dance and drum as a graduate student observing initiation ceremonies in African villages.

Morris, the Howard professor, says that "father hunger" is a common theme for both black and white men, but that a wide gap remains between the two groups. "I'm not terribly comfortable with a lot of the terms," he says. "I'm not sure what they mean—the Warrior, and the Wild Man. In a small retreat he conducted with Craver, he says, "I used black poetry and prose and things out of African literature, but Bly and those guys don't do that enough. The movement needs to be more inclusive if it's not to be a lilly-white, segregated experience."

At one point, he says, a white movement leader shared an article with him about "Glory," the movie. "He was really excited about it, how the essayist looked at 'Glory' from some of these mythopoetic viewpoints. I was not as excited, and he said, 'Why?' And I said, 'What the guy does is focus 98 percent of the article on Colonel Shaw, who is the white commander of the black regiment. He didn't deal with the courage and dynamism and perseverance of the black soldiers.' For me, that was too narrow."

Charles Herring, founder of the Black Men's Health Project in New Jersey, puts it more starkly. Although his "Afro-American Males at Risk" seminar is listed in *Wingspan,* Herring says he's never heard of the mythopoetic men's movement. "We're dealing with real issues," he says, "like education, health, employment: and the criminal "justice system."

The Feminist Critique

Mystic brotherhoods with elaborate initiations have long held a fascination for American men. W.S. Harwood, writing in the *North American Review* in 1987, estimated that as many as one in five men belonged to at least one of the nation's 70,000 fraternal lodges, such as tne Odd Fellows, Freemasons and Knights of Pythias. They felt, he wrote, a "strange and powerful attraction" to the ritual. In his recent book, "Secret Ritual and Manhood in Victorian America" (Yale), Mark C. Carnes notes that this movement was primarily an urban middle-class phenomenon.

Most of those fraternities died out as America moved into the Depression and war in the '30s and '40s. As the iron grip of the patriarchal system came under siege from the feminist movement in the '60s, the men's movements that arose in support of feminism (still in business as the National Organization of Men Against Sexism, or NOMAS) and as a backlash to it (various men's and fathers' rights groups) were different—men banded together in support of a cause, not primarily to enjoy ritual and one another's friendship.

One starting point of today's mythopoetic movement was Bly's realization in the early '80s, after a decade of studying and teaching ancient matriarchal litera-ture— "the Goddess thing and the Great Mother," as he puts it—that his personal quest had less to do with women than with his hunger for a bonding he'd never had with his alcoholic father. After seeking out his father during the man's last years, Bly felt happier and began sharing his new theories on the lecture circuit. He struck a chord: Others had felt the same.

Many women have a lot to gain, according to Honnold, if their men can break away from all-too-typical patterns of alternating passivity and rage through "nurturing associations" with other men. "The vitality and enthusiasm for life that they experience increases their capacity for love with their wives and families," he says. "A man in touch with his own grief, and also with his exuberance, can be a more compassionate and loving man."

Theoretically, perhaps. But many women react with mild puzzlement, suspicion or shock. "Oh God, sick," says Betty Friedan, whose 1963 book "The Feminine Mystique" helped launch the feminist movement. "If I've ever heard a demonstration of threatened macho—this Wild Man thing—I mean, honestly. I'd hoped by now that men were strong enough to accept their vulnerability and to be authentic without aping Neanderthal cavemen." And Carol Bly, Robert's ex-wife, told the *Utne Reader* that she considers the movement "frightening. The goal of invoking 'exhilaration' through regressive behavior isn't what's needed."

Jean O'Barr, director of women's studies at Duke University, is skeptical of the mythopoetic approach, calling it intellectually "weak because the power anal-ysis is missing" and men still largely run the world. On the other hand, Molly Yard of the National Organization for Women says that "men reaching for community" in this way "is probably a good thing as long as they're a support group for one an-other and not hurting women."

Women professionals who counsel men tend to be more positive. "This Wild Man and Warrior stuff, I think it needs to be done," says Ruth Meaders, a psy-chotherapist at the Austin Men's Center in Texas. "It's a hell of a lot better than beating your wife or kicking your kids. That men are bonding with other men in a nonsexual way, instead of looking to women to complete them emotionally, is very healthy. It's opening up the anima in men, making them more approachable, more human, more honest."

Anima is the Jungian term for the feminine side of the male psyche, and Bly says male flowering includes nurturing it. In his theory, the final stage of male de-velopment (after bonding and breaking with mother, father and mentor in that or-der) is "marriage with the interior Queen. To marry the Queen you have to be a

King. To be a King means you're not accepting other people's opinions any more as to how you should run your own life."

Bly's daughters, he says, insisted on vetting his "Iron John" manuscript, and that he write, as he did in the preface, that his book "does not constitute a challenge to the women's movement. The two movements are related to each other, but each moves on a separate timetable." (According to *Wingspan* editor Harding, there's a "gender reconciliation movement" afoot, mainly in California, but so far the results aren't in.)

How, exactly, they relate remains a mystery that Bly doesn't explain, but Michael Kimmel, a sociology professor at the State University of New York and spokesman for NOAS, thinks "the mythopoetic movement has everything to do with women and feminism. It's a retreat from strong, powerful, assertive women. Many men at these gatherings that I've spoken to suggest that a significant amount of anger is expressed at mothers and ex-wives."

In Kimmel's view, Bly is right when he says that men feel powerless on an individual level, and that their feelings can lead to rage and violence against women. "But we don't want," he says, "to support each other in how valid is our anger against women. We need to work it out in a context that says the anger is inappropriate, not that it's appropriate." Bly, for his part, says this is what the mythopoetic movement does.

NOMAS co-chair Jack Straton, a physics professor at California State University, recalls attending a Bly workshop in Washington a few years ago and being disturbed that, among other things, "there was no mention that a considerable number of us are gay. ... And at one point Bly was saying that women criticize men for being too aggressive, but that 30,000 years ago if men hadn't been aggressive against lions, there wouldn't be any women today. And the entire room of 500 men roared like lions at that point. It scared the hell out of me. I sat there with my jaw open."

Another self-described "feminist man," Robert C. Brannon, professor of social psychology and director of the Center for Sex Role Research at Brooklyn College, says he was concerned at first about the apparent "nuttiness" of the mythopoetic movement, then surprised when it caught on big, but finally decided that it is "harmless as long as they're not buying into separatism. It's a matter of taste and style—our movement is more of a politically correct, lefty type atmosphere where people want to eat vegetarian."

Seriously, though, Brannon objects to this "soft male" stuff.

"I mean, the guy's a poet—what's so tough about him? We have the guts to stand up and oppose male privilege and power, so who are we calling 'soft,' and why?"

Into the Woods He loved me; from a swarm of rosy boys
Singled me out, as he in sport would say,
For my grave looks, too thoughtful for my years.

As I grew up, it was my best delight
To be his chosen comrade. Many a time
On holidays, we wandered through the woods . . . .
—Wordsworth, "The Excursion"

Bly quotes Wordsworth's tender memory of an old man who befriended him to underscore his point that, nowadays, "Grandfathers live in Phoenix or the old people's home," as he writes in "Iron John," "and many boys experience only the companionship of other boys their age who, from the point of view of the old initiators, know nothing at all."

In men's gatherings like today's, he says, "nothing happens unless there's some older men there. Nothing happens if there's just one or two generations." Typically, at some point during these gatherings, the older men are called forward to be applauded and honored.

"There's father hunger and grandfather hunger," Bly observes over his bacon and eggs, "and the grandfather hunger is so deep that we will even hire a total fake like Reagan because he looks like a grandfather. Actually, he's a regressed child."

As for his own father, "I was 55 years old and my father was in an old people's home before I bonded with him," he says. "He was off the bottle then, and I went to see him. ... Initiation was a little slow with us, wouldn't you say?"

The old boy is really getting going now, you might say. Good night's sleep. Full belly. "Often in our culture a bonding with the father begins in adolescence and then often is broken," he says. "In traditional cultures, adolescence is where the father teaches his son a craft. The son gets tuned to the frequencies of the adult male body. For thousands of years, our father was an incompetent arrowhead maker, and we sit with him watching him ruin all these arrowheads. Heh heh heh! He's taking a long time, then he finally gets one done! And all that time we're learning what it's like.

"But that's not happening today. In our culture, adolescence is where we decide our father is crazy and there's a big break. And we go into our work life and it stagnates for 20 years or so, and then at 48 or 50 the man begins to realize he doesn't know his father. I don't know how many men have said to me, 'My father's on his deathbed and I want him to tell me that he loves me.' And we have to say, 'It's very likely that you're not going to receive that.. . . '"

But you can always go out and roar in the woods.

Bly says: "Guy stood up in Colorado the other day and he said, 'I'm having a hard time with my wife' or 'my girlfriend' or something like that, 'and I'm 48 years old and I'm always getting put down. And, well, I went out in the forest a week ago and took off all my clothes and started to roar, I was going to look for a mountain lion and kill him.' "

He laughs again.

Continues: "Well, he never found a mountain lion, but something happened there when he took off his clothes and roared, and then the men clapped and men came up and hugged him. That Wild Man that Christianity and Judaism had tried to kill came out in that kind of form. It sounds silly. It wasn't silly. He broke through a whole lot of negative software by doing that.

"What's amazing about it is the men come up to him and say, 'That was fantastic what you did.' They'll support him. They don't shame him."

February 3, 1991

The Bachelors

They Say Power Corrupts—In Washington, it Also Seduces

ROXANNE ROBERTS

He's a bookworm who looks like Pat Paulsen. His idea of excitement is a long hike in the woods. He does impressions, for God's sake. He wears extremely bad ties.

David Souter is not your standard hunka hunka burning love. News that the 51-year-old judge had never married set off a flurry of speculation that the Supreme Court might be getting its first gay justice. When reporters unearthed three former girlfriends, it appeared instead that he is simply a scholarly workaholic too busy for romance.

Okay, so he's no Tom Cruise. No matter. He's a bachelor; more important, now he's a confirmed one. That makes him a hot ticket, the catch of the day, a Power Date. In short, Washington's idea of Extremely Eligible.

"His position will make him handsome to a lot of people," says Washington hostess Buffy Cafritz. "I can hear the footsteps marching already."

"David Souter better fasten his seat belt because this ain't New Hampshire—and it ain't like living with Mama," whooped Rep. Charlie Wilson of Texas, one of the Hill's legendary ladies' men. "They're going to burn his door down. I can't think of anyone—except a single president—who would be more of a prize."

Judge Souter's sudden appeal has nothing to do with the trappings typically associated with eligibility. It's not about looks, money or sex. Once you cross the Beltway, it's about power, influence and the ability to look presentable in a tuxedo.

"The trappings of their power are seductive to anyone," says tennis coach Kathy Kemper, who recently married an investment banker after years of dating high-profile bachelors. "It's very heady to be at a party with the person that everybody wants to talk to. You can get very spoiled if you're dating one of these guys."

Women used to come to Washington to marry a senator; now they come to run their campaigns. But dating a high-profile bachelor is still a shortcut to the best tables, the biggest parties, the stretch limos, the power networking—a personal and professional entree to haute Washington and beyond.

"A lot of women treat me differently," says single Rep. Dana Rohrabacher of California. "You're a star. It's like being a member of the football team in high school. You're part of the varsity team."

Which makes Souter Rookie of the Year.

Supreme Court Justice William Douglas went through four wives during his 36 years on the bench: He was unattached for 17 months after his first divorce, less than a year after his second. His third marriage, to 23-year-old Joan Martin, lasted three years; three weeks later, the 67-year-old Douglas married wife No. 4, Cathleen Heffernan, a 23-year-old cocktail waitress.

During the Nixon administration, Henry Kissinger, who was called the "world's most eligible bachelor" (Prince Charles notwithstanding), created a sensation every time he appeared in public with one of his celebrity dates—Gloria Steinem and Jill St. John. "After work I try to be with a beautiful girl—if possible not too intelligent," he once teased. His 1974 marriage to New York socialite Nancy Maggines made front-page headlines and retired his infamous little black book.

Washington's dating game changed in 1987 with the Gary Hart scandal. The presidential hopeful's fling with Donna Rice wasn't just a question of adultery—the press decided that the "character issue" was a part of the public's right to know, a fair test of political judgment. Everyone became fair game, even single men. John Tower's cabinet nomination battle last year turned into a referendum on wine, women and fooling around, despite the presence of his current girlfriend loyally at his side during the tussle. The message was not lost. Even bachelors buttoned up.

To hear today's bachelors tell it, life is all work and no monkey business. Most of them show up at social affairs without dates. Ask a question about their private lives and they get that deer-in-the-headlights panicked look in the eyes.

"I work when I'm in Washington," says Massachusetts Sen. John Kerry. "I'm at my desk at 11 at night. You can call me there."

"None of them—with the exception of one ... and Gary Hart, of course—are great womanizers," says Kemper. "They could be because they have so many women available to them. They could be the Warren Beattys of Washington. But they're really nice guys."

"In Washington," says Rohrabacher, "people are much more interested in politics than sex."

The Top Ten

Who's eligible?

The short answer: Any man still breathing, legally unattached, with privileged parking at National Airport.

The long answer is a complicated socio-political continuum, with variables:

Size of the club. The fewer members, the better. A single president or vice president would be considered the biggest catch (there hasn't been one since 1949, when Truman's 71-year-old veep, Alben Barkley, married 38-year-old Jane Hadley). A Supreme Court justice ranks slightly higher than a Cabinet member, followed by senators, representatives and everybody else.

Contender quotient. Is his star rising or falling?

Flutter factor. What kind of media attention does a public romance generate? Handicappers rank the 1990 lineup:

1. Souter. New kid on the block. Long-term job security. Former girlfriend Ellanor Stengel Fink describes him as "very funny, loves to tell stories, loves Robert Frost." Has one season to prove he's not a nerd.
2. Sen. Ted Kennedy. Keeper of the flame. Works hard and plays harder; he makes headlines just for breathing. Case in point: In a widely reprinted photograph, Kennedy was caught up close and personal with an unidentified brunette in a boat off St. Tropez, which prompted one wag to crack: "Well, Teddy, I see you've changed your position on offshore drilling."
3. Virginia Gov. Doug Wilder. Not only the nation's first elected black governor and oft-dropped name for the No. 2 spot on the 1992 Democratic presidential ticket, but cute, charming and funny to boot. Rumors of a romance with Patricia Kluge, glamorous barely-ex-wife of billionaire John Kluge, dominated Richmond cocktail parties this summer. "We're just friends," he tells reporters.
4. Nebraska Sen. Bob Kerrey. The ex-governor is a handsome Vietnam veteran with a yuppie presidential resumé. Flutter factor is up-up-up now that he's back together with his off-again, on-again love, actress Debra Winger; she makes him, potentially, an even bigger catch ("He used to go out with Debra, now he goes out with me").
5. Massachusetts Rep. Joe Kennedy II. Live the fantasy. Play touch football. Have kids with an overbite.
6. Virginia Sen. John Warner. The sixth husband of Elizabeth Taylor is considered a catch for ambitious socialites ("He used to be married to Liz, now ..."). Not noted for sparkling conversation, which doesn't appear to be a detriment.
7. Marlin Fitzwater. President Bush's press secretary is charming, self-effacing, a hotshot tennis player, and knows Gorby. Forget dessert: The once roly-poly Fitz is always loudly on a diet.
8. Maryland Rep. Tom McMillen. The former Rhodes scholar and pro basketball star is known for his height (6-11) and his penchant for willowy, awed young models. Issued a statement in March denying any romantic relationship with Trump Toy Marla Maples after it was revealed that Maples had lived at McMillen's Atlanta condominium for several months in 1985. Dates said to revolve around fund-raisers and other free food.
9. Massachusetts Sen. John Kerry. Heartthrob of the Left. Known for un-abashed ego and killer office hours; dates start at midnight. A tad forgetful—his divorce became final four years after his separation, a fact that reportedly came as a surprise to some of his frequent companions.

10.   Connecticut Sen. Chris Dodd. Smart, hip, likes to play. Gets invited to the good parties: "Saturday Night Live's" 15th-anniversary bash, for example, which he attended with buddy John Kerry. "He's the only guy in Congress who's a bad influence on Ted Kennedy," says Washington writer Bill Thomas.

The upcoming nuptials of CIA Director William Webster, 66, who was finally snagged by 33-year-old marketing executive Linda Clugston, took one of Washington's most popular bachelors off the market. Senate Majority Leader George Mitchell would normally make a "most eligible" list, but he keeps such a low, low profile that few know he's divorced—much less dating a senior administration official. Ditto for White House Counsel Boyden Gray.

It's hard to even name 10 high-profile single women in Washlngton. And as for other professions, even celebrity bachelors such as journalists George Will and Michael Kinsley still can't match the name-dropping allure of political bigwigs.

"Is Paul Nitze on the list?" asked journalist Nancy Dickerson. "He's a honey. He's rich, 83 and still skis."

Barracudas

They don't mind spending money. They throw dinner parties in honor of men they hope to meet. They muscle their way into glitzy parties. There is even rumor of a woman who bought an apartment at the Watergate in her campaign to snag Warner, who has a pied-a-terre in the complex.

"The guys refer to them as 'barracudas,' " says Kathy Kemper. "They usually tend to be middle-aged women, very well turned out, and they make a beeline for the powerful, eligible bachelor."

Georgetown hairdresser Robin Weir had three clients who wanted to meet and date Washington's Most Eligibles. All three women were over 40, loaded with money and afflicted with a serious flush of Power Hormones.

"My advice to them was to attach themselves to a cause—animal rights, beautify the city—that would give them a social conscience," says Weir. "Of course, buy seats or tables at balls and fund-raisers and invite anyone single who they want to get their little clutches into. And it doesn't hurt to drop by their offices to say hi."

He told them it was just like lobbying: "You go after an issue, you go after a man."

None of this is news to Alma Viator, spokeswoman for the National Theatre, who determines the guest lists and seating for opening-night performances and parties. She has had women call to ask for invitations—providing the perfect excuse to ask VIP bachelors to be their escorts. ("That way they can go fishing with an invitation to a high-profile event.") She has watched women change place cards at dinner.

But Viator's most memorable barracuda was a socialite who, already included on the guest list, would inevitably telephone before opening night.

"She would call me and ask which of these high-profile bachelors were coming—particularly Ted Kennedy, Chris Dodd or, if they weren't coming, John Warner," she says. "Then she would ask if she could sit by them during the show."

Viator says she usually sat her near if not next to the senators.

"Why not?" she says. "I'm a romantic."

The Dating Game Most women who date Top Ten bachelors bristle at any suggestion of political gold digging. Any motivation other than a quest for True Love is dismissed as sexist, dated and demeaning.

Okay, okay. What follows are some examples of how some really romantic women ran into really swell guys who just happen to be powerful, famous politicians—not that it matters, of course.

Passion for Politics: Lobbyists and staff members spend 12 hours a day hanging around politicians. The experience either sours them completely or makes anyone else dull by comparison. First-year staffers, says one Hill assistant, are always falling in love with their bosses.

Nancy Dickerson arrived in Washington in 1953 and landed a job as a secretary for the Senate Foreign Relations Committee. She met and dated Scoop Jackson, John Kennedy and Jack Brooks before her marriage to real estate tycoon C. Wyatt Dickerson; they were divorced in 1983. Nancy Dickerson was seated next to former deputy secretary of state John Whitehead at a dinner party at the Canadian Embassy in 1986. Turns out they had a lot in common. The couple married last year.

South Dakota Sen. Larry Pressler was considered a big catch before his 1982 marriage to Harriet Dent, a public relations secretary and volunteer on his Senate campaign. Ditto for Senate Minority Leader Robert Dole when he met Elizabeth Hanford, then deputy director of the White House Office of Consumer Affairs, in 1972. Hanford, already highly regarded in her own right, married Dole three years later; the two now preside as the quintessential Power Couple.

Current bipartisan alliances include Jackie Clegg—a legislative assistant to Sen. Jake Garn—and Dodd, who attended the "Les Miserables" opening with her; and Bush administration official Janet Mullins and Senate Majority Leader George Mitchell.

Mutual Interests: "Of course, tennis is always a great meeting ground," says Buffy Cafritz. "If the woman is a good tennis player, there's an opportunity there."

Tennis coach Kathy Kemper served and volleyed with a number of power bachelors and met most of Washington's big names as a result. The guest list for her Easter wedding to investment banker Jim Valentine included best man Pressler, who introduced the couple, and NBC White House correspondent Andrea Mitchell as her maid of honor.

Warner's frequent companion, Cathleen Magennis, rarely appears in public with the senator but is said to share his interest in both horses and politics.

Star Power: "I like Hollywood starlets," Henry Kissinger once observed. "They are even greater egomaniacs than I am. They talk about themselves all the time and I don't have to talk about myself."

Debra Winger met then-Gov. Kerrey while filming "Terms of Endearment" in Lincoln, Neb. Winger was a frequent visitor at the governor's mansion, then the couple split and the actress married and divorced actor Timothy Hutton. Kerrey and Winger are now back together and she is a financial backer of Kerrey's new health club in Omaha.

Both Alan Cranston and John Kerry have been spotted with actress Morgan Fairchild, who is frequently in Washinyton testifying on women's issues. Gossip columns most recently linked Kerry with actress/author/dolphin advocate/former First Daughter Patti Davis.

Hunting Grounds

Cozying up to Washington's top hostesses used to be the one sure-fire method of meeting the best single men. The importance of private dinner parties decreased, however, as women entered the work force and developed more social outlets. Nonetheless, an introduction over creme brule'e and brandy has sparked more than one romance.

Buffy Cafritz says she invites bachelors to bring a date to her dinner parties if she knows about a current relationship; otherwise, she asks them to come alone. After all, there are so few eligible men and so many women trying to meet them. A few of her friends have casually dropped a hint or two.

"They say, 'If you invite so and so, please include me,' " she says. "They say it with a laugh but it's a serious laugh."

When the Eligibles do venture out in public, they tend to favor haunts where they will be protected from their adoring public and the prying eyes of the media.

Private clubs such as Pisces in Georgetown and Desiree in the Four Seasons Hotel have launched more than one assignation and plenty of rumors. Hill bachelors have also been spotted living it up at the River Club and Anton's 1201 Club, both open to the public.

Watering holes near the Capitol are usually filled with Hill staffers. When congressmen do drop by, it's during the week; they fly to their districts on the weekends. Bullfeathers, on the House side of the Hill, gets a lot of representatives; the Tortilla Coast, on the Senate side, gets congressmen and an occasional senator.

Restaurants are traditional stalking grounds for both business and pleasure. The Monocle restaurant has served senators and representatives for the past 30 years; New Hampshire Sen. Warren Rudman brought in Souter the night his nomination was announced.

For the most part, his customers "want to be left alone," says owner John Valanos. "We make sure they're not bothered by outsiders."

Valanos admits that some low-key flirting does take place, but meeting a high-powered bachelor in a public place is more difficult now than it was a few years ago. "Senators are more discreet," he says. "Their faces are more recognizable than most of the members."

Or perhaps they were sobered by the GQ magazine article published in February. La Brasserie restaurant was named as the site of not one but two bachelor bacchanals: In 1985, Kennedy and Dodd allegedly made drunken advances to one of the waitresses; in 1987, a waitress said she discovered Kennedy and an attractive blond lobbyist in flagrante delicto on the floor of a private dining room.

Kennedy's office always issues a standard response: "It is our policy never to comment on this endless gossip and speculation."

Sacrifices

There are women who complain that the press "goes wild" when they show up on the arm of a VIP bachelor, which they consider an invasion of privacy for both the man and the woman.

"If the public official makes a public announcement, then it's fair game," snapped one woman dating a prominent senator. "The rest is no one's business."

The press attention, she charges, discourages "positive" relationships. "It destroys any sense of private self they have. I think it really borders on indecent."

Still, the Most Eligibles are out there, smiling bravely for the cameras.

"I get tired of my colleagues saying they sacrifice for the common good," says Charlie Wilson. "When, in fact, you couldn't blow them out of office with dynamite."

October 3, 1990

The Flings Of Summer

What Looks Delicious on the Boardwalk May
Seem Ridiculous Back in the Boardroom

RON GASBARRO

Summer love. Or sometimes, as the Beach Boys would say, a bummer love. Would someone be so kind as to softly hum Percy Faith's "Theme From a Summer Place"?

Now, many of you will fall in love over the summer. Typically, this will occur in a mountain resort, behind a sand dune or when you stop at the top of the Ferris wheel. In other words, while you are on summer vacation.

Many of you do not get three months off as you did when you were younger. Many of you are lucky to get two weeks off with pay—and hope your boss does not hang a beeper to your bikini. So—if single and over 30—you will want to find true love at least once before your first heart attack.

Excuse me? You've been hurt, you say? You've been lied to?

You end up spending all your money keeping in touch via long-distance telephone after a summer fling. Add in someone's brilliant idea to fly to Akron to visit this person and there goes your IRA contribution for the year and three payments on your Volvo.

And for what?

Can a summer romance ripen into true love? The answer is, yes.

Mr. Right vs. Mr. Right-Now

During non-vacation times, we have to be more pragmatic than romantic. We do not blow our mortgage money sending roses and bottles of French champagne to paramours. If we do, our charge card gets revoked.

But on vacation, we throw aside our shoulder pads and power ties for a bottle of suntan lotion and a daiquiri. Throw in a goofy smile and the stage is set to meet someone new.

"When we go on vacation, we psych ourselves up to get away from our routines and our schedules," says Alvin S. Baraff, a clinical psychologist and director of Washington's MensCenter. "That feeling of freedom is like when we were kids, sprung from school for the summer," he says. "Only people don't have much time today and try to cram in as much as possible on vacation."

And the hopes of a summer romance can lurk in the backs of our brains as well as Points South.

"The fact that you are meeting people wearing a minimal amount of clothes, in itself, is a turn-on," says Baraff, author of the soon-to-be-released book "Men Talk" (Dutton).

"Summer romances can be so addictive," says romance novelist Donna Hill, who has written such scorchers as "Indiscretions" and "Last Year, Last Chance,"and who pens articles for *True Romance* magazine. "In the summer, one is less inhibited. The sun brings out the best in people, makes them more attractive, whether it's because they are more vibrant or because the clothes are skimpier."

Our urban persona might define Mr. (or Ms.) Right as, say, a dermatologist with a BMW. On vacation, our fantasies take over.

"It's wonderful to come in from the hot city and suddenly start dating somebody totally different, like a fisherman," says Robin Soslow, author of the cookbook, "It Was on Fire the Last Time I Checked It." Soslow lives in Ocean City and has seen much of what goes on, romantically, in a resort setting.

"To you, this fisherman is so down-to-earth and he captures his own food and lives on his boat," continues Soslow. "And he really wants to live this all-natural type of life. If you can accept this, fine. But the problems begin when your corporate mentality takes over and you start wanting him to be the Head Fisherman or to start His Own Fisherman Company."

So, be aware that you have met somebody very different from your regular life. Sometimes it's that difference that is zingy and alluring. And sometimes these charming idiosyncrasies can later become major irritations. Ever try to get the smell of freshly caught bluefish out of satin sheets?

She Lusts You, Yeah, Yeah, Yeah

On vacation, what are your criteria in evaluating a potential date? Try: 1) Does he/she look good? 2) Does he/she like margaritas? 3) If male, has he mooned anyone in the last week? If female, has she lost her top in the surf at least once?

If, 24 hours after meeting, you stupidly murmur the "L" word, remember you don't mean "I love you," but rather "I lust you." Then quickly jam a flip-flop in your mouth.

"I know this woman lawyer who once fell in love with a dude at the beach,"says Rick Lippman, president of Corkscrew Press, a Los Angeles publishing company. "He made her howl with his recycled Greaseman routines. She told him and all her friends that she was terminally in love. She insisted that this Mr. Right meet her K Street crowd the next week. Out of his natural environment, his hippie-dippy antics went over about as well as month-old Thrasher's french fries."

Where do people go wrong when it comes to summer romances? How come what looks delicious on the boardwalk looks ridiculous back in the boardroom?

"The problem is that summer flings are usually based solely on a physical attraction," says Baraff. "The two people don't really get to know about the other's backgrounds and interests. And when the summer romance quickly develops into a more exclusive relationship, like an engagement, the relationship can get into real trouble."

Like the man who shared a beach house with a female friend. By the end of the summer, he asked her to date only him, even though he lived in Philadelphia and she in Washington. By Christmas, they were married and the bad feelings began. Two years later, he is in therapy, finally getting enough self-confidence to get a divorce.

"It would have been better for them to continue to date and have summer fun, but to take a much longer time to go steady and even longer to get engaged," suggests Baraff.

Don't Let the Sun Catch You Crying

On vacation, you are more daring and thus willing to take more chances. That's usually not the way you are in real life and any lifelong relationship—should you want one—is based on how the two of you are in real life.

"You meet someone the first day, have sex with them all week long and now you're back in your office starry-eyed and ready to make a life-change based on that meeting," says Baraff.

What's the right thing to do?

"Before you go away, realize that you're going away to have fun, not to meet the person of your dreams," says Baraff. "Second, do not make lifelong decisions based on a very brief meeting. Third, if you think something is clicking, allow some time after vacation to get to know each other."

And on the darker side.

"Before you get in over your head, find out about the guy," says Robin Soslow. "How does he relate to his friends? What do they think of him? There's also drug addictions and alcoholism to worry about in resort areas. Such things are easy to hide in party-till-you-drop atmospheres."

Use the autumn to your advantage in getting to know the other person. Meet for a rainy weekend in Manhattan and tour museums. Be romantic but have no expectations based on the summer before.

Should you fly off to his or her city for a rendezvous?

"If your expectations are realistic, why not?" says Donna Hill. "But if your expectations are greater than the reality of the situation—the reality being that you met him or her briefly on vacation and that's all—you can end up being disappointed."

"Sometimes you are so in love, it's like you're on a drug," says Rich Lippman. "Then she calls you at your office the next week and you think, 'Do I really know this person?'"

The best advice Lippman gives is, "Go into any summer fling with your eyes open—and your zipper shut."

July 8, 1991

The Ecstasy and the Agony

MARJORIE WILLIAMS

You, he said. You think of getting married like you start out with a certain amount of capital, and that's all you're ever going to get, and you start to spend it the day you get married.

By which he meant emotional capital, of course, and he was right: It was exactly what I believed. My parents had divorced after 35 years together. I must not get married, I thought, until I found myself in a relationship so manifestly rich that 35, 40 years, a lifetime could not spend it.

It was a new idea to me that marriage could be a source of capital, instead of the thief of my hard-won store. It was the concept that changed everything.

I've been to a wedding on a farm, in 1969, where the bride wore a diaphanous white dress and no shoes and the groom wore a mismatching suit and no shoes and a funny Daniel Boone hat, and the service took place in a cornfield. The couple were friends of my best friend Julie's parents, and after the ceremony the groom took me and then Julie on motorcycle rides. I was 11, and the day's novelties—seeing what I took to be actual hippies, and being alone with the groom, holding loosely as I dared to the warmth of his back, and riding a motorcycle, which would surely have horrified my mother—still carry a wild romance for me.

I've been to a wedding on a golf course newly carved out of a bluff overlooking the San Diego Freeway, with golf carts still whirring toward the clubhouse as the bride and groom came down the aisle, and a stiff Santa Ana worrying the huppah. Later, inside the clubhouse, the groom's mother gave a toast, holding microphone and cigarette in the same manicured hand.

I've been to the wedding of my former high school boyfriend, who got married a year out of college on the bank of a lake in Upstate New York. Everyone, including me, seemed to think it made fine sense for me to be his best man: The bride and I had become friends by then too, and he was something like family. Hours after the ceremony I found myself sitting alone on the damp grass, drunk, under a whirling sky. I carefully timed my retreat to bed so I wouldn't have to talk to anyone on the way.

I've been to the wedding of close, close friends radiant with the rightness of their marriage. The wedding of my college roommate, who married her boyfriend of seven or eight years with her usual air of having known since she was 6 exactly what she was destined for. The wedding of my sister, 13 years ago; of my father, only two years back; of near-strangers who assumed an immediate definition for me through the intimacy of their celebration.

But a lifetime of going to weddings, I am learning, is scant preparation for having one. Doing one? Throwing one? There is not even a verb that relates the bride and groom to their wedding, except for planning, a correct but wildly incomplete description.

As I write this, our wedding is five months off. We allowed 10, from the time we got engaged: Tim and I have lived together for two years—there was no rush, and we had a shared instinct that we would need the time. To assemble all those details without having to drop the other threads of our lives, for one thing. But also to enjoy the planning, to meet each piece of it consciously and with care.

We learned, quickly, that there is a genial conspiracy in the world toward nuptial hysteria. Not until October? people said. That hardly counts as engaged. There was something . . . plodding, it was implied, about allowing time to experience this promise we were making. You should do what we did, they said, and:

Elope.

Get married next week at a friend's house.

Run away and get married in a cave in Hawaii.

Decide not to get married.

For some couples, the decision to strip their wedding to essentials may be their own way of preserving or heightening its meaning. But the advice cones through as a call to urgency. Hurry up, hurry past; the covert message is that marriage is just too frightening an undertaking to enter into deliberately.

Paradoxically, these scoffers-at-ceremony have a lot in common with the camp that favors drowning a wedding in oceans of ritual and formality: They share the urge to avert their eyes from the occasion's meaning.

All weddings, I think, are ruled by the tension between ritual and meaning. Rituals hold meanings, of course: You cut the cake, you dance the first dance, in the South you send guests home with a boxed piece of groom's cake, to slip under their pillows for dreams; you say the vows, you break the glass, you toss the flowers. All of these practices are containers of meaning, but every person who gets married has a choice: to use the ritual to keep the meaning contained, or to pour out the meaning, and taste it.

For a man, the invitation to evade his wedding's meaning comes wrapped in the generic packaging of stereotype: the near-universal suggestion that men's lives aren't supposed to be all that rich in emotional meaning. Tim is routinely told by friends (especially married ones) that he should resign himself to being a pawn at his own wedding.

For a woman, the invitation to distraction is more lavishly seductive. There is the tradition that brides should fret, making up in a surfeit of nervous feeling for the groom's supposed stoicism; there is all the pressing hokum of the bridal magazines: I am urged to "start working on" my choice of bouquet three months in advance.

I still can't make up my mind about the bridal magazines. I've bought them, to be sure, skulking compulsively into magazine stores, approaching the cash register with the studied nonchalance of the porn store habitue. And they are a kind of pornography, promoting as they do the whole aspect of weddings that objectifies the happy pair on the most important day of your life; that especially objectifies the bride, her beauty (brides are always beautiful) and her body.

On the other hand, you can find between all those ads, as you find it few other places, the earnest message that something important is afoot.

But of course, I buy them for the ads. For a woman in her thirties, marrying more than 10 years after she first read *The Second Sex,* wedding porn has a certain added charm—the one-time-only offer of legitimacy for the abandoned, forbidden sweets of girl-dom.

Peau de soie, I find myself saying, the words hilarious but tasty on my tongue. And tulle, and stephanotis. Will I buy little white shoes swathed in satin? How preposterous. With little covered buttons, maybe? What fun.

At the bridal salon, mothers and daughters contend over dresses in the international language of mother-daughter aggravation. Over necklines, to be specific, the daughters yanking the bodices down to the cleavage, the mothers turning to the saleswomen, those masters of diplomacy, to suggest that the lines of the dress are lovely, but perhaps a little veiling . . . here, above the bodice—and up to the neck—like so. Sit there long enough, waiting your turn to be conducted into one of the dressing rooms and back to another century, and these exchanges take on an uncanny sameness. A daughter tries on confection after confection, all of them designed to make her look gorgeous, until finally she is unlucky enough to hit on one that does nothing for her. Nine times out of 10, this is the one that brings the other out of her chair in admiration.

Standing in front of a long mirror, surrounded by other brides-to-be, I can usually remember that this part is simply the costume.

At other times, it seems to me the ultimate act of self-definition: As I marry this person, who am I? I know I am not ruffles, not beads; I know I am exposed shoulders, a bit of swagger. This one is definitely too fussy, this one perhaps too severe. Goldilocks in the dressing room, I seek the one just right.

My older sister, like my mother, got married at 23. My sharpest memory is of knocking over a Coke bottle while helping her with her hair, nearly splashing it down the front of her dress. She jumped out of range in the nick of time, but when I think of it, more than a decade later, my heart can still beat faster with fear.

Such is the terrible weight of weddings. I've watched perfectly level-headed friends unravel under the pressure; I've watched as the smallest things began to take on otherworldly significance for them. (Can you believe my sister-in-law wants to buy bridesmaids' shoes with a lower heel?) I never understood until now that it is because there is no easily found seam between the two meanings of marrying, the day's events and the life's commitment. Hence the parade of bridal anxieties: The trivia of menu planning (and we are talking trivial here—two kinds of mustard or three, to go with the ham?) gives way to the largest issues in our relationship, now out on the table as the first work of our marriage; in the next moment, these seem less pressing than how long the musicians should play.

There's only so much meaning, it seems, a person can stand.

Since I got engaged, I've learned that people—intimates, acquaintances, near-strangers, family —have large reactions to the inherent emotional power of this thing Tim and I are doing. Tides of response rush at or past us, some of it very intimate and dear to us, some of it absurdly misplaced. It seems a function of people's own marriages or weddings, of the unknown roles in which people have cast us, as people always will. But for every sudden sting or acid comment that must be turned aside, every Don't worry, you can always get divorced, there is an assertion of love, a claim on my friendship or his, that cannot go unmet.

Of course, any wedding is two weddings, if you add in the social event taking place for the four or 60 or 300 guests. Weddings are one of our last great vessels of clannishness, rigorous schools of cultural education.

What's more, even if the bride and groom marry by themselves, in a Vegas wedding chapel or a lean-to on the tundra, they never marry alone. Every wedding is at least a little haunted by the children they were. Whether or not they avail themselves of it, a wedding is each bride and groom's most explicit chance at our common, three-word heart's desire: Look at me. And the child's experience of that wish—whether it was expressed or fulfilled, whether it was answered too much or too little—is present in the decision to elope as surely as it is present in the happy exhibitionism of a couple who marry before a throng.

One friend, the radiant one, confided that she hated the idea of holding her reception in a single large room. For her, and the child she had been, there was unbearable tension in demanding that her guests focus so constantly on her and her business of the day; far better to give them choices, other rooms, other (possibly more interesting?) things to do.

But she and her groom did it anyway, deliberately, making themselves the shining center of a great big room full of their pasts. And so her ghost of former years was only a very faint presence and, I thought, a grateful one.

Halfway toward October, the tide of wedding hysteria sucks ever more strongly at our ankles. With each decision we make that successfully steers away from reflex, whether over a grand or a trivial matter, we feel a surge of pleasure to find ourselves still in control, still masters of the event instead of its objects.

One decision I made was to ask a very close but relatively new friend to be my only attendant. An old friend from college would have been an easier choice (I was her maid of honor four years ago), but I wanted with me someone who knows me exactly as I am today. Another, mutual, decision was that we would serve at the reception only food Tim and I both liked. (Whether the salmon constitutes an exception is a whole other story.) A third was to find a site only blocks from our house, for the sake of making our promise with feet planted in the center of our lives—not in some glade, however gorgeous, unrelated to our every day.

In each decision there is a moment of stopping to will away the automatic impulse: to try to look beyond what background or family tradition or social convenience or sex stereotypes or Checklist for a Perfect Wedding say we should do.

Sometimes our decisions coincide with the advice of these oracles. Some wedding ritual, I have decided, may help me by remaining just that: an underpinning of custom to lift us all past the anxiety of family reunion. For part of what my wedding will mean to me is seeing my parents together, in the same room, for the first time in more than four years; a room in which my stepmother will also be a welcome guest. Everyone will behave well. But the prospect touches in me, as weddings always do, every familiar bruise. I am astonished at my hubris in marrying as long as we both shall live. I have to concentrate to remember my confidence that I have learned how to compound interest.

If it will ease this reunion to rely sometimes on what the rule book says, so be it. But I want to know that in making each decision, I have at least uncorked the bottle and sniffed at the essence inside. We have not decided what vows to say, for example, but we liked the advice we got from the old friend who has agreed to marry us: Even if couples want a standard ceremony, he asks that they also, privately, write their own vows, to make sure they can articulate to themselves and each other what promise they are making. In the same way, I want to know I have teased what meaning I can from all the other rituals of the day.

When I think about my wedding, some of my wishes are things that are only partly in my control. Ways I would like people to be with me, and connections I hope to make—with my sisters, for example, or with particular friends. But my biggest wish is one whose fulfillment is entirely up to me. It is that between now and October, I cultivate in myself a generous enough appetite that I can take it, or let it, all in.

June 3, 1990

Sisterly Connections

BARBARA MATHIAS

Bonnie Dommert says she will never forget when she was 7 years old and she received a letter that congratulated her for being accepted to a school for the mentally retarded.

"The letter was typed on official paper, so I didn't catch on until I read the P.S.—'Are you potty trained?'"

By that time, the authors of the prank, her two older sisters, were falling on the floor laughing and Bonnie was in tears. "It was so demeaning," says Bonnie with more wisdom than hard feelings. "They always treated me like I was the baby."

With 20-some years of such tricks and intimidations, Bonnie never felt she was very close to her two sisters until recently, when she moved to Washington after college. Now she feels an emotional bond that tugs and stretches all the way to Pennsylvania and back to South Carolina where her sisters live.

Sisters. They can be as mean as any big brother or as loving as the most endearing mother. They can be so alike in personality and style that folks can't tell them apart, or so totally opposite that everyone swears they came from different households. No matter what the discrepancies may be, most are still, as Rudyard Kipling put it, "sisters under their skin."

Ruth Shapiro from Silver Spring has felt different from her sisters for most of her 75 years. Whether she was waterskiing or playing hockey as a young woman, Ruth's daring would frighten her mother and "particularly put off" her two older sisters, Shirley and Esther.

The second youngest of six children, Ruth grew up near Coney Island and was a competitive swimmer like her younger brother. "My sisters could swim, but they would never consider competing," says Shapiro, who five years ago won the 500-yard freestyle in the Maryland Senior Olympics.

They also didn't like her excelling in school or her independence in electing to go to college, something unheard of for the older girls. "And yet it was Esther who paid my lab fee in college," notes Ruth, who now holds a master's degree in social work from Columbia University.

There were smaller, nagging differences over lifestyles and personalities that lasted many years: Esther and Shirley put more emphasis on money and how they dressed and decorated their homes; Ruth couldn't have cared less. And there was that certain edge, a coolness that is too hurtful to recall or describe.

Then shortly before Esther's death seven years ago, the relationship between Ruth and Shirley began to noticeably improve.

"Shirley had such a hard time growing up," explains Ruth. "Neither of my parents were well and she had to work with my father, who lost his job in the Depression. When he died, Shirley was left without a job and a lot of responsibility was on her shoulders.

"She never had the nurturing in the early years from our parents like I did from her and Esther. That's all that I can remember now, the wonderful nurturing those two gave me."

Gail Fisher, a clinical social worker in Silver Spring, is fascinated with the bond between sisters. "There's relatively little written about it," says Fisher, who conducts evening workshops on adult-sister relationships at A Woman's Place, a women's counseling and resource center in Rockville, "and yet it is often central to a woman's present-day relationship at home, with friends or in her job.

"It helps when a woman looks at her relationship with her sister and she sees patterns in her life. It also helps her to open up and allow herself to change." For example, says Fisher, a woman whose husband always harasses her recalls that when her sister constantly harassed her she had the same timid response she has now.

Sister relationships (like all sibling relationships) are formed by a combination of many factors, one of the most important being whether the parents were involved, absent or living in an emotional vacuum.

"From birth to 18 months, trust is made for the child, often according to how much time the parent had to give," explains Fisher. "We know those who are always seeking what they didn't have, that it is often derived from those formative months. These are usually needy people who do not have good sibling relationships. It is considered a rivalry that never stops."

Sisters may experience totally different parenting, simultaneously or at other times in their upbringing. The oldest daughter, for example, may have enjoyed her parents when there were fewer worries, while the younger daughter had to fend for herself because of her parents' growing estrangement over money, infidelity, or whatever the issue may have been.

Other factors for producing different sisters, according to Fisher, are family size, placement and geographic or cultural differences.

There are exceptions, but generally in large families, the oldest girl is more likely to be the nurturer and more responsible. Often, unlike her younger sisters, she isn't interested in marrying and having a family, says Fisher, because she feels she already has done her work. As adults, this may cause problems when one sister is career-minded and the other wants to stay home and raise a family. They may feel worlds apart and threatened by each other's different goals in life.

As for geographic/cultural influences, Fisher cites the example of a sister raised in Europe, where her father was stationed with the Army, who is significantly different from her sister who grew up in a small town in the United States years later.

"Sisters also play different roles at different times in their lives," says Fisher. "As children or adults they can identify with each other or separate from each other. They assign tasks to each other, such as 'You are in charge of housework, I do gardening.'

"Or they translate for each other, such as 'Don't talk to Dad when he chews his cigar; stay away from mom, she looks depressed.' "

It's also not uncommon for the most differing sisters to suddenly commiserate over their mother and father, especially when they both feel their parents "are off the wall," says Fisher.

Though Fisher's aim is to teach women how to be comfortable with themselves and their sisters, she emphasizes that, "A healthy sister relationship is not intensely loyal or intensely giving. If it's too much, it doesn't work well."

That's a difficult lesson that even Florence Nightingale, the greatest of givers, was slow to realize. Through much of her adult life, "Flo" was emotionally smothered by her older sister Parthe and her hysterics when she didn't get Flo's attention.

Whenever Flo became too independent, working in the hospitals away from home, Parthe's health would fail and her sister would unhappily have to come running home—mostly because their father insisted on it. Parthe's whole sense of being was wrapped up in Flo, whose life she adored, but couldn't emulate. Neither sister benefited from such neediness.

Sisters also can cause embarrassment, especially those in and out of the limelight. Oprah Winfrey recently made the gossip columns, admitting that at age 14 she had a baby that died right after birth. It was a painful experience then and now, but Oprah gained some dignity by reportedly revealing it before her half-sister, Patricia Lloyd, planned to spread the news herself.

Most of us marvel at and love to watch the famous sisters: Anne Landers and Dear Abby giving advice without stepping on each other's egos; the lifelong rivalry between Olivia de Havilland and Joan Fontaine (when they were youngsters, Olivia broke Joan's collarbone in a wrestling scrap); the temptation team of Joan and Jackie Collins, and the beautiful Hemingway sisters, who do as they please and still remain friends, one posing nude for Playboy, the other staying home with her babies.

But one woman's fame isn't necessarily shared by her sister. British Prime Minister Margaret Thatcher has a sister, Muriel, who apparently lives a much quieter life. It's not surprising to learn that Muriel spent much time with Mommy in the garden, while Margaret was favored by her father, a local politician. Muriel is a trained physiotherapist, but that's about all outsiders know of her. One isn't even sure where she lives or what her political leanings might be. But perhaps that's the way Muriel prefers it.

Whether sisters are 10 months or 10 years apart they can perceive themselves differently, especially in relation to their parents and each other, says Fisher.

Anne Sexton, the beautiful, troubled poet who took her life at 46, always felt she was the "unwanted third daughter," abandoned and unloved by her parents. her older sister Beatrice, however, describes Anne as the one who was the center of attention and was even over-indulged by their parents.

Whether accurate or not, families like to label their children, says Fisher, and those labels can remain far into adulthood, often affecting the quality of the relationship between sisters. Sisters at 3 years or 55 can be "the little devil," "the big talker," or "the responsible one." Heaven help them if they should try to switch or change these roles.

A Washington woman in her middle-forties recalls that all her life she was "the bookworm" and her sister, who is six years older, was "the pretty one."

"We drifted further apart when my sister married right out of high school and started a family and I went to college. Later she was intimidated by my having a career, I was intimidated by her good looks."

Finally, five years ago, the two sisters planned a vacation together where they shared an ocean cottage with their families. Both were extremely apprehensive—after all, they thought they were total strangers, but they discovered differently.

"Every night we took long walks along the beach and somehow we were able to put the past behind us. We actually talked about our parents objectively and were able to tell each other how we felt."

Unfortunately sisterly amends often aren't possible until there is a great loss or a major change in the family. Katharine Hepburn was a carefree tomboy at age 13, then she discovered the body of her 15-year-old brother, Tom, who had hung himself, and her whole identity changed.

With her parents devastated for years to come, Katharine took over the parenting role, creating a bond between her younger sisters and brothers that persisted through a lifetime.

A Maryland woman grieving from her father's sudden death a month ago is stunned by how helpful her sister was the last days of his life.

"I was always the close one to my father. Now she did all this for him and I realize how much I care for her, but I am also struggling with how envious I am. I couldn't get there in time for him and she could."

Changes in family patterns also can be threatening to sisters. One Washington woman believes her mother's early death contributed to her not being close to her two older sisters. "I was only 19 when mother died, but by that time none of us had been close to our father and we all drifted apart. I don't think it's a coincidence that we've all had problems with our marriages and intimacy."

Self-described as "the hinge" between one sister who is "hot-headed" and the other who considers herself "the black sheep and an outsider," this woman is tired of the family labels that have kept them apart for nearly 40 years.

"We've all changed over the years, but it's as if we are afraid to get close. As if we think it would invade on our individuality."

With a little bit of work, sisters can not only change roles, they can equalize them. Katie Schultz from Chevy Chase, Md., always had felt like a parent to her sister, Karen, who is six years younger. While growing up in South Bend, Ind., Katie was "the one who knew where the ribbons were to do the ponytail," and who always included Karen when she went to the movies with her friends.

"I grew up guarded," says Ratie. "Karen felt more freedom to shout family secrets to the wind."

When the two sisters married within a year of each other, their closeness was replaced by their spouses. Soon the gap widened as their differences became markedly geographic and economical. As an IBM manager working in Washington, Katie has an attractive wardrobe, a full-time housekeeper and a hectic travel schedule. Karen, who is a speech pathologist and midwife in Oklahoma City, spends most of her leisure time enjoying the outdoors.

The sisters soon realized they had different rules and expectations of their children, a sore point at times, but clearly a function of economics.

"Her children's allowances are conditional on the chores they do," explains Katie. "Not my children. I don't like it, but it's difficult to make children do things when there's always been a housekeeper around to do it.

"For years there were real tensions and problems, but somehow we have integrated all the differences and we're finally relating adult-to-adult," observes Katie.

Much of that change is due to their decision to meet every June at a women's fitness camp in Colorado, where the two sisters hike and climb mountains for a week.

"It took us 13 years of marriage to give ourselves permission to do that," says Katie. "And it's been great ever since.

"We've been through difficult times of irritating each other. But I know that if I ever needed Karen, she would never let me down. She's the best friend I've ever had."

May 15, 1990

Looking For 'Higher Love'

DON OLDENBURG

Craig Comstock describes himself sexually in rather ordinary terms. Nothing kinky. No earthshaking boasts. No risky business. "I'm kind of a normal heterosexual," says the 52-year-old writer, who lives in Mill Valley, Calif., across the Golden Gate Bridge from San Francisco. "Pretty normal background. Married for 13 years and then was single after that....I lead a very monogamous sexual life.

But don't let the modesty fool you. When pressed, Comstock admits matter-of-factly that his sexual beliefs will arouse "utter fascination" among friends and acquaintances; women especially catch on to the possibilities. His sexual savoir-faire leaves most people feeling as though they learned about sex from the birds and the bees. There are those who contend that the sexual philosophy he espouses may be the antidote to the confusion, danger and dysfunction that taint sexuality in the '90s.

Comstock's sexual conquests, you see, aren't so much of the flesh as of the spirit. He is one of a small but growing number of American aficionados who embrace a sexual way of life that is being called by various names, among them "sacred sexuality," "enlightened sexuality and spirituality" and "higher sex."

In simpler terms, it is a trend toward holism in the bedroom. Its devotees seek full integration of mind and spirit in intercourse. In a culture that creates a mythos of multiple orgasms, fulfillment for them comes beyond orgasm, where sexuality and spirituality are momentary united in rapture.

"You don't have to have any special gifts or any arcane belief or unusual prowess of any kind," reassures Comstock, whose education in higher sex began in 1984 while coaching one of its leading practitioners, Margo Anand, on writing a manual about sexual ecstasy. Defined as "extreme emotional exaltation" that overpowers the senses, and lifts one into a trancelike state, ecstasy has since become almost second nature in his sex life, he says.

"That's the way it can be for any one who wants to do it," says Comstock. "It offers a wonderful alternative to puritanical avoidance or fascination with sex on the one hand and mindless sleeping around on the other hand.

For Anand, the sacred sexuality trend is the Western love child of tantra.

Ancient mystical Hindu teachings that include sex as a path to enlightenment, tantra often scandalized mainstream Eastern society in its day by rebelling against sexual repression. Anand, a French psychologist who has studied self-development, yoga and meditation, felt an affinity to the tantric tradition. "I had a very high experience in my love life early on," she says, "so I knew sexuality was going to be a path to liberation for me."

Keeping the tantra's ecstatic goal and some of its techniques, Anand designed Western-oriented training she calls "SkyDancing Tantra." It teaches methods of massage, visualization, breathing, ritual, movement, fantasy and lovemaking to enhance the pleasure of sex and deepen intimacy. The detailed manual that resulted from her research, titled "The Art of Sexual Ecstasy," has sold "very well, exceeding all expectations, and has gone into paperback now," says a spokesman for its publisher, Jeremy P. Tarcher Inc. He adds that the book also has transcended the initial stigma that had some bookstores displaying it behind the counter or in shrink wrapping.

Anand says more than 3,000 people have learned how to find bliss in sexuality at workshops offered through five SkyDancing Institutes in Europe and and California. last week, she led a three-day session with 70 participants in North California, where the lessions ranged from duplicating the orgasmic effect without sexual contact to relaxation during intense states of arousal. But despite techniques with names such as "Riding the Tiger" and "The Butterfly," she emphasizes that her seminars aren't orgies—there's no nudity and participants aren't pushed beyond the limits of comfort, she says.

"They begin to understand that sexuality is a holistic event," says Anand. "The body is relaxed, the heart is open and trusting, and the mind is at peace. Then you can move from phsyiological pleasure to delight in the heart to ecstasy in the spirit."

Interviewing people about their experience of "mystical union" during sexual intercourse for his upcoming book, Georg Feuerstein heard such descriptions as: "I fell into the fullness that had arisen in and between us" and "my body was disappearing." That kind of ecstasy, he says, is the real sexual revolution, not the liberation of libidos that occurred in the '60s.

"I feel the sexual revolution has been exremely incomplete," says Feuerstein, a Sanskrit scholar whose book "Sacred Sexuality: Living the Vision of the Erotic Spirit" (Tarcher, $19.95) is due out in March. "It gave us all kinds of new optins and did away with Victorian constraints in our sexual expression. But after all the gadgets and permissions were given, we really weren't told how to integrate that with the rest of our lives. What it didn't show us was how to integrate sex with higher values."

As "immensely terrible and terrifying" as it is, says Feuerstein, the AIDS epidemic is facilitating that transformation. "Sexuality is out of the cupboard," he says. "This is a good time in our culture to look at what sex can do apart from giving us a momentary thrill. How are we going to manage our sexuality? What are our primary values?"

This questioning, he says, coincides with a renewed interest in spirituality. Like others drawn to sacred sexuality workshops and books, Liliana Cane's fascination originated from her metaphysical rather than her sexual interests. "I was very interested in sprituality, and this made like a bridge for me," says the Montreal clinical psychologist who met her husband at her first workshop 10 years ago.

"I think there's a new consciousness about sexuality," says Cane, 38. "Couples are having to learn more about intimacy. It makes you be honest with yourself, know about yourself, learn how to express your needs and be respectful of others' needs. It has to do with the whole development of the person."

"Attitude and Sex." "The Birth of Universe and Cosmic Sex." "Love at First Scent." Articles that have appeared in Ecstasy: The Journal of Divine Eroticism during the first year have mostly had a cerebral tone to them. To say John Elfers has sex on his mind is literally correct.

Last year, he and his wife, Deborah Crews, began publishing the quarterly journal from their Ojai, Calif., home. So far 4,000 subscribers pay $20 a year for its distinctly un-Playboy and un-Penthouse content. Elfers is confident there are another 25,000 would-be subscribers out there.

"I think people are seeing the limits of their techniques," says Elfers, 39, an educator who has taught sex education, counseled pregnant teens and instructed parents on how to talk to their children about sex. "People are seeing that there's got to be something more to this, that sex is a lot more powerful than even mainstream psychology recognizes."

That doesn't mean Ecstasy has found easy acceptance. The journal goes too far for some people who've let Elfers know they don't want smut in their mailboxes. And then there were the four subscribers who wanted refunds because Ecstasy was too tame. "We live in a very sex-negative society," says Elfers. "What Ecstasy is about is a shift in attitude. It has nothing to do with having sex more frequently, or with different positions. It has to do with attitude—that sex is beautiful, wonderful, a legitimate way of realizing more about our spiritual selves. . . . I think we have a lot to gain by helping people see there's much more to sexuality than meets the eye."

Probably the best evidence that sacred sexuality is more than a glint in a visionary perspective is its concurrent emergence in other fields. "It is out belief that sexuality is one of God's greatest gifts to mankind," says Morton Kelsey, who faults some of the fathers of early Christianity, an overzealous patriarchal church and Victorian prudery for desecrating sexuality in Western culture.

Kelsey, an Episcopal priest and professor emeritus in theology at the University of Notre Dame, dares to envision what Christianity might have been like had it not, as he puts it, "strayed from its roots." He has written 10 books on other controversial religious subjects, from speaking in tongues to communiques from God through dreams. In 1986, he and his wife, Barbara, co-authored "Sacrament of Sexuality: The Spirituality and Psychology of Sex," a book that attempts to leap the aybss between sex and soul in Christian terms.

Borrowing from sources seemingly as disparate as Masters and Johnson and the Rev. Andrew Greeley, Kelsey peaches basic guidelines to sacred sexuality: "Human love, when it is really intimate, caring, genuine and equal, gives an intimation of an infinitely greater love. When two people can communicate on all levels of their being, there is openness to divine love."

And what about tantric sex and enlightenming? "If it helps the people they are addressing, bless them," he says. "You might say sex is one exstasy that can lead us to greater ecstasy. As Plato said, first you fall in love with the body, then you fall in love with the soul, and then you fall in love with the one who made the soul."

Parallel thought is also emerging in a field that previously focused on sexual pathology and not potential. Sex and marriage therapists, professionals who've attempted to create a problem-solving science to address sexuality, are starting to couple science and spirituality. "Counting orgasms is only part of the picture; family therapists are bringing intimacy back into the relationship," reports Virginia Rutter, spokeswoman for the American Association for Marriage and Family Therapy.

Sex therapist David Schnarch believes his profession— and Western culture at large—may be on the thereshold of "a paradigm shift," a perceptual change so fundamental as to redraw the blueprint of sex therapy, and of our intimate lives.

"Reproductive sex is a natural function, intimate sex is not. Intimacy. . . is a learned behavior." says Schnarch, who is also a professor of psychiatry and urology at Louisiana State University Medical Center in New Orleans. He is the author of "Constructing the Sexual Crucible: An Integration of Sexual and Marital Therapy" (W.W. Norton & Co., $39.95), a text whose insurgent approach has stirred debate in his profession and heightened public interest since its release two weeks ago.

"Most people never reach their sexual potential," says Schnarch, who proposes to add to sex therapy's two sexual designations, "functional" and "dysunctional," a third—the "blessed few" who have profoundly erotic and intimate experiences. Couples who "know each other" at that level of intimacy, he says, have reached one of the pinnacles of human development.

The difficulty getting there, Schnarch says, is due to modern views of intimacy and sex that are rife with contradiction. Orgasm, for instance, is understood as a momentary "dimming of consciousness," which thereby undermines intimacy during sex, he says. The commonly held notion that couples must compromise and negotiate their sexual styles tends to produce a lowest-common-denominator experience—meaning boredom rather than what Schnarch calls wall-socket sex.

"If you have normal views about sex, in many ways you are set up to have boredom in the relationship, which is exactly what we believe about marriage" he says. "Most people believe that sex declines in marriage."

Schnarch believes it doesn't have to be that way. He warns that the chapter in his book titled "In Pursuit of Sexual Potential" is "adults only" reading "by virtue of the personal maturation and tolerances it requires." The same, he says, is required to pursue our potential in intimacy and sex.

The case study he uses in the chapter—a couple in their early sixties pursuing their own erotic and intimate potential—reveals another contradiction in our beliefs. Most people assume the best sex happens for teenagers and young adults when the opposite is true, says Schnarch. It is through experience, struggles and triumphs that a couple are better able to "differentiate from ill-fitting social values and adopt their own sexual behavior.

"It takes a long time for people to come to grips with their own eroticism and then introduce that to somebody else," Schnarch says. "I would venture to say this retirement-age couple is having better, more meaningful and more salient sex than many young people are experiencing."

Schnarch also has a theory on why people's desire for fulfillment in their lives is now beginning to spill over into their sexuality. "What we are seeing is human beings as a species maturing," he says of Western culture overcoming its myopic and mistaken views of sex and sexuality. "We are talking about an evolutionary development."

November 26, 1991

Pee-Wee's Nightmare

The Kiddie Star and the Ancient Taboo

JOEL ACHENBACH

Paul Reubens is living out every man's and every boy's worst nightmare. He is alleged to have been seen touching himself.

The police claim Reubens was caught in the act. The case is all the more sensational because Paul Reubens is better known as Pee-wee Herman, the TV manchild, entertainer of children, someone presumably sexless, a squeaky-voiced character who cannot be easily reconciled with the disheveled figure who admits that he patronized a porno parlor. The simple equation of fame plus alleged sex crime equals news, requiring that the entire clammy story be exposed to the world.

This case is not just about masturbation, of course. Indeed, the average person who has read or heard about it probably thinks the allegation against Pee-wee is something much worse— flashing, perhaps. he was, after all, charged with "exposing himself" in public, which raises the image of a guy in a raincoat prowling outside a schoolyard. The moral of the story so far, to judge from office banter the past couple of days, is that Pee-wee's a pervert.

The Pee-wee jokes started circulating within a day: "Q: What's Pee-wee Herman's favorite baseball team? A: The Expos.

The truth is so much more mundane.

According to the Sarasota County Sheriff's Office, Paul Reubens sat alone Friday night in a darkened adult movie house during a pornographic film and "did begin to masterbate {sic}."

Reubens denies the allegation, his publicist said Monday. "Paul, who is emotionally devastated by the embarrassment of the situation, is currently in seclusion with friends and eagerly anticipating his complete vindication," publicist Richard Grant said in the only statement so far from the Reubens camp.

There were no witnesses to the event other than one of the undercover officers assigned to stake out the theater—masturbation is apparently such a grave public threat in Sarasota that the Sheriff's Office assigned not one but three detectives to infiltrate the place and watch for flapping elbows. The arrest report gives no indication that Reubens wanted anyone to see what he allegedly was doing.

As Reubens was walking out, he was confronted by an officer and arrested for indecent exposure, in violation of Florida statute 800.03, Exposure of Sexual Organs. It was hardly a novel thing to happen in an X-rated porn palace; three other men were spotted doing the same thing that night and were arrested as well, police said. Reubens, a Sarasota native, was released from jail later that night after posting a $219 bond.

"As long as these laws are on the books, we're going to enforce them," said Lt. Bill Stookey, spokesman for the Sheriff's Office.

All laws, he said, are enforced identically.

Stookey added that the South Trail Cinema has been targeted in the past for "this type of criminal or unlawful activity."

Would that crime be masturbation?

"I like to use the term 'manipulating the genitalia,'" the lieutenant said. "Don't ask me why."

Perhaps, says sexuality educator Debra Haffner, the executive director of the Sex Information and Education Council of the United States, the real problem here is that society is "anti-pleasure."

Solo sex, in particular, is an ancient taboo.

It is the sin of Onan. In the Book of Genesis, Onan violates Jewish law by spilling his seed rather than inseminating his brother's widow. The biblical passage implies that Onan withdrew before ejaculation, but history, as always, got confused about the story, and onanism became known as the crime of self-pollution. (God punished Onan, by the way. Slew him.)

Since then, masturbation has been linked to all manner of deviancy, disease and bodily mutation—it makes you blind, puts hair on your palm, causes syphilis and generally weakens the body against the invasion of malign humors and spirits.

The American doctor John Harvey Kellogg invented cornflakes so people wouldn't eat meat and get carnal desires. He recommended that a father sneak into his son's bedroom, rip off the covers, and, if the boy had an erection, beat him up.

Samuel Pepys put a secret symbol in his diary to designate each time he masturbated. Freud called masturbation the only real addiction; smoking and all other addictions, he said, were mere substitutes for it. In the early 20th century, parents seeking more drastic prevention could outfit their boy with the McCormick "Male Chastity Belt," patented in 1897. It was designed to "prevent self-abuse" and "control waking thoughts."

The 1934 edition of the Boy Scout Handbook had a paragraph on "sex fluid conservation" and implied that losing "fluid" would weaken a boy and invite disease. Even in the enlightened 1990s, masturbation remains taboo. Husbands and wives deny to each other that they do it. Focus groups, according to sex educator Haffner, will talk of all manner of unusual sexual activity, but not that. It is universally practiced, and it is universally considered vile.

Which brings us to Pee-wee.

Haffner asks, "What do they expect happens in those movie theaters? I certainly don't advocate public masturbation in any way, but my understanding of why people, men in particular, attend those movies is to become aroused. That the police in this area spent their time patrolling this area makes me wonder what they're not doing."

Police said Reubens did not try to keep his identity a secret. He admitted in the patrol car on the way to the station that he was the actor who played Pee-wee Herman. His lawyer told a reporter before the story broke that Reubens's career would be ruined if the arrest were publicized. Certainly the situation raises the question of whether the very real punishment of national humiliation (the press doesn't hesitate to pounce on sex scandals of the rich and famous) fits the merely alleged crime of masturbating in an adult movie theater.

John Money, professor of medical psychology and pediatrics emeritus at Johns Hopkins Hospital, says Reubens's alleged behavior might have been foolish, but is not necessarily abnormal in any medical sense.

"Pee-wee Herman's behavior was ideologically abnormal because other people had more power than him and they could arrest him for doing it," says Money. "Is it harmless? Yes, except for the person who gets caught. And it would be purely harmless were it not considered criminal and illegal."

It is also sensational. Sarasota police say they received more than 100 media inquiries Monday. The Pee-wee Herman story seems to have inspired more publicity than, to pick an example, the one about boxer Mike Tyson, who has been accused by a Miss Black America contestant of raping her July 19. Tyson hasn't been charged, but police are investigating. The corporate sponsors of Tyson's championship fight against Evander Holyfield in November say they won't cancel the bout if Tyson is arrested and tried for rape.

But Pee-wee's career may be finished.

CBS canceled Reubens's Emmy-winning Saturday morning TV show, "Pee-wee's Playhouse," in April, and Monday the network said that reruns are being pulled as well. Disney-MGM Studios in Florida has stopped showing a video starring Pee-wee on its theme park tour.

The sex crime allegation stings so much because he is not just any actor, he's one who prances around and talks in a squeaky voice and entertains children. It does not help that, to an extent unusual among major stars—he had about 3 million adult viewers on Saturday mornings in addition to all the kids—Reubens has had no public persona outside that of his fictional character. He was almost always Pee-wee in an interview, never Paul Reubens.

He gets arrested, and now a person can say, "Oh, I always knew there was something weird about that guy." People cast a jaundiced eye at any adult who makes a living around children; witness the Mr. Rogers jokes that have endured for decades despite the man's record of professionalism and decency.

Reubens apparently was tiring of the Pee-wee character anyway—he'd been playing him since 1979—so perhaps this oversize pre-adolescent figure was already destined to be a 1980s novelty.

"When you work 12 hours a day, you literally have no (personal} life," he said in an interview with *Newsday* in 1989. "I'm up at five in the morning and on the set by seven. By the time I get home at eight, take a shower and eat dinner, it's already past my bedtime. It's built into this schedule that I can't get enough sleep. One is forced to be disciplined."

Since the show was canceled he grew his hair long, down to his shoulder blades. He adopted a scraggly goatee. Friends have said in interviews that Reubens wanted to travel and take it easy for a while. Last weekend he was visiting his parents in Sarasota—which may answer anyone's question as to why a 38-year-old man who wanted to see a skin flick wouldn't just rent a video and bring it home.

His mother, Judy Rubenfeld, declined yesterday to talk about what happened. But Reubens admitted through his publicist that he did go Friday night to the South Trail Cinema the XXX-rated movie house on Tamiami Trail, just down from the Red Lobster family restaurant.

The movies that night included "Nancy Nurse." Starring Sandra Scream.

Later he was photographed, as all suspects are, from both the front and the side. The look on his face is of a man condemned to death. The punishment of Onan.

July 31, 1991

Study Questions

Chapter Three

1. The story concept of eligible bachelors in Washington is a list in rank order of status in the social world. Create other lists of influential people that could serve as an organizational structure for a feature article. Eg. Behind-the-scenes power brokers.
2. Can you think of other story ideas reflecting family relationship issues?
3. What is your most powerful memory? Could it be turned into a feature story?
4. Take a sensationalized event in the news and devise research strategies to shed more light on the topic,

Art of Living 4

One objective of the media is to help readers lead better, more satisfying lives. These articles on comfort, food, the environment, health, safety and medicine address that goal.

Critic Tom Shales' paean to room service links travel, food and comfort. The writer's confessional voice expresses a passion for self-indulgence. The humor of the piece is based on that candid attitude, one others may hold but not be bold enough to state.

The creativity in Peter Carlson's tribute to Barcaloungers is also amusing. He formulates his own definition of lounging: "that semi-vegetative state that's somewhere between the comfortable and the comatose." And he's playful with language, creating such terms as "sit-ability" and "Sitman." Even his interpretation, that the fetal position one assumes in a lounge chair mimics the primal joy of a newborn babe, is a funny, clever insight.

The inventive structure of Linton Week's article about barbecue employs the disciplines of a university to illustrate a variety of aspects of that well-known Southern delicacy. Seeing a topic from a number of different perspectives is invaluable for readers.

The title, "Armchair Activism," may be an oxymoron, but many citizens no doubt look for shortcuts to political correctness. Writer Dan Oldenburg capitalizes on the conflict between lazy participation and the image of being good. The article is cheeky and amusing, yet offers useful service information and resources, Oldenburg perceptively constructs a sociological typology of activists, even though his categories are couched in populist terms—sprouts, grousers and greenback greens.

Sweating is a universal activity that Henry Allen elaborates on in a clever, nonoffensive way. Despite sweat's potential as a social problem, Allen guides readers to appreciate its healthy aspects.

Controversial issues are perfect grist for feature article writers. David Streitfeld tackles the legality and effectiveness of Mace as a form of self-defense. In another piece on public safety, Streitfeld raises questions and informs readers about scientific studies involving the potential health hazards linked to electro-magnetic fields.

Feature articles about medical topics are increasingly important to readers. The doctor in this profile has turned writing about his work into a second career. Oliver

Sacks is a curious phenomenon in his profession: a scientist who is compassionate and a doctor who wants to share stories about strange maladies and miracle drugs with the public. The tag on Judith Weinraub's article, "Hero of the Hopeless," helps readers identify with her subject.

Knock! Knock! Who's There?

Waiter-Borne, Heaven-Sent Repast in the Hotel Room

TOM SHALES

Rumble-rumble-rumble, tinkle-tinkle-tinkle . . . Is that what I think it is? Tinkle-tinkle-tinkle, rumble-rumble-rumble . . . Yes, yes—and it's getting closer. Ding-dong. Ding-dong. Knock knock knock.

Hosanna, eureka, excelsior, ay caramba! He's here—the man in the white coat pushing the rolling table with the clinking glasses and dishware! But before opening the door, if you haven't heard the clarion call already, you have to make it official:

"Yes? Who is it?"

There followeth the response—two of the sweetest little ol' words in the English language:

"Room service."

What balm, what succor, what sweet repast for the weary traveler, and what traveler doesn't get weary? Room service is one of the saving graces of life on the road, and perhaps of life on earth. You dial a number on a telephone, place an order, and half an hour later a meal is delivered to your room or, better still, your suite.

One of the few remaining classic examples of desire and fulfillment easily and painlessly accomplished.

Ugh, wilderness! Who needs that? Room service remains an eminently civilized constant in the decreasingly civilized urban world. It's basic, yet somehow luxurious, a pampering nicety available to everybody, but most enjoyable at the proudly pricey big-city hotels catering to the rich, the near-rich, and those who just want to feel rich for a night.

Never mind the French-milled soap in the bathroom or the soft plushy terry-cloth robes or the mints on the pillow that you forget about anyway and wake up with a chocolate ear, or worse. Those little amenities don't really add up to much. It's the quality of room service that separates the real hotels from the mere places to stay.

"We call it a loss leader," says Stan Bromley, general manager of the Four Seasons Hotel in Georgetown. "It's the backbone of a hotel in terms of what the upscale traveler really needs. The most important things to a guest at that level are the valet and the room service."

The reason room service is not a big money-maker per se, Bromley says, is that such a large staff is required to keep impatient guests happy: "They'll rip my throat out if the food's not there in 20 or 25 minutes." Should there be an unforeseen catastrophe and more than half an hour passes, Bromley says, the hotel will offer the guest free drinks or free dessert or a free something to make amends.

Two widely held notions about room service in hotels are that the food is overpriced and that it is not very good. Overpriced? A relative term. At the shady, cushy Hotel Bel-Air in Los Angeles, considered by many veteran travelers the best hotel in the world, you can order a shrimp cocktail, Caesar salad and soft drink and get a bill for more than $30, without the tip.

But it's worth it to sit in your suite by the fireplace and enjoy your dinner and not have to get up, dress up or go out. The suites at the Bel-Air are so airy and homey you hate to leave them anyway.

As for the idea that room-service food isn't very good, no one could reasonably say that after enjoying one of the chicken piccata sandwiches at the Beverly Hills Hotel. This prosaic delicacy is only on the room service menu, not on the menu of the hotel's restaurants.

At luxury hotels now the rule—once the exception—is room service available 24 hours a day. At 4 a.m., in a good hotel, you should be able to get a cheeseburger or a Cobb salad or a Western omelet sent up. Room-service receptionists at better hotels will speak to you by name when they answer the phone (a computer clues them in as to who's in which room) and will make every effort to comply with the oddest request.

London's historic Savoy Hotel, which celebrated its 100th birthday last year, claims to have invented 24-hour room service and certainly has refined it to an art. You can dial a number on the phone, yes, but you can also merely push a button in your room and then, moments later, with an audible whoosh, a gentleman IN TAILS arrives to take your order.

Years ago, when Diet Coke had just been introduced, I asked if the Savoy stocked it. The answer was, "No, but we can get it for you." Diet Cokes arrived with the meal; someone had obviously been dispatched to a grocery store to buy them.

Certainly the management has complied with stranger requests than this. When the Beatles visited Bob Dylan at the Savoy in 1965, they asked for, and received, porridge and peas sandwiches. Steve McQueen, on the other hand, was supposedly thrown out of the Savoy for cooking in his room. It appears he almost set it on fire with his hot plate and was seen running nearly naked down a corridor clutching a fire extinguisher.

Room service waiters must, of course, be models of discretion. It's key among the requirements for the job. "People do in their rooms what they do at home," says Bromley. "Under the influence of alcohol and other great feelings, they forget they're in a public place. They answer the door in their underwear—both men and women—and that sort of thing."

Sander Vanocur, anchor for the weekly ABC News "Business World" report, tells the story of a famous network correspondent who, with his wife, checked into the Ritz in Paris, then left the room on business. He sent his wife a dozen roses in his absence. When, some time later, the wife heard a knock at the door, she assumed her husband had returned. Throwing off her nightgown, tucking one rose between her knees and flinging open the door, she shouted a frisky, "Ooh, la-la!"

"Madame," she heard a voice say. "It's room service."

The great Jack Paar, a champion traveler as well as champion talker, remembers the time he took the "Tonight" show to Hawaii and was getting ready for a black-tie event that evening. He called room service and told them to send up a sandwich and a glass of milk. "Bring it in and put it on the table, because I'll be in the bath," Paar instructed.

He undressed as he ran the bath water and at that point decided to tie his black tie to get it just right. He also decided that the air conditioning was too drafty, but to get to the machine and turn it down, he had to put a stool on top of the bed, then climb up and reach for the controls.

It was at this point that the room-service waiter entered. "There I was, nude as I could be, with the tie around my neck, naked on a foot stool on top of the bed," Paar says. "All I could think of to say was, 'Aloha!' "

Room-service waiters not only have to be adept at dealing with such awkward situations, they also have to pick up vibrations from guests about how much attention they really want in their rooms. "They have to know whether a guest is saying they want a lot of service or 'Get out now,'" says Bromley. "You need people who are sensitive to this kind of thing."

At the Bel-Air, the room service waiters usually seem to catch the hints guests throw. But to solve the age-old nagging problem of cold toast in the morning (when will the media ever address this pressing issue?), the Bel-Air has waiters bring the toasters with them to guest rooms during breakfast hours.

This means you have to make an awful lot of small talk and chitchat while waiting for the toast to pop. It's almost easier to forget the whole thing and go for a croissant.

For several years I was under the impression that the proper tip for a room-service waiter was three or five dollars, what you might give to a bellperson for bringing the bags around or similar convenience. Oh, the naiveté! Room-service waiters are to be tipped just like restaurant waiters, 15 to 20 per cent of the bill.

Who knows how many of those waiters left hotel rooms muttering curses because I had undertipped them? And yet, to their credit, I don't recall any of them being surly or snappish about it.

Strangely, perhaps, considering how many other fields have changed their gender complexions in the past few decades, room serving appears to remain exclu sively a male occupation, at least in this country. But some things about room service are changing. Bromley says that today's guests want "more informal, fun foods" from room service, not necessarily big official meals under silver domes.

For this reason, the Four Seasons here has added pizza to its room-service menu. For $6.50, not really much more than it costs at movie theaters, you can get a bucket of popcorn. One recent celebrity guest at the Four Seasons ordered popcorn and caviar late one night.

Bromley doesn't want to divulge the room service eccentricities of famous guests, but he does say that really super superstars like Michael Jackson and Prince bring their own chefs with them as part of their entourages, so anything they order is custom made.

"Entertainers all ask for weird things," Bromley says. "Rock stars generally tend to love bologna sandwiches on white bread with tomatoes and French mustard. Also popcorn, and big thick steaks." They'll eat macrobiotic health food and drink carrot juice in the daytime and then, returning to the hotel after a concert, pig out on pizza and steaks into the wild wee hours.

That the phrase "room service" summons up soothing images is borne out by the new home-delivery outfits that spirit gourmet meals to customers' waiting doors in Chicago and Los Angeles and go by the name Room Service. New York has one called Dial-A-Dinner and San Francisco offers Waiters on Wheels, but these names don't stir the romantic associations that "room service" does.

The phrase was also used as the title of a play by John Murray and Allen Boretz that was a hit on Broadway in 1937 and, the next year, under the same title, a movie vehicle for the Marx Brothers. Lucille Ball was also in the cast.

And then there's Ray Thompson's immortal Eloise, the fictitious 6-year-old who lived, with her nanny, her dog and her turtle, in the Plaza Hotel and who, in Thompson's first book about her, exclaims, "Ooooooooo, I absolutely love Room Service. They always know it's me and they say 'Yes, Eloise?' And I always say, 'Hello, this is me Eloise and would you kindly send one roast-beef bone, one raisin, and seven spoons to the top floor and charge it please. Thank you very much.'

"Then I hang up and look at the ceiling for a while and think of a way to get a present."

However it has changed over the years, the elegant central concept of room service remains the same. You want food, you get it. Rumble-rumble-rumble, tinkle-tinkle-tinkle. "There is no such thing as room service in the Soviet Union," notes the well-traveled Vanocur, offering another example of a gap the Russians will be hard-pressed to close. Of course, they have a few other priorities.

Vanocur also remembers a particularly pleasant meal on wheels he shared with his wife, Virginia, during a visit to Honolulu. It was 4 o'clock in the morning and the Vanocurs, having freshly arrived, found themselves unable to sleep because of the time zone change.

"Virginia said, 'Let's have room service and watch the sun come up over Diamond Head,'" Vanocur recalls.

And they did.

Is there room service in heaven? Yes. That's part of what makes it heaven. And another good reason you should try your damnedest to end up there.

May 16, 1990

The Big Easy

PETER CARLSON

Billy Shepherd gazed around the firehouse in Rocky Mount, N.C., looking for a man to match his chair.

He needed a big man, a huge man, a giant among men because his chair was a monster. It looked like King Kong. It was humongous—45 inches high, a full yard wide, and built like a nose tackle gone to flab. Its arms bulged with padding, and on its back were four foam-filled pouches that hung down like potbellies lopping over belt buckles. It looked like a sumo wrestler encased in black vinyl.

The chair was named Titan. It was the new "Big Man's Chair" from Barcalounger, and Shepherd, who is Barcalounger's manager of upholstery and frame operations, had hauled it a few miles from the factory to the firehouse, and then, with the help of a burly fireman, humped it into this place of honor in front of the house TV. Now he needed somebody to test it out. Somebody large.

"We got one right here," said one of the firemen, who promptly hustled off down the hallway.

Shepherd has been delivering Barcaloungers to the firehouse for years. It's the best place to test their durability. Whenever the firefighters aren't fighting fires, they're plopping down in the Barcaloungers, three shifts a day, 365 days a year. In the life span of a chair, Shepherd said, "a month in a fire station is like a year in a home." He inspected one of the other Barcaloungers in the room, a model called the Dynamite, which is only slightly smaller than the mighty Titan. The chair was well used, but it obviously had plenty of butt-hours still left in it. Shepherd tipped it on its back, knelt down and peered into its innards, looking for the sticker that reveals the chair's birthday. It said March 3, 1983. When he tipped it back up, a green grape rolled out onto the floor, symbol of the thousands of snacks consumed in it over the last eight years by firemen sitting in front of the tube, waiting for an inferno.

At that point, a certified Big Man entered the room—Capt. C.R. Webb, all 280 pounds of him.

Capt. Webb obeyed. He sat down. He reached over and pulled the Titan's handle. His feet popped up, his head eased back, and his eyes closed involuntarily, like those dolls whose eyelids automatically shut when you lay them on their backs.

"Oh, man," he said softly. He uttered a long, slow, satisfied sigh and lay there with his eyes closed and a manila file folder balanced on his chest. For a minute, it looked as if he might never get up. "Sure sits great," he said.

It sure does. Your basic Barcalounger may not be elegant enough for, say, the Elysee Palace, but it sure is comfortable. Dangerously comfortable, in fact. Hardworking, hard-charging, Type-A guys have been known to lie down in one and immediately lose all desire to ever get vertical again. They slip into a semi-vegetative state that's somewhere between the comfortable and the comatose. At that point, all movement ceases, except for the minimal effort required to click the remote control or holler, "Honey, get me another beer, willya?"

The Barcalounger is not just a comfortable chair, it's a mystical experience. Lying in one produces something akin to the pure spiritual bliss long sought by Indian swamis and opium smokers. Nobody understood just how this humble chair could produce the "peace that passeth all understanding" until I myself accidentally stumbled upon the underlying scientific reason during my tour of the Barcalounger factory.

Well, actually, it was after my tour of the factory, when I was hanging out in the offices of the Barcalounger bureaucrats, who were gathered around an employee who was showing off her 3-week-old baby. The bureaucrats were kitchycooing as the new mom cradled her sleeping babe in her arms. And then it hit me: The blissed-out bambino was lying in the exact same position as the inhabitant of a Barcalounger in full tilt! That explains it: Lying in the Barcalounger reproduces the primal joy of the newborn babe. We drowse in the Barcalounger's plump arms! We nuzzle in its voluptuous Naugahyde bosom!

What a concept: the Barcalounger as upholstered Earth Mother!

But maybe I'm getting too metaphysical here. Maybe we should get back to the mundane facts of the matter. Technically, the Barcalounger is merely one of dozens of brands of recliners, which are known in the furniture industry's oxymoronic phrase as "action furniture." There are Stratoloungers and La-Z-Boys and Action Recliners and many others, but over the years, as the *Los Angeles Times* once noted, "the Barcalounger has emerged in the same league with Band-Aid and Xerox: It has become generic, the word people use when they mean recliner."

"Barcalounger was America's First Recliner," claims a company brochure, but Thomas Hine is dubious about that. "The history of the reclining chair is a very long one," Hine wrote in Populuxe, his study of American style in the 1950s. "Recognizable American forebears date to the beginning of the nineteenth century, and the Winterthur Museum has a 1810 New England example that is functionally the same as the 1950s La-Z-Boy, foldout footrest and all."

But by 1947, when furniture manufacturer Edward Joel Barcolo (of the Buffalo Barcolos) began peddling his Barcalounger, America was ready to tilt back and doze off en masse. "The recliner," Hine wrote, "was transformed from a gimmick to a respectable part of the household."

In the 50's the recliner became the porch swing of the postwar era: a chair to sit in while watching the world go by—not on the street anymore but on a TV screen. And the massive, mammoth Barcalounger beecame a philosophical alternative to that other classic American seat, the Shaker chair. Built by a communal

Christian sect that rejected all earthly pleasures, the Shaker chair of the 1800s was straight, austere, unpadded and uncomfortable. By contrast, the Barcalounger, built for secular suburbanites eager for all earthly pleasures, was round, sprawling and plush—a little bit of heaven right here in the living room.

Soon, the Barcalounger and other recliners added all kinds of space-age devices designed to soothe and pamper their occupants. There were recliners that rocked and recliners that swiveled and recliners that massaged and reclineers that had little stereo speakers into them, sort of like a Walkman for the sedentary set—a Sitman.

And then there was the air-conditioned Barcalounger. Or was there?

The Barcalounger training manual refers to it in the official company chronology: "1964—Air conditioned upholstered chairs introduced." But Stan Harwood, Barcalounger's personnel manager, had never heard of them.

"It's got my curiosity up," he said. "I talked to a guy who's been here with the company since 1961, and he doesn't know anything about air-conditioned chairs. So I gotta find out what that is."

An air-conditioned Barcalounger? I was intrigued. "Could a Barcalounger really pump out cool air?"

"I guess it could, " he said. "But my thinking is it might be something more along the lines of an open arm to allow air to come through. I might be way off base, but it's hard to imagine some type of hookup where you got air running through the chair." He paused and pondered. "One time we did make a chair with a heating pad in the back. But we got concerned about maybe some problems with the heat source—electrocution or whatever—and we abandoned that project."

Harwood was the man deputized to tell me all about the Barcalounger, and he did. The company, he said, produces dozens of styles of recliners—the Titan, the Greenbriar, the Stealth and the best-selling Dynamite, among others-and they retail from about $400 to oveer $1,500. Those prices are higher than the competitors' he said, but that's because the chairs are better. "Our market niche is in the mid-upper to upper range," he said. "We don't compete head-to-head with Stratolounger or La-Z-Boy."

Not that he was maligning the La-Z-Boy. He wasn't. "Matter of fact, I owned one before I came to work at Barcalounger," he said. "I had to sell it before the plant manager came over to the house."

Quickly, I changed the subject to sex. Barcaloungers have incited some minor skirmishes in the battle of the sexes, I suggested. Generally speaking, men seem to think they're gloriously comfortable and women think they're hideously ugly. In fact, bitching about Barcaloungers has become a minor sub-genre of Women's Literature:

"I've never quite reconciled myself to a Baralounger, " one woman wrote in the *Chicago Tribune* a few years back, "in part because I am not comfortable with furniture that looks as though it is going to eat me for dinner. . . "

". . . Historically, of course, women's relation to the recliner was to dust under it or to decorate around it," another woman wrote in the *New York Times*. "Women also carried food and beverages to the chairs . ."

Harwood shrugged off such sentiments as archaic. "It was more of a male-dominated chair years and years ago," he said. More recently, the company has begun wooing the fair sex with recliners like the First Lady, which is designed for petite women, and the Registry, an elegant wingback model that looks like something a judge would have in his chambers. Call them Barcalounger Lites.

The good news about these chairs is that they don't look like Barcaloungers. The bad news is that they don't feel like Barcaloungers either. If lying in one of the old behemoths is like being cradled by your mother, then lying in the Lites is like being cradled by your uncle Fred. Nice enough, perhaps, but not quite the same.

Harwood reached down and picked up a huge black leather scrapbook, which turned out to contain the Barcalounger archives. There was an old ad showing Slammin' Sammy Snead slumbering in a Barcalounger. There was a picture of the Barcalounger given to composer Quincy Jones for being the "successful man of action for 1965." There was a photo of Wilhelmina, "America's top model," perched in a Barcalounger that was perched on a Tunisian zebra skin. And there was a news item revealing that the employees of Barcalounger had donated a red leather recliner Cardinal Spellman and a "specially designed white leather" one to Pope John XXIII.

The pope in a Barcalounqer! My mind reeled! I was overcome by a vision: A couple of Italian workmen heft the white leather throne into the Sistine Chapel. His Holiness sits down. he pulls the handle. He reclines. He smiles. He's always wanted to study Michelangelo's ceiling paint job without hurting his neck and now, by God, he can!

Harwood led me on a tour of the Barcalounger factory, a 365,000-square-foot facility where 400 workers create about 425 chairs a day. They were hustling like hungry ants, cutting cloth, bolting frames, stapling fabrics and stuffing cushions to the bursting point with comfy foam. It was an inspiring sight: all these folks busting butt so that their fellow Americans might drowse and doze in motionless rapture. And at the end of the whole complex process was a woman who inspected every fabric, checked every seam and, yes, sat down in every chair, pulling the handle and leaning back to make sure that each and every Barcalounger met the company's strict standards of sit-ability.

After we'd made the rounds of the factory, Harwood escorted me into the product development office, where designers were hunched over drawing boards, sketching out the Barcaloungers of the future. But Harwood wasn't interested in future Barcaloungers; he was itching to find out about past Barcaloungers—namely that mysterious air-conditioned model allegedly introduced in 1964.

He buttonholed Ben Potter—the product development manager, a weather-beaten old veteran who's worked for Barcalounger since 1960—and asked if he knew anything about the air-conditioned chair. Potter furrowed his brow in thought.

He rubbed his chin in contemplation. Finally, he shook his head in sad negation. No, it wasn't the chair that was air-conditioned in 1964, he said, it was the factory.

Finally, the mystery was solved!

But Stan Harwood wasn't completely satisfied. For the next couple of days, he kept asking around. Finally, he grudgingly concluded that Potter was right, that there had, alas, never been an air-conditioned Barcalounger. But you could tell it kind of bothered him. He was obviously still captivated by the concept of an air-conditioned recliner, which is, after all, some sort of ultimate, a veritable Everest of upholstered hedonism.

"You know, it might be a good idea," he told me on the phone. "Put some ice packs in there or something. If anybody could do it, we could."

October 6, 1991

Barbecue U

LINTON WEEKS

You won't find Barbecue Law offered in the catalogues of the nation's prestige law schools—at least not yet. But if the paper chasers need instruction in that arcane science, they can turn to a recent case from the annals of the Lone Star State: Texas Pig Stands Inc. v. Hard Rock Cafe International Inc.

Though the suit was filed in February 1988 by Texas Pig Stands owner Richard Hailey—who likes his barbecue with a reddish, slightly sweet-flavored sauce and sour dill relish—the roots of the controversy go back to 1921, when the first Pig Stand was opened in Dallas. The small stand, which Hailey claims was the first drive-in restaurant in the country, featured a "pig sandwich" on its menu. The tasty sandwich and the curbside concept were so successful that other Pig Stands were opened throughout the United States; at its zenith, the chain was more than 100 restaurants strong. The company logo, then and now, was the profile of a hog with the words "Pig Sandwich" stretching from ear to tail. In the latter half of the century, however, the business began to shrink, and today there are only seven Pig Stands left. All are in Texas.

Still, Texas Pig Stands has a proud tradition. So when the Hard Rock Cafe opened in Dallas in 1986, Hailey was chagrined to find that it too served a "pig sandwich." He took the matter to court, seeking restitution for all of the profits that the Dallas Hard Rock had made on its version of the entree.

The Hard Rock lawyers argued that the company's founder, Isaac Tigrett—who likes his sauce hot and vinegary—grew up in Jackson, Tenn., just a few miles from the barbecue mecca of Memphis. According to Tigrett's testimony, Memphis and other cities across the South were for years dotted with small barbecue shacks known to one and all as pig stands, and the sandwiches they served were called, generically, pig sandwiches. So he was within his rights to put the pair of words on his menu.

"It was one of the most extraordinary cases I've ever seen," said Hard Rock attorney Ralph Kalish Sr.—who doesn't even like barbecue sauce all that much—"and I've been practicing law for 43 years." Kalish took depositions from people all over the country who testified that sticking barbecue between two pieces of white bread was sure enough a pig sandwich.

The presiding U.S. magistrate, John Primomo, must have felt the weight of the matter as he dismissed the jury for a weekend break prior to deliberations. With great solemnity he instructed them not to talk to their families or each other about the case. Not to watch television. Not to read the newspapers. And, above all, not to eat any barbecue.

Lest you think this was an isolated incident, a quick scroll through an index of recent lawsuits provides a number of other juicy examples, most notably a $1 billion breach-of-contract suit filed against entertainer Redd Foxx in 1986. In the suit, Foxx was accused of backing out of an agreement to endorse a line of barbecue products.

If barbecue has begun to spice up the bar, surely it's only a matter of time before the Southern delicacy insinuates itself into other aspects of our culture—medicine, sociology, education—so the more we know about the subject, the better off we'll be. To that end, perhaps the time is right for a college entirely devoted to the study of barbecue culture, a sort of Barbecue U.

The president of the college would have to be Nashville's John Egerton, author of the definitive opus, Southern Food, who knows barbecue the way Bo Jackson knows everything else. The deans would be Greg Johnson and Vince Staten, two reporters for the Louisville Courier-Journal who wrote the book on barbecue, called Real Barbecue. The school colors would be red and brown. The nickname would be the Chefs. And with no apologies to the University of Arkansas, the mascot would be a razorback. The course list might look something like this:

World History

By way of introduction, President Egerton will explain to students how Spanish explorers discovered Indians in the Caribbean who roasted meat on wooden frames. The Spanish called the framework barbacoa and from that word comes the present-day barbecue. The reading list will include numerous treatises on pork preparation through the ages, including Charles Lamb's 1822 essay on roasting pigs.

In his essay, Lamb speculates that barbecue was first discovered in the Far East when a villager's hut burned down, charring the pigs and chickens in the yard. The distraught villager, looking for a morsel of food, pulled the roasted meat from the ashen rubble and discovered that it was very tasty. Word of the newfound delicacy spread, and soon people throughout the land were burning down their houses and enjoying barbecued pigs and chickens.

American History

Students will learn that pork was the meat most commonly eaten by colonial southerners because it was easy to preserve. But pork could get a little tough, so a great deal of energy was spent on the sauces that were believed to enhance the flavor of an otherwise unappetizing dish.

Guest lecturers will include celebrity chef Paul Prudhomme, who once wrote that while growing up in Opelousas, La., he didn't know what the word "rare" meant when applied to food. "My mother never served anything that wasn't really cooked, because you never killed an animal that was still productive." As a result, when an animal finally was slaughtered on the Prudhomme farm, it was fairly old. And what made it tasty was the sauce.

Literature

You've heard about people who talk about reading cookbooks the way others read novels. In this course students will receive credit for doing just that. The reading list will include works by Craig Claiborne, Julia Child and James Beard. Prose works by Calvin Trillin and William Faulkner, on the other hand, will be read as cookbooks.

Visiting poets will drop by to delight students with samples of their works. For instance, Roy Blount Jr. might read "Song to Barbecue Sauce" from his book One Fell Soup, or I'm a Just a Bug on the Windshield of Life: Hot and sweet and red and greasy,

I could eat a gallon easy:
Barbecue sauce!
Lay it on, hoss.
Nothing is dross
Under barbecue sauce. Brush it on chicken, slosh it on pork,
  Eat it with fingers, not with a fork.
  I could eat barbecued turtle or squash—
I could eat tar paper cooked and awash
  In barbecue sauce.
I'd eat Spanish moss
With barbecue sauce . . .

Philosophy

A course that studies people, such as Bobby Seale, who've raised barbecue to a higher plane. "There was a time," wrote Seale (who believes that barbecue should be spelled with a "q") in his book Barbeque'n With Bobby, "when 20 million liberals and left radicals across the country were saying 'Free Bobby Seale.' Now they're grown up and have their own barbeque grills and pits in their backyard. This is an American pastime. I love it. Barbequing can change a grumpy attitude to a pleasant kind of sereneness."

Geography

Calvin Trillin was right when he said, "Barbecue is a touchy subject all over the country." The college hopes to foster understanding among regions by bringing together a group of cartographers and geographers who believe that America can be divided into regions according to barbecue preferences. Students will learn from visiting scholars that Texans barbecue beef as well as pork and prefer a tomato-based sauce, while North Carolinians live by pork alone and tend toward a sweet, vinegar-based sauce.

Guest speakers might include University of South Carolina professors Charles Rovacik and John Winberry, who wrote a 200-plus-page geographic treatment of their state in 1988. One of the ways they divvied up the state was by pointing out which region uses which sauce. According to the authors, the Low Country loves mustard-based sauce; along the western side the sauce resembles ketchup; tomato-based sauce is found in the northwest; and up around Myrtle Beach the shag dancers go for a pepper and vinegar sauce.

Business

Students will spend their spring term in Memphis, observing preparations for the Memphis in May International Festival, the centerpiece of which is the annual World Championship Barbecue Cooking Contest. This year the contest will draw 175 teams—with names such as the Pot Bellied Porkers and the Porky Pilots, competing for over $10,000 in prizes before 100,000 spectators. The real money, however—more than $350,000—goes to the festival in the form of corporate sponsorships, and the citywide economic impact of the barbecue contest alone is about $1.8 million.

Politics

Politics and barbecue have gone hand in hand since before the founding of the nation. Readings from the textbook Real Barbecue will include the Acts of the Virginia Burgesses in 1610, which forbade "the shooting of firearms for sport at barbecues, else how shall we know when the Indians are coming,," and an entry from the 1769 diary of George Washington, which reads, "Went up to Alexandria to a barbecue. Back in three nights."

Students will take field trips to political barbecues in most of the 50 states. And a barbecue lobbyist from South Carolina will explain why in 1986 his state legislature passed a Truth in Barbecue law, which requires barbecue restaurants to advise patrons how the barbecue is cooked and what parts of the hog are used.

Music

Guest artists will perform various renditions of Louis Armstrong's 1927 hit "Struttin' With Some Barbecue" and "B.B.Q.U.S.A," written by Mojo Nixon in 1987.

Ethnography

Participants will include John Marshall, whose 1981 master's thesis "Barbecue in Western Kentucky: An Ethnographic Study" is the first and last word on the subject.

Alas, Barbecue U doesn't exist yet, so in preparing to make legal war against Hard Rock Cafe International, Ralph Kalish Sr. had to put together his own curriculum. In the end, after all the depositions were taken and the issues presented, the jury found in favor of Texas Pig Stands. The case will probably be appealed, so until a final decision is reached, the pig sandwich will continue to appear on the Dallas Hard Rock Cafe menu. Hard Rocks outside of Texas, such as the Washington cafe, have not been affected by the suit.

But for the attorneys in another barbecue lawsuit, there's still time to learn a thing or two. It seems that Christopher Carroll, owner of the Spring Creek Bar-B-Que in Arlington, Tex., has filed suit against former employee Londell Fisher, owner of the newly opened Stage Coach Bar-B-Que. Carroll—who likes his sauce very red and a little sweet—is charging that Fisher—who also likes his sauce very red and a little sweet—has stolen his recipe. "I was shocked and disappointed," Carroll told the *New York Times*. "I treated him like family."

April 1, 1990

Environment

Armchair Activism—For Couch Potatoes, Easy Ways to Save the Earth

DON OLDENBURG

Activism is making a comeback, even among ordinarily inactlve Americans.

Well, kind of. Like the way democracy is rehabilitating the Soviet Union: So far the prospect outshines the reality. A lot of people are just warming up to the idea that they might take personally such seemingly distant problems as ozone depletion and rain forest destruction.

Last summer, the Roper Organization reported that more than three-quarters of the American people now believe that we (presumably meaning all of us) should be making a major effort to improve environmental quality. But the same poll also reflected the Downside of '90s activism: passivity. Put simply, most Americans aren't acting on their beliefs. Only 22 percent polled by Roper said they actually were doing much of anything—not even a third of those who insisted we all should be doing more.

This is not surprising. Spouting off one's beliefs is one thing, taking action another. "How to Make the World a Better Place: A Guide to Doing Good" (Morrow, $22.95), one of a caboodle of such "quick and easy" activist books published last year to satisfy what was perceived to be a growing public desire "to make a difference," identifies the usual pitfalls to activism. Among them, misguided thinking such as: Don't worry because someone else knows what to do and is in control; or, if I can't commit totally, I won't do anything; or, technology and the free market will straighten out everything in time.

Inhibitions like these paint the profile of the 26 percent of respondents the Roper folks label "Sprouts." Not as apathetic as stick-in-the-sludge "Basic Browns" (28 percent), nor as paranoid as "Grousers" (24 percent, who do nothing because they're sure no one else is), Sprouts are concerned about the environment but aren't convinced individuals can make a difference.

The remaining 22 percent? Equally divided between "True-Blue Greens," who are community activists, real leaders whose lives are filled with commitment and involvement and environmentally appropriate activities; and the politically correct "Greenback Greens," who drag their feet on involvement but are willing to foot more of the bill for a cleaner environment than the average American.

A tidy bit of pigeonholing. But common sense says there's another category out there, one that's not so neatly tabulated in opinion polls, because it consists of people who would never complete a survey and therefore never be reflected in one.

Somewhere among the Sprouts and Grousers and Greenback Greens is a group of would-be activists whose reluctance in such matters has more to do with inertia than ignorance or misconception. Unlike Sprouts, individual empowerment isn't the issue for this group. Effort is. Gumption is. They comprehend the consequences of unrestrained appetites converging with limited resources, all right. They know that the planet needs rescue, that "there's no way to peace because peace is the way," that baby seals deserve a better fate than a bloody whack on the noggin, that tea pickers in India get rooked and babies in Africa starve. But before they can move on any of these issues, they first must contend with the forces of gravity. For Reluctant Activists (as we shall call them) to take a stand requires firsr that they stand up—which may be asking too much.

No grand revelation, this. They are the reason why the overwhelming majority of how-to activism books emphasize "easy things you can do" on their covers, meant to encourage couch potatoes of social consciousness. But these activist authors overestimate the Reluctant Activists. Easy isn't good enough. "How to Save Mother Earth Without Lifting a Finger" is a title that might get their attention.

Fortunately for Reluctant Activists, and for the future of the planet, low-energy, minimal-demand tasks do exist that produce decent payoffs. Gleaning them from the pages of pro-environment chores and from the long lists of recommended actions is a bigger challenge than doing them.

Instant Ecology

Take the book "Two Minutes a Day for a Greener Planet" (Harper San Francisco, $7.95), promoted as "the easiest 235 steps everyone can take to save the Earth." This would seem tailor-made for effortless activism; two minutes a day, arguably, isn't much.

Marjorie Lamb, the Canadian environmental adviser who wrote the book, suggests, for instance, that people "fill the coffee pot with water the night before." Logic: The water warms overnight to room temperature, reducing the energy needed the next morning to crank out a hot cup of joe. A small gain? Yes. But this suits Reluctant Activists nicely, inasmuch as it requires only a few extra memory cells and absolutely no extra effort. Yet it scores a big plus on surveys, such as the Roper poll, as "regular activity at home to conserve energy."

Using biodegradable laundry soap instead of detergent is another do-nothing doable. The price is right and it saves water resources from dangerous pollutants. And even if the laundry doesn't come out smelling like a chemist's rendition of springtime fresh, the clothes get clean enough.

The No-Action Action

Probably the most effortless of the recommended actions are the ones that require doing nothing—the modus operandi of Reluctant Activists. Enter the boycott, a powerful tool in the hands of passive personalities, yet a strategy time-honored by the most active of activists.

Simply by not buying a particular product manufactured by a company whose policies or practices are unfair or endanger people or abuse the planet, one can all at once make a statement of principle, affect the coffers of major corporations, inlprove the world in a small way, and do so with no cost, no sacrifice and no effort. All that's required is to find out what products or companiex to boycott—and hardcore activists are hard at work compiling those lists already.

Consider the recent boycott tha forced canners to market "dolphin-safe" tuna. Or the simple aside at a party: "I don't buy ivory products." That positions a Reluctant Activist in the middle of a worldwide Save-the-Elephants action that began more than a year ago and has practically closed down ivory-carving factories in Beijing and Canton, according to the Animals' Agenda magazine. Boycotts can offer an added dividend: When the spouse says, "Time to dig peat moss into the flower beds," Reluctant Activists can answer, "Sorry, not buying peat moss anyrnore. The international boycott to save the Irish bogs, you know."

War machine makers? Racist governments? Global polluters? Whatever the offense or issue, boycotts are probably underway. One easy and cheap (about $10) source of information on the status of dozens of such boycotts is the Nation Boycott Newsletter (NBN), in Seattle. (Phone: 206-523-0421.)

Spreading the Word

Activism, no matter how passive, includes some evangelism—spreading the word, gaining new allies. Because propagation requires at least some exertion and more than a superficial understanding of an issue, this can be a real problem for Reluctant Activists. But there are ways. Promoted as "the Green gift of the '90s," the Earth Basket is an alternative to sending flowers or fruits-and-cheeses on special occasions. Besides bolstering one's activist self-esteem, it painlessly encourages others to energetic levels of activism.

The basket is lined with Eco-pack, an environment-friendly packing material, and stuffed with an assortment of consciousness-raising products, including a copy of "The Recycler's Handbook"; a nondisposable shopping tote; a vegetable scrubber to remove pesticides; a cedar sachet to substitute for mothballs; a tire gauge to help save on gas mileage; "Save the Whale" soap; and a box of Rainforest Crunch candies, among other pro-planet stuff.

"Designed to make the transition to an ecological lifestyle attractive, convenient and enjoyable," says the promo. And it can be delivered anywhere in the country.

Prices range upward from $39.99—no more expensive than a dozen long-stems that would wilt in a week anyway. To order, call 1-800-EARTH 49.

Speaking of rain forests, this is one more cause that poses some low-exertion possibilities for Reluctant Activists. Start with "The Rainforest Book: How You Can Save the World's Rainforests" (Living Planet Press, $5.95), a nice little volume that wedges plenty of suitable tasks between the more demanding ones. Skim past hard-core suggestions such as "Organize a 'Rainforest Awareness Week' at your children's school" and "Build a back-yard wildlife refuge," both of which require getting out of the recliner.

Instead, adopt an acre of rain forest through the Adopt-an-Acre program of the Nature Conservancy (1815 Lynn St., Arlington, Va. 22209). This helps to pay for protection of threatened territory and supports the acquisition of these drippy but ecologically beneficial jungles for safekeeping. And the honorary land deed the Conservancy folks send can be displayed prominently, all this for only $30.

Too much? For $5 less, Reluctant Activists can add "Guardian of the Amazon" to their credentials, via the World Wildlife Fund (60 St. Clair Ave. E., Suite 201, Toronto, Ontario M4T 1N5). The money goes toward guarding the land and teaching locals how to harvest without destroying it. But no deed to hang on the wall.

Other cheap ways to make sure the rain stays mainly in the rain forest: Disposable chopsticks, this book informs us, are made from tropical timber—much of it from these very rain forests. So for home use, Reluctant Activists eat with reusable chopsticks—and know why. And when carrying out Chinese, they say "no thanks" to the throw-away sticks, and wink at the person in line behind them, adding, "To save the rain forests, you know."

There are brands of commonly purchased products that help to support the rain forests—and enviromnentalism in general—either through contributions from profits or by being produced in a nondestructive manner. Ben & Jerry's Homemade Ice Cream, for example, features one flavor called Rain Forest Buttercrunch, made from Brazil nuts harvested properly in the Amazon. And The Body Shop cosmetics chain is developing a line of products made from rain forest flora. More expensive? Perhaps. But spending a little extra for "environmentally friendly products" would promote Reluctant Activists to what Roper calls the Green minority.

Saving Their Skins

Animal rights isn't everybody's pet project. But you don't have to wear a "Rats Have Rights" T-shirt (for $15 plus $2 shipping from RAGE Products of Protest, P.O. Box 86837, Portland, Ore. 97206) to acknowledge that some animals are getting a raw deal these days.

Refusing to buy a high-ticket chinchilla is one convenient way to join forces with the animal liberalion front—and save big bucks as well. But to make it a principled decision, the reluctant Activist needs to bone up a little on some facts and philosophy. "Animal LIberation" by Peter Singer has been the primer on this for 15 years and is a real conversation-provoker for your bookshelf. The new, second printing is updated and priced at $19.95—a substantial discount over a visit to the furrier's and a much better karmic deal.

For other low-impact ways of breaking into the animal lib movement, consult "Save the Animals: 101 Easy Things You Can Do" (Warner Books, $4.95). Though the Reluctant Activists will probably have to haul out the Webster's to look up "vivisection," it does contain a few ideas on helping animal friends by doing virtually nothing.

For example, for a self-addressed and stamped envelope, the D.C.-based People for the Ethical Treatment of Animals (PETA, P.O. Box 42516, Washington, D.C. 20015) will send you a handy wallet-size, cruelty-free shopping guide that separates companies into those that hurt animals to make their product:, and those that don't. And for that child in Reluctant Activists' lives, the "I Love Animals and Broccoli Coloring Book" is free for two first class stamps from the Vegetarian Resource Group (P.O. Box 1463, Baltimore, Md. 21203).

Animal rights is territory where expressing the right opinion at the right moment goes a long way. Again, this doesn't take much effort but does require basic knowledge. But even that can be minimized by expressing opinions to those who really don't want to hear more about it: "Save the Animals!" has a chapter titled "Dial 1-800 . . .", which provides easy-chair activists the toll-free numbers of major corporations that use animal experiments to test products, and companies that sponsor rodeos or promote hunting and furs. A few minutes spent provoking them might make a difference.

Which came first, the chicken or the egg? The argument itself is too taxing for Reluctant Activists, but as it turns out, doing something to save both the chicken and the egg isn't. In his book "How to Make the World a Better Place," Jeffrey Hollender proposes that people eat brown-shelled eggs. "Protect the diversity of a species and fight reduction of the gene pool at breakfast," he declares, explaining that 95 percent of people in the United States who eat eggs eat white ones—those laid by White Leghorn hens—creating the possibility of a genetic catastrophe should that species ever be attacked by disease.

"If you're a passionate or even occasional egg lover there's no reason to quit your job and launch a 24-hour-a-day vigil outside the nearest chicken farm," he writes. "The problem of a declining egg gene pool can be addressed simply by buying brown eggs . . . If a fair number of people were to make just one small adjustment in their lives and buy brown eggs, they could drastically alter the gene pool {and} create a new market that justifies farmers raising another breed."

Eating as a political act is a Reluctant Activist's cup of tea, which, by the way, is one of many Third World grocery products that can be purchased through alternative trade organizations. These are groups that try to minimize economic and environmental rape of Third World producers and support socially responsible companies. One such organization is Co-op America, which will send a free catalogue on request (locally call 202-872-5307; long distance call 1-800-424-2667). This group makes responsible consumerism a breeze by locating and marketing such products as organic cashews that help to reforest Honduras, coffee that helps support. farmers' cooperatives in Nicaragua, and wool hats that provide income for a cooperative of women in Nepal.

Dial-a-Cause

As in most things today, the telephone has made the activist world so much smaller and manageable. Enter the era of 900-number activism. USA-EARTH (1-900-872-3278) mails out boilerplate letters of protest to designated government officials and corporate heads on a variety of issues. Cost: $1.99 the first minute and 99 cents each subsequent minute. And for 99 cents a minute, GreenLine (1-900-446-4761) provides daily updates on environmental topics.

Another company targeting the Reluctant Activist is The Write Cause (P.O. Box 751328, Petaluma, Calif. 94975). For $35 annually, Reluctant Activists receive a monthly newsletter summarizing the hottest issues relating to animal treatment and environmental protection. They check off the issues that get them hot, return the form to The Write Cause in the stamped and addressed envelope provided, and within two weeks, get "personalized" letters, pre-addressed to the offending corporations or agency, awaiting a signature.

Almost as easy is a new product called "EarthCards" (Conari Press, $6.95), which includes 32 postcards with preprinted messages on a range of environmental issues: rain forest preservation, global warming, toxic waste. They are pre-addressed to movers and shakers, CEOs and politicians, who are in positions to make a difference. All one need do is choose the message, sign a name, lick a stamp and drop a card in the mailbox. As the "EarthCards" booklet says, to be an effective activist "you don't have to research the issues in depth . . . or write a whole letter or look up any addresses." In fact, you don't have to do much at all.

January 14, 1991

Sweat

The Mercury's Rising, So Work Up a Lather and Let the Good Times Roll

HENRY ALLEN

Think of a droplet of sweat arising from your forehead. Think of the tiniest waterlily of worry blossoming on your brow, or arriving like a kindly postcard from the Mother Ocean inside us all, perhaps a freckling of sweat, sweat scattered across your face like a sort of Protestant work-ethic confetti, like thrown rice at a wedding of Animal and Heat, sprouting, burgeoning, gathering into dank little mule trains that skid down the mountainsides of your face, your neck, collapsing down your thorax like the rain on a movie windowpane just before the flashback, starting and stopping, rappelling down your rib cage while an outraged mob streams through the fever ports of your armpits—flooding, leaking, turning the hair on your arms into low-tide seaweed, turning your bellybutton into a jolly little hot tub, igniting your mosquito bites, turning your shirt into something that feels like chain mail made out of fresh pasta, making your clothes soggy and stiff, your skin slippery and sticky at the same time, making you feel both befouled and cleansed, as it happens, an odd combination, part of the moral ambiguity of sweat, a frantic and pathetic quality about it all, like an overcooked duck falling apart in its own grease.

> She liked the sweat, liked the way it felt, slick as oil, in all the joints of her body, her bones, in the firm sliding muscles, tensed and locked now, ready to spring—to strike—when the band behind her fired up the school song: "Fight On Dead Rattlers of Old Mystic High."—Harry Crews, in "Feast of Snakes"

People do like to sweat. Admittedly, some don't, particularly women, but there are those who like it, who think that a big sweat is a good sweat, that sweat means power, health, authenticity and saintliness.

A good, big sweat may not make you feel ready for a speech or a job interview, but it does set you up for whatever primal challenges life might throw at you—boxers like to come into the ring in a full sweat before the fight has even started. If you pay the big money for ringside seats, you can get it on you too. Maybe that's why people buy those seats.

122

In 1882, one F. Blumentritt reported in a German-language journal that "In Tud, or Warrior Island, in the Torres Straits, men would drink the sweat of renowned warriors . . . in order to make themselves 'strong like stone, no afraid.' " The rest of us only have to watch Sly Stallone and Arnold Schwarzenegger movies to get our fill of warrior sweat.

As air conditioning becomes standard in stores, buses, cars, houses and offices, and as more and more people work indoors in service jobs, good sweats are getting harder to find. They are becoming a discretionary luxury, like horses after the invention of the automobile, like wood stoves after the triumph of central heating. Sweat is becoming quaint and reassuringly authentic. Maybe you'll be able to order it from the L.L. Bean catalogue soon.

You jog, you row, you play at physical work in order to sweat. Once you got paid to grunt and lather over rows of dark machines in factories—now you pay to grunt and lather over dark machines in Nautilus rooms. A good sweat makes you feel purged, prepared, virtuous. It is the true altar wine of Calvinism. On the other hand, you tend to associate it with the lower classes, with brutality, with a failure to be "feminine," a semi-mystical advertising concept that gets linked with other semi-mystical concepts such as "freshness." They all preclude sweating.

A good sweat can make you feel healthy, make you feel you've lost weight, and you have—Brooklyn Dodgers pitching great Don Newcombe once claimed he lost 20 pounds in one game. In the 17th century, according to a history of sweat in *Sports Illustrated,* an Italian physician named Sanctorius "built a large metal arm balanced on a fulcrum. He placed weights equal to his body weight on one end of the arm and sat on a platform on the other end for hours at a time—his slow ascension proving beyond doubt that his body was losing weight through so-called 'insensible perspiration.'"

Just about everybody in America thinks there are times when it's healthy to sweat, according to a Research & Forecasts Inc. report on stress for Mitchum Anti-Perspirant and Deodorant.

Seven out of 10 find it pleasurable to sweat when they're doing hard work or sitting in a sauna. And eight out of 10 Americans think it's "very acceptable" to sweat when exercising. Also on the "very acceptable" list: "on a hot day" at 70 percent, "at the beach" at 57 percent, "when dancing at parties" at 32 percent, and "in romantic situations" at 18 percent.

It depends on what you mean by "romantic situations."

You might be thinking of a verse by Aldous Huxley: But when the wearied band

Swoons to a waltz, I take her hand,
And then we sit in peaceful calm,
Quietly sweating, palm to palm.
You might also be thinking of "Fish, Chips and Sweat," by Funkadelic:
Sweat was dropping off of my face,
Fish and chips were all over the place.

You should've seen my baby move.
Hey, hey, hey, we got us a groove.

Black music seems to have more references to sweat than white music. Think of: James Brown's great "Cold Sweat" (1967), "Sweat (Til You Get Wet)" by Brick (1981) and Aretha Franklin's new album, "What You See Is What You Sweat."

White music has the band Blood, Sweat and Tears, a name taken from a speech by Winston Churchill. It's hard to think of other references. In 1945, Stan Renton's big band did "Easy Street," with June Christy singing: "If the sun makes you perspire/ There's a man that you can hire/ To plant trees so you can have some shade/ On Easy Street."

"Perspire" is a euphemism for "sweat," as in the old saw: "Animals sweat, men perspire, ladies glow." This euphemism is a tradition. So is complaining about it. In 1791, a British magazine complained that "it is well known that for some time past, neither man, woman nor child . . . has been subject to that gross kind of exudation which was formerly known by the name of sweat; . . . now every mortal, except carters, coal-heavers and Irish chairmen . . . merely perspires."

Men like to sweat more than women do. Women worry more than men that they're going to sweat, and they get more embarrassed when they do, according to the Mitchum survey. Men take such pride in all their fluid output, though, the spitting and writing of initials in the snow and so on. Maybe it's a case of fluid envy—their production is so tiny when you compare it with women's feeding and breeding of the human race.

Why aren't women proud of it?

"For many women, to have any wetness break through is to lose their femininity," says Connie Comstock, a group leader in antiperspirant and deodorant product development at Procter & Gamble. It's also to ruin clothes, not just with the sweat but with the chemicals from the stuff they put on to stop the sweat, those bad scenes where a blue dress turns pink under the arms or a dress gets concentric rings of sweat, salt, chemicals or dye descending down the sides. Men don't have these problems, wearing cotton shirts. They also wear T-shirts, which women don't, for whatever reason.

Also, somewhere in the race memory lurks the reminder that it was Eve who ate the forbidden fruit, thus condemning mankind to sweat. God said: "In the sweat of thy face shalt thou eat bread, till thou return unto the ground."

In any case, toiletries manufacturers say that more than 90 percent of adult women in America use antiperspirants at least once a week and usually daily, while half of men settle for a deodorant only. Sweat by itself is odorless, by the way. But when bacteria under your arms eat sweat, they put out funky acids.

Some women "love to sweat, but if they're new to it they're uneasy," says Tracy Smyth McMullan, an instructor at the BodyLine Exercise Studio and Boutique in Bethesda. "I remember when I started eight years ago, people weren't accepting of sweat—a lot of people are apprehensive about the appearance of sweat. My mother would have said that sweat is not clean, you need deodorant, fans, changing clothes."

There even seems to be a subtle sweat competition among some instructors, the ones who wear light-colored leotards to show that they're not trying to look thinner, the way the clients do. Lighter leotards show the sweat too. But the instructors don't care, that's the message. They're free of those old mamma-lore taboos.

"They'll say, 'I sweat like a dog,' " McMullan says.

Some aerobics instructors tell their clients that they're sweating out toxins. This is part of the lore of steam baths, saunas and Indian sweat lodges too. And there's an odd sense of peace that comes with waking up after a night sweat—the fever has broken, you feel released. Somewhere, Hunter Thompson writes of asking a doctor about his constant and profuse sweating. The doctor inquires about Thompson's drug and alcohol intake. Thompson describes it. The doctor tells him the only problem would be if he stopped sweating.

Sweat researchers tell us that this is hooey, that sweat bears off little in the way of impurities. It's mostly water with a few salts in it. Still, you feel cleansed.

Even blessed. During the day of her appealing religious crisis in the ladies' room of Sickler's restaurant, J.D. Salinger's Franny Glass does a lot of sweating. Her date, the awful Lane Coutell, says to her:

"You're sweating. Not sweating, but I mean your forehead's perspiring quite a bit."

"It is? How horrible! I'm sorry . . . . "

But we readers are proud of her. Her sweat proves her authenticity in a world of phonies.

On the other hand, wasn't that Richard "I am not a crook" Nixon sweating away on television, back in the old days? Then he stopped. Word went around that he was putting antiperspirants on his face.

People who are physically fit sweat more, and sooner, than couch potatos. People who worry sweat more than those who don't. We sweat for two reasons— heat and emotion. The emotional sweat gives us clammy palms, wet feet and wet armpits. It gives us the cold sweats referred to by poets from Sappho to James Brown.

An absence of sweat can be a sign that something is wrong, evil wrong. Sweat has a morality to it. In "The Big Sleep," Raymond Chandler describes the ancient, half-dead and all-rotten General Sternwood sitting in an overheated greenhouse, surrounded by dripping orchids and wrapped in a traveling rug, hardly warm, reminiscing about a son-in-law of wonderful vitality, a man capable of "sweating like a pig."

Actually, animals don't come close to our capacity for sweat. "The development of sweat glands and of the associated nervous apparatus has been most highly attained in man," according to Yas Runo, who published the benchmark "Human Perspiration" in 1956. It's a human thing. Hence its association with Original Sin, work, worry and truth-telling—sweat is one of the things that lie detectors measure.

The climax of "The Great Gatsby," with its terrible truth-telling, happens on a hot day, everyone sweating except Gatsby, that gorgeous fraud. Daisy says to him: "You always look so cool."

In "On the Road," Jack Kerouac's Dean Moriarty never stops sweating. Sweat is water from the rock of hipness. Dean goes to hear George Shearing play the piano, "innumerable choruses with amazing chords that mounted higher and higher till the sweat splashed all over the piano and everybody listened in awe and fright."

We like to watch performers sweat. It means they're working and they care.

The American public can even rank movies by how much sweating goes on in them. Given a list of "Rocky," "Body Heat," "Fatal Attraction," "Sea of Love," "Broadcast News" and "Who Framed Roger Rabbit," they will rank them in precisely that order for containing "the most memorable sweaty scene," according to the Mitchum report.

Work up a sweat. Sweat it out. Sweat bullets. Sweat blood. Ride 'em till they sweat.

On the other hand: No sweat. Don't sweat it. Thoreau, the great cosmic wise guy of the 19th century, said: "It is not necessary that a man should earn his living by the sweat of his brow unless he sweats easier than I do."

If you don't like to sweat, imagine what life would be like if you couldn't. Imagine those high-tension occasions when you dread sweating, and think of the alternatives—giving a speech, say, and having to periodically pick up the pitcher of ice water and pour it over your head, like an elephant. Or doing a job interview while slavering like a Saint Bernard.

Better to sweat.

July 20, 1991

Issues; Safety In A Can?

Controversy Over Self-Defense Sprays

DAVID STREITFELD

Murder is never easy to understand, but the slaying of two University of Florida college students June 6 has produced more questions than most—especially after Alan Robert Davis, a 29-year-old carpet cleaner, was arrested.

The young Gainesville women had renewed their lease for another year, and shampooed carpets were the reward. What happened after Davis arrived is still unclear. According to police and prosecutors' accounts in the local media, Davis said or did something that caused 20-year-old Eleanor Anne Grace to shoot him with Mace. The spray hit Davis in the face, whereupon he became so enraged he knocked her out.

The other roommate, 22-year-old Carla McRishnie, tried to defend Grace, causing Davis to choke her until she stopped breathing. He then finished off Grace. The bodies were discovered the next day, one in a bathroom, one hidden under a bed.

Davis, who submitted a bill for cleaning the carpets to the apartment manager, was arrested June 8. He had been routinely sought out for questioning as one of the last to see them alive. After a lengthy interrogation, police say he confessed to the strangulations.

For the manufacturers of Mace, it was a nightmare. The two victims reportedly were given their little tear-gas canisters by their parents after the still-unexplained slayings last year of five Gainesville students. What had been hoped to make the two women safer may have played a role in their deaths.

MSI Mace, manufacturer of the spray for the last five years, released a statement saying "there is currently no evidence that tear gas was discharged . . . The determination that Chemical Mace was involved . . . is premature and, most likely, inaccurate."

At the least, matters are murky. Lt. Spencer Mann of the Alachua County Sheriff's Department said Friday that "a couple of containers" of chemical repellent were found at the scene, but "we're still awaiting lab results" as to whether they were used at the scene. He also said he didn't know whether the canisters were Mace, which tends to be used as a generic for all chemical sprays, or one of its less-well-known competitors.

James Kardas, creative director of MSI, notes that "any weapon you choose to use could cause an individual who's intent on doing you harm to become more upset. It could get the adrenaline up. If you shoot someone in the shoulder with a handgun, better watch out. He could come after you, use the gun on you." Mace warns on its label that people with "reduced sensitivity to pain" are difficult to stop.

The question remains: Is it better to carry Mace or not? In the District, you can't do it legally, which could tend to complicate matters for those who, say, carry a canister in their glove compartment and drive across the District line frequently. It's legal in Virginia and Maryland, as indeed it is everywhere except New York and Wisconsin.

The manufacturer says sales are booming. MSI, a privately held Vermont company, bought Mace from Smith and Wesson in 1986. It's doing some aggressive marketing, including an ad that plays on CNN twice a day. That, coupled with the ever-increasing public awareness of violent crime, has resulted in sales being up 570 percent over where they were 18 months ago. It's generally thought that Mace accounts for half of all sales of personal tear gas products.

While MSI won't give specific figures, it's clear there's a lot of Mace out there somewhere. But no one really knows just how much, or where.

If you try to take a canister on an airplane at National Airport, for instance, the security people will either give it to a non-boarding member of your party or, if that isn't possible, confiscate it. A spokeswoman says there hasn't really been any upswing in such seizures, however.

Similarly, at the University of Maryland at College Park, a member of the campus police doesn't recall any recent incidents involving Mace at the school. "There's no evidence one way or the other" that there's an increased amount on campus, he says.

The question of efficacy is even hazier. Independent studies seem in short supply. MSI says it doesn't have any, and no one else seems to know of any either. It's likely, of course, that if you foil a mugging with Mace, no one's ever going to know about it except your friends.

Out of every 100 canisters of Mace that are sold, Kardas estimates that "maybe one" ever gets used. "I would hope," he says, "that none do."

Mark Lollar and Larry Denny are in business to sell you something, a fact that shouldn't be forgotten while reading the following. But the odd thing is, they don't quite agree on what you should be buying.

Denny owns the Cop Shop in Arlington. His philosophy: "I don't believe you should turn the other cheek. You run out of cheeks." He sells an increasing amount of Mace, currently about a dozen canisters a week. Other chemical sprays are hot too: He does about 20 or 30 cans a week of those. "You print a murder story, and all of a sudden sales rise. Especially every time you print a story about a serial murderer. Isn't that terrible? This is a growth business, I have to say."

He doesn't think Mace is strong enough to be effective, tries to dissuade customers from pistols, but is enthusiastic about stun guns, which work by applying an electrical charge to the person at the wrong end. This takes some convincing of the potential customer. "I get this complaint: 'Oh, I don't want to get that close.' Who the hell asked you? I'm the armed robber, I set the rules, we're going to do things my way."

Another protest: "That's a lot of money." Denny has an answer for that too. "Out here in Virginia, if you get your butt whipped, it's going to cost $100 to ride the ambulance to the hospital. Ninety dollars for a stun gun is chump change."

Lollar, general manager of Knight Tactics in Alexandria, doesn't even sell Mace or similar products. "They don't work consistently enough," he says. He also doesn't sell stun guns. "You have to get too close to use them. Unless you know follow-up techniques—what most folks know as martial arts—the chances of it being taken away are very good."

Lollar is instead most enthusiastic about Cap-Stun, a pepper spray now produced by Zarc International in Bethesda. He sells about 100 canisters every week or 10 days. An inflammatory agent that works at a range of four to six feet, Cap-Stun is touted as a micro-droplet that will hang in the air if it doesn't immediately hit a target.

"If someone's moving toward you," Lollar says, "they move right into it." Breathing soon becomes very difficult, courtesy of the pepper, and your eyes tend to shut. Damage is not permanent, but the immediate effect is said to be impressive.

Again, though, substantiated evidence of it saving people's lives is in short supply. "You never hear about when it works," says Lollar. "You hear when it doesn't." There's also a controversial incident in which Cap-Stun worked too well. Two New York police officers last August were trying to subdue a 14-year-old who was attacking them with a knife. So they sprayed him with Cap-Stun. They sprayed him again. Then they used a stun gun.

At this point, according to the New York Daily News, "an explosion occurred, touching off a small fire that burned the teen and ignited wallpaper." A sergeant was quoted: "We had no idea it was flammable. The manufacturer never gave us a warning."

Gardner Whitcomb, the developer of Cap-Stun, says that news accounts were over-dramatized, the product is no more flammable than a hair spray, and that the version of the spray used was more powerful than the commercially available stuff. Yet he concedes that "training is very much necessary—because it's so different."

Not different enough, say the makers of Mace, who think as little of Cap-Stun as the Cap-Stun people think of Mace.

"The pepper-based products require proximity to be effective," asserts MSI's Rardas. "A woman in a situation where someone is coming after her, maybe in a jerky manner, is going to find it hard to be accurate. You need to hit someone directly in the face, and need to be close to do that. With Mace, the only requirement is hitting in the upper torso." MSI is, nevertheless, coming out very soon with its own pepper-based product. Gotta keep up with the competition.

Like Mace, Cap-Stun is illegal in D.C. "Everything's illegal in the District, except you can scream as loud as you like," complains the Cop Shop's Denny. Which doesn't mean that people in the city aren't carrying his sprays anyway. "Look for the ladies carrying a little leather case, about the size of a roll of nickels, with a ring of keys on the bottom. They're my customers."

It's very American, very high-tech, to think that technology is going to save you. Patricia Occhiuzzo Giggans has seen more self-defense products than most. The executive director of a Los Angeles rape crisis center and chair of the National Coalition Against Sexual Assault's self-defense task force, she is sent the stuff regularly. She doesn't think much of most of it.

"There was the perfume that smelled bad—you broke a vial and there was going to be this odor," she remembers. "Then there's the latest new siren. They always say, 'This is the loudest noise ever,' but they're never that bad."

She's not overly enthused about Mace or other sprays. "We know of too many incidents where the canister didn't go off, or the woman goes to get it and realizes it isn't in her purse. 'I don't have my Mace!' You become dependent on it, and then it short-circuits the brain and paralyzes you."

There's a larger point here. "I don't know of anything that works 100 percent of the time. When it comes to your life, I wouldn't believe any product or person or method which says, 'We guarantee it.' You need to be able to depend on yourself, because that's who's going to be with you. Your German shepherd, the police, Mace, your husband might not be there."

The products are nevertheless popular because people want the quick and easy way. It's an understandable impulse, this desire for a magic bullet that will painlessly defend you from all comers. But it's unrealistic and could be dangerous. Even those who opt for carrying Mace or another spray should test out a canister—Mace sells for about $18 each—to get some idea of the angle of fire.

Self-defense courses are another option encouraged by Giggans. These can be found through rape crisis centers, martial arts schools, newspaper advertisements, sports clubs, YWCAs and similar organizations. Her advice:

Learn the difference between self-defense and a martial art. Despite what happens in the movies, you've got to be very, very good to use karate or judo on an attacker.

Are the moves being taught simple but still effective? Does the instructor work on mind and attitude as well as body?

Is the instructor and atmosphere respectful, or do they put down women's fears? "I've seen instructors say, 'You don't have to be afraid,' and do something fancy. They're trying to impress you rather than help you acquire skills. But they can also go wrong by trying to frighten you."

The amount of time needed in a self-defense course differs with each person. Just don't think it only takes half an hour. And be careful of gadgets. There is, says Giggans, "no quick fix to safety. If there were I would have gotten rich a long time ago."

July 16, 1991

Consummate Consumer

Fields Of Power—Old Town Going
Under Amid Electromagnetic Debate

DAVID STREITFELD

The meeting at the Alexandria city hall had the atmosphere of a family get-together, where you don't have to be explicit about unpleasant facts like Uncle Bill's drinking or Cousin Susan's shoplifting because everyone knows them anyway. So instead you refer to "the situation" and "the problem," which was the way things went for most of the status report on the wldergrounding of the Old Town power lines.

Ken Schutz from Virginia Power detailed what he called "a conceptual plan for the beginning of what will be a long-term project." A map was displayed of the rewired seven-block area, and a chart shown that ticked off various stages of the prcocess: acquiring land rights, developing conduits and so on. It was all very informal, right down to passing around a package of Pepperidge Farm shortbread cookies.

Supposedly, the wires are being put underground as part of the continued sprucing up of historic Old Town. That's what Schutz says, and that's what it says on official documents. But for the 10 people in the audience there was a much more important motivation, even if for the longest time no one mentioned it.

Finally, Catherine Webster grew impatient. "It's important to remember why we all came together a year ago: the potential health hazards of electromagnetic fields," she said. "This isn't a beautification project. Citizens of Alexandria have a basic right not to have health hazards six feet from their houses."

Welcome to the controversial world of electromagnetism. After years on the scientific and media fringes, the idea of electricity as the source of a potential problem is heating up. What's happening in Alexandria is on tha forefront of the issue: This is apparently the first time a local government has told a power company to take existing distribution lines and sink them into the ground for health reasons.

Says Alexandria Mayor Patricia S. Ticer: "The Old Town residents have convinced us, and we have convinced Virginia Power, that there is too much risk associated with the high level of power on these narrow streets. We wouldn't ever think of committing that kind of money"—the city's share of the bill in the first year will come to $500,000—"unless we were convinced there was this danger."

As such, the case is likely to prove influential. "However much you think {Virginia Power} can get away with calling this an historic-preservation decision, there are plenty of people who will see it as a precedent for reducing neighborhood magnetic fields," says Louis Slesin, editor of Microwave News and a close observer of the issue.

The problem is, even those who concede there is a legitimate risk disagree that putting the wires underground is going to solve it. Warns Martin Halper of the Environmental Protection Agency (EPA): "The people on these blocks may very well be spending a lot of money to increase their level of risk."

To understand why, it's necessary to start with the basics. Every time an electrical current flows through a wire, an electromagnetic field, or EMF, is produced that radiates in all directions. This is true for power-distribution lines like Alexandria's, as well as electrical appliances.

While the strength of the field is important, equally significant is the duration of the exposure. An electric razor, for example, produces an extremely high EMF rating, but you only use it for a minute or two a day. Consequently, says Robert Becker, a longtime researcher in biological effects of electrical fields, "We have no indication whatsoever from anecdotal evidence that use of an electric razor is more hazardous than use of a blade razor. The tentative conclusion is that short-term exposures to very strong fields are probably—underline 'probably'—not associated with any harmful effect."

But Becker believes that "exposure of six hours or greater to these fields is bad for you. So you look around your home and say, 'What could my kids sit in front of for several hours a day that plugs into the wall socket?' You come down to the computer and the television set."

Those who don't believe in taking any chances can sit farther back from both. (Thirty inches is a good guess for an absolutely safe minimum, which most people do with a TV anyway.) Then there are things you don't sit in front of, but which the cautious might feel are too close for comfort anyway. If your bedroom clock has a dial face—the type that uses a motor to make the hands move—it doesn't take much effort to make sure it's more than 18 inches from your sleeping head.

Similar recommendations—don't stand in front of an operating microwave for long periods; use an electric blanket only to warm the bed if you're pregnant—have been devised under the label "prudent avoidance." That means they're stress-free and simple, even if the extent that the overlapping electric and magnetic fields influence the body is still not understood.

"There's a broad spectrum of natural magnetic fields, and they probably have a lot to do with the evolution of living forms," says Ross Adey, a professor of neurology at Loma Linda University in California and leading researcher in this area. "Now we come along and, in less than 100 years, have distorted the whole electromagnetic experience by exposing the human organism from the moment of conception to a vastly different set of fields."

Says Becker, whose book "Cross Currents" explores "the perils of electropollution and the promise of electromedicine": "If you have a small cancer beginning, say, in your skin, the body senses it and under normal circumstances kills them." But, Becker speculates, "this kind of field may make the cancer cells grow faster than your body can destroy them."

Studies have shown that workers who are constantly exposed to EMFs also have higher levels of cancer: in an '89 study, electrical engineers had over four times as much brain cancer as unexposed workers; in another '89 study, cable splicers (a speciality among telephone-line repairmen) had 1.8 times as much cancer as other telephone workers, including seven times as much leukemia.

As for the risk to the general public, the spectrum of opinion ranges from *New Yorker* science writer Paul Brodeur, whose feelings on the topic can be gathered from the title of his 1989 book, "Currents of Death: Power Lines, Computer Terminals and the Attempt to Cover Up Their Threat to Your Health," to John Bailar.

A faculty member of the McGill School of Medicine, Bailar summed up his feelings to a reporter when he was in Los Angeles last year, leading a discussion on the subject at the American Statistical Association convention.

"There's enough evidence," he fiaid, "to say it's unlikely there's a health problem related to the power lines, and even if we're wrong and there is a health problem, then it's small."

In December, the EPA weighed in with its "Evaluation of the Potential Carcinogenicity of Electromagnetic Fields." This created a stir because, first, a dispute erupted between the EPA and White House science adviser D. Allan Bromley, who said at the time he was worried about "whether the report might be open to very reasonable misinterpretation that would raise unnecessary fears."

The report's conclusion: There is a "consistent pattern of response which suggests a causal link" between electric field exposures and leukemia, lymphoma and cancer of the nervous system in both children and adults. An earlier draft of the report suggested that EMF was a probable carcinogen—i.e., a cancer-causing agent.

The EPA says more research is needed, but Bob Webster isn't in the mood to wait. A lawyer who lives on South Lee Street in Old Town, Webster discovered EMF via his neighbors. He was sufficiently concerned to ask Virginia Power to take some gauss meter readings, and eventually to buy his own meter.

On one occasion, he got a measurement of over 100 milligauss. Typically, they run between 3 1/2 and 28 milligauss, with a mean of at least 15 at all times—five times the threshold of what many experts consider the danger zone! Some studies have indicated an association with cancer at the 5-7 milligauss level.) The Websters changed the front room closest to the power lines from a bedroom to a storage area.

Others who looked into the situation began to discover the same thing—the result of the streets in question suffering from an unfortunate combination of circumst:ances. There are no front yards, which places the power lines close to the front windows. In addition, two of the lines are carrying enough juice not only to take care of their houses but some of the commercial properties on King Street as well.

The affected homeowners took their complaint to the city, which happened to be renegotiating Virginia Power's franchise to provide electricity to Alexandria. Under the old deal, 100 percent of any undergrounding would have to be paid for by the city. This time around, the renegotiation was used as leverage to get the costs split on a roughly equal basis. The franchise agreement now is in the hands of the lawyers; if matters proceed as expected, work will start this summer.

From Virginia Power's point of view, it's all a matter of aesthetics. "This is an area that has significant historic value. The undergrounding does not have anything to do with EMF," says consumer representative Schutz. Technically, contractually, he's right.

Schutz adds: "We don't know if more is good or less is good. The biologic effects of EMF are not dose-responsive." What this means is that EMF doesn't have linear toxicity. If it did, things would be much simpler.

Some researchers believe that if EMF is toxic, it doesn't work the way sugar does in coffee: two spoonfuls produce a cup that is twice as sweet as one spoonful. Instead it's as if one spoonful of sugar produced sweet coffee, a spoonful-and-a-half yielded an extremely sweet brew, but with two spoonfuls you're back to only a trace of sweetness.

"All the data we have to date show a degree of peculiarity of action with EMFs," says the EPA's Halper. "Where you would intuitively say, 'When I go from 4 to 40 milligauss, I would have a 10-fold increase in risk,' the data indicate that not only is that not the case, but you may have a decrease."

Halper is the EPA's national program manager for EMFs. He's not unsympathetic to the Old Towners' problems, but says, "If the exposure in my home was, let's say, 30 milligauss and burying the lines was going to reduce it to 6 or 7, I would really have to think very, very hard, and probably come to the conclusion that was not a wise thing to do."

Why won't these houses be able to reduce their EMF readings below any possible danger levels? Perhaps they can; it's a point of dispute. Bob Webster argues that the affected homes already fall into "exposure windows." Those readings of 15 milligauss in the front of the house decrease as you move into the back rooms. What if a bedroom, or a bed, ends up where the level is 5 milligauss?

Tom O'Cane doesn't know what to think. The director of environmental services for Alexandria, he has a mountain of information on EMF. "I am confused by conflicting data. It all depends on whom you talk to . . . We've disconnected services to find out what is contributed by the wires outside, and found some of the EMF comes from the grounding of the house itself. It's just baffling."

If rewiring the blocks doesn't reduce the EMF levels to the homeowners' satisfaction, it's going to be a different ballgame.

"They were getting an inequitable share," says O'Kane. "But once the city does the undergrounding, if there is still an elevated reading within the houses, it's up to the individual property owners to take action." This can include putting in a new grounding system or rewiring.

It's a chance they're willing to take. At the meeting last month, the clearest sentiment was urgency. "Let's do it," was the attitude. "We're worried about ourselves and our children."

Even Halper, uncertain as he is about the result, believes, "The money may be well spent in this case, because the people may have such enormous levels of anxiety." And that, he adds, can be detrimental to health all by itself.

"You will never, ever get into a scientific issue that is more complicated or confusing than this one," says the Environmental Protection Agency's Martin Halper. One of the very few things people agree on is the importance of the following three studies:

The groundbreaking work was done in 1979 by the team of Nancy Wertheimer and Ed Leeper, which compared 344 children in the Denver area who had died of cancer with a control group of 344 disease-free kids. The wiring code was then examined for each child's house, which means the power lines were studied to determine the amount of current being provided. Conclusion: "The homes of children who developed cancer were found unduly often near electric lines carrying high currents."

In 1987, there was a follow-up by David Savitz of the University of North Carolina. This study also was done in Denver, but with a different group of children. Savitz not only measured the wire codes but also looked at the magnetic fields inside the homes.

What he discovered was puzzling: While he again found that prolonged exposure to low-level magnetic fields "may increase the risk of developing cancer in children," the presence of the power lines showed a much stronger correlation to disease than the in-home measurements.

Was the equipment Savitz was using—which measured the magnetic fields on a one-time basis—inadequate, or were perhaps the power lines simply a confounding factor? Possibly, it was suggested, the wiring codes simply accompanied Some other problem, and was not itself the instigator of the cancer.

Last month came the first news of a University of Southern California study of 232 cases of childhood leukemia. Information was collected from three sources: the wire codes, and both instantaneous and 24- to 72-hour measurements in the homes.

The full study hasn't been released, but it has been announced that, just as in the Denver studies, the wire codes "were associated with risk of leukemia": a statistically significant 2.5 times increase in the odds ratio. But there was no similar association with the 24-hour or the spot measurements.

If the wires are really at fault, why don't the fields they produce show up on the recording meters?

Savitz offers this analogy: "If we want to know about long-term diet and disease, one thing we can ask is what you ate yesterday, and examine it carefully and see if that predicts whether you have colon cancer.

"Alternatively, we can ask about your diet through adulthood. That method sounds much cruder, and it is, but it's probably a better measure over the period of interest."

Consequently, says Savitz—who does not have a reputation as being an alarmist on this issue—his initial conclusion about the USC study is that "it could only move you in a positive direction. It seems more likely that these fields pose a hazard."

March 11, 1990

Oliver Sacks, Hero of the Hopeless

The Doctor of 'Awakenings,' with Compassion for the Chronically Ill

JUDITH WEINRAUB

"I had a dream about manganese the other night," says Oliver Sacks, chortling over the idea. "I can't think of all the details, but I felt so good when I woke up.

"It was a dream about a stable mental object," he continues with delight. "You know, people may come and go, but manganese is forever. Its electrons behave themselves. They've got Pauli's exclusion principle. They can't leave orbits. You know where you are with manganese."

As a source of inspiration for dreams, the periodic table of elements isn't exactly standard. But for writer-neurologist Sacks, it's a natural.

A shy, burly Santa Claus of a man, Sacks, 57, is a consummate scientist, a compassionate clinician. He is also the model for the brilliant, caring doctor whose work with seemingly hopeless patients in a Bronx hospital for the chronically ill is described in the new movie "Awakenings."

And today, huddled self-protectively at his desk in his office in a Greenwich Village apartment building, he is not at all comfortable with finding himself at the wrong end of a microscope. "Celebrity is not a word I use or a concept I'm very interested in," he says.

He has been avoiding the spotlight all his life, preferring instead to define himself through his work with communities of outsiders: the strangely "frozen" post-encephalitic patients described in "Awakenings"; the neurologically damaged ones he detailed in "The Man Who Mistook His Wife for a Hat"; the deaf culture he wrote about in "Seeing Voices." He works with them, studies them, and then, through his best-selling books, interprets their worlds to the world at large.

It is with these people whom society has shunted aside that Sacks is more at ease. An erudite, expressive man, he is not married. He lives alone. "I feel I don't have any identity," he says simply. "I'm a resident alien, a kindly resident alien."

So it was with considerable trepidation that Sacks approached the personal exposure involved—both for him and his patients—in seeing his 1973 book translated to the big screen. (He is the film's technical consultant. The screenplay was written by Steven Zaillian.) His book—essentially a compilation of case studies from the spring and summer of 1969—had been adapted many times before, as a documentary film, a radio drama, a stage play, a one-act play by Harold Pinter. But the idea of a flat-out commercial film with mega-movie-stars Robin Williams and Robert De Niro at first was disturbing.

"I was worried about the relation of fact to fiction—particularly the fictional me," says Sacks, his voice still full of stammers and the accent of an upper-class English Jewish childhood. "I wondered very much if it was possible to act a neurological disorder.

"I finally decided that the plot and character and story were not quite my business but that representing neurological and medical and historical reality was. As long as I could imagine it, it was okay."

In the fall of 1989 while the film was being shot, Sacks traveled to the Brooklyn set at 6:30 every morning before starting his ordinary workday. The company members took him to their hearts. "Oliver was invaluable," says director Penny Marshall. "If we had any medical questions at all, I would turn to him and say, 'Would this happen? Is this okay?' and he'd say, 'Well, maybe a little more like that.' Robin and Bobby both loved talking to him. He was terrific."

What allowed Sacks to relax a little was his decision not to allow his name to be used (his character, played by Robin Williams, is called Dr. Malcolm Sayer). And by Williams's ability to observe him unobtrusively, in order to incorporate some of the doctor's mannerisms in his performance. Says Sacks, "Robin was infinitely tactful and never gave me a feeling of watching me. I think he has created a credible, real person. Who is not me."

No Happy Endings

"I wanted happy endings," says Sacks wistfully.

They were not to be.

Sacks first discovered the patients whose poignant odyssey is chronicled in "Awakenings" in 1966 at Beth Abraham Hospital, a chronic care facility in the Bronx. Frozen in a variety of physically distorted, trancelike states for decades, they were all victims of an international outbreak of encephalitis lethargica (familiarly known as sleeping sickness) in the years after World War I. Thought to be retarded, mad or simply undecipherable medical puzzles, they had been stashed away, forgotten.

Young Sacks, Oxford- and UCLA-trained, saw a similarity in his patients' symptoms and those of Parkinson's disease, and was intrigued by the possibility of trying out L-dopa, a new drug that had been helpful to victims of Parkinson's. For two years he hesitated.

"Partly I didn't know what would come out of it—they were so complex physiologically," he recalls. "And partly these patients had been so out of the world, so turned away from the world, I didn't know how bearable it might be for them. I didn't know what sort of Pandora's box would be let out."

The hot New York summer of 1968 made his decision for him. There was no air conditioning, and many of them died. "I thought, Ollie, you'll spend a lifetime procrastinating and hesitating, and the rest of these poor patients will die."

He administered the drug, first on one (played by De Niro), then gradually on the others, and found that, miraculously, it woke them up. But the awakenings were of limited durations. In some cases sooner, in others later, things started to go wrong and the L-dopa produced a tic-ridden manic behavior, even with reduced doses. When taken off the drug, the patients returned to their former state. And each one responded to the drug—and to its inevitable failure—differently.

Sacks was despondent. Between March and July, although his apartment was only 100 yards away, he spent 20-hour days at the hospital, trying to stabilize the patients. "I wondered what the hell had I got them into," he says. "I couldn't understand the fluctuations and I didn't know what to do. I worried that I was doing something wrong."

But those concerns were medical. It was the ethical side that really tormented him. The L-dopa experience had caused the patients great suffering. "Did I have the right to meddle," he remembers asking himself.

The patients asked that question too. Says Sacks, "One or two of them said to me, you open the window and you raise unbearable hopes and prospects. And now you close it."

Traumatic Childhood

The reliability of science was what had attracted Sacks to it in the first place. As a child in London, he'd been separated from his family and sent away to boarding school to avoid the dangers of World War II. He rarely saw his parents or knew when he would see them next. To make matters worse, he remembers the couple who ran the school as "a disturbed pair, abusers."

Whatever the impact of the situation ("I probably have something of a traumatic sort of blur about the period, which years of analysis haven't dissipated," he says), he connects his desire for stability and predictability to the experience.

"All I can be certain of," he recalls, "is that when I returned to London a month short of 10, I almost immediately developed a passion for science, and in particular for chemistry and the periodic table."

And for numbers. Unlike the location of the first bubble in a boiling liquid or the variations in the flow of water from a tap, numbers were predictable. "As a child I would feel numbers as my friends," he says. "They wouldn't deceive or slip away."

His interests seemed natural to his parents, both doctors: his father, who had given up academic life to become the Yiddish-speaking general practitioner in London's East End in the 1920s, and his mother, a professor of anatomy who was the first woman to be allowed to join the Royal College of Physicians and Surgeons.

Sacks seems to share both parents' skills, the humanity of his father (who died last summer at 94 after having spent the previous four years making daily house calls via taxi), and the acuity of his mother (who died in 1972).

He refers to both as "medical storytellers." His father, who he estimates probably saw more than 100,000 patients, could recall family medical tendencies for generations back. And his mother reveled in sharing her ideas. "She loved telling stories to everyone, the butcher, the milkman," says Sacks. "She didn't have two forms of discourse. Whether it was the colleague or the gardener, the same sort of narrative was given to both."

Sacks's destiny seemed fixed. By 1958, he has gotten his medical degree and was on his way to a series of internships. His father wanted him to join his practice. Not knowing quite what he was going to do next, Sacks found himself "between continents and between lives." Then in 1960, he came to Canada and the United States for a holiday, and soon after he arrived sent home a one-word telegram: "Staying."

He is not sure what he meant by it. "I wished not to belong, and I wished to belong," he ventures. In any case, he had promised himself California. So, putting away "the soft European name of Oliver," he headed west, where, embracing his legitimate middle name, he became Wolf Sacks, the "lycanthropic creature of the freeways." Tall and lean, his hair slicked back, riding a motorcycle. For a time, he was an unofficial physician to a chapter of the Hell's Angels.

From the fall of 1960 until the summer of 1961, he was footloose. With the arrival of his green card (he'd applied for it when he came to America), he became employable, and continued along the neurological path that led him from California hospitals to the patients at Beth Abraham.

"It was a complete accident I went to work with post-encephalitics," he says. "But we were made for each other."

Criticism and Chaos

In the summer of 1970, in a letter to the *Journal of the American Medical Association,* Sacks published his findings on 60 patients he had maintained on L-dopa (sometimes on, sometimes off, sometimes combined with other drugs) for more than a year. The letter explained that all of the patients had done well at first, but then all of them got into trouble. He had found no easy way of controlling or predicting their reactions though the condition of many of them improved.

His letter caused a furor. An entire issue of *JAMA* was devoted to letters Sacks describes as "abusive."

"I was publicly roasted," he says. "I think a lot of my colleagues really felt threatened by notions of uncontrollability and unpredictability that reflected on their own power and reflected on the power of science."

He was wildly upset. "I'm a genuine neurologist and observer," he says. "And these were my patients. I cared for them, and I passionately wanted things to be right. And if they couldn't be right, I at least wanted them to be intelligible." Sacks wrote to each of the respondents, asking them to come to the hospital and see the patients for themselves. None of them came.

Over the years, as he turned his attention to other subjects, he has continued to treat post-encephalitic patients. And continued to brood over the question of what went wrong.

And now a major motion picture has brought his work to the public. Does it give him a feeling of vindication?

It's a question he avoids answering directly. Instead he points to an international conference on Parkinson's that was held in Rome last summer. He was asked to open the conference by presenting his most recent theories on the subject, which have evolved from some of the concepts of contemporary chaos and catastrophe theory.

He describes his report as "an attempt to model many different factors simultaneously in a way somewhat similar to weather forecasting—weather forecasting itself being an interesting example of a kind of chaotic system," he says. Factors such as "the absorption of L-dopa from the gut, the way L-dopa is treated in the bloodstream, the levels of dopa in the perceptors in the brain and an attempt to put everything together instead of trying to seek an increasingly elusive relation between just two things like dose and response."

"What I did do was to introduce this chaos theory thing which tried to embrace what everyone was doing," he says. "And I didn't want to do it in a retaliatory way.

"But myself, I'm rather pleased that 20 years later, in clumsy terms, I'm able to have an attempt at some sort of model or theory."

Does he still feel a need to explain what happened?

"I think it needs to be explained," he says. "But it is currently not in my power to go any farther than I have."

Has he ever regretted using L-dopa in the first place?

"Not at all," he says briskly I regret we didn't have it sooner. For many of my patients it made the difference between living and not living."

Resident Alien

Oliver Sacks really is a resident alien. He has maintained that legal status since he came to the United States in 1960. And since 1967, he has been based in New York, where he lives in a red-shingle house on City Island, a mostly working-class, waterfront enclave of the Bronx. He spotted the house and its pleasant gazebo while he was swimming around City Island one day. (He is a champion swimmer.)

He hates the city. He loves open spaces, and the most he can do in New York is walk in the Botanical Gardens, which he tries to do every day.

"I don't know how I ended up in New York," he says. "For years it didn't matter. I was absorbed in my work and thought, and I hardly noticed where I was."

If he is no longer at home in England or New York or California, he is at home with his patients, whether they are deaf or neurologically damaged or Tourettic (he is hoping to get going on a "an endlessly incubated and procrastinated book on Tourette's syndrome") or post-encephalitic.

"I wanted to be one of the patients, to be among them, to be both a participant and an observer," he says of the group he awakened. "It has to do with community and identity. I wanted to know more and more what it was like to be them, to actually know what it felt like to have the sensations."

It affected him with the deaf too. And with Touretters. "I'm an honorary Touretter, one of the few they can bear to be with."

Not everyone welcomes him at first, this large, bespectacled, bearded man in a short-sleeved shirt and seersucker trousers—he gets overheated easily—looking for a group of patients to immerse himself in.

"I think originally the deaf community was quite supicious," he laughs. "Who is this weird person? Where does he come from? What does he want? What does he have up his sleeve? Well, I don't have any sleeves. And I don't want to do any more than try and understand them to some extent."

"There are a million people with chronic neurological disease locked away in this country," he says. "They are sort of dismissed and regarded as defective. But it isn't so. I've been in their world myself for a quarter of a century and I find it full of unexpected life and resource and courage and humor and just the sheer capacity to survive—and often without bitterness."

A few years ago Sacks was introduced to a new post-encephalitic patient who had been brought to Beth Abraham. She had been in a state hospital for 45 years. "Somehow, and I don't know why," he says "I looked at her and I wanted to kiss her and embrace her because she was post-encephalitic. I thought, 'you dear old thing.' "

What is there about these patients that attracts him so much? Why build his life around them?

"I'm not sure," he says, venturing that his choices must have something to do with his ambivalence about belonging, and identity, and being an outsider, and his feeling that for him, his way is the safe way, the way he needs.

"And yet sometimes," he says, "I have an image of myself as a little boy with my nose pressed against the window, looking in. I sometimes feel like a sort of Martian. But then I'm a resident alien, you see. Looking in."

January 13, 1991

Study Questions

Chapter Four

1. Tom Shales' passion for room service makes an amusing feature. Do you have a passion that could become the basis for an article. Explain.
2. In "The Big Easy," Peter Carlson refers to a lounge chair as a "Sitman." What's the source of his word invention? Can you make other variations using other items?
3. People often attempt to project an image that is inconsistent with their true lifestyle (i.e. having a diet drink with a large, calorie-rich meal). Think of some paradoxical images (such as armchair activists) that could be used as examples of this self-delusional practice.
4. Hair care is a universal activity. Think of three story ideas related to hair.

5 *World of Work*

Feature writers find more to write about in the workday world than corporate statistics. They probe case studies, trends and interviews for fresh ideas and strive to offer interpretive viewpoints that are original.

Warren Brown's article on "feel engineering" shows that he is as perceptive of consumer standards as marketing experts are. "Building a Feel Good Car" explains Japanese competitiveness and concern for quality products. It also describes changing audience tastes and the lengths companies must go to satisfy those preferences. Details, such as the image of flat vs. shiny-finished plastic, help affirm Brown's thesis.

The expanding world of advertising is Paula Span's topic in "Ads, They're Everywhere." Her coverage not only describes new strategies for reaching mass audiences and now specialized media forms, but also explores the emerging issues of clutter, saturation and consumer backlash. The hot-dog example at the end illustrates how absurd the trend has already become.

Sexy lingerie and boudoir decor are sales tools of Victoria's Secret, an American company profiled by James Morgan in "Frisky Business." Morgan theorizes that the firm's popularity and success are linked to significant societal shifts involving sensuality, pleasure and self-indulgence. Morgan also constructs a selective timeline of fashion and looks beyond the frilly merchandise and clever marketing to reveal the company's real product—hope.

Martha Sherrill's article on swimming pool maintenance men is a delightful example of a seasonal feature. Her reporting blends a daily round with a poolman and his tales of experiences with clients. She bolsters her description of "an archipelago of pools across town" with statistics. She also recalls scenes of poolside action in movies and makes the point that pools used to stand for suburban indolence, money and alcohol, but now represent a lifestyle of exercise and health.

No topic, including technology and science, is inherently boring. Henry Allen looks behind the statistics of America's eroding technological edge to inventors and the creative process. Using a historical approach, Allen ties in two current events as a news peg and illustrates how invention is now linked to consumer products like sneakers.

The question-and-answer interview is occasionally used as a feature format when the topic is important and the subject is candid. This lively exchange explores the futuristic ideas of computer whiz William Gates.

Building a 'Feel Good' Car

'Out-Thonking' a Mercedes and Other Feats of Detail Auto Salesmanship

WARREN BROWN

Carol Jones, a 50-year-old Arlington real estate agent, is shopping for a car that will make her feel younger. Mechanical reliability, vehicle safety and decent mileage top the list of her purchase concerns, but those are basic needs that any automaker should be able to meet. Jones wants a car that feels right, that's fun to drive.

"I like to drive, and what I really want is a car that feels tight when it's going around curves, and that looks good and has good seats," she said.

Jones used to buy American cars. Now she's shopping Japanese, and therein lies much of the explanation for why companies like Toyota and Honda are expanding in a U.S. auto market where their American and European rivals are losing ground.

The Japanese have become masters of what the industry calls "feel engineering"—the ability to enhance consumer perceptions of vehicle quality by perfecting everything readily visible to the buyer, and everything that the buyer can immediately touch, smell and hear.

Done right, feel engineering yields doors that close with an authoritative "thonk" instead of a flimsy metallic "ting." It places minivan cup holders where they are most likely to be used in the vehicle's passenger cabin. It chooses interior plastics, fabric colors and dashboard design as much for emotional appeal and style as it does for their durability.

"It is the difference between shiny plastic and flat-finished plastic," said Francesca J. Giaimo, a 36-year-old assistant manager at the Kennedy Center who owns a 1985 Mazda RX-7. "If plastic is shiny, it screams at you that it's plastic and that it's cheap. The Japanese use a lot of flat-finished plastic, which looks more classy," Giaimo said.

All major automakers do feel engineering, a key element of which involves extensive and expensive market research—the surveying of thousands of current and prospective customers on everything from the way they feel about exterior paint colors to what they think about the feel of buttons and levers used to operate a car's radio or heater.

For competitive reasons, the car manufacturers are hesitant to specify how much money they spend on feel engineering. But according to some auto industry analysts, as much as one-third of a $2 billion product-development budget might be dedicated to pursuing just the right ride, color, dashboard illumination, ventilation and passenger-cabin feel of a car.

The declining fortunes of many American and European car companies can be pinned in part to their reluctance to take the notion of feel engineering seriously, according to many auto industry officials, analysts, sales people and customers.

"General Motors will tell you that their customers aren't interested in that sort of thing—flat-black plastic versus shiny-black plastic, or some richer feeling vinyl," said Ronald E. Harbour, with the auto consulting firm Harbour & Associates Inc. in Troy, Mich. "That's why the people who are interested in that kind of thing are not GM customers. They are Honda's customers, and Toyota's customers, and Mazda's and Mitsubishi's."

No need to persuade Giaimo of that.

She eventually dumped her Ford Fairmont, not so much because of its intermittent mechanical failures as for its flops in the feeling department: "Crushed velvet seats! Tacky, tacky, tacky. They reminded me of the kinds of sofas people used to have in apartments in my old neighborhood in New York. You know? The kind they always covered with clear plastic. Why are American car companies so tacky?"

A 'Reputational Lag'

The question rankles Joel Pitcoff, Ford Motor Co.'s in-house market analyst. It bespeaks a stereotypical view of American car companies that is contrary to the facts, Pitcoff said.

"People can be too generous in the way they heap praise on the Japanese auto industry," he said.

Pitcoff believes the whole idea of feel engineering is overrated. Feel engineering "is more a perception of car aficionados than it is of the general public," Pitcoff said. The general public is more concerned about a car's future trade-in value, durability and reliability, he said.

"In reality, we have narrowed the gap in product quality with the Japanese to the point where the difference in quality is minuscule," said Pitcoff. "But we have a reputational lag, which is bound to be. You can't change history. If a guy owns a three- or-four-year-old car that's a lemon, he's going to remember that."

Christopher Cedergren, an analyst with J.D. Power and Associates in Agoura Hills, Calif., said that Pitcoff's comments miss the point.

Basic quality—good durability and reliability—"is the basic price of admission" for an automaker's presence in today's highly competitive auto market, Cedergren said. That means car companies must concentrate on product image, which means paying attention to detail.

Accordingly, fake wood grain that looks fake—a trademark of many American cars—cheapens a product's image. But good vinyl that looks like leather conveys a stronger sense of quality, Cedergren said.

U.S. automakers say that they put in fake wood grain because their buyers want fake wood grain.

"The perception that a Japanese-built car is a better car is misleading," said Terry Sullivan, GM's director of sales and financial reporting. "It's a question of customer base," what a manufacturer's customers want, he said.

"I don't think it's that the plastic in the Japanese cars is better than the plastic in ours," Sullivan said.

"We have communicated to our customers that we are making better, more attractive cars," he said.

Catching Up With Japan

Still, the Americans have a lot of catching up to do if they are to reverse their decades-long slide in the U.S. market.

As a group, American carmakers have seen their share of U.S. sales drop to about 62 percent today from 95 percent in 1955. Japanese automakers, which barely existed in the U.S. auto market in the 1950s, now hold a 30 percent share. Perhaps even more telling, in the currently sluggish U.S. auto market, Japanese car companies have increased their sales 4 percent over last year's levels, compared with an 11 percent drop for American automakers and a 5 percent decline for the Europeans.

Some Japanese companies, notably Subaru, lost sales. But as a group, the Japanese are successful "because they are doing the basic task of designing a car a lot better and faster" than the Americans and Europeans, said James P. Womack, research director of the International Motor Vehicle Program at the Massachusetts Institute of Technology.

A key element of Womack's research, published last week in a report called, "The Machine that Changed the World," was the determination that Japan uses "lean production systems" in its auto and other major manufacturing industries.

Simply put, lean production allows a manufacturer to turn out a variety of quality products quickly by eliminating 50 percent of the design and development steps used in mass-production programs.

As a result, automakers like Toyota Motor Corp. and Honda Motor Co. can act on market-research information faster than their competitors—turning out completely new products quickly and making fast "touch" and "feel" changes on existing model lines, Womack said.

Jack Rowe, president of Precision Toyota Inc. in Tucson agrees.

"We are constantly being visited by Toyota factory representatives who are asking us about what the customers feel about our products," said Rowe. "But the beautiful thing is that they're serious. I've been them change some things within 90 days after they found out about it," said Rowe, referring to some cosmetic changes, such as the type of levers used.

Several Washington area dealers who sell Japanese and domestic cars supported Rowe's assessment of dealing with Japanese automakers.

"I don't want to appear disloyal to my domestic manufacturers," said one Washington-area dealer who sells Nissan and a variety of other domestic and foreign nameplates. "But the truth is that they are not as responsive as the Japanese," he said.

Where to Put CDs?

That apparent lack of responsiveness has left some customers with factory-installed compact-disc players in 1990 Cadillac Eldorado Touring Coupes that have no compartments for storing compact discs, another Washington-area dealer said.

"It's a little thing. But it's damned irritating to a customer who pays that kind of money for a car," the dealer said of the $30,000 auto.

One GM source said that the oversight in the Eldorado stemmed from a lack of coordination between the people who designed the car's sound system and those who outfitted its interior.

"The sound system was ready to go before a disc storage compartment was ready," the source said.

It is those kinds of seemingly innocuous missteps that most Japanese car companies are trying to avoid in their pursuit of larger pieces of the American market, said Kiyoshi Eguchi, general manager of DCA Advertising in New York, which markets for Mazda and a host of other Japanese companies.

Mazda calls feel engineering kansai, or total sensory experience, Eguchi said. Mazda officials said that the term is more than a slogan.

For example, when Mazda was redesigning its 929 sedan in the mid-1980s, the company spent much money and time trying to determine the right sound the car's doors should make when they closed, Eguchi said. Mazda wanted a "thonk," similar to the sound made by the substantially more expensive Mercedes-Benz 300 cars.

To get that sound, with a Mazda "identity," the company made numerous recordings of sounds made by different car doors, compared them with the Mercedes-Benz 300, and then tried to come up with a way to "out-thonk" the "thonk" of the Mercedes, Mazda officials said.

Chrysler Corp., the smallest of the three native American car companies, also has shown a willingness to make major investments in feel engineering. To hold on to its increasingly challenged lead in the minivan market, Chrysler surveyed its buyers to come up with what the company said was the most ideal way to locate cup holders in its 1991 minivans .

That research also gave Chrysler ideas for changing its minivan instrument panels—for example, equipping them with switches that are "rounded and improved to provide a world-class, silky, satisfying feeling," the company said in a manual describing its new products.

Nissan Motor Co. pursued feel engineering to dizzying heights in its development of its 1990 Infiniti cars. For example, leather interiors for Infiniti Q45 cars were selected from the same breed of cattle to minimize deviations in the texture of the skins.

Nissan officials also spent several months with prospective Infiniti buyers in California to help determine what weight and shape of exterior door handles should be used on the cars. Not even the "new-car fragrance" of the flagship Infiniti Q45 sedan was left to chance, according to a report by Nissan equipment design engineer Nobuo Saegusa.

The result is a new-car smell that mixes sandalwood with rich leather, alternatively sensuous and spiritual, Nissan believes.

Philosophical Concern

Why are the Japanese so obsessed with these matters?

"For the Japanese, it's a matter of philosophy," said Cedergren. "It's why the domestic car companies are not winning over the Japanese car buyer with domestic products. Domestic car quality is good; but in this light, it's not good enough."

Such comments are mixtures of jingoism and truth, said Nathaniel B. Thayer, director of Asian studies in the School of Advanced International Studies at Johns Hopkins University.

"All of this talk about 'feel engineering' and 'kansai' really does not mean much of anything, I think, except as a way for the Japanese to communicate with the American market," Thayer said.

The truth is that Japanese automakers are not competing with American car companies, because "they won that competition a long time ago," Thayer said.

"Fear is driving the Japanese attention to detail," said Thayer. "The Japanese have an ancient tradition of perfection of craftsmanship, but they are really afraid of one another."

In Japan, Thayer said, "customer loyalty lasts 10 minutes."

If you consistently make a good product, "Japanese consumers stick with you," he said. But if you make a bad one, he said, they'll be the first to leave you.

September 30, 1990

Ads, They're Everywhere!

PAULA SPAN

It's not just your imagination. They're stalking you.

Advertisers no longer trust you to keep your twitchy fingers off the remote control or settle back to spend an hour with a favorite magazine. They're afraid you're insufficiently engrossed in such traditional media. They're going to hound you, pop up with commercials where you don't expect them, track you while you commute and shop and catch a movie and schuss down a mountain.

They're everywhere.

The phrase that recurs, among the entrepreneurs unleashing these new ad media, is "captive audience." If you're grabbed at the right time and place, "there's no zipping, no zapping, no ability to change screens," says Al Babinicz, president of Metro Vision Media Network. "People are almost forced to pay attention."

Three-year-old Metro Vision, by way of example, is installing dozens of large video monitors in subway stations in Chicago and Philadelphia, bus shelters in Rochester, the airport in Syracuse.

The lure for commuters, already confronted with numerous but static subway and bus ads, is that Metro Vision provides frequently updated transit information— delays, reroutings, cancellations—along with news headlines, weather reports, stock prices and sports scores. Besides, there's not much competition for one's attention on a train platform.

The catch is that 40 percent of what appears on the high-resolution monitors is commercials. A national advertiser—NBC, Miller Beer and the Wall Street Journal are among those that have signed on—pays $75,000 a month to have its 15-second spots shown every 10 minutes on 300 screens. Metro Vision gives the local transit agency a sliver, typically 5 percent, of the revenue. Washington's Metro, be advised, is among the systems the company lusts after.

This is what the trade calls "out of home" advertising, a proliferating category.

A new company called MallVision, for instance, wants to capitalize on its finding that more than 85 percent of the population, presumably with consumption in its collective heart, visits a shopping mall at least monthly. "Any time you get numbers like that," says Ned A'Bell, MallVision president, "{advertisers} get excited." He expects 40 to 50 malls this year to accept unspecified financial inducements to place multi-screen "video walls" and/or 50 to 60 free-standing monitors along their glossy corridors. Each screen will flash loops of "programming" (i.e., beauty tips, fashion updates, fitness shows) and, naturally, commercials.

POP Radio Corp.—the abbreviation suggests the lulling soft rock it plays, but actually stands for "point of purchase"—has staked out supermarkets, pharmacies, home centers and mass merchandisers, 18,000 of them. Its format apes a radio station's: You hear a smooth-voiced deejay, a little Ronnie Milsap, a little the Schmaltz Strings Play Lynyrd Skynyrd, a few consumer features and a lot of ads for "sponsors" like Alka-Seltzer, Sara Lee and Wisk, as well as for the store itself.

Not even recreational time is immune. Close to half the ski resorts in the country have signed on with Ski View, which puts 4-by-2-foot ads for the likes of Chevrolet, Rodak and Lipton Tea on the support towers of ski lifts. Skiers have a good 30 seconds to gaze at each billboard; the advertisers pay $100,000 to $350,000 a season. Many of them also sponsor promotions—giveaways, events, sweepstakes—until, as Ski View's project manager Lisa Cooperstein brightly puts it, "that whole day in the mountains is just plastered with signage and samples and headbands and contests."

Why this relentless pursuit? It reflects the way the splintering of once-mass media has made reaching a national audience more difficult. "You used to be able to go into one of the three TV networks and move product in a short time," says Bernie Newman, vice president and director of media resources for DDB Needham.

Now, a car maker that wants you to know about its sporty new Fabuloso Coupe faces a vastly multiplied media world. With double the number of radio and TV stations of 20 years ago, with only 66 percent of television households tuned to the three networks (it was 91 percent in 1978), with a growing number of cable networks and two-thirds of U.S. homes equipped with VCRs, with scores of new magazines launched every year, advertisers either have to spend a fortune (and don't seem pleased at that prospect) or find new ways of commanding consumers' attention.

"There probably are 100 or more new specialized media," Newman says. "You see more of a willingness on the part of advertisers to experiment. And there are entrepreneurs out there who recognize these changes and want to exploit them."

Like former adman Eric S. Medney, who invented a board game called "It's Only Money." His ESM Marketing Group sold more than 200,000 of the games, at $20 to $30 retail, in part because a sweepstakes entry form was enclosed in each box. But Medney also found 25 national advertisers (Courvoisier, HBO, Revlon) willing to buy spaces on the game board at $30,000 per. "It allows advertising to get into the relaxed environment of the home," says ESM spokesman Steve Goldberg. "This game is in front of someone for an hour or two at a time."

Not all such notions will catch on, of course. There's constant churn in the area, new ideas popping up and old ones fading out," says Pete Riordan, vice president and out-of-home media manager at BBDO. "Most of these new ventures will bomb." The practice of attaching commercials to rental videos, for instance, has not really taken off. And who knows how many takers there will be for the improved blimp technology (soon, instead of videotex messages running across its belly, a blimp may be lighted from within to become a giant logo, a glowing Pepsi sign drifting across the nocturnal sky) under development on the West Coast?

Nevertheless, "there are more formats now than yesterday, and there'll probably be more tomorrow," Riordan predicts.

And there has been rather little measurable resistance to the onslaught. The most significant scuffle has involved movie theaters, where ads shown before films have become the second biggest profit maker (next to popcorn, far ahead of ticket sales) for theater owners. Screenvision Cinema Network, the largest purveyor of theater advertising, places spots for Toyota, Sprite and the U.S. Marines on more than 6,000 of the 17,000 first-run movie screens in the country. It's a pricey ad buy, at $650,000 for a 28-day nationwide run, but Screenvision claims a demographically desirable audience unarmed with zappers.

A few weeks ago, however, the Disney people upset this cozy arrangement by announcing that the studio would prohibit paid screen advertising at theaters bidding to show its movies. Warner Bros. followed suit, the policy to take effect with the May 18 opening of "Gremlins 2: The New Batch." Both studios contended that commercials detracted from the moviegoing experience and were unpopular with ticket-buyers.

Screenvision argues that its research, conducted by Certified Marketing Services Inc., shows very little negative audience reaction, only about 4 percent, down from 6 to 8 percent a decade ago. (Certified doesn't poll audiences; a "negative" reaction means that one of its monitors, visiting a movie theater on a weekend, heard someone complain or boo. The lesson here, if you don't appreciate screen commercials, is not to suffer in silence.)

Disney, however, citing a national survey it commissioned from the National Research Group, retorted that 90 percent of the nearly 19,000 moviegoers polled on March 31 said they did not want commercials shown in theaters. Whether other studios will join the intensifying revolt is unclear.

Meanwhile, a Federal Trade Commission spokesperson declined to confirm or deny published reports of an FTC investigation of whether the Disney and Warner bans may constitute restraint of trade.

Another mini-flap arose when Whittle Communications (headed by the man of whom Vanity Fair recently asked, "Is Chris Whittle the Devil?") announced that ads were about to invade the previously pristine pages of hardcover books. Whittle's "Larger Agenda" series of nonfiction books, commissioned from reasonably well-known authors, each contain about 75 pages of text and 18 pages of Federal Express ads. The company, which signed a two-year contract with Whittle in order to bathe in this quasi-literary glow, also ships the books to its nonpaying audience: 150,000 "opinion leaders," including business execs, legislators, media types and assorted policy-making hangers-on.

A certain disgruntlement surfaced on op-ed pages and in the publishing industry when this marketing venture was first announced. "There were people who were sort of hostile, on a knee-jerk level," says Tony Kiser, who edits the series. But many publications (including the *New York Times Book Review* and *The Washington Post's Book World*) reviewed the first volume—"The Trouble With Money," by Rolling Stone national editor William Greider—as they would have more traditional economic treatises. And when Kiser approached 35 established writers, only two turned him down because of discomfort at coexisting with ads. At a "representative" $60,000 fee for a 25,000-word manuscript—a standard book manuscript is at least twice that long—Whittle was offering a very sweet deal.

So far, Whittle has not made much of an effort to sell the "Larger Agenda" books to the general public, shipping just a few thousand copies sans ads to bookstores, since the Fed-Ex contract more than assures its profits. But, never one to overlook a potential moneymaker (this is the company beaming Channel One news programming for kids, complete with commercials, into public schools), the company is rethinking this nonchalant practice.

Won't overwhelmed consumers grow inured to the blitz, so accustomed to seeing advertising everywhere that, eventually, they stop paying attention to any of it? Madison Avenue sorts already talk about "clutter" in television; now the clutter seems to be seeping into the general environment. Starting this month, Screenvision is supplementing its movie-theater ads for Volkswagen with "promotional materials" (i.e., brochures and contest entry forms), to be pressed directly into the hands of its captive audience.

But ad people, not surprisingly, insist that consumers get tired only of bad advertising. BBDO has done "commercial wear-out studies" and found that "if you have a terrific commercial, people never forget it," Riordan reports. Even if you're annoyed by three minutes of soda pop and raisin commercials when you've just paid seven bucks for a movie, "I don't know that a negative response to the commercial actually animates any animus against the product," he says. "You may remember the commercial and forget where you saw it." When it comes to new avenues of advertising, "I don't see any drop-off."

Prepare yourselves, therefore, for the coming baseball season. You already see ads on the video scoreboard and around the perimeters of the field. This year, thanks to a technological breakthrough from the Chicago-based Viskase Corp., the world's largest manufacturer of cellulose casings, you'll find advertising on the hot dogs.

That's right—using a "food colorant" that transfers onto the frank during cooking, Viskase can now stencil commercial messages on behalf of anyone who orders a minimum of 100,000 dogs. A graphic arts department is standing by. Only one color so far ("we call it 'toast'; it's, well, it's brown," says the manager of technical services), hut the Viskase people are working on that.

Among the expected early customers are baseball franchises themselves, radio stations ordering edible call letters for summer concerts, a governor running for reelection—Viskase won't say which or where—who's considering a Vote for So-

and-So dog. There could be designer dogs with little polo players. Dogs plugging the antacids they'll necessitate. Anti-drug dogs urging "Just Say No."

But no insults or cuss words, says Viskase. Some things are sacred.

April 28, 1990

Frisky Business

JAMES L. MORGAN

For almost 50 years, Hugh Hefner has thought that the sexiest word in the English language is nude. He's wrong. The word is panties.

Roll those two words on your tongue and let them pique your senses. Nude: What image does that evoke? The picture isn't altogether unpleasant, but unless you're an adolescent male who still believes the destination is different from the journey, there's a certain fait accompli quality about it. Even the word itself is abrupt, like rude or thud. Now consider panties, a dainty, silken, infinitely unfolding word: You men, notice how the diminutive -ies makes you feel big and strong? Sense the tactile pleasure of silk between thumb and forefinger? Feel your mind wandering to forbidden bureaus fragrant with sachet? From my male point of view, it's obvious: If God hadn't wanted us to take pleasure in presents, She wouldn't have invented gift wrap.

All of which is why the Victoria's Secret catalogue, and not Mr. Hefner's magazine, is widely considered by men to be the sexiest publication in America today. Women may not call it sexy (though some do), but they certainly find the pictures and lingerie provocative, a delicious menu of self-indulgence, a healthy celebration of femininity.

For you three or four ex-'60s-radicals-in-hiding who've somehow avoided getting on any catalogue mailing lists, maybe I should explain that the Victoria's Secret catalogue is a 15-times-a-year mail-order "store" for lingerie and women's ready-to-wear. There are also, of course, Victoria's Secret shops—at this writing 450 of them in shopping malls all over the country, 13 here in the Washington area alone. The shops feature lingerie, perfumes and a line of bath goods.

Victoria's Secret shops are so astoundingly successful that management is predicting annual gross sales of $1.5 billion by the mid-'90s. The catalogue, gross sales of which have doubled each of the past two years, aims at $1 billion a year by mid-decade. In just nine years, the number of shops has increased from fewer than 10 to the present number, and there'll be 63 more of them, up to 513, by the end of 1991. The catalogue is already the most successful catalogue in the country.

Considering the utter ubiquitousness of Victoria's Secret in our culture, it may seem quixotic to stop and wonder, as I have, how it got here and what its presence means; how, to put a finer point on it, a chain of stores selling if not sex then pure sensuality has come to be an accepted part of the Everytown mall scene here in good old Republican America; and how what is arguably the raciest publication in the country arrives at our doorsteps unprotested, thence to be displayed on coffee tables, while books with less sizzle (but more flesh) sulk plain-wrapped in 7-Eleven racks.

If you want to know the answer to those questions, you must be prepared to pay the price. First, you have to log many hours in dusty library stacks. Second, you have to struggle through myriad interviews with supposed cultural observers. Third, you have to transcribe countless tapes to see what they said.

And fourth, and maybe most important, you have to spend innumerable days and nights thinking about panties.

A brief social history of the United States, late '50s to late '70s:

* 1957—Three and a half billion pairs of panties are manufactured in the United States, but panties are still just underwear. Retailers are trying to push panties and other lingerie as fashion, but the country isn't ready. In this year of Sputnik, a trade journal admonishes salespeople to "Ask customer what type girdle she wears—long, short, all-in-one, etc. Show panty that fits most comfortably over customer's reqular girdle."

* Circa 1960—Still pushing, this time slips. "Bouffants especially, but petticoats too, sell much better when attractively displayed. Get them up on racks showing at least one of each color. Use your bright taffeta styles as a magnet to draw customers to your department."

Fast-forward to the mid-'60s. The Beatles and long hair are already breakfast-table topics. Baby boomers are hitting their twenties, a fact not lost on Madison Avenue.

* 1966—In a speech to the American Apparel Manufacturers Association, Charles Burg, vice president of sales for Vanity Fair Mills, predicts 1967 will be the best year yet for lingerie. "Fashion," he says, "has been our blood transfusion. We haven't been in the underwear business for the past ten years. Lingerie is a fashion accessory. The need for this change was rather simple. It was a case of survival."

* 1970—A cover story in *Clothes,* a trade magazine, lambastes intimate-apparel retailers for thinking old: "The first step toward change is to view the merchandise as it really is today, instead of as it was fifty or thirty years ago. Foundations . . . are no longer desired as girders to hold the body-structure rigid. The ready-to-wear looks have precluded this need for some time now. First the sack and then the A-line concealed a multitude of sins . . . Then, shorter skirts paved the way for pantyhose, which . . . lopped off the need for garters . . . Now, along has come the 'natural look' to change the concept of bras—either don't wear a bra at all, or wear one that makes the bust look unfettered."

* 1971—"Whatever happened to modesty?"—Stores, a trade journal.

* 1973—"Who," asks *Women's Wear Daily,* "is the 'contemporary' lingerie customer? Each buyer has her own opinion. But many agree the future of their departments rests with the career woman in her 20s and early 30s who has more

disposable income than the young junior and a less traditional outlook than the older misses customer."

* 1974—"There's a feeling for the sexy, trollopy thing. You know, the Frederick's of Hollywood thing. People remember the beautiful French lingerie of the thirties. The current generation never had anything like that"—John Kloss, designer, in the *New York Times*.

* 1977—"Teen-agers in Chicago have switched from T shirts to laced-up camisoles to wear with their blue jeans"—*Newsweek*.

* 1978—"Disco fever has hit the intimate apparel scene"—*WWD*.

Whoops, too far.

* 1977—The first Victoria's Secret shop opens.

Well, thanks for the memories.

What was happening, of course, though we didn't know it at the time, was that the culture was getting itself ready for Victoria's Secret. The culture had to become a pop culture. Movies and TV and Madison Avenue and fashion had to dominate. Fantasy and self-indulgence had to play major roles in people's lives. Ralph Lauren had to show us how to re-create ourselves.

All of which I have divined from reading between the lines in that short history of lingerie marketing. Do you doubt me? "Buying lingerie is something women do all their lives," magazine journalist Mimi Swartz once wrote, in relation to Victoria's Secret, "and as such, it's a perpetual marker of both internal and external changes—the way we view our times and the way we view ourselves."

That being the case, what I think has happened is this: Victoria is Barbie for grown-up baby boomers. Someone to dress. Someone to play make-believe with.

In her earliest incarnation, Vicky, as she's called by insiders, was the creation of a man named Roy Raymond, who thought up the idea of Victoria's Secret shops and catalogue back in 1977 in Palo Alto, Calif. "It was really out of my own frustration of trying to buy lingerie for my wife in a department store setting," says Raymond, who at the time held a marketing job with a wine company. Raymond recalls stern salesladies—"corsetieres," he calls them—responding with disdain to the notion of a man hanging around the lingerie department. Upon discovering that friends of his had experienced the same problem, Raymond says the proverbial light bulb appeared above his head. "My God," he said to himself, "here are people spending money and not having fun at it."

Instead of cold chrome fixtures, such as the kind department stores featured at the time, Raymond, then 30 and exactly in tune with his generation's penchant for fantasy, visualized a Victorian boudoir stage set, a make-believe world of warm wood and warmer welcomes. The name Victoria's Secret came later, born of the unified mood Raymond had created. The name itself is a delicious exercise in creative tension. If he had called it Kandi's Secret, there wouldn't have been much of a secret, would there? But Victoria? She's proper, refined, respectable, the woman in the office next door—not the kind you might expect to be wearing a pair of turquoise thong-back panties. "There must've been a couple hundred names we came up with," Raymond says, "but only that one seemed to have all the elements for the character we were trying to portray."

The "secret" of this character called Victoria was that this self-contained, upwardly mobile, assertively trained, late-'70s businesswoman in the tailored wool suit liked to stay in touch with her femininity by wearing frilly feminine things underneath. She was really Attila the Honey. Somehow, Raymond managed to avoid the wrath of feminists, who, you'll recall, spent the late '70s angry at men for any number of sins, not the least of which was objectifying women; they eyed Raymond's operation with some suspicion, but never objected. Maybe Roy Raymond truly did discover a secret.

By the early '80s, Raymond's creation had expanded to six stores, all in California, and a catalogue that was mailed twice a year. That's when Leslie Wexner, widely known as the country's premier merchandiser of women's apparel, decided to make a pass at Victoria. Wexner is founder and chairman of the Limited Inc., owner of a large chunk of just about any given mall in the country today. His empire includes Limited Stores, Lerner, Lane Bryant, Express, Structure, Limited Too, Abercrombie & Fitch, Henri Bendel, Cacique, Bath & Body Works, Penhaligon's . . . and, since 1982, Victoria's Secret.

Listening to people talk about Les Wexner, you have no choice but to believe the man is an artist. He's a dreamer of such prolific visions that he has no time for a spouse; in fact, one of his pet theories is that most people retire when they're 30 and buy a home and have children. No such fate for Les Wexner. He has worlds to conjure. By all accounts, he's a very visually oriented person. "He would have been an interior decorator if he was not in this business," a friend of his told writer Julie Baumgold.

But I like to think Wexner would've been a movie director. Both see worlds inside their heads—and then are able to bring those worlds to life.

"With Victoria's Secret," says an associate of Wexner's (all employees of the Limited Inc. are known as "associates"), "he thought there was a good idea there, a chance to reinvent the lingerie business. He let the concept simmer for a long time. He just thought about it and experimented. That's the way he works." And then Les Wexner began turning Roy Raymond's character Victoria into a major motion picture.

Not literally, of course, but in effect. Movies are created by skilled fabricators, people so adept at benign manipulation that, once they get you there in the dark of the theater, alone with your dreams and hopes and insecurities, they can induce fantasy—they can make you believe, for a little while, that some part of you could be someone else in some other place. Didn't every man squint his eyes and try to see himself as suave as 007? Didn't every woman stretch her neck an elegant inch longer after watching Audrey Hepburn? Wexner simply took the stuff of movies and applied it to marketing women's intimate apparel.

Wexner wasn't the first to do this. In our time—that is, in the age of the baby boomer—the master of the auteur theory of merchandising has been Ralph Lauren, born Ralph Lifshitz, who first reinvented his own world according to his fantasies, and then proved that his fantasies were a generation's fantasies as well. Says a woman who works in this "hidden persuader" field, and therefore wishes to remain anonymous: "Ralph became who he wanted to be by taking England and running it through Brooks Brothers and straining that through the American West." With his elaborate props—instant-antique perfume bottles, tarnished silver table frames, burnished riding boots—Lauren has created worlds most of us would Like to claim as our own: Be they West or East or African Explorer, they're easygoing upper-class worlds of taste and money and tradition. If Lauren had a liquor license, he'd sell martinis.

"Wexner," says Hidden Persuader, "is an Anglophile. Victoria's Secret is Wexner's vision of what an English store of its type would be. "First of all, it has a London address—No. 10 Margaret Street. (Never mind that headquarters is a brand-new building in Columbus, Ohio, USA.) Wallpaper is English floral, circa 1890s. Rugs are mock needlepoint. Perfume bottles that look like your grand-mothers' crystal convey just the proper weight. And if all these visual tricks aren't enough, as soon as you walk through the door you're enveloped in romantic music and the scent of old-fashioned sachet—Wexner's answer to Hollywood's Sensurround.

"It's a movie," says Hidden Persuader, "and Wexner tries to get you to speak a part."

These days, he has delegated that job to two extremely capable associates, Grace Nichols, president of the Victoria's Secret stores, and Cynthia Fedus, president of the catalogue. Wexner divided the business for a couple of reasons—one, he likes to keep his divisions small and agile, so they'll be more innovative and competitive; and two, because running a chain of stores and running a catalogue aren't necessarily compatible exercises.

Both executives travel constantly. Nichols, based in Columbus, estimates that she's gone from her husband and family 50 percent of the time. She visits one of her shops somewhere one day a week, mostly to stay in touch with the customers and what they're looking for. She also makes regular trips to Europe and the Far East, gathering ideas, meeting suppliers and checking on production.

Fedus, who is single, lives and works in Manhattan. There she and some 30 associates do the merchandising, select the product and manage the creation of the catalogue. (The day I was there, most of the floor space was littered with shopping bags filled with clothes being sent back to suppliers—bag lady nirvana.) The catalogue also has some 1,800 associates in Columbus who handle all other parts of the business—receiving merchandise, checking quality, taking phone orders, processing mail orders, shipping merchandise to customers, paying the bills, running the computer system. When she's not presiding over this madness—which she calls "a wedding of art and science"—Fedus also makes regular scouting trips to Europe, Asia and through the United States looking for product ideas.

The brilliance of Victoria's Secret is that Wexner et al. have refined the notion of lingerie as fashion better than anyone else. "If I asked you the color of most women's bras," says Fedus, "you'd probably say white, pink, beige, black—a basic palette. We believe the innerwear should be as exciting as the outerwear. I have on a navy blue suit today, I had on a pink one yesterday, I may have on an orange one tomorrow. We take that same mentality and apply it to lingerie."

"When we look at the customer," says Nichols, "we start with the idea that most women wear underwear on a regular basis. Our appeal is to women who respond to the indulgence of lingerie. Age isn't a primary focus; it's more psychographic than demographic."

But what sets Victoria's Secret apart from the pack of lingerie manufacturers and retailers is the unity of image, the illusion of Victoria that positions the product squarely within the realm of the emotions. While the details of running the two sides of the business are different, in order for Wexner's carefully crafted script to hang together, Nichols and Fedus must somehow share an understanding of that image, that illusion. Mostly, they don't like to entertain such discussions. "That's not the kind of thing we talk about," a PR woman told me at the outset ("The Oz syndrome," says Hidden Persuader. "To talk about the magic is to destroy it"). When pressed, Nichols doubles back into a more comfortable patter about fashion ("We're appealing to the fact that people respond to the emotion of the product").

Fedus, however, talks about Victoria and make-believe in the way a young girl might talk about playing with Barbie. "The aspirational aspect of the Victoria image is very important," she says. "I live in an apartment in New York. I don't live in an English manor house. But I might aspire to that. The idea of quality, tastefulness, classiness, while at the same time being sensual and maybe a little self-indulgent. I think that's the image of both the stores and the catalogue. We both work very hard so the image is consistent." Neither of them, you'll notice, mentions the word sex. In fact, it seems to be a very bad word indeed within Victoria's Secret, as though it had nothing whatsoever to do with the company's success. "Obviously," says Nichols, "the lingerie business places you in the bedroom. But we never use that word in our merchandising and marketing meetings."

Wexner, however, once used an even more vivid form of that word to a *Fortune* magazine writer: "Revson said women all hope they get laid," Wexner said, referring to one of his prime influences, Charles Revson of Revlon Inc., "and I agree. They're sensuous. They're different from men. They dress to please men. You're not selling utility. That's why uptight women stockbrokers will put on a G-string when they get home. Like Revson said, we're selling hope in a bottle."

Nichols and Fedus adamantly advertise a different label. "Sex is not what these businesses are all about," says Fedus. In fact, she points out, the catalogue used to be much sexier, back in the mid-'80s. The models chosen then were younger—more "teeny-bopperish," one associate says—and they were photographed in twos, in threes, sometimes with men in boxer shorts and robes, sometimes touching, always looking very . . sexy. "We modified the image of the catalogue, beginning in the spring of 1988," says Fedus. "The business was profitable, but there was a leadership change at that time. Les felt the image had strayed, and he said, 'Bring it back.' I'll tell you, when we modified the image, brought it back from that risqueness that had crept into it, the response from customers was terrific."

"We concentrate on the appeal of this merchandise to the woman, and how it will make her feel," says Nichols, putting this subject to rest. "And I think that's our success, so people feel good when they buy."

We have a story. We have a script. We have beautiful sets. Now all that remains is to cast the title role.

That process begins on the second floor of a row house in downtown Manhattan, home of Elite Model Management. The people at Victoria's Secret know precisely what kind of image they're looking for—elegant, sensuous, sophisticated. At Elite, president Monique Pillard, a motherly Frenchwoman with a graying pixie haircut and an eye trained to spot the elusive quality in women known only as "It," dips into her model book and selects a candidate. Pillard has been extraordinarily successful, placing three women as prominent regulars in the Victoria's Secret catalogue and one of them as the focus of a stunning national ad campaign for Victoria's Secret stores. "It's a very sexy, sensual look," says Pillard, "yet not a vulgar look. Classy but sensual. The Victoria's Secret woman is the woman every woman wants to be."

If you had to choose one model and decree that she, more than anyone else, represents Victoria, you might well start by narrowing the field to Jill Goodacre, Frederique and Famke. Famke is the smoldering brunette whose classic form has graced the pages of numerous magazines over the past year in a generic ad campaign for both the shops and the catalogue. In that sense, she is Victoria.

Jill Goodacre and Frederique, on the other hand, have played major roles in nudging the ubiquitous catalogue into the "must-read" category. Goodacre's chiseled Greek-goddess features have appeared on the covers of the catalogue. Frederique, a statuesque Dutch beauty (Famke is also Dutch), displays the lingerie to great effect, using what one Washington professional woman says is "the working definition of bedroom eyes."

Monique Pillard reports that these models have indeed become stars of Les Wexner's movie. They command top salaries, they receive love letters from thousands of adoring fans, they travel in a star-studded universe. Stuck to Pillard's bulletin board in her office is a picture postcard from Jill Goodacre. The photo on the postcard shows Jill, her boyfriend—singer Harry Connick Jr.—and Frank Sinatra at what appears to be a glamorous holiday party. The message is, "For Monique, Happy New Year, Love, Jill, Harry and Frank."

Alas, these women also have in common another of today's manifestations of stardom—they're being pursued by *Playboy* magazine. The proposed feature would be called "The Girls of Victoria's Secret." The problem," says Jeff Cohen, Playboy's managing photo editor, "is that some of these models are booked up with lucrative contracts and they're tied to the Limited exclusively for lingerie. We've even talked about shooting them in lingerie that you can order." Only in America. Only in this America, in which illusions openly cavort with other illusions. In which you can't tell where the package ends and the product begins. Call it MediaMerge. Today, Hollywood's principle of "high concept" ("Miami Vice = MTV cops") has been turned to merchandising ("Banana Republic = L.L. Bean meets Indiana Jones"), and we all get to be in our own movie. Our clothes are costumes, our music's a soundtrack. Barbie as Vicky? Believe it. Didn't we always know Barbie would end up in the movies?

Meanwhile, will Vicky hang out with Hef? Will Hef learn to appreciate women in panties? Will millions of catalogue readers finally admit that they don't just read it for the articles of clothing?

Anything could happen, and probably will. As for Victoria, she promises to continue doing remarkable box office. "The way we see the lingerie business," says a Victoria's Secret associate, sounding for all the world like a producer on the make, "it could be a $15-, $16-, $17-billion business."

And it's playing now at a mall near you.

September 8, 1991

Summertime, and the Poolman is Busy

MARTHA SHERRILL

It's another day of empty pools—lots of water but no people. This one's an indoor pool, a pale-blue rectangle sitting in Bethesda under a retractable skylight. There's also a terra cotta-tile deck. Ten plastic plants. A sauna. Stereo speakers. Silver inflatable rafts and boats. The sliding door has been left open for him. He's Paul Wahler. Poolman.

The automatic sweeper-cleaner is running. There's something poetic about it because it doesn't seem to know where it's going. It circles the pool like a stupid robot, a renegade without direction. Three skinny hoses are flailing around, trying to clean the bottom. "One customer did complain after I fixed her sweeper that it was going too fast," says Wahler, "that it bothered her nerves."

Wahler takes off his cap. He takes off his shirt too. He knew this would happen because he's brought a beach towel. He spreads it out. He drops flat on his gut, down on the towel, and hangs over the side. He reaches into the deep end. He reaches his arms right in—like a surgeon, like an obstetrician—and pulls it out: The dead underwater light bulb. His Shakespearean beard almost touches the glassy surface.

"It happens. It happens," he says sheepishly. "Sometimes in extremely hot weather . . .

The sentence hangs. Poolman looks pained.

"I'll drop my screwdriver in the pool. I won't be able to get it out."

And, and . . .

"And I'll have to go in."

There's an archipelago of pools across town—kidneys, ovals, rectangles, Classical Romans, Grecians, free-forms, L-shapes. There are jet pools, lap pools, hot tubs, Jacuzzis and spas—made of wood, concrete, gunite, shotcrete, fiberglass, concrete and masonry block—across McLean, Potomac, Chevy Chase, Cleveland Park, Kalorama, Georgetown.

Montgomery County is flooded with them, and Great Falls is getting more. Wahler's firm, Poolservice Company—the largest by far in the area—maintains 300 residential pools a week, but there are about 1,700 in-ground residential pools in the District alone, according to the National Spa and Pool Institute (NSPI). Maryland has about 63,600 in-ground residentials and 67,800 above-ground. Virginia's got about 51,600 in-ground and 25,000 above.

Pools. Welcome to summer in America. No matter how much chlorine you pour into them, they stand for desire and danger, for Greco-Roman decadence, for the vanity of a tan and for the pursuit of pecs. And they stand for Zen contemplation too, and for the excesses of the rich. They call to mind lifeguards with lips burned stiff as Tupperware and arm hair bleached white as aspirin, poolmen who look like Jimmy Buffett. They give relief to arthritics, excuses for decorating with Tiki torches, green hair to blonds.

In Hollywood, you make deals by them. In books and movies, it's where you fall in love or—almost the same thing—get shot to death. Jay Gatsby dies in one, after all, and William Holden's dead body floating in a pool gives us the opening shot of "Sunset Boulevard." It's where Katharine Hepburn winds up with Jimmy Stewart in "The Philadelphia Story" after she gets drunk enough to think she wants to marry him, where Daniel Day-Lewis first sees Juliette Binoche in "The Unbearable Lightness of Being," where Geena Davis first sees Jeff Goldblum in "Earth Girls Are Easy," and where Mel Gibson is introduced to Sigourney Weaver over gin and tonics in "The Year of Living Dangerously."

Violence and nudity. At the White House, JFK and Johnson both swam naked indoors, then Nixon filled in the pool and created the press room. A rat was swimming in the outside White House pool on the south lawn a year ago and George Bush drowned it in front of Barbara.

In the '80s pools meant health and exercise, but before—in the '60s and '70s— they stood for suburban indolence, money, alcohol. In "The Graduate," Dustin Hoffman tries out a new wet suit and later spends the summer floating around on a raft wearing his sunglasses. There are L.A. pools in David Hockney paintings, New York pools in Alex Katz paintings and Connecticut pools in John Cheever stories. In the movie version of Cheever's "The Swimmer," Burt Lancaster swims a lap in pools across his county—and is offered a cocktail at each one. "Pool by pool," he says, "they form a river all the way to my house."

People and their pools. Paul Wahler, Poolman, has been skimming the surface for over 20 years, and repairing pool heaters, restoring old concrete, pulling sludge from filters. He thinks pool chemicals get a bad rap. "Some people do get freaked out—they overreact—about them," he says. "Like chlorine. Ever since World War I. Sure, once a season somebody at home mixes the chlorine with something else and gets gassed, but it's like everything else. Handling is the key."

His truck takes a turn down Foxhall Road. He stops by a retired diplomat's pool with white marble deck. He checks the automatic pool cover. He stops by another one, a huge rectangular pool—22 by 66 feet—designed by Philip Johnson with 34 underwater lights, an overflow gutter and some outdoor sculpture.

He's drawn to a Zen-style pool in Cleveland Park. It's a free-form shape with a black bottom—landscaped with natural rocks, flagstone and a weepy-looking pine. There's also a hutlike pool house. The bottom of the pool isn't really black-black. It just looks splotchy and watery and dark. The plaster is dyed black before it's poured, not painted. Gray pools, he says, are the "in-thing now." Also, real boulders stuck into the concrete.

Wahler cruises through Kalorama, big house by big house. Pool by pool. He finds his way into any back yard that he wants, it seems. Sometimes Wahler's hand finds a clob of muck floating like a jellyfish in the skimmer basket, or gum. There are mats of tangled hair to find too, and pine needles, leaves, pollen, flowers, slime. "Your basic grease scum," he says. "Just like a bathtub. Grease. Body oil. Suntan oil. All that."

Dead things also have a way of winding up in pools, especially when they're opened after winter. "In the spring, you'll find dead possums all the time," he says, "because they're very stupid. And very rarely, you'll find squirrels and raccoons and cats—the ones who weren't smart enough to get out before they froze."

What do you find in the summer?

"In order of appearance? First there's chipmunks," he says. "Second, frogs, then snakes." The pools around Rock Creek Park, especially, get the chipmunks. "An old lady client of mine devised a wire-mesh chipmunk ladder to save the ones that landed in her pool. Worked great. I've used it a number of times for other clients."

Through a locked gate, Wahler finds an overgrown yard—the family's away someplace better. The grass needs to be cut. This is the tragedy—so many empty pools belonging to people who can also afford summer houses. Wahler points to a birdhouse full of white pigeons. "This is where I was attacked once," he says. "Right in the middle of Kalorama. By a rooster."

Wahler comes to another Kalorama house—of another retired diplomat—with a small, white, oval pool. There are two white chairs facing the sun like Easter tourists. Some white gravel. A closed umbrella. A bamboo grove.

"Old money," Wahler says.

Black squiggly things sit at the bottom of the old-money pool, like lines drawn by Hockney, like the pair of eyeglasses in the salt-water pool in "Chinatown." Dead worms, these turn out to be. "After a heavy rain," he says, "they float up from the soil, get washed into the pool and drown. Worms don't swim, despite what you may have heard."

The worms and the mire aren't exactly Wahler's calling. Does he have a calling? Like so many Poolmen, he fell into this. Wahler was a fine arts major at Rice University. He knows the Monets, Manets, Frank Stellas on the walls of some of his clients' houses. He was a theater technician before too, but he got tired of "not making any money," he says. The pool gig started as a summer job—first lifeguarding, then pool management, then pool maintenance and repair. Since 1968, he's been one of four working partners of Poolservice Company. What holds him to it?

"You get to work outside," he says. "You don't have anybody hanging over your head. You're on your own. The clothing is casual. There's a variety in what you do—a different job at every pool."

The Poolservice headquarters in Arlington is a fun, free-wheeling place. The metal desks are painted to look like rattan. The door is open. There's a breeze of a kind. A collection of ceramic and plastic frogs—the company mascot—sits on a ledge. A computer screen has a paper fortune from a Chinese cookie taped to it: You're soon going to change your present line of work. The 30 poolmen and pool-women are calling in from their truck radios.

The trucks—have they been mentioned yet? There's a fleet of blue, one-ton trucks—like laundry trucks or ice cream trucks—that say "Poolservice Company" in white letters. There's a big green frog too, painted on the side. It's a frog sitting on a diving board. He's holding a martini glass.

"That's been our logo since Day 1," says Wahler. "Since Day 1. I like to think that the frog is one of our customers. It's like he's thinking, Do I want to drink this drink or jump in the pool? It's open, of course, to interpretation."

Wahler's got good legs for shorts, calloused knees from kneeling on concrete, a khaki polo shirt with the frog-and-cocktail logo, sunglasses, Reeboks and a black NSPI baseball cap. There's great camaraderie among pool people.

"There are lots of neat people in the industry," says Kelly Reed, business manager of Contemporary Waterworks in Montgomery County, another pool service company. She knows Wahler and the rest of them.

They fall into this. Ron Callaghan at Capital Pool Service is a Georgetown University graduate—a political science major—who gave up politics for pools in 1976. "He was friends with someone," says his wife, Beth, "and they wanted to go into business together. They just bought a truck and a pool pole."

Wahler enjoys visiting with people's dogs. "I've only been bitten once," he says, "but I've been chewed out and spit out by several customers."

Columnist Carl Rowan has the most famous pool in Washington, Wahler says, and Rowan is a longtime client.

"Some of our guys went to open his pool," says Wahler. "When they knocked on the gate, Rowan said, 'Come on in, I won't shoot you.' He's great."

Wahler's got stories of nakedness too. There's some of it at the University Club's all-male pool. ("Hey," says Wahler, "it's casual, you know. It used to be like that at the Pentagon until they went coed.") He mentions a senator who's always sitting naked in his hot tub, and then, the occasional topless woman. ("It happens," he says. "You just say you're sorry and back out the gate quickly.") He's got a couple of stories about the Soviets' Olympic-size pool at their complex on Wisconsin Avenue. ("They were draining all the water out every three weeks," he says. "They have a big commercial filter, but just didn't know what they were doing. It was like, 'Hey! You don't dump all the water out in America?'") He was paid to train the Soviets to use their filter, to not dump the water, and got a bottle of Stoli as a present.

Stories. "Sit around with a group of pool guys," he says, "and they'll all admit to having cleaned the neighbor's pool by mistake."

Stories. He has heard "that in California, the poolman's like the milkman. Am I right?"

Yes.

"Not here. In all my years, I've only known one guy who was servicing more than the pool."

He's tired of people always asking what he does in the winter. Some pool companies sell Christmas decorations, or deliver firewood, or push snow. "We've just tried to expand our pool renovation business," he says. Wahler mostly fixes pools and spas, but there are fountains, fish ponds, other water things. "I don't like to do baptismal fonts," he says. "No money in it at all."

It's time to move on. Another pool, another client. "This one," he says, "has more money than brains." They've built an indoor swim-spa—12 by 18 feet. "The latest thing," he shrugs, "is swimming in place. There's a soaring ceiling-high waterfall with three openings, real boulders, lava rocks, computer controls, remote controls, redwood walls, two-story windows—all designed by a Japanese architect for the back of a bland-looking tract house in Bethesda.

Swimming in place. Something to contemplate. ("Not everybody's a swimmer," says Jack Cergol at the NSPI. "Some people just like to look at a body of water. It's very soothing and relaxing. Your blood pressure drops, some say, when people just look at oceans and lakes and a body of water that's moving.")

Wahler seems relaxed enough, and think of all the bodies of water he's seen. "I'm not that big on swimming—to tell you the truth," says the former lifeguard.

Got a pool at home, Paul?

"No way."

August 29, 1990

The Patent Truth of a Bygone Age

After 200 Years, America's Inventiveness Has Ebbed

HENRY ALLEN

Oh lost paradise of gizmo gods, oh broken dream of Gyro Gearloose and mad inventors, oh forgotten eurekas of basement geniuses becoming the next Edison, Salk, Fulton, Carver, Wilbur Wright, Orville Wright, Morse, Franklin, Goddard, Tesla, Colt, Marconi, Ford, Goodyear . . .

Once, these men were giants in our land. They built better mousetraps. We beat paths to their doors. "The American invents as the Italian paints and the Greek sculpted. It is genius," a European visitor to the Centennial Exposition of 1876 is said to have said.

Last year, almost half of the 102,712 patents issued in America were issued to foreigners, up from about a quarter 20 years ago. The four companies getting the most patents were Japanese.

"We feel the increase is an indication that American technological leadership is slipping," says Herbert Wamsley, executive director of Intellectual Property Owners Inc., a Washington foundation that helped put together the bicentennial celebration of U.S. patent and copyright law this week.

Nowadays, our giants build better bodies or reputations or cases for the defense. Our celebrated inventors are people like Sylvester Stallone, who invented the hairless chest of Rambo, or Michael Milken, who invented the junk bond, or Donald Trump, who invented himself. Our famous inventions are $125 sneakers, the fax machine, the home equity loan and elevators that talk. But we don't know who invented them. Companies invent things. Marketing people invent things. The insane Tokyo salarymen invent things.

"Invention now is done by teams of people," says Ellen Cardwell, executive director of the Foundation for a Creative America, which organized the symposiums, dinners and museum shows of the celebration. "They are faceless. You never get to see the physical person."

If one pops up, a lone genius from the old mold, he may face years of lawsuits over patent infringement by corporations. In a piece in *Popular Mechanics,* Tom Wolfe quoted the testimony of robotics inventor Jerome H. Lemelson before Congress in 1979: "Company managers know that the odds of an inventor being able to afford the costly litigation are less than one in ten; and even if the suit is brought, four times out of five the courts will hold the patent invalid. When the royalties are expected to exceed the legal expense, it makes good business sense to attack the patent . . . . What all this means to the inventor is that he either quits inventing or he licenses foreign."

Our giants are anonymous. You wonder if they vanished at about the same time Americans began telling each other that the corporations were buying up all the inventions and hiding them, wild tales of Gillette suppressing the thousand-shave razor blade or Standard Oil keeping the plans for a hundred-miles-per-gallon carburetor in a safe deposit box—none of it more than folk wisdom, but an indication that an old faith was dying. Still, the dream gets dreamed—witness the panic of hope that erupted last spring when the two cold-fusion guys in Utah said they'd figured out a way to make unlimited electricity in a fish tank. And witness the events of this week in Washington.

Since Tuesday we've had much talk, many galas, museum shows, youth awards, discussions of women inventors and minority inventors, a laser show and the U.S. Marine Corps Band.

Last night at the Pension Building, the Third Century Award was given to Leonard Bernstein, James Michener, Stephen Sondheim, Steven Spielberg and Stevie Wonder, among others.

But they're not inventors, you say. Indeed, they are celebrity artists known for their copyrights, which cover things like songs, designs, books, poems, pictures, puzzles, maps, souvenir kerchiefs, movies, videotapes of movies, even the colorization of the movies, and so on. More power to them, but they are not inventors.

"We need to get back to where as many people have heard of John Bardeen as have heard of Steven Spielberg," says Wamsley.

The Third Century Award was also given to John Bardeen, co-inventor of the transistor; Lloyd Conover, inventor of tetracycline; Gertrude Elion, holder of 45 medical patents including one for AZT, the AIDS drug; Jack Kilby and Robert Noyce, co-inventors of the semiconductor chip; and Edwin Land, inventor of the Polaroid camera. They are inventors, but with the possible exception of Land, you probably haven't heard of any of them. You may not know for sure what a semiconductor is.

You may not care. "An era of technological enthusiasm in the United States," historian Thomas Hughes says, is "an era now passing into history."

No more miracle tales and creation myths.

No more Thomas Edison, the Wizard of Menlo Park, working so hard he had to catnap on the laboratory floor. No more Samuel F.B. Morse, abandoning a brilliant but unrewarding career as a painter to send "What hath God wrought" in dots and dashes from Washington to Baltimore in the first telegraph message. No more horses bolting as Nikola Tesla's generators sent lightning ripping out for 10 miles from his laboratory. And, after decades of being milled down to homogenized and socialized pabulum by American public schools, no more Teslas epitomizing the ideal of the 19th-century romantic genius by saying, "Originality thrives in seclusion free of outside influences beating upon us to cripple the creative mind. Be alone—that is the secret of invention: Be alone, that is when ideas are born."

It's hard to imagine picking up *Scientific American* and seelng someone say, as a writer said in 1896, that this is "an epoch of invention and progress unique in the history of the world"; that there has been "a gigantic tidal wave of human ingenuity and resource, so stupendous in its magnitude, so complex in its diversity, so profound in its thought, so fruitful in its wealth, so beneficent in its results, that the mind is strained and embarrassed in its effort to expand to a full appreciation of it."

Once, the patent office was one of the biggest tourist attractions in Washington, but that was a century ago when they still had a hall full of working models in the space that now holds the National Portrait Gallery. It was called the Museum of Models then. It had pillars and groined ceilings, like a shrine. There was no dream too big or small—endless variations on the theme of steam engine, typesetter, drill, still, valve, sled, reel, camera, fire alarm, gin, press, reaper, lock, lathe, lamp, sewing machine, automobile, adding machine, pinball machine, stove, phonograph, telephone, pump, playpen, paper bag maker, unicycle, bicycle, tricycle, washing machine, clothespin. The period from 1864 to 1873 may have been the golden age of the clothespin, in fact, with 62 patents issued.

You can see a selection of these clothespins, along with model steam engines, etc., at a show called "Icons of Invention" at the Portrait Gallery, in the very hall that once held thousands of patent models—the hall that for a horrible time in 1863 held not just the patent models in all their curlicued Victorian gadget gloom, but the wounded soldiers from the battle of Antietam, moaning and rotting in the aisles. Technology and its victims! What a tableau!

Anyway, the current show is just a smattering of the old model—the patent office stopped requiring them in 1880 and most were sold in 1926. On a recent weekday morning the aisles were populated with a few dozen schoolchildren, fidgeting while their teachers told them how amazing and thrilling these things were.

Such as clothespins. Remember clothespins, those wooden gadgets that fastened clothes to clotheslines before the electric dryer came along, and before hideous respectability led planned communities to ban the hanging out of laundry?(Oh spontaneous back yard banners of washday glory!) You would think that a clothespin would be self-evident, that its form would follow so clearly from its function that it would be obvious. But it wasn't and didn't. There are enough clothespins on display here that you can see how long it took humanity to get it right. It took a while.

Little credit that Dexter Pierce, of Sunapee, N.H., gets for coming up with the simple split piece of wood in 1858, but there he is, the Thomas Edison of hanging it out to dry. The other pins look like the sort of complicated wooden, organic, non-aggressive toys that children of the worrying class get for Christmas.

The clothespins are in the same case with a model washing machine. It seems that all the washing machine inventors kept trying to imitate the action of hands on cloth, when what they needed to do was make the paradigmatic leap to the action of a machine on cloth—rotary agitation! Eureka!

There's an Elias Howe sewing machine that looks nothing like a sewing machine. There's a Singer from the same period that looks exactly like a sewing machine—it would end up paying for a 31-passenger canary-yellow carriage with smoking compartment, nursery and water closet that Singer would drive through Manhattan. There's a rocking chair that harnesses the wasted power from the rocking motion to operate a fan. Nearby is a violin with a brass horn sticking out from the fret end, to amplify it—one of those strange mutant devices that populated the imagination of the time. And 40 yards away down each of the hall's two aisles are two old cases of inventions, perhaps the original cases from Antietam days, unlit, filled with technological freaks and fossils that all start to look the same after a while—all those flywheels and cogs and brass cranks and iron wheels rendered with the coy, unnerving quality of miniatures. But miniature whats? The same model might be a threshing machine, a chiropractic device, a loom for the blind.

"It is the obviousness and simplicity of the machine as a symbol of progress that accounts for its astonishing power," Leo Marx writes in "The Machine in the Garden."

These things were brought to Washington as offerings to the great god of Progress, and preserved past their usefulness as relics of a bygone saintliness. The world was not ignited by the ideas that most of them represented. A caption on a steam engine patented on July 29, 1837, says that the inventor "produced a long line of curiosities that, for all their novelty, were no more efficient than the machines they were intended to supersede."

Why didn't the Portrait Gallery fill the hall with them, instead of providing this cursory smattering? Well, their power has dwindled.

If you want to savor the spirit of the last decades when America had the inventing faith, walk down to the art gallery on the same floor and look at the social realist paintings from the 1930s: Paul Kelpe's "Machinery No. 2," for instance.

The first patent in America was granted on July 31, 1790, to Samuel Hopkins for his improvement in "the making of Pot Ash and Pearl Ash." It was signed by George Washington, and a copy is on display at a lively little exhibit of both patent and copyright history at the Library of Congress.

Copyrights are tricky. You can copyright blueprints but not buildings, a doll of Mickey Mouse but not the character himself, calendars and software programs but not recipes or formulas such as $E=MC^2$. You could copyright the music for "He's So Fine," the big Chiffons hit of the '60s, but it turned out you couldn't copyright the music for George Harrison's "My Sweet Lord" because it was the same song, a court ruled. You can hear the difference by pushing buttons in the exhibit.

You can't copyright natural sounds on a record but you can patent a peach, as Luther Burbank did. The Duncan Hines people patented a chocolate chip cookie. Coca-Cola could probably patent its secret formula, but then it wouldn't be secret anymore, the exhibit points out.

Patent leather shoes are patented.

If the old American religion was invention, progress, the better mousetrap, what is the new religion? One could venture guesses along the cosmic lines of "yourself," or "greed," but on a lesser level, somewhere below the cult of the Mazda Miata, is the nationwide sect of the sneaker. Nike Airs! Reebok Pumps! Technology at work, harnessing American teenage spending power for the greater good of shopping malls! The library has a sneaker exhibit with patented cleats, patented stabilizer bars, patented air bladders, patented waffle outsoles. It even has a sneaker time line, showing sneaker genius at work building a better tomorrow, from the rubber sole of 1917 to the heel wedge of 1952 to the waffle sole of 1962, on and on. This is important. Kids kill each other over these things.

The age of production has long since become an age of consumption. Meanwhile, we've used the powers of public and private sectors to keep the inventor in his place. "Get over there with them nerds, boy, that's where you belong." Once, artists, writers and political thinkers were inventors and scientific tinkerers: Leonardo, Samuel Johnson, Thomas Jefferson. Abraham Lincoln patented a device to float ships off sand bars. Actress Lillian Russell patented a trunk. Maybe what we need is celebrities taking up inventing as their new cause, sort of like the environment or homelessness.

Environmentalism and modern warfare have taken a lot of the glamour away from technology. It is now ecological heresy to say, as the *American Journal of Science* said in 1840, that "Man is indeed lord of creation; and all nature, as though daily more sensible of the conquest, is progressively making less and less resistance to his dominion." Modern architecture no longer aspires to build Le Corbusier's "machine to live in." Literature worried about what science hath wrought, starting with the romantics, such as Mary Shelley with "Frankenstein." The Wizard of Oz ends up exposed and belittled as a mere . . . inventor. As it stands among the ordinary people of America, the last believers in the power of the individual engineer may be the girls who spend Saturday mornings watching their boyfriends writhe around under cars.

Then again, up in Monroeville, Pa., last weekend, the Invention-New Product Exposition featured American inventions such as a noiseless alarm clock (it vibrates under your pillow) and a guitar strap for both left- and right-handed musicians. And there was a throwback to the old days—a water-powered engine designed by the man who invented the computer floppy disk and the digital watch. His name is Yoshiro Nakamutsu. He is known as "the Edison of Japan."

May 11, 1990

Putting a New Spin on Software

Microsoft's William Gates Talks About the Age of 'Fingertip Information'

EVELYN RICHARDS

William H. Gates III, one of the upstart pioneers of the personal computer industry a dozen years ago, has persevered to become one of its giants today, a 35-year-old multibillionaire with the potential power to influence the course of the entire industry.

His Microsoft Corp. is the world's largest producer of personal computer software, led by the MS-DOS disk operating system for IBM and other personal computers, Macintosh software and the fast-selling Windows program that permits personal computer users to handle different jobs quickly and simply on a single screen.

Gates's goal for the 1990s is a new generation of software that would dramatically expand the amount and variety of information available to computer users, while simplifying access to the material at the same time—an approach Microsoft calls "information at your fingertips."

In a recent meeting with *Washington Post* reporters and editors, Gates had this to say about the future of personal computers.

Q: What has to happen for your notion of "information at your fingertips" to become a reality?

A: The software requires a mix of skills that no existing company can claim to have. It's not just writing code {the detailed instructions that enable computers to carry out human instructions}. Code is part of it, but so are images and sound and animation.

We've spent five years now putting together the rights to images {of well-known paintings and photographs} and maps and music scores and sound to serve as our master database.

It's a new thing and it will enable home and office computing to get into a broader set of uses and will play a fairly significant role in education—something the computer has not yet done, you'd have to say.

Getting the rights to build a product like this is very hard.

Q: It's not just software that has to evolve?

A: Screens are going to improve dramatically. We're going to get big, flat screens. In fact, the question will be, in any office, what part of the surface area do you want to be a screen. You can touch any piece of information displayed on that screen and ask for more detail or use some kind pointing device, a stylus or laser gun, whatever you like, to zoom in on the data that's there . . .

Q: You're banking on the computer and its screen as the vehicle for displaying this information. The data will be stored on compact discs. . .

A: If this happens in one to three years, it's the CD. If you're more patient, there will be other kinds of technologies . . . .

Let's say, for example, you put the Sears catalogue onto a CD. The first thing you see when turn the computer on {and ask for the catalogue} is the home. You walk around this home and say, you want to buy a rake, so you go over to the garage, open it up, see all these rakes. It shows you all the choices. Maybe it's hooked up through a phone connection to Sears to show you the specials available for rakes at that time or to let you place an order.

Q: What does this say about the future of newspapers and magazines?

A: Hopefully, this broad availability of information preserves curiosity in people and makes them more interested in what's going on.

Q: That sounds like the right answer for this group. Now, give us the truthful one.

A: No, this is the truth. Paper has such huge advantages in terms of its cost and portability . . . . A computer screen today is such an ugly little thing to look at. Even at Microsoft, any memo over two pages, it's considered rude to send it on the computer screen. Well, not necessarily rude, but you're going to print it out and look at it to read. So the computer may be transmitting it, but we're going to print the thing out . . . .

Let's get far out. Suppose you have in your house large surface areas for screens, so whatever art you want to see, whatever pictures of the world you want to see, or let's say every morning whatever news you're interested in will come up.

Supposedly, based on articles that you browsed in the past or specific indication of interest, you're seeing a newspaper—that's your newspaper with the basketball scores at the front, certain stocks in the middle, that kind of thing. This narrow casting concept may be possible and that's quite different than newspapers are today.

Then again, part of the value of the newspaper is sort of a norm—what everybody else is reading: not only do I want to know what other people know, I sort of want to have something to talk to them about . . . . The idea of having customized newspapers, news alerts for people—that will start at the very high-end of the business markets.

Q: You operate a very elevated level of technology. Where do you get your people from?

A: They come from science. In order to prove to us you have the crisp thinking and IQ level that we want, except in very rare cases, you have to have worked in some kind of science—physics, chemistry, math or computer science. We're willing to take people who haven't done much computer stuff who've worked in the pure sciences just because a lot of our very best people were PhDs in physics and math. Then when they move over to computers, it's just simple stuff.

In the United States, we have 15 target schools. In Canada, there are four target schools. Japan has six. Target means we actually go on campus, we know professors there. Every year we're asking the professors, 'Who should we be after?' We're hiring people from those universities everywhere. We hire more from the University of Waterloo, in {Ontario} Canada, than anywhere else.

This recruiting effort is one of the most fun things we do.

We interview them on campus, or if you're not at one of the target schools, you have to send a sample of your science work or your coding work . . . .

Q: How much competition do you see from Japan in, say, 10 years from now?

A: We're in an unusual part of the software industry, which is this packaged software for personal computers. The only country in the world where we're not the largest personal computer software company is Japan. That is because we fail to do a Japanese word processor, which is by far the largest application category in Japan.

I actually don't see much direct competition in that area. We got into Japan early enough. The way they do capital formation over there hasn't created companies like ours, really . . . . So we don't see that much competition.

Japan does great software. There was this crazy myth that {the} Japanese couldn't write good software. I never knew where that came from, because all the good video games—not all, but a high percentage, a majority—were invented in Japan by individual creative programmers . . .. Software requires sticking with something, working hard, lots of engineers. That's . . . you're talking about Japan now.

But our business is so dominated by U.S. companies, it's strange.

Q: Most of the people who come here from your industry talk about what they want the government to do, why the U.S. is falling behind Japan in competitiveness and you haven't mentioned any of that. Are these important issues? Are they irrelevant? Is there just not that much that Washington can do that's helpful in this industry?

A: Something the government can do to help is to get copyright laws passed in different countries {to protect against pirated copies of American-made software}. The U.S. government is doing a great job of that. They made it their top agenda.

Beyond that, the question is, are you suppose to have somebody to worry about when you wake up in the morning? Sure, I think so. Well, it happens to be the Japanese. They're very good—across the board—they seem to be hard-working, they have good companies. Who else is preventing America from getting lazier and lazier? I mean, if {the government} put the fix in, maybe we would just get lazy. I don't believe there is a grand conspiracy against us, you know, that these guys were going to get together against us in some way. That's Japanaphobia, which I don't believe in.

Now when you look at a particular industry like the {computer} chip industry, then I agree, it's not as easy to just say, well, too bad, our guys didn't do a good job. We were the creators of so many of the innovations. It would be disappointing to see it essentially disappear.

Q: So you're not interested in government support for important new technologies, like advanced computer screens, for instance, or high-definition television?

A: There's some very poor thinking going on when we think {high quality screens} are going to be made in the United States. I don't care how much money the government throws at it, they're not going to be made here.

I believe in this thing called digital transmission. {Television signals would be converted into computer language and then transmitted electronically, creating the possibility for dramatic improvements in viewing quality and enhancements.} Digital transmission, which would probably take 10 years to catch on, no, 10 to 20 years. It is very chip-intensive and it's cool. That's going to be great and the U.S. chip companies should find a way to get involved with it. But the screens themselves, we got out of that a long time ago and there's no reason to get back in.

Q: Listening to you today, you seem like such a nice guy, but some people say you are not at all nice to your competitors. Is there a Jekyll and Hyde quality there?

A: Well, you can interview me after midnight. We have never sued anyone. Ever. . . . I think that with the level of success we've had there are pretty positive feelings toward us.

Q: What is wrong with the world from where you sit?

A: Oh, I have a very positive attitude . . . . The fact that we might go into a recession, that's not the end of the world. At Microsoft, we have five-year product cycles, tons of cash. A majority of the company is owned by two people who can afford to think very, very long term, so that's not a huge concern.

I tend to be pretty upbeat because of the number of new companies that are being started in our business, the number of new ideas that are coming along, the way that we feel our products are affecting people's jobs. The potential to create tools that help in education is very significant.

Q: Is it still an industry where a couple of people can quit their jobs and go out and do a prototype idea and . . .

A: Absolutely. That's happening all the time. They're not starting in writing a word processor but they have some wild ideas about how to write the words for you. They do something new.

There's so much opportunity and it's happening all the time. They don't have to worry about training people, three or four really great programmers are so productive and if you're focused on what you're doing. That kind of thing is happening. It'll continue to happen.

THOUGHTS ON APPLE AND JOBS

Gates on Apple Computer Inc.:

In terms of doing radical things, Apple hasn't had anything since 1984. And in fact, some people—not me, but some people—have criticized them for that. If Apple doesn't show something they've done with that {profits}, their market share certainly in some areas will drop off. But I have faith that Apple will do new things.

Gates on Steve Jobs, former Apple Computer founder who is producing a new computer called NEXT:

Well, he has a great product. Now his product comes with an interesting feature called incompatibility. That is, it doesn't run any of the existing {IBM or Apple} software. Not joking around, it's a super-nice computer. I don't think if I went out to design an incompatible computer I would have done as well as he did.

Now he's made signigicant improvements in the machines, so the question has to be asked again: Will he sell the quantities that justify, {Microsoft and others} writing software for it?

Steve is a unique individual. Very high talent. People pay attention to what he does in a way that is an asset as well. And so I spend time talking to Steve—I'm going to go down and see him in January. I still am taking the posture that I'd like to focus on Mac {Apple's Macintosh} and Windows and not divert time off for the Next machine. But I'm going to go down and hear what he can tell me about it. Who's buying this machine, where is he taking it in the future? And see, because if I'm wrong, it's very bad business judgement.

But it is kind of an awkward thing, because Steve and I worked so closely together on the Mac, and that was a lot of fun.

December 30, 1990

Study Questions

CHAPTER FIVE

1. Look at the development of a particular product over time and note how its change in design and function have reflected evolving audience tastes.
2. What lessons can be learned from success stories, such as the tale of Victoria's Secret? What else could be learned from a feature story about a failure?
3. Profile a type of character by constructing his or her image from movies, the press and books. For examples, think about scientists, secretaries or college professors. How might that image change if you spent a day with a typical case study?

Land of the Free 6

Joel Achenbach's feature examines the Christopher Columbus legacy in light of a controversy over whether America should "celebrate" or "commemorate" the Discoverer. Using a revisionist approach, Achenbach explores the political waves still being created 500 years after the voyage, by using interviews with historians and scholarly analysis of earlier biographies. By including the point of view of Native Americans, he presents a multi-cultural perspective on a familiar historical tale.

Memories of life before air-conditioning are the focus of vignettes by different writers, who vividly recall images, attitudes and experiences. The pervasive sentiment of "When You Were Hot, You Were Hot" is pure nostalgia for the bad old days.

Antics and anecdotes are the heart of Peter Carlson's profile of the U.S. House of Representatives, titled "The Least Exclusive Club in the World." Told in eleven sections, the article contrasts the bizarre ideas and activities of some Representatives to the staid ways of Senators and employs funny stories to affirm the eccentricities and goofiness of the former.

The newsroom values of fairness and balance apply to feature sections and magazines as well. It's the media's responsibility to keep coverage even-handed. Since the views of proponents of labeling record albums had already been frequently reported, Richard Harrington concentrated on the First Amendment rights of rap artists in his article on a free speech advocate. The story is a roundup of censorship struggles across the nation.

A consumer story with a legal angle turns up a new privacy issue: a citizen's right to protection from being involuntarily placed on computerized mailing lists used in mass marketing. In a jointly bylined article, Daniel Mendel-Black and Evelyn Richards observe that personal information is now being treated as a commodity and that the marketplace is increasingly invading people's lives.

In the wake of the mass murder of college students in Gainesville, Florida, Joel Achenbach looked into the American fascination with serial killers. His coverage of the phenomenon extended to new movies and books, in which he found a cultural glorification of evil and the monstrous. Serial killers are being viewed as "an American Original, a romantic icon, like a cowboy," he concluded. To increase public understanding of these psychopaths, Achenbach cited psychologists who link serial killing to sexual maladjustment and the dissolution of community.

Columbus Rediscovered

In Nineteen Hundred And Ninety-Two, the Admiral Is Sailing into One Hell of a Political Squall

JOEL ACHENBACH

History does not know the name of the Discoverer. But he, or she, was probably one of the children of the fisherfolk, some sharp-eyed sprite swimming in the tropical blue water or collecting shells on an island called Guanahani. The Discoverer would have seen, early in the morning, a strange object on the horizon, gradually coming closer. An enormous watercraft. With vast white squares of cloth.

The vessel came into the lagoon, and then six large men rowed to the shore in a skiff. They had sickly pale skin, and colorful hair that sprouted from, of all places, their chins and cheeks. They had a hard shiny covering around their bodies. They looked like gigantic beetles.

The fisherfolk gathered peacefully, and welcomed these bizarre visitors.

The leader, the "Captain General," as he called himself, was completely unintelligible.

Cristobal Colon stepped on land and proclaimed, in Spanish, that this would henceforth be the property of the king and queen of Spain. He asked that his five colleagues bear witness to the deed. One took notes. Three flags were planted in the sand.

Then came the cultural exchanges. The sailors gave the "Indians," as they eventually misnamed them, some trinkets, in return for cotton balls and parrots. One of the fisherfolk tried to pick up a sword and cut his hand on the blade. Colon wrote in his journal that these people clearly had no knowledge of warfare.

"They must make good servants," he wrote on that Oct. 12 of 1492. Two days later, he penned a letter to his royal sponsor: "Your Highness may, whenever you so wish, have them all sent to Castille or keep them all captives in the island, for with fifty armed men you will keep them all under your sway and will make them do all you may desire."

To Colon, a k a Christopher Columbus, this new land was ripe for exploitation. He figured he was in some islands in the Sea of China, not far from the kingdom of the Grand Khan, or perhaps in the Indies. He didn't care, really, so long as there were riches to be plundered. He'd already claimed the royal reward for being the first to sight land, even though another sailor, the lookout, had first shouted

"Tierra!" Such are the discretions of being the Captain General—soon to be the Admiral.

As for the natives, he wrote, "I say that Christendom shall make good business with them, especially Spain, to which all must be subjected."

In the end, the fate of the islanders, and the fate of all the diverse nations of indigenous people in the Western Hemisphere, was to be worse than mere subjugation. If indeed a child had first seen the caravel of Columbus, he or she probably did not live to see adulthood. The "Indians" endured a holocaust, a disease-borne extermination unlike anything since in human history. There were as many as 3 million Tainos on the Caribbean islands in 1492. Within a generation, there were virtually none.

In the years leading up to 1892, the 400th anniversary of the "Discovery," there was a movement to canonize Columbus. But he was ultimately deemed no saint. The movement was derailed not because Columbus exploited and abused other human beings, or because his immediate legacy included the creation of a vast African slave trade, or because his vision of what could be done with these new lands was mercenary to the point of rapacity.

It was because he had a son out of wedlock.

The Quincentenary is a razor-sharp spike rising from the calendar, a hazard by which every thinking person must carefully navigate. It is sheer perverse coincidence that the mega-anniversary for Western civilization is about to pop up right when Western civilization itself, its values and prejudices and dead-white-guy heroics, is on trial, argued over in every publication from *Newsweek* to the *New Republic* to the *Nation,* a cause celebre made no less passionate for being purely cerebral.

Columbus is in for a rough ride. The Columbus promoters find themselves not so much promoting the man as defending him.

"Yes, Columbus was a less than perfect individual. So what else is new?" says Frank Donatelli, chairman of the Christopher Columbus Quincentenary Jubilee Commission. "Let's not forget the fact that what Christopher Columbus accomplished was possibly the most important thing that had happened to the world since the birth of Christ."

"If you put down Columbus, you put down the entire Renaissance," says Anne Paolucci, president of Columbus: Countdown 1992. She says the "wonderful festivities" of the 400th anniversary added up to a "marvelous celebration," but adds ruefully, "This time around, for whatever reasons, suddenly the factionalism, which is a political thing, has reared its ugly head, and now we are faced with a Quincentenary that could easily fall apart."

No, not fall apart. But the Quincentenary (or Quincentennial) is going to be a messy business. Only at great peril of ridicule will any event take on a triumphalist, celebratory tone. Columbus is being held up to new, exacting standards, a test of political and moral correctness that will be hard to pass for someone who was not particularly humane even by the standards of the medieval world, someone who once wrote that he had been given "seven heads of women," as though the female Indians were cattle.

And this time around the Indians themselves will be something more than mere sideshow attractions, as they were at the Chicago World's Fair of 1893, where they were exhibited as objects of curiosity. In one of many planned protests, a group of Indians will sail to Spain and present a list of grievances at the World's Fair in Seville.

Columbus, says Alex Ewen, editor of the journal *Native Nations* and a member of the Purepecha Indian nation of northern Mexico, "was possessed by an ethic of destruction. The idea that people could be property, that the earth could be property, was an idea alien to Indians. We see him sort of like a creature out of science fiction, an alien from another planet who sort of zipped down and imposed a new way of life, against which there has been a guerrilla struggle to this very day."

The guerrilla struggle has mainstream assistance. To take merely one example: The American Library Association has passed a resolution urging libraries to approach the Quincentenary with materials that "examine the event from an authentic Native American perspective, dealing directly with topics like cultural imperialism, colonialism and the Native American holocaust."

The Smithsonian is following the revisionist line by calling the discovery an "encounter." The New World is "the Western Hemisphere." This is not a celebration but a "commemoration."

There are backlashes to the Columbus backlash. Sen. Ted Stevens (R-Alaska) has attacked the Smithsonian in public hearings for, among other things, the institution's first major Quincentenary exhibition, "The West as America" which appalled traditionalists with its dismissive, heavily politicized commentary on the romanticization of the West by 19th-century painters. The National Endowment for the Humanities has also taken up a conservative position, declining to give funding to two separate TV programs that attack Columbus. One program, NEH huffed, accuses Columbus of genocide.

Call it the Orthodoxy War.

Just as the Indians were stick figures to Columbus, so too has Columbus become a stick figure in the middle of the fight between those who embrace and those who reject Western civilization.

The old orthodoxy holds that Western civilization is self-evidently a great achievement of the human mind, a linear progression from the state of barbarism toward the state of individual freedom and intellectual utopia. Columbus represents enlightenment, liberty, the catalyst for that exceptional nation, the United States.

The new orthodoxy, however, claims that Western civilization is racist, sexist, imperialist, exclusivist and generally contemptuous of anything that smacks of otherness. Columbus is no longer just a resourceful sailor; he represents the White Man. He is capitalism. He is Eurocentrism.

The peculiar thing about all this is that history is already fixed, it has already happened—and yet both sides treat the rigid past as though it were flexible, unshapen, something to be redesigned, something to be won. Perhaps the idea, unstated but implicit, is that whoever controls the past also controls the future. Perhaps the argument is not about the past 500 years, but the next 500.

History is a progressive march from barbarism.

History is a cruel joke on the meek and powerless.

History is . . . up for grabs.

Stories About Columbus

At the main public library in Washington, named after Martin Luther King, the weathered, colorful children's books about Columbus paint him as a clever boy who grew up into a great hero. A daredevil. He's a medieval Evel Knievel.

Ingri and Edgar D'Aulaire's 1955 children's book "Columbus" gives the sailor credit for figuring out that the world is round, not "flat as a platter." (The truth is that every educated person on the planet in the 1400s knew the world was round.) When Columbus arrived in the Caribbean, the authors say, "All he could see were naked, red-skinned savages. They threw themselves to the ground and worshiped Columbus and his bearded men. The Spaniards did not mind being treated like gods by these gentle heathens to whom they had come to bring the Christian faith." The book has only two passing references to Spanish greed and nothing about murder or slavery. Columbus's decision to kidnap six Indians and take them back to Spain is described in the most benign of terms: "He had even brought along some Indians to show."

Adult biographies are more realistic. The standard volume on Columbus has been Samuel Eliot Morison's acclaimed 1942 opus "Admiral of the Ocean Sea: A Life of Christopher Columbus." Morison does not hesitate to note that Columbus enslaved and exploited the natives he encountered, but the historian's greater fascination is with Columbus's nautical achievement. At the time, Morison's work was regarded as a daring piece of revisionism, mainly because the previous standard work was Washington Irving's four-part biography published in 1828. The Irving account is still in print around the world, and says of Columbus, "His conduct was characterized by the grandeur of his views and the magnanimity of his spirit."

Now, in some circles, even Morison is thought of as an apologist for Columbus.

John Yewell, a Minnesota writer, is editing one of the many anti-Columbus books that are in the works, and the first line of his introduction states flatly, "The United States honors only two people with holidays bearing their names: Martin Luther King Jr., who gave his life combating the legacy of slavery, and Christopher Columbus, who initiated it."

Yewell said in an interview, "We're not striving for balance here, by the way, we're striving for truth."

This "truth," however, is hardly original. The first Columbus critic was his own contemporary, Bartolome de las Casas, a friar who documented and protested the awful process by which the Indian population of the New World was wiped out. Las Casas wrote that Columbus's exploitative behavior "was very far from the purpose of God and His Church."

Ever since, there has been vibrant intellectual debate as to whether the cost of the Discovery was worth the reward. Among true historians (as opposed to, say, Washington Irving) there was never much doubt that Columbus and his followers were in many ways unsavory and despicable. Columbus's men were rapists and killers. The conquistadors Cortes and Pizarro were butchers. The debate is still not really about what happened. There's only a debate about what politically oriented people call "spin."

The spin has been such that, for 500 years now, Columbus has remained an untarnished icon at the popular level, the level of Columbus Day parades, of children's books, of that George Gershwin song that goes, "Everyone laughed when Columbus said the world was round."

If there is a single person armed with more tarnish than anyone else, it's Kirkpatrick Sale. Sale's vitriolic, immensely readable book "The Conquest of Paradise: Christopher Columbus and the Columbian Legacy" is the Holy Koran of Columbus-bashers.

The book's title is not meant to be merely lyrical. Sale thinks that the New World was a kind of Paradise on Earth, despoiled by Europe. Sale writes with a post-Earth Day sensibility. He faults the Europeans for exploiting the natural world rather than living in harmony with it, as the Native Americans did. The New World was just another resource to be mined. This attitude has remained a part of the American culture and contributed to the dire (in Sale's opinion) prospects of the modern, polluted, denatured planet.

"I regard it as a desperately sick and inwardly miserable society that doesn't realize that it is suffering from the terminal disease I would call affluenza," Sale said in an interview. "It is the most powerful and successful civilization the world has ever seen, you've got to give it credit for that, but it is founded on a set of ideas that are fundamentally pernicious, and they have to do with rationalism and humanism and materialism and nationalism and science and progress. These are, to my mind, just pernicious concepts."

Rationalism is bad. Science is bad. Progress is bad.

Mankind must reject its decadent, materialistic ways.

"Imagine if it had singing, dancing, laughing and sex as its regular components," he says.

For radical environmentalists, Columbus is the guy who began the process of the world's destruction. Europe and its progeny are the ones who created the Industrial Revolution and thus Global Warming. Sale's view of Columbus is informed by his conviction that the planet is in peril of total annihilation.

"I am firmly of the opinion that ecocide is our certain future, and probably in the next 20 or 30 years if we do not discard those values," Sale says. "At my most optimistic I can believe that there will be some humans that survive the eco-catastrophe when it comes, and those humans will have to start thinking about new values, and discarding the old ones, and so I will hope that books like mine will be there to assist them at that. That's the most optimistic, of course."

"Realistically," he says, "I think it's unlikely that oxygen-dependent life will survive."

WHAT HATH COLUMBUS WROUGHT?

Commercial or Controversial?

Until recently, the biggest Columbus controversy was over whether he was really the first. (He obviously wasn't. It has been well established that, nearly 500 years before Columbus's voyage, Vikings settled for a few years on what is now Newfoundland. Some scholars argue that European fishermen knew of the continents across the sea for many years prior to 1492 but did not want to reveal the location of their secret fishing grounds. There are even cases made that ancient Phoenicians or Africans first crossed the Atlantic.) But this is all irrelevant. Uncontestably, Columbus's voyages started something big.

In the mid-1980s, it appeared that the Quincentenary would be a totally uncontroversial conduit of hype for corporate America. *Ad Week* magazine called it an "Olympic-sized marketing opportunity."

And the U.S. government called it a "jubilee."

The Christopher Columbus Quincentenary Jubilee commission was created by Congress in 1984 to coordinate all the Columbus-related events throughout the nation. Seven years later, by February of this year, it had managed to put together only two projects, and the chairman, Republican fund-raiser John Goudie of Miami, had resigned after questions were raised about his personal financial dealings.

Goudie was replaced in February by Donatelli. That an Italian American would be put in charge is in keeping with tradition in the United States. Italian Americans are the biggest boosters of Columbus Day. (In the "Old World," it is Spain that leads the hype.)

Donatelli quickly realized that, in addition to all the other problems, the commission's board of directors didn't include a single American Indian.

"It is clearly an oversight," sighs Donatelli. "In 1984 this sounded like a good idea, did not seem to be controversial, so I don't think the attention was paid to having a good balance on the board so that everyone who has a stake in the Quincentenary was represented."

He promises that a man named Bill Ray will join the 30-person board soon. He's an Indian.

Genocide or Germs?

Herman Viola is caught in the Middle.

Viola is curator of "Seeds of Change," the Museum of Natural History's major offering on behalf of the Quincentenary, a huge exhibition. He wants to avoid friction. His show is carefully scrubbed of any political markings. He has chosen to focus on the geographical transfer of horses, potatoes, sugar, corn and diseases.

"I think if you get in a politically charged debate you are going to miss the fundamental issues that we should be talking about," he says.

Such as?

"A lot of good came out of 1492. We wouldn't be here today."

Viola likes to point out that Italian food was prepared without tomatoes prior to 1492.

"Can you imagine Italian cuisine today without tomato sauce?"

And: "If it weren't for Columbus, we wouldn't have Swiss chocolate."

This detached, scientific view is not going to please either the Columbus bashers or the Columbus boosters. But in many ways it is the most authentic account of what happened. Despite all the rhetoric, the conquest of "Paradise" was affected not by Europe's superior technology but by a biological quirk. The Old World had many large animals that could be easily domesticated. Those animals, in turn, transferred diseases to humans. While the Old World genetic pool developed immunity to those diseases, there was no such immunity in the New World. The Europeans were killers, it's true, but they conquered the diverse and powerful nations of the Western Hemisphere because the indigenous people sickened and died right in front of them. The holocaust can hardly be described as genocide. It was an accident caused by things unseen, by microbes, transferred across the ocean in an era when no one even knew that germs existed.

Nor did Columbus change merely the Western Hemisphere. The corn imported into Africa led to a tripling of the population there, despite the burgeoning slave trade. The existence of the new continents and of the Indians also provoked a philosophical revolution in Europe. There was no place in the biblical explanation of the world for these new, racially ambiguous people.

The medieval world disintegrated—the first achievement, one might argue, of what would centuries later be called "multiculturalism."

Multiculturalism

The rejection of modern America requires a kind of intellectual surgery in which society is carefully tweezed apart into incompatible and confrontational elements. The idea of the "melting pot" is considered reactionary; it robs people of their ethnic heritage.

"The history of the past 500 years demonstrates a commonality of oppression and also resistance on the part of all the minority groups," says Sanford Berman, a

Minnesota librarian who helped draft the American Library Association letter on the Quincentenary.

Berman says the Quincentenary is a protest opportunity for many groups, not just Native Americans. He runs down the whole list: African Americans can point to Columbus as the catalyst for the New World slave trade; Asian Americans came to America as exploited, underpaid laborers; working-class people have suffered from the greed of capitalists who emerged from the European economic system; Jews and Moslems have a special interest in 1492 because that year they were expelled from Spain as the Catholic monarchs solidified their rule; and so on.

But what about people who don't fit into those category? What about "European Americans," as whites are sometimes labeled?

"I think white or European American people, no matter what their station, need at some level to recognize that they have been the beneficiaries of a racist system, if you will, an exploitative system, that has over these 500 years oppressed people of color," Berman says.

In other words, whites can feel lucky, and guilty.

The irony is that a few decades ago the liberal agenda was based on the belief that people were similar and deserving of equal rights regardless of their skin color or national origin or religion. Now the liberal agenda, or at least the multiculturalist appendix, requires that everyone be labeled by race, ethnicity, sex, economic status, sexual preference, religion etc. Everyone can thereby be categorized as either oppressor or oppressed. Who you are matters less than what you are.

Multiculturalism has an ally in the form of the Smithsonian Institution. "The West as America" was not an aberration. Alicia Maria Gonzalez, director of the Smithsonian Quincentenary Program, applauds that exhibition for "making people think." She says that in the past, minority viewpoints haven't been adequately represented by the Smithsonian. "Hispanics that come in don't see themselves at all. There's nothing that speaks to them. African Americans see almost nothing at all," she says.

She says the Smithsonian will have a number of "mainstream events." Her long list of projects also includes the following:

Chicano Art: Resistance and Affirmation (exhibition)

Golden Threads: A Tapestry of Sephardic Experience (exhibition)

Images: Women in the Americas (symposium)

Algonquin Heritage Garden (exhibition)

Will the Circle be Unbroken? Historical Perspectives on the African Diaspora (conference)

Perhaps the biggest danger of multiculturalism is that, when adopted by previously conservative institutions, it might become simply dull. In the hands of a fire-breather like Kirkpatrick Sale, multiculturalism is intensely provocative. But in the hands of an institution that wants to make everyone happy—and the Smithsonian did tone down the wall plaques in "The West as America" after critics made noise—multiculturalism can turn into the blandest of ideologies, something little more than a census of opinions in which the only ambition is to go around the room and let everyone talk for five minutes. The glorious concept of "inclusiveness" becomes not the means to an end, but the end itself. It's just an intellectual head count. Who's here? What's on yer mind?

The idea of Difference can become fetishistic. Even the peoples of the so-called Old and New worlds were not so terribly different as one might expect. They were eons apart biologically—isolated from one another for at least 10,000 years, probably much longer—and yet they independently developed agriculture, astronomy, mathematics. Both hemispheres had great empires. Both hemispheres had wars. Both hemispheres had environmental catastrophes caused by such misguided human practices as excessive irrigation of cropland.

It is true that many of the natives in the Western Hemisphere were peaceful, but they were not incapable of violence. Columbus left 39 sailors on the island of Hispaniola after the Santa Maria was shipwrecked. All 39 were killed by natives (probably with good reason, say many historians).

The historian Doug Foard, who edited the special Quincentenary edition of the *Magazine of History,* says that although Europe conquered the new lands, "Does that mean there's something fundamentally flawed in the European character? I think it just means that given this great disparity of power, people can be very cruel to each other."

It's human nature, he says. And he adds, "I don't think human nature has changed very much."

Native Sensibilities

Perhaps it is also human nature to fight over the meaning of history, to try to impart the spin that best serves the interest of your own kind. The people hurt worst will fight hardest.

For Suzan Shown Harjo, a member of the Cheyenne and Arapaho Indian nations, a woman who grew up on a reservation in Oklahoma, who hauled water from a well and burned kerosene lamps for light and used an outdoor john, who saw her people suffering from poor diets and high rates of disease and suicide—for her, the Columbus quincentenary is not just a matter of abstract debate.

"We're not talking about being a skunk at someone's tea party or spoiling someone's parade. We're talking about life-or-death matters," she says, sitting in her office at the Morning Star Foundation on Capitol Hill.

What Harjo wants is fundamental: She wants to be treated as fully human. She points out that Indians are still treated as archaeological artifacts, their bones dug up and exhibited in museums; tons of human remains are kept in storage at the Smithsonian. She is tired of her people being used as brand names, like the Jeep Cherokee or the Winnebago. She is appalled that Washington's football team is called the Redskins, the most derogatory name for her people. She is slightly annoyed that Kirkpatrick Sale, a "European American," has gained so much attention for presenting the Indian viewpoint—"People aren't being authentic when they're telling other people's stories," she says. There is also the nagging fact that the Bureau of Indian Affairs is in the Interior Department, the agency that handles inanimate resources, like National Parks and offshore oil deposits.

"We are always where the nonhumans are," she says. "That's what we're up against, the entire perception that we aren't human."

A perception that goes back to that first day, long ago, on the shore of the island called Guanahani.

"We're beginning in 1991 to mark the Quincentenary of 1491, which we call the last good year," she says. "The good old days!"

July 14, 1991

When You Were Hot, You Were Hot

Life Before AC Wasn't Always Uncool—
Recalling Sweat Surrender.

PAUL RICHARD, EVE ZIBART,

JOEL ACHENBACH AND KEN RINGLE

The midnights were the worst, especially the breezeless ones when, in the heavy darkness, you'd find yourself awake enough to recognize again that it was just too hot to sleep. On those August nights you'd resort to the full bathtub, the bathtub filled at bedtime. Nothing else would do. You'd sit up very slowly, without switching on the light or opening your eyes, and stagger to the bathroom, stumbling through the dark. The trick was to stay un-alert. Eyes still closed, still half asleep, you'd slip into the water and submerge yourself completely, and float there for a moment. Then, streaming with cool water, you'd squish back to the bedroom and flop down on the sodden sheets, and, with your eyes still closed, and your inter-rupted dreams still partly recollected, pray that you would find yourself—before the fading chill of the evaporating wetness had vanished from your skin—once again asleep.

Paul Richard

Air conditioning has stripped antiseptic the smell of Southern nights.

When I was small, sleeping with the bed pushed up to the open windows and my pillow on the sill, nighttime had the warm, heavy odor of humid wood, the dusty sweetness of old lead paint and the masculine must of rusty window screens—the same scent I always thought lightning bugs would have. The breeze carried in whispers of clover and cut grass and hard green pears and magnolia from spots so precisely familiar that I could trace the perfumes coming from the corners of the yard like smoke in the rain.

And there were strange, quick waftings to be puzzled over: birds' nests under the eaves and hot tar from the roof and papery moth wings singed in the lamps. On the holidays the gunpowder smell of fireworks and the acrid burn of sparklers would linger for hours. Curtains recalled the iron, the newly washed venetian blinds smelled of wet cord—even the motes in the moonlight seemed to have a smell back then.

The richest odors came from the long screened-in sleeping porches that ran across the upper backs of old houses and were swept with a clean tang when the rain blew through; afterward the thick, languid honeysuckle and the flat asphalt smell of the wet roads would swell up dense as muslin in the humidity.

And there were those most wondrous comforts of all—the smell of sun-warmed flesh, sweetish reminders of the day's baking, my mother's perfume. I would give all the air conditioning in the world to smell it again.

Eve Zibart

The two crucial scientific concepts for cooling off during summer, and I'm speaking here as a congenital Floridian, are:

1. Conductivity.
2. Specific heat.

Dirt, for example, has decent but unspectacular conductivity and respectably high specific heat, which is to say, it's actually cool. This can be determined by digging a hole in the ground and then either laying down in the hole or lying down in it, depending on what is grammatically correct. The soil is refreshing against your bare summery flesh. You can cover up everything but your head and chill out for hours. It takes a while for the dirt to warm to your level, which, as you know, is what high specific heat is all about.

The only problem with this is that by laying or lying in a shallow grave you can be mistaken for the victim of a serial killer, which is why you might instead employ a different technique, deepening the hole by several feet and then adding water. Water is extremely amazingly high in both conductivity and in specific heat. As you lounge in the murk, you can think of yourself as a swimming pool owner. I have tested this myself, once upon a pathetic time.

We didn't even have ice. We were like aboriginal people. Ice is, for my money, the substance with the greatest conductivity and specific heat, but we had none, because we forgot the recipe. The recipe. Because we forgot the recipe. Thank you.

Really, the freezer was busted for what seemed like my entire childhood. So I'd ride my bike down to the Howard Johnson's, half a mile away, and raid the ice machine in the motel breezeway, lugging back a towelful. What one cannot create, one can steal. The ice would go in tall perspiring schooners of very iced tea. Sipped, naturally, poolside.

Joel Achenbach

In New Orleans, where the climate in August approximates that of Rangoon, people really did dress in seersucker and white linen and straw hats, wilting with their garments as the day went on. And at night, when unlike Washington it is almost never cooler, there was one accepted strategy. That was to close all the windows except the ones on the other side of your bed, then turn on the giant, house-exhausting attic fan. This move, if it didn't immediately suck out your eardrums, would create a wind-tunnel effect, which left the curtains flying horizontal from the windows, launched tornadoes of loose papers on the desk and made you feel like

Dorothy heading Ozward. Then you took off all your clothes, lay spread-eagled on the sheet and went peacefully to sleep like a babe amid the cyclone's roar.

Ken Ringle

In the summer in the South Bronx during the second Eisenhower administration, the preferred method of coping with the heat was complaining about it in loud sputtering soliloquies that wafted out open casement windows and into the gutters where I was playing stickball. If you were male and between 8 and 18, you played stickball from morning to evening, your only concession to the heat being continual trips to the nearest public fountain, where the water pressure was so feeble you wound up licking warm moisture from the spout like a poodle in a pet store.

It was only on spectacularly hot days that one's parents actually did anything about the weather, invariably by escaping into either of the two air-conditioned venues that anyone who happened to live in the South Bronx could remotely afford: bowling and movies. Both places had signs outside advertising their air conditioning in words with descending icicles.

The problem was, the decision to go was spontaneous, made without warning or planning, usually by one's father, whose judgment in high heat was notoriously impaired. Though this posed no problem at the bowling alley, at the movies it meant walking in whenever you arrived, watching the film in progress until it ended, watching the second feature in its entirety, and then watching the first feature to the point you had walked in on three hours before. The movie was irrelevant; you were there to get cool. In those days, at movies in the South Bronx, there was never a real line to get inside, but always a shuffling procession of people filing in, shouting "Down in front!" and filing out with puzzled expressions, trying to recall which character died in the end.

To this day, against all reason, I harbor a secret enthusiasm for that most Ozzie of sports, bowling. And to this day, I won't go inside if the credits have so much as started.

Gene Weingarten

You think this is hot? Try New Delhi after May. Life was organized around the heat, however, which to a child, at least, seemed very sensible.

Our bedrooms were air-conditioned, but the hallway was a brutal slam of hot air and a smell like stale orange juice that is with me still. You wore loose cotton clothing and sandals and retired from any activity more strenuous than reading during the afternoon, by which time the temperature would be in the 100s and the streets would burn through your shoes.

In some houses (not ours) children were hired as punkah-wallahs to pull the string that moved a wide strip of a fan back and forth on the ceiling. We had electric ceiling fans that my brothers liked to run at high speed, flushing down a gust of hot air and dust. All the ashtrays had water in them to keep the ashes from blowing away.

But the khaskhas were the best invention, huge blinds made of woven grass that covered the entire front of the house. These were hosed down regularly by the gardener, which cooled the air coming into the house, and cut down on dust and light. They gave off a great dark wet smell that came to mean comfort and a kind of safety.

One heard about people fainting from the heat every now and then. I fainted once, but the mothers all said it was just the onset of adolescence. I preferred to think it was the heat.

Megan Rosenfeld

What I did in those Bethesda summer mornings was lie indoors in a slung backyard chaise in my little-girl underwear with cotton in my ears because I always seemed to have an earache, maybe from jumping in the pond at the big picnic at the Naval Hospital, where there were so many tiny green frogs that when they swarmed across the sand it looked like wind through grass, and watch "The Life of Riley" in black-and-white on our color TV, reruns even then.

What my mother did in those summer afternoons was spread a sheet on the living room floor, in front of the screen door, so we could all take our naps together, my beautiful mother and her three daughters, all dreaming on that cool white island.

Janet Duckworth

As a suburban, climate-controlled boy, I held haughty scorn for the family cottage in the woods, since it didn't even have screens on the windows, much less air conditioning. But my young summer memories are filled fondly with the wet weight of those humid nights—and the smell of whiskey.

Many nights I spent restless, sunk in the feather bed, flipping the pillow endlessly and wishing that even the slightest breeze would slide through the open window. Instead, in came the screech of owls, the trickle of the creek and mosquitoes as big as bats (or so I remember them). Eventually, my struggle against the heat exhausted me and I slept, but too often I woke with red, tingling bites all over those parts I had foolishly bared to the wild. That's when my grandmother went into the chest on the porch and took out a vial of Old Crow. With a few dabs of whiskey on the welts, the sting went away.

I had all but forgotten those nights until I moved to Washington not long ago. Now I live in a humble apartment that has no air conditioning and, indeed, no screens. So this summer, like those long ago, the humid nights are on me, and so is the Old Crow.

Blake de Pastino

Summer in the '50s was when our already superheated house filled up with visiting relatives, mostly uncles who smoked noxious cigars, played the numbers and ran around with what our grandmother called "cheap waitresses." We couldn't afford a week at the beach, but on the hottest days, we would head for Glen Echo

Amusement Park for a swim in the immense art deco pool there. My mother wore the locker room key around her ankle.

I would choose one hour with those people by that pool over a summer in St.-Tropez.

Marianne Kyriakos

We may be the only yuppies in Takoma Park still without air conditioning. My husband almost bought a window unit this summer, but I convinced him that prices will never be higher.

What I like best about riding out the heat waves is the finely tuned sensitivity one develops to the subtlest change for the better. I knew the minute the last cool front came through—I felt the difference in the air from the fan on my back. Sure enough, the temperature outside had dropped to 80, and moments later the dining room was a cool 85. That's another thing I like, discovering the body has acclimated to the point where it thinks 85 is cool.

Of course, when it's 101 outside, 85 really is cool, and 90 isn't so bad either. Another thing I like is walking into my house at noon, full of disgust for summer and sun, and feeling . . . relief. The house itself is protection, shade, insulation. It's doing what it was designed to do, and just with bricks and shingles and window blinds. It's a lot cooler than outside, even before I turn on the fans.

And it's no small benefit to discover that friendship with one's husband is still easy, even when he's lobbying for an air conditioner and I'm resisting. He'll probably win before next summer.

Elizabeth Dahlslien

The end of a high summer day in Washington still reminds me of a '60s science fiction paperback cover: Stark against a red blasting sun, the cityscape looks sentient, exhausted, aware of the heat that is parching it, wearily aware that it has no escape.

The whole solar system sizzling out; heat as destiny, everybody fried. I read a shelf of those end-of-the-world paperbacks at Hains Point, Washington's single site of summertime hope, the city's open sleeping porch. I guess it was cooler down there in my non-air-conditioned days; I suppose it was breezy in a riverside sort of way. But what I actually liked about it then—and what still draws me there—was that Washington's Southern summers seemed more intensely themselves on the old sandbar.

A Washington summer day there eased by slowly. No Crystal City then. No jets. Just a big lazy if toxic river and lots of bank to look at. Patient fishermen, their catfish dinners twitching in the grass; willows to catch the breezes you couldn't feel, so that at least you saw them; sleepy cicada lullabies. There was a little white building near Hains Point's tip that was once a teahouse. I can't remember that it ever served tea in my lifetime, but I wish I could. A few old guys in boaters would have been about right.

What's the good of air conditioning in the face of a supernova? I still believe the last sentient beings on doomed, heat-blasted planets must be willow trees, drooping sadly as they wait in vain for the rivers to flow again.

Charles Paul Freund

September 1, 1991

The Least Exclusive Club in the World

PETER CARLSON

In the last few months alone, members of the House of Representatives have compared themselves to thieves, zombies, dope fiends, Donald Duck and babies in need of toilet training. We wouldn't dream of disagreeing—but hey, they still put on the best shown in town.

Part 1: On the Soybean Standard

The federal budget had run out, the government had shut down, and now, late on the night of October 7, the House of Representatives was meeting in a special emergency session to ponder some way to solve the crisis. The galleries were packec and the crowd hushed and leaned forward to listen as Neal Smith (D-Iowa) rose to address the House:

"Mr. Speaker, you know, you cannot eat gold, but you can eat soybeans," he said. "Would it not make more sense to go on the soybean standard?"

On the House floor, the representatives were laughing. But up in the galleries, the citizens were confused: "Did he say the soybean standard?"

Only two days earlier, House members had dramatically defeated the budget summit deficit-reduction package. They'd passed a resolution to keep the government going for another week, but President Bush had vetoed it. Now, the government had shut down "non-essential" functions, including the Washington Monument and the Smithsonian museums, and so hundreds of disappointed tourists had come to the House, which was about the only show in town.

But what they saw there was a bit, well, bizarre.

At 1 p.m. House members convened and then immediately recessed until 4 to give a committee time to draw up a new budget plan. At 4, they reconvened, learned that the committee hadn't finished its work and immediately recessed until 6—provoking a chorus of boos from the galleries. At 6, they reconvened, made a few quick speeches and recessed until 8:30. At 8:30, they reconvened, talked about why the committee hadn't finished its work yet and recessed until 9:30. At 9:45, they reconvened and the speaker pro tempore, John Murtha (D-Pa.), urged members to get up and make some speeches—please!—because the committee still hadn't produced a budget plan.

He didn't have to ask twice. House members are good that way. Called upon to speak, they'll gladly get up and say a few words. Or more.

Robert Torricelli (D-N.J.) launched into a scathing attack on House Republicans. E. "Kika" de la Garza (D-Tex.), chairman of the Agriculture Committee, told a long story about his trip on a nuclear submarine, a story designed to illustrate the idea that nuclear submarines had won the Cold War and that the crews on nuclear submarines ate food, and that food was grown by farmers and therefore the House should not cut the agriculture budget. Then William Dannemeyer (R-Calif.) rose to denounce Torricelli for being "on the political left" and for being a danger to American taxpayers and . . .

"Will the gentleman yield?" asked Sam Gejdenson (D-Conn.), who was grinning mischievously under his bushy moustache.

"I yield to the gentleman from Connecticut," said Dannemeyer.

"I thank the gentleman for yielding," said Gejdenson. "I'm surprised the gentleman did not bring in the gold standard at some point."

The Democrats giggled and tittered and laughed aloud. They were privy to a private joke: Encouraging Dannemeyer to talk about the gold standard is akin to asking your most boring in-law to show slides of his trip to Niagara Falls.

"Would you like for me to talk about that" asked Dannemeyer. He was only too happy to oblige, and he was soon soaring into an impassioned oration on how America's financial problems—and the Soviet Union's too—stemmed from the fact that its money was no longer backed by gold.

And then Neal Smith rose to ask his question about the soybean standard.

"I admire the taste and utility of soybeans," Dannemeyer replied, "but I do not think they qualify as a storehouse of value."

Besides, he added, "gold does not grow mold."

Finally, James Bilbray (D-Nev.) rose to inject a little reality into the proceedings. "I would like to point out one thing, in case the public is out there watching everything that is going on," he said. "They may wonder where we are at, what we are doing talking about the gold standard . . ." This talk was mere "filler," Bilbray informed the viewers, something to pass the time while the House waited to work on the budget.

"'So, please,'" he begged, "do not think we are a bunch of fools tonight."

Part 2: "A Little More Raucous, a Little More Fun"

Thank you for clearing that up, Congressman Bilbray.

Sometimes it's difficult to tell when House members are acting foolish on purpose and when they're doing it inadvertently. So it helps to get the inside scoop.

Bilbray could have added another tip for citizens watching the House for the first time: No matter how serious the issues being discussed—and they're frequently quite crucial to the fate of mankind—the House is always poised on the verge of low comedy, strange stunts or just plain wackiness.

On the day of the great budget debate, for example, the House was pondering its biennial pre-election anti-crime package, and there were so many amendments designed to expand the list of crimes punishable by death that House liberals could no longer control themselves. So they started a satirical chant: "Kill! Kill! Kill!"

And one of the liberals, David Obey (D-Wis.), rose to make a sardonic inquiry: "Mr. Chairman, would it be possible to bring the guillotines directly to the House floor?"

They don't do stuff like that in the Senate. The Senate is too stodgy, too stately, too . . . well, senatorial for such stunts. But the House has never been accused of stateliness, at least not by anybody who has seen it in action. The House's charm lies precisely in its wonderful lack of stateliness, pretension, even dignity. It's a funny, funky place populated by an eclectic collection of eccentric American characters. It's also a mecca for connoisseurs of the human comedy and aficionados of the Theater of the Absurd.

"The House is a little more raucous, a little more fun," says Andy Jacobs (D-Ind.). He ought to know. In the late '70s, he and John Dingell (D-Mich.) nearly came to blows on the House floor while debating whether the peregrine falcon should be included on the official list of endangered species. A few years later, Jacobs distributed hand-held portable urinals to his fellow members of the House Ways and Means Committee so they wouldn't have to wade through the hordes of lobbyists encamped between them and the men's room.

The Senate is known as "the most exclusive club in the world," and its 100 members are inevitably addressed as "Senator." The House is known as "the people's chamber," and many of its 435 members officially encourage people to call them "Sonny" or "Jimmy"' or "Chip" or "'Buddy" or "Buz."

Senators run every six years and are generally questioned about the Great Issues of Our Time. House members run every two years—the voters will choose all 435 on Tuesday—and the questions tend to be less lofty. "With the Senate, they expect them to be statesmanlike," says Patricia Schroeder (D-Colo.). "With us, it's, 'Hey, I called you at 11 o'clock on Christmas Eve and you didn't unstop my drain.' "

Sometimes it helps to think of our bicameral national legislature this way:

The Senate is a gentleman's club. The House is a fraternity.

The Senate is the *New York Times*. The House is the *New York Post*.

The Senate is "Washington Week in Review." The House is "The Morton Downey Jr. Show."

Part 3: Is The House Representative"

The Senate is composed of 98 white men and two white women. The House has plenty of white men too, Lord knows, but it also has 28 women, 24 blacks, 13 Hispanics and one American Indian. The American Indian is Ben Nighthorse Campbell (D-Colo.), a jewelry maker, horse trainer, former member of the Olympic judo team and great-grandson of Black Horse, who fought on the winning side at the Battle of Little Bighorn and whose fierce-looking battle knife hangs on the wall of Campbell's House office.

Campbell remembers when he was sworn in with the congressional class of 1987. He looked around and saw Joe Kennedy (D-Mass.)—son of a senator, nephew of another senator and a president—and John Lewis (D-Ga.), who was arrested and beaten countless times during his days as a civil rights activist. The three of us, Campbell thought proudly, represent a pretty wide slice of America.

The House, unlike the Senate, has five non-voting members from far-flung corners of the American empire—such exotic places as the Virgin Islands, Puerto Rico, Guam, American Samoa and the District of Columbia. The delegate from American Samoa is Eni F.H. Faleomavaega, who can be seen performing a Polynesian dance in the Elvis Presley movie "Paradise, Hawaiian Style" and who has an elaborate tattoo that goes from his navel to his knees—a tattoo created when needles made from the tusks of wild boars were hammered into his flesh over 12 excruciatingly painful days in a ritual that was designed to teach Samoan men to appreciate the pain of childbirth.

No one in the Senate has anything that can match it.

The House, like the rest of America, suffers from a plague of lawyers—more than 180 of them—and at least one self-proclaimed non-lawyer. "I am not a lawyer," Fred Grandy (R-Iowa) once announced on the House floor. "If God is good, I will never be a lawyer." Grandy, who played Gopher on "The Love Boat," is one of two former TV sitcom stars in the House, the other being Ben Jones (D-Ga.), who played Cooter on "The Dukes of Hazzard." The House is also the home of three former talk show hosts, three public relations consultants, several real estate salesmen, a car dealer, three sheriffs, a riverboat captain, a psychiatrist, two preachers (one of them currently under indictment), a beer distributor, two former pro basketball players, one former big league pitcher, one ex-boxer and Charles Hayes (D-Ill.), who once labored in the pork department of a Chicago slaughterhouse and has thus witnessed both of the sights that the old American proverb warns against watching—the making of sausage and the making of laws.

Demographically, the House of Representatives is hardly representative of America—it is whiter, richer, older and maler than the rest of the country—but in some odd, idiosyncratic way, its disparate membership reflects some of the quirkier psychic corners of this grand and goofy land.

Gun nuts? Charlie Wilson (D-Tex.) has a gun collection that includes a Soviet grenade launcher, a Soviet submachine gun, an Israeli Galil assault rifle, an American M-16, a British Enfield rifle, a .44 Winchester rifle and two AK-47s—not to mention the gripstock of a Stinger missile, which hangs on the wall of his House office.

Homosexuals? Barney Frank (D-Mass.) hired a male prostitute based on a newspaper ad that read: "Hot bottom plus large endowment equals good time."

Homophobes? William Dannemeyer took to the House floor to denounce gays in a speech that contained a rather graphic section titled "What Homosexuals Do."

New Age proselytizers? Claudine Schneider (R-R.I.) appeared in a half-hour TV commercial endorsing a $179.95 self-help audiotape called "Personal Power."

Ex-drunks? Ben Jones was arrested at least 10 times during the wild days before he stopped drinking 13 years ago.

Rap artists? Major Owens (D-N.Y.) composes rap songs on the major issues of the day, including one called "The Budget Summit" that begins like this:

In the big white D.C. mansion
There's a meeting of the mob
And the question on the table
Is which beggars they will rob . . .

"We do reflect the American public," says Tom Downey (D-N.Y.). "We have a lot of dolts here, but there are also a lot of very capable people. We reflect the good and the bad of the American public."

"Truly," agrees Faleomavaega, "the House does reflect what America is about."

As he says this, he's sitting in his House office in his white shirt and tie, with his big bare feet propped up on his coffee table.

Part 4: The One-Minute Orators

Jim Traficant stood at the House lectern, bellowing angrily and gesticulating wildly.

That wasn't unusual. Traficant (D-Ohio) bellows angrily and gesticulates wildly almost every morning, during the period when the House recognizes any member who wants to give a one-minute speech. Traficant is Congress's answer to Howard Beale, the "mad prophet of the airwaves" in the movie "Network." Nearly every morning, Traficant has something he wants to get off his polyester-clad chest. On the morning of August 3—the day after the invasion of Kuwait—Traficant was outraged that a former member of the Joint Chiefs of Staff had announced that America didn't have the capability to react militarily in the Persian Gulf.

"Now I want my colleagues to think about that," Traficant said indignantly. "After spending trillions of dollars on Star Wars and war games, Congress may be forced to send in the Capitol Police—and they are underpaid."

That got a laugh, but Traficar wasn't through yet. "I say to my colleagues, let's face it, maybe we can hire generals a hell of a lot cheaper from Korea . . ." By this time, he was flailing his arms like a drunk fighting a mosquito. "Let's start using that trillion-dollar budget before we have to drive to Iraq to buy a gallon of gas!"

Traficant lumbered off, and Robert Dornan (R-Calif.) stepped to the lectern, carrying a couple of props. As he made the routine request for permission to "revise and extend" his remarks, Dornan, a former actor and TV talk show host, started flailing his arms and bellowing in an uncanny imitation of Traficant. That too got a laugh.

"My colleagues," Dornan said, "in Ashqelon, just within the last week, they found the golden calf, the idol that the heretics worshiped. What we are worshiping in this country today, unfortunately, is the god Baal. They fed him children. They threw them into the fire."

Dornan was talking about one of his favorite topics—abortion. He showed some *Life* magazine photographs of fetuses, then held up a model of a 12-week-old fetus. "Call it Michelle, call it Michael," he said, and then he made his colleagues an offer: "Come up and ask me about it," he said. "I will let you touch it and handle it."

As he left the lectern, Dornar dropped something. It was only the model's carrying case, but some House members thought it was Michelle or Michael, and they started hooting and jeering, and somebody yelled, "You killed it!"

Ah, another morning of stimulating debate in the House of Representatives.

And that wasn't all. There were other one-minute speeches. Silvio Conte (R-Mass.) urged House members to forgo their summer vacation, turn off the House air conditioners and sweat out a budget. Andy Jacobs complained that he was misquoted in *The Washington Post*. Ron Wyden (D-Ore.) denounced the rise in the price of infant formula. Dan Burton (R-Ind.) denounced the specter of a tax increase and concluded with the immortal lines: "Read my lips. No new taxes." House Minority Leader Robert Michel (R-Ill.) denounced Fortney "Pete" Stark (D-Calif.), who had been quoted in the newspaper calling Louis Sullivan, the black Secretary of Health and Human Services, "a disgrace to his race." Then Stark, who is white, got up and apologized to Sullivan—sort of. He started out apologizing: "To the secretary, I have to say I blew it; I should not have brought into the discussion his race"—but then he turned on an oratorical dime and his apology abruptly became an attack—"because it obscures the fact that he is carrying a bankrupt policy for an administration which has been impacting the poor and the minorities of this country by denying them decent medical care . . ." He went on in that vein, whacking the administration's policies toward minorities, then concluded: "And I apologize for obscuring that."

Whew! All that—and much, much more—within just half an hour!

Bob Dornan likes to compare the House's one-minute speeches to radio call-in shows. Both serve as a "steam pressure release valve," he says, for people who "want to scream out." Both also tend to attract obsessives. Helen Delich Bentley (R-Md.) likes to use one-minutes to bash Japan. Bob Walker (R-Pa.) likes to use them to bash House Democrats. Frank Annunzio (D-Ill.)—a powerful member of the House Banking Committee, which failed to prevent the multi-mega-billion-dollar savings-and-loan debacle—rises almost daily to demand the jailing of "S&L crooks." Dornan denounces abortion and defends the B-1 bomber. And Traficant denounces the big shots who are "screwing"—his favorite word—the little guys of this world.

Some House members, like Downey, see the one-minutes as mere grandstanding for the TV cameras. Schroeder disagrees. Before the House was televised, she says, one-minutes tended to be recitations of a constituent's recipe for pickles or chocolate chip cookies. They may be less practical now, she says, but they're a lot more fun: "I love them. Can you think of anyplace else where you can see a debate between Traficant and Dornan?"

Occasionally, a one-minute speech can inspire poetry. Last June, on the eve of Nelson Mandela's address to a joint session of Congress, Dannemeyer delivered a one-minute attack on the African National Congress leader. "Nelson Mandela is no Martin Luther King," he said. "He is more like H. Rap Brown or Willie Horton . . ."

That enraged Major Owens, the House's unofficial rap poet laureate, who banged out an angry attack or Dannemeyer and inserted it into the Congressional Record:

. . . Fascist go home"
For you the House chamber
Is nowhere to roam.
Let's put all Nazis to bed,
Let's make Hitler real dead.
Go tell the headline-hunting scavenger
That Willie Horton is more like his mama!

Part 5: *In the Decade of the Brain*

Hochbrueckner and Hammerschmidt, Gonzalez and Martinez, Rleczka and Mrazek, Levin and Levine, Kennedy and Kennelly, Fazio and DeFazio—the roll call of the House reflects the great ethnic stew that simmers in America's melting pot.

The House roster is also a lyrical compendium of great American names that roll off the tongue like poetry: Schaefer and Scheuer and Schneider and Schroeder. Baker and Boxer and Archer and Hunter. Horton and Houghton and Hoyer and Hughes. Brooks and Boggs and Fields and Wheat. Slaughter and Savage and Pickle and Fish. Green and Gray and Brown and Clay. Hatcher and Natcher and Bonior and Conyers. Harris and Parris, Mazzoli and Foley. And Smith and Smith and Smith and Smith and Smith and Smith and Smith and Smith and Smith.

Nine Smiths in the House of Representatives: What could be more American than that?

Congressman Tom Sawyer, that's what.

Thomas C. Sawyer (D-Ohio) serves an important function in the House. As chairman of the Post Office and Civil Service Committee's subcommittee on census and population, it is his responsibility to rise on the House floor during lulls in the action and ask unanimous consent to pass the resolutions that carve America's calendar into a quilt of tributes to various causes, professions, ethnic groups, art forms and battles against dread diseases.

It happens like this: When the sponsor of the resolution has collected 218 cosponsors—in other words, a majority of the House—Sawyer rises to say, as he did on May 25, 1989, "Mr. Speaker, I ask unanimous consent that the Committee on Post Office and Civil Service be discharged from further consideration of the joint resolution to designate May 25, 1989 as National Tap Dance Day and ask for its immediate consideration." And then the speaker asks if there are any objections, and Tom Ridge (R-Pa.), the ranking Republican on Sawyer's subcommittee, rises and introduces the sponsor of the resolution. In this case it was John Conyers (D-Mich.), who proceeded to praise it as "one of the most significant resolutions that I have been able to bring forward to this body in the 101st session of the Congress."

This is the ritual that gave America Children's Day, Senior Citizens Day, German-American Day, Arab-American Day, Ducks and Wetlands Day, Patient Account Management Day, Federal Employees Recognition Week, Organ and Tissue Donors Awareness Week, Correctional Officers Week, Give Kids a Fighting Chance Week, Quality Month, Digestive Disease Awareness Month, Irish-American Heritage Month, Italian-American Heritage and Cultural Month, and Take Pride in America Month, among many others.

Not to mention the Decade of the Brain.

These resolutions probably don't have a profound impact on the republic, but they do give House members an excuse to praise some constituents in the pages of the Congressional Record. On May 16, for example, Chester Atkins (D-Mass.) inserted an undelivered speech into the Congressional Record. "Mr. Speaker," it began, "I rise today on the occasion of National Police Week to pay tribute to the Littleton Police Department for their dedicated and outstanding service . . ."

On the same day, Atkins also inserted into the Record identical undelivered speeches in praise of the police departments of Boxborough, Dracut, Pepperell, Lowell, Dunstable, Tyngsboro . . . and every other police department in his district, each of them, it turns out, equally "dedicated and outstanding."

Part 6: The Rhetoric Bazaar

When President Bush finished addressing the joint session of Congress on the subject of Iraq, the members rose to their feet and gave him a rousing ovation. Then they hustled out of the House chamber and scooted to Statuary Hall, where the really important events of the night were occurring: their TV interviews.

After every presidential address, Statuary Hall is packed with TV cameras—21 of them on this particular night—all of them eager for quotes from their local pols. The pols, needless to say, are equally eager. They hustle into the hall and line up like schoolchildren, fussing with their hair and waiting to go on-air, while the room echoes with the cacophony of pontification.

"It's sort of like a rhetoric bazaar," said Ben Jones as he gazed at the chaos around him.

"It's like the Easter egg hunt," said John Lewis.

Jones and Lewis were standing in line, waiting to be interviewed by three camera crews from Georgia. "The first question," said Jones, "is always, 'What did you think of the president's speech' " Then he rolled up a piece of paper and held it up to Lewis's lips. "What did you think of the president's speech?" he asked.

Lewis laughed.

Up ahead of them on line, Newt Gingrich (R-Ga.) was not laughing. He looked very serious. He was facing a terrible dilemma: A reporter from PBS's "Nightly Business Report" had asked him for an interview. Which was fine: Gingrich never met a TV camera he didn't want to talk to. But to do this interview he would have to move to another place, which would cost him his spot in line. He looked at his feet, which were occupying that spot. He frowned, furrowed his brow in thought, and finally referred the reporter to his press secretary, Sheila Ward.

"Talk to Sheila," he said. "I stand where she tells me to stand."

Like most Americans, most House members love being on TV. Unlike most Americans, though, they don't have to paint their chests and strip off their shirts at sub-freezing football games to get on the tube. House members have their own tax-payer-financed TV studio, where they can record their wisdom and beam it via satellite to the folks back home. They also have a studio where they hold press conferences while standing in front of a bookcase filled with serious-looking books, including the Holy Bible. The books give the representatives an air of intellectuality—unless you happen to notice that the bookcase is only a few inches deep and consequently all the bocks, including the Holy Bible, have been sliced off a couple of inches from the binding.

Like contestants on "Let's Make a Deal," House members sometimes use weird props to attract the TV cameras. Helen Delich Bentley once demonstrated her displeasure with the Toshiba Corp. by smashing a Toshiba TV with a sledgehammer while the cameras churned. Silvio Conte once wore a Miss Piggy mask to a press conference at which he denounced a pork barrel bill: "The congressmen have their nostrils right in the trough," he said, "and they're slurping it up for their districts at the expense of all the taxpayers."

During the House debate over the proposed constitutional amendment to outlaw flag desecration, Gary Ackerman (D-N.Y.) pulled out an American flag bathing suit. "Is that desecration" he asked. He also produced a flag scarf, flag socks, flag pantyhose, flag napkins, flag slippers and flag paper plates. "If you put your spaghetti on them, have you violated the Constitution?" he asked. "And what do you do when you're finished with them?"

Some props don't work quite so well, though. Last spring, after President Bush blithely abandoned his "no new taxes" pledge, House Minority Leader Bob Michel and several other Republicans appeared before the cameras carrying a chain saw with the blade covered by a piece of paper that read "SPENDING." The idea, of course, was that they thought Congress should cut spending instead of raise taxes. Unfortunately, although the chain saw produced plenty of sound and fury, it failed to cut the paper.

Which was, come to think of it, a brilliant metaphor for congress's chronic inability to cut spending.

Part 7: Backslapping and Begetting

It's true: House members really do slap each other on the back. They also shake hands a lot and throw their arms over each others shoulders and refer to each other as "the distinguished gentleman" and "my esteemed colleague." Sometimes they go a tad overboard with this, like the time William Hughes (D-N.J.) referred to E. Clay Shaw Jr. (R-Fla.) as "my distinguished colleague from Florida, whom I love."

When the bells go off around Capitol Hill, indicating a vote, the representatives hustle to the House floor, stick their cards into the machines that record the votes and then start wandering around, shaking hands, slapping backs and schmoozing. Votes are supposed to take 15 minutes, but they inevitably take longer because nobody wants to stop shooting the breeze—except Charles Hayes, who inevitably starts yelling, "Regular order! Regular order!" His colleagues ignore him, just as they ignore the speaker pro tempore when he starts banging the gavel and calling for order. They're a sociable crew. In a lot of ways, the House is like a small town. Everybody knows everybody else and there are a lot of little cliques. Members hang out with other members from their state, or from their committees, or the members they eat dinner with every Tuesday night. Some members share apartments in Washington, some travel back home together, some campaign for each other, some vacation at each other's houses. The House is a chummy place, a nice place to work, a way of life you'd like to pass on to your children. And many members do:

John J. Duncan Sr. (R-Tenn.) begat John J. Duncan Jr. (R-Tenn.).

Andrew Jacobs Sr. (D-Ind.) begat Andrew Jacobs Jr. (D-Ind.).

John D. Dingell Sr. (D-Mich.) begat John D. Dingell Jr. (D-Mich.).

John J. Rhodes (R-Ariz.) begat John J. Rhodes III (R-Ariz.).

Carl D. Perkins (D-Ky.) begat Carl C. Perkins (D-Ky.).

Guy Molinari (R-N.Y.) begat Susan Molinari (R-N.Y.).

Thomas J. D'Alesandro Jr. (D-Md.) begat Nancy Pelosi (D-Calif.).

Hamilton Fish (R-N.Y.) begat Hamilton Fish Sr. (R-N.Y.), who begat Hamilton Fish Jr. (R-N.Y.).

And Thomas Luken (D-Ohio), who is retiring this year, begat Charles Luken, who is the Democratic cancidate for his House seat.

Then there's the amazing Byron dynasty. Rep. William D. Byron (D-Md.) died in a plane crash in 1941 and his wife, Katherine E. Byron (D-Md.), won election to serve out his unexpired term. William and Katherine begat Goodloe E. Byron Sr. (D-Md.), who was elected to the House in 1970 and died while jogging in 1978. He was succeeded by his wife, Beverly Byron (D-Md.), who still holds the seat. Beverly and Goodloe Sr. begat Goodloe E. Byron Jr., who recently ran for the state Senate. And lost. But he's still a local Democratic leader, and very few people would be surprised if he someday succeeded his mother, father, grandmother and grandfather in the House.

In the 202-year history of Congress, there has been only one marriage between House members, probably due to the paucity of congresswomen. In 1976, Andy Jacobs (D-Ind.) married Martha Reys (then D-Kan.). They'd met on the Ways and Means Committee, and their romance blossomed on plane rides home. "TWA served Indianapolis and Kansas City on the same flight," Jacobs says. "It was like being on the same bus line."

Their coalition proved to be a temporary one, alas, and they divorced in 1981 without begetting anybody.

Part 8: The Battle of $19.90

The now-famous fight over the now-deceased budget-summit package was not the first fiscal battle in the House this year. Far from it.

Congress has the solemn constitutional responsibility for raising and spending the government's money; last year, for example, it raised $1,123,000,000,000 and spent $1,355,000,000,000. Such a solemn constitutional responsibility quite frequently results in a lot of silly squabbling in the House. On July 18, for example, Bob Walker rose to offer an amendment to cut the agriculture appropriations bill by 0.0000000002 percent.

"In total," Walker announced, "this amendment will cut $19.90 from the $50 billion appropriation."

Walker's fellow Republicans laughed and cheered. The Democrats hooted and hissed.

Nobody bothered to check Walker's math. But then again, the bill wasn't really about $19.90 anyway. It was part of House members' continuing effort to pass the hot potato of blame for the deficit to the other party. The previous day, the Republicans had pushed for a constitutional amendment requiring a balanced budget—an idea supported by Ronald Reagan and George Bush, two Republican presidents who have never submitted a balanced budget to Congress. The amendment was defeated in the House, but not before scads of Democrats rose to say that the real way to balance the budget was for the House to vote for sensible spending cuts. But that was yesterday, and this was today, and the Democrats had defeated bills to cut the agriculture appropriations bill by 7 percent, by 5 percent, by 2 percent. Now, Walker's tongue-in-cheek amendment was designed to show that Democrats wouldn't even cut a lousy 20 bucks out of the bill.

"This amendment will be an across-the-board cut," Walker said, "'and I have to tell members, it will hurt . . . There are several major programs under this amendment that may be cut by a dollar or more."

He was being sarcastic, of course, but several Democrats rose to attack the amendment as if it were a serious threat to the republic.

"Mr. Chairman, I take a back seat to no one in trying to have a balanced budget,'" said Jamie Whitten (D-Miss.), the ancient chairman of the Appropriations

Committee, "but I do not believe in doing it at the expense of programs that are absolutely essential to the well-being of the American people."

Cardiss Collins (D-Ill.) took another tack. She rose and offered to pay the $20 out of her own pocket. Walker declined the offer.

"Vote!" the Democrats bellowed. "Vote!"

"The gentleman from Pennsylvania purports to save $19.90," said Dennis Eckart (D-Ohio), "but I would like to point out to my colleague that it costs $480 to print a page in the Congressional Record. So far, the gentleman is saving the taxpayers $20 but costing them $480."

Several $480 pages of debate later, Mickey Edwards (R-Okla.) used the same argument against the Democrats: "I would just like to point out to my colleagues across the aisle how much money they have spent desperately trying to prevent a $19 cut."

At that point, Timothy Penny (D-Minn.) asked Walker to withdraw the amendment. "If we proceed to a recorded vote, we will spend far more to print that vote in the Record than this amendment would save."

But Walker declined to withdraw the amendment, and he did indeed demand a recorded vote, which resulted in a 214-175 defeat, and which took about half of a $480 page to print.

Then the Democrats came up with their own potato-passing vehicle: a bill requiring the president—who happens to be a Republican—to submit a balanced budget to Congress. It passed 251-173, but has gone nowhere in the Senate.

Part 9: The Gym Committee, Among Others

The House of Representatives is a highly competitive place, and one area of the most intense competition these days is, of course, leg lifts. Nobody's sure exactly how this competition started, but Tom Downey figures that one of the denizens of the House gym must have been bragging about how many leg lifts he'd done, and pretty soon there was an intense competition going, complete with a chart on the wall for members to record their daily leg-lift tallies.

"If you want to start a competition," Downey says, "all you have to do is tell a few people what you did. It's as close to college as you can get in that sort of thing." In the old days, stories of male bonding in the overwhelmingly male House of Representatives tended to involve bourbon bottles and poker games and rooms full of cigar smoke. These days, they involve leg lifts and basketball games and rooms full of weights. "It's more of a jockocracy now," says Patricia Schroeder, a veteran observer of male culture in the House. "There's kind of a golf caucus and a basketball caucus and a tennis caucus." Not to mention the weight-lifting caucus, the pool caucus, the karate caucus, and, in the women's gym, the treadmill caucus and exercycle caucus.

Downey is an avid "gym rat," one of about 30 House members who play basketball almost every afternoon. "The games are played as if we were winning money at the end," he says. "I mean, people get killed going to the hoop."

That hoop is the hard-won trophy of a generational battle in the House. When Downey, one of the House's Watergate babies, arrived in 1975, the hoop was mounted right on the wall, which tended to inhibit a member's ability to drive in for a layup. The older House members never cared much about layups. They spent most of their gym time lying down under sun lamps, cooking themselves to a precancerous glow while snoozing in a room full of beds. But the younger generation of House members was more interested in aerobic exercise than in power napping. Soon they were using their political savvy and their growing clout to pressure the House Gym Committee to move the backboard out on the court and to turn the old tanning parlor into a weight room, where they now do their competitive leg-lifting.

"The speaker said that he had more requests to be on the Gym Committee," Downey says, "than he had to get on the Intelligence Committee."

Wait a minute. The Gym Committee?

Of course. The House has committees and subcommittees and task forces and caucuses for just about everything. Like most Americans, House members are great joiners. They embody Alexis de Tocqueville's observation that "Americans of all ages, all conditions and all dispositions constantly form associations." This urge to join might explain why 49 white House members became associate members of the Black Caucus, why 64 non-Hispanic House members became associate members of the Hispanic caucus and why 119 male House members joined the Women's Caucus, which is now known as the Caucus for Women's Issues.

The House has 27 official committees, which encompass no fewer than 139 subcommittees and 11 task forces. Consequently, just about every House member with any seniority whatsoever gets to be the chairman of something—except the Republicans, of course. Outnumbered 258-176, House Republicans never get the psychic thrill of being addressed as "Mr. Chairman." Maybe that's why they get cranky and offer amendments to cut $19.90 out of $50 billion appropriations. Of course, the Republicans do have their own party-run committees, four of them, including the poetically titled Committee on Committees.

One of the perks of being chairman of a big, important committee, such as Ways and Means, is that an artist is hired to immortalize your countenance in an oil painting. This is one kind of government-sponsored art that is not controversial in Congress, but perhaps ought to be. When the painting is completed, it is hung in the committee's room, in a rogues gallery of previous chairmen. Often, there's an official unveiling ceremony, which is often quite solemn: "It's like going to church," says Andy Jacobs.

Jacobs vividly remembers one such ceremony about a decade ago, when the portrait of Al Ullman, then chairman of Ways and Means, was unveiled. Jacobs, a member of the committee, arrived early and got a sneak preview of the painting, which portrayed the chairman "with a wild look in his eye," Jacobs says, "and a halo of light surrounding his head." Jacobs possesses an impish sense of humor and he was suddenly seized with a strange compulsion. He started going through the pile of official programs and adding the phrase: "A Portrait of Dorian Who?"

"'Poor Al,'" he says, "it was unfair of me." Then he bursts out laughing.

Part 10: Saddam and Leona

Like most Americans, House members were irate, aghast and incensed at the Iraqi invasion of Kuwait. Unlike most Americans, House members could actually do something about the invasion—namely, send out press releases and make angry one-minute speeches in the House. Which they did, in great profusion.

Some of the one-minute speeches were particularly memorable. Bob Dornan announced that the invasion had caused him to change his nickname from "B-1 Bob" to "B-2 Bob," in honor of the bomber he thought might make a good weapon in the Persian Gulf. Jacobs expressed skepticism about Operation Desert Shield: "Uncle Sam is in Saudi Arabia to defend everything he does not believe in and one thing he wants." Pat Schroeder denounced the idea that "the world thinks all they have to do is dial 1-800-USA and we come free of charge." And William Broomfield (R-Mich.) denounced Saddam Hussein: "He has stuck his thumb in our eye. I say we should break his arm."

Several House members used the invasion as an opportunity to take a verbal whack at their favorite targets. Like liberals: "The Kuwaiti ambassador is serving crow over in the Kuwaiti Embassy right now," Dornan said. "I hope some of my liberal colleagues have the common decency to eat a little of it." Or Japan: "The Japanese have been acting totally the way they usually do," said Carroll Hubbard (D-Ry.). "If there's no profit in it for Japan, forget it." Or environmentalists: "The greenies have led us into the crisis in the Middle East," said Tom DeLay (R-Tex.). ". . . The rabid environmentalists felt it was more important to jeopardize the lives of our brave American servicemen than risk the death of a single snail darter."

Jim Traficant—the Babe Ruth of the one-minute speech—rose on the House floor to read an anti-Saddam advertisement that Leona Helmsley had taken out in the *New York Times:* "Mr. Hussein, the people that you hold in your grasp are not guests, they are hostages." Traficant took that little nugget of information and ran with it. "I have a suggestion," he said. "I recommend to the president that he send both Leona Helmsley and Judge David Souter to the Gulf. After Judge David Souter completely confuses Saddam Hussein, Leona Helmsley can get close enough to maybe kick him in the crotch and end this thing." But House members did more than just talk about the Gulf crisis, of course. They also took action. On September 14, Charles Hayes rose to urge the House to pass a bill granting free mailing privileges to American troops in Saudi Arabia. The idea proved popular, and member after member lauded it as "a good morale booster" and a "token of our esteem for our armed forces."

Then Tom Ridge (R-Pa.) rose with a motion to change the bill slightly: The troops would still get free mail, but it would be paid for, not by the Pentagon as in other wars, but out of Congress's "franking" fund, which pays for House members' mailings.

Needless to say, that kicked up some controversy. "It has always been paid out of the Defense Department," protested John Myers (R-Ind.). ". . . I urge this be defeated."

"This motion is completely out of order," said Hayes, "and we ought to vote it down."

And vote it down they did, 43-24. Then Ridge reminded his colleagues that they didn't have a quorum. So the vote was postponed until the following Monday.

By then, the Senate had passed its version of the bill, which authorized the Pentagon to pay for the postage. So the House members voted on the Senate bill, passed it 368-0 and sent it to the president. Then they took up Ridge's bill, safe in the knowledge that the issue was moot and their mail money was safe. It passed 227-142.

Part 11: Congress R Us

"Reader, suppose you were an idiot," wrote Mark Twain, "and suppose you were a member of Congress; but I repeat myself."

In the 1860s, Twain worked for a senator, then covered Congress for several newspapers. He was not impressed. "'It could probably be shown by facts and figures," he wrote, "that there is no distinctly native American criminal class except Congress.'"

Twain is just one in a long line of great American Congress-bashers, a tradition as old as Congress itself. Today, Congress-bashing is as popular as ever. The current Congress has drawn more flak than nearly any of its hundred predecessors, perhaps because of the budget debacle, or the ethics scandals, or the sex scandals, or the indictments, or the power of PAC money, or the pay raise fiasco. Or perhaps it has something to do with the various problems that Congress has failed to solve despite decades of posturing—the deficit, the S&L crisis, homelessness, poverty, crime, drugs . . .

Whatever the cause, the result is an unprecedented outpouring of scorn: *Business Week* recently compared Congress to "'the legislature of a banana republic." Ralph Nader attacked its "leadership by self-enriching sleights of hand." Former Treasury Secretary William Simon denounced it as "totally unwilling to halt its selfish indulgence." And author Philip Stern denounced it as a pawn of its contributors—The Best Congress Money Can Buy.

Nobody's madder at Congress than Jack Gargan, a retired insurance man who founded an organization called "Throw the Hypocritical Rascals Out." Gargan built his organization—which now has more than 40,000 members, he says—through a series of anti-Congress ads he has purchased in more than 60 newspapers across the country since June. The ads denounce the pay raise, the PAC money and the S&L scandal, among other issues, in paragraphs that begin with descriptions of Gargan's state of mind on these matters: "I'M APPALLED . . . I'M BITTER . . . I'M OUTRAGED . . . I'M ANGRY . . . I'M INCENSED . . . I'M LIVID . . . I'M EVEN MORE LIVID . . . I'M ENRAGED . . . I'M DISGUSTED . . . I'M FED UP . . . I'M SHOCKED . . . I'M REALLY HACKED-OFF . . .'

But not too hacked-off, apparently, to come up with a calm and rational solution to the problem: "VOTE EVERY INCUMBENT SENATOR AND CONGRESSMAN OUT OF OFFICE!"

That seems unlikely. Despite the perennial torrents of Congress-bashing, when Americans enter the sacred privacy of the voting booth, they generally choose to vote for the same House members they elected last time. It's a strange paradox: Although Congress's approval rating hovers down below 25 percent, the reelection rate of House incumbents is above 98 percent.

Why? The conventional wisdom points to the power of incumbency. House membership has its privileges, which pay off in a campaign—the free mailings, the access to TV, the PAC money, the publicly paid staffers working on constituent services. All of which are, no doubt, potent factors. But the power of incumbency has obvious limits: When the voters get mad, really mad, incumbency is a liability. Just ask Jimmy Carter.

Perhaps there is another reason. Perhaps our representatives keep getting reelected because they are truly representative. Perhaps America, like the House, is a cacophonous collection of contentious characters—gun nuts and gym rats, homosexuals and homophobes, ex-drunks and ex-jocks, big spenders and cheapskates, rap poets and one-minute blowhards, backslappers and leg-lifters, publicity hounds and shameless hams, gold standard theorists and the wise guys who mock them, talk show hosts and sitcom stars and lawyers and lawyers and lawyers and lawyers . . .

Perhaps they really are us.

Think about it: We Americans love getting federal benefits but we hate paying federal taxes. So we elect representatives who love funding federal programs but hate raising taxes. And then we blame the deficit on Congress.

Which is, by the way, exactly what members of Congress do too.

House members bash Congress at least as hard as Jack Gargan does. They too are appalled, bitter, outraged, angry, incensed, livid, disgusted, fed up, shocked and really hacked-off at Congress—and they're not shy about saying it, either. In fact, some of America's best Congress-bashers are congressmen.

Groomed by the goofy give-and-take of House debate and the intellectual rigors of the one-minute speech, House members bash Congress with more pizazz than mere citizens. They use better metaphors too. In the last few months alone, House members have compared Congress to all sorts of nasty things:

Thieves: "Mr. Chairman, we are all thieves," said Bill Sarpalius (D-Tex.) during the debate over the balanced budget amendment. "If we were on trial today, we would be found guilty of stealing . . ."

The non-toilet-trained: "A tax-and- spend Congress acts a lot like feeding babies," said Dennis Hastert (R-Ill.). "Irresponsibility on one end and no accountability on the other."

Zombies: During the debate on the textile tariff bill, Tom DeLay called the bill's backers "Zuppies—Zombies Under Protectionist Influence" and described their symptoms: "They're walking around the halls of Congress with their eyeballs swirling, their knees locked and their arms out like this . . ."

Donald Duck: During the debate over flag desecration, David Obey looked around the House and said: "I see too many people who remind me more of Donald Duck than they do of Thomas Jefferson."

Dope fiends: "Money is a substance," said Dannemeyer, "and Congress is a substance abuser, an addict out of control . . ." Jim Traficant used another dope metaphor during a one-minute speech denouncing the horrors of raising the beer tax: "I think that members of Congress and the Cabinet should take a drug test. Everybody must be high for screwing this country up like they have."

And then, during the interminable battle over the deficit-reduction package, Silvio Conte turned Congress-bashing into poetry.

It happened just a few hours after that bizarre moment when Dannemeyer touted the gold standzrd and Neal Smith countered by touting the soybean standard. The House had finally begun debating a new budget plan around midnight, when October 7 became October 8, which just happened to be Columbus Day. That fact inspired Conte to write a poem.

Unlike Major Owens, the House's urban Democratic rap poet, Conte, a rural Republican, works in a more traditional poetic form. So he began his verse the same way the great American poet Anonymous began his most famous work:

In fourteen hundred ninety-two,
Columbus sailed the ocean blue.

After hymning the heroism of Columbus and his crew, Conte contrasted their bravery with Congress's craven cowardice:

In nineteen ninety, here we are;
I don't think we have come so far.
We scream and boo and moan and hiss;
We don't have time to take a—break.
We shout and jeer and fuss and bark;
We blame each other in the dark.
Although we've had five centuries,
We see no forest for the trees.
We're frightened by the interest groups;
We act like silly nincompoops . . .

When Conte finished, the objects of his scorn gave him a wild ovation. Say what you want about the House of Representatives, it does put on a good show.

November 4, 1990

Exercising The Right to Censor the Censors

One Man's Tactics to Ensure Freedom of Speech and Rap

RICHARD HARRINGTON

"A wave of vulgar, filthy and suggestive music has inundated the land . . . with its obscene posturings, its lewd gestures. Our children, our young men and women, are continually exposed . . . to the monotonous attrition of this vulgarizing music. It is artistically and morally depressing and should be suppressed by press and pulpit."

The *American Spectator* on N.W.A.? No, the *Musical Courier* on ragtime, back in 1899, toward the end of a decade-long war declared on ragtime by press, pulpit and "women organized to be of service to some worthy cause," as Russell Sanjek notes in "American Popular Music and Its Business: The First 400 Years."

Yes, we're now closing in on a full century of attacks on popular music styles. Usually, the styles originate in African American culture, and are decried for their moral, intellectual and physical threat, and dismissed for their musical inferiority. The names change—blues, rhythm and blues, rock-and-roll, rap—but the approach remains the same: Equate vernacular music with the debauching of children and the debasement of traditional values.

Since 1984, the focus has been on explicit lyrics, and as recently as a year ago there were bills in more than two dozen states to require labeling of albums with explicit lyrics, to prevent minors from purchasing such albums, or threatening fines and jail terms for retailers and manufacturers handling such albums. Most of those bills were tabled, defeated or withdrawn after the Recording Industry Association of America introduced a voluntary but uniform label warning consumers (and parents) that certain albums did in fact contain explicit lyrics.

However, Louisiana became the first state to approve a mandatory labeling bill, only to have it vetoed on constitutional grounds by Gov. Buddy Roemer. Recently, a new bill requiring a government warning on songs sold to adults, prohibiting children from buying certain records (even with parental permission) and penalizing store owners for selling certain albums to minors (stickered or unstickered) passed the Louisiana House and a Senate committee. It must be voted on by tomorrow, Louisiana's constitutionally set adjournment date. Should the bill pass, music industry observers believe Gov. Roemer will simply veto it again, on the same grounds he did last year.

Such action at the highest level of state government may provide relief for the music industry, but author Dave Marsh suggests grass-roots activism is even more

214

important. In fact, he's written a 128-page guide called "50 Ways to Fight Censorship" (Thunder Mouth Press). Marsh does not focus solely on censorship issues in music, of course, insisting that in light of attacks on Salman Rushdie, Bret Easton Ellis, Robert Mapplethorpe, 2 Live Crew, movies and NEA grants, "There is no way to separate the censorship of one form of expression from that of any other. The indivisibility among different kinds of censorship is a hard lesson to learn. . . . No matter how vile you may find what that other guy has to say, there is always a better way to disarm the message than by silencing it."

"If I have a vision, it's of a rainbow coalition of anti-censorship people—but that's tough," Marsh admits. It's possible, though. Witness the Media Coalition that has come together to oppose the Pornography Victims Compensation Act of 1991 (S. 983), which would allow victims of sex crimes to sue retailers if they allege the criminal was influenced by a sound or video recording the dealer sold or rented. It has brought together 18 groups, including the American Civil Liberties Union, the Motion Picture Association of America, the RIAA, the American Booksellers Association, the American Association of Journalists and the Video Software Dealers Association, to oppose a bill the Media Coalition says embodies "an unconstitutional theory of incitement."

Censorship, Marsh points out, "isn't about intentions—it's about consequences. Whether they're presented as 'consumer information' or 'child protection' or 'public safety,' regulations and activities that deny the right to speak are forms of censorship, no matter what name their sponsors give them."

Marsh, author of two best-selling biographies about Bruce Springsteen and editor of *Rock and Roll Confidential,* suggests that the United States is full of freelance censors and that the most effective countermeasures are likely to be rooted in adapting some of their tactics. In fact, Marsh says his book was inspired not by Paul Simon's "50 Ways to Leave Your Lover" or the flood of environmental tip-sheets, but "from pro-censorship handbooks on how their people should act."

"50 Ways to Fight Censorship" is subtitled "& Important Facts to Know About the Censors," and it gleefully identifies the fundamentalists, right-wingers, government officials and business leaders who are the adversaries in this battle (such as Focus on the Family, American Family Association, Parents Music Resource Center, Truth About Rock Ministries and the National Coalition on Television Violence).

Marsh suggests his troops get to know these groups, study their literature, and then expose them to public scrutiny—such as investigating the tax-exempt status of pro-censorship lobbying groups. The book also lists anti-censorship resources and organizations. It urges people to put pressure on lawmakers and retailers; patronize those that carry controversial material; write movie moguls and tell them to eliminate the MPAA Ratings Code; boycott products made and marketed by companies that feed the censors; and speak out ("the single most important thing you can do").

And, naturally, fight record labeling. Marsh finds it disturbing that many new bands—"say those younger than Fishbone"—cannot imagine being unlabeled. "In five years you've had this massive erasure of freedom and people don't even remember that this was a controversy, or they think the controversy was over laws, not pseudo-voluntarism."

The pressure, Marsh suggests, comes from the system's arbitrariness: The challenge is not at the higher levels—most superstars can contractually keep warning labels off their product—but "down in the ranks with people who have relatively less control over their product. What you find is that not only is there the imposition of labels, but that sometimes the reason that there's not a label is because a song was modified or was taken off a record by whatever star-chamber proceeding exists at the record company."

The ultimate argument against censorship, Marsh adds, is that "from a moral point of view, it won't work. What works is dialogue, education. More speech works; less speech fails."

To that end, Marsh would like to see the Senate hold another hearing on lyrics, "to show how the music has been slandered and all this stuff isn't true and the government's involvement. If they refuse, we'll hold hearings ourselves in Los Angeles, a Bertrand Russell-type Vietnam war crimes trial."

Speaking of trials, Marsh also is concerned about the end result of 2 Live Crew's conviction on obscenity charges in Florida. If the group's appeal reaches the new, conservative Supreme Court, there's already speculation that the majority will hold that "community standards by themselves are indeed sufficient grounds for going after certain works," Marsh says.

Being an advocate of free speech has not turned Marsh into a defender of 2 Live Crew—he finds much of the group's canon reprehensible—just of their right to rap freely. Racism, according to Marsh, is a familiar component in censorship, particularly on the musical side of things. He points to 1911 and an Irving Berlin song, "Everybody's Doing It Now," written soon after his first hit, "Alexander's Ragtime Band."

"It" was inspired by the vigorous, sexually charged dances popular in the African American community, dances with names like turkey-trot, monkey, lame duck, humpback rag, bunny hug, come-to-me-tommy, dances where partners actually pressed their loins together on the dance floor in full view of the public (long before the tango and lambada!).

The ever practical Berlin chose the generic "it" to avoid identification with a particular dance that might quickly go out of style, but the mere suggestive connotations of "it" drove the authorities crazy. Newspapers ran editorials asking "Where Is Your Daughter This Afternoon?" and the New York Commission on Amusements and Vacation Resources for Working Girls found evidence that "reckless and uncontrolled dances" could create "an opportunity for license and debauch."

"The Catholic Church, the big censorship group at the time, and the city grand jury came right straight after Berlin; "he was corrupting the morals of women," Marsh explained. "You see {this pattern} all the time and it's when it hits the white audience that it becomes a controversy. . . . If it's black enough, you get into trouble.

July 7, 1991

Peering into Private Lives

Computer Lists Now Profile Consumers
by Their Personal Habits

DANIEL MENDEL-BLACK AND EVELYN RICHARDS

Vacuumed into huge databases around the country is information about how many times you went out to eat last month, about whether your dog prefers Alpo to Purina, about the kinds of videotapes you rent.

Details like these are sorted, digested and compiled so that computers can plop you into neatly defined categories to help determine the likelihood that you'll pay your Visa bill on time or buy a new brand of detergent or cigarettes within the next few months.

Until recently, such profiles have been available only to a few big retailers, banks and other credit services willing to pay handsomely for the right to take advantage of them.

But that could change dramatically this spring if Lotus Development Corp. follows through on plans to bring out a controversial product that has the potential to put lifestyle, demographic and income estimates of about 80 million American households into the hands of almost anyone who wants it.

A joint effort with the credit agency Equifax Inc., the product is a compact disc that would hold the names, addresses, approximate income levels and personal buying habits of people nationwide. It would mark the first time that the mammoth databases of credit bureaus and marketing powerhouses would be married with the personal computer—a combination that is fueling questions about individuals' rights to privacy because it vastly expands how and by whom such data can be used.

Lotus says it has been barraged by some 30,000 callers and letter-writers who believe the product is a clear invasion of their privacy and don't want their names included in its data bases. The outcry has fueled industry speculation that the Cambridge, Mass., software company could be forced to pull or delay the product.

What has privacy advocates concerned is that the Lotus product appears to be moving the nation a bit closer to a day when all the information available on one person could be gathered in one place and then easily retrieved, sold or manipulated by virtually anyone.

Today, there is no simple way to retrieve all the information stored about a single individual simply by punching that person's name into a computer. While data about a specific person's creditworthines, criminal record or driving history can be easily obtained electronically, information about an individual's lifestyle and other personal buying habits usually is retrieved only as part of a group of people with like characteristics.

The new compact disc product, to be sold by Lotus, opens the "window of vulnerability,'" said Evan Hendricks, the Washington publisher of Privacy Times, a newsletter on privacy issues. "Once they have established this precedent, there is nothing to stop the next guy from selling anything he wants {for use on personal computers}, from your Christmas purchases to your genetic history."

With the Lotus disc, a small business essentially would build a profile of the type of customers most likely to respond to its sales pitch. A new restaurant, for example, would specify a certain income range, age group and other criteria of people it believes would be most apt to frequent its establishment. The computer would digest all these desired traits and then spew out a tailor-made list of residents in a certain neighborhood, including their addresses.

Information for the disc was gleaned from 40 different sources, including the U.S. Census, Internal Revenue Service, Postal Service and surveys taken at 8,500 shopping centers and retailers nationwide. As one of the country's largest credit bureaus, Equifax has also drawn on its own records, which contain specific information about a person's marital status, sex, age range and likely income level.

In essence, the company creates "a profile of an individual based on their credit files," said Robert Hilles, an Equifax vice president. The most sensitive information—estimated income and lifestyle—is blended with that of nearby households to build a general profile for each neighborhood. And users would not be able to seek out a specific person. In other words, a user could not look up John Q. Smith on Aurora Drive, but Smith's name and address would pop up as part of a larger group of people fitting a certain profile.

The companies say this and other measures will help protect privacy. Lotus vows to sell "Marketplace: Households," as the product is known, only to businesses and nonprofit groups, although it admits policing that process will be a difficult task.

Still, privacy advocates worry that the product is a dangerous step toward the mass-marketing of personal data.

"As we go into 1991, there is no such thing in the marketer's mind as too much information,'" said Elgie Holstein, executive director of Bankcard Holders of America, a consumer advocacy group in Herndon. "The trend toward developing products which massage and gather information about people is irreversible."

Compuserve, a computer network of information to which anyone with a personal computer can subscribe, also has found itself vulnerable to the attack of privacy advocates with its new Phone File service.

Users of this service, which contains the names, addresses and phone numbers of millions of Americans nationwide, can type in a telephone number and learn to whom it belongs. Or, they can search for a person's exact address and phone number by designating only a name and city, or name with a state.

Computers also accelerate the gathering of data by enabling companies to more easily obtain, sort and trade information on specific people. Americans unwittingly feed he cycle simply by going about the innocuous business of everyday life. Today, dialing an 800 number can put your name and address on a list. So can cashing in a coupon—some that arrive at your home are encoded with digits that will identify you when you trade them in. Filling out warranty cards, subscribing to magazines and booking a hotel room will likely get you into a database that will be used to pitch you more products or deluge you with solicitations.

Certain supermarkets now electronically monitor the purchases of customers who agree to participate in return for discounts.

As goods pass over the counter, scanners record the universal product code of each item, providing retailers and manufacturers feedback about their customers. Because the computer can determine which people are repeat buyers of diapers, granola or certain brands of dog food, for example, manufacturers and stores can target coupons for such items directly to those customers, thereby skirting costly mailings to uninterested consumers.

A unit of Citicorp collects purchasing data on 2 million participating shoppers at supermarket chains around the country. In one test scheme, it used the data to assemble individualized bundles of coupons for households. When the encoded coupons are turned in, manufacturers can determine who responded to what type of pitch. Coca-Cola, for example, could use such a technique to try and win over Pepsi devotees.

One Southern California supermarket chain, Vons Cos., uses the Citicorp system to lure customers into departments where they're not shopping, like the fish counter or juice bar. It also cross-tabulates its customer list against larger databases to find the names and addresses of residents who don't shop at Vons—and then it mails them special offers.

Particularly useful for marketers are the handful of huge databases that profile nearly all adult Americans. In the computers of TRW Inc., which operates both a credit bureau and a marketing information service, for example, any one of 150 million Americans can be characterized in up to 600 different categories. Some categories describe easily obtainable data, like your age and how long you've lived at your current address. Other traits are more personal. Based on previous mail-order purchases you've made, TRW may classify you as a health and fitness fanatic, a fishing enthusiast or a literary scholar.

This kind of information comes in handy for marketers like the Sharper Image, the upscale catalogue and store-front retailer. The firm keeps one list of its own 800,000 mail-order buyers and another of 1.2 million people who have shopped at its retail stores. Every 18 months, the company learns considerably more about who these people are by supplying the names to National Demographics & Lifestyles, a Denver outfit with detailed characterizations of 30 million people gleaned from product registration forms returnecl by buyers. National Demographics matches Sharper Image's customer's against names in its own database, then concocts a statistical description.

The most recent finding was something like this: The typical Sharper Image buyer is male, between the ages of 45 and 55, with a household income of $70,000. National Demographics then reaches into its database and supplies the retailer with the names of thousands more Americans who fit that description.

To build its roster of prospective customers even further, Sharper Image selects three dozen narrower lists every few months from the more than 10,000 specialized mailing lists for rent. Among those it has found fruitful: the list of mail-order and retail buyers of Hoffritz cutlery and the list of 427,315 mail-order buyers of motor-vehicle radar detectors.

List owners also can take their screening a step further by turning to a credit bureau like TRW, which can winnow down a list to include only people who hold a certain number of credit cards or maintain specified balances. The resulting names would go to a third-party mailer so the credit information is not revealed to the business that requested the screening.

All these methods of manipulating profiles are popular with advertisers, who say computerization helps ensure that you'll get pitches that are more carefully attuned to your tastes. At worst, they say, the new schemes will cause an added clutter of gift catalogues and shampoo samples.

"Privacy advocates have been so busy fighting for privacy that they don't always realize that the most this will result in is an extra bit of mail," said professor Alan F. Westin, a Columbia University privacy expert who advises Equifax.

Such arguments are small comfort to those who have already fallen victim to abuse or errors made by mailing-list hustlers. Michael Riley, a Washington-based Time magazine reporter, jumped at the mail solicitatlon he received in late 1989 for a pre-approved Citibank Visa card. A few weeks later, his wife, Arline, was about to buy a blouse when the cashier told her the card was no good.

When the Rileys checked further with Citibank, they were told that their car had been repossessed, they faced $70,000 in tax liens and that they had filed for bankruptcy. As it turned out, Citibank, which had purchased its credit information from TRW, according to Riley, had confused Michael George Riley with a Michael Gilbert Riley.

Riley's problem may be more common than it seems. According to Bankcard Holders of America's Holstein, 35 percent of the people who pay to see their own credit reports find their credit information had somehow been confused with someone else's.

It is this type of horror story that has raised concerns in Europe, where a draft directive would require companies to gain explicit consent from individuals before processing any information about them.

The European movement is likely to stir up privacy concerns on Capitol Hill. Rep. Robert Wise (D-W.Va.), plans to reintroduce legislation to create a Data

Protection Board that would oversee federal privacy policies and guide the private sector. And Rep. Richard H. Lehman (D-Calif.) has championed a proposal to revise the 1971 fair credit act to give consumers more control over what's in their credit files and how the data is used. Lehman, however, is relinquishing his chairmanship of the consumer affairs subcommittee.

January 20, 1991

Serial Killers

Shattering the Myth—They're an American Phenomenon, and They're not What You Think

JOEL ACHENBACH

The campus killer used a knife enthusiastically, to create a picture, to manipulate the human form, to alter for his own delight the appearance of the female nude. He proudly placed mirrors next to one body, at disparate angles, to intensify the visual impact of the deed.

But there was no artistry in his work. He was just a butcher. He mutilated his first victim. At his second stop, he was even more frenzied: he left his victim's head on a shelf. At his third and final visit he was sloppier, his fantasy—whatever its macabre storyline—punctured by the presence of his victim's athletic 200-pound boyfriend. The boyfriend, too, was stabbed to death.

This was more than seven months ago. The case remains unsolved. The police were faced with five bodies at three separate murder scenes, and once they dealt with the initial shock, and contained their overpowering nausea, they had to figure out what it all meant. They had to find the message.

Gainesville Police Lt. Sadie Darnell saw the first two bodies.

"It was a much different murder scene than I had ever experienced before," she says. I was only in there maybe 10 or 15 minutes but it seemed much longer. It was as if I was absorbing things in slow motion, because there was so much on a sensory level to absorb. It was an eerie feeling and very much a feeling of the presence of evil."

She pronounces the last word cautiously, aware of its power.

"That all sounds so trite, I know, but it was a feeling I had never had before," she says. "The only thing that could have caused that was something that was evil."

He's a genius, he quotes poetry, he kills and eats his fellow human beings. His name is Hannibal "the Cannibal" Lecter, and he's the star of the novel and the movie "The Silence of the Lambs," the current top-grosser in both mediums. Lecter has a series of tense discussions with Clarice Starling, a pretty young FBI trainee who has come to prison to interview him. She says she wants to find out what "happened" to him.

"Nothing happened to me, Officer Starling," Lecter lectures. "I happened. You can't reduce me to a set of influences. You've given up good and evil for behaviorism, Officer Starling. You've got everybody in moral dignity pants—nothing is ever anybody's fault. Look at me, Officer Starling. Can you stand to say I'm evil? Am I evil?"

Something curious is going on in America. Murder is a growth industry, particularly this special kind of murder, the bogeyman homicide, the sadistic slaying by a stranger who, without comprehensible motive, steps out of the shadows and savages.

Before the 1970s, they were the rarest of creatures. In most countries, they still are. But in America, they have become so commonplace that criminologists estimate there are as many as 20 serial killers roaming the country at any given time—not to mention those who inhabit the bookstores and movie theaters. The serial killer has become an American Original, a romantic icon, like the cowboy.

"The Silence of the Lambs" is no aberration. On Thursday Simon & Schuster and Pocket Books paid a staggering sum—nearly $1 million—for an author's first novel. It went to a still-unnamed Washingtonian who has written the book pseudonymously. It's about a serial killer.

Between the fact and fiction of serial killing is an enormous gulf, a chasm of ridiculous romanticization.

The imaginary serial killer is a powerful creature, brilliant at his craft, an implacable death machine. He's like a shark, driven not by mindless hunger but by an elaborate malevolence—evil, if you will.

Real life is not so gothic. When police bag a serial killer, he is usually a weak man, cowardly, not terribly savvy and a failure at most everything he's ever done in life. He's a loser. He manages to get away with multiple murders not because he's smart, but because he kills strangers and keeps moving; in real life, unlike on "Murder, She Wrote" or any other TV drama, such crimes are always hard to solve. "The bottom line is that most of these serial killers are not that clever," says Vernon Geberth, a former New York City cop and author of an authoritative text on homicide investigations.

This confusion between the real and the fake may explain the peculiar reaction of the people in Gainesville in recent months to the announcement that police have a prime suspect in the murders.

His name is Danny Harold Rolling. He's in jail, charged for the moment only with an unrelated armed robbery. He was identified in newspaper stories in January as the main suspect in the case, and on Thursday the *Gainesville Sun* reported that investigators feel they have enough physical evidence to seek an indictment of Rolling for the murders.

You would think Gainesville might collectively untense, would gratefully accept an end to its terror. It hasn't happened. In recent weeks, when you listened to the talk at off-campus hangouts like the Purple Porpoise and P.J. O'Riley's sports bar and the Market Street Pub, you find hardly a soul who thinks the police have cracked the case.

"Whoever did it is probably in another state by now," says Marti Sullivan, a University of Florida senior standing warily in the dark parking lot of the Gatorwood Apartments, where the last two bodies were found.

The problem is Rolling himself. He is a two-bit grocery-store robber, a nondescript 36-year-old drifter from Shreveport, La., where he is wanted for allegedly shooting his father in the face last May. Police say that on Aug. 30, two days after the last bodies were found in Gainesville, Rolling stole a car from a university student, drove south to Tampa, held up a grocery store, crashed the car when chased by the cops, escaped on foot and then four days later got nabbed in a similarly bungled robbery at a supermarket in Ocala.

He's inept. He's uneducated. He's a zero.

"We don't want it to be someone, who is, say, less intelligent than we are," theorizes police officer Darnell. "We don't want it to be someone who is ordinary."

People aren't satisfied. They expected Hannibal the Cannibal.

There is something reassuring in imagining our killers to be driven by an almost supernatural monstrousness. Perhaps our attempt to make them larger than life is a way of distancing ourselves from them, of making sure that we share nothing in common with these creatures. It is almost too terrifying to think that they are merely a diseased product of human nature, that they are driven by the same forces that are in every human being: Aggression and lust.

This is the dirty secret of serial killers. They are horribly twisted, but they are us.

The Real Thing

The Gainesville killer was fastidious. The bodies were scrubbed with a cleanser. There were signs he had used masking tape to bind the victims, then removed it later.

One investigator told reporters that it was as though the killer created a "play" for the cops, that he was leaving messages. This remark helped foster the image of the killer as a demonic fiend who was toying with the police.

Police did find some important physical evidence. It has been mentioned in some of the news accounts of the killings, but often in passing, a minor detail.

Not fingerprints. Semen.

The typical serial killer, criminologists say, is a sexually dysfunctional man who lives alone or with a parent. He is not capable of a healthy sexual relationship with another person. He is likely to treasure pornography and those detective magazines with the staged pictures of women being menaced by knives, with impotency relief ads in the back. He gets drunk before he kills.

His immediate motive is hardly grand: He wants sexual gratification. Killing is a characteristic of the way he rapes. Torture and murder arouse him.

Ed Kemper, a California killer in the early '70s, had sex with the headless corpses of his victims. A few years later and not far away, Leonard Lake video-taped himself raping and torturing his captives.

Floridian Christopher Wilder asked pretty women if he could take their pictures, then kidnapped, raped and killed them. Some writers have suggested that serial killing has arisen in response to the growing economic and political power of women, but in fact the victims are often male. John Gacy of Indiana raped and tortured to death 33 boys and buried them in his basement. Randy Steven Kraft drove around the freeways of Los Angeles picking up young men, whom he then drugged, sodomized, tortured, killed and mutilated. Juan Corona raped and murdered 25 migrant farm workers in California in 1970. The grisly list goes on.

"I have yet to see a serial killing that didn't have some sexual motivation," says Bob Ressler, a former FBI agent who was a leading figure in developing profiles of serial killers at the FBI academy at Quantico. "I have never seen a serial killer who is a happily married family man, or who had a long-term successful relationship with a woman."

In recent years it has been popular among psychologists and some law enforcement authorities to say that these crimes are not acts of sex but of violence and power and domination. It is a peculiar argument, downplaying the sexual aspect, because there are very few cases in which violence, power and dominance are wielded without an accompanying sexual climax. Maybe the Son of Sam case falls into that category, because David Berkowitz didn't rape his victims, but his choice of young lovers in parked cars indicates a sexual element.

"It became vogue to say this was just an act of violence," says Ressler, but "it's an act of violence that's based on a sexual maladjustment."

When people think about America's most famous serial killer, Ted Bundy, they think of how diabolically clever he supposedly was, how he went to law school, how he easily blended into normal society for so long. In a movie he was played by Mark Harmon, once labeled the Sexiest Man Alive by *People* magazine. What people don't think about is the fact that Bundy was a necrophiliac. He craved sex with the dead.

Bundy was a failure in his normal life and a cowardly brand of killer. He would wear a cast or a sling on one arm and lure young college students into helping him carry his books to his car. Then, when the woman turned her back, he'd pick up a tire iron from the ground and kill her with a blow to the back of the head. Upon reaching a safe location he would have sex with the corpse. This would sometimes continue for several days—he would wash the hair and apply makeup.

Yet these details are often deleted from Ted Bundy's public image. One consequence is that his cell on Death Row in Florida filled up with love letters. He received literally thousands of them. During one of his murder trials an admirer married him in the courtroom. She now claims that she bore him a child after a Death Row visit.

"I've been contacted by all these Bundy aficionados, all women, they're either in love with him, they want to talk to the person who was last with him, they have some feeling of attachment to him, many of them wrote to him in prison," says Bob Keppel, a Seattle prosecutor who tracked Bundy and spoke to him near the end. He is dismayed by the glorification of serial killers. "They are not romantic at all. They are just the lowest level slimeball you would ever want to run across. They're the lowest dregs of society."

In a sense, the serial killing phenomenon is an extension of this country's rape problem, which is growing faster even than the homicide rate. Per capita, the United States has 15 times as many reported rapes as England, 23 times as many as Italy, and 26 times as many as Japan.

But people don't like to think about rape. It is too low, too vulgar, too crass.

"We are fascinated by murder. We are not fascinated by rape," says James Alan Fox, co-author of the book "Mass Murder: America's Growing Menace." "Crime stories focus on murder, not on rape. Rape has never been fashionable, it's always been seen as disgusting and demented. We can be fascinated by murder, it's so extreme, it's so bizarre, but we're only sickened by rape."

Steven Egger, author of "Serial Murder: An Elusive Phenomenon," mentions in his book that in all of the academic literature on the subject, there is almost no mention that nearly all serial killers are men. It is as though people want to steer away from any explanation for these crimes that addresses a hormonal factor—people don't want to think of it as a testosterone explosion. But the behavior of serial killers is an exaggeration of the kinds of behavior found throughout the male population—predatory sexuality, treating women as objects, aggressiveness, desiring immediate gratification, narcissism, and so on.

The novelist Norman Mailer is one of the many writers who have been fascinated by killers and crazies. He wrote in his essay "The White Negro," "At bottom, the drama of the psychopath is that he seeks love. Not love as the search for a mate, but love as the search for an orgasm more apocalyptic than the one which preceded it."

The Myths

Fictional serial killers don't tend to rape anyone. Orgasm via sadism is never a motive. That would not be sufficiently entertaining.

Instead, they're just plain evil.

One absurd creature is Patrick Bateman, the murderous yuppie of "American Psycho," the bestseller by Bret Easton Ellis. Bateman is handsome, Harvard-educated, works on Wall Street, buys expensive clothes and goes to all the trendy night clubs. He also tortures and kills people in the most ghastly ways. The reader is led to believe that Bateman is the product of the excessively commercial, shallow, greed-infested era of the 1980s. He cares about things but not people. In one breath he says, "I'm wearing a wool suit by Armani, shoes by Allen-Edmonds, pocket square by Brooks Brothers" and the next he says, "Today I was obsessed with the idea of faxing Sarah's blood . . . over to her office in the mergers division at Chase Manhattan."

Bateman is not merely fictional, he's totally improbable. Serial killers are invariably professional failures—even the ones like Ted Bundy and Christopher Wilder whose few minor achievements were exaggerated by the news media. No known serial killer in America has ever been remotely as well-educated, affluent and successful as Ellis's murderer.

"I have never seen a person like that," says Ressler, the former FBI agent.

Thomas Harris, author of the novel "The Silence of the Lambs," did a lot of research. The FBI was cooperative. Ressler, among others, gave Harris advice. Nonetheless, the two psychos of the novel and movie are not on the whole very realistic.

Hannibal Lecter is just a vampire. The second-string psycho is Jame "Buffalo Bill" Gumb, who captures women and flays them so he can make clothing out of their skin. The character is based on three real serial killers: Ted Bundy, Ed Gein and Gary Heidnik.

From Bundy, Buffalo Bill gets his cleverness, including the technique of using an arm cast to attract sympathy from women.

From Gein he gets his interest in skin. Gein, a madman, dug up graves and took the corpses back to his lonely Wisconsin farmhouse. He did "experiments" with the body parts; one favorite activity was making masks out of human faces and skulls. He toyed with sexual organs. One day in 1957 he went into a nearby town and murdered a middle-aged woman, then killed another, both resembling his deceased mother. He wanted fresher material for his experiments. Upon his arrest he acted offended that he was accused of taking money from the store where his first victim worked. "I'm no robber," he protested. He died in a mental institution in 1984, his actions immortalized by Alfred Hitchcock's 1960 film "Psycho."

From Heidnik, Buffalo Bill gets his basement dungeon. In March 1987 police raided Heidnik's house in Philadelphia and found three women in chains in the basement, emaciated. Two others were already dead. The body parts of one were found in pots on a stove and in the freezer. Heidnik had fed the human remains to his captives.

The FBI looks at these three killers and puts them in two separate categories: Organized and unorganized. Gein was unorganized. Bundy and, to a lesser extent, Heidnik were organized.

What the FBI does not find, however, is someone like Jame "Buffalo Bill" Gumb: Extremely clever, but also interested in something incredibly bizarre, in this case making dresses out of human skin. It's not realistic. It has never happened.

"The reality of a person like Gumb is just not possible, because he has very psychotic tendencies and at the same time he's very organized and premediating," says Ressler. "The movie is a joke. It's a joke on society and it's a joke on the FBI."

The Misperception

"You know what's funny?" says Annie Hunter. She's a senior at the University of Florida. "Nobody talks about it anymore. People call it 'the incident.' "

It's over. People go on. They absorb the horror into their daily risk calculus.

"Now it's not even a topic of discussion anymore," says Spencer Mann, spokesman for the sheriff's office.

"I haven't thought about it recently because I prefer not to think about it," says Amy Barnard, a 27-year-old bartender in downtown Gainesville. "I'm tired of it."

The psyche heals, the fear subsides, and life goes back to normal.

Only now, normal has a new definition. Normal incorporates an astonishing glut of violence throughout American society. More violence in the media, more violence in real life: They seem to feed on one another.

Park Dietz, a psychiatrist in Long Beach, Calif., and a consultant to the FBI, says, "The psycho killer public relations industry depends on real offenders for its fodder, and the real offenders draw ideas, inspiration and hope of historical importance from their public relations industry."

The crime statistics are ominous. Despite great leaps in forensic technology to solve murders, the clearance rate has fallen from 86 percent in 1970 to 68 percent by 1989. The reason, in part, is that more and more murders are "stranger homicides," says Jim Wright, an FBI agent who analyzes violent crime. Another disturbing trend is that serial killers are racking up larger and larger body counts; there are more cases like that of Randy Kraft, who may have slain as many as 65 people in Los Angeles. "They learn from their mistakes. Every time they commit a crime, they learn. And they get better," says Wright.

Celebrated, probed, fussed over, the rapist-killer is now a familiar figure on the American landscape. He is probably here to stay. He is beyond the bounds of governance, beyond social engineering, beyond control. Perhaps he is the price we pay for slavish devotion to individualism, mobility, the right to buy smut, the right to ignore one's neighbors even when they seem weird. He can come through town and no one will ask him any questions. This is the way it is going to be, as long as this remains a nation of strangers.

Norman Mailer once made a prediction:

"The psychopath may indeed be the perverted and dangerous front-runner of a new kind of personality which could become the central expression of human nature before the twentieth century is over.

He wrote that in 1959. At the time it seemed preposterous.

April 14, 1991

Study Questions

Chapter Six

1. How does Joel Achenbach express the point of view of Native Americans toward Christopher Columbus? Would they consider him heroic? Discuss other luminaries in light of a multi-cultural perspective.

2. What are people doing with their vinyl record collections now that that form of recorded music has become obsolete? Is there nostalgia for old records? Who could you interview for a story on this topic?

3. As Peter Carlson did with the U.S. House of Representatives choose any institution and contrast its good aspects with its negative. Could your two lists become the basis for a feature story?

4. Do you know someone who champions a cause with little support, but keeps going anyway? What motivates such action? Is their cause worthy? Lost? What point of view would you adopt in writing about this person?

5. Feature stories are often constructed around a news peg, such as the examination of serial killers in the wake of the mass murder of college students in Gainesville, Florida. Look though a metropolitan daily newspaper and select several current events that could generate broader feature treatment. Justify.

A Sampler of Popular Culture 7

Covering the popular culture represents a significant challenge for feature article writers because they are writing about people, events and ideas which most readers will already know about, so they must strive to tell them something new about the topic. Popular culture is an expansive term which includes the popular arts, but also covers a wide spectrum of other cultural activity.

Summer Jobs, writes Elizabeth Kastor, are a teenage rite of passage into adulthood. In her story, "Hard Knocks 101," she reports anecdotes from former interns and reflects that summer jobs can be viewed as a window into character. Kastor concludes that while temporary jobs are often exploitive, it's easy to quit if it's too bad.

Roxanne Roberts calls senior proms both "the last blast of high school" and young people's first formal event and taste of adult luxury. She chronicles the growing excesses in prom-going, from pricey formal dresses and tuxedo rentals to hiring stretch limousines and helicopters for dramatic entrances. Her reporting is impressionistic and her viewpoint interpretive.

Rita Kempley's profile and interview with actor Jack Nicholson is meta-journalism, a form which calls attention to its own reporting process. It's ironic that Nicholson admits he hates the press, but needs it to publicize his movies. He also claims he lies in interviews so he won't get bored, calling into question the credibility of the story. Kempley tries to cope with Nicholson's attitude, but tells readers explicitly that "Conversation (with him) is a duel." She cleverly tags him "Jack of All Tirades" and then explores a range of topics—censorship and civil liberties, his liberal politics, his pro-choice stance on abortion and the eternal battle of the sexes. The story also traces his career history, shares some personal information about his children and identifies a few of his eccentricities. The ending is pure Nicholson!

Television critic Tom Shales' appreciation and assessment of the late Jim Henson's career recognizes the Muppeteer's contributions to TV and puppetry and serves as an eloquent tribute. Shales personalizes his comments and takes readers behind the scenes into Henson's famous alter-ego, Kermit the Frog.

The half-naked, on-stage antics of the band, the Red Hot Chili Peppers, had stirred up notoriety as their concert tour rolled into town. Writer Richard Harrington investigated the reported incidents, interviewed the band and tried to define their musical genre (white funk) and its phenomenal audience appeal. In tracking the group over its nine-year history, he describes the development of both the physical and cerebral aspects of their show. Part of the fun of the piece comes from Harrington's straight-forward writing about off-beat and colorful performers.

In a feature article on Nashville's annual Country Music Fan Fairs, writer Linda Chion-Kenney discusses the important role these events play in the industry and in people's lives. She observes the connections both fans and performers make and their emotional interaction. She also probes the psychological role of music in fans' lives, especially the dominant country music theme of "going home," which includes nostalgia for one's childhood. The story also offers service information so readers can make their own connections.

The bizarre sensibility reflected in "The Far Side" comic strip would likely spring from a twisted mind. But James Kindall's profile and interview with cartoonist Gary Larson surprises readers by depicting a normal lifestyle. Larson's success and impact are documented by statistics and ratings in polls. Kindall delves into Larson's insights into human nature, his macabre humor, political iconoclasm and off-beat view of life. It's a success story that's entertaining and far out.

Coping articles offer readers advice about timely topics. Marcela Kogan's piece talks to parents about negotiating their children's fashion limits. "When Your Kids Go Punk" presents cases that reassure parents and helps them tolerate adolescents' struggles to win independence from parental control.

In an article about a commonly shared childhood activity, Henry Allen alerts readers to subtle shade shifts in the color palette of Crayola boxes and ponders the significance of these minor alterations.

Hard Knocks 101

The Summer Job—Lessons in Life for a Minimum Wage

ELIZABETH KASTOR

It is the thing your parents make you do. It is the place where you first fall in love. It is the way you learn the disturbing truth that many people's work is tedious. It is what you will be nostalgic about—but not for many, many years. It is the last time you will have to know how to make a lanyard.

It is the Summer Job, that moderately distorted Introduction to Adulthood—accurate to the extent that it introduces kids to paychecks, taxes and getting up early, false to the extent that come Labor Day it is over.

Like many rites of passage, summer jobs go badly more often than they go well. Just ask any of the 3 million 16-to-24-year-olds who joined the labor force after school let out. Too many lawns mowed. Too many hours spent scooping ice cream (resulting in frostbitten fingers and weight gain). Too many waves of heat rising off the french fry vats. The right summer job pays okay-to-well, gets you outside, keeps you awake through the afternoon. The wrong job makes you stink.

"My worst summer job was when I was 16," says Montgomery County school Superintendent Harry Pitt. "I worked in a fish store. I cleaned fish, scaled fish. Every night I came home and the whole neighborhood smelled me coming."

But everyone knows if Pitt had had the good job—the Real Summer Job—he would have avoided that smelly humiliation. The Real Summer Job is, of course, lifeguarding, that classic endeavor that keeps you close to water and away from all scents other than coconut oil. The lifeguard bestrides the pinnacle of summer employment: outdoor work, opportunities for romance, strong element of boredom, chance to show off your body, most likely will not be pursued as an adult career path.

But not everyone can be a lifeguard—just one more example of the essential unfairness of life, one more lesson summer employment can teach.

What Parents Suspect About Summer Jobs

There are no reliable statistics on how many teenagers make a summer job of looking for a summer job, but anecdotal reporting suggests that the numbers are high.

The Awful Ones

Paul Ruffins, who now works for the International Union of Bricklayers and Allied Craftsmen, remembers one youthful spring spent laboring at a Friendly's. When he was not scooping, he was stationed in the zero-degree freezer, hefting newly arrived 35-pound cartons of ice cream.

"First of all, when you work with ice cream you get chocolate forearm and strawberry elbow," he says. Second of all, there was the prospect of the upcoming summer increase in ice cream deliveries. "You stood there, in your hat and mittens, and if you were going to do it well, you had to rotate the ice cream when the new deliveries came in—lift the old cartons down in front and put the new ones on the shelves.

"As the summer started, I decided it was time to move on."

Chris London, 21, is a camp counselor this summer. He has had enough of retail work. "I worked all over Georgetown," he says. At one record store, the managers discovered some thefts, decided it was someone on the staff, and went about dealing with it as they saw best. "Because it was the type of music it was, they thought it was a black person," says the young black man. "And I worked in classical. They accused all the black staff. I just quit."

The Moral

Summer jobs are made to quit.

The Interns

They blanket the city every summer, jangling with enthusiasm and newly found expertise, secure in the knowledge that they have the kind of jobs that are made for the resumé. On buses to the Hill from Georgetown and Clover Park they speak loudly—"Well, my member thinks that . . ." As if guided by some mysterious intern pheromone, they are drawn to obscure receptions and happy hours, seeking free food. They live in group houses furnished with milk crates and piles of newspapers and play frisbee in the living room. They read constituent mail. They make photocopies. They mill about. They are almost all unpaid volunteers (thank you, Mommy and Daddy). But of course at the end of the summer they do get pictures of themselves with their members. And then they are gone.

"You go out after work, and it's just interns everywhere," says Natalie Fousekis, a recent college graduate volunteering in the office of Sen. Pete Wilson (R-Calif.). With 40 of her kind working in his office each summer, Wilson is believed to be the most-interned senator.

About 4,000 work on the Hill each year, 2,500 of them in the summer. "Thank God they don't drive," says Hilary Lieber, director of the Congressional Intern Office. "The traffic would be terrible."

The Summer Job as Window Into Character I

"The summer job which made me a psychologist was at the age of 21," says Dr. Joyce Brothers. "I took a job for which I had no working papers, as a counselor at a camp for 'problem boys'—boys who had been in trouble with the law for rape, arson, beating people up. I took care of a dozen 14-year-old boys.

"For the boys to go to the bathroom, they had to walk through my bedroom—it wasn't a very well-organized camp. One night I had a sense something was cooking—you hear a lot of giggling. The boys all walked in totally nude, all with erections"—there the thoughtful and media-wise psychologist pauses to advise, "If you can't say erections, say 'in a state of excitement.'

"Should I have freaked out or panicked, we would have been in big trouble. I just went on painting my nails and as they walked into the bathroom I said in my normal voice, 'Boys, make sure you flush the toilets.' When they came back through, they weren't excited anymore. That was the end of the problems for the summer."

How to Make the Best Of a Bad Job

Find a larger meaning in it.

Rep. Fred Grandy (R-Iowa) spent one youthful summer doing "retail espionage." According to his spokeswoman, Georgia Dunn, he visited department stores and cased the prices on "specialty men's work clothes—shoes, engineer's caps, overalls."

"This was an experience that paid dividends when he moved back to Iowa," says Dunn. "He told me, 'When I campaigned through rural Iowa, I knew exactly where to look for the best pair of work shoes.' And to sum up the experience in a more existential light, there is a purpose for everything we do in our life, even though we may not realize it at the time."

Natalie Fousekis has spent her share of time in Sen. Wilson's mail room opening and sorting the tens of thousands of constituent letters that arrive each week. "That's not one of my favorite tasks, but you can still learn something," she says.

Oh really?

"Well, you see what the big issues are to people," she offers, then laughs. "If you're going to do it for three hours, you've got to get something positive out of it."

Kids, Kids Everywhere

At a roller-skating rink in Prince George's County the counselors stand and watch their charges. Small children skate over and drape themselves from the counselors' arms like hanging moss. They stare up at the giants and beg for money, or candy, or attention, or something, anything. Their eyes are filled with yearning and love and imminent boredom.

Being a camp counselor is like being a senior in high school. You are bigger than everyone else. You know how life works. You are perfect.

"The impact you have on these kids!" says Delores Colbert, director of the older camper program at the Southeast YMCA Camp. "You get out of the car and they're, like, 'DELORES!!' They'll do anything for you."

It is a position of sweet and frightening responsibility, and the fear is drummed into counselors along with the idea that this is not a Job, this is a Calling. Listen to Tracey Williams, 22 and the director of the Southeast Camp younger camper program: "I always tell people I'm interviewing, you can work anyplace else—the drugstore, the mall—and you can burn the store down and the insurance will pay for it. But if anything happens to these kids, you'll be on the news that night."

It is a responsibility that some find daunting. "I look on this as a test," says Marni Mintener, a 19-year-old Howard University student. "I'm not positive I want to go into education, but I figure if I can survive this summer with these crazy kids I can do it."

Mintener is a willowy and graceful and disciplined former gymnast who has worked with children before, but that was at a gymnastics camp in Wisconsin, where her charges were willowy and graceful and disciplined current gymnasts. Here, the kids are just kids. They lose their shoes and socks, they talk back, they form rowdy clumps and race around rooms.

They also offer painful moments of insight into small lives. "One kid came up to me and said his father is in prison," remembers Mintener. "That crushes you. One boy was crying, and he said, 'I miss my daddy!' I said, 'Don't worry, you'll see him when you get home.' He said, 'He's dead. He died two weeks before camp started.' You can get depressed too, and you have to shake that off."

The Summer Job as a Window Into Character II

Phyllis Schlafly makes it clear—the job wasn't just for the summer, she did it during the year too as she worked her way through college. But if you want to know, yes, she'll tell you. "I fired machine guns and rifles, testing ammunition on the night shift."

The Fruit Man

Sam Jannotta reads Noam Chomsky. He reads "The Unbearable Lightness of Being." Between chapters, he sells fruit.

Seated at a card table covered with neatly stacked pyramids of fruit at 17th and L streets NW, Sam Jarnotta has managed to make street vending an intellectual pursuit. A graduate of St. Mary's College recently back from a trip to Costa Rica, he is figuring life out, deciding his future, selling plums.

"A friend of the family did this and she made a good amount of money over the summer," he says. "She worked this corner and said it was very good."

Jannotta has his books to keep him company, but he also has made friends with the other vendors. "The Ben and Jerry's ice cream guy, he comes by and hangs around. It's a great summer job. You get to meet people. You get to be outside. The weather hasn't been so bad. The worst thing is you have to get up at 5 every morning to buy the fruit."

The Catch-22 of Summer Jobs

You cannot be a waitress until you have waitressing experience. This is the adolescent equivalent of a Zen koan.

The Sad Fact About Summer Jobs

You are young. You are strong. You can work like a horse. You are slave labor.

"I worked in a fast-food pizza place," says Mintener. "The management was awful and they expected me to run basically the whole store. I was at the counter dealing with customers, I had to bus the tables and wash the dishes and keep the salad bar filled. I lasted almost a month."

Sometimes they try to make you forget you are slave labor. Do not be fooled.

At Kings Dominion, for example, the 3,500 summer workers can choose from a variety of jobs from retailing to landscaping. Some choose to be "area hosts."

"It's basically street-sweeping," says the somewhat embarrassed spokeswoman, Serena Barry. "They get the message sooner or later."

Final Words of Advice

Just remember, the best thing about a bad summer job is this: It is a summer job.

August 13, 1990

The Selling of the Prom

Big Bucks for High School's Last Bash

ROXANNE ROBERTS

They call it Prom Fever. Temporary insanity is more like it. How else to explain this seasonal mania?

A giggling mother pulls out her checkbook to pay for a strapless, sequined get-up that transforms her sweet darling into a Pageant Queen Gone Bad. She writes a check for $125, then forks over another $100 in cash. "Don't you dare tell your father how much this costs."

A 16-year-old self-described "dude"—whose idea of formal attire is a clean Bart Simpson T-shirt—develops a sudden obsession with tails, top hats and gold lamé cummerbunds.

A senior in an advanced marketing class describes a limousine that rents for $345 as "a really good deal."

Prom night is the last blast of high school, the first taste of adult luxury, the night to remember—bigger, better, badder than ever before—and a multimillion-dollar Dress Rehearsal from the same folks who made weddings a $30 billion-a-year industry.

The Magazine

What started out as a gym dance has evolved into an elaborate rite of passage, complete with all the ceremonial trappings formerly reserved for weddings. Prom is a chip off the block; the Big Day, Junior Division. All the glamour of a wedding without the gamble of marriage.

The dress, tuxedo, limousine, flowers and the photographer—if all the details are perfect, then prom night will be perfect and the memories will be perfect. And the bridal business is eager to share in the fantasy.

The latest salvo is *Your Prom* magazine, published by *Modern Bride* magazine. The premiere issue, a teenage orgy of rhinestone sophistication, hit the stands in February and sold out within days.

"This magazine is special because it is devoted to the one subject so intensely important to you at this special time in your life," writes editor Cele Goldsmith Lalli in her message to readers.

According to a reader survey, the magazine's average customer is a 16.7-year-old girl who spends almost two hours poring over the 132 pages that include: How

238

to Say No and Still Get to Go," ads for dresses, "Creative Corsaging," ads for dresses, "No Dream Date?," ads for dresses, "Sex: Why It's Your Call" . . . you get the idea.

She starts shopping for her prom dress—which she expects to pay $200 for and will wear only once—four months before the dance, long before she has a date. She flips through the magazine 10 more times before it is passed on to nine of her friends. That is advertisers' heaven.

The success of the debut issue means *Your Prom* will be back next year, complete with ads from the prom dress manufacturers who market their creations through bridal salons, as well as ads for limousine companies and men's formal wear companies.

The booming prom industry is "directly reflective of what happened in the '80s," says Lalli. Today's prom is "a return to things that are traditional, elegant. It's the first formal event in their lives."

The Dress

Danielle Unger casts a critical eye at her reflection in the three-way mirror. The 17-year-old cheerleader at West Springfield High School has selected a ruby red, strapless floor-length gown—instead of the shorter versions popular this year—to conceal her knee brace. She breaks into a smile. Torn ligaments and broken bones, souvenirs of a cheer gone awry, are no match for the perfect prom dress.

Gone are the soft, flowing visions of yesteryear. Today's prom dress—average price $200—is shorter, tighter, strapless and usually sequined. Shoes ($50) are dyed to match, and the most popular accessories are matching gloves ($20) and long, shoulder-dusting rhinestone earrings ($30).

Unger, who paid $250 for her dress and $50 for a slip to keep the skirt poufed, is just one of the customers at Katherine's Boutique & Bridal in Alexandria on this busy Saturday afternoon. Mothers and daughters sift through the racks crowded with sequined confections. Brides argue with their best friends about bridesmaids' dresses. They all wait for their turn at the raised, mirrored platform to model The Dress.

The pink, pocket-size boutique, normally the domain of women, is filled with couples during prom season. Fernando Baez pulls a black velvet dress off the rack and slips into one of the tiny dressing rooms where his girlfriend, 18-year-old Elizabeth Patrick, tries it on. A giddy chaos reigns. Prom business accounts for 30 percent of the boutique's revenues from March through June.

"Girls don't want a dress everybody else has," says owner Katherine Larson. "Girls will come in with a magazine and say, 'I want this dress.' Some shops keep logs—what girl at which school buys which dress." This year's most popular dress was a $450 white sequined floor-length gown by Alyce. "It flew out of the store."

Department stores, short on formal romantic fantasy appeal, are striking back with more elaborate in-store promotions. Garfinckels threw an extravagant prom fashion show—complete with smoke machine—at Springfield Mall and asked high school students to model dresses in the show and at six stores the following day. "Modeling in this show will make the students feel that much more special and confident on that important evening," said Garfinckels's Aniko Gaal.

"Malls all have the same dresses," says Unger, who searched for a month before finding her dress at the boutique. She leaves and then returns a half hour later. "I forgot to get a swatch for my boyfriend."

Matching Cummerbunds

"The cummerbund matching the dress is extremely important," says Ira Adler, district manager of Royal Formal & Bridal's 14 local branches. "Guys will come in with swatches from their dates' dresses. Very often, they come in with their dates to pick out the color."

Royal has 50 different colors for cummerbunds and bow ties to choose from: "light pink, dark pink, magenta, lilac." Adler ticks them off. "Metallics, gold lamé, silver lamé—you name it."

Adler's stores rent 5,000 tuxedos each weekend during prom season, at an average rental of $80 including the shirt, studs and that all-important bow tie and cummerbund. "We've had requests for black bicycle shorts with stripes down the side," says a salesman, sighing. "Not this year, but probably next year."

The walls are lined, floor to ceiling, with rows of top hats, canes and wedding and prom dresses for sale. Royal has its own photographers to go to weddings and proms and, new this year, limousine rentals. Flip on any Top-40 radio station and you're likely to hear a Royal prom ad. As one radio advertising executive told a reporter: "No offense, but the target audience is not a heavy reader."

Dan Redman, 19, comes in to pick up a classic tux for the Madison High School prom later that night at the Marriott Hotel in Tysons Corner. His cummerbund is classic too—black, an increasingly popular color for prom dresses. The bleached blond streak in his hair, however, places him definitely left of preppie. "My girlfriend wanted me to spike my hair up," he says. "I used to have a mohawk two years ago." He's going to wear it slicked back in a ponytail.

Yorktown seniors Greg Keish and Mike Myers wander in for a preliminary peek at the latest styles. Even though his parents will pay for his tuxedo rental and dinner, Keish figures he will have to come up with $400 for prom tickets, a corsage and his share of the eight-hour limousine rental.

"You only do it once," he says. "You only have one prom."

Car Talk

"It's expensive and kind of a silly thing to spend your money on," says Violeta Chapin, a freshman at Georgetown Day School. "But I'd appreciate a limo."

"I wouldn't be embarrassed if he didn't have one, but I think I'd like a limo," offers Becky Lasky, her 15-year-old classmate. "Like an old Rolls-Royce or something. I'd love to go in an old Rolls-Royce. That would be amazing."

"I think I'd be kind of irked if someone showed up in a dumpy old Pinto or something," Violeta says. "I would be, like, 'Oh.' But I wouldn't really mind as long as I got there. I think the dress is more important than the car."

If getting there in style is the priority, getting home in one piece is the pitch.

Prom night is traditionally the night for seniors to do everything they haven't had a chance to do in the past four years. It's the first night with no curfew. Parents used to worry about sex. Now they worry about drunk drivers.

"Adult ethical concerns for the prom-goers have been reduced to a prayer for survival: Dear God, bring 'em back alive sometime within the next 48 hours," wrote T.C. Williams teacher Patrick Welsh.

Until the early '80s, high school students borrowed Dad's car and treated drinking on prom night as a part of the festivities. Even gym screenings of "The Last Prom," a grisly anti-drunk-driving film about a prom that ends on the pavement, failed to keep the champagne corked.

The combination of the Reagan Era opulence and Mothers Against Drunk Driving (MADD) turned the limousine from a seldom-seen extravagance to a common sight on prom night. It's the one luxury parents will bankroll in an effort to keep their kids off the road and safely delivered to the all-night, after-prom parties.

"Every weekend in March through June, you cannot get a limo," says Wayne J. Smith, executive director of the National Limousine Association. Prom rentals bring in up to 25 percent of the annual income for an operator; 65 percent of all the rentals are paid by the parents, 35 percent by the students.

There are strict rules against alcohol in the car. Many companies ask parents who are renting to sign a contract that entitles the operator—if the students drink while in the limousine—to cut short the evening, return the students home, and still collect the full rental fee. While the rules can't eliminate drinking completely, says Smith, "for that six-hour period, consumption overall is less."

Typically, a prom night limousine is rented for a six-hour period for $300, although local costs are slightly higher. The super-stretch, which seats up to 10 and includes a TV, VCR, phone and mini-fridge stocked with soft drinks, rents for $550 to $600 and is snapped up faster than you can say "Home, James."

"It's almost like a party within the car," says Smith. "In their minds, they're sitting in the seat and being attended to. It's a Cinderella story."

The Castle

"They're king and queen for the night and they try to act it," says Kathy Summers, sales manager of Martin's Crosswinds in Greenbelt. "They want to prove they're grown up. They're extremely well behaved."

Royalty needs a castle. Susan Ford's 1975 prom at the White House came close, but the average high school prom committee doesn't have executive privileges.

Martin's Crosswinds, with three mirrored ballrooms, crystal chandeliers and a fireplace in the lobby, not only is a favorite choice for wedding receptions but also will play host to 20 proms this year. The catering facility offers four different prom packages for the students: the 5 1/2-hour full package, which includes a sit-down dinner and four hours of dancing to the band or deejay of choice, goes for $25-$27 a person. Since most students have dinner somewhere else first, the most popular choice is the cabaret package at $23—four hours of dancing with a two-hour hot buffet.

Food, of course, is not really a serious part of prom night. The band, the decorations, the theme matter much more. And making an entrance—now that's serious.

"It's quite an event to stand on the balcony and watch these kids come in," says Summers. And before that, there is the scene outside. For the past two years, a few would-be Trumps have arrived in helicopters. They touch down in the parking lot. Of course, they have to get permission to land first.

Of course.

"It amounts to wanting to outdo everybody else," says Summers.

Prom Videos

Steve Mosseau of Video Specialists Inc. is kind of bummed out. Given the popularity of wedding videos, Mosseau was expecting to make big bucks when he placed a full-page ad in *Your Prom*.

"The prom end of the business never materialized," he said. "I was really surprised."

Oh, he got a few calls from individual couples, but Mosseau had his eye on greener pastures—big contracts from the school prom committees. They never called.

Mosseau forgot about the star system. Wedding videos have two stars and a supporting cast. A prom video is full of bit players on the one night everybody wants to be a star. Besides, students are already paying $50 for prom pictures.

"I think it's a couple of years away from being an integral part of the event," he said.

The Survey

Dana Chinn, a senior at West Springfield High School, just completed the 1990 Prom Survey, answered by almost 300 of her classmates. The survey, which breaks down the prom into cost estimates for each expense, will be published in the student newspaper before the June 2 prom.

"It's so students can compare notes and so parents won't be totally shocked at the prices," she explains. "So parents know what to expect."

The survey reveals that most of the girls (or their parents) will pay for a dress, accessories and a boutonniere for the escort, for a grand total of approximately $245. More than 75 percent said it is worth the expense.

The guys (or their folks) will pay for the tux, a corsage, transportation, dinner and after-prom entertainment, for a grander total of $420. Despite the additional costs, more than 50 percent of the males said it is worth the money.

Heavy breathing notwithstanding, the trend toward going to the prom with a friend, rather than a True Love, also eases the financial burden a bit. More students are attending in groups of six or eight, splitting more of the costs equally.

"If you want to go in style, you have to pay for it," says Chinn, who is taking her boyfriend, who's in college, to her prom and sharing the cost with her parents. "It's the last time the class will be together, to dress up, to say 'This is me.' It's the last time you're going to see each other. It's what people are going to remember."

Divorce Court, Prom Division

Memories? Ask Tomontra Mangrum about her Dream Date. Ask the Palm Beach Lakes (Fla.) High School student about Marlon Shadd, who stood her up on prom night last year.

What Mangrum wanted was a public apology from the 17-year-old basketball star. What she got was silence. So she sued him for $49.53—$26 for shoes that could not be returned, $23 for her prom hairdo and 53 cents for the flowers in her hair.

"I can't believe this," said Shadd, when he learned of the lawsuit. "She said she didn't believe me when I told her I fractured my ankle." Shadd, as it turns out, was out of town that night seeing a college basketball recruiter.

Mangrum settled out of court for $81.28—the $49.53 she asked for, $19.50 to file the case in court and $12.25 to have it served by the sheriff's deputies.

Shadd got off cheap. Mangrum could have sued for intentional infliction of emotional distress, said her lawyer. "She could have collected more."

"I felt it was worth it, all of it," she said. "If this is what you have to do, you might as well go all the way. No one knows what I went through on that Friday night."

May 20, 1990

Jack Nicholson, Unleashed

The Profundities and Profanities of the Joker and One of 'Two Jakes'

RITA KEMPLEY

The sky is porridge, a thick soup of grit and humidity that struggles up 27 stories and seeps through Jack Nicholson's open window. He lights up a Camel, drags, pauses and decides he hates the press even more than usual. The brain whirs, there's an audible click. He has decided to do his impersonation of the Big Bad Wolf, and Mr. Wolfie is in a grumpy mood. Jack Nicholson claims at least half of what's been written about him is off the wall. For him, an interview is an exercise in put-downs, self-deprecation and foul language. It's sadomasochism with Evian water. He leans forward, picks up the bottle and slugs it back in a manly fashion. He hates publicity, but it's a necessary evil, part of the game when you're launching a movie, especially a troubled one.

It took him five years or more and cost him his best friend, but Nicholson did it, he finished "The Two Jakes." "You're going to love it," said the *Los Angeles Times* of this convoluted sequel to "Chinatown." "A masterpiece," raved the Thumb Twins. Nicholson, who starred in, directed and rewrote buddy Robert Towne's script, is about the only other living soul in agreement. "Are people going to like a flawless, thoughtful, intelligent movie?" he asks, flashing the notorious grin, vivid as an acid flashback.

Nicholson reprises the role of detective Jake Gittes in this return to old Los Angeles. Set in 1948, 11 years after "Chinatown," "The Two Jakes" gives us a golf-playing, prosperous, porky Jake. "He's comfortable," allows the actor, who points out that he's now "a lot thinner than I was in the movie." Indeed Nicholson, whose Jake II looks like the Nutri-System poster child, is waisted, paunchless even.

His performance is heavy too, like a wide-load trailer taking hairpins through the San Gabriel Mountains. Gittes is having a midlife crisis in slo-motion, crying over spilled blood at the end of "Chinatown." He finds his current case, murder-adultery-orange grove abuse, is intricately related to the past. A voice-over was added to clarify the plot.

"The Two Jakes," Nicholson's third directorial effort, was a problematic production that was revised, re-shot, postponed again and again. Nicholson worries that "gibbering" about all that will hurt the movie's reception. (In fact the opening weekend grosses were puny.) "I wake up and here's this article and all they said is,

'Robert Towne blah blah blah,'" he says of his Tinseltown tiff with his erstwhile comrade. "And I think, 'Uuuhh Jack, you don't need to do interviews. They're just going to make you make a fool of yourself. . . . Are you ever going to grow up and say, Look, shut up?"

Nicholson, at 53, remains a rascal, trying to shock the girls, impress the boys with his devilish manner and syncopated eyebrows. Like a kid who's just learned to curse, he is free with four-letter words. With a double-dog-dare-you look in his eyes, he watches for a cringe. Conversation is a duel.

A reference to censorship lights his fuse. "Remember, it was only 15 years ago that you couldn't say 'for unlawful carnal knowledge,' so the fact that you can say {bleep} and {bleep} now does not represent a large progression to me . . . . You know, the first {bleep} is much more important than the sixth {bleep} and {bleep} and . . . ."

Reassured that you can indeed say bleep in modern times, he fumes, "Well, okay, I don't want us to get into a conflict over definitions and context. In fact, let me tell you where censorship has actually gone so that you won't be just reflecting the conventional wisdom. What I always said is you could slice a {breast} in the movies but you couldn't kiss one. And that's the real issue, you know.

"I'm fearless. Even in an interview, I dare to be realistic. Heh, heh, heh."

The Jack of All Tirades has no patience with puritans. Profanity is not merely chest-beating but his way of exercising his civil liberties. He is what he is, the same as the parts that he plays—the catalytic outsiders, the system-buckers, the rugged individualists. He's "Mr. Smith Goes to Washington" without the apple pie and the starry eyes. The world is his cuckoo's nest.

The topic of censorship continues to worry him. "You've got to know that individuality is under fire. I'm not even interested in any system that isn't specifically designed to expand personal liberty. I think everything is simply the dog police. It's as though human beings were to be kenneled and fed and leashed. They're not. And certainly if America is about anything it's about, you know, the Magna Carta.

Ah, the mind unleashed.

Nicholson lights up another Camel, drags, grins, looks really proud of himself. "You know," he tells a reporter confidentially, expounding on his theory on the battle between the sexes, "you have more in common with a female cat than you do a human man."

When it comes to women, he has three guidelines: "They're smarter, meaner and they don't play fair." He means that as a compliment. Nicholson grew up in Neptune, N.J., believing himself to be the son of a beautician, Ethel May Nicholson, and the sign painter, John, who abandoned them. Some 38 years passed before he learned that his older sister, June, the showgirl with whom he had so much in common, was really his mother. And this he learned as the result of a magazine article.

The truth was confirmed by his aunt, Lorraine, whose name he gave to his 4-month-old child, born to actress Rebecca Brousard. His affair with Brousard—a spunky gal Friday in "The Jakes"—reportedly brought the curtain down on his 17-year relationship with Angelica Huston. "I feel very blessed," he says of his second daughter. His first, Jennifer, 26, was born to his actress-wife Sandra Knight in the early '60s.

Life is dear to Nicholson. He gets all fuzzy, smiles tenderly over his favorite line in "The Jakes," delivered by costar Harvey Keitel: "Remember, the children are watching. They're watching." There's a hush. "I don't mean to act it out for you," he apologizes.

Nicholson's appreciation for his life fights with his "ultra-liberal" politics. "I'm pro-choice, but against abortion because I'm an illegitimate child myself and it would be hypocritical to take any other position. I'd be dead, I wouldn't exist," he says. "And I have nothing but total admiration, gratitude and respect for the strength of the women who made the decision they made in my individual case. But as I say, I believe this is the choice of the woman. And, you know, I walk it like I talk it."

Beyond that, he believes that at some super-conscious level, guilt and self-loathing keep us from reproducing. "See, I don't mind the idea of abortion, you know, I mean I'm not a metaphysical person." Fast forward. "But being the man in the situation, I find that they're choosing between their ability to have lunch versus their ability to have a baby. And I fear that this is some self-hypnotic mantra. These are my fears. I always fear for all of us but not the future.

"Remember, we come from a species that lived under the water. To come out of the water, if you breathed in the water, represents death more certain than any kind of radiation. And we've already overcome that." Which brings him to:

"If you've ever been involved in athletics, you see coaching gets people to just simply understand, 'You can do this.' It's one of the positive elements of the military. God, I hated being in the Air Force, but it saved the mimbly-pimbly momma's boys. I had to say, now this is very good that this guy's being told someday you're going to live with other people. You might want to know how to pick up your socks. You know what I mean?"

Incongruous against a floral-print sofa, Nicholson sports loud, checkered socks that could be used to declare the winner of the Indy 500. His loafers, appaloosa-hide and dandified, are a made-for-strutting fashion statement. Rivaling Imelda Marcos when it comes to footwear, he purportedly owns 74 more pairs, as well as 25 pairs of sunglasses. Today his eyes are naked under the boomerang eyebrows. And his skin, loose as a camel's lips, shows the wear of the 16 years that have passed since the premiere of "Chinatown."

Towne and Nicholson always planned to do a series of films based on Gittes and the screenwriter's memories of his family's real estate business. "As a non-native I always have looked at Los Angeles as the city of the future. It has, you know, more to do with building than decay . . . . I love Los Angeles. It's paradise in its way. Certainly I'm not a country boy. My model for living is I live in a two-bedroom apartment—one bedroom's in L.A., one's in Aspen, and I don't have to pay the gardeners in between.

"And you know in today's world, over-identifying geographically with home is arcane. But of course, you mourn {the pollution}. I mean I fight all the time up where I live with developers, trying to keep things in my own back yard ecologically nice, but you can't stop other people from living where you live. That's not America. That's not democratic. It's not right. But you can try and intensify their sensitivity to the situation, and in that sense the movie is an appeal to that sensibility."

Unlike Gittes, who is given to hard-boiled homilies, Nicholson is anything but succinct. His conversation rambles, lurches and gets tangled as a yard dog wrapped in his own leash. He explains the symbolism in the earthquakes that shake "The Jakes" from time to time. "The earth is moving under your feet, the globe is hurtling through space. You can never be where you were, and yet where you were still is there where it was and that's what the movie is saying and the earthquake is this, you know, as I say the metaphoric feeling of the earth rumbling."

Nicholson, the high school sophomore, took up acting when he was kicked out of Manasquan High's sports program—"and all the chicks that I liked were doing plays." A Jeff Corey-trained method actor, he calls his work autobiographical in that it comes from his gut.

Before "Easy Rider" brought him acclaim in 1969, he earned a buck doing episodes of "Divorce Court," and a living as an actor, writer and producer in Roger Corman's B-movie factory. His directorial debut came with "Drive, He Said," a countercultural tale, in 1971, followed by "Goin' South" in 1978. A western romp, the latter was trounced as a Gabby Hayesian nose-candy spoof.

"I have always kinda been ticked off that they always start reviews of movies I directed by saying, 'Well of course all the performances are brilliant—however,' as though this were the case in every movie that came down the block. I mean, you know, 'Goin' South' produced more million-dollar actors from obscurity than any movie in history. Mary Steenburgen, John Belushi, Chris Lloyd, Danny DeVito.

"I was doing 'The Shining' in England {at the time it came out} so I didn't get the full brunt of the criticism, but I resented that it was this kind of claptrap view . . . . And I think that wanting to grab that easy handle kept them from seeing what I extremely modestly say is a comic masterpiece. Remember, this is a singular complaint. If anything, I've been overly praised {by critics}."

He has high hopes for "The Jakes." "You know, this is action painting, this movie. It's not linear painting. It's a diptych," says Nicholson the art collector. Colleagues who have worked with the sometime director in the past have said that he was more assured, easier-going this time. "I matured somewhat, is the most self-congratulatory term I can come up with at the moment," he says wickedly.

According to the *World Almanac, Who's Who* and the rest of the world, Jack Nicholson was born April 28, 1937, in Neptune, N.J. "I was born in Manhattan," he says firmly. "You know the press." Grrr. Suddenly there's more beard stubble on the ruggedly fascinating face.

Surely he gets tired of hearing the same questions.

"Ah, that's okay," he says pleasantly. "Mrs. Vreeland cautioned me on this when I first started. She said never tell the truth in an interview, you'll get bored with your own life. One of the lines that was cut out of 'The Two Jakes' is, 'The wise man is never bored.' It was said in Chinese so it wasn't going to last into infinity, but it is something I believe, yeah. I've never been bored."

Then he never tells the truth?

"Well, there's a big difference between telling lies and telling the truth. A lot of ground in between.

"I don't tell many lies. I just don't tell that much."

Nicholson is supporting a Colorado ecologist for the Senate—"Give Josie Keaton a plug," he urges—but says, "Look, I don't want to really be labeled. I mean I'm for a strong police force, liberals are not. I'm for legalizing drugs, conservatives are not. That's why I'm not more systematically political, because I don't really fit. And I'm not interested in homogenizing. I do what I do. I know from my interchanges with the public, half of 'em think I'm a raving lunatic. And you know nothing could be further from the truth. I feel myself I'm ultra-rational."

He is relieved to hear that his driver has arrived with a sandwich. Tonight he's making his annual pilgrimage to the House That Ruth Built. A sportsman in his own right, he says, "I like basketball because it's played at night. I like 'Batman' because it was the only comic that took place at night. I liked the darkness as a kid, the wild, deranged complexity of the Joker."

He was attracted to the Gittes films because they were noir, but he didn't want to make a movie that could be classified. "Everyone is in some kind of ethical conflict, everyone in the picture. So this to me is a successful twist on the genre. It's dark and appears light. Darkness is shaking under the ground, the fuel of the pollution of the future. And that's the reason to refer to the past, learn from it. Those fossils were formerly living creatures. That's what fossil fuel is, you know.

"I don't mean to be precious. We don't consider things at this depth {in the movie}. That's part of what I do for my livelihood and I don't do it all the time. I'm just as capable of being bizarre and flimsy and falling down and out of line as the next guy . . . . I don't just cruise through life, devil-may-care. In fact just the opposite. My friends say, 'Oh God, you just worry too much.'"

Another Camel in his mouth, the dim sun streaming in, he explains himself. "In interviews, we just talk dreams. You see what I'm saying. But normally since directors are control freaks, this to me is threatening but stimulating. I think it's good. Because after all is said and done you know I became an actor so I didn't have to be a salesman. I'm a natural salesman. From childhood people wanted to buy what old little Jackie's selling."

Old little Jackie. He's off to the Yankees game. "George Steinbrenner did overlook pitching for a mighty long time," he says of the morning's headlines. He walks the reporter to the door. A short man with more hair than you'd imagine. "Never say you're sorry, babe," he advises.

August 15, 1990

The Voice and Soul of the Muppets

TOM SHALES

It's not as if this is a world into which happiness is easily brought. Bringing even a little can be a major undertaking. Jim Henson brought a lot. The precise amount is immeasurable.

A visionary, a magician, a comedian and a technician—part Hans Christian Andersen and part Thomas Edison—Jim Henson revolutionized puppetry and helped reinvent children's television. He did it through craftsmanship and showmanship and even salesmanship, but he also did it by keeping alive within himself the child he once had been.

When death took Jim Henson yesterday, at the age of 53, it took that child as well. How do we explain this to the other children, and to ourselves?

Jim Henson presided over a national theater in miniature. His repertory company, global in impact, had among its principals a vain blond pig, a cookie-craving monster, a grouch who lived in a garbage can, and a shy and ungainly yellow bird. And Bert and Ernie and Grover and Scooter and Gonzo and Statler and Waldorf, and ducks and penguins and cows.

When he fathered the immortal Kermit in 1957, Jim Henson created a Frogenstein. His world would never be the same. Neither would ours. There would be more happiness in it. There would be Muppets.

Nearly as tall and nearly as shy as Big Bird, Jim Henson had the puttery, distracted air of a scientist, a softspoken tinkerer who loved manipulating the technologies of Muppetry and television to wreak clever effects and imaginative illusions. A Muppet was, he explained, a crossbreed of marionette and puppet, more agile and antic than either had been before.

Over the years, Muppets rushed in where puppets feared to tread. They rode bicycles, they swam, they flew through the air. And they starred in motion pictures, a first for a bunch of actors made of felt and foam rubber.

When they branched out from "Sesame Street" and started "The Muppet Show" in the late '70s, the Muppets were able to lure big stars (make that other big stars) to appear with them, from Linda Ronstadt to Sylvester Stallone to Milton Berle to Ethel Merman. Rudolf Nureyev appeared on the show and, with a gigantic pig, danced the "Swine Lake" ballet.

Soon after launching "The Muppet Show," which is still in circulation all over the planet, Henson agreed to show a reporter around his New York workshop.

250

There was Kermit T. Frog, painlessly impaled on a stand, alarmingly limp and lifeless, his green head bowed solemnly.

Henson picked him up, slipped the frog onto his hand, raised his voice a little so that it became Kermit's, and brought that froggie to life.

And the reporter, without a blink, instantly turned in his tracks and addressed his next question to the frog, as if Henson himself had vanished. As the mild-mannered Henson animated the frog, however, the frog animated him.

Looking around the cluttered workshop a little later, one could see other copies of Kermit designed to be used in various kinds of scenes.

Which one was the real one?

"They're all the real one," Jim Henson said.

What Henson and his associates brought to televised puppetry wasn't just cuteness, which was already there in abundance, but also a raucous irreverence. Early Henson TV shows in Washington were full of playful rowdiness, and his hilarious commercials for Wilkins Coffee usually ended with one Muppet dispatched abruptly to a cartoonish kingdom come: Blam!

Later, the Muppets made audiences roar on "The Jack Paar Show" and "The Ed Sullivan Show" by blowing each other up or, on some occasions, swallowing each other up.

They were furry, funny, stylized slapstickers. Then, when "Sesame Street" came along in 1969, they became something more. They developed soul. They had subtexts and complexes and inner selves. In Kermit's plaintive eyes, one can even sense a haunted angst. Despite the existence of the "Muppet Babies" cartoon series on CBS, Kermit really seems to be a character with no youth behind him and no dotage ahead.

Ageless and unattached, sometimes encountered alone and contemplative in his home pond, Kermit emerged as an existential hero for our time. For him, it was no easier being green than it was for others to be black or white or shades in between.

"Kermit is the closest one to me," Henson said of his alter ego in 1977. "He's the easiest to talk with. He's the only one who can't be worked by anyone else— only by me. See, Kermit is just a piece of cloth with a mouthpiece in it. The character is literally my right hand."

That he remained mostly behind the scenes didn't seem to bother Jim Henson any more than it had bothered Burr Tillstrom, the creator of "Kukla, Fran and Ollie" and one of Henson's inspirations. Occasionally he showed his face, however, as in one of those American Express "do-you-know-me?" commercials. "Nobody knows my face," he said in the ad, surrounded by his antic progeny.

Kermit and Miss Piggy, of course, have worldwide recognition.

"We are grief-stricken," said Joan Ganz Cooney, president of the Children's Television Workshop, yesterday. CTW produces "Sesame Street," and Cooney hailed Henson as "an authentic American genius." He was an authentic American success story too, and a determined American dreamer.

He was able to realize an ideal—to make a living, and indeed build an empire, doing precisely what he most enjoyed doing. Unlike most of us, he never had to stop playing with his toys. His toys were his fortune. He did the playing; we had the fun.

Jim Henson and his wife, Jane, who met in the '50s and manipulated the original Muppets, had five children. And, in effect, millions more. We all feel a little orphaned this morning, and we worry about that "piece of cloth with a mouthpiece in it" perched somewhere on a stand. Head bowed. Eyes plaintive.

The fortunate thing is, the happiness Jim Henson brought into the world remains behind. Today the kids may cry. Tomorrow, they will laugh again.

May 17, 1990

The Medium is the Mayhem
Red Hot Chili Peppers, Rocking Their Socks Off

RICHARD HARRINGTON

Singer Anthony Kiedis has developed an engagingly allusive description of the music his band, the Red Hot Chili Peppers, plays: "hard-core-bone-crunching-mayhem-psychedelic-sex-funk-from-heaven."

Whatever the name, it's visceral, a flying wedge of sound that connects the frenetic stage antics of the Peppers—truth in packaging would require they be called the Red Hot Mexican Jumping Beans—to frantic audiences that seem to convulse in roiling rhythm.

Over the last few years, the Peppers have been getting gradually hotter, and their increased visibility has occasionally landed them in the hot seat.

"A lot of our venues are getting quite nice, with the exception of this bunker," Kiedis jokes backstage at the University of Maryland's Ritchie Coliseum. Ritchie is a celebration of concrete, that rare hall where the seats—slabs, actually—are likely to do more damage to the audience than the audience could possibly do to them. It's packed for the Peppers' recent concert, and for 90 minutes the area in front of the stage is jammed with hopping fans and slam-dancers, some of whom catch a human wave and body-surf forward, only to be turned around at the lip of the stage by security guards. All night they keep coming, energized by the Pepper's half-naked on-stage antics.

"Since we started seven years ago, the perception has been a frantic, aggressive enjoyment of our band," Kiedis, 27, says proudly. "Our fans have always been very intense, loyal and emotionally moved by us. It's just the numbers are increasing."

It's not just the fan-base that's growing. So is the band's reputation as the Red Hot Chili Perpetrators. In April, Kiedis was convicted of sexual battery and indecent exposure resulting from a backstage incident a year before at George Mason University's Patriot Center. He was fined $1,000 on each misdemeanor charge.

In March of this year, bassist Michael "Flea" Balzary, 28, and drummer Chad Smith, 27, were arrested in Daytona Beach, Fla., after a spring break taping for "Club MTV." Balzary faces misdemeanor charges of battery, disorderly conduct and solicitation to commit an unnatural act after grabbing a woman in the audience, trying to remove part of her clothing and simulating a sex act after she refused to perform a sex act with him. Smith was charged with battery. A trial has not yet been scheduled, and though the Peppers insist the incident was a jest, there are already repercussions: The State University of New York's College at New Paltz banned them from playing a free concert there. In an attempt to salvage the situation, the Peppers sent a videotape of the incident to SUNY, offered to discuss it and said they would sign a contract promising to be on their best behavior. The concert remained canceled.

Kiedis insists the Virginia incident was "blown way out of proportion by both the media and the prosecution. It was a playful thing that happened backstage— there was never any harmful intention. Speaking for my band and myself, we're all very friendly people who would never want to hurt anybody or make people uncomfortable."

In the Florida incident, the band was lip-syncing the song "Knock Me Down," which deals with the 1988 death by heroin overdose of original Pepper guitarist Hillel Slovak.

"We don't enjoy lip-syncing," says Kiedis. "It's not a very musical experience, and it doesn't make sense to us, and the nature of that song didn't lend itself to being phony. It's a very honest song about a very emotional experience when someone that we loved very much died."

On those occasions that they do lip-sync, the band members often undermine the situation by trading instruments and acting up, out of sync. "We started serious, but towards the end, we looked at each other, thought it was stupid, put instruments down and dove into audience," Kiedis says. "Chad and Flea picked up a couple of girls on their shoulders, thinking they would like that—let's dance around on the beach. Someone fell over, a girl was knocked down, and there was some friendly profanity in the exchange—it was a show."

Suddenly, after years without the glare of publicity or the attention of MTV, the Peppers have found perhaps a bit too much of both.

"The climate is terrible right now," Kiedis says, "but the way we've dealt with that in the past is basically to ignore it, and that's always worked for us. We do what we do and we believe in it and we're not going to change what we do for anybody. Somehow we've always managed to slip through the cracks and we've never been hassled up until now with these court cases.

"Once people have experienced us face to face, they know that we're not villains."

Kiedis's father, on the other hand, is a villain—professionally only. One of the mainstays of the Sunset Strip scene in the late '60s and early '70s, Blackie Dammett is a character actor most often cast as "a psychopath or villain," Kiedis says.

"My dad was my hero and idol {when I was} a young teenager," Kiedis recalls. "I wanted to be just like him. We both had real long hair in the early '70s. Then he cut it all off and went to slicked-back, changed his look, and I did the same thing. He studied with Lee Strasberg, and so did I when I was still in high school." In 1978, Kiedis was cast as Sylvester Stallone's son in the punchless "F.I.S.T.," "but then I just got too crazy to handle the responsibility of being a young actor."

Soon afterward, the younger Kiedis's hair was growing out again and he became part of a scene fueled by the "attack-oriented punk rock energy" of bands like Black Flag, The Circle Jerks and Fear. "We grew up listening to these bands, going to see them play," he says, adding that those bands' maelstrom of punk fashion and sledge-hammer rhythms sounded at breakneck pace "are what inspired us to be so physical in our approach to playing music.

"Our sound and our energy is fairly unique to a specific area of Los Angeles—Hollywood," Kiedis explains. "We all went to high school together—Flea, {drummer} Jack Irons, Hillel Slovak and myself. We all met at Fairfax High, we all shared our lives together as kids. The growing-up experience in Hollywood is very intense because there is so much going on there, so much beauty and so much tragedy at the same time, that the sensory input is phenomenal. You've also got the deserts to the east and the ocean to the west, and so the energy in the air is very intense and electric. People are attracted to Los Angeles like a magnet. It was just a matter of time before the pot got to boil."

Kiedis, who sports an Indian totem tattoo on his back and portraits of chief Tecumshe and Sitting Bull (on the credits for the band's latest album, he thanks the latter for killing Gen. Custer) says he had no intention of being a musician until hearing a Defunkt record at age 19. "I used to spin around the house, and I thought how wonderful it would be to make other people feel the way I feel. Then I heard {rapper} Grandmaster Flash and it dawned on me: I can write poetry, and this is my chance to get into a band. I had no training or experience as a singer, but I knew I could hang with the rap. It all kind of took off from there."

Slovak, Irons and Balzary had all been playing music since their early teens; the multi-color mohawked Balzary is also an actor, having costarred in Penelope Spheeris's L.A.-punk epic "Suburbia" and played several other minor roles, including Michael J. Fox's boss in "Back to the Future II."

In 1983 the Peppers finally came together, almost as an afterthought. Someone asked them to create a single song for a punk club happening. The afternoon rehearsal was basically a cappella, with Flea offering a bass line and Kiedis fitting in a sudden rap. "We took the stage and didn't know what to expect," Kiedis recalls. "It was complete anarchy and mayhem, and we destroyed the whole stage."

Obviously, they couldn't do an encore. "We didn't have one. But the owner asked us to come back next week with two songs. We said, 'Yeah,' and we did." That first song, "Out in L.A.," remains the Peppers' show opener.

Since then there have been thousands of shows for loyal and increasingly larger legions of fans, and four albums, each selling better than its predecessors. Along the way, the Peppers have become purveyors of what some have called "white funk," a reference to the band's appreciation of the legacy of George Clinton. "It took us by surprise because we were so unexposed to that kind of music," Kiedis notes. "When we began the band we didn't know anything about Parliament-Funkadelic at all, and it wasn't until after our first record, when people kept coming up to us and said, 'You guys must be totally down with the Funk,' that we looked into it, studied it and realized that it was some of the most beautiful music of the century. And that's when we started to educate ourselves to that music." They also got Clinton to produce their 1986 album, "Freaky Styley."

Then as now, Peppers music is a startling meld of the physical and cerebral. "That's really the challenge," Kiedis says. "The type of music that we play propels us into physical gyrations." There's also a lot of practice. These guys are all great musicians, and they spend enough time with their instruments that it's second nature and they are able to release themselves physically on stage without having to think too much about what they're doing. The tornado starts from the second we get on stage, and we don't fight it, we go with it. It's the combination of precision and anarchy that makes us viable."

Since MTV was slow in opening up to the Peppers, they found other ways to become visable. Their 1988 album featured a cover parody of the Beatles' "Abbey Road," with the Peppers crossing the street naked except for socks on their genitals. They've also been known to perform encores in similar undress. In fact, fans hope, and sometimes expect, to attend a sock hop.

"If you have too many expectations, you can be disappointed," Kiedis says with a shrug."The thing with the socks, it's such a small part of what we're all about. It's just part of the showmanship, a joke. It's a good feeling for us to be on stage naked playing a song, but we usually only do it for an encore. The energy rises, people get a good laugh, but it's really all about the magic that we play, the songs that we write. The ideology and philosophy and the approach or the band is what we prefer people focus on."

The band itself had to refocus after the June 1988 death of Slovak. Irons, the drummer, ended up leaving the band, and it was then that Smith and 19-year-old guitarist John Frusciante joined the group. Kiedis is very direct when he talks about Slovak, with whom he first became friends in junior high school.

"Although he died specifically of a drug overdose, the real cause of Hillel's death was the disease of drug addiction, and when people are afflicted with that particular disease there's very little that an outside force can do, other than suggest possible alternatives for treatment or for help, and we had done all that, especially since I had gone through that myself.

"I've been clean for 21 months now" he adds, "and trying for a year before that to get clean. I was always saying to Hillel, 'I want to spend my life with you and I think we should both be totally clean. There's no room for drugs or alcohol in our life anymore. We've been through that and we've gotten all the good things out of it, and now it's only going to lead to bad things.'

"But until you really have the desire from within to make what at the time seems like a sacrifice and later turns out to be the greatest thing you could have ever done for yourself, until you really have that inner desire to change your life, there's nothing that anybody can say to you. But there's no way you're going to listen to anybody until it gets bad enough that you decide you're willing to do what needs to be done.

"And Hillel hadn't gotten to that point. Still, no one ever expected {his death} because though everyone knew it was a serious problem, Hillel always gave the illusion that he had it under control—he always maintained his business affairs and kept playing music. It was unexpected, and if anybody was going to die, everybody pretty much thought it was going to be me."

The swirl of emotions surrounding Slovak's death is evident in the song "Knock Me Down," in which Kiedis sings, "If you see me getting high . . . knock me down."

"It's basically a love song about a friend, about the madness of missing somebody that you really enjoyed being with, and it actually feels good to talk about it, sing about it and to be able to express it in music. It would be more painful if it was bottled up inside, and I know it's having an effect on people that listen to it."

The updated Peppers have a ritual before each show: In their dressing room at Ritchie Coliseum they form a small circle of four, lock hands and swing their arms in small circles, shouting encouragement at each other, very much like a sports team. "We are four people aiming for the same goal at the same time, and our energy is derived from that," says Riedis.

In fact, a song on the new "Mother's Milk" album celebrates fellow Angeleno Magic Johnson. "We use the Lakers as a guideline for our own team," says Kiedis. The band was supposed to meet with Johnson recently for a news-video shoot, but "just like us, before Magic gets ready to play, he doesn't want to meet anybody because he's focusing all his concentration on what has to be come for the task on hand, which is to win the game."

Meanwhile, don't look for trials, tribulations or criticism to damper the Peppers' on-stage celebration of the physical, the sensual and the sexual.

"In America too many people look at sex and violence as one and the same thing," says Kiedis. "We're here to break down that barrier, because the sexuality or physically of a human being is something that does deserve to be celebrated. It's a very beautiful part of our lives and the lives of many people in this country, but for people to associate sex with something lurid and lascivious doesn't make sense to us, especially when it's done in a good-natured fashion.

"There is a distinct correlation between sex and certain kinds of music, especially in funk, where the rhythmic correlations are undeniable," Kiedis adds. "And there is a celebration of that and that's what it should be, and that's what we promote, not something twisted and devious. It's a very positive energy reflected in the music. Woody Allen said it best: The brain is probably the most overrated organ. Without the physical capacity to enjoy that aspect of life, you're really only getting the half of it."

May 13, 1990

Focus: Country's Faithful Followers

LINDA CHION-KENNEY

Gary Daniels remembers who helped him heal the hurt that tore his heart almost 20 years ago. It was Ray Price, a man he never met, who sang a song he'll never forget.

"I was in the Navy," Daniels says, "and I was married to a very pretty little gal, my high school sweetheart. We split and it just devastated me. I sat and I listened to this song over and over and over on the jukebox, in Virginia Beach, in a little club called the Lamplighter."

Daniels, who is now working on his own country music career, recounts the song, "It Should Be Easier Now," in which Price sings: "The wound in my heart you carved deep and wide, followed and washed by the tears I've cried, but now there'll be more room for love inside, it should be easier now."

Those words, Daniels says, "gave me a light at the end of the tunnel. Here I'm 19 years old, and this is my first love, my true love, and I don't think there will ever be anybody else that could even compare. And all of a sudden this song is telling me: 'Hang on. Just hang on.' It carried me through."

And that, country music fans say, is country's draw: The words and the music carry them through the pain to a place of hope and greater understanding.

At least this was the consensus of dozens of country music lovers interviewed at the 19th annual International Country Music Fan Fair in Nashville last month. They were among the 24,000 performers, fans, promoters, managers, disc jockeys and roadies who attended the up-close, down-home fan appreciation week.

The event, sponsored by the Grand Ole Opry and the Country Music Association and held at the Tennessee Fairgrounds, included 13 shows featuring more than 90 acts—among them Randy Travis, Waylon Jemlings, the Judds, Charley Pride and Charlie Daniels. Seven buildings housed more than 260 exhibit booths, mostly manned by fan club organizers. And many stars hosted breakfasts, luncheons and barbecues for their faithful followers.

Loretta Lynn headlined a 14-act dinner show sponsored by the International Fan Club Organization, a group founded by Loudilla Johnson of Wild Horse, Colo., and her sisters Ray and Loretta. Johnson says it was her idea for "some kind of party for all the fan club people" that led to the first Fan Fair.

"We envisioned it was going to be this huge success," Johnson says, "because we had worked with fans of country music enough to know that if the artist would devote the time, the fans would be there to support them."

Number among them Julie Sbraccia of Boston, who attended her first Fan Fair this year. "It's just something I thought I really should do, even just once," Sbraccia says. "So many stars participate and they stand behind their fan club booths and talk to you. You can actually walk up to someone you really admire, meet them, shake their hand. In rock-and-roll, I don't think you'll ever see something like this."

For Sbraccia, and fans like her, it's all about connection.

"When you listen to somebody's music over and over, you kind of feel like you know him," Sbraccia says. "And then you come here and you meet him, it's almost like you feel you have a friendship. This person whose singing has done something for your life. And it's almost like: 'I finally got to meet that person who contributed to my life.' I might never do it again but I made a memory this time."

Sbraccia is among 30 million people nationwide (an industry estimate) among them President Bush, who listen to country music.

The misconception is that country music "is hayseed, but it's not," says Ronald Cotton, a concert promoter. "And it's not the 'Hee Haw' you see on television."

The stereotype is "twangy and hillbilly," says Lucy Grant, a Cleveland disc jockey who grew up in Bethesda. "And it's so much more contemporary now, with kind of a rock feel to it. It has a lot more mass appeal."

Country music "is everybody from k.d. lang to Hank Williams Jr., with the Kentucky Headhunters somewhere in between. Now you define that," says singer Larry Gatlin. "You can't. It's impossible. And it isn't important."

What is important, Gatlin says, is what country stands for in the minds of those on both sides of the jukebox. And there, some common themes emerge.

"It's the 'Green, Green Grass of Home,' " Cotton says, citing the title of his favorite cut. "It's going back home. We'll never be able to. None of us will. But we try to remember the times as great."

"It's music for the people, everyday people," says Roy Wakely, a disc jockey in Dayton, Ohio. "People can relate to it in the way they live their lives: their love affairs, their ups and downs, their jobs, the hard times and the good times and the bad times."

"When you're down and out," says Michael Powell, of Michigan and a member of country singer Gary Morris's fan club, "you can listen to the music and say, 'Hey, I'm not alone. There's other people out there, maybe not in the same boat I am, but close enough. And they're making it. So I can make it too.' "

That's the key, says Jim Ibbotson of the Nitty Gritty Dirt Band, whose favorite self-penned lyric is: "Dance, little Jean, this day is for you, two people you love stood up to say, 'I do.' Today your mama's marrying your dad."

"We write songs that deal with the events of our lives," Ibbotson says, "and we present them in an easy-to-swallow melody. It's nothing real challenging for anybody to listen to. Plus, if the song is any good, it will touch a chord inside the listener. I think that's why most people tune in day after day, 'cause they find out that somebody else hurts as much as they hurt or felt as elated as they felt."

In other words, country music is about "real people in real situations in a real world," says Jim London, co-host of the morning show on country music radio WMZQ-AM/FM (1390/98.7), the area's third-highest ranked station. And many of the listeners, says news director Kim Leslie, "look at the songs and the artists behind them as their own personal support group."

Support groups provide courage and encouragement from people who share a similar plight, "and you're saying the same thing goes on with a country music song," says Dan Hammer, president-elect of the Tennessee division of the Association for Marriage and Family Therapy. "The finger tells his story, and it's not exactly like my story, but it's close enough for me to say: 'Gee, I hadn't thought about telling my story in those words, but I can really relate.' "

This innate need for identification, for connection, magnifies in times of trouble.

"We listen to music all the time, even just walking around the mall, but we're not always feeling that particular need for support," Hammer says. "But when I'm experiencing a loss, I'm more heightened to words from anywhere. I'm not claiming country music is always artistic. But if it's in a form that can reach past some of our usual blocks, then we'll feel supported. We'll identify with the words."

Some people make the connection through other forms of artistic expression: an opera, a rock song, a poem, a painting, a dance. To focus on country is to "take a piece of Americana to show some very common, ordinary traits that happen to do, with being human," says Esco McBay, a family therapist in Nashville. "They're simply being expressed in this particular way in this particular setting.

"Obviously, behind every piece of art there is a person who expresses that thought or feeling," McBay says. "The music, then the song, becomes a connecting link between that person and the receiver. And so when I respond to that message, when I respond to that song, at some level I'm connecting to that person."

In today's "society of strangers," he says, "you see it even more. We're looking for a person to connect with, a person who understands us."

Garth Brooks, one of those peo ple, found at Fan Fair a connection to the "real people" country music attracts.

"It's people who have started with nothing and built it," says Brooks, 26, whose debut album went gold in May. "They're chasing their dream, you've chased yours. They've given you your dream and now it's time to give something back."

Fan and star alike feel bonded by the values and memories they hold most dear. Fans talk about the stars almost as friends. Stars talk of fans who work hard, take pride in their families, believe in America and make it possible for the stars to live their dreams. And each sees in the other a reflection of himself.

"Hey, I slop hogs, I shovel horse manure and I change diapers," says Pam Perry, singer and mandolin player for Wild Rose, an all-woman band. "I know what that part of life is about."

"It hasn't been that long that I remember being a fan, wanting to meet somebody," adds Kathy Mac, bass player for Wild Rose. "It's the American dream. It really is. Because you've seen somebody come from humble beginnings and suddenly become popular, and people want to meet them and they want to be around them. To people who are trying to get ahead in this world, that gives them hope."

It's a matter of "taking courage in our own lives by the examples of others," McBay says. "The way that I can relate to that is the mentor concept. Most people develop mentors . . . people who . . . in a sense become a model."

Wendell Cox, lead guitarist for the Travis Tritt band, sees that with "I'm Gonna Be Somebody," a song the band sings "about this guy" everybody looks down on "so he wants to make something of himself."

And "most teenagers go through a hard time," he adds. "You get depressed or think about suicide and things like that. I think this song would probably give them a little bit different view of things and maybe help them to go for it, some kind of goal to have in mind, instead of sitting back and being depressed."

To tell a story that inspires, enlightens or entertains, someone needs to put pen to paper. And that's when country comes alive.

Our lives are better left to chance, I could have missed the pain, but I'd have had to miss the dance.

Those words, from a Garth Brooks song, "The Dance," written by Tony Arata, describe a dance "shared underneath the stars above" that for a moment made the world right. But the dance ends and the romance fades, and the song, says Janet Williams of Nashville, begs the greater question: "If you knew something was gonna hurt and break your heart and be painful, would you avoid it? If you did, then you'd never know the sweet part, the good things, the pleasure. And so the pleasure is worth the pain."

If you're gonna throw stones and put on an act, you better move out of your house made of glass.

Those lyrics come from "It Takes One to Know One," a song about a woman who leaves her man because he's been cheating, which "is kind of typical country," says songwriter and singer Robbin Linda Brown, 34. Brown says while she has "a knack for rhyming and timing," she "had to live some life" to give heart to her songs. "I had to hurt a little."

I've looked to the stars, tried all of the bars, and I've nearly gone up in smoke. Now my hand's on the wheel of something that's real and I feel like I'm goin' home.—from "Hands on the Wheel" by Willie Nelson

This theme of going home is a staple of country music.

"We wouldn't need to go back to childhood if our childhood were so perfect that it prepared us for everything that life was going to give us. And so there are some gaps," says family therapist Hammer.

For some people, he adds, a country music song provides "a retreat to a place where things were more secure. And there may be some things we would like to go back and experience because we'd like to have some more out of those experiences."

Such was the case for Ruth B. Swift of Baltimore, who was reminded at Fan Fair of good times with her father.

"He was a balladeer," Swift says, "and I remember as a child growing up, Daddy taking us to see a lot of the old performers." While walking the grounds at Fan Fair, the sound of country in the air, Swift says, the memories washed over her, "and I looked at my sister and said: 'Wouldn't Daddy love this?'

"And so it's personal," she says of her attraction to country music, tears welling in her eyes. "It's personal."

Making Connections

Those interested in country music or country music fan clubs can connect through the following:

The International Fan Club Organization, run by Loudilla Johnson and her sisters, Kay and Loretta, furnishes assistance and information on joining, forming or learning more about country music fan clubs: IFCO at P.O. Box 177, Wild Horse, Colo. 80862-0177.

Country Club, a subsidiary of the Country Music Association. Annual membership is $20, and includes a bimonthly newsletter, VIP concert seating, a toll-free concert hot-line number, and a tape of new artists and a merchandise catalogue. CMA Country Club, 507 Maple Leaf Dr., Nashville, Tenn. 37210-9861. Or call 1-800-767-2900.

Smithsonian Recordings has scheduled an October release for "Classic Country Music," 100 selections recorded from the late 1920s to the mid-1980s. Included is an 84-page book written by Bill Malone, with notes on the selections, photographs of the performers and a reading list. Send $59.96 for records or cassettes, $64.96 for CDs, and $5.09 for postage to: Smithsonian Recordings, P.O. Box 23345, Dept. WT, Washington, D.C. 20026; (202) 287-3738, ext. 369. (Smithsonian Associates, $5 discount.)

For Fans, 30 Seconds of Heaven

Ann Scalise of Brentwood, Tenn., had one goal in mind: to get Randy Travis's autograph to give to her mentally retarded sister.

"I know why I do it," she said in her fifth hour in line for the autograph at Fan Fair in Nashville last month. "But I don't know why people come and stand in these incredible lines for less than 30 seconds in front of this guy. I guess it's their one moment of glory. If they can't get famous, they're going to get close to somebody who is."

"Oh, it's worth it, just to set to meet them," says Sherry Hunt of Greenfield, Ohio, who waited hours at Loretta Lynn's fan club booth. "It's like being a part of their world for a little while."

An autograph, says Esco McBay, a family therapist in Nashville, is evidence of that contact, "reminders of a moment, a piece of time."

Says Tommy Daniel, who researches fan attraction for the Country Music Association: "It's like they {entertainers} live a life that's different from me, and I want to get close to them, to touch them, even if it's just for a moment."

Dozens of fans interviewed in Nashville say they see in the stars living proof that "real" and "down-home" people can, with sacrifice, humility, faith and hard work, overcome formidable odds. And many fans see in the stars a realization of the dreams they treasure.

"Everybody thinks they can sing to a certain extent," says Roy Wakely, a disc jockey in Dayton, Ohio. "They think: 'I can be a singer, but I don't want to because I've got a good job and a family. But that's me, Garth Brooks, if I would have pushed it. He's lived the life for me, and I'm staying home with my safe and secure job with my family.' People think like that."

July 24, 1990

Gary Larson's Re-entry in the World of the Weird

Refreshing New Insights as 'The Far Side' Returns

JAMES KINDALL

A particular look appears on Gary Larson's face as he takes another bite of his steak in an intimate Seattle restaurant.

The expression, something akin to a baby catching sight of its first soap bubble, materializes as the creator of "The Far Side" begins a tale about a type of catfish found in the Amazon, one of the spots he and his wife visited during his recent sabbatical.

The 39-year-old cartoonist explains that this spiny-finned specimen swims into the privates of animals to plant its eggs. "Humans, too," he adds with delight. Once inside, the creature cannot be extracted without an excruciatingly painful operation. Here he stops transfixed, looking like his own drawing of Einstein before a blackboard filled with formulas proving that time actually is money.

Ah, yes. Nature.

"Ha," he says with a satisfied smile. "And they say there's no God."

Of course there's a God. It is the same omnipotent being who pulls a simmering Earth out of a cosmic oven in a Larson drawing while musing, "Something tells me this thing's only half-baked." And it is the same one who returns to his heaven today, New Year's Day, with the appearance of the first new Larson cartoon after a 14-month hiatus.

Refrigerator doors will be populated by fresh absurdities—cows that stand on hind legs, lions that attack tourists' car doors with coat hangers, and dinosaur seminars ("The picture's pretty bleak, gentlemen . . . . The world's climates are changing, the mammals are taking over, and we all have a brain about the size of a walnut.").

Once again, morning silence in offices across the nation will be disrupted by bursts of laughter and the refrain, "Have you seen 'The Far Side' today?"

Larson's lifestyle only hints at the bizarre brilliance that has led to his cartoon's syndication in more than 900 newspapers. His modest, Tudor-style home, in a neighborhood ringing Lake Washington, has a Persian rug, a fireplace, a comfortable couch; all in all, a habitat more cozy than ostentatious.

Gone are the 20 pet king snakes and the 150-pound python he used to have around the house. But evidence of his creature fixation is still present. In one corner is a brass lamp in the shape of a giant cobra. On the wall is a petrified crocodile, a gift from Smithsonian friends trying out a new preservation process. Upstairs in his study are charts of spiders, a stuffed hammerhead shark. Placed affectionately on his drawing board is a chillingly lifelike cast of a coiled rattlesnake.

In person, his manner is the jeans and T-shirt persona of relaxed anticipation. Wire-rim glasses and thinning, collar-length hair grant him grad student chic. Shy and soft-spoken (he rarely gives interviews), he seems flustered by the confines of speech as well as befuddled by the practicalities of life. He seems the kind of guy who might discover cold fusion and, when you pointed out that he had altered the course of history, would reply, "Hum, guess so."

His wife of two years, Toni, has gotten used to the glassy looks associated with his actively wandering mind. She has suggested a stencil for his forehead—"Back in a Moment."

Heading for the kitchen to fetch coffee, Larson returns to announce a "slight disaster" because "I forgot to put the carafe under the coffee maker."

His humor takes quantum leaps at odd moments when it seems like someone has placed a crowbar at the edge of his mind and given it a sudden, sharp tilt. On the way back to the kitchen to clean up the mess, he pauses at the threshold, throws up his hands and mumbles, "Oh no, now my wife's dead!"

Over dinner, he confides that he has always wanted to start a restaurant that serves only cereal. High concept; he loves it. "You'd, like, have the special of the day be Rice Chex or something. And you'd offer a variety of milk from whole to 2 percent to skim."

Discussing the flowers on the table, Toni takes a guess they are freesias, although they might be a false variety, she adds. Her husband is intrigued by the comment. "You know, there's a whole variety of false things in nature like that. Like there's a false killer whale, for insurance." The look appears. "I suppose it's too anthropomorphic to think they're bummed out about that."

No wonder Joseph Boskin, author of "Humor and Social Change in 20th Century America," remarks that Larson has "a peculiar view of life that most of us don't have."

Boskin, a Boston University history professor, recalls, "I was at a seminar with him one time where we both were speaking. He said to me beforehand he didn't know what he was going to talk about. I suggested he talk about where his ideas come from. He said, 'I don't know where my ideas come from.' "

Few cartoonists have made such an impact in a single decade. A man whose 14 cartoon collections have sold 15 million copies here and abroad, Larson is a publishing gold mine.

His creations are copied on T-shirts, cups, calendars and, for the first time this year, Christmas cards. Three of his publications have appeared simultaneously on the *New York Times* Paperback Best Seller list "The Pre-History of the Far Side" is there at present. He won the National Cartoonists Society's award for best syndicated panel of 1985 and 1988. A museum exhibit organized four years ago by the

California Academy of Sciences, featuring more than 400 of his cartoons, just completed its tour of the nation.

What other cartoonist can claim an insect named in his honor? In this case, Strigiphilus garylarsoni.

"The biting louse," Larson explains. "I didn't figure they'd give me a swan."

Newspaper polls regarding comics pages repeatedly show him among the top five in the country. But opinions vary. A South Carolina newspaper subscriber complained in a survey that Larson " . . . is definitely demented." A pair of *Chicago Tribune* readers in a poll countered, " . . . we love the cows, the nerdy kids, the insects, everything. Whatever drugs Gary Larson is on, keep them coming."

That he should be earning a living with a pencil is more the result of fate than calculation. He was raised in Tacoma, Wash., where, he says, he was a nondescript child who collected snakes, lizards, a monkey, a boa constrictor. He and his brother Dan created swamps in their back yard. Such pastimes were encouraged by their father, a retired car salesman, and tolerated by their mother, a secretary.

At Washington State University in Pullman, he rejected biology to study communications, hoping eventually to go into advertising. He has also been employed, as they say, as a Humane Society investigator, half of a banjo duo, and a salesman in a music store. The last job so depressed him that in 1976 he took two days off, sketched a half-dozen cartoons and, to his surprise, sold them for $90 to a wilderness magazine.

Introduced to the world in a panel called "Nature's Way" in the *Seattle Times,* he was dropped after one year because of subscriber complaints. Three days later, the strip was picked up by the *San Francisco Chronicle,* the result of a previous trip in which Larson threw all his work together and was given an interview with an intrigued editor.

Even he is sometimes rocked by the immensity of what his mind has spawned: "I wanted it to be fun, but this whole thing has become such a little empire."

Burnout from nine years of a cartoon-a-day deadline finally drove Larson away from the drawing board, he says. His new obligations will be restricted to turning out five originals a week; papers will also publish "classic" (he blanches at the term) reruns.

The hiatus with Toni included a month-long trip to Africa, two weeks in the Amazon and a four-month stint studying jazz guitar in Greenwich Village, where he roamed unrecognized. Aside from an album cover for jazz guitarist Herb Ellis (jazz is a private passion), he didn't draw a thing. His creative batteries are restored, he says. But where does one find the electricity for an imagination that could conceive of "Custer's Last View"—a ground's-eye shot of a half-dozen grinning Indians? Frankly, he doesn't want to know.

"Why go into therapy to try to understand something that's paying the bills?"

Aware that others who have taken time off from their strips—such as "Doonesbury's" Garry Trudeau—have returned changed artists, Larson says he doesn't know yet what the ramifications of his time off will be.

He may do fewer cows, he says.

But millions of people have been waiting for a new batch of cows for 14 months, he is reminded. The term millions is particularly odious to him. He wavers, then capitulates.

"Well, maybe I'll do more cows."

Unlike the social commentary of a Trudeau or the former "Bloom County's" Berke Breathed, Larson humor deals in sheer, apolitical weirdness that both shocks and tickles with obtuse perspective. Who else would draw disappointed sharks suddenly finding out why swimmers have been fleeing? ("Whoa! Our dorsal fins are sticking out! I wonder how many times that's screwed things up?")

His unique, sometimes macabre humor also has generated controversy. To Larson, this is just the way the buffalo chips have fallen.

"I never sat down and said, you know, what the world needs is a good, sick cartoonist," he says. "This is just the kind of humor that was in my family when I grew up. My Mom and Dad and brother laugh at my work when they understand it. Or when I understand it. It wasn't until later that I was described in words like 'offbeat' and 'bizarre.' "

He still cringes when he remembers a heartfelt letter from a woman who thought one of his drawings made fun of schizophrenics—like her son. But he cheerfully discounts most criticism. His first complaint came from a woman upset with a drawing of Santa Claus studying a cookbook titled "Nine Ways to Serve Venison."

"She was very offended and wanted to know how she was supposed to explain this to her 5-year-old. I thought, come on, lady. It's like, now this 5-year-old is going to grow up and take a shot at the president."

He takes solace now, knowing that none of it matters against the grandeur of environments such as Africa.

Ah, yes. Nature.

"It's wonderful that there's still a place in the world where you can't step out of a vehicle without the risk of being eaten," he says. "I'm glad there's still a place like that. It puts things in perspective."

January 1, 1990

Coping

When Your Kids Go Punk

MARCELA KOGAN

When her 7-year-old son said he wanted to wear an earring, one-time '60s hippie Marilou Legge was horrified. The Silver Spring resident imagined her firstborn turning into a Punk—spiking his hair, boasting metal studs, shooting drugs. Was he hanging out with the wrong crowd? Or was it just a fad? She asked Matthew why he was suddenly turned on to this latest style.

"He said he thought {earrings} were cool," says the 36-year-old manager at Arbitron. "At that time he also wanted to dress surf-ish—long, funny-colored pants. . . . I assumed he was expressing a desire for freedom. So I gave him a dangling clip-on with a green flower that was kind of tacky-looking. No damage was done, and he grew out of it."

Initially, Legge was afraid that Matthew would embrace the punk philosophy, the "violent music, nihilistic attitude." But she watched him closely and didn't notice any drastic change in his behavior. A clean-cut dresser right out of a Bugle Boy ad, 12-year-old Matthew now is competitive in athletics.

Some experts agree that kids who feel loved and frequently interact with parents tend to explore fashionable trends but usually return to family values as grown-ups.

"Engaging in unusual fashion shows the child is independent," says Oklahoma psychiatry professor Wanda Draper. "It's a way for kids to say 'I'm making a passage from child to adolescence, making my exit from parental control.'"

The style, spun off from Britain's punk musicians, sought to shock the establishment in the early '80s by wearing dog-collars, sticking safety pins through their ears, sporting nose rings, and dyeing their hair dayglow orange. By now, portions of the punk style have become chic, even touted by magazines and ad agencies.

"I like being different," says Guadalupe Quinteros, 17, from the District. "One day I may wear jeans with patches, another day I may try a wild hairstyle," she says.

It's when a child's behavior changes drastically, says Draper, that parents "should be concerned. But if they do well in school and continue to participate in appropriate activities, it doesn't really matter what they wear. The fad will give way and kids will go back to wearing conservative clothes."

Former hippies who are now sitting at corporate helms should understand what their kids are going through, since they went through similar phases before they bought suits to fit in with the mainstream. So why are they shocked when they criticize their own kids for trying to be "different?"

The fact is that yuppies are just as embarrassed about their kids' "nonconformity" as their parents were with their style during the '60s. Instead of instituting the rules of childhood—'Do what I say because I'm your father'—moms and dads should find more subtle ways to influence their children's choice in fashion.

Sometimes kids listen to their parents' suggestions; other times they do the exact opposite. Debbie Bailey of Oxon Hill dissuaded her 13-year-old from getting an asymmetric hair cut. "I told her tomorrow there will be something different and she'll want her hair longer. Plus, it could damage her hair."

That was practical advice, which came in handy since Bailey thinks those haircuts look vulgar and uncouth. But Bailey also dislikes heavy makeup and was shocked to see her daughter Davida wearing bright red lipstick, mascara and eye shadow. They talked about this later, and Bailey felt reassured that Davida was just experimenting.

Talking about fashion and negotiating limits gives kids a chance to think about what they are doing and helps parents determine whether their kids' desire to wear tire chains as necklaces is just a fad or a sign of trouble. Also, such discussions reinforce family values.

The parents' goal should be to "restore mutual respect in the relationship" and not control or cave in to the teen, says Bethesda Youth Services counselor Rob Guttenberg. "Say to your kid: 'I see how much you want to have your nose pierced; I'm not crazy about it and would feel uncomfortable being seen with you,' As opposed to: 'You look stupid with that hole in your nose.'

"Parents should move away from the attitude of right and wrong and say, 'As a fellow human being I need to let you know what I believe about what you are doing.' " The kid may still get a nose ring, but the excitement probably will wear out quickly and parents can relax knowing their child is not in trouble.

Contrary to what most adults think, "Teens like to talk things over with parents when they don't feel controlled." William Harris of the District let his mom trim his hair—three inches high—after she suggested that his style probably gave people the wrong impressiion.

"They thought people may associate my hair with Jamaican drug dealers," says the park ranger, also a freshmen at UDC. "I know I'm not a drug dealer. But I take into consideration what they are saying."

Being open-minded and reasonable is easy when someone else's kid looks like a punk. But Paula Jensen of Woodlawn has no intention of letting her 8-year-old wear earrings. "I don't care where he puts them," says Jensen, who swaddles her kid in polo shirts even though he yearns to wear T-shirts. "They connote a different style. We consider ourselves average, middle-class. It was instilled in me that you dress nicely when you go to school."

Like many parents, Jensen. equates "Mohawk" styles, dyed hair and outlandish fashion with low-achievers who get in trouble, even though there is little evidence that links fashion to behavior or intelligence. A study conducted by Jean Larsen and Barbara White of Utah State University compared behavior of college males who wore "deviant hair-length" (long) and those with crew cuts. No difference was found between the two groups regarding psychological security.

Some schools have taken a hard line against nonconforming hairstyle. Eight-year-old Zachariah Toungate of Austin, Tex., has been banished from class since October because he refused to cut his nine-inch wisp of hair, a length that violated his school's dress code. "He couldn't sit with kids at lunch, go to choir or even to Christmas parties," says the child's aunt Jane Toungate.

The family went to court but lost the temporary injunction that would have let Zachariah return to class until the dress-code issue was resolved. The case is on appeal. "Teachers who raise a stink over rattails should be dropped out of the profession," says District educator Leon Leiberg. "Just because someone has a weird hairdo doesn't mean they'll make a beeline to the nearest crack dealer or cause problems. What people find and don't find acceptable beats me."

Parents should examine childrens' behavior, not their dress, to ensure they are okay. If kids eat dinner with family, pay attention, come home at night and don't have glassy eyes, they are probably fine. But if they start hanging out with a different crowd, become totally irresponsible and refuse to pull up their shirt sleeves (to hide needle marks), they could be in trouble.

Margie Weiner of Rockville was nervous when her 16-year-old daughter started hanging out with kids that "are kind of sleazy-looking, with spiked hair and skateboards." She was getting good grades, so Weiner didn't harass her.

"I don't want to be saying no all the time so they don't hear it when I mean it," says Weiner, who is the marketing director of a Rosslyn-based publisher. "You have to fight the right battles."

Margie Lidoff of Bethesda Youth Services spends a lot of time helping parents identify the battles and calming frantic moms and dads alarmed that their kids are shaving their heads, playing loud, heavy-metal music and dressing strangely.

"Our goal is not to change the way teens dress," she says, which is what parents usually want. "I get into the relationship, 'How do you and Suzy communicate about her appearance?' I ask teens: 'Is your dress style interfering with your life, do people look at you and roll their eyes? Is everything okay even though you happen to have pink hair?' "

Sometimes, things are not okay. Says Guttenberg: "If you've got a teen who is into heavy Satanic music, I'm going to explore that because it's not just a power struggle between parents and children. This teen is discouraged."

But most parents Guttenberg talks to just need tips on how to deal with teens who caused few problems before and are suddenly argumentative, defensive and intolerable. "I tell them, 'Welcome to adolescence and let's talk about boundaries you can set. But beware: This is part of the roller-coaster ride.'"

Aprill 11, 1991

Crayola, Changing the Colors of Childhood

HENRY ALLEN

Not that anybody was frightened or outraged to learn that Binney & Smith, the maker of Crayola crayons, is replacing eight colors, but in the manner of sleeping dogs lifting their heads at the first sound of thunder, we paid attention.

TV news was all over this story, and *USA Today* put it on the front page. No wonder. Messing with Crayola crayons is like messing with the rainbow or the spectrum, with the prism of the American psyche.

The facts: Binney & Smith is replacing blue gray, green blue, violet blue, orange red, orange yellow, lemon yellow, maize and raw umber, which will go into the Crayola Crayon Hall of Fame in Easton, Pa., according to company spokeswoman Lina Striglia. In fact, they will be the only things in the Hall of Fame.

They will be replaced by fuchsia, vivid tangerine, jungle green, cerulean, dandelion, teal blue, wild strawberry and royal purple. Only the first four will go into the box of 24, five in the box of 32, six in the box of 48 and all of them in the box of 64—the one with the sharpener—and, of course, in the box of 72, which includes the fluorescents and pastels, though not the legendary flesh, which was renamed peach in 1962 when the company recognized that flesh comes in different colors.

Not all change is bad.

The new ones sound better, to judge from the names. Besides, even if they weren't, it's not as if the company were replacing the original eight crayons introduced in 1903, ones you can still buy today in boxes that say "different, brilliant colors": red, blue, green, yellow, orange, brown, violet and black, double-wrapped in that soft, grippable paper and smelling of rainy days and car trips, a smell of paraffin so memorable it's one of the 20 most recognizable smells among American adults, according to Binney & Smith (the first two being peanut butter and coffee), though it's strange that something that smells as distinct as a crayon has almost no taste, just the feel of those waxy crumbs in your mouth.

We don't need lots of the colors in the bigger crayon boxes—think of what a disappointment silver and gold always were. They looked great, you figured you could do great ray guns and browns with them, and then they just came out shiny gray and brown, really. Though the company says that the "metallics," as it calls them, are often mentioned by adults as their childhood favorites.

We have all crayoned.

Think of this the next time you see some pin-striped executive heavy cruiser gliding down the sidewalk toward you in all his dignity—picture him working away at a spaceship/monster shootout. Know that he felt bad just as you did when he broke one and said to himself he shouldn't have pressed so hard, and tried to pretend it hadn't happened. Finally he had to tear the paper in half and make it two short crayons. These always fell to the bottom of the box when he put them back, which made the other ones stick up too high and so those perfect rows of crayons that were lined up in the fresh box like organ pipes or a choir were ruined.

Ah, the pristinity, the virginity, the infinity offered by a brand-new box of crayons—and then you'd look around the floor of your room at the end of an afternoon of coloring and see the squalid mess of paper and crayons and the stuff your kid brother had scribbled on the wall just as you heard your mother say the three sentences that awoke you from so many reveries:

"Oh.

"My.

"God."

Anyway, after the shock of hearing about the new colors—the first since the fluorescents (hot magenta, ultra green, ultra orange, ultra red, ultra blue, ultra yellow, chartreuse and ultra pink) of 1972—they sound okay. They come out of interviews with 150 kids. The discarded colors are not apt to be missed—they tended to be the ones you used when you ran out of another color, except they never quite matched unless you colored the whole thing over.

"Violet purple—who cares?" says Peter Dunne, 46, a corporate communications manager who lives in North Haledon, N.J.

He learned how to color in his cousins' apartment in Brooklyn. "They had a shoe box full of crayon pieces, two girls. Girls color better than boys. It was there that I learned how to outline areas in the same color. As you get older you learn to color in the same direction, instead of like an asterisk. If you had to fill in big areas it was best to color in circles that overlapped. If you colored until there were layers built up, the crayon clicked when you took it off the paper. When you grow up, you can use oil pastels—they're more like lipstick. The color saturation is great but you don't have the edge control. Grease pencils are fun. When you were a kid, remember how you'd always pull that string back one dot too far? I still like to color. If it rains at the beach and you've already bought sandals you go to the Ben Franklin and get crayons and a coloring book, except they call them activity books now. I leave them behind at the house, and the next tenants come in and their kids say, 'Wow, a major leaguer was here.' "

Binney & Smith makes 2 billion crayons a year. They begin life when you open the box and see that gorgeous chord of color in 72-part harmony (or that perfect octet of the original eight). They end up in dusty cacophony under car seats, behind bookcases, under porches. They melt on sidewalks and windowsills, and they are never the same again.

Your mother carried them in her purse, and after you got tired of looking at the tropical fish at the dentist's office, she'd take them out with a coloring book and say: "Color me a picture."

You'd come back and show it to her.

"I went outside the lines," you'd say.

"That's the best part," she'd say. You still thought it looked stupid.

Your parents told you not to sharpen them in the pencil sharpener, they would ruin it, and you did, and they ruined it.

You could take a fistful of them and draw a whole bunch of colors all at once, and it would look like when the fighters go over at the air show and let out the different-colored streams of smoke.

When they got small enough, you peeled the paper off and pushed them sideways across the page, but without the label you couldn't be sure what color they were anymore.

"If you take off the paper you'll be unhappy when you use purple for black," says Nicholas Isaac DeWolf Allen, 9, of Takoma Park.

These things will not change.

Why doesn't Binney & Smith give us extra red and black ones instead of vivid tangerine? Red and black are the most popular. You always run out of them. They'll still be slipping under back seats when vivid tangerine has gone to the Hall of Fame.

June 14, 1990

Study Questions

Chapter Seven

1. If you are what you eat, as some contend; what do other aspects of life tell us about people's character? Examples, the cars we own (and drive)? The show styles we prefer? Others?
2. Who is the most intriguing person you know (or know about)? Why would you want to write a profile about him or her? What would your first five questions be in an interview with this person?
3. Tom Shales' article on the late Muppeteer Jim Hanson is rich in assessment. Is there someone's talent you admire? Could you write an appreciation of their skill and contributions to their field?
4. Think about the funniest person you know and analyze why he or she amuses you. Share his or her humor with others.
5. Coping articles are a form of service journalism. How would you advise others to deal with a social problem such as discrimination? Loneliness? Offensive behavior?
6. Is there a childhood memory that you treasure that others might share or enjoy? Car games? Fantasies?

8 *Pleasures of the Mind*

In a reflective essay on aesthetics, Henry Allen judiciously selects street observations to set up his thesis that "things are ugly right now." The writer's ability to get incensed springs from a heightened awareness of sordid urban surroundings, including specific examples plucked from a walk, movie, photography show and the news. Intent on making a philosophical statement, Allen posits that bland may be the only alternative to ugly, but it's still a long way from beauty and truth. He often repeats the word "ugly" to make his contention stronger.

Pamela Sommers' article, "'Phantom's' Moveable Feats," literally taken readers behind the scenery of a touring show and helps them appreciate the craft of dramatic production and the intricacies of transportation logistics. Sommers doesn't assume her audience will know much about theatre, so she addresses readers directly ("Whoa, slow down. Too much jargon.") and explains terms in common language.

The profile of author Ishmael Reed captures some of the complexity of an outrageous, funny and decent man. Feature writer Elizabeth Kastor lets Reed explain himself and rant about his paranoia, literary politics, gender, ethnic and multicultural issues. Kastor spins diverse images of Reed: as a creator of highly original work, a compassionate teacher, a confrontational figure in public and in the press and a supportive mentor for young writers.

In the lead to "Artist of the Portrait," writer Judith Weinraub turns the tables on celebrity photographer Annie Liebovitz and has her in a quandary on how to have her picture taken. It's a vulnerable moment for someone obsessed with her career and phenomenally successful. This profile shares insights into Liebovitz's drive and artistic style, raising the aesthetic question of whether her prodigious output is more artistic or photojournalistic.

The devastating affect of AIDS on the arts community is chronicled in this roundup feature, "Fear and Fury" by Paula Span. She traces the brief history of the pandemic and reports on artists' reactions, from benefits to support groups. Span's sensitive coverage touches on economic loss and emotional pain. The article creates a sense of urgency in dealing with this disease as Span begins and ends with the mounting death toll.

Henry Allen's critical essay on the late artist Thomas Hart Benton reports on a long-brewing intellectual controversy over Benton's ranking in American art. Allen's article is persuasive because it draws on his rich knowledge of art and vast vocabulary. The thoughtful piece deftly profiles Benton as a public figure and authoritatively assesses his art and ideas in a long-term context.

Essay: Ugly Ugly Ugly Ugly Ugly— and the Only Alternative is Bland

HENRY ALLEN

Things are ugly right now.

They are also exhausted, fatalistic, sterile, beleaguered and loud, but what you notice is the ugly.

For instance, you decide to catch a matinee of "Total Recall."

On the way to the theater in Dupont Circle you see: four half-shaved heads, a guy urinating in a stairwell and an utter-obscenity T-shirt printed in colors that make you think of a nerve gas factory blowing up. You hear a car a block away erupting with rap music, a sort of sustained grand mal seizure of sound that reminds you of 2 Live Crew and their numbers about ripping apart women's vaginas. You see a man with five days' growth of beard and a pair of fluorescent plastic reflecting sunglasses that make him look like a mutant 1950s starlet. You see a woman with orange hair. "Hey, look at me!" a guy yells at her. He keeps yelling it: "Look at me! Look at me!"

Ugly.

You are puzzled, you are depressed, but you are going to the movies.

In the theater, the K-B Janus, the guy behind you keeps kicking your seat. You look at him but he keeps kicking it. Through the screen you can see a light bulb burning. The movie flutters for a while and then the credits roll, minute after minute of names you've never heard of, but you have to look at them.

"Total Recall" is a sci-fi movie with Arnold Schwarzenegger. He would be ugly too if it weren't for his sense of humor, which makes him coyly grotesque instead. He plays a crazed and vengeful loner, which means he is the hero.

A woman says to Schwarzenegger: "No wonder you're having nightmares— you're always watching the news."

Indeed. How timely. The news is very ugly these days.

Americans like it ugly, apparently. They probably don't like looking at the Romanian AIDS children or the dead, frothing lakes of East Germany or gay activists pelting Secretary of Health and Human Services Louis Sullivan with condoms. But judging from the ratings, Americans like people of the Sam Donaldson sort asking ugly questions that really aren't questions at all because they really say nothing more than "Look at me." And Americans are making "Total Recall" one of the biggest movies of the summer.

Schwarzenegger turns off the news, and then in a few minutes the woman is kicking him in the crotch. Look at him knock her down. Actually, it hardly gets your attention. It's like vomiting, the shouting of obscenities and the gurgling of exotic wounds—you get used to it if you go to the big movies.

Bad guys shoot at Schwarzenegger on an escalator. Our hero grabs a bystandar and uses him as a shield. Then he jams a machine up his own nose until cartilage crunches. This is a high-tech joke about nose picking. The machine picks a high-tech implant out of his nose, thus enabling him to meet a three-breasted whore on Mars and see a guy's hands chopped off by an elevator, thus saving a mutant revolution led by a slime-covered baby who erupts halfway from a man's stomach.

Look at this. Has there ever been anything like it in the history of Western art?

Bosch and Gruenewald, eat your hearts out. Goya, forget it. The history you have to look back to would be something like public flogging or the medieval pastime of cat butting, in which a cat was nailed up and people tried to butt it to death with their foreheads before it tore their faces off. Or maybe you have to look back only as far as cable news last week, where you could watch dwarf tossing, people picking up a dwarf and throwing him across a room, a sporting event. Or to the sort of performance art that Sen. Jesse Helms has found to be a target of opportunity lately—a guy urincting on stage or a woman with an act involving sticking yams in herself.

You leave the movie. You think: There must be finer things in the American arts just now.

The beautiful flower photographs by Robert Mapplethorpe come to mind. If you went to the Mapplethorpe show at the Washington Project for the Arts when Helms et al. were complaining about the govermnent paying for obscenity, you saw beautiful flowers and beautiful nudes. Perhaps they were a little overwrought, but they were beautiful. There was room after empty room of them. Why were the rooms empty when there were people waiting outside with umbrellas—the educated, thoughtful, art-loving people of America, the people who aspire to the finer things in life and will stand in the rain to see them?

As it turned out, these people wanted mostly to see the Mapplethorpe pictures of subjects such as himself with a whip handle stuck up his rectum. Of course. That was what all the scandal was about. They were such upstanding and progressive citizens, huddled there in the room with the whip-and-rectum stuff, they made you wonder if you were doing something wrong by looking at the flowers.

Anyway, you leave the theater. After the movie, Dupont Circle looks good by comparison, you can say that much.

Later the same afternoon, you turn away from the gross commercial opportunism of Hollywood and seek respite in modern literature, high-art stuff. The first thing you pick up is *The Quarterly,* Summer 1990. It is an anthology of short stories, poetry and drawings published by Random House and edited by Gordon Lish, whose stock is high among the literati.

The first line of the first story reads: "She was out of practice and he wanted practice, so they started kissing one another."

This sounds promising. The boy puts his tongue in the woman's mouth and it tastes of "warm sweet water," which is good too. Then it turns out the boy is kissing his mother. In the next story a daughter sexually impales herself on her father. Skipping around reveals a poem about a boy who wets his pants: "Stinking cotton at my crotch/ which neither time nor heat could wash." Another story is about a woman who keeps sneezing in the direction of her husband. "I felt it all over, dampening my hair and dripping down my forehead and wetting my eyebrows, all these prickles of gooey snot sticking to my cheek and chin." There is a drawing of oral sex in the back, along with a story in which the characters talk about Gordon Lish, the editor. Look at him.

Not everything right now is ugly, but the other choice is not beautiful, it is bland, and you can't look at it for very long.

Bland is the triumph of taste over style. Bland is the world according to home decorating magazines, Valium, shopping malls and managers of all the bureaucracies of this country—the corporations, colleges and governments. It is all personality and no character, all consumer, no producer. It is a spiritual condition akin to having a psyche that is sanitized for your protection, maybe with one of those chemical canisters of the sort that turn the water in your toilet blue.

Bland is life lived in a fog, a cloud of unknowing that perhaps can be penetrated only by ugly:

By Andrew Dice Clay, who is the adult version of the kid in sixth grade who knew more dirty words than anyone; by Madonna, with her nun-flouting fetish costumes and an audience that will pay to see a female Donald Trump in a 1950s push-up bra; by the funny, sad and perceptive but ugly squalor of "The Simpsons" on television; by the maniacal speed-crazed screaming of "Who Framed Roger Rabbit"; by the University of the District of Columbia, trying to spend more than $1 million for a sculpture called "The Dinner Party," in which each of 39 place settings is set with a representation of a vulva; by "Modern Primitives," a book that shows genitals split, mutilated, transfixed with pins and punctured by rings, all of this described and photographed as "anthropology"; by all the television dramas in which people simply shout at each other with indignant fury—"If you think I'm letting one rotten egomaniac like you destroy this whole damn investigation, mister, you've got another think coming . . ."

Look at them all.

There has always been ugliness in the arts, much of it in this century. Moderns have demanded the real thing, the truth, in a tone that suggested they really believed they could get it. They wanted "authenticity." Ugliness delivers authenticity, all right. Think about Hemingway's night thoughts in a story called "Now I Lay Me," or T.S. Eliot's "The Waste Land," or Paul Cadmus's paintings of 1930s social realist squalor, or Stanley Kubrick's movie "A Clockwork Orange" with its futurist rape and sadism, or Alberto Giacometti's molten-drip sculptures that look like incinerated ghosts.

The old ugliness was there to show the truth we had lost and could only hope for. Now, there is an exhahsted, end-of-the-world feeling that suggests we've moved on to a place where truth and beauty are irrelevant.

Oooh, truth. Beauty.

Look at them. It makes you squirm a little to say them, doesn't it? Things are ugly right now.

July 29, 1990

'Phantom's' Moveable Feats

The Logistics of Taking a Spectacle on the Road

PAMELA SOMMERS

The driven, disfigured Phantom and the young opera singer Christine Daae, with whom he is obsessed, have embarked on one of the most magical journeys in theatrical history.

Wending their way across and down a labyrinthine passageway that runs from ceiling to floor, they descend to the shore of a moonlit, underground lake. All at once, the two are in a Venetian gondola bedecked with richly tapestried pillows, drifting through clouds of mist. Great clusters of flaming candles and ornate candelabra rise dreamily from this watery expanse, and the boat swirls languorously around them until it arrives at the Phantom's lair.

As miraculous as that scene from "The Phantom of the Opera" may be, it is even more of a miracle that it can be re-created at the Kennedy Center and other theaters around the world—with all its Broadway spectacle intact. For taking a show such as "Phantom" on the road is rather like dismantling Mount Rushmore—and reassembling it on the East Coast.

"Most shows you can set up in a couple of days, maybe a week," says Robert Could, production manager for the Washington incarnation of "Phantom," now in previews at the center's Opera House in preparation for its 97 percent sold-out, 14-week run that officially begins next Thursday. "In this case it's taking four weeks. There are so many more pieces to put together," he says—the understatement of the season.

"Every time the show is rebuilt, there are new ideas that go into play," Gould says. For instance, when "Phantom" premiered in October 1986 at Her Majesty's Theatre in London, there were sequences in which stagehands actually cranked some of the show's scenery by hand from a basement machine room.

For "Phantom's" Broadway run, producer Cameron Mackintosh and composer Andrew Lloyd Webber and their associates decided that New York's Majestic Theater would have to be thoroughly refurbished to suit the show's needs. At a cost of $1 million (paid by the Shubert Organization), the theater was enlarged, its basement excavated to make way for—among other things—102 trapdoors that allowed the candles to rise out of the underground lake; the dressing rooms were moved; and a fire curtain and sprinklers were added. Before the show opened two years ago in Los Angeles, that city's Ahmanson Theatre weathered substantial alterations as well.

It was Gould's task to supervise the transformation of the Kennedy Center Opera House into set and costume designer Maria Bjornson and lighting designer Andrew Bridge's replica of that other, Belle Epoque venue—the 1880s Paris Opera House that is the physical and spiritual center of "Phantom." To understand the immensity of the $10 million project, one had only to visit the production manager backstage during this month's preparations. There, crew members, drilling and hammering like crazy, installed thick bunches of cables in the floor, putting down an entire stage covering specially designed for touring purposes, and setting up the special rigging needed for the famed 1,200-pound plummeting chandelier (of which more later). An ornate proscenium arch encrusted with immense golden figures was constructed around the Opera House stage.

But for the chandelier, those items are, in fact, duplicates, so that "Phantom" can be simultaneously performed and readied for performance. When the show closed in Fort Lauderdale, Fla., two weeks ago, a raft of stagehands pulled an all-nighter loading the remainder of the equipment needed for the Washington engagement—the chandelier, costumes, props—into 13 semis.

In Washington, "we began with a couple days of 'pre-advance'—putting special structural steel up in the ceiling that makes it able to hold on to the chandelier and the proscenium," Gould says. "Then the major pieces of the show—the 'travelator,' the deck, the proscenium, the opera boxes—started loading in.

Whoa, slow down. Too much jargon.

The travelator, he explains, is the part of the set that moves both vertically and horizontally and allows the characters to travel on various levels, rather like a bridge suspended between two towers. The deck is the movable stage cover that is transformed into the candlelighted underground lake. Though it took two years for Mackintosh's staff to develop and fine-tune it, this essential part of the touring machinery has eliminated the need to dig up theaters hosting the show. "In New York and L.A.," says Gould, "the candelabra are down in the basement and rise up out of the floor. But in this touring production, they ride in on a track from the wings. It's the same number and type of candles, but it's so much easier technically."

He is quick to add that the effect is identical to the original.

There are other refinements for the touring show. For his dramatic appearance perched inside the arch atop the proscenium frame, the actor playing the Phantom on Broadway is required to climb a precarious set of steps; at the Kennedy Center, though, he simply rides an elevator to the top. For the lavish "Masquerade" number—in which dozens of gorgeously costumed singers and mannequins seem to float down an immense staircase—the New York stage crew was required to accordion-fold the staircase immediately after the scene; in the spacious Opera House, it is simply pushed back.

"The Kennedy Center has been an unbelievable pleasure," says Gould, who joined the "Phantom" tour eight months ago. "The facility is wonderful and the stagehands are among the best in the country."

Rather than celebrate its state-of-the-art computerized light and sound boards, Mackintosh, the most contemporary and media-wise of producers, prefers you to perceive "Phantom" as a mystery-laden ode to a bygone era. "Illusion has always held a fascination for people," Mackintosh said during an interview by phone last week from his London office. "Indeed, the sort of technology that we use in this show is patterned after 19th-century technology, only we have the electric motor to replace 20 sweating stagehands."

Mackintosh cites the chandelier and the travelator—which he refers to as the "moving bridge" as the two "really special effects," describing the latter as "a sort of black-box illusion, in which highly decorated props float about and connect with the eye rather than the stage."

He describes "Phantom's" endless flying swags of brocade drapes as wiping away one scene and introducing the next, rather like the technique used in early films. The effect of the candles rising from the floor is based on the old trapdoors in Victorian theaters. And he points out the show's broken mirror and the odd angle of Christine's dressing room are components of a mythic, Gothic world, where everything looks real but isn't quite.

Back in Washington, Gould takes a less romantic approach to the subject.

"Technology is a big part of the show," he says. "It is a lot of what people come to see and what they hear about. There's no denying it, it's something the American public likes these days."

And it's also a major part of the production crew's responsibilities.

"Phantom," Gould says, "is a very complicated show. And it has been intricately choreographed—every automation piece, every timed sequence. . . . We have all these computers set up in this corner backstage, and it's like a nerve center. I did 'Dreamgirls' for a 61-city tour and that was a fairly complicated show, and 'Legs Diamond,' that was extremely complicated—there were two very large restaurant sets that turned and danced around the stage. But there are only a couple of shows that are in 'Phantom's' class—'Starlight Express' and 'Les Miserables.' "

So what happens if the nerve center fails? If the chandelier comes unhinged?

"The way this automation has been designed, it doesn't really break," says Gould confidently. "And there are so many safety precautions hooked into the chandelier that it's very rare that anything might go wrong. Once in a while, the boat—which is radio-controlled—may not work, and the Phantom has to drag it around. But nothing of major proportions has happened since I've been around."

Mackintosh, however, remembers a few technical snafus: the time the candles rose out of the lake and blew up simultaneously; the time when, during a test run in Vienna, the chandelier shattered in the middle. But he points out that these incidents did not occur in American productions.

"Touch wood," he chuckles.

May 30, 1991

The Writer and the Joys of Paranoia

*Ishmael Reed, Agitating and Satirizing
in His Barry-Inspired Play*

Elizabeth Kastor

Ishmael Reed is pulling documents out of his blue nylon bag and examples out of his memory. Articles from the *New York Times, The Washington Post.* Interviews on NPR, ABC. Exchanges of letters in *Ms., the Nation.* Here, he says as he offers each new reference—one more example of the duplicity of government, the bias of reporters, one more clue to the reality hidden behind the obfuscations of white culture. Evasions, secret societies, official lies and inconsistencies are everywhere. Here—just look.

"I think paranoia is a good thing," the novelist, essayist and publisher is saying. "I think for women and minorities in this country—they've earned their paranoia. Some of the things they felt were happening, were happening. In the '60s, there was secret surveillance by the government."

He does this part so smoothly now—defending himself against a charge of paranoia—because he's done it so many times before. A lecturer in English at the University of California-Berkeley, Reed is a highly praised novelist who for two decades has been writing wild, satirical novels and saying wild, confrontational things. He knows people think he is excessively prone to seeing demons. He knows and he does not mind.

"Paranoia—someone once called it a heightened sensitivity." He laughs, a sharp gust halfway between amusement and sardonic punctuation. Reed's heightened sensitivity has found its latest outlet in a play. "Savage Wilds II" is a one-act satire about two female television producers who are so desperate to succeed in their careers that they agree to assist an obsessed U.S. attorney in constructing a "honey trap" to catch—yes, you guessed it—the black mayor of Washington.

"This Barry thing, I really studied it in a hermeneutic fashion—cabalistic," says the longtime resident of the academic world. "I could see what was coming." Sex, drugs, a secret government plan against a black man—the Barry sting might as well have been crafted for Ishmael Reed. The play is currently being performed by the BMT Theater in Emeryville, Calif., and its Oakland-based author has hopes it will someday see Washington.

"Using fiction, I'm able to speculate and raise questions about the Barry case," he says. "When Marion Barry bragged about his sexual prowess in a *Los Angeles Times* article—that's an ancient thing, there's a sexual competition between white men and black men in this society. I thought he would be bagged for that kind of comment. In my tradition, the Afro-American tradition, you raise issues that people may feel uncomfortable with, but they should be raised nevertheless. I think all our great American artists—Lenny Bruce, for example—have done this, because I think too often the truth is shielded by protocol."

Reed has been hailed as a strikingly original writer and is routinely listed among the preeminent black authors of his day. His eight novels, which include the highly praised "Mumbo Jumbo" and "Flight to Canada," are part parody, part voodoo, part black vernacular, part comic book. "They call it postmodern," he says, smiling, of the critical descriptions of his work. Personally he thinks his style was formed by the television and comic books of his youth, but if They want to give it any number of fancy labels, he's not objecting—with the critical tags come invitations to a perpetual round of international conferences and symposiums.

"If they call it postmodern, I get a trip to Italy," he says. "They call it post-structuralist, and I get a trip to France. They call me an African American Writer, and I get a trip to Washington."

But he has received other labels as well: a misogynist, a troublemaker, an artist who sometimes draws with a stroke so broad his works get lost in blots of exaggerations. In fact, his satire can occasionally veer into the merely nasty. But when he reads his work out loud, the giddy joy he takes in his own outrageousness is contagious.

That's how it was last week when Reed read "Savage Wilds II" for about 150 people at the Smithsonian Institution's Resident Associate Program. Dialogue that seems fatally heavy-handed on the page takes on a loopy, comic logic when shot out by the fast-talking author. The Smithsonian audience roared and croaned, and Reed laughed along.

Nobody comes off well in "Savage Wilds II," from the preening, drug-and-sex-hungry mayor to the knee-jerk feminists who set him up. The president of the country, for example, borrows FBI tapes of Martin Luther King's sex life for private listening. But the villain is clearly the U.S. attorney, who is so determined to trap the mayor he has set up a video camera in the mayor's bathroom. ("Yellow toilet paper," one character muses. "I wonder what that means?")

"This is not based on anyone you know," Reed interjected to general amusement while reading a scene between the mayor and his wife. "This is all fiction."

And scatological fiction at that, so don't look for many quotes in this family newspaper. Much of what is funny is the fact that these things are being said by a pudgy, graying author standing behind a podium in the marble-lined Hirshhorn

Museum auditorium. This is the stuff of jokes traded among friends. The listeners giggle like children scribbling dirty jokes on the walls of the school bathroom.

"The critics always tell me I shouldn't write plays," Reed says and pauses, a comedian teasing the crowd. Then—"Which only encourages me to write them."

Score: Reed 1, Critics 0.

"The critics always tell me to retire," he says.

The audience laughs, dismissing all who oppose this author.

Score: Reed 2, Critics 0.

Reed's relationship with critics has become particularly testy over the past few years, especially following the 1986 publication of "Reckless Eyeballing," a scathing story about two feminists who torment a black male playwright. A number of critics dismissed the book, which appeared around the same time as the film of Alice Walker's "The Color Purple." Because Reed—like many other African Americans—was offended by the portrayal of black men in that movie, his soon became a familiar voice in a tense public debate. He was unafraid to criticize black women writers for their depictions of black men, or to accuse white feminists and the publishirg industry of encouraging such works out of less than honorable intentions.

"I hate to say this, but we're in a very bland period in American culture because of all the power that white middle-class women have acquired," he told *Publishers Weekly* last year. "What we have now—I call it 'Men Stink' literature—comes from women who grew up in privileged situations; their creative work doesn't have the kind of hunger, the drama, of people who have real problems. These women turn out melodramas in which the women are all good and the men are all bad."

Soon, women were meeting him and saying things like this: "I heard from a friend in Chicago that you hate women."

He doesn't care what friends in Chicago think. "Black feminists in private will say what I say, but not in public. They'll set me up in the newspapers and then ask for job recommendations. It's all a performance. I finally saw it as a performance and decided I can go to town and be the villain to someone's Hulk Hogan—'Intellectual Wrestling Mania!' "

Just how much of the public Ishmael Reed is a performance remains open to question. Despite his statements about feminism, through his various literary magazines and publishing ventures he has supported many black women writers. "I was the first to publish Terry McMillan," he says. "I have good relations with Toni Morrison and Toni Cade Bambara."

But he will not stop the verbal agitation. "It's good to raise the temperature, because if you raise the temperature, maybe you'll have a cure."

After all, he has written, God "is a trickster." And God, apparently, created a world full of shifting, fooling creatures. "In our tradition we have a figure of satire—guije," he explains. "His job is to show each man his devil. He's a trickster figure. He comes from Haiti, but maybe originally from Africa."

Haiti. Africa. Perhaps he now resides in Oakland.

Surely it would take a trickster nature to enjoy so fully the shock with which Reed's opinions are often received. With his books and statements, he pokes at American culture, daring people either to keep up with him or through their defensive reactions to provide him with future ammunition.

But at the moment, Reed the trickster is not in Oakland but in a Washington hotel. The phone rings and he becomes the multicultural czar of California, the man to whom authors of all hyphenations—African-American, Japanese-American, You-Name-It-American—turn to seek publication, introductions and other forms of help.

"Just send her out there," he is saying about an anonymous writer. "We can put her in touch with some Native American writers we have in Alaska."

Reed's interest in the varied cultures of the United States is decades old and led to his creation of the Before Columbus Foundation, which honors and supports minority authors, and I. Reed Books, which publishes them. His new magazine, the latest in a series, is called *Conch* and has a similar goal. "I've found the problem in the United States is that not only are whites not acquainted with black history, but also with their own ethnic history. That influenced the polarization in this city over Barry. Whites didn't know the problems blacks have had with this Justice Department since the '30s."

By now his individual tastes have spawned a bureaucracy that has overtaken him. ("At the Before Columbus Foundation they don't even want me anymore," says the 52-year-old author. "I'm too old.") He often speaks in the plural, as if expressing the opinions of a movement rather than those of a single author. That movement now includes two daughters who write, a 29-year-old fledgling novelist and a 13-year-old poet whose second book is being published by a Native American press.

Much of America is now waking up to the realities of multiculturalism, but it should probably come as no surprise that Ishmael Reed is not satisfied with whatever progress there has been. "The word 'multicultural' has been co-opted," he says. "We think it's interchangeable with multiethnic, but I think what's happening is the well-heeled cultural groups like the opera and the symphony have been co-opting it to receive funds. You get a big grant and get two black students to come to Verdi."

Although Reed is unlikely to publish anything by an underappreciated male WASP, his definition of multiethnic is a broad one. Irish Americans, he thinks, and Italian Americans are often as poorly educated about their past as any other citizens. His social scope is broad, and he intends to broaden his literary reach as well. Reed is now studying Japanese and working on a novel that will be bilingual, or perhaps trilingual, with the addition of Yoruba. How's that for a multicultural experiment?

"I'd like to write a novel that transcends the border," he says. "Many black novelists have gone to Europe. We have a great expatriate tradition. But instead of going into exile in the '60s, I thought I'd go into exile in my own country. I went to Seattle and then California. And so, firmly exiled in his own land, he continues his tricks.

August 31, 1990

Artist of the Portrait

Photographer Annie Leibovitz Shooting Through Life

JUDITH WEINRAUB

Annie Leibovitz strides out of the National Portrait Gallery searching for a place to pose, looking for all the world as confident as the celebrities she photographs. In charge. Electric. Her handsome profile plucked off a Picasso vase. Ready to do the weird things for art that her subjects have been happy to do. Bette Midler under a bed of roses. Lauren Hutton in the mud. The Rev. Al Sharpton getting a permanent.

But wait.

How should she stand? And where? "Is this right?" she asks. "Is this good enough? What should I do?"

Leibovitz, 41, has solved the eternal what-should-I-do problem by working as fast as she can. The result: a 20-year body of work chronicling everybody who's anybody in American popular culture of the '70s and '80s—and a life that is her work.

Today, when an 80-portrait retrospective, "Annie Leibovitz Photographs 1970-1990," opens at the Portrait Gallery, that body of work will be celebrated. The exhibition continues through Aug. 11. A second, larger exhibition opens at the International Center of Photography in New York in September and will travel around the United States and Europe after that. A book she always hoped to do when she was 40 (which inspired both exhibitions and will bring her a reported $1 million) will be published in the fall.

But the question is still one that nags at her—and one that reporters don't let her forget.

Should she be the record-every-minute mirror of pop culture that led her to become the first chief photographer of *Rolling Stone* at 22 and the darling of *Vanity Fair* a decade later? Should she be the let-everything-loose impetus of her startling set-up shots of the '70s? The photojournalist? The serious photographer? And just what is she going to do in the '90s, anyway?

It's enough to make a legend weep. Instead, she is courteous, accommodating, eager to please.

This has been an amazing week for the 1967 graduate of Silver Spring's now-closed Northwood High. TV cameras rolling. Friends and family flying in from all directions to join the festivities. Every day she's been on display—for a time, as famous as her subjects.

"This is the highest honor that my work can possibly have," she said, choking back embarrassed tears at the Portrait Gallery press conference midweek. "It's a wonderful moment."

Ever since Leibovitz started taking her photography seriously 20 years ago, she hoped that moment of recognition would come. "But I didn't know if it would happen in my lifetime," she says softly.

She bought her first camera in Japan in 1968, on her way to the Philippines where her father, an Air Force colonel, was stationed. At the San Francisco Art Institute, where she went to college, she switched her major from painting to photography, partly because she had started taking pictures for *Rolling Stone* and partly because she realized her adolescent dream of being a painting teacher during the day and an artist at night did not represent success. "I always wanted to do things really well," she says.

Rolling Stone was a great adventure. "I didn't take it lightly," she says, of the world that allowed her to photograph John Lennon for the first time in 1970 and the last time just two hours before his death. "There was a seriousness and an obsession about the work I really loved." Like one of her idols, French photographer Jacques-Henri Lartigue, she wanted to spend her whole life taking pictures.

Leibovitz was successful from the start—only 25 when she was commissioned by the Rolling Stones to document their concert tour in 1975—though she had little self-awareness and not much of a sense of self. (Before an assignment in Italy early on, she recalls, a friend took her aside and advised her to get a bra. "She was right," says the lanky six-footer. "But living in San Francisco, what did I know?")

Nevertheless she had a strong sense of what she was doing, and she plunged headlong into doing it, giving her personal life little thought. "Home" was not a concept she thought about.

"I had the camera with me all the time," she recalls. "I was young and impressionable and I lived inside each photo assignment. I wanted to photograph everything I saw and did—to really report my life. I had a great time. It was hard to give up—being on the road with the Rolling Stones, turning up in Bar Harbor to camp out at Norman Mailer's house—I never went home."

She measured herself then—as she does now—by her own high standards. And the self-criticism is relentless. "If I get five great photographs a year, I feel good," she says tentatively, clearly believing the number is nowhere near enough. Her 1983 book came too early, she worries. It represented only one segment of her work and technique. What on earth was she doing in 1977-78, she asks herself. The years looked a little thin when she went through her files for her new book. "Am I too serious," she frets. What should I do?

The difference, of course, is that now she's become a very big deal—not only a major name in magazines but also the creator of a portrait campaign for American Express (which underwrote her retrospective) and a major contributor to the Gap's celebrity ad campaign.

So on the downside, there's her reputation to worry about. But on the upside, she's in a position to hold others to her standards. A staff frees her from worrying about the logistics of her life. She can build a backup day into her contracts in case she needs it for just the right shot. She can even demand specific and tight parameters for using transparencies from the Portrait Gallery press kit. It's simply too risky otherwise.

After all, she confesses, she's more comfortable when she knows the drill—"I like the rules," she says. "There's work being done. I have a hard enough time going out to dinner and having a conversation."

Though, rules or not, she can't help but try to take charge. Two icons of popular publishing (*Rolling Stone's* Jann Wenner and *Vanity Fair's* Tina Brown) have tried to give her instruction. "I pretty much end up doing what I want to do," she says. "I rely on myself a lot. . . . I was taught or figured out early on that it was nice if a photograph had a little piece of news or information or told a little story."

She also relies on the instincts of her subjects, and quibbles with the notion that she gets people to do unnatural things. "In everything that I do—even in the more produced photos—the ideas are derived from real life," she says. "My ideas are always heightened reality from the person's life. . . . I don't feel like I'm asking anyone to do things they don't want to do or wouldn't do.

"And I always manage to get done what I want—though I don't think it works to push your point of view."

Intimacy with her subjects is not a part of it. She prepares, of course ("you can't count on other people to have an idea. I know enough to know what I need to do"), but she mostly knows people through their work, their image. "The days of making people relax are over," she says. "It's all about work. We develop a relationship through work."

Work is, after all, where she feels most comfortable. She doesn't hang out with the celebrities she shoots. (When she was younger, people like Jerry Garcia and Linda Ronstadt were friends, but she's less comfortable with crossing the line now. "It's left over from the journalistic creed," she says. "You're on the other side. I'm there just to take the photograph. It protects me.")

And even when she works with someone she thinks might be really nice to know, there is little time for such a luxury. Or for the friends she already has. "I'm not a good person for 'friend' friends. My friends know that," says Leibovitz, who gave her pals portrait photographs of themselves for Christmas. "My work is first, and I see them when I can."

In her rare free time, she admits to a passion for taking care of herself, something she's learned to do only recently. She's gone off to a health spa a few times after she finished *Vanity Fair's* yearly Hall of Fame photos, and went this year after she finished her book. "I knew if I didn't go, I was going to die," she says. But even that, she admits, is for the work. "I really need legs when I work," she says, "so what I'm doing is rebuilding my strength."

She still doesn't spend much time at home. When she returned to her Upper Fifth Avenue apartment in Manhattan last veek, she knew she'd be heading to Milan on May 4 to supervise the printing of her book. But before then, she has to shoot two assignments for Vanity Fair, one album cover for Bruce Springsteen ("we've had two sessions but I don't think I have the picture yet"), one group of portraits for the Gap and something for American Express.

"Sometimes it feels like I'm visiting New York," she says. "For whatever psychological reasons, I like to keep busy. I like to keep moving. It's worked for me." So she rushes back and forth across the Atlantic, in and out of New York, to Florida, Japan, Germany. And when she's really lucky, she steals time to go to a rented house on Long Island. "I see it maybe eight days a year, but knowing it's there is really nice."

Leibovitz says she is learning that she needs life to feed the work, but she knows full well that's hard for her. So far the work has always come first.

And with luck, it can nurture as well. Recently, her work (in the form of her portrait campaign for American Express) took her to Europe and Asia, and whole new ideas opened up for her. "I've been very fortunate in my commercial work," she says. "It helps feed the editorial work that is my first love."

Because she's interested in ideas for simpler portrait work now. In photojournalism too. And for new ideas for the set-up, very theatrical photos that made her famous.

"I want to learn to do more in order to have it all available to bring with me," she says. "I'd like to have a palette of styles. I don't want to be stuck."

It's unlikely of course that will happen—not that she's really worried.

"I'm happy doing exactly what I'm doing," she says. "It only reinforces the idea that if I keep on doing it, it gets more interesting. I always saw the work lasting a long time. I can do this the rest of my life. It's only going to get better."

April 19, 1991

Fear and Fury

AIDS in the Arts—The Context; Living Through the Losses

PAULA SPAN

The mail arrives at Simon Watson's gallery in SoHo in the early afternoon, usually. Each day's delivery brings a few more rectangular slips of paper for the Witness Project, the blanks filled in with ballpoint or pencil.

Last name, first name. Date of death. Sculptor, poet, curator, musician—circle all that apply.

This day's mail adds five artists to the growing list. A couple from Maine submits the name of their son, a painter and photographer who died on Halloween. A man from Jersey City remembers his dancer friend who died two years ago. Since the forms were mailed out in December, with instructions to photocopy them and pass them on like a sorrowful chain letter, more than 1,500 torn-off slips have made their way back to this art-project space on Lafayette Street.

Any number of events could have prompted Watson to begin collecting the names of those in the arts who've died of AIDS. It might have been the phone call from his shaken father, who at 63 had lost his first close friend, to cancer. "My friends started dying about nine years ago," the younger Watson realized afterward. "There hasn't been a day that's gone by that someone hasn't told me he's seropositive, or gone to the hospital, or died. That's an extraordinary thing for someone who's 35."

In fact, however, the Witness Project came into being because curators had begun to select artworks for the Whitney Biennial and Watson urged that the last biennial of the '80s ought to recognize the impact of AIDS. When he went to see the exhibit, he was so infuriated at what seemed to him a willful evasion that he went through the catalogue with a rubber stamp, every few pages stamping DENIAL, in red letters. DENIAL. DENIAL.

He and his friend Jerry Saltz, an art critic and editor, began talking about what Saltz calls "a sense of loss, palpable but unmeasured."

"There was no handle for it," Watson adds. "When I talked to curators or artists, there was no way to say who or how many."

"Let's collect the names," Saltz suggested to him. "No one else is keeping track of us; we'll do it ourselves."

New York's cultural community—its dance troupes and opera companies, theaters and museums and galleries—has suffered grievously from AIDS. In trying to describe this time, people resort to metaphors of war. They talk of feeling under siege; they use the word "devastation."

Yet as Watson found, the toll remains difficult to calculate. Numbers from the New York City Health Department indicate that, based on a subset of cases, at least 13 percent of the AIDS cases for which occupation is known have occurred in what may be loosely defined as the arts, but that figure is likely to be an underestimate.

There are other benchmarks as well, lacking in scientific validity yet full of meaning:

LaMaMa, one of the city's prime wellsprings of experimental theater, has counted close to 60 deaths among people who've worked with it at various times—playwrights, set designers, performers, stagehands.

Beverly Sills, former general director of the New York City Opera, recalls delivering a dozen eulogies (and attending many more funerals) over three years for company members, employees and associates. "I don't do eulogies anymore," she says. "I felt almost ghoulish. I attend but I don't speak . . . . I can't."

Anne Livet, whose arts-oriented special events firm, Livet Reichard Co., staged the first Art Against AIDS benefit in 1987 (it raised $2.5 million), can page through its catalogue and see who's gone. The introduction she wrote thanks curator Bill Olander, who died 21 months later at 38; Peter Krueger of Christie's, who died at 32; Nathan Kolodner, director of the Andre Emmerich Gallery, who was 38. The donating artists included printmaker Brian Buczak, sculptor Scott Burton, multimedia artist Max Pestalozzi di Corcia, painter Keith Haring, photographers Peter Hujar and Robert Mapplethorpe and Mark Morrisroe—all have since died of AIDS. Art Against AIDS was also the last big project for Stephen Reichard, Livet's partner of 10 years, who died a year later at 39. "Anyone in the art world can rattle off a long list," Livet says. "It's cast a pall over life in New York."

Forty people step out of a bitter winter night into a church in the theater district to remember dancer Tim Wengerd. "A wonderful new boy from the West," Martha Graham had called him in 1973 when a visitor, spotting him at rehearsal, wondered who he was. Wengerd was winning accolades for his choreography after his celebrated years with the Graham Company when he died in Albuquerque at 44.

Just as AIDS benefits have constituted some of New York's most glittering cultural events these past years, memorial services for artists have themselves become multimedia art forms. This one like others features the tribute to a talent prematurely stilled, the funny anecdotes, the keening expressions of pain—and the remembrance of the work. Slides on a screen behind the speakers show Tim Wengerd hurling himself across a stage, raising his partners aloft; in some pictures he is a blur, moving too swiftly for the shutter to capture.

At first, AIDS caused shudders of fear in the artistic community, as it did outside. Its name was still new in the early '80s, its etiology unclear.

"It snuck up on everybody and there was so little information," says Donald Moore, executive director of the national service organization Dance/USA. He remembers the disorientation: " 'People are dropping dead. What's going on?' . . .

To really understand how many people would die within five years, of a particular generation—it took a while to come to grips with."

Theater people wondered nervously if the hugging and kissing endemic in their circles were spreading the disease. At City Opera, Sills recalls, "all the old wives' tales swept the company. There was great fear of sharing makeup sponges." As late as 1986 at American Ballet Theatre, the physician who worked with the company had to reassure dancers that no, they couldn't contract the infection from the sweat on other dancers' bodies.

Beyond the anxiety caused by the disease itself, a fear that the arts would be stigmatized by homosexuality was at work. When dance companies were struggling to organize the 1987 Dancing for Life benefit, they encountered some reluctance to associate dance with what was then seen as a gay disease. "It never happened that blatantly; I couldn't prove it in a court of law," says Les Schoof, general manager of ABT. But I certainly believe those were the underlying feelings at the time."

Because gay men constitute the largest group among New York's and the nation's AIDS cases (though the greatest number of new diagnoses now occurs among IV drug-users), to talk about AIDS and the arts raises consideration of the role of gays. It remains a touchy and ultimately unanswerable question. There are those who dismiss the notion that AIDS is more prevalent in the arts than in any other field. And those, like opera impresario Matthew Epstein, who believe that the arts appear more affected because "people in the arts perhaps have reached a greater level of fame. . . . In insurance, I'm sure there've been losses, but we don't know those people." And also those like dancer-choreographer Bill T. Jones, who says, simply, "Gays dominate the arts" and therefore, "the arts feel a greater loss." Arnie Zane, with whom he founded the Bill T. Jones-Arnie Zane Company, died in 1988.

Newspaper obituaries serve as evidence of some residual discomfort. The deaths of a number of major figures in American culture who died in the late '80s were described euphemistically as their survivors tried to avoid the acronym AIDS.

For the most part, however, the initial fright and avoidance swiftly yielded to campaigns of self-education, followed by impressive mobilization. One has to look back to the anti-Vietnam War activism of the '60s, or further, to the WPA in the '30s, to find comparable galvanization in the arts. "Somehow," says curator and critic Henry Geldzahler, "we've been made generous by this."

A series of starry benefits—1985's "The Best of the Best," Art Against AIDS (since replicated in other cities and currently underway in Washington), Music for Life in 1987, Dancing for Life—has raised millions.

At Sotheby's, the glossy uptown auction house, Senior Vice President Robert Woolley has become known in-house as "vice president in charge of benefits": He supervised 16 last year. Fund-raising against AIDS became something of a personal mission after his lover of 14 years, art dealer Jeffrey Childs, died in 1987.

Smaller, more personal benefits take place almost weekly around the city. A few dozen friends and colleagues gathered recently at the Dia Foundation downtown for a hastily organized dance evening that raised $4,000 to help pay the medical expenses of Demian Acquavella, a Jones-Zane dancer with AIDS.

The theater world in particular, with a long history of taking-care-of-its-own, has organized both fund-raising groups—like Broadway Cares and the union-sponsored Equity Fights AIDS—and a comprehensive service program under the auspices of the Actors Fund, which will spend a million dollars this year providing everything from rent to insurance to funeral expenses for about 200 people with AIDS. "I'd rather be an actor with AIDS than a plumber or a teacher with AIDS; I'll be better taken care of," muses Broadway Cares Executive Director Roger McFarlane. "God, what a sick thing to say."

But no other American industry, with the possible exception of the fashion and design business, seems to have responded to AIDS with such urgency. Individual artists join the Actors Fund volunteer program and go off bearing copies of Variety to visit the sick; they answer phones for Gay Men's Health Crisis; they demonstrate with ACT-UP.

Other emotions also percolate through this fairly small community, in which everybody knows somebody, or five or 20, who has or had AIDS. Anger, for instance. McFarlane of Broadway Cares, a former GMHC president, calls the show business anti-AIDS effort "heroic" but adds, "It's done one-tenth of what it could've done, and a lot of people will pay for that one day."

People grapple, sometimes, with a kind of malaise. "My friend who is in Broadway said to me, 'Why am I so depressed all the time?' " recalls mezzo-soprano Marilyn Horne, a veteran of many AIDS benefits. "I pointed out to him, 'You're in constant mourning.' "

Has any other generation of young artists descended onto New York and been confronted with anything like this? Bill T. Jones describes the way his small troupe responded as co-founder Arnie Zane, his lover for 17 years, grew ill: "How does a young dancer relate to seeing the artistic director lose energy, lose vitality, be inaccessible? . . . Be unable to sit on a chair, lie on the floor? They didn't know they were allowed to cry, be angry, be upset or frightened—the usual things people go to support groups to learn. The group became a support group.. . .

"The people in the company now are used to expecting the unexpected . . . . They expect things to be emotional and passionate. They expect people to die."

In the small, dark Nat Horne Theater on 42nd Street, 30 people hold hands silently and think of Alan Bowne, an off-Broadway playwright and screenwriter who died a few weeks earlier in California at 44. A friend recalls his plays staged, his conviction that "what was essential in life was being with the people you love; the rest is just fixing up the second act."

The strongest tribute comes from the scenes performed from his plays, particularly "Beirut," which takes place in an AIDS-ridden future in which bodies are burned on Sundays in Tompkins Square Park. "I used to think," one of the characters says, "that life was over here and death was way over there. But now, they're joined at the hip."

The challenges now, with the disease seemingly part of the landscape, grow more specific. Employment. Insurance. Money.

Eric Stamm, the social worker who coordinates AIDS services for the Actors Fund, has witnessed a remarkable commitment, in theater, to keep people working as long as they can, even "finding people to substitute four days a week so a performer can work the fifth." But he also sees clients' fears, despite guarantees of confidentiality, that the infection could threaten their future jobs.

How to accommodate, but not discriminate against, people with AIDS has become a staple of the agenda at arts symposiums and conferences.

Soaring health insurance premiums are also preoccupying arts groups, many of them small and struggling to pay. American Ballet Theatre has seen its rates jump 30 percent to 40 percent in some years; it has had to reduce its benefits and increase deductibles.

Suspicions that the arts are being redlined, at least in states with fewer legal safeguards, are rampant though unproven. "There's no doubt that there's discrimination against arts and entertainment groups, and I think it's because of the presumed risk of AIDS," says Barbara Janowitz of Theatre Communications Group. "There are too many instances of our theaters being unable to purchase premiums."

The costs of AIDS frighten everyone. The Actors Fund will spend a quarter of its 1990 program budget on AIDS services and expects annual increases of 20 to 25 percent. Some artists seethe at the way they are scrambling to provide what they think government should—and would, if the disease affected a different population.

Small organizations, often the most innovative, may be most vulnerable to the turmoil the disease can unleash. The Ridiculous Theatrical Company in Greenwich Village, since 1967 a spark plug of the comic avant-garde, was the invention and expression of playwright-director-actor Charles Ludlam. When Ludlam died of AIDS in 1987, his lover, Everett Quinton, a longtime company actor and costumer who'd never directed a play, took the helm. "I kept the company going because I was afraid to lose that too," he says.

Quinton found the first year post-Ludlam "devastating, on all fronts." One production was critically panned; another closed when Quinton was injured; a third was scrapped on what was to have been opening night when he decided it wasn't ready. Some company members, shaken, no longer accepted casting offers; the state arts council put the Ridiculous on notice that it had to demonstrate viability in order to continue receiving grants.

The Ridiculous survives, flourishes in fact. Its state funding continues and Quinton, now a veteran of a bereavement group for those who've lost people to AIDS, has reaped critical praise for his stewardship. "I was clinging to the past as my flotation cushion," he says. "Charles was a great playwright and a great comedian. . . . And it dawned on me that there was no more Charles."

The memorial service for sculptor Scott Burton fills an auditorium in the Museum of Modern Art, which displays a pair of his chairs in its sculpture garden.

Museum officials and well-known critics affectionately recall Burton's caustic brilliance and his artistic importance.

It's Charles Stuckey, an Art Institute of Chicago curator, who raises the question, considerinq Burton's death at 50, of a creative gap. "With Scott, with other artists of his generation who were cut down so young, there'll be a relatively new approach all of us will be obliged to take," he says, "wondering what some of these artists would have done if they'd been able to fulfill their lives and careers."

People think about this, as the disease enters its second decade. Fifty years hence, will art historians look back on the '80s and '90s and see a kind of dimming, the result of the paint never put on canvas, the words never put on paper, the music never composed? "Think of the years you'll wait for the next Balanchine," Les Schoof of American Ballet Theatre muses. "And what if the next Balanchine died at 18? In the most bleak terms, it is an insurmountable loss."

Artists, other artists are fond of saying, are like fingerprints: No two are alike and one is not replaceable by another. "We don't shrivel up and cease to exist," says Ellen Stewart of LaMaMa. "But we are crippled. Weakened."

Keith Haring, who began by drawing on blank placards in the New York subways and was internationally known as a painter by his mid-twenties, illustrated something of the way artists live in the shadow of AIDS.

When *The Washington Post* was preparing a profile of him in 1985, Haring urged that the reporter refrain from printing that his roommate was his lover. That Haring was gay was no secret in the New York art community, he acknowledged, but publishing it in a major newspaper would imperil his art projects with children. Haring, in good health at the time (he would not be diagnosed HIV-positive until 1987) was frequently invited to paint murals with children in museums, schools and playgrounds, and he treasured those experiences. At the height of the AIDS panic, he feared, any gay man would be barred from working with kids. The article, which focused on Haring's professional life, not his personal one, did not refer to his sexuality.

But last year, after Haring developed Kaposi's sarcoma, he gave a remarkably frank interview about his life, his illness and his thoughts on dying to *Rolling Stone*. "His friend Henry Geldzahler called it "a last reaching out, being honest." Always generous with his artwork for anti-AIDS causes, Haring "really began to focus on {AIDS} more than he ever had before," according to his longtime assistant, Julia Gruen. He joined the activist group ACT-UP. "He underwent an enormous catharsis," Gruen says.

When Haring died in February at 31, friends and admirers suffered not only grief but haunting questions of what might have been. What art might Haring have made had he lived to be 51, or 71?

Within a week, Simon Watson received a slip of paper adding Keith Haring to the roster being collected, name by name, for the Witness Project.

May 20, 1990

Our Artist, Right or Wrong

A Hundred Years After His Birth, Thomas Hart Benton Is Still Coming on Strong

HENRY ALLEN

We prefer our artists to be disturbed but not disturbing, messianic but not pugnacious, confessional but not vulgar. Hence our distaste for Thomas Hart Benton, who was cranky but not neurotic, egotistical but not martyred, lurid but not decadent.

Then again, as Tonto said to the Lone Ranger, who's this "we" you're talking about, white man?

"We" is the weight of established opinion—big-media and little-review heaviosity. A century after his birth, with a huge show hanging at the Whitney Museum in New York until Feb. 11, Benton is still getting it dropped on his foot. *Time* magazine's Robert Hughes, who has defied established opinion with muscular glee on other occasions, recently joined it to call Benton "the Michelangelo of Neosho, Mo. . . . flat-out, lapel-grabbing vulgar, incapable of touching a pictorial sensation without pumping and tarting it up to the point where the eye wants to cry uncle."

Hilton Kramer, editor of the *New Criterion,* wrote: "The sad tale of Tom Benton has long been a familiar one in American art history. After a brave start in Paris and New York, as a votary of the avant-garde, Benton lost his nerve, abandoned the modernist ideas that allowed him to produce a handful of serious paintings and settled into a long and successful career as a Regional mediocrity."

Still, here he is in a traveling show at the Whitney, with easel paintings and murals exalting American arts and industries and the common man. He is the subject of a lavish new biography from Knopf. He doesn't go away. Maybe someday he'll be our Bruegel or our Bosch, the national painter of common people in a country that believes anything worth doing is worth overdoing. Now, though, he is one of those figures who doesn't quite fit into the canon of art history, like Walt Disney or R. Crumb. A hundred years after his birth, he remains outlandish, in every sense of the word.

Benton was born in 1889. He was named for his great uncle, the Missouri western expansionist and duelist who was a senator from 1821 to 1851.

Benton's father was a Confederate veteran who made a lot of money as a lawyer and spent four terms in the House of Representatives. His mother, 19 years younger, was a culture-climber from Waxahachie, Tex. It was not a happy family. Dad was a crude little populist, 5-foot-3 and 200 pounds. Mother kept a carriage and socialized when the family lived in Washington. Benton would always remember her screams and protests when his father would take his crudeness into her bedroom at night.

Benton grew up to be a 5-foot-3 picker of fistfights and then a young poseur in the latest Paris vie-Boheme styles. He was stubborn and ineducable. He believed deeply in his own genius. He bounced from classroom to classroom, depending on the teacher or the model on any given day. His first lessons were at the Corcoran Gallery in Washington. Then he cartooned for a newspaper in Joplin, Mo. He went to the Art Institute of Chicago, where he decided he was meant for art, not illustration. He talked his parents into sending him to Paris. He disliked formal drawing classes, but did nicely at a number of modern styles—impressionism, neo-impressionism, fauvism, cubism, synchromism. He got hauled back to Neosho when his mother found out he was keeping a mistress in his Left Bank studio.

In 1914, he ended up in New York. He decorated ceramics. He designed movie sets. He strove to be a modernist. The modernist efforts of this period are "serious," all right, admirable for their earnestness, but they are dead-end pastiches, failed attempts to reconcile modernism with instincts that had driven Benton for his whole life. The problem was Benton had always been fascinated with perspective—when he was 9, untaught, he was drawing railroad trains, always a favorite subject, steaming away from him into the distance. Modernism, on the other hand, had little interest in perspective and was on its way to making a fetish of flatness.

Benton never escaped his fascination with depth, and never stopped trying to get the effects of three-dimensional sculpture from two-dimensional canvases. The contradiction was heresy, in the canon of modernism. Benton didn't care. Modernism was a means to him, not an end. When he saw cubism, he saw a way of thinking about pattern in depth, rather than a way of disassembling three dimensions and reassembling them into two. From the impressionists he learned to shape objects with color, but he studied Tintoretto and Michelangelo and never stopped shaping things with tone as well. In the early pictures he uses both techniques, and they don't quite work together.

Then there was the problem of subject matter.

After declaring himself an abstractionist in his early studies, and dismissing subject matter in the best modernist fashion, Benton had two major moments of conversion.

The first came in the Navy during World War I. He was an architectural draftsman. He later wrote, in his pugnacious styles "My interests became, in a flash, of an objective nature. The mechanical contrivances of building, the new airplanes, the blimps, the dredges, the ships of the base, because they were so interesting in themselves, tore me away from all my grooved habits, from my play with colored cubes and classic attenuations, from my aesthetic drivelings and morbid self-concerns. I . . . opened thereby a way to a world which, though always around me, I had not seen. That was the world of America."

He read a history of America and began work on a huge, unfinished project called "American Historical Epic." Flatness was forgotten—he even modeled his paintings in clay to heighten the sculptural quality of his scenes.

He also began spending summers in Martha's Vineyard. This was back before the rich arrived, and the natives were so isolated that their inbreeding had left many of them deaf, like the couple portrayed in the 1926 dinner-table scene called "The Lord Is My Shepherd." Note the cartoony hugeness of the hands, the cubist foreshortening of the table and the hint of de Chirico surrealism in the self-conscious artificiality of the jarful of spoons. Also, the drapery has the simplified massiness that would mark social realism between the world wars, and then revive with all its doughy, tonal roundings when commercial artists such as Robert Grossman took up their airbrushes in the '60s and '70s.

"Self-Portrait with Rita," a Vineyard scene from 1922, has a touch of the surreal in the handless wristwatch and the otherworldly face of his wife, an Italian immigrant. This painting also begins to unleash the sinuous, rhythmic line that was not just the result of his sculptural perspective, but a curvilinear signature you can see in drawings he made as a Paris art student, or in his newspaper caricatures, a gesture that was there from the beginning, just as Gauguin's acute, thorny little twist to things was there from the beginning.

This line would blazon everything the mature Benton painted. It warms and enlivens, but it also writhes and alarms. There's an obsessive quality to it, like the doodles on high-school notebook covers, with odd fetishy exaggerations of feet and hands in the manner of cartoonist Bill Davis in the EC horror comics of the 1950s. Locomotives lean forward like the *Little Engine That Could*. Clouds curl around like a combination of a snake and an unmade bed. It's the world the way it looks when you're very, very young and everything's alive, or you can't tell the difference between what is and what isn't—the world that makes movie cartoons so charming, with their grinning trees and dancing brooms.

The triumph of 19th century science had left the spirit of the world for dead on microscope slides, like Snow White in her glass coffin. Benton brought her back alive, animating everything from clouds to blast furnaces with a sentiment that appealed to both the child and tree-worshipping pagan in all of us.

Benton's second epiphany was much like the first. It came in 1924, while he sat by his father's deathbed and watched the old Missouri pols pay their respects. "I know that when, after his death, I went back East I was moved by a great desire to know more of the America which I had glimpsed in the suggestive words of his old cronies. . . . I was moved by a desire to pick up again the threads of my childhood."

From 1925 to 1928, Benton spent each summer on the road, sketching cotton pickers, fiddlers, mules, cowboys, holy rollers, oilmen in boom towns. Meanwhile, the house of modernism was making a temporary loan of its guest bedroom to social realism and regionalism, thanks to the writings of the Southern agrarians, and cultural doyens such as Lewis Mumford, who published "The Theory and Practice of Regionalism," when he still supported Benton. Other regionalist heroes included Grant Wood with his satiric "American Gothic," and John Steuart Curry with his Kansas tornadoes and baptisms. The movement appealed to the right with its patriotism and the left with its exaltation of the common man—this being an age when both communism and fascism appealed to the culture-bearing elite, and political debate dealt not just with funding highway expansion but with the nature of America and mankind.

Anyway, this land is your land, as Woody Guthrie sang. Franklin Roosevelt's Works Progress Administration would soon be setting countless artists to painting murals in post offices. *Time* magazine put a Benton self-portrait on its cover in 1934. As late as 1940, a book called "Modern American Painting," published in part by Time-Life, would state: "America today is developing a School of Painting which promises to be the most important movement in the world of art since the days of the Italian Renaissance. . . . Under the banner of Henry Luce, publisher of Time and Life, and his associates and assistants, the work of carrying appreciation and knowledge of art to the far corners of the land has been wisely guided." What a lost world, where such things could be written!

The book made much of Benton, and put him next to other artists who exemplified the American and regional spirit as defined by Luce: Raphael Soyer, Charles Sheeler, Georgia O'Reeffe, Peter Hurd, Doris Lee, Edward Hopper, Charles Burchfield, Paul Cadmus.

By this time, though, Benton had begun to lose favor with the intellectual establishment. He shared little of the messianism of pre-war politics, a messianism that ranged from the Communists to D.H. Lawrence's blood-and-soil fascism to Mumford's city planning. He announced he was a collectivist, but he said he didn't think that collectivism should be enforced, thus demonstrating his naivete. He was less interested in the dilemma posed by T.S. Eliot's "Wasteland" than he was worried about soil erosion in the South. He never seriously questioned the value of electoral democracy.

His cranky politics were a bit like those of Katherine Anne Porter, come to think of it, with her hatred of New York's political intellectuals, and his art had things in common with that of Georgia O'Keeffe, but, perhaps, being a male, he was not eligible for that canonization we confer on selected women in our arts— Diane Arbus, Sylvia Plath or Lillian Hellman (before she turned out to be a liar).

In 1935, Mumford had looked at Benton's murals at the New School and the Whitney museum, and written in the New Yorker: "In order to do a big canvas, it is not enough to have big figures. One must also embody significant ideas. . . . Afraid of being highbrow, he takes refuge in puerility. . . . The fact is that much of Benton's larger studies of the American scene, like 'Lord, Heal the Child,' and 'Preparing the Bill,' belong to the level of journalism."

Indeed, when compared to Diego Rivera and Jose Clemente Orozco, two other great muralists of that great, brief moment of social-realist mural painting, Benton lacks something. Rivera's murals, in contrast to Benton's, were full of political purpose, of the inevitability of history, of communism, as it happened. Benton's murals were full of people who riveted big steel and dove from crashing locomotives and played country fiddles. But there was no head of Lenin, no political iconography. None of Benton's raw-boned caricatures of the common man seemed to share any of American intellectuals' ongoing grief that our democracy is a splendid means to no defined end. Instead, they merely reflected an America full of vitality, going everywhere and nowhere at warp speed, as if Benton were trying to convert the energy of our arts and industries into the mass of culture in a sort of nuclear reaction: Culture = Art x Publicity.

He had no modesty. He liked to paint in front of audiences. Life photographed him painting the great, huge nude "Persephone." He cultivated the press. He bragged about the authenticity of his research, saying that the fingers of his guitarists and violinists were placed to be in tune, but in "The Suntreader (Portrait of Carl Ruggles)" he shows a piano with a bottom note of E, not A. The same top-hatted plutocrat appears in both "American Historical Epic" and "'The Arts of Life in America," where a harmonica player in overalls is a ringer for the one in "The Ballad of the Jealous Lover of Lone Green Valley." In the same mural, are the boxers an homage to George Bellows's "Stag at Sharkey's" or a lift from it?

These are questions, but not condemnations, particularly when you consider the speed he painted at. After doing the drawings and clay models for a mural commissioned by Indiana, he painted the whole thing in 63 days—it was 14 feet high and 230 feet long.

He said: "The very thought of large spaces puts me in an exalted state of mind, strings up my energies and heightens the color of the world. . . . I get cocksure of mind and temperamentally youthful. I run easily into childish egomania or adolescent emotionalism."

The Indiana mural, like his mural in the Missouri state Capitol, aroused the fury of those who feared vulgarity and wanted their states portrayed as bastions of high culture, rather than places where black slaves got whipped and babies' bottoms got wiped, where Abraham Lincoln leaned on an ax in his grotesque homeliness, and the Ku Klux Klan burned crosses, all of it writhing and glowing with Benton's dizzying line, palette and scattershot vanishing points.

In a comment that would foreshadow the attack by *Time's* Hughes, Missouri state Senator John Christy said: "They looked like they was jumpin' out at me." And they're both right, if you think of art as something to live with for years or contemplate for hours. Benton's paintings come on like "Roger Rabbit," wildly exciting at first, but after a while you start to feel like you're trapped in Toon Town.

The *Tulsa* (Okla.) *Tribune* said: "Shame on you, Thomas Hart Benton {for} declaring that Missouri's social history is one of utter depravity."

Benton might not have minded either criticism that much. He once said he wanted people to look at his paintings the way they looked at the funnies. He also liked to say his stuff should be hung in bars, and when "Persephone" caused a scandal, promoter and man-about-town Billy Rose hung it in his New York bar, the Diamond Horseshoe, for a month.

Like his art, Benton came on strong, and became one of those American heroes who by their works or their very presence leave you feeling that the circus is in town; a public figure in the American tradition of Everett Dirksen, Mohammed Ali, Buffalo Bill, Walt Whitman, Douglas MacArthur, Frank Lloyd Wright, Louis Armstrong, H.L. Mencken, J. Edgar Hoover, Allen Ginsberg, John Huston, Huey Long . . . people who come to seem like flesh-and-blood stand-ins for theme park robots of themselves.

Benton is vulgar. His vulgarity disturbs people. In Europe, where the class system is publicly accepted, and true aristocracy exists, vulgarity doesn't disturb the upper classes the way it does here—witness Britain's smutty tabloids. In America, vulgarity is not only a threat to the social-climber's religion of culture, but a reminder of the alarming vigor and pride in the lower classes.

Uppers fear lowers' energy. This has been most conspicuously true of America's treatment of black men, but equally true of its treatment of lower-class white ones, the rebellious populist farmers, the moonshining hillbillies, striking miners and rednecks with shotgun racks in their pickup trucks out there in America, a country as close as your neighborhood tavern. Just as the urban elite moved out to the suburbs, Benton's rural folk moved into them from an America that has dwindled since Benton's day—the Dust Bowl driving the Okies and Arkies to the aircraft factories of California, and Roosevelt driving thousands of people off their land so he could create a park in the Shenandoah. But the spirit remains.

Benton showed these people for good and ill, and he showed them as moral beings, not the muscular economic entities of socialist propaganda about the proletariat.

Critic Malcolm Cowley talked about "the heads that Benton has sketched in his travels—miners, plantation overseers, field hands, old back-country fiddlers, done so that each of them is a complete individual and yet at the same time a representative of his class and section. But apparently Benton takes no such pleasure in drawing the human body. His figures have clubfeet and hands that look as if they were encased in thick Canton-flannel gloves. . . . Of course it may be that Benton never learned how to draw bodies but it seems to me that what he reveals is a sort of Midwestern puritanism that still, subconsciously, finds the body sinful and therefore wants it to be ugly."

He was no kinder to the upper classes. Ultimately, he exhausted the capital of his fame on picking endless, needless fights with the Eastern art establishment. He bullied. He red-baited. He gay-baited, stating that "precious fairies get into positions of power and judge, buy, and exhibit American pictures on a base of nervous whim . . . ."

In a 1935 newspaper interview, he said he was leaving New York for Kansas City. "On the upswing New York is grand—when it is building buildings, tearing down buildings, making and spending money, its life is irresistible and in its drive it's a grand show. But when it is on the downswing it gets feeble and querulous and touchy. . . . Principles . . . That's what the town has come to. It don't act anymore, it talks. The place has gone completely verbal." We would hear this charge again in the 1970s, when Tom Wolfe wrote "The Painted Word," attacking a New York art establishment dominated by theory.

Once back in Kansas City, teaching at the Art Institute, he claimed Eastern decadence had infected Missouri: "Our museums are full of ballet dancers, retired businessmen and boys from the Fogg Institute at Harvard. . . . They hate my pictures and talk against them." He ended up getting fired at the beginning of World War II.

By the end of it, he was part of the past. He had no place in the high culture of an America that suddenly discovered it was running the world—abstract expressionism, existentialism, the metaphysics of be-bop, the Partisan Review, Samuel Beckett, Jackson Pollock, Charlie Parker, art according to principle, aesthetics as theology.

Benton had been Pollock's teacher and mentor for years, and they ended up railing at each other. Social realism vanished as utterly as running boards on cars. It was an art form that sought to include all of America, to create context in the tradition of Whitman. But modernism was about decontextualization and alienation—Georgia O'Keeffe's gardenless flowers, architecture's vast empty plazas, photographs not just of parts of machines, but of the gleams on those parts, Andy Warhol's Brillo box installed in a museum, Jasper Johns's gloomy, stolid, ironic paintings of the American flag.

After World War II, high art didn't worry much about what it meant to be an American. This is a question that means a lot to a country so young that it still has to invent and reinvent itself every morning, a country where you sense that a windstorm could blow everything away in an hour (with possible exceptions such as the Golden Gate Bridge and the great gray greedy Protestant-work-ethic cathedrals of Wall Street). Hence the affection and outrage that Benton can produce 50 years after he went out of fashion and 100 years after his birth.

Benton kept painting up till the end. His colors got soft, his figures got sentimental, but he kept painting. He did a mural for the Truman Library in Independence, Mo., between 1959 and 1962, and Truman called him "the best damned painter in America." He lived on in Kansas City. For all his homophobia, he was a fan of Allen Ginsberg's epic "Howl." In 1975, he finished a mural for the Country Music Hall of Fame in Nashville. On Jan. 18, he went out to his studio to chew tobacco and look at his work. He told his wife Rita that if he liked it, he'd sign it. He died with a paintbrush in his hand, and the mural was left unsigned. He was 85.

Now, 15 years later, New York critics are still railing at him, and the public is still looking at him. He still comes on strong. He is very American—our artist, right or wrong.

January 21, 1990

Study Questions
Chapter Eight

1. Is there some societal practice (i.e. rock lyric censorship) that enrages you? What ton points of evidence could you cite to persuade others of your view in an essay?
2. Writers help define their subject by using similes to compare what something is like. For example, Pamela Sommers compares the logistics of moving the musical production of "Phantom of the Opera" around the country to "rather like dismantling Mount Rushmore—and reassembling it on the East Coast." Can you think of other similes that indicate such stale and movement?
3. Complex characters say and do things that appear contradictory. Can you define conflicts in someone you know well? Cite examples.

9 *Habits of Being*

Magazine-style features are more likely to cover ideas and trends than events or places. Whether the story concept is esoteric or commonplace, writers strive to generate enough research so that their articles are not one-dimensional, but substantive in content and rich in reader interest. Features here are clustered by topics related to sociology, psychology, ethnicity or religion.

Staff writers collectively concocted a fun-to-read trend story on political correctness, titled "To Be PC, or Not to Be." To define the guidelines, they devised two lists: PC behavior and incorrect, retro activities and attitudes. Although brief, the piece says a lot about changing lifestyles and values in the "oh-so-correct 1990s."

The concept of Henry Allen's humorous essay is well-expressed in the title, "Omens; You Know You're In Trouble When . . ." Reading like a seamless monologue, the piece is an impressive litany of minute observations, personal conjectures and social analyses. Its ending may be the most significant portent of all.

The feature, "Whatever Happened to the Hero?" follows up the news of the downfall of former Washington mayor Marion Barry and emphasized its local impact. Elizabeth Kastor found that while people expressed a basic need to admire and be inspired by others, they were jaded enough now not to expect perfection in role models. It's a timely, lively analysis of people's needs and a sad, sobering reflection on a changing world.

Form follows content in the article, "The Time of Her Life." Madeleine Blais' account of the maelstrom in one single working mother's daily life is recreated with precision and non-stop flow.

Phil McCombs' views from city park benches in "The Grass Menagerie" capture an incredible spectrum of people and activities. His slice-of-life reporting snares mothers with children, senior citizens, drag queens, dog walkers, sports enthusiasts and drug dealers.

In a profile of Charlottesville, Virginia, writer Martha Sherrill reports on how a small town earns its chic. Spotlighting the former wife of the richest man in America, Patricia (and John) Kluge, Sherrill gives readers a sense of shared local concerns, not just those of the resident jet setters, literati, native horsey set or mobile home dwellers. To describe the tony little burg, Sherrill often repeats the phrase: "It's a place . . ."

The societal depression that accompanies economic gloom is the topic of Henry Allen's spritely article, "Red, White and Truly Blue." Allen amasses an array of evidence to substantiate the national neurosis: polls and statistics, cultural observations and primary and secondary quotations from astute observers, economists, authors, diplomats and professors. Rich in ideas and specificity of language, Allen's point of view is conclusively stated at the end when the metaphoric question of half-full or half-empty is answered.

"Sarah's Story," by writer Cynthia Gorney, briefs readers on a court case determining whether or not a woman with multiple personalities was legally mentally ill and, therefore, a rape victim. Gorney interviews a number of the woman's personae and uses courtroom scenes and testimony to build her complex profile. In "Stepping Lively," writer Jill Nelson reports on the growing popularity of a revived black dance tradition and examines its ethnic roots. Her article documents a local competition, describes its action and utilizes interviews to interpret the value of the activity to its young enthusiasts.

Phil McCombs takes the bedeviling question of "Angels Among Us?" seriously by examining the spiritual beliefs of two leaders of an angelology seminar, a local author and a Catholic pastor. McCombs evenly blends holy and secular views into his article.

Trends: To Be PC, or Not to Be?

A Guide to Correct Behavior in the Oh-So-Correct 1990s

DAVID STREITFELD

It's all so confusing, this business of having to be politically correct. What are the boundaries? How must one live? Can you still get away with referring to your wife as "the rib"? Is it okay to express a preference for vanilla ice cream? All-white-meat chicken? Must one eat multicultural yogurt?

Some things are easy. Jokes that use stereotypes are no longer funny, of course, unless they begin with "There were these two white guys, see . . ." But if you watch reruns of "All in the Family," are you laughing at the purveyors of racist and sexist material, or actually participating in their jokes?

What are the faux pas you need to know about, the potholes on the path to PC-dom? Read this list—which started out and to some extent remains a Knight-Ridder dispatch, but which has also been heavily worked over by various friends of Style Plus—and live accordingly.

Politically Correct (PC) meal: Anything cooked in triple virgin, cold-pressed, $15-a-bottle olive oil. Balsamic vinegar. Canola oil. Organic fruits or vegetables. Water-processed decaf. Free-range anything. High fiber. Conspicuous sprouts.

Politically Incorrect (PI) meal: Chicken-fried steak. Palm oil. Eggs. Mayo. Cool Whip. "Meat-lover's pizza." Fruits and vegetables harvested by slave-wage immigrants. Veal Oscar or any other dish made from mistreated calves. Any dish that once had a face.

PC restaurant: Serves veggie dishes. Donates leftovers to a food bank or shelter. Special Chinese restaurant political correctness: no MSG.

PI restaurant: Waitresses in abbreviated costumes. No waitresses at all (just waiters). All-you-can-eat anything. Gives parties of women the worst seats. For couples, gives woman menus without prices. Gives wine menu to man. At the meal's end, hands him the bill.

PC makeup: Not tested on animals. No aerosols.

PI makeup: Made from whales.

PC pets: Neutered. Rescued from the pound. Extra credit if saved from animal testing labs.

PI pets: Rare or endangered species. Parrots kidnapped from the Amazon. Wolf-dog hybrids. Pit bulls and Rottweilers. A dog without a yard.

PC TV shows: Anything with Bill Moyers. "This Old House." "Wild Kingdom," "Living Planet," "Wild America" and "Mister Ed." Of course, the most politically correct thing is not to watch television at all and then go around telling everyone you don't watch television.

PI TV shows: "Father Knows Best." Hunting and fishing shows. "Wall Street Week." "Married . . . With Children." Geraldo and Oprah.

PC radio: Anything on NPR.

PI radio: Howard Stern, Rush Limbaugh. Is Paul Harvey still on the air?

PC music: Obscure choirs from the Soviet bloc. Rap, reggae and trash metal—any reflection of the anger, frustration and simmering hate resulting from long-term political and social disenfranchisement (i.e., Boogie Down Productions, Ice Cube).

PI music: Any rap, reggae or trash metal that demeans women, gays or ethnic groups (whites excepted); rock-and-roll; country; and pop (unless it's by some sort of minority representative).

PC medication: Prozac.

PI medication: Valium.

PC movies: "Robin Hood: Prince of Thieves" (Kevin Costner exudes PC attitudes toward his Moorish sidekick and toward poor Saxons. And the women fight alongside the men—although Marian becomes a PI wimp at the end). "Dances With Wolves." All John Sayles movies. Woody Allen's. Oliver Stone would have been PC in the '70s, but we're not stoned anymore.

PI movies: All Brian De Palma movies (sexist). Ditto any Kim Basinger film where she's handcuffed. Double ditto any Julia Roberts film where some guy solves all her problems, which so far is all of them. The unreconstructed Sylvester Stallone. Andrew Dice Clay, with his "Ford Fairlane," is a veritable PI-17—but we don't have him to kick around anymore.

PC birth control: Condoms.

PI birth control: The Pill.

PC shoes: Birkenstock sandals. Reds.

PI shoes: Sneakers with sequins. Crocodile loafers and alligator cowboy boots.

PC song: Anything by Phil Collins.

PI song: N.W.A.'s "One Less Bitch."

PC mail-order catalogue: Anything made from recycled paper. Those that use popcorn to pack their material. Extra credit for those that market environmentally safe products that return profits to Third World workers rather than factory lords.

PC grocery bag: Washable, reusable string bag carried from home.

Less correct: Brown paper.

Not at all correct: Plastic. As for "degradable" trash bags—nice try.

PC vehicle: A bicycle. Rollerblades. But if you must drive, make sure the car's got air bags and uses almost no gas. Geos are geopolitically correct and get 52 miles to the gallon on the highway. Wear that seat belt and use that kid's car seat! (However, if you're more into saving whales, dolphins and tapes of the show "thirtysomething" than the jobs of assembly line workers—all politically correct acts among certain subsets—we'll be seeing you in your Volvo or Saab. As for us, we'll cut in front of you.)

PI vehicle: Anything fun to drive. If you're running for public office, anything imported. Anything that belches opaque smoke from the exhaust pipe. Anything with fins or that requires more than one parking place. Whatever Pete Rose or Jose Canseco is driving these days.

PC patio furniture: Anything made from recycled redwood or trees that are not from the rain forest.

PI lawn ornaments: Jockeys. Slumbering Mexican peasants. Come to think of it, anything other than a birdbath.

PC garden: Manure driven. No chemical fertilizers or pesticides. Uses natural predators and organic lures to fight pests. Weeds are increasingly lauded. Extra points for turning lawn into a meadow.

PI garden: Marijuana crop. (Being pro-legalization is passe these days. So is smoking the stuff.)

PC jewelry: Friendship bracelets.

PI jewelry: Ivory.

PC cigarette: Virginia Slims would like you to think so, but there's no such thing. It's not PC to smoke anymore. Particularly incorrect cigarette: Uptown.

PC beverage: Mineral water. Domestic bottled spring water. Nonalcoholic brews.

PI beverage: Cisco. PowerMaster. Shooters.

PC snack: Rainforest Crunch candy and anything else homemade by the very PC Ben and Jerry.

PI snack: Twinkies and fried pork rinds.

PC clothes: Union-made. Natural fibers. Those that make an ethnic or racial pride statement. And, lately, Desert Storm stuff, although it could also be argued that it's all PI, too. Stay tuned.

PI clothes: Anything that needs dry cleaning. Leather coats. Fur coats. Jeans with American flags on the behind or anyplace else. T-shirts that say "Master" and "Slave," or "Captain" and "First Mate," or "Boogie Till You Puke."

PC excuses for turning down a date Saturday night:

"Sorry. I'm in a walkathon for chronic fatigue syndrome."

"That's my night with my {fill in the addiction} 12-step group."

"I have an Amnesty meeting."

"That's the night I tutor Bob. He's 31 and just learning to read."

PI excuses for not accepting a date Saturday night:

"My book group is discussing Dinesh D'Souza that night."

"I never miss 'Empty Nest.' "

"I have a National Rifle Association pep rally."

PC Kennedys: Patrick Kennedy, a Rhode Island legislator; Caroline Kennedy Schlossberg, lawyer and author of a book on the Bill of Rights.

PI Kennedy: William Kennedy Smith. And now—JFK.

PC reasons for not going to the shore:
A wish to avoid skin cancer.
A wish to avoid cataracts.
A wish to avoid polluted water.
A wish to avoid polluting the water.
PI reason for not going to the shore:
Going power-boating and fishing on ecologically fragile lake instead.

July 2, 1991

Omens:You Know You're in Trouble When . . .

HENRY ALLEN

There is decline. There is fall. There are omens of these things.

You sense these omens, much like the Chinese farm animals that go berserk just before the earthquake. With the millennium coming, with real estate prices softening, with the population aging, you will be sensing more and more of them.

Little things. But unmistakable.

A veteran Redskins quarterback opens a restaurant with his name on it. An established actress like Mariel Hemingway gets breast implants. An aging shopping mall seems to be all shoe stores, and then a wig store appears.

Somewhere, you hear something. Footsteps? A clock ticking?

Your husband heads for the hardware store and your best friend sees him in a phone booth. Suddenly, it feels like a small wind on the back of your neck. Your boss starts bringing his kids into the office a lot, a whole lot, and uses them to Xerox stuff for him. He's already felt the wind on his neck.

Donald Trump (or any real estate developer) denies rumors of financial woes and insists he's selling off properties because he wants cash to "go and bargain hunt." A network advertises a new series as "critically acclaimed"—witness the late "Capital News" on ABC. You notice these things. You know that sooner or later, you'll think of them and say: I knew right then. I saw it coming.

Actresses who aren't Jane Fonda do exercise tapes—Debbie Reynolds, Raquel Welch. Dan Rather wears a sweater to read the "CBS Evening News." Rap music gets an NBC special and a Saturday morning cartoon show. A politician's friends start saying loudly that if you only knew him in private, one on one . . . . Actors publish poetry—Suzanne Somers, say. A poet tries acting—James Dickey in "Deliverance," say. Television talk shows, particularly the political sort known as "food-fight journalism," can be dangerous—only the doomed argue with Pat Buchanan, says Hunter Thompson. And whatever it meant when that swimming rabbit attacked Jimmy Carter's canoe, it wasn't good.

A presidential campaign is in trouble, says political columnist Mark Shields, when congressional candidates from the same party "say they'd love to be with him at the rally but they have a taxidermist appointment or their nephew is graduating from driving school. Any candidate is in trouble when he says he wants to spend more time with his family. That means the polls are running 2 to 1 against him."

You know the girl of the year has already peaked when she's the big guest at the White House correspondents dinner—Fawn Hall, Donna Rice, Marla Maples.

Or is it that the White House press corps has peaked when its big guest is the girl of the year?

Democratic consultant Carter Eskew says a secret art of divination has arisen in Washington with computers. Big guys and players get on the keyboard "and they do Lexis/Nexis searches for their own name." If they don't find it in the last month, they can expect headwaiter snubs, although with the downtown restaurant business falling apart, what difference does it make?

And what good can it augur for Washington that the downtown restaurant business is falling apart?

Whatever it means, it's not nearly as bad as the pheasants people have spotted inside the Detroit city limits. A nasty sign for New York was when you heard the phrase "gold coast" to describe the condos across the Hudson River in Jersey City.

Sometimes you should shrug these things off.

Just because the flight attendant is laughing uncontrollably, there's no certainty that the plane is going to crash. The fact that you can't find your car keys doesn't mean you have Alzheimer's. And why do Washingtonians tend to feel something terrible has happened to their neighborhood when a congressman moves in?

Still, something inside you knows that it means little good when your child comes home with a tattoo, or, worse, comes home with half a tattoo. And perhaps you should worry about your job as a spot welder if the president of the Weldspot Corp. gives a lecture on competitiveness to the local Junior Chamber of Commerce, or, worse, he offers to sell the company to the employees.

Bad love omens:

When you fly out to see him, and you don't want to get off the plane.

When the girl you're driving home starts chewing bubble gum; when she makes a call on your car phone, asks for someone named "Todd" and tells him what you bought her for dinner; when she tries to sell you an Amway dealership.

When middle-aged couples buy big new televisions and start watching "Doogie Howser" together.

When either spouse keeps quoting a shrink during arguments, or uses words like "space" or "growth," or in any other way talks like a rock musician explaining why he's leaving the group to start a solo career.

Celebrities occupy a special place in our divinations. If you are one, you know you're in trouble when:

You find yourself appearing on more than one Christmas special.

You appear on "Hollywood Squares" and people think that's what you're famous for.

People talk about your "great courage" or refer to you as a "survivor." If they say you're "one brave lady," you're ready to move on to the next omen, which is the *People* magazine cover story full of references to God and Betty Ford.

All that's left is the Polident ads, recliner ads and, finally, becoming an ironic nostalgia curio in a John Waters movie, like Troy Donahue or Joey Heatherton.

You worry about musicians when they go to a Latin sound, like Linda Ronstadt and Talking Heads' David Byrne. You know something is ended when they do reunion concerts with the old group.

When TV actors get into politics, you may not be seeing them in a prime-time slot for a while: "Lou Grant's" Ed Asner, "The Man From U.N.C.L.E.'s" Robert Vaughn. And, in one of the great career collapses in Hollywood history, General Electric Theater's Ronald Reagan. Is it possible that Clint Eastwood's acting career had peaked just before he became mayor of Carmel, Calif.?

When writers get into cultural exchanges, or, worse, become PEN presidents, watch for their books on bookshelves at Ikea.

When tennis players have babies (John McEnroe) or even talk about having babies (Chris Evert), don't plan to watch them in the finals. When any athlete over 30 says: "As long as it's fun, I'm going to keep on playing," watch for his coach to say: "Hey, he's family" just before he gets put on waivers.

You have learned that any trend is headed for ridicule and oblivion when it appears on the cover of *Time* or *Newsweek*. The hot new food—sun-dried tomatoes, blackened anything—has cooled when you see it at Bennigan's, then your company cafeteria.

So many things are dying or dead when New York City turns them into institutions: any artist under 40 who gets a retrospective show, novelist Jay McInerney, a social life that revolves around nightclubs.

You know any business is shaky when the trade publication that covers it gets a new name, as in the *National Thrift News,* a journal of the savings-and-loan industry, becoming the *National Mortgage News.*

And you. What about you?

Aren't you the one who threw the party where the guests kept lining up to use the phone? Have you begun to hate reading the alumni news because of all your classmates getting rich and famous? (Years later, of course, the tragedy will be complete when you find yourself eagerly opening it to see if they've died of something unpleasant.)

It is a particularly nasty portent, of course, if you've read this far. And we will not even discuss what it means if you read it in a clipping that your mother cut out and mailed to you.

June 11, 1990

Whatever Happened to the Hero?

Finding Someone to Look Up to
Reflections Of A Changing World

ELIZABETH KASTOR

Superman. Martin Luther King. George Washington. Wonder Woman. Abraham Lincoln. Mother Teresa. Eleanor Roosevelt. Rambo. Joan of Arc. Malcolm X.

Nicole Tobias is silent, as if trying to remember someone who lived in her house once but long ago moved away.

"I don't think I have heroes," Tobias, a graduating senior at Washington's McKinley High School, says at last. "Maybe I should, but I don't."

She is not alone. More than two decades after the deaths of John and Robert Kennedy and Martin Luther King, it has become a cliche to say we live in anti-heroic times. Nelson Mandela's visit to the United States is one more reminder that we now find ourselves seeking inspiration in faraway places. The charismatic American presidents, the glistening war heroes, the magical, supreme figures who society agreed were somehow beyond taint have disappeared. We are jaded, we say, no longer expecting perfection from anyone, searching in fact for the dirt behind the glitter.

And often enough it is there. Pete Rose gambles on sports. American University President Richard Berendzen makes obscene phone calls. Four members of the Washington Capitals are accused of rape. Barney Frank befriends a prostitute. Gary Hart lies about his involvement with women. Lillian Hellman invents dramas for her much-praised memoirs. Again and again the tawdry reports emerge and the image is punctured. As the air rushes out, we experience those by-now-familiar sensations—curiosity, titillation, disappointment and ultimately exhaustion. Again, we think. There goes another one.

With the arrest and trial of Mayor Marion Barry, this city has been reminded once more of the pain and anger that accompany the fall of a hero.

When Barry was arrested, Prince George's County high school teacher Jerome Deshields says, he watched his students at Forestville High School react as they have when others fell. "The response at first seems to be one of fear. It is this fear—'if you pull down my hero, what am I going to do now?' For those who had a slight dependence on him through their feelings, it's very frightening."

There are those who bridle at the very idea of Barry as an object of admiration, but for many he has long been a source of pride and inspiration. Defiant, strong,

Barry was the warrior. There was magic there. Loyal believers still cling to him, the need for Barry and what he symbolizes is so strong they will not let go.

"Mayor Barry is one of my favorites," says 14-year-old Alonzo Washington. The revelations about Barry, he says, have not disturbed him. "Everyone isn't perfect. Everyone makes big mistakes all the time. I just like him—I just like him for being a black American mayor."

But for others, Barry's arrest is one more argument against having heroes.

"I was disappointed," Nicole Tobias says. "Somebody at our school had gotten killed—Sammy Unger—and at his memorial service Barry came and was holding up Sammy's jersey, and when he got arrested they showed that picture on television. I thought that was tacky."

With the decline of myth and the rise of social science, the age of heroes has faded into the era of role models, a more practical culture in which singers and actors and athletes are shipped into schools to deliver brief inspirational talks and then disappear once again into their limousines. They are famous, they are rich, and it is the fame and the riches that are supposed to spur children on, not some superhuman prowess or crusade or vision.

Ask adults about heroes today and the very word elicits a surprised smile and an extended struggle to come up with some name, any name. Although they want their children to have figures to look up to, for themselves the concept has become irrelevant. But behind *their* skepticism there is often a certainty that, like Nicole Tobias, they should believe—if only they could—and a nostalgia for the time when that was possible.

"I think you have to have heroes," says Sandra Plourd, a teacher at Columbia Park Elementary School. "We have so many negative things bombarding us, it's essential to have something positive."

To his fans Oliver North possesses a heroic gleam. Mikhail Gorbachev drew huge crowds and was dubbed a man capable of remaking the world. And every day the lines outside "Teenage Mutant Ninja Turtles" are a scrabbling mass of excited kids desperate to sit in the dark and adore their favorite reptiles. The need to admire—to idealize the distant idol—remains as basic an urge as the small child's adoration of the parent.

So what can be done with that hunger?

Kneeling around a low table at the Capital Children's Museum, small children fold tissue paper into flowers and talk about their heroes.

"A hero," says one 6-year-old girl, "is someone who *saves you*—saves you from something like if you spill some hot tea on yourself and you say, 'Help! Help!' your hero will come."

"Batman," says a boy. He has the tape of the movie, and he likes him, he says, " 'cause he can't die."

The classic definition of a hero requires something more than immortality or the ability to save a child from a hot drink. At a 1987 Smithsonian symposium called "The Superhero in America," historian Barbara Tuchman offered her interpretation of that tradition: "A hero is one who possesses a noble task and who performs it for the sake of his country or his fellow man or for humanity and, in doing that, becomes a larger figure."

For many people that definition still holds, at least in theory. Finding the person to whom it can be applied, however, is a different matter.

"I think in order to become a hero you have to have some sense of the danger you're facing, and then you decide, you make a conscious decision, to go ahead and face it," says arts activist Peggy Cooper Cafritz. "It was clear during the civil rights movement that Martin Luther King could be killed. It was clear that Muhammad Ali could have been sent to jail."

But now, she looks around and sees only one person who qualifies for that definition: Nelson Mandela.

"For a large segment of the black community, Jesse Jackson of all national people has that status because he seemed to go more against the grain—going against the grain embodies more risk-taking than a Doug Wilder," she says. "But even Jesse Jackson doesn't come close to a Nelson Mandela, because in Mandela you not only have someone who has stood up for what he believes in, but he has made it really clear he's willing to risk his life. Not that a Jesse Jackson wouldn't be willing to do that, but there has been nothing about his life that demands that, and there is very little in our society that demands that kind of sacrifice."

Like any dream, each person's definition of a hero is shot through with memories, with expectations of what is possible, with childhood fantasies and adult disappointments. When they talk about heroes, people open small doors to reveal private visions of the world. A child says he likes Batman " 'cause he can't die," and you learn something about his fears. A woman says she never thought of having a hero—heroes were for boys—and you learn something about her thoughts on gender.

Wendy Frank listens to two boys talk about Superman and baseball players in her Wheaton Plaza store. "I don't think girls need those kinds of heroes," she says. "From a young age they teach boys they have to be the strong one—you know, it's corny, but they're told they're going to have to earn the money, protect the family. So they have to have those strong people to look up to." Women, she thinks, look closer to home: "I think a lot of girls would say their mothers."

Oftentimes the vision is bleak. A.J. Grennon, a D.C. resident who works in an appliance shop on upper Georgia Avenue, sees little to admire around her. "The military is out for itself, politicians are corrupt, normal people are living paycheck to paycheck if they're lucky—who the hell can find a hero?" she says, the words rolling out with the unstinting certainty of ideas expressed before. "When I was young, I looked up to people who were loners and did what they want. If you can make it on your own, you're set. I learned that early. I'm country down to the bone and that's all you hear in country songs, that loners win."

There are those, however, who do not share the general ambivalence. A middle-aged man who works in Northwest Washington does not hesitate to offer a name: "Minister Farrakhan," he says. "He's for the downtrodden. He's the only person I know who's trying to lift up the black race." He has admired Muslim leaders since the days of Elijah Muhammad, and although he was hurt by the split between Muhammad and Malcolm X in the '60s, in his mind he has reconciled the two men so that they can both retain their power for him.

Not to believe in someone, he says, is "sad—you don't trust anybody. I try to teach my children that, but you can only teach so much and then they go on their own way."

And often enough, parents feel, those children gravitate toward figures who can only hurt them.

"A lot of people are going to need heroes. A lot of people who can't do these things for themselves need somebody good to imitate," says Allan Schwartz, a parent of grown children who works with A.J. Grennon. "But most of these people out on the streets, all they see are people selling dope. Those are their heroes."

Other figures are almost as troubling to parents. Years after historian Daniel Boorstin declared that celebrities are well known for being well known, the cult of celebrity continues to grow. Michael Jordan and Bart Simpson, Michael Jackson and the New Kids on the Block remain the heroes of schoolchildren. "The besetting sin of the age is impatience, and television panders to that sin, and so does journalism," says Roger Kennedy, director of the National Museum of American History. "Today we have the synthetic or instant hero, which is a characteristic of Hollywood and Washington, but the ebb and flow of celebrity is not heroism. Heroism today is heroic persistence. It's not a spasm of virtue. Any klutz can do the right thing once."

But heroic persistence is not what matters to many people, especially children. Angela Frizzell, who lives in Silver Spring, thinks frequently about the inadequacy of her children's heroes and is not surprised when her four blond boys call out their favorites: Rambo, Indiana Jones, Teenage Mutant Ninja Turtles, Eric Clapton (the 14-year-old likes oldies). "Children and people today look at football—athletic people—the rock singers, people who are in the bright lights," she says, "and they mimic them, they copy them."

Of course entertainers and invented characters have always commanded fascination—Frizzell's husband, Gerald, remembers loving Roy Rogers and Dale Evans. "I like adventure movies and I always like the good guy," says Starr Karaveloas of Annapolis, just as her 5-year-old daughter likes the Ninja Turtles and the Little Mermaid. "I guess we never really thought of heroes as real-life people," she says. "It's an ideal thing, really."

But now, with what Peggy Cooper Cafritz calls the "undressing of our heroes," the cowboys and singers and baseball players strike some as hollow and dangerously untrustworthy.

"There's this one girl in my school, she's in love with all these singers and stuff," says Nicole Tobias. "I think she's in a fantasy world, and she needs to fall in love with the things around her."

In his own quiet way, Renard Wood has made a journey that mirrors one taken by his society. Long ago he abandoned heroes. Now, as a seventh-grader, he has a role model instead: Louis Farrakhan. "I go myself to all the times when he speaks," he says. "He's trying to stop the drugs, and he's talking to the black people about using the drugs, and what the drugs do to you." He likes that, and although his mother also admires Farrakhan, "I picked him out myself."

Years ago Wood followed another. "Superman," he says. "I really thought I would be able to fly with him. When I was young I thought that."

No more. Heroes and the hope for flight have faded. The Man of Steel has been replaced with someone who can offer more pragmatic guidance in the ways of the world.

But role models raise problems. They can fall just as easily as heroes, which Barry himself acknowledged recently when he said, "I may be a poor role model, but . . . being a poor role model is not a crime." They can be as distant as any hero. And their pragmatism can leave a soul yearning for the poetry of heroes.

"Role models aren't going to do a damn bit of good if the kids leave that session with the role model and go back to their miserable, oppressed, undereducated life," says Robert Alexander, director of Living Stage, the community outreach branch of Arena Stage. "It can inspire you, but if there's no support system, after a while you're going to crash and get more bitter. Unless that role model is accessible it won't work—if that role model's phone number isn't known to the whole school."

Historian Phyllis Rose, who writes about women's lives and most recently published a biography of dancer Josephine Baker, regrets the growing popularity of the term for other reasons: It offends her desire to be inspired without offering enough in return. "Hero is much more stately, dignified and perhaps even inspiring," she says. "Role model—it's a small, puny sort of word. It doesn't have the grandeur."

But many have grown wary of grandeur and skeptical of any relationship that demands a vast distance between the admired and the admirer.

"I think people ought to respect each other, but I think verticality in relationships is not healthy and hero worship implies that," says Randall Robinson, executive director of TransAfrica. "That kind of adulation means self-denial—when you have the kind of respect you must have to do well in life, then your relations with most people are essentially horizontal. I think also hero worship tends to blind you so you don't see well—when problems arise, then the disillusionment is all the more devastating."

Robinson is certain that "the things you really need to know" are learned as children through "intimate contact," from parents, close family. There is also safety in choosing to admire those people close at hand—a safety from surprises. It is among people we know personally that most of us both find our first heroes and discover they are not without limitations. To young children, a parent towers over everything, flawless and omnipotent. But slowly the infallible figure is replaced by something a little more realistic, a little smaller. "All of us remember that day as a child when a friend said, 'Your mommy and daddy do it,' " says Spencer Hammond, a former D.C. Schools psychologist and the new director of the Center for Educating African-American Males at Morgan State University. "First you said, 'My mommy and daddy? No way!' " But then finally one of them said, 'Where do you think you came from?' and you have to accept it. And then that purity is gone."

That naivete is about not just sex but all the truths of adult life. It is something that every child must lose in order to grow up, and one that biographer Rose believes a society should probably lose as well.

Rose says her biography of Josephine Baker was criticized because she presented the dancer as "promiscuous and irresponsible in some ways. Well, it's true she was, but you can't expect everyone to be perfect in order to be inspired by them. What's inspiring about her is her resilience, her idealism, her courage. I think, in fact, that this generation of people who are being written about now are more inspiring for being believable, for having feet of clay."

Discovering those frailties and reconciling herself to them, she says, is an essential part of her work, and over the years she has learned how to find heroism in that process. "You start out in love with the person in some way, and then comes the stage of disillusionment," she says, "and then comes the stage after that of reasoned acceptance and a love that's less blinded than the initial love."

It is a love that allows for flaws, a love that finds heroism in the known, familiar, imperfect world.

June 20, 1990

The Time of Her Life

MADELEINE BLAIS

There is no way to take a true picture of time, the blur of hours and motion of minutes. I used to think of myself as a champion keeper of the calendar, expert at knowing as far in advance as possible the precise destiny of every second. This was my kingdom, a place I could control. But then I made a new friend, another mother, with children the same ages as mine, a boy of 8 and girl of 4, who put me to shame. Here was a true maven, a marvel of efficiency in using up time before it even exists. I asked if she would take me on a time tour of her week. She said fine, but in order to do this, I had to make a phone appointment: Thursday morning at 11:05. "Which do you want?" she asked. "A week that's maxed out, or just a week week?"

Be wild, I thought, be a gypsy: Go for broke.

"Maxed out," I said. "Definitely."

So here goes, if not a full portrait of time itself, at least a kind of snapshot of the way some of us live: On a typical maxed-out Monday, my friend wakes up at 6:30. She leaves at 7:45 to bring the children to school. Her son is dropped off at 8 and her daughter at 8:15. She goes to her gym at 8:30, changes, swims until 9 and then aerobicizes until 10. Then she showers, does her hair and dresses for work, having picked out her outfit, stockings and jewelry the night before. From 10:45 to 11 she drives to her therapist, stopping to pick up a muffin (usually something whole-grain) and a bottle of water. The food she eats in the car, the liquid she drinks during therapy. She leaves at 11:50 and arrives at her office at 12:10, making one stop at the florist to pick up her standing weekly order of a $5 bouquet for the office. Because she's a regular customer, the bouquet she gets is usually worth much more. She counts on hitting enough red lights to be able to put on her makeup; she doesn't put it on earlier because she generally cries in therapy. In her job as a therapist, she sees individual patients from 12:30 to 7:30 and then leads a group from 7:30 until 8:45. Meanwhile, her son takes the bus home after school and is met by a sitter. Together they pick up his sister at her child care at 4. The sitter helps them pack clothes and their special blankets for the overnight at their father's house. My friend hires good dependable sitters with cars and pays them $8 an hour. (Her top-paying patients pay her $80.) When my friend leaves work on Monday night, she either goes to the grocery store to shop for the week's provisions, or meets someone for dinner. Either way, she is home by 10:30 or 11. Tuesdays are her early day; she gets up at 6 in order to run 4 1/2 miles in 45 minutes, a double loop around a small lake, and still be out of the house by 8. At 8:30 she starts seeing patients, all day, until 5: nine in all, straight through, without a break. Lunch is always a sandwich packed the night before, not just a hunk of bread and slab of meat slapped together but, because she is a gifted cook, usually something inventive, tenderly compiled, say a half-piece of pita bread with munster cheese, sprouts and a dab of gourmet salsa. On Tuesdays at 5:01 she leaves the office in an absolute dash to get to her daughter's day care before it closes. Wednesdays are structured so that she gets a break in the middle of the morning for her weekly manicure. A patient finishes at 9:50; she goes for the appointment from 10 to 10:30 and is back in the office for the next patient at 10:40. This is a recent indulgence. She never used to worry about her nails because she never really worried about her looks at all. She is a tall, slender, beautiful woman with thoughtful blue-gray eyes. When she tries on clothes, almost everything looks great. She is out of her office by 2:30. This is her son's early day for getting out of school, and often he beats her home. He lets himself in with his own key: Usually he is not alone for more than 15 minutes. They then spend from 2:30 until 5 on a special outing, at the arcade, the comic book store or the library. Together they pick up her daughter, and when they get back shortly after 5, she starts dinner, and during the warm months she often mows the lawn, though once in a while, lately, because there is no other time for exercise that day, she leaves the children in front of the TV and does an abbreviated 22-minute jog. There are tenants on the bottom floor of their house, and she does not leave the children unless she is sure the tenants are at home. Because she is never confident that the children ate as well as she would like at their father's on Monday, she likes to insist on a good dinner on Tuesday and Wednesday nights: no pizza, no hot dogs, nothing gobbled on the run. Ideally this is a civilized interlude when they all sit down and eat together, though sometimes the meal degenerates into a pitched battle between the children as to who is going to tell her what first, with her daughter sabotaging her son's conversation by putting her feet on the table and with her son sabotaging her daughter's conversation by opening his mouth to reveal half-eaten food, saying, "Train wreck." The temptation, she says, is "to drink 12 glasses of wine." A standard good dinner might include roast chicken, a fresh vegetable, rice or pasta. After dinner, she bathes the children, helps them with homework and puts them to bed (she calms the children with a book, a board game or some quiet conversation) and then her time to herself begins. From 10 to about 12:30 is for phone calls, correspondence, TV or just sitting in an armchair, zoned out, home, happy enough, cossetted by fatigue.

Sometimes she has trouble sleeping; it was hardest when she and her husband first separated. One or the other of her children woke up every hour. Oddly, the less sleep she gets, the less she needs, and sometimes she is up until 1 in the morning, fussing, cleaning. "You'd think my house would be immaculate." On Thursdays, she sees five patients from 8:30 to 1:35. At 11:05, she has half an hour free, and unless her husband is out of town, that is their time to talk about the children and also their divorce settlement. They used to talk at night, but she found that when they talked late at night, she felt depleted, snappish, vulnerable. That is why she carved out of her schedule a time during the workday for them to talk, a few sunlit minutes, crisp and efficient. Thursday afternoons, she picks up her children and brings them back to the house, where they are met by a sitter at 3:30. She returns to work by 4:10 in order to meet with two more patients and lead a group that gets out at 7:30. At 5 or so, the children's father picks them up for an overnight. Friday morning, she gets up at 6 and goes for a long run. Fridays are devoted to professional consultations as well as sessions with patients. She finishes up at 6:30. A sitter has met her son when he gets home from school, and as on Mondays, the two of them pick up her daughter. Friday nights are for puttering. Sometimes she will get a home video for her children, and usually Fridays are when she gets to open her mail. Saturday mornings at 7:30, the cleaning woman comes. The minute she arrives, my friend dashes out of the house to go for a quick run in order to be back and showered in time to take her daughter to ballet from 9 to 10. The cleaning woman stays with her son while he plays Nintendo. Every other Saturday, her husband comes at 11 and the children spend the next 24 hours with him. If the children are with their father, she spends the day on errands: dry cleaner, hairdresser, florist again, picking up her own personal bouquet for the house, $7 on a regular weekend, $9 if she's having a dinner party. Sometimes on Saturdays she goes to the Power Pack aerobics class at 4 at the health club, where she pays reduced membership fees because she has agreed to use it only on weekday mornings and weekend afternoons. In the warm months, she loves the beach: all that warmth, just pouring down. She used to read all the time when she was married; she liked that aspect of herself, the part of her that delivered her psyche to a wash of words and imagined the lives of others. But now she is too distracted to read; her life is its own surfeit of plots and subplots. There is no use reading about invented lives when she is spending so much energy reinventing her own. She sometimes thinks that the orgy of reading was really just a way of being alone, and now she is alone enough. Besides, books are filled with unexpected twists and turns, and she feels she cannot take any more emotional surprises. Sometimes, despite her better intentions to have an active, productive Saturday on her own, she is overcome by the absence of her children. She often feels a horrible pang when she sees them disappearing out the front door with their father. It is, she says, as if all the meaning in her life has just walked off.

Sundays are a late day, a luxury of sleep. Sometimes she stays in bed until 8.

On Monday, the week begins anew. At least summer, with its odious, preening spontaneity is finally over. What chaos it is to accommodate vacations, hers, her patients', her soon-to-be-former husband's, plus all those camp schedules, and the baseball games, especially the ones that are rained out and must be rescheduled, and then the usual epidemic of potluck picnics and last-minute invitations to someone's cottage for an all-day barbecue. There comes a moment every summer when she finds herself filled with longing for the peace of the school year, when every week she launches the same vessel with its cargo of hours, borne ceaselessly into a maelstrom consoling in its very predictability.

Madeleine Blais, who-teaches three university courses a semester, has two children, one husband and no time.

June 20, 1990

The Grass Menagerie

Views from the Park Bench—Transvestite to Dog Lover, a Space for Every Taste

PHIL MCCOMBS

Washington is such an amazing city for parks—8,559 acres in all, more per capita than in New York, Geneva, Kuala Lumpur. Every neighborhood has its island of green. And like all islands, each has its own indigenous, idiosyncratic, inexplicable wildlife.

The Cat in the Tap, the Mouse in the Ear and the Car in the Tree

Bald Eagle Park, Joliet Street and Martin Luther King Jr. Avenue SW:

"That water fountain," says Martina Garces, 11, who is holdinq her doll, "is off-limits, because they put a cat in it."

Further explanation is not needed, nor in fact is it available, here at the Bald Eagle Urban Day Camp, a city operation where Anita Fitzgerald, the assistant director, and several counselors teach sign language, arts and crafts, creative writing and other things to 50 kids each summer weekday.

The kids are taking a break, relaxing on a bench in the deep shade of tall trees. A few of the girls are jumping double Dutch.

"Hey, you got a Mickey Mouse earring in your ear," says Lawanda Chase, 11, to counselor Anthony Love, 19. In fact, he does. It is small and gold in color, though perhaps it is not actual gold. He laughs.

Oscar Sharp, 10, is from Oakland, visiting relatives. "Hot out here in Washington," he says. "Too many bugs. And a little bit violent out here. This drunk driver crashed into a car where I stay." Behind him, there's a big gap torn in the chain-link fence, and a trail leading down into the thick, untended woods where vines hang from the trees.

"Someone stole a car and drove it through the fence," explains Fitzgerald. "The police had to come and take it out. The car was up in the tree, like."

Hell's Bells, Son, It's the American Way

Gompers Park, Massachusetts Avenue at L Street NW:

Undoubtedly the city has some name for this tiny verdant wedge amid busy boulevards, but for now call it Samuel Gompers Park for its imposing statue of the labor leader, from behind which into the noon sun emerges a man in a mini skirt with blue fingernails, long blond hair and lipstick. "The heat is killing me," he says.

He identifies himself as one Chris T. Arpe, 20, and deposes thus: "I don't like this park so much at night because we're bothered by boys throwing bottles and stuff. The police chase us out of the park, but when the boys are here throwing bottles and selling dope, you can't find the police." Indicating a group of feminine figures lying in the shade, Arpe explains: "We're considered drag queens because we dress up as women. There's butch queens, they dress up as boys but act real feminine. There's another park over at 13th and K where all the butch queens hang."

Here we have a new approach to Special Purpose Parks.

"Thats a queen over there, her name is Diamond. The guy next to her with his shirt off, he's a construction worker. You ought to see her at night— she's got great big breasts, you'd never know she's not a woman. That security guard over there, he mainly dates Diamond.

Across the street, the security guard seems to be straining, craning his neck to see what is going on in the park.

Arpe admits to being "addicted" to the action in the park. He says it can get hairy. "I got shot in the head three months ago—guy shot me and then backed up over me with his pickup. I was lying on the ground bleeding to death and a woman was holding me." And one night last winter there was an altercation in the park and Arpe, in a fur coat and high heels, was interviewed. "When I got home my mom said, 'I saw you on Channel 5. I didn't know you did this.' Then she accepted it.

"My dad has his own construction company. I'm his only son. He says, 'Well, if you do it, be the best at it.' "

Where Else but the Hill?

Stanton Park, Fifth and C streets NE:

Every evening around dusk, the neighborhood doggies gather here with their humans. This particular evening, there are a dozen or so of each. The rule is that the humans have to address one another by the names of their doggies. There is a list for cross-checking, but it can't be released to the press, for privacy reasons, you understand. The humans carry little plastic sandwich bags, which is thoughtful because the doggies could hardly be expected to clean up after themselves. Over in Lincoln Park there's a doggy costume party at Halloween, but here they think that's overdoing it. They're just here because their humans need a place to run and socialize. There are complaints from some unruly neighbors about their children being chased in the park, and in fact an officer was here just a little while ago, so the doggies quickly put their humans on leashes.

"Maybe the Park Service could put up a fence. We pay our taxes," complains Chuck, an Irish terrier.

"There's never been a real problem with the kids," sniffs Sheba, a German shepherd-pit bull.

"In fact," says Baby Bess, part Pekingese, "a lot of children without dogs come here to play with them." But, she adds sadly, "a lot of people have babies, and then you see them with baby carriages walking on the fringe of the park, with their dog walking obediently along, their freedom gone."

Mama!

Fort Stevens Park, 13th and Van Buren streets NW :
On Monday, ceramics, bridge, bowling. On Wednesday, water exercise. On Thursday, pinochle lessons. On this particular hot afternoon, the seniors at the center here are having a flea market, lazy laughter and conversation around heaped tables. Glassware, a food processor, a Therm-a-Jug, a stainless steel chandelier.

"Shhhhh, Lenny!" orders a wife as her husband attempts to crack a joke. In an aside, she adds, "Fifty-two years of marriage in September and we're still together, unfortunately, ha ha, and I don't understand him yet."

Theresa Crawford, the director, drives her charges here and there, even if it means staying up late at night. "I do not allow my seniors to go home alone," she says. "I have to make sure they're safe."

Anna Willard, 87, confirms this. "This woman," she says, "is a dedicated director, with a heart of gold. She's very lovely, and compassionate, and kind. She's always trying to do something for someone else, and when you need her, she's there.

Why?

I lost my mother," says Crawford, "and I devote myself to making elders happy, these same seniors who made my mother happy. She was 94. I've wrapped myself around them, and made them all my moms. "

Out of Bulgaria

Rose Park, 26th and O streets NW:
Here, on the edge of Georgetown, where power tennis is played on the public courts, Daniela Stefanova, 20, waits. She is the daughter of a Bulgarian diplomat, and she waits to use the tennis wall. She is learning this game, even as her country, whose Communist government was ousted in 1989, is learning a new game. "I love sports," she says. "I don't know about 'power tennis.' It's great for fitness as well. After I get my master's in literature, I'll return to Bulgaria, which is trying to establish a market economy and democratic institutions. There are lots of changes, and sometimes it's difficult to keep up with them.

Nearby some people from Ghana are cooking fish and rice. A cop car is pulled up on the grass. The smiling cop is being given a Styrofoam container of fish and rice. Some kids are playing chess. The guy volleying against the wall finishes. Stefanova steps forward, and tentatively hits.

Prayer Warriors

North Michigan Park, 13th and Emerson streets NE:

The mayor had sworn up and down that the pools in the parks would be full this summer, or anyway, as she said, "will have water in them" by June 15—so of course the one in this park was empty during one midsummer visit, its white sides gleaming in the heat haze of late afternoon like a whale belly turned inside out and bleaching in the sun. No doubt it did have water in it June 15.

In any case, Anthony Weaver, 26, and Relvin Foster, 33, are playing basketball with three kids—Dion, Bryant and Dave, ages 9 to 13. The eternal thump of the ball. Weaver and Foster are doing this on their own time, after work, before going home to their own families. They say they believe in God, and that they can help save these kids from drugs and violence, from which they themselves were saved with the help of caring adults. They became friends at Boward, where they study social work on Saturdays.

"I tell kids, 'Leave drugs alone, and don't blame anyone else,'" says Weaver. "I tell them, 'Jesus Christ made me go back to school to help the youth out.' I've got three prayer partners at church, and I call them up before I do anything—go out at night or anything."

Foster: "Somebody gave me a chance once. Somebody worked with me. I'd say I had problems. The Lord has been with me since I was a kid—you stray away, and then you come back to Him. If I can help out just one kid, that gives me satisfaction."

Foster is a clerk at Wilmer, Cutler and Pickering, where he's coached the law firm's basketball team, Brief Emotion. What a wonderful name! Upon inquiry, unfortunately, it turns out to be a more carefully enunciated Briefs in Motion.

No matter. One day, a fax arrives from that firm stating that the values of many youths "are the wrong ones—owning a pair of expensive sneakers. . . . Whenever a person needs material things or someone else to change their mood, they suffer from low self-esteem."

It's Foster's term paper.

Down, but Not Quite Out, In Old Anacostia

Martin Malcolm Marcus Park, 14th and U streets SE:

Dirty paper everywhere. Broken benches. 'alf a dozen guys, unemployed, sitting there, saying they want work, want a chance, a life.

"The shooting and the crime and the crack," says Terry Bryant, 30, "most of us are not like that. We're trying to do the right thing, but we get put in that category."

"We're not about violence," says Donald Jordan, 33.

"We don't have a 9-millimeter in our hand," says Bryant.

"We just want a pen in our hand, a shovel in our hand," says Jeffrey Foster, 28.

"We aren't crying on anybody's shoulder," says Milton Carter, 28.

"They won't give a brother a chance," says Foster.

It is 4 p.m. Earlier, they looked for work. Now they've repaired to their park to socialize, compare notes. Up walks Chester Smith, 28, who speaks long and eloquently on these same subjects, with such oratorical flair that his buddies kid him about becoming a political candidate. "I speak for all of our brothers here," he says. "We're not bad guys. I'm married with two children, I live with my wife and children. I just enrolled in school today. I know I can accomplish something!" He tells how he got shot one day, was at a pay phone calling home and got caught in a drug revenge scene.

He pulls up his shirt to reveal terrible scars on his belly where the bullet fragments came out, turns to show the round scar where it entered, three centimeters to the left of his spine.

"I woke up in the hospital," he says, "with my intestines in a bag."

Designer Park Guilt

Bureaucrat Park, Sixth and I streets SW:

This may be the most exquisite park ever, though nameless on maps. One square block of immaculately manicured foliage, beetle traps on the trees, a lake with mini-islands and fountains, little walkways and cozy hidden areas with benches that look as if they were designed by Sam Maloof, all set gemlike amid the Southwest renewal area. The Environmental Protection Agency headquarters is next to it, and the bureaucrats lunch there.

One day, two uniformed workers are cleaning the park. Already it seems spotless, but they sweep and trim and clean anyway, aided by plenty of clean-looking equipment loaded aboard their sparkling official white Chevy Custom Deluxe pickup, which is parked in the middle of the park.

"It's maintained by the National Park Service, I don't understand why," says Robin Cornwell, an EPA management intern with a degree in public administration. She is seated on one of the benches, eating a bagel, thinking.

"These guys are out here every day, and they really do a good job," she says. "And it's always like this, it's always clean and well maintained. I've thought about this. It's nice to have pleasant parks to sit in and eat lunch, but one wonders whether the priorities are in the right place, when you see the truck here so many days."

Vive la Tradition, If Not la Difference Turtle Park, 45th and Van Ness streets NW:

Three young women are chatting as their tots romp.

"I gained 45 pounds," says Sarah Rass, "but you lose it."

"I gained 50, and I'm five feet," says Patricia Beggiato. "I had fat over the knees. It was incredible."

"Did you swell?" asks Anne Farkas.

"The nursing," observes Kass, "helps you lose the weight and get your figure back." With one eye, she's watching her 18-month-old son, Jacob, who is climbing on the train. Suddenly she shouts cheerfully, "Chugga chugga choo-choo!"

Kass herself as a child used to play here in Turtle Park, so named for the big cement mommy turtle followed by little cement baby turtles in the sandbox, which have been here for decades at least. Turtle Park has lots of shade over the playground, and on the basketball court a sprinkler showers the shrieking toddlers just as it has done for these many years.

They talk about their husbands. Their friends. Their kids. Their jobs, which they once had, and liked, but don't want now and may never want again.

"We have the toughest job in the world," says Beggiato. "I'm enjoying staying home, definitely.

Farkas: "It's the most wonderful job in your life."

Kass: "Who knows when I can go back to teaching? I definitely want to be doing what I'm doing. It's exciting, and he's the best student I ever had. He's a really independent, happy, self-confident little guy, and I think it's because I'm with him."

Amid the women and children is a father, Malcolm MacPherson, former Newsweek foreign correspondent and now book author. He lounges upon a bench with his wife, Charlie, and their two children.

He has a book coming out next year and says his last, "Time Bomb," a history of the race for the atom bomb, "was in '86. You can see I haven't been exactly productive in the last couple years, but these things do take time, as far as books are concerned, anyway. You get started on something and think it will take a year, and all of a sudden three years have gone by in a blink. And then you have a couple of children, and come out to these playgrounds, and time goes by faster.

Surviving Grant Park

50th Street and Nannie Helen Burroughs Avenue NE:

The woman sucks on her beer through a straw. It's not even in a paper bag.

"All right, Pooper!" she shouts at her kid on the slide. "Don't do that, you'll break a leg!"

A pair of cops walk by. The other woman slides their beers out of sight. The cops don't care anyway, they're busy talking to each other.

It's tough in the apartment where she lives, the first woman says. "They won't fix anything up for me. There isn't enough room for us—two boys and a girl, and I haven't got but two bedrooms. I'm on Social Security, they're trying to get me for welfare fraud. They think I get welfare and Social Security, but I only get the Social Security."

She sucks on the straw. "Every time I come out here, all these kids come. They're here like sardines, starting when the sun goes down. There's been a lot of shooting and raping in that park over there"—she points across the avenue, where the cops have gone. "I don't go that way."

"I told my daughter to walk over there and wait for my son," says the other woman. "She said no."

"Some of these spots give me the creeps," says the woman. "Here, at least, I'm in the open and everybody can see you."

She looks around.

"I wouldn't mind having a house out here, in the park."

August 31, 1991

Charlottesville's Web

Posh, Polo and Shabby Chic

MARTHA SHERRILL

The night air is thick. The wind brings mint and grass and skunk. Trees rustle. The entrance to Patricia Kluge's place—in the dark middle of nowhere—says Albemarle Farms on little white stanchions by the gatekeeper's hut. Two little lions face each other with frozen roars. A lone light is burning. A million moths circle around the bulb. Far away, past the "No Trespassing, No Hunting" signs, past her golf course designed by Arnold Palmer, her swimming swans, her three-story stable with big brass chandeliers, past her tournament croquet lawn, is the 45-room mansion, the gothic-style chapel, the crypt, the tennis court, the pool house, the sculpture garden, the outdoor fountains, the helicopter landing pad and the herb garden that John Kluge left in April when he moved to the historic estate he owns next door called Morven Stud Farm.

It's 2.2 miles between them on the country road, but it seems longer in the dark. At Patricia Kluge's gate, there are stone walls and moths. At John Kluge's gate, there's a corral of mailboxes, ivy and a grand painted sign that says Morven, where the neighbors used to line up for the tulip garden tour every spring.

The neighbors wonder, now, if the gardens at Morven will ever be open again, or what will happen to the antique carriage museum that Pat Kluge wanted to build there. Nobody seems to care about whether she's dating Doug Wilder, has ever dated him, or has ever thought about dating him. They ask about the garden.

Pat Kluge laughs and laughs and laughs. "You do get questions like that, which is what makes the place so endearing," she says from Albemarle Farms. "Of course the gardens at Morven will be open in spring."

Passing commentary. Just passing-the-time commentary. Horse people wonder what Pat might to do with all her warmbloods—her glorious dressage horses—even though she's gotten the biggest divorce settlement in history. Nearly $2 million a week. The antiques people are thinking deaccession time. The university community wonders whether she'll remain on the University of Virginia Board of Visitors. But most-most-most of all, people in Charlottesville this summer are hoping for rain because their grass is dry.

They care, they don't care. "'They created a little English village, you know," shrugs one nearby horse farmer, "'with a chapel and a family crypt and everything, but they couldn't even stay married long enough to enjoy it."

The carriage museum project, by the way, has been canned. And Pat Kluge isn't selling her horses, but John Kluge is selling his. Otherwise, "life goes on as usual," she says. "The only thing different is that Morven has an occupant."

And of her friendship with Virginia Gov. L. Douglas Wilder? "When John and I decided to support Doug Wilder for governor, we had a hunch that he was a great man, that he'd make a wonderful governor who'd bring national attention to the state of Virginia. Our hunch was right," she says. "We didn't look on him as a black man. We looked on him as a man who would make a great governor. And so he has."

Passing commentary. "It's kind of like watching a soap opera," says antiques dealer Butch Elder in his Virginia drawl. "But it's not important. There's only a certain fascination for what's going to happen next. That's all. Charlottesville was a great place to live before Kluge got here. And it will be after he leaves."

Gentle Slopes

A great place to live. It's where a bad perm and baggy clothes don't stand out. It's where farmhouses aren't air-conditioned, where people don't have call waiting. It's a place that's small enough to have the white and yellow pages bound together in one slim phonebook—and in big type. It's a place for old and new hippies, where a pair of Birkenstock sandals can show up at a polo match. "'The only people I know who still smoke dope," says one observer, "live here."

It's a place where the fox hunting is "more egalitarian" than in Middleburg or Piedmont or Orange, according to Jill Summers, master of Farmington Hunt for 23 years. It's where her father, writer William Faulkner, rode until he dropped off. It's where U-Va. professors fox-hunt with students, with playwright Sam Shepard, with doctor's wives, with Old Virginia Types, with gas station attendants, and with writer Rita Mae Brown, who also plays polo. It's where many blacks have ridden, but none is a member. "None have applied," says Summers—who's also on the Farmington board. "I don't think there'd be any problem. I don't think so. But I could be mistaken."

It's a place where the roadside boxes for the *Charlottesville Daily Progress*— the town paper started in 1892—are stuffed with back issues. Nobody seems to care much for news. Or television. It's a place where 7-year-old John Kluge Jr. shouts "They have baseball card shops here!" in the background while his mom's on the phone. It's where small cottages in town have empty porch swings. It's where hundreds of old farms outside of town have white fences and emerald pastures and broken backhoes in the barn.

It's a place for vegetarians, and people who drive Chevy Blazers and four-wheel-drive station wagons powerful enough to lug trailers. It's where, in four days of driving, you can go without seeing one Mercedes-Benz. It's a place of gentle slopes—you're always driving uphill or downhill—and where you feel embarrassed to honk even though there's always a sleepy five-second delay before the cars move on a new green light. It's a place where actresses Sissy Spacek and Jessica Lange look just like all the other blond mothers with blond children walking on the mall. It's a place with a junky shopping strip (Route 29) with a pancake house and a view of the Blue Ridge mountains.

It's where people claim that the bones of Redcoats are buried in their back yards. It's where huge boxwoods as old as Earth grow. It's a place with scrub pines and maples, oaks and dogwood, wild cherry and ash. It's a place where you keep your dogs outside because they're covered with ticks. It's a place where a bookstore owner says she sells lots of fiction. It's a place where you can park illegally next to City Hall for three hours and not be ticketed.

It's a place for people who want farms but not rednecks. It's where horse farmer Cindy Schauer, a recent transplant from Minneapolis, says, "I barely run into any Virginians," but Thomas Jefferson probably designed her house. It's where Chuck Beegle, a professor of education at U-Va. who moved here 20 years ago, says, "I have to pinch myself sometimes. I grew up during the depression and my mother raised us. It was a tough life. I never thought I'd be around anything like this. It's really wonderful." And it's a place where Pat Kluge says, "This is my home. Absolutely. I'm staying here until they carry me out—in an attractive box, I hope."

It's a place for refugees of glamour too. It's where Peter Taylor and Ann Beattie write their stories, where Steven Soderbergh writes his screenplays, where Lincoln Perry paints. It's where Burt Reynolds and Lee Majors recently fought over a piece of land and where Kate Jackson has bought a farm. It's where members of the Scripps-Howard newspaper family and the Bronfman (Seagrams) family dwell, plus a son of Augie Busch and the Champion spark plugs heiress. It's where John Kluge—the richest man in America—still lives, and the "number one" spot in the country for "affluentials," according to the National Demographics and Lifestyles. It's where Art Garfunkel and Muhammad Ali and Martina Navratilova have lived, and where Rita Mae Brown, a lesbian writer with a cult following to rival Hemingway's, has become an absolute pillar of society.

"It's just getting so chic," Brown gripes, "I'm moving to the next county."

Girls' Polo

A couple hours away from sundown—when the birds are still yakking but the crickets have started up—the Piedmont Polo Team practices. It's women on horses in the arena. All women. It's all women but for the coach, Brian Barquin, who's calling them "you girls." He's either got the guts to do that or he doesn't know to call them "you women." Welcome to Charlottesville, the progressively backward paradise.

A blond 10 year-old girl in neon colors wanders around too, with a mammy doll in her hands. The New Old South?

Rita Mae Brown has a red tank top, a tattoo on her back, a tan. Her teammates wear T-shirts that say: In a perfect world, men would ride sidesaddle.

"Go faster, Rita Mae!" the coach shouts.

"If I go faster," Brown shouts back, "I'll get scared and stiffen up and fall off."

"Rita Mae . . ."

"I'm better than I was last year, Brian."

"I know you are," he says, "and you're still not fast enough."

If the Witches of Eastwick decided to leave New England, they'd move to this place. Brown puts up her mallet. She's poking at her eye. "Wait a minute, I've got a problem," she shouts. "I've got to take my contact out."

One player has stopped to get a Band-Aid. Someone else has been offered an Advil. "We're really learning the game," says Brown. "We may go slow, but we're being careful. Men aren't careful. I mean, they're over-mounted, usually, and are always being thrown.

"We may go slow," she says, "'but at least we stay on."

There are 17 members. It costs the team $10,000 a season to play. They sell parking spots for the matches, and T-shirts with the team motto, and little huggies for drink cans. They started in the summer of 1987. "When people ask me about summer in Charlottesville," says player Beth Seawell, "I say it's just polo and opera."

"Most of us fox-hunt," says Brown, who's lived in the area since 1949, "but that's hardly the same."

In the back of her pickup after the practice, she asks what other people are talking about in Charlottesville. Renovating houses. Development. Route 29. The Kluges.

"Mostly we don't talk about development," she says. "We talk about who's sleeping with whom—all that stuff. Don't you talk about that in Washington?"

Nobody seems to be sleeping with anybody in Washington, Rita Mae.

"You should move here, then.'"

How about Pat Kluge, do people talk about her?

"She's one of the most generous, loving people I've ever met," says Brown. "And in the brief time she's been here, she's done more for this town than families who've lived here for six generations. I can't believe anybody complains about her. Everybody I know, who knows her, loves her. She's always helping people, helping friends. She's always looking after people. Always."

Heading off to her truck, a Swedish-looking blond shouts out, "Hey! You didn't ask us anything about Sissy and Jessica."

What's there to know?

"Sissy keeps saying that she wants to join our team," says Brown. "Every year, she says that. Who knows? But she's great. And so is Jessica. They are good people—not snots."

"There's just more to Charlottesville," says the blond, "than them."

The Happy Stripper

More to Charlottesville. A sign on High Street reads "The Happy Stripper," and this turns out to be a furniture refinishing store. Refinishing, renovations—this part of the world is crowded with people freshening up the past, inhaling history like fumes. "I remember trying to buy furniture in 1969,"' says one PhD. "If you wanted something that wasn't old reproduction Sheraton or Hepplewhite, forget it. There were only two stores in the whole city that sold anything made in the 20th century."

There's a futon shop now and Scandinavian Interiors, but the focus on old things hasn't changed. "There's a real antiques-oriented market here in Charlottesville," says Butch Elder, who owns 1740 House Antiques with his wife, Mary Ann. The 1740 House is also a Virginia Landmark and on the National Register, since it was a tavern once belonging to John Marshall. The Elders have restored it. They've also sold furniture to "Sissy and Jack" and "Jessica and Sam." They sell "period" pieces. Period. They specialize in 18th-century American. They've got 12 rooms of it. It's spare, simple stuff. Jokes are cracked about Victorian furniture, or about the Empire style that people like in New Orleans.

Butch Elder is wearing a short-sleeved button-down. Polished brown shoes. Navy socks. There's a fan going in his office. "We don't see Sam as much as Jessica," he says. "But they both like horses and period houses, antiques, a ranch-type operation at home. Sissy is much more open about how much she loves it in Charlottesville, but I think they'll all remain here."

Development is the big issue in town, the Elders agree. Then, maybe, the Kluge Divorce and the tackiness of Route 29. "Although I think it's the fox hunters,"' says Butch, "who gripe about development the most. They are very conservative people. A little too conservative.

Sharing the Wealth

Verdant, people always call the Charlottesville countryside. But here and there you see houses and old barns being bulldozed. You see tractors and dirt movers up Barracks Road. You see quarter-acre lots out by Farmington Country Club (separate from the hunt club) with pricey new houses on them. There's traffic at rush hour on Route 29, especially near the pancake house.

In 1980, there were 55,000 people in Albemarle county, according to the Census. There were 40,000 people in the town of Charlottesville. The Visitors Bureau for the county predicts the 1990 figures for Albemarle County will jump to 73,000 and the town figures will remain the same.

"The town's the town," says the bureau spokeswoman. "It can't really grow."

Heading out on Barracks Road, you see small trees and dying grass. There are cookie-cutter attached town houses, Northern Virginia style. The tracts have names. There's "Huntwood" and "Old Salem" on the right. There are apartments that look like brick dorms with green shutter" for that Old South feeling, called "Hessian Hills" for the soldiers who were captured and housed near there.

"Much of the land where we once fox-hunted,'" says Chuck Beegle, "has now become developed. A few years ago we had to move the Farmington Hunt further out of town, but I don't think it was far enough."

The university owns nearly 2,500 acres in the county—and its University Real Estate Foundation has been at the center of several hotly disputed developments, particularly when it tried to build near Monticello, and when it announced a "research park" on a 500-acre site near the Charlottesville-Albemarle Airport.

For $2.45 million, real estate broker Steve McLean's got "Tall Oaks" for sale, a 96-acre farm. Everything has a name—which usually doesn't change from owner to owner. "Most of the people who buy the larger residences are from out of town," McLean says. "There've been so many articles about what a great place this is to live, some people just show up with their bags packed.'"

Charles Hurt, with his Virginia Land Co. of Charlottesville, is believed by many to be the biggest landowner in Albemarle County. "I've got about 4,000 or 5,000 acres," says Hurt—most of being developed. "I'm not the biggest landowner, but I guess I sell the most land," he says. He bought his first bit of land before he graduated from U-Va in 1954.

"I think the community is anti-development," he says. "That's always the way it is. People don't like to see things change. People come to town, buy a developed lot and house from me, then get mad when more are built. They don't really want to share the wealth."

Who is the biggest landowner;

"John Kluge", Hurt says. "John Kluge by far."

Citizen Kluge

The place the Kluges bought in 1982, the year after they married, was called "Short Hills Estate" and cost $2.97 million. Just four miles up the road from Monticello, it was an 18-room Georgian-style mansion built in 1948 on 1,000 acres of cattle farm. It had originally been an estate of 9,350 acres—a 1730 land grant from King George II to John Carter, secretary of the Virginia Colony.

After three years of renovation ending in 1985, the Kluges had demolished Short Hills and built Albemarle Farms. "It's a Kluge creation," says Pat, "and I plan to live here until my son takes over. The creation is a rambling house—45 rooms full of new marble and columns, upholstered walls, Portuguese rugs, painted plaster ceilings. They built the glass conservatory, the chapel, the crypt, stables, helicopter pad and golf course. Year by year, they bought neighboring farms—several of them historic properties. After the acquisition of Morven's 3,000 acres—for $9 million— the Kluges were sitting on nearly 9,000 acres.

It became a San Simeon of sorts. And John Kluge, the man who started Metromedia, who once owned the Harlem Globetrotters, the Ice Capades and 35,000 outdoor billboards, became something of a mystery.

People say they like Pat Kluge for sometimes walking around Charlottesville without makeup. Rita Mae Brown says everybody who meets Pat Kluge likes her, but most here, of course, haven't met her.

"I'm very happy that they take me as their own," says Pat Kluge of the locals, "that they scrutinize everything I do, how I must feel, where I go. It's like having a huge, extended family. But it's an invisible involvement, and it doesn't bother me. And I guess if it was gone, I'd miss it.

"I just wish," she says, "I had the time to be so interested in their lives."

Since moving into the area, there's no question that the Kluges—according to long-timers—have affected life here. Some good. Some bad. The pluses are the $3 million they've given U-Va. for the Kluge Children's Rehabilitation Center and their initiation and support of the Virginia Festival of American Film—going on its third year. Pat Kluge has helped out a local sexual assault rehabilitation center, and set up a minority internship at St. Anne's Belfield School in the name of Frances D. Hooks, and has also donated to the restoration fund for the old Paramont Theater downtown.

The Kluges cleared carriage paths and riding trails on their property, and offered use of them to neighbors. They invited friends and their large staff (more than 100) to use their private chapel. Daughters of friends were married there, and receptions were thrown. They raised campaign money for Douglas Wilder, a man who seems extremely popular in town. And they infused the county with glamour—perhaps unwanted by some. Their dinner parties and weekend house parties brought Frank Sinatra, King Juan Carlos of Spain, Barbara Walters, Tony Bennett, Rupert Murdoch, former King Constantine II of Greece and former attorney general William French Smith, among many others, to Albemarle County.

"It hasn't hurt the town," says Butch Elder. "It says something that the richest man in America would choose to live here."

Early on, Pat Kluge came up with the idea of building the finest English-style shooting preserve in America. She hired a chef d'equipe from Ireland, a baronet called Sir Richard Musgrave, to run it. Friends were asked to shooting parties until it was discovered that Musgrave and his two gameskeepers had been killing perhaps hundreds of federally protected hawks and owls that preyed on game birds. In 1988, the three were charged, convicted, fined. Musgrave returned to Ireland.

It is this and a *Town and Country* magazine article that local people mention to show their disapproval of the Kluges' lifestyle. In the 1987 article, Albemarle Farms was described as "the grandest estate to have been built in America since the Twenties." There were pictures of Pat Kluge standing in one drawing room—36 feet long with a 22-foot ceiling. She sat with John in a rare 1920 Bugatti coach. In her dining room, she posed in a ball gown with two servants. The servants were dressed in period costume. The article said the estate was "decorated with a grandeur previously unknown to the Virginia countryside."

Nothing could have been truer. "The South appreciates shabby genteel," says Farmington Hunt's Jill Summers. "They came to town, expected to be the social kingpins, and it didn't work."

"I saw pictures of those period costumes in *Town and Country*," says one academic. "I couldn't get them out of my mind." Another horse farmer just put it this way: "Marie Antoinette."

While gas station attendants and U-Va. undergrads ride with the Farmington Hunt, Summers says the Kluges were not accepted. "They attempted to take up fox-hunting, but they went about it the wrong way," she says. "You don't just say 'I'm a fox hunter' because you've got the proper clothes and a $100,000 horse."

William Faulkner said he liked Virginians because they were snobs, and snobs left him alone. Does his daughter still find this true? "Yes," says Summers. "But I think Pappy meant the word 'snob' to mean a self-contained person. A confident group who felt they didn't need to impress people. In Virginia, you don't make a big splash for the neighbors."

"Imagine," says Pat Kluge, "in a little town like Charlottesville, here comes a new family, with new wealth, who make contributions to the arts, to medicine, who build one the largest estates ever built by a family. Of course it makes an impression. We understand the feelings of the town. We can't help it, though. It has happened to the other families of great new money—to the Vanderbilts, the Rockefellers, everybody. We understand and we sympathize.'"

Southwood Mobile Homes

There's some laundry hanging outside to dry. There's a couple hundred mobile homes here, and plenty of speed bumps. The trailers are settled sweetly in the shade of big trees, but still, most of them—like the $3 million farmhouses up in the hills—are not air-conditioned, and it's up past 90.

Two women are standing in the Southwood Mobile Home Park office. There's a desk and some filing cabinets. There's a big painting hanging behind them. It's of a thunderstorm with a black horse and a white horse bolting off together. A conversation starts up. Just passing the time.

"I can't imagine why anybody'd move here," says Catherine Minor, 27. Her mom owns the park, where trailers are rented out for $275 to $300 a month. She's wearing a blue print cotton summer dress and pumps. "It's a nice place," she says. "I mean, it's got Monticello and everything, but I don't see the attraction."

"And people aren't so nice here," says Judith Tillman, 28. She was born in Charlottesville. She's got four kids and a husband trying to keep cool in a mobile home down the way. She's wearing the town uniform—baggy shorts and a huge T-shirt that's not tucked in. "Out in the country they are real nice, though. In Scottsville."

Minor: "It's the U-Va. students who are the worst."

Tillman: "Yep."

Minor: "They're cocky. They're arrogant and egotistical. They act like the city's supposed to stop when they arrive. They take over the town."

Tillman: "And it's harder to find jobs and homes when they're here."

Minor: "They're no better than us. They're just the same as we are."

Tillman: "John Kluge moved here, and he's just like we are."

Minor: "That's right. So is Pat Kluge."

Tillman: "Yep. She puts pantyhose on just the way we do.

Minor: "Yep. One leg at a time."

July 22, 1990

Red, White and Truly Blue

With Depression the Sigh of the Times, Gloom and Doom Are Sweeping Across America

HENRY ALLEN

America is like a barroom drunk. One minute it brags about its money and muscle, and then for the next hour it bleats into its beer about failure and hopelessness— from Mr. Big to a pitiful helpless giant, half-full to half-empty, strutting to fretting, a huge, lumbering manic-depressive going from Carter's malaise to Reagan's morning again in America to Bush warning us on Nov. 3: "You face a choice, whether to turn the clock back and return to . . . the malaise days."

Right now America is in one of its bleating phases, an ugly spasm of guilt, dread and nostalgia. Once more, America is depressed. Like a barroom drunk, it almost seems to be enjoying it.

A *Time* magazine cover story warns of a "national sense of uncertainty and malaise."

Money magazine's Consumer Comfort poll said in October that "gloom reigns" with an index rating of minus 24, lower even than the minus 19 of April when the headline was "Americans sink into a deep funk."

The *Economist* reports: "The American dream is in danger, as incomes stand still."

A recent *Wall Street Journal* story from Kansas City begin": "Here on Polish Hill, where Frank's Place tavern flies the Polish flag beside the Stars and Stripes, they celebrate the rebirth of Poland" democracy—and fear the decline of America's."

The outlook is bleak, the insights are bleaker. We may very well have nothing to fear but fear itself, but we do have fear itself.

According to a *New York Times*/CBS poll, about 4 in 10 Americans say things will get worse in the next five years, compared with 2 in 10 in 1984. ABC says that 8 in 10 Americans see the economy as worsening. Seven in 10 predict war with Iraq, and *USA Today* says fewer and fewer of them like the idea. Though the October jobless rate was only 5.7 percent, up from 5.2 percent in June, CBS News recently ran a week-long series called "Bad Times." Was this because 1990's bad times seem to be hitting unusually hard among the professional class—neighbors of media types?

In *Harper's,* Lewis Lapham exerts his prerogative as editor to write: "Although I know that Jefferson once said that it is never permissible 'to despair of the commonwealth,' I find myself wondering whether the American experiment with democracy may not have run its course."

Everything becomes a sign that things are getting worse. At recent fashion shows, some designers explained bright, sexy, playful new clothes as a response to pessimism and unhappiness, the same way they might have explained a fad for black veils. This is how America thinks when it gets depressed. When the gross national product grew at a rate of 1.8 percent in the third quarter of this year, the *Wall Street Journal* called it "surprising," and said in the same issue that much of the country was in a state of "clinical depression."

Economists don't expect a big recession, but "you never expect a big one," said Stephen McNees of the Federal Reserve Bank of Boston. A CBS News report reveals the tragedy of the "hidden homeless"—people who are forced to live with relatives. Once we called these situations "families," but now we see them for what they are—a sign of decline.

Fears of American decline have produced the declinists (Paul Kennedy, Richard Lamm et al.), who in turn have goaded into being the anti-declinists (Joseph Nye, Richard Rosecrance et al.). The problem for the anti-declinists is that while they may be right that we're not declining, they have to admit that so many of us are pessimistic that they had to write books to keep us from hurting ourselves with self-fulfilling prophecies.

Welcome, Mr. and Mrs. Front Porch U.S.A., to Sector D.

In Sector D you find: depression, decline, depravity, doom, denial, decay, debacle, dementia, Dukakis, debt, dysphoria, deconstruction, desuetude, dog days, distrust, drugs, dilly-dallying, despair, drivel, devolution, dissipation, danger, dysfunction, downers, degradation, divisiveness, deprivation, deficiency, dilemma, dwindling, dilettantism, dullness, darkness, deep doo-doo, damnation, dearth, death, doubt and disgust.

In Sector D, depression is fashionable. The drug that people urge on their friends is Prozac, but you have to be depressed to get a prescription for it. Being depressed has always had a certain glamour—it means that you are sensitive, serious, suffering, you are Hamlet, you are Joan Didion. With Robert Bly's seminars for men and John Bradshaw's family workshops, weeping is once more a public sacrament. The fashionable television shows for the intelligentsia are "The Simpsons," a cartoon about futility and ugliness, and "Twin Peaks,'" in which an entire town is sinking into madness, degeneracy and weeping. It is hard to imagine that only a couple of years ago we were humming "Don't Worry, Be Happy."

The *Village Voice Literary Supplement* for November ran a group of reviews under the title: "Everything You Wanted to Know About Depression but Were Too Bummed Out to Ask."

In one of the more celebrated books of the fall, John Updike's "Rabbit at Rest," the protagonist considers that "there has been a lot of death in the newspapers lately . . . everything falling apart, airplanes, bridges, eight years under Reagan of nobody minding the store, making money out of nothing, running up debt, trusting in God." The good news is that as he lies dying of a massive heart attack, he tells his son what it feels like: "All I can tell you is, it isn't so bad."

Another bestseller is "Darkness Visible: A Memoir of Madness," by William Styron. It chronicles his depression, and the depressions of famous friends and acquaintances (he doesn't seem to have any other kind), a condition so painful as "to verge close to being beyond description," and one that can be fatal, it should be added, in 15 percent of untreated sufferers of major medical depression. Once you get over the pain provoked by paying $15.95 for 83 pages, you can sample the strange faux-Augustan tone of Styron's prose, a style you may remember from your high school literary magazine when somebody wrote a short story narrated by a brooding duke, lines like: "It had been my custom of a near-lifetime, like that of vast numbers of people, to settle myself into a soothing nap in the late afternoon."

America's depression is not brought on by plague, flood, famine or war (actually, psychiatrists say the incidence of clinical depression goes down during wars). Instead, it is marked by fear of them, along with either a belief that things were once much better but never will be again (the conservative line), or a belief that things could and should be better, but won't be because of some flaw in the American character, or at least the character of America's white males (the liberal line).

We are guilty, guilty, guilty. We have raped Mother Nature, dishonored the Founding Fathers, abused our children, forgotten our past and mortgaged our future. In other countries, the press takes sides. Here, our value-free, fair-minded, statistics-obsessed media have met the enemy, and it is not one side or the other as much as it is all of us. We don't have problems, we have national crises, which keep adding up in commission reports and media woe-saying to "a nation at risk," as if a quarter of a billion people living in the strongest, richest, freest, most generous and most peaceful country in history were going to vanish tomorrow into the La Brea Tar Pits.

"When you watch the European media and the American media, you realize that everything is a crisis the way the Americans describe it," says an American diplomat in Bonn.

We have bred a governing class—media, academia, appointive politicians, lawyers—that is whipsawed by a nasty combination of both puritan dread and WASP-rot nostalgia; a class that can brood simultaneously about auto safety and how expensive Adirondack chairs have gotten; pallid proponents of skinless chicken and historic preservation, of no-smoking laws and the stories of John Cheever. They think that we deserve whatever punishment is coming to us, but like many of their fellow Americans, they also believe that happiness is the normal state of affairs, a belief that is contradicted by most of philosophy and all of history, although unhappy countries, like unhappy families, are unhappy in their own ways.

"America is an underachiever in happiness, when you compare us to countries who are poorer than we are," says the University of Michigan's Ronald Inglehart, author of "Culture Shift in Advanced Industrial Society."

He points out that according to life-satisfaction surveys, "the Irish are happier than Americans, even though they're much poorer." So are a lot of countries. In fact, some Americans get more unhappy the richer they get. "Once protests were a working-class phenomenon. Now it's the upper-middle and upper classes who do the protesting, particularly the post-materialists for whom quality of life and self-expression are important issues—younger, more educated people."

Newsweek reports that in the last decade the disease once known as "yuppie flu" has spread throughout the population—"2 million to 5 million Americans have been stricken" with chronic fatigue syndrome, a disease in which fevers, lymph-node swellings, night sweats, diarrhea and muscle pain get together with mood swings and panic attack." One woman with CFS had a dog who'd gotten it too. It seems like only yesterday that so many of us were suffering from hypoglycemia, not to mention post-traumatic stress disorder, premenstrual syndrome, postpartum depression, seasonal affective disorder, psychic numbing, holiday depression syndrome and midlife crisis.

In "The Diseasing of America," author Stanton Peele asks: "What has given us the idea that we are so impotent and helpless? Why have we become enmeshed in dysfunctional, exaggerated fears about our environment? Why have we decided that we—and our children—cannot control even our own emotions and behavior? . . . Why have we become so afraid that addiction is everywhere and that we are out of control of our eating, shopping, lovemaking, gambling, smoking, drug taking, menstrual cramps, feelings after birth, anxieties and depressions, and moods of all kinds?"

Is it possible that something has utterly changed in the national psyche? We are led by media reports to wonder if America is in the midst of a unique nervous breakdown suffered by a generation grown so narcissistic and selfish, "so enamored of ourselves, that we are dissatisfied if our explorations bring us face to face with any image but our own." A generation marked by "desire for stimulants and narcotics . . . fear of responsibility, of open places or closed places, fear of society, fear of being alone, fear of fears, fear of contamination, fear of everything, deficient mental control, lack of decision in trifling matters, hopelessness . . ."

As it happens, the quotations in the last paragraph were taken from popular publications of the 1880s and the 1890s. In short, we have been depressed before.

"There is that chronic strain in America," says Rutgers cultural historian Jackson Lears, pointing to decade after decade of fears for the republic.

Tocqueville looked at America's best and brightest in the 1830s and saw that "a cloud habitually hung on their brow, and they seemed serious and almost sad even in their pleasures" because they "never stop thinking of the good things they have not got."

In 1854, Thoreau assured his place in *Bartlett's Familiar Quotations* with: "The mass of men lead lives of quiet desperation."

In 1881, a book called "American Nervousness" popularized the term "neurasthenia," a disease that affected "civilized, refined and educated" people, said the author, George M. Beard, with a set of symptoms that sound like a combination of depression and chronic fatigue syndrome.

After World War II, we picked up W.H. Auden's phrase, "age of anxiety."

Nowadays, are we depressed because the future looks bleak, or does the future look bleak because we are depressed." Popular prophecies of hard economic times are pretty reliable, but how many of them are self-fulfilling? Do the media describe Americans as disgruntled because media people—precisely the class at risk for everything from neurasthenia to mood disorder—are disgruntled?" Do Americans tell pollsters they're worried because it's gotten hipper to be worried, a sign of one's intellect and social commitment? Are they angrier because they've been taught to let it all hang out?

Is there a melancholy that is part of the American psyche? Being American means being prey to a sense of being overwhelmed by time, space and opportunity, of failing to think big enough, of having missed your chance, a sense that produces the astonished fatalism of Faulkner, the bewildered corruptions of "The Great Gatsby," the ending of the '60s movie "Easy Rider" where Captain America says to Billy, "We blew it." Are things worse in 1990?

"In general, people are more pessimistic now," says Gerald Klerman, a professor of psychiatry at Cornell University Medical College. "People get depressed when there's a gap between expectation and fulfillment. This is particularly bad for females—the women's movement raised expectations very high for women. Reality has not fulfilled these expectations."

Even after allowing for changes in the way we diagnose clinical depression, and for the fact that mental illness isn't kept a shameful secret the way it once was, a lot of psychiatric epidemiologlsts think there's a lot more depression in America since World War II, an increase of two to three times, an increase far greater than increases in schizophrenia, panic disorder and phobias.

"Who knows?" says Klerman. "It could be almost anything. It could be something in the air from radioactive testing. It could be food additives. It could be a virus—if there was a virus, we could have a vaccine."

And if there was a virus, we might find that chronic fatigue syndrome and depression are part of the same thing. "I think that when all is said and done, the increase in fatigue will be seen as an increase in depression," Klerman says.

Reality, oh grim reality: In the last few years, we've heard the depressing news that depressives tend to be more realistic than normal people. They see themselves as others see them, they predict their performance on tests better, psychologists report. This is the depressive's equivalent of Hunter Thompson's First Law of Paranoia:

"There is no such thing as paranoia. Your worst fears always come true."

As the most beautiful sunset in the history of the world unfurls, glitters, blooms, stabs and generally spreads out against the sky like everything but a patient etherized upon a table "to quote one of the poems that has glamorized depression for generations of American students), Frederick Goodwin, the psychiatrist who runs the Alcohol, Drug Abuse and Mental Health Administration, sits in his 12th-floor office overlooking greater Rockville and says:

"Vulnerability to depression is a constant. It doesn't change. But the incidence of depression has increased since the 1960s and the age of onset has lowered. What might explain it? There were the traumas of the early and mid-1960s, and fundamental changes in society. There was a loss of the compact between people and government. Gender differentiation broke down. There was a doubling in the divorce rate. We now are seeing the first generation of kids coming to adulthood who were not raised by their mothers. We are seeing adults who survived because of advances for kids who used to die in infancy, adults who might have survived with somewhat compromised nervous systems.

"We've had a decreased impact of religion and patriotism, and an increase of cynicism about public institutions. We had a tremendous increase in mobility after World War II. External sources of self-esteem were stripped away. Allan Bloom {author of "The Closing of the American Mind"} has cited increasing moral and cultural relativism. It's hard to get an anchor. A lot of depressed patients cannot forget injuries, and the legal system plays into that with its concept of injury liability, and there is the politics of victim empowerment that runs the risk of reinforcing that way of thinking."

Goodwin turns out the office lights, the better to study the crepuscular glory over Montgomery County.

"It is useful to say there is a certain contagion factor here, and it affects the whole society. Hopelessness and inability to believe you can change things are part of depression too, and since 1964 we've seen a tremendous drop in research and development as a percentage of gross national product, a drop in investment in roads, bridges and education. That would reflect a general loss of confidence in the future."

However, Goodwin is the first to point out that the sunset is very pretty indeed.

"We're bombarding people more and they're responding to things they hear," says Everett Ladd, director of the Roper Center for Public Opinion Research at the University of Connecticut. "There's more volatility than 15 years ago. You turn on the tube every night and there's somebody screaming—if you go back to the '50s, the days of the Camel Caravan, the tone was a lot different. Something has come along, a cynical or skeptical thing has become more fashionable. You see it in assessments of presidents in polls. Back in the '50s, even members of the out party were much more reluctant to be critical of the president, but there's been a change in public rhetoric."

In 1952, according to Gallup, 47 percent of Americans said they were very happy, and in 1982 the number was 50 percent. The highest it got was 57 percent in

1973, the lowest was 40 percent in 1976, but over the long haul, the satisfaction and happiness numbers stay remarkably level. Or the dissatisfaction and unhappiness numbers stay level, depending on whether you see the glass as half full or half empty.

Robert Reich, a liberal philosopher at Harvard, writes about the manic-depressive mentality of America:

"Celebrate our triumph over savages and evil abroad! Rejoice in the opportunity open to each of us to gain fame and fortune! Admire our generosity and compassion! See how we have overcome vested privilege! But the same stories can be cast as rebukes, exposing the great gulf separating what we are from what we want to become, or how far we have fallen from an ideal we once achieved. The world is succumbing to tyranny, barbarism, and devastation while we stand idly by! Hard work and merit are sabotaged by convention, chicanery, and prejudice! We are selfish, narcissistic, racist, indifferent—look at the poor and hungry in our midst! Our democracy is a sham, and everything important is controlled by a cabal at the top!"

Half-full, half-empty. Right now, we seem to be running on half-empty.

November 26, 1990

Sarah's Story

Voices from a Fractured Past—Wisconsin Woman Describes the Origin of Her Selves

CYNTHIA GORNEY

Two blocks from the courthouse, waiting for the verdict, Sarah was smoking a cigarette. She held her arms oddly, a stiff angle to the elbows, and when the reporters came in she smiled and sat carefully in a dining chair in the middle of the room. She had invited three reporters, summoning them as a group to the small hotel where she had decided to spend Thursday afternoon, and she received them in the sober dress of a promising young executive—stockings, smooth gray blouse, navy pin-striped suit.

"Castration," Sarah said, with precision. A reporter had just asked for her view on a suitable punishment for Mark Peterson, the unemployed grocery store bagger charged with raping her in an Oshkosh park. "Life in prison," Sarah said.

She was asked to elaborate.

"What he did was unforgivable," Sarah said. She had put on eyeliner, neatly, upper and lower lids. Her hair was combed smooth and straight to her shoulders. She said she did not object to being described in some detail, as long as the description was not unkind; "terrible" was the word Sarah used, and she laughed. "Don't say I look terrible."

She said it was all right to put her first name in the newspaper, even though she believed herself to be a rape victim. "The name Sarah," a reporter said, sounding uncertain. "Are we talking to Sarah now?"

"Actually," Sarah said briskly, "I'm not sure if she—Franny? Are you still here?"

For an instant she sat, her eyes open, her gaze fixed a short way off. Her eyebrows lifted. A fleeting animation swelled her face. "Yes, dear!" she cried. Then the eyebrows lowered again, and she nodded. "She's here," she said.

Did you believe it? From his bench, Judge Robert Hawley faced the jury Thursday morning, reading aloud from the printed instruction" he had prepared to guide their deliberations. "Second-degree sexual assault, as defined in Section 940.225 (2) (c) of the Criminal Code of Wisconsin, is committed by one who has sexual intercourse with a person who suffers from a mental illness which renders that person temporarily or permanently incapable of appraising his conduct," Hawley read, "'and the defendant knows of such condition."

He read clearly, enunciating each word, the papers held before him in both hands. He told the jurors they must disregard any testimony stricken from the record. He said the burden of proof rested entirely with the state. He said it did not matter whether the woman named Sarah had in any way consented to sexual intercourse; what the jurors must determine, Hawley said, was whether Sarah was mentally ill on June 11, 1990, the day Mark Peterson and Sarah—or Jennifer, or Franny, or Emily, or Leslie, or Leona, or any of the other names that Sarah gave to what she described as dozens of alternate personalities—had sex in the front seat of his car.

Did you believe it? On Main Street, in Oshkosh, in the Daun-town Cafe, an older man sauntered gaily Thursday morning toward a booth of younger women. "Can't help myself," he cried, as he leaned forward to wink suggestively at them. "'I'm just one of those dual personality guys."

The women laughed and poked him in the arm. "I think they ought to give her an Academy Award," someone said at another table. "There's an idea for you, Tony," a third man said. "If you ever get caught with another woman, just tell your wife you've got multiple personalities."

There were multiple personality jokes in the courthouse pressroom too, and reporters turning uneasily to each other the day the extraordinary Sarah took the stand and appeared to shift in and out of personality on request: What did you think? You buy it? The experts had insisted, when news people called them for comment, that *State of Wisconsin v. Mark A. Peterson* was not forging law on the question of multiple personality disorder; the jurors were simply obliged to decide, they said, whether Peterson knew Sarah was mentally ill before he drove her from her apartment and seduced her in an Oshkosh park. "*National Enquirer* story," a University of Wisconsin law professor snorted, as he disposed of yet another request for comment on the Multiple Personality Rape Case. "Not the kind of thing you guys should be covering."

But of course the courthouse halls were crisscrossed with television camera wires, and two motion picture people took notes from the front rows, and when spectators arrived outside court on Wednesday at 7 in the morning, they found a lengthy line already waiting to get in. A court of law is a place of public display, and the 27-year-old woman who brought charges against Mark Peterson was promising a display so memorable that District Attorney Joseph Paulus screened his jury pool Monday by asking for a show of hands from those who thought it too bizarre to contemplate.

"You will get the chance to observe her transform from one personality to another," Paulus said. "It is somewhat dramatic, and most unusual. Is there anyone who feels they could not be a part of that process?"

To no one's surprise, no hands went up. From the day last August when the Winnebago County prosecutor's office first drafted the criminal complaint against Peterson, this case had stirred interest and argument about a good deal more than a date-rape report and a subsection of the Wisconsin criminal code. If the allegations were true, then ordinary people in one Midwestern city were about to watch a courtroom demonstration of something that might without undue hyperbole be called the splitting of a human mind. And if the allegations were true, then Peterson had managed almost literally to do what men and women have for decades made the subject of raw anger and raucous jokes: Deliberately, planning it, figuring it out beforehand, he had reached into a woman of great self-control and pulled out a woman with none.

Growing Up 'Multiple'

"I know from Leona that I was at least multiple since I was a baby," Sarah said. "She remembers being with me in the orphanage—arriving there. She was the first one."

The psychiatrists who now diagnose multiple personality cases frequently believe severe childhood trauma causes the young mind to split apart to protect itself. Did Sarah know whether she had been traumatized too?

"For one thing, I had no maternal or paternal care of any kind," she said. "I was not touched or picked up, except to be fed or changed. And Leona reports—Leona is an empath . . ."

An empath?

"She can sense the emotions of the insiders, and of myself," Sarah said. "She reports that I was a very angry, lonely, sad and confused baby. And the reason she finally emerged was as a comforting presence. She could not communicate at the time."

Sarah's voice was extremely firm and clear. "I know that my father was probably a soldier, Caucasian of some sort," she said. "My mother was Korean. That a neighbor brought me to the orphanage."

Here she stopped, and gazed at her knees and breathed. When she spoke again, her voice was unchanged. "That round-eyed, half-breed babies are not accepted in countries like that, at least in that country, and that had I remained there I probably would have been killed, murdered or ended up in prostitution, forced prostitution, drugs, slavery, something like that. Bad. That they want to keep the race pure."

There were reasons, Sarah said, that she did not elaborate during the trial on the particular troubles of her upbringing. "For my parents' sake," she said, meaning the Americans who adopted her and raised her in Iowa City. "Not all of it was their fault. There was a lot of confuslon, because they did not realize what they had in me. And because I believe my father was ill and could not help himself." Her father's illness appeared to her to be manic depression, she said. "They did not realize I was multiple," Sarah said. "All they knew, for all I know, was that they had a child they couldn't cope with."

When she was 20, Sarah said, her father was crushed to death when the jack collapsed under a car he was repairing. Sarah and her mother found the body, she said, and she believes a personality named Evan was created to manage the emotion of the discovery. "Justin and Richard came about when I went to a private school," she said. "So did Ginger. That one was formed specifically to take in the sexual abuse that I suffered at the private school, and from the hands of a 32-year-old that I did not know."

A teacher?

"No," Sarah said, her voice still firm. "A stranger. And to learn to like it, in order for the body to cope with it."

Was there any possibility, she was asked, of talking to Ginger?

"No," Sarah said quickly. "The last time she went on a bender, she nearly killed the body. I'm on medication that does not mix with alcohol. She nearly killed us. I ended up in the hospital. As a punishment, and to protect the body, Leona took her down very deep into my mind, and dropped her in some sort of a well and left her there, with a massive headache. She cannot come out unless Leona brings her out, and I strongly recommend that not be done except under a doctor's supervision, with Thorazine close by."

The reporters nodded and put writing on their note pads. There was a moment's silence. "Would it be possible," a reporter asked, "for us to meet one of your male personalities?"

"Which one?" Sarah asked quickly. "How about Evan? Do you have any Marlboros? Evan believes Marlboros are the only real cigarette. Typical male. No offense meant."

The reporter said none was taken. "L&Ms are the best I can do," he said.

"I'll see what I can do," Sarah said. "I can ask them out. They don't know you. Whether or not they come out is entirely up to them. Perhaps if Sheila calls them out."

Sheila Carmichael, the county victim's assistance coordinator, went to look for a pack of Marlboros. "Evan is 19," Sarah said. "He is mainly meant to cope with crises. He went to college with me, where we got an associate of arts degree in law enforcement, and he wants very badly to be a cop. But he realizes that as long as we are multiple, we cannot."

Carmichael came back with the Marlboros. "Okay, Evan, let's get ready," Sarah said. She opended the package and tapped a cigarette into her palm. "Can you stand so that he can see you?" she asked Carmichael.

"Sure," Carmichael said, and moved closer. Sarah closed her eyes. "Can you call him?" she asked.

"Evan," Carmichael called, wheedling a little, as though coaxing someone from the next room. "I got something for you. Marlboros."

Sarah opened her eyes. She looked at the cigarettes. She looked up at Carmichael. Heartily, with a voice that now had chest in it, she cried, "Bless your heart! How you doing?"

"I'm doing fine," Carmichael said. Sarah held up the cigarettes. "Can I have one? Are these mine? Hot damn."

"Evan," Carmichael said. "These people are from several different newspapers. Tom Richards, he's from the *Post-Crescent*."

Sarah lunged across the table to shake hands, and then gazed down at herself. "Oh, God," she said. "I'm wearing a dress. I hate it when that happens."

She looked at her feet, and started. "What the hell are those?" she cried.

"Pumps," Carmichael said.

"Jesus Christ," Sarah said. She lifted one heel. "They're 10 feet off the ground."

Scenes From a Courtroom The criminal complaint itself, written in dry police officer's prose, has about it the tone of unnerved sobriety that marked nearly all of the four-day trial. "While driving in the car, Sarah was still experiencing the 'Franny' personality. Mark A. Peterson then asked Franny if he could talk to Jennifer, at which time the 'Jennifer' personality appeared. Sarah described the 'Jennifer' personality as a 20-year-old female who likes to dance and have fun. Sarah indicated that neither her 'Franny' personality nor her 'Sarah' personality were present after the 'Jennifer' personality appeared. Therefore, neither 'Franny' nor 'Sarah' had personal knowledge of what subsequently transpired."

Mark A. Peterson, according to the complaint, had introduced himself on the evening of June 9 to a woman fishing at an Oshkosh park. The complaint declares that the woman identified herself as "Franny," and that Peterson was told, both by the woman and by a neighbor who was fishing with her, that the woman had "multiple personalities and a mental disorder." Following these warnings and additional information about the woman's many personalities, the complaint charges, Peterson took the young woman out in his car two days later and waited until she had turned into "Jennifer" before proposing that they have sex. Edward Salzsieder, Peterson's attorney, asked Sarah on the stand about what happened next. "You did not like the sex?" Salzsieder asked.

Sarah, in the voice she had introduced as Jennifer's, asked Salzsieder what he was talking about.

"The sex," he said.

"What's that?" Sarah-Jennifer asked. Sarah-Jennifer, Sarah-Sarah had already explained, is 20 and shows up at the sound of rock music. She very much likes to dance, Sarah-Sarah had testified. But she does not know about much of anything else.

"Didn't the two of you have sex?" Salzsieder asked.

"I dunno," Sarah-Jennifer said, her voice rising. "What's sex?"

It was a moment of such utter illogic that Salzsieder stopped for a moment, looking at the witness, collecting himself. In the courtroom he was a plodder, with his ill-fitting jackets and his hair awry over his forehead; for the first two days he carried his notes and files to the defense table in a cardboard box that read "Schweppes Seltzer" on the side, and there he would sit, bent over his legal pads, while the younger prosecutor in the good dark suits brought witness after witness to the stand and then chatted amiably with the television reporters during recess.

Salzsieder was defending a rapist whose alleged victim was testifying that she put her arms around him and told him it felt good, but he appeared to be making no headway at all.

"Did you tell him before you got to the park that you were multiple?" Salzsieder asked.

"I'm not multiple," Sarah-Jennifer snapped.

"Did you tell him you were seeing a doctor?" Salzsieder asked.

"No," Sarah-Jennifer said.

"Did you tell him you were in treatment with a therapist?" Salzsieder asked.

"No," Sarah-Jennifer said.

When the exchanges like this were complete, Paulus would get up and propose to the jury that it was obvious Sarah's personalities had no mental illnesses; they were her mental illness, or at least the plainest symptoms of it. The argument began to suggest a passage from "Through the Looking Glass": Every time the judge entertained motions outside the presence of the jury, Salzsieder would reason that his client had sex with Jennifer, that Jennifer was "in touch with reality" that even if Sarah didn't know what she was doing in the front seat of Peterson's car, Jennifer did.

Some personality along the way had arranged for a tubal ligation too, either Sarah or Jennifer or one of the others; Jennifer herself had let that slip under Paulus's questioning, and Salzsieder kept trying to convince the judge to let him inquire further about that, or the hints that during one period in her life Sarah had gone out as the alcoholic Ginger and picked up men in bars while becoming, as Sarah-Sarah testified, "totally toasted."

But the judge would have none of it. "The rape shield law prevents any questioning of that type," Judge Hawley would say, citing state law preventing the introduction of evidence about a rape victim's past sexual history. Hawley himself evinced no change of expression each time he swore in a new Sarah; her head would sink, she would look up again, her eyes would fly open, and out of her mouth would come a voice whose inflection and language were different from the one just before.

Not very different, though—just different. After a few minutes the difference would flatten, as though the vocal cords were abandoning the effort. Her vocabulary stayed consistent from one personality to the other, and toward the end of her testimony much of the courtroom had fallen into a kind of hypnotic confusion of grammar, with attorneys and reporters variously referring to her as Jennifer, or Jennifer-and-Franny, or Franny-and-Emily, or "them."

Along the open courtroom benches, where the seats were so jealously guarded that Hawley had warned that anybody going to the bathroom might be displaced by someone in line outside, the onlookers thrashed it around. "She consented," said a retired restaurant owner named Dennis Hughes. "She gave him her telephone number."

"But Jennifer didn't give him her telephone number," said a retired business-man named Dan Sullivan. "Franny did."

"Same person," Hughes said.

"Not really," Sullivan said.

"When I hear a Sousa march, my foot goes tap, tap, tap," an elderly man said. "Does that mean I have an additional personality?"

"Want to see me do it?" asked a woman in the back row. "Watch. I'll reemerge as Jennifer. I'm a good actress. I could do that."

An Illness or an Act

When she is Evan, Sarah explained to the reporters, she uses the toilet sitting down. But she hates It. "It's just annoying," Sarah said, in the voice she introduced as Evan. "I have to sit down. I tried it standing up, and I missed the john."

Was there a reason for this?

"It's the way the body is built," Sarah-Evan said. She sounded matter-of-fact.

What if she were sick, she was asked, but not the way the doctors said she was? What if some ordinary guy from the courtroom back row thought her sickness were a frantic and brilliantly realized need for public attention? What if her entire court testimony, not to be overly rude about it, was one, long, mad stretch of the-ater?

A reporter wondered if this was a question best handed off to Sarah. "You can ask me," Sarah said. "Sarah."

So Sarah answered.

"The majority of people are totally unaware of MPD, or its nature," she said. "Even doctors and psychiatrists are only recently beginning to acknowledge this as a legitimate disorder. They have been unable to recognize it. I would not expect the average layperson to understand it, because I believe it's a difficult concept to ac-cept, even for me. But I have it."

She was certain about this?

"Oh, yes," Sarah said. She had put out the Marlboro. Her arms still had the odd tense angle to them, as though she were recovering from surgery. "Oh, yes. No doubts."

The prosecution-introduced psychiatrists who examined Sarah over the past year, both in Oshkosh and at the medical centers where she was sent for confirma-tion of the multiple personality diagnosis, testified that her personalities appear to have varied in number from 18 to at least 46. Some of these are "fragments," the doctors said, holding only certain emotions, and some of them, like the ones that pushed burning cigarettes into the backs of her hands, are self-destructive. On the stand, as Paulus examined her, Sarah testified that she sometimes entered into con-tracts with personalities whose behavior she needed to control; she had given her car keys to her neighbors so that Ginger would not drive drunk, she said, and for a time she kept her hands bandaged because the personality called Shadow kept jamming her hands through glass windows.

She kept small signs by her apartment windows, according to the trial testimony, that read, "Do Not Break These." This was not Sarah's testimony; it was Peterson's. Peterson said he was in her apartment when he saw the signs. He was at her house when he learned everything he was to know about Sarah's illness, Peterson testified; he did he see her change personality, as he said to the police in his statement, and he did have knowledge that she engaged in sex with him as someone named Jennifer. But he said all this knowledge came after the sex act, not before.

"I thought I was having sex with Franny," Peterson testified.

When he first heard about Jennifer, Peterson testified, he thought she was another person entirely. He said Sarah, whom he thought was called Franny, was talking about someone named Jennifer in the cafe where they spoke before they drove off and had sex in his car.

"A possible promunctuous person," Peterson said, referring to Jennifer.

"What?" Paulus asked.

"Promunctuous," Peterson said. "Bold."

"Promiscuous?" Paulus asked.

"Whatever,'" Peterson said.

He gave his testimony placidly, his head slightly cocked toward the lawyers' tables, without looking at the jury. He said that much of what he had said in June in the police affidavit he signed was wrong—"screwed up." He said he never heard Sarah's neighbors warn him early on that she was, in Paulus's word, "mental." He said Sarah never explained to him before their drive to the park that she was, in her word, "multiple." He said his co-workers were "mistaken" when they testified that Peterson told them he had engaged in sex in his car with a 20-year-old named Jennifer who had seemed unusually innocent and who "turned him on."

He said that after he brought Sarah home and learned about her mental disorder, he left the house quickly because he "had to get ready to get to work."

"You weren't due at work for three hours," Paulus said.

"I had to freshen up," Peterson said. "I couldn't go to work smelling like some bull in a pigpen."

Before supper on Thursday, when the jury had been debating for a few hours, they called the judge to ask for a copy of the police affidavit Peterson had signed. The affidavit was sent to the jury room. Cameramen went out to dinner; reporters slouched across the tables in the pressroom; outside, in the nearly deserted courthouse parking lot, it started to snow.

"Verdict!" someone said.

When the judge read the verdict Peterson looked ahead, with no discernible expression on his face. The judge polled the jurors, one by one: You find him guilty, the judge repeated, all of you, each and every one.

"I don't want to say he was lying, but he was all contradictory," one of the jurors said afterward. "Personally, I believe that she is a very sick woman, and I do not myself believe that she has MPD. . . . But we didn't need to recognize MPD. We just needed to recognize that there was, and is, an illness."

Peterson tried to walk quickly from the courtroom, but the cameras were faster than he was, and when he broke into a trot the cameramen began trotting too, and calling his name. The lights were brilliant in the darkened hallway. "Come on, Mark," somebody shouted, and when he turned around he was standing in a corner, his arms crossed in front of his body, with all the cameras at him and his back to the courthouse walls.

"'Could this happen to anybody?" somebody yelled.

"Oh, definitely," Peterson said. "It could, again, anybody can, if they're not aware of this person. Somebody else could be the next one. "Mark!" a reporter shouted. "Do you feel sorry for anything?"

"What's there to feel sorry about?" he asked.

The microphones came forward, closer to Peterson's mouth.

Did he think she was lying?

"You be the judge," Peterson said. "Do you think she was?"

November 10, 1990

Stepping Lively

At Black Frats and Sororities, the Dance that Unites

JILL NELSON

"This step has never been performed before by women in these United States," a young woman intoned as eight members of Zeta Phi Beta sorority tied blindfolds across their eyes.

"Please, please, don't try this at home," the woman teased.

The eight women stood on a dimly lit, unadorned stage. They were all wearing white shorts, multicolored T-shirts, black patent-leather shoes with blue ribbon, and white socks—the Zeta colors. Then they coupled off and were into it. Feet intersected with feet, hands slapped hands, knees linked but never knocked. They created danceable rhythms with hands and feet. When it was over, the crowd conferred its version of a standing ovation, a mixture of barking, clapping and ululating. Or was it meowing?

A few routines later, chanting "Zetas are the only ones licensed to groove," the women stood with their legs apart. Then each tapped the left foot twice, the right once, clapped hands, jumped on the left foot, slapped the sole of the right, pivoted, turned 360 degrees and did the whole sequence again.

Or something like that, the foot and hand often being quicker than the eye in "stepping," a ritual already familiar to the 200,000 African American college students who belong to fraternities and sororities, their 2 million alumni, and anyone who saw Spike Lee's 1988 film, "School Daze."

Stepping is tap dancing without tap shoes, James Brown without the music of the JB's, Cab Calloway sans piano, a marching band without John Philip Sousa. It is jazz, funk, rhythm and blues, and rap without instruments.

Stepping is lean and mean. The music comes from the synchronized interplay of hands and feet, from chants and hollers. It is a way to make music using the body as instrument. Stepping has been a part of the rituals of African American fraternities and sororities for a half century, but its roots reach all the way back to Africa.

"The actual stepping is based on African dance, especially West Africa," said Maurice Henderson, whose book "'Black Greek Letter Organizations: A Lesson in Egyptology and African American Heritage" will be published in July by Civilized Publications.

The first African American fraternity, Alpha Phi Alpha, was founded in 1906 at Cornell University. According to Henderson, step shows originated in fraternities in the mid-1940s. Women didn't start stepping until the 1950s.

"When I first joined a frat and I was stepping, they showed a film in anthropology class that showed Africans dancing, and I said, 'Hey, that's stepping!' " recalled Henderson, who declines to identify his fraternity.

"Stepping started . . . as celebration, but it is subconsciously rooted in the African tradition of celebrating culture and heritage," Henderson said. "'The hand motions, like the hambone, came from people who joined the frats who were from New Orleans, or other parts of the Southern region. The pitapat that's created with hands and feet comes from the patty-cake, hopscotch and other childhood games. It also comes from black marching bands and drill teams, things that little children do. Stepping just made it more complex.

"The step shows have call and response, toasts, dozens and signification. All these things are deep-seated in African American history," said Henderson. "If you listen to different jazz artists, when they scat, the sounds made in step shows are almost the same as scatting. It's basically a combination of African and African American history."

While stepping and other recreational activities are an important part of fraternity life, these organizations continue to play another, more important role in the African American community. "Fraternities provide black male bonding and black male role models, which is really important today, when more than 50 percent of black families are headed by black women," said Henderson. "They provide nurturing for upwardly mobile blacks.'"

They also can provide a forum for political discussion. "During the 1960s, the fraternity memberships totally decreased," said Henderson, explaining that fraternities seemed anachronistic during the political upheaval of the time. "During the '70s there was a simmering period, with slight interest. Then when the 1980s came around, there was a growing interest, because fraternities and sororities started to use more things in their step shows that talked about black culture, African history and the community, and people were interested in that."

Elements of stepping have moved from the college campus to the choreography of some singers, particularly rappers. "That's because some of the new up-and-coming rappers were college-educated, and that environment had to influence their choreography," said Henderson. "Another influence was rappers being asked to perform on college campuses. From there, some of the basic step movements went into rap dancers. Now you can see stepping in the work of all the major rap artists, especially M.C. Hammer."

Stepping is spontaneous, creative, competitive. It is a physical manifestation of celebration and the fun part of pledging. Once pledges have crossed over, stepping is most often done because they feel like it.

"StepFest 90" at the D.C. Convention Center late last month was a way of bringing together Greeks from area colleges for one big competition and show.

Along with the Zetas, there were members of Delta Sigma Theta sorority and of fraternities Alpha Phi Alpha, Omega Psi Phi and Phi Beta Sigma. Several hundred students attended, part of the show as much as spectators.

The show was the brainchild of George Washington University students Kent Cushenberry II and Chuck Baker, who formed an events production company, jokingly named it C.N. Bank ("seein' bank" means making money) and brought in four friends as assistants. They looked around for a business venture and decided that this area, with a number of historically black colleges and black students, would support a step show.

Baker and Cushenberry are smooth, which is good, not slick, which is bad. They exude confidence and success, so much so that, when near them, one can almost hear the strains of the O'Jays singing "Money, Money, Money." They're also clean, in gray suits, roaming the Convention Center, greeting friends, averting minidisasters, chill at all times.

"I'm a stepper myself," said Baker, 21, a finance and philosophy student and an Omega who handled the publicity and outreach to contestants. "Stepping actually originated to unify the people stepping and those in the chapter. Everyone works on the choreography. When we step, we step tight, real close to each other. It kind of creates the atmosphere that we're one. It signifies unity, of everyone stepping as one."

Cushenberry, 20, a management major, said "StepFest," which planned to donate some of the proceeds to charity, didn't break even. Undaunted, he and Baker plan to keep on steppin'. They're already looking for the best location and date for next year.

During the not-so-brief breaks between steppers, the audience, mostly people under 25, crowded the floor and the steps leading up to the bleachers. A conga line snaked down one aisle, a group of male voguers dominated another, free-form dancers did their thing someplace else. The more inhibited stood at their seats, elbows bent and hands in fists, and simply shook. Everyone sized everyone else up, in a nice way.

The crowd, smaller than anticipated, made up for size with enthusiasm. They booed, barked, meowed and hissed when the Deltas, dressed in white overalls, red blouses and red-and-white saddle shoes" chanted, "What is a Delta?/ A Delta is what a Zeta ain't/ What an Alpha wants to be/ And what a Sigma Rho can't." Their rap was bad, but their stepping was lackadaisical and several times—the kiss of death for a step show—off beat. Afterward, Dee Cunningham, a 21-year-old junior, acknowledged, "We've done better in the previous two shows. We just got a little off beat tonight."

After the women stepped, it was time for the men. Twelve Alphas from the University of Virginia took the stage, dressed in loose gold shirts and billowing black pants, looking like the Giorgio Armanis of step.

The Alphas kicked it off with a brief speech about entering the 1990s and the struggles ahead. Mention that "Nelson Mandela is free but South Africa is not"' brought applause and the now-familiar barks and meows, but it was the Alphas' stepping that really turned it out. Chanting, "Ice, ice, baby. Too cold, too cold," the Alphas blended the traditional and the contemporary into a pounding stampede.

Imagine 12 young black men moving their hands, feet, legs and bodies in graceful, rhythmic unison. Then add a few Bobby Brown gyrations, some Watusi-like crouches with arms outstretched, winglike, and some deep-voiced chanting, and you'll have an inkling, but only an inkling, of how the Alphas stepped.

They stepped so high, they almost flew.

Backstage afterward, the Alphas hugged and sweated. "We're a business organization, not a social club," said stepmaster Leonard Spady, 21, a third-year government major. "The stepping isn't the important thing; the focus is. The stepping is just a sideshow. We focus on service, brotherhood, scholarship, love for all mankind."

If the Alphas looked as if they were dressed by Armani, the brothers of Omega Psi Phi, from Virginia State, 1988 national step champions, looked uncomfortably stiff in purple shirts, gold ties and black slacks from like maybe Robert Hall.

It wasn't until the end of their set, ties awry and belts coming undone, that the Omegas loosened up. They paired off, one Omega lying on the floor with his knees up, another sitting on his midriff facing his knees. Then, simultaneously, one Omega worked his arms, the other his legs, clapping, stamping, creating rhythms as if they were one person.

Finally came the Sigmas from Howard, the university's 1990 Homecoming Step Champions and favorite sons. Reflecting the new Afro-centricity of black fraternities, the festive attitude on some college campuses and the power of popular culture, they were dressed in white dashiki-like shirts, long baggy shorts trimmed with kente cloth and matching hats.

Their show began with vogueing, in which one stepper struck model-like poses while a tape of a speech by Malcolm X that ended "The price of freedom is death" played in the background.

The Sigmas' winning move involved eight brothers lying opposite each other on the floor, holding hands—or was it ankles?—and then, somehow, still prone, each pair leaped over and under each other to exchange places. Kind of pick-up sticks with humans.

Again, the crowd barked, meowed, ululated, applauded and stomped. Then it was over and time for the judges, WRC's Susan Ridd, Redskin Alvin Walton, ex-Redskin Vernon Dean and Miss D.C. 1989 Donya Baker, to decide who were the best steppers.

It wasn't too much of a surprise when it was announced that Howard's Zetas took first place. But there was some suspense and tension when it came to the men, to who deserved first place, the Alphas or the Sigmas. There was little disagreement that the Omegas were third.

When it was announced that the Alphas came in second, the audience went wild, flowing like a tidal wave down from the bleachers to the stage, hundreds of feet creating their own spontaneous step show of celebration as they ran to embrace the men of Phi Beta Sigma, the winners.

"Homeboy! Homeboy!" shouted a young man as he ran to hug a friend, flinging his legs around the othor man's waist. Lifting him, his homeboy spun him around in a weird, insectlike, four-legged dance. After a few turns, the man lowered his feet to the floor. He and his friend began jumping up in the air, fists clenched, screaming, "You know! You know!" which for some reason is the Sigmas' chant.

When their feet hit the ground they tapped away in a spontaneous step show of their own. Around them, many others danced similar spontaneous dances of celebration, culture, heritage."

June 17, 1990

Angels Among Us?

On the Bedeviling Question of their Existence, We Wing it

PHIL MCCOMBS

Be not forgetful to entertain strangers: for thereby some have entertained angels unawares.
    —The Apostle Paul

When Washington writer Sophy Burnham had a contractor over the other day for an estimate on painting her Georgetown row house, she mentioned that she's just done a book on angels. The man became "very excited and said that when his wife was a little girl she and her sister used to play with an angel in the bedroom. They bounced on the bed with this little being of light, and their mother saw light pouring from under the door."

Burnham put the story down in her notebook, as she has repeatedly over the years—another of those "common, everyday, garden variety mystical experiences shared by millions of people" that can sometimes seem out of place in busy Washington, but perhaps not quite so out of place in this season of joy for both Christians and Jews.

Polls have shown that more than half of Americans believe in angels. Gallup found last year that 74 percent of teenagers believe in them, up from 64 percent a decade earlier. Interest in the subject has prompted at least one local priest, the Rev. Karl Chimiak, associate pastor of St. Michael the Archangel Catholic Church in Silver Spring, to teach two-day angelology seminars with a special focus on guardian angels. (Perhaps the most beloved example in popular American culture being fretful little Clarence in Frank Capra's "It's a Wonderful Life"—Capra has said he believes in them.)

"People are thirsty for knowledge of their angels," says Chimiak, explaining that every person has one. "I've had Smithsonian bureau directors, school principals, 90-year-olds, children—all wanting to find out about these dear creatures whose main role is to give honor and glory to God."

In a recent session attended by 40 students, the priest told them that angels "are among the first creations of God, so they are fellow creatures with us. They have sharp intellects and free wills, and while they've taken human form, generally they're invisible, working through our consciences."

Burnham came to believe in angels, she says, because she has seen them more than once. Years ago, she recounts, a guardian angel dressed in black and with "beautiful, luminous eyes" saved her life.

364

And as she notes in "A Book of Angels," her charming, eclectic paperback published by Ballantine just in time for Holy Week and Passover—her publisher having one eye on the bottom line, the author spent last week on a nationwide book tour—angels are of critical importance in the Judeo-Christian tradition as messengers of God and protectors of humankind. It was an "angel of the Lord," according to St. Matthew, who rolled back the stone in front of the sepulcher on the third day after the Crucifixion "and sat upon it. His countenance was like lightning, and his raiment white as snow." He announced the resurrection to Mary and Mary Magdalene, telling them to "go quickly, and tell his disciples that He is risen from the dead."

The archangel Gabriel, Chimiak says, was an early feminist of sorts, in keeping with the Christian doctrine of free will. After announcing to Mary that she had been chosen to bear the son of God, "he waited for her to say 'yes.' " Which of course she did, telling the angel: "Be it unto me according to thy word."

In the Old Testament—which Burnham also examines in detail—the angel Michael is described by Daniel as the "prince" of Israel, considered to be the special guardian and defender of the Jews in their struggle against godlessness. According to Rabbi Harold S. White, a chaplain and lecturer in theology at Georgetown University, "Angels in the Old Testament serve as messengers, they do the bidding of God. In Exodus, 'the angel of the Lord' appears to Moses in the burning bush, communicating to him that he is going to be a prophet."

Apparently, White says with a chuckle, that wasn't quite enough for Moses, since God then spoke directly to him to make the point that he was going to be the deliverer and lawgiver of the Israelites. Later in Exodus, when the Lord lays down the law for him, Moses is told reassuringly that "mine angel shall go before thee."

As for guardian angels, White suggests that those who protected Jacob while he slept, as recounted in Genesis, were going "up and down the ladder because of the change of shift. Angels don't work for more than 12 hours."

Another chuckle.

While it has often been stated in newspapers—including this one recently—that Passover has something to do with "angels of death," White points out that this is untrue. It was the Lord himself, according to Exodus, who "passed over the houses of the children of Israel" and killed the firstborn Egyptians, finally forcing the Pharaoh to let Moses and his people go.

"In the narrative of the Haggadah, which we read at the Seder table," says White, "it says that 'the Eternal brought us forth from Egypt, not by a ministering angel, not by a fiery angel, not by a messenger, but by Himself in His glory.' "

As for angels of death, he adds, Jewish mystics "believe that when we are conceived, an angel places our soul in the body, and during the nine months of pregnancy takes the child on a mysterious journey to gain knowledge. When the child is born, that angel slaps him on the upper lip . . . and all that knowledge goes into his subconscious. The only other time we see that angel is at the moment of death, when he is seen carrying a sword with poisonous gall on it. A drop of gall enters our mouth, and we die."

On the subject of death, it shouldn't be forgotten that Satan was, according to the Revelation, a fallen angel who battled Michael in Heaven and took with him a third of the angels to do devilry among men. His sin was pride, and Christian theologians think he balked at God's plan to exalt human nature through the incarnation.

While Satan doesn't appear as a distinct personality in the Old Testament, White says that some Judaic scholars speculated that angels rebelled because "they didn't want God to create human beings. Human beings can have fun, sexual intercourse and so on, and the angels became jealous. They said to God, 'You're doing all this for humans, what about us?' "

Sophy Burnham didn't grow up in a household where speculation about angels was encouraged. Her father was a well-to-do Maryland attorney who "had no truck with the mysterious" and once told her, "I have no reason to believe in God. On the other hand, I've noticed throughout my life that all of the most brilliant minds of every generation believe in God—Tolstoy, Einstein, Marcus Aurelius—and who am I to say there's not?"

Her own epiphany came after a difficult operation and hospital stay in 1972, when she began "a long spiritual journey through Buddhism and Hinduism and eventually back to Christianity." She came to realize that many of her experiences, which she had explained away for one reason or another, were mystical.

Particularly the man in black with the luminous eyes:

She and her then-husband David Burnham, a former *New York Times* reporter and author of the recently published "A Law Unto Itself: Power, Politics and the IRS," were skiing in France when she was 28. She fell mid-schuss and was heading for a cliff, she writes, when the angel skied out of nowhere at enormous speed and positioned himself between her and the cliff. "I fell against his legs," she writes. "It didn't hurt. Neither did he fall with the impact or even apparently stumble and have to catch his weight as 120 pounds plowed into him . . . 'Merci beaucoup,' I said."

Not answering, he skied off and disappeared over the top of the hill, never to be seen again.

For a long time, it didn't occur to her what he might have been. However, her mother, hearing the story, said simply: "Oh, you saw an angel."

Then there were other mystical experiences: Burnham saw the friendly ghost of a former occupant of her New York apartment, her mother visited her three times after dying, an angel appeared as a swan to save her in a stormy boating incident, and so on.

She could, of course, have seen the swan and not thought it an angel. "Why is it," she writes, "that angels like disguise? It seems they take whatever form the visited person is willing to accept; and sometimes no form at all—a dream, a thought, a surge of power, a sense of guidance. They don't seem far removed from natural events. This explains why angels are easily explained away, and why skeptics can pad down the corridors of their intellect, unhindered by the intrusion of the inexplicable . . ."

Chimiak's view is that "angels don't want notoriety. They want to give the news of God and then fade out." An excessive interest in angels—at least for Christians—he teaches—is spiritually dangerous since it may tend to obscure Christ as the center of the history of salvation.

Angels come "most commonly," Burnham writes, " . . . to children, saints, and primitive people, to the innocents, who perhaps can perceive more clearly than we." She tells of 8-year-old Bridget, who "has an angel that accompanies her everywhere. She has pink wings, says Bridget, a yellow gown, and wings for feet. She has been with Bridget since about the age of three; and when Bridget goes to sleep at night, the angel envelops her body in a spiraling rainbow to protect her when she sleeps."

Many popes have spoken openly of guardian angels, and John XXIII, says Chimiak, "recommended that parents teach their children that they will never be alone, because they have an angel with them, and he taught them to converse on familiar terms with the angel."

Burnham's book is a wide-ranging exploration, touching on angels and angel-figures in Islam, Hinduism, Buddhism, Zoroastrianism and other religions. While she considers herself Christian and regularly attends an Episcopal church, she tends to talk of "spirits," and her interests and experiences have led her to include in the book discussions of ghosts and paranormal phenomena such as telepathy and faith healing.

"It doesn't matter how you worship," she believes, "as long as you pray and give thanks. It can be done in a mosque and a beggar's hut and a Christian church. It doesn't make any difference as long as it's done with the heart. An angel, after all, is only an idea of God."

Burnham calls herself a "healer" as well as a writer, and practices professionally a form of massage that is essentially a soothing laying-on of hands. Her previous work includes a nonfiction book, "The Art Crowd," and a children's novel, "The Dogwalker." She has kept a notebook on angels for years, which made writing "A Book of Angels" easier and gave it a pleasant jumbled quality, full of quotations from holy and secular literature. You can, she says, "pick it up and read any page."

The one sure mark of an angel, she writes, is that it "brings a calm and peaceful serenity that descends sweetly over you, and this is true even when the angel is not seen . . . Their message is always: 'Fear not!' Don't worry, they say."

Chimiak teaches his students too that encountering an angel will bring a feeling of deep peace in "the knowledge that we have a guardian companion to console us and guide us through this world from the moment we're born until the moment we die." He notes that Christ himself, according to St. Luke, was consoled by an angel during his agony in the garden of Gethsemane.

A clothing salesman before entering seminary, Chimiak became interested in angels while reading St. Thomas Aquinas—known as "the angelic doctor" for his extensive writings on the subject—and "The Angels and Their Mission" by the late Cardinal Jean Danielou, a modern text that Chimiak now uses in his seminars.

After becoming familiar with the subject, the Silver Spring priest found that "it gave me easier access to God, and everything in my ministry has improved since then." And it can be handy too, he adds, because when necessary "we can send, in the name of Jesus Christ, our guardian angel to the guardian angel of another person."

Chimiak has found that talking of such things will cause "people without faith to laugh at you," and Burnham says she had to break down barriers with people to gather the angel stories for her book. Always she found people were afraid to talk at first, but would open up when she revealed her own beliefs.

"Over and over they would say, 'I've never told anyone this, because people would think I'm a kook.' Last year I was on my way to LaGuardia and I told the cab driver I was writing a book on angels. He said, 'Oh yes, when I was 5 years old in Greece I saw little baby angels, a whole flock of them playing up and down a staircase of a woman who had just died.' "

Having come to believe in angels, Burnham now perceives their actions almost daily.

Recently, when her editor asked her to check a quotation from the Koran ("Then angels and revelations waft down"), she went to Second Story Books near Dupont Circle and looked at the huge, unfamiliar tome in despair, wondering how she would ever find the right passage.

"Finally I said 'God, you've got to find it for me,' and I just rippled through the pages and there it was! It took 30 seconds."

Special correspondent Marianne Kyriakos co-reported this story.

April 15, 1990

Study Questions
Chapter Nine

1. Interior monologues—what you say to yourself about people, places, events—can become the basis for feature stories. Do you have a pet peeve that's unusual? Do you instinctively not like things that are popular? Turn your off-beat views or confessions into a story idea.
2. Could you construct a stream-of-consciousness feature about the most traumatic day in your life, detailing events and mind-sets?
3. Slice-of-life stories can be generated from any place, not just park benches. Where would you go to people watch? What kind of folks would you expect to see and what observations seem likely?
4. In the Charlottesville profile, writer Martha Sherrill reposts the sentence pattern "It's a place where..." to give readers a sense of being there. Complete the phrase with ten original statements describing a town (or city) of your choice.
5. Analyze the sources used in Henry Allen's article, "Red, White and Truly Blue." What does each contribute to the story?

"New York: The Reel Thing" is a travel article with a strong story concept. Writer Barbara Ann Curcio invites visitors to recall movie memories about a particular landmark or part of the city while encountering the real site. From her exhaustive research, readers see New York through different lenses. For film buffs who want more information, Curcio provides a resource bibliography.

Christopher Corbett's profile of the Ohio State Fair is full of delightful, gentle whimsy. Corbett sets readers up by calling the event a wholesome and timeless Midwestern ritual and then points out the bizarre midway sideshows. A wide-eyed observer, he slips into first person to record his own experiences and quirky sensibility. His wry sense of humor extends to identifying one celebrity performer as Willie "Chapter 11" Nelson. Another clever aspect of Corbett's style is mimicking the verbal mannerisms of Midwesterners.

Feature writing about the outdoors is another popular type of travel story. In "American Way," John F. Cullicott writes in first person to describe a hike he and his young adult son took along the Appalachian Trail. In addition to writing about a particular trip, Cullicott touches on his changing relationship with his son and the sublime rewards of being outdoors. At the end, he supplies advice and sources for adventurous readers.

Magazine-style features afford sportswriters such as Thomas Boswell an opportunity to wax philosophical and to place their obsession in a larger context. In his article, "What We Talk About When We Talk About Sports," Boswell insists that sports have become central to what remains of our American sense of community, and are part of a national debate about mores: how we act and how we should act. Loosely organized, his article ranges over societal issues such as racism, media intimacy and common-sense ethics. Boswell pierces trivial sports babble to help readers understand the significant role sports play in many people's lives.

Jim Naughton's profile, "The Slam Jam Joy of Michael Jordan," explores why the basketball star is considered America's number-one role model and favorite athlete. Co-mingling the language of religion and sports, Naughton says Jordan represents excellence on and off the court. The article claims Jordan's soaring to the basket is literally transcendent, bringing ecstasy to fans and millions of dollars in endorsements to the player.

Peter Carlson's article on skateboarding culture captures the scene, its tattooed characters and their ragin' style through observant reporting and the use of vernacular lingo. He doesn't miss the irony of the location of the Xanadu of skating ramps in a country club. Rad.

The psychology of hobbyists who collect things is probed in "A Congregation of Collectors." From case studies, writer Ron Gassbarro identifies escapism as the motivation of people who collect sugar packets, bricks, cookie cutters and spark plugs. He also provides service information so collectors can connect with one another.

In "Major Meows & Kitty Glitter," Martha Sherrill describes the pampered show animals, their masters and activities at a typical cat show. The article also compiles odd information in a list labeled "Things to Know." Her feline profiles and reporting on cat products heighten the realism and absurdity of the event.

A curious twist of nature is chronicled in William Booth's short feature "The Day the Ants Lost their Head." The seriousness with which this microcosmic tale at the zoo is treated is part of its pathos and fun.

New York

The Reel Thing—In Every Corner
of the City, You Get the Picture

BARBARA ANN CURCIO

The way I figure it, the best stories about New York are the celluloid kind—of which there have been at least a thousand, sayeth the Mayor's Office of Film, Theatre and Broadcasting. Movies have been made here since the turn of the century, when the film over in Thomas Edison's labs in New Jersey, and "Hollywood on the Hudson" is showing no signs of slowing down.

With four of the last five Oscar nominees for Best Picture filmed here—"Awakenings," "GoodFellas," "The Godfather Part III" and "Ghost"—and with the mayor's office issuing 10 feature-film permits a month on average, despite the on-going film-workers dispute, moviegoers and filmmakers obviously concur.

Okay, so "Dances With Wolves" won the Best Picture Oscar . . . about as far as you can get from the megalopolis physically, spiritually and just about every other way you can think of. But that film said something about the American spirit—and so do New York movies, obviously, or there wouldn't be so many. So when it comes to movies, I'll take Manhattan.

Now, no matter where you go in New York City, you can't avoid being reminded of some movie. Is there a bridge or a building or a street that doesn't recall a New York story? So what better, more memorable way to visit New York than to visit the places where the stories were set that have been so indelibly etched on our imaginations, that have become a part of American folklore?

And there have been some real gems—screen gems—robbers, mobsters and their molls, wise guys and working girls, urban romances, comedies of manners and cautionary tales of life on the make in the big city. "King Kong," "Tootsie," the "Godfather" "Taxi Driver," "On the Waterfront," "Wall Street," "Working Girl," "Annie Hall" . . . . These are movies whose stories have implanted New York City on the international consciousness to such a degree that New York, not Washington, is the capital of the country—not Hollywood, the reigning Dream Factory.

Thanks to New York movies, we've all been there, even if we've never been there. What other city has so many instantly recognizable landmarks, used to such advantage by filmmakers? There's the Staten Island ferry ("Working Girl"). The Empire State Building ("King Kong" and "An Affair to Remember"). Ellis Island

("The Godfather Part II"). Central Park ("Marathon Man" "Alice"). Wall Street ("Wall Street"). Greenwich Village ("Next Stop, Greenwich Village," "Barefoot in the Park"). The Brooklyn Bridge ("Manhattan," "Sophie's Choice"). And they're only a handful of the film locations and only a few of the films shot there. The Empire State Building alone has made cameo and feature appearances in some 90 films.

Thanks to the movies, New York belongs to us all. We know where we'd go to eat, having had sneak previews of its restaurants—whether the Russian Tea Room ("Tootsie," with Dustin Hoffman in drag); Elaine's, which so often appears in Woody Allen's films; or Ratz's, site of the infamous deli scene in "When Harry Met Sally." They are ours, as are the city's shops and department stores. We've been to Broadway, "On the Town," to the opera (the Met), the museums (the other Met) and all the other places New Yorkers eat, shop, play, romance, live and work. The seedy and the sublime, the awful and the wonderful are all here.

Everything in New York is larger than life, like in a movie. And with New York as one giant movie set, we are the extras. Stand at the fountain at Lincoln Center at the Met, like Cher and Nicolas Cage in "Moonstruck," transformed by love and the romance of opera; hear Bobby Short at the Cafe Carlyle, like Woody Allen and Dianne Wiest in "Hannah and Her Sisters" (and hopefully have a better time); play in Central Park like "Alice," stopping in at the zoo to see the penguins and polar bears; visit the Planetarium, like Diane Keaton and Woody Allen in "Manhattan."

How could you not feel like Audrey Hepburn, standing at Tiffany's on Fifth Avenue, with that incredible view up and down the street from the corner of 57th Street? She had it right: Tiffany's is still the cheapest place for breakfast—with takeout, gawking at the windows.

How could you not cherish dreams of meeting someone special and falling desperately in love, but agreeing to wait six months as a test—like Cary Grant and Deborah Kerr in "An Affair to Remember"? Meet at the top of the Empire State Building like they did—but watch out crossing the street.

A trip to New York is a constant tango between real New York and movie New York. On your next trip, just try to figure out whether you first experienced the movie version, or the real thing—whether your New York haunts first entered your consciousness from movies, or whether you discovered them, casting them in your own movie version of New York.

Movie lovers who love New York and New York lovers who love movies don't just simply "arrive" in New York. They land at LaGuardia to a rousing rendition (if only in the mind) of Liza Minnelli (or Frank Sinatra—pick your version) belting out "New York, New York" in the movie of the same name. Or they might arrive more inauspiciously, by bus, like Joe in "Midnight Cowboy." Or by train—at Pennsylvania Station, as countless Washington commuters do, or at Grand Central Terminal, whence Cary Grant departed on his harrowing journey in

Hitchcock's "North by Northwest." Unfortunately, these days you're more likely to find yourself negotiating the vagrants at these stations.

From Penn Station in a taxi, on the way to an East Side hotel, movie New York reels by—more familiar settings and magical places. Here are Times Square and the Winter Garden bathed in neon. "CATS!" screams a sign with six-foot-high letters. "Still starring the Rockettes," shouts back the marquee at Radio City, and around the side, billboards herald the coming of "Ella," "Liza" and "Julio"—no last names required. You pass the Time Life Building and Rockefeller Center, with its flags and fountains, where Woody Allen chews out his movie ex, Meryl Streep, for her tell-all book about their marriage in "Manhattan."

As you rhapsodize about movie New York, you careen past streets that appear to have had large chunks ripped out of them, the soil exposed, as if by rabid movie monsters. Has Godzilla just been here? You listen to the traffic reports, detailing the day-long gridlock downtown today, where a steam pipe burst and shot a column of asbestos a few hundred feet in the air, causing a several-block area to be closed off. An asbestos geyser!

New York, New York.

Now, the less tough and romantic might say you could save yourself a lot of time, expense and asbestos exposure just by sticking with video tours of New York City—the people who think that the quintessential New York movie is "Escape From New York." But they won't get to take that cab ride from Penn Station and gasp at how much New York reminds them of the opening of "Manhattan," the overwhelming elegance and grandeur and excitement of Fifth Avenue and all the rest of it. This is the city that Woody Allen's narrator idealized out of all proportion, the town that still "existed in black and white and pulsated to the great tunes of George Gershwin."

This unabashedly romantic New York does not always appear even to inveterate New York lovers—sometimes resembling more the nightmarish city of "The Out-of-Towners," when the innocents Jack Lemmon and Sandy Dennis get mugged in Central Park, or "Where's Poppa?," where one character gets mugged almost nightly.

New Yorkers also seem to hold the reasonable view that there is no one quintessential New York movie—that trying to answer that question would be like deciding which New York eatery you'd most want to transport intact to a desert island with you. Like there is no one best cuisine, there is no one movie version of New York.

There is the New York of musicals—countless editions of "Broadway Melodies" (from '29, '36, '38 and '40), and mind-boggling production numbers—"On the Town," "West Side Story," "All That Jazz" and "New York, New York." There is contemporary New York, more or less romantic, as best represented by films like "When Harry Met Sally," "Green Card," "Tootsie" and "An Unmarried

Woman." In this category, see anything by Woody Allen, but especially "Manhattan," "Annie Hall," "Hannah and Her Sisters" and, most recently, "Alice."

For SoHo, where Manhattanites live in lofts big enough for their kids to roller-skate inside (what with the traffic, never mind the crime, they can't skate outside), watch "After Hours" and the vignette "Life Lessons" from "New York Stories."

Then there are the postwar New York movies that baby boomers remember, like "How to Marry a Millionaire," "Splendor in the Grass," "The Sweet Smell of Success" and "All About Eve." For criminal and hard-edged New York, try anything by Martin Scorsese—"Mean Streets," "Taxi Driver," "GoodFellas" and the "Godfather" films—and Al Pacino films such as "Serpico" and "Dog Day Afternoon." There are also the Spike Lee ("Do the Right Thing") and Brian De Palma ("Dressed to Kill") versions, and New York according to Sydney Pollack ("Tootsie") and Sidney Lumet ("The Verdict" and "Prince of the City").

Design your own tour, depending on which version you prefer. How about the movie deli tour—Carnegie Deli (857 Seventh Ave., "Broadway Danny Rose") and Katz's (205 E. Houston St., "When Harry Met Sally")? Or the "Alice" shopping tour (Chanel, 5 E. 57th St., and Krizia, B05 Madison Ave.)? Or focus on one movie: You could spend the weekend going to "Bright Lights, Big City" sights, or maybe "Kramer vs. Kramer."

Or choose a director. You could follow Martin Scorsese's film career, from his early "Mean Streets" to the recent "GoodFellas," by trudging around the Little Italy where Scorsese grew up and where he now sets his films.

You could, on the other hand, just scout out the locations of your favorite films. Pay your respects to the exteriors of the "Ghostbusters" apartment (55 Central Park West) and to the houses featured in "The Godfather" (110 and 120 Longfellow Rd., Staten Island), "Sophie's Choice" "101 Rugby Rd., Brooklyn) and "Saturday Night Fever" (221 79th St., in the Bay Ridge section of Brooklyn). Or stop by the subway grill where Marilyn Monroe stood to catch a breeze in "The Seven-Year Itch" on the northwest corner of Lexington Avenue and 52nd Street (wear pants, unless you want to attract a crowd).

But for me, the ultimate New York tour combines shopping and films. True, it's easier on the credit limit to shop vicariously—say, by watching "Alice" trying and wearing thousands of dollars worth of Chanel. But if you're on Fifth Avenue, why not go into Tiffany's (727 Fifth Ave.), site of the classic Audrey Hepburn film, and more recently "Betsy's Wedding" with Molly Ringwald. The elevators are jammed here—and they're not all tourists. Wander into Rizzoli (31 W. 57th St.), the sleek Italian bookstore with its beautiful artful displays of even more beautiful artful books. The store appears in both "Manhattan" and "Falling in Love."

If you remember "Miracle on 34th Street" from Christmases, for nostalgia's sake you'll want to make the pilgrimage to Macy's Herald Square (151 W. 34th St.). Then there is the cosmetic counter at Bloomingdale's (1000 Third Ave.), which figured in a tryst between Diane Keaton and Michael Murphy in "Manhattan," and was the unforgettable scene of Robin Williams's defection in

"Moscow on the Hudson." And the elegant Bergdorf Goodman (754 Fifth Ave.) appears in "Someone to Watch Over Me" and "Just Tell Me What You Want," with Ali MacGraw.

Cut.

After a morning of shopping and browsing, have lunch at the Cafe Des Artistes (1 W. 67th St.), with its Howard Chandler Christy murals of 1930s nymphs who look like they spend all their time in the gym. "My Dinner With Andre," the ultimate talkie—a film whose entire action consists of one dinner conversation—was filmed here. As was the scene in "9 1/2 Weeks" with Kim Basinger dressed as a man.

After lunch, head back over to the East Side to Polo, Ralph Lauren's flagship store (867 Madison Ave.). The former Rhinelander mansion was built in 1895 for Gertrude Rhinelander Waldo and modeled after a Loire Valley chateau. One of the "invisible" scenes in Woody Allen's "Alice" was filmed here (where Joe Mantegna follows a famous model into a dressing room and upsets her with his heavy breathing). Allen and his crew took over the store for three mornings, from 4 a.m. to 10 a.m., soundproofing the cash registers and building ramps to move equipment around. With Lauren taking inspiration from the star aristocracy of the '30s and from old movies, it seems that his store should itself become a movie set. Is that life imitating art imitating life?

What all these settings have in common is that they could not make more perfect movie sets. Nor could you duplicate what New York has to offer visually, for the variety of architecture and scenery—from skyscrapers to tenements, urban to bucolic, back alleys to storefronts. New York's unique street sound, what the mayor's office calls a "liveness," cannot be duplicated in post-production. And the city's special quality of light captivates cinematographers.

On a movie tour of New York, you can't help but conclude that it is really New York that is the star—sometimes it plays cameos, and sometimes starring roles. And if New York is a star, its agent is the mayor's film office, which coordinates all film production in the city, granting permits, providing police protection and worrying over traffic flow and congestion.

You want to know what film shoots are upcoming, and where? The mayor's office won't reveal its production schedule, but it will say that among the most popular locations for filming in the city are Central Park, especially the softball fields and the Great Lawn; the corner of Prince and Thompson in SoHo; Greenwich Village; the Upper West Side, especially Central Park West between Amsterdam and Columbus and 66th and 80th streets; Rockefeller Center; and Little Italy (Mott, Elizabeth and Mulberry streets). The Brooklyn Bridge is featured in the new Bruce Willis movie, "Hudson Hawk," due out this summer (the Brooklyn-bound lanes of the bridge were closed for three nights during filming).

Other upcoming films featuring New York, according to the mayor's office: "The Butcher's Wife," with Jeff Daniels and Lena Olin; "The Fisher King," with

Robin Williams, due out this fall; "Prince of Tides," with Barbra Streisand (she also directs) and Nick Nolte.

If you've been keeping count of New York movies, that makes it 1,004 . . .

For help in designing your own New York movie tour, get "The Movie Lover's Guide to New York," by Richard Alleman (perennial Library, Harper and Row), crammed with lists of movie locations and movie-related sites, including sound stages, museums and stars' hangouts and home addresses for Manhattan.

Or head over to the American Museum of the Moving Image in Astoria, Queens (35th Avenue at 36th Street, 718-784-4520), which is dedicated exclusively to film, television and video, with exhibitions (some interactive) and screenings. Exhibits emphasize the craft of film and examine how movies have influenced our society—what we wear, how we dress and, arguably, our values. You can even "become" Judy Garland in "The Wizard of Oz," Marilyn Monroe at the subway grating on Lex and 52nd or Sylvester Stallone as Rocky, thanks to the magic of holography and a projector. The museum is open Tuesdays through Fridays from noon to 4 p.m., Saturdays and Sundays from noon to 6 p.m. Admission is $5 for adults, $4 for seniors, $2.50 for children and students, and free for members.

If all this inspires you to do some research, stop in at the New York Public Library for the Performing Arts at Lincoln Center (111 Amsterdam Ave., 212-870-1630) to do your own digging about your favorite films. Or check out the Museum of Modern Art's (11 W. 53rd St., 212-708-9400) regular screenings: The museum has one of the best film collections anywhere.

April 21, 1991

Along Miles of Midway

In Ohio, an Extravaganza of Things Midwestern

CHRISTOPHER CORBETT

The 137th Ohio State Fair still had more than two weeks to run when the fat man died. The sideshow workers took down the sign advertising 529-pound Big Billy Pork Chop, and with considerable effort the mortal remains of Big Billy were removed too.

But the show—one of America's largest and longest-running state fairs—must go on and so, a good fat man being hard to find, Zoma the Deranged from South America was brought in to replace Mr. Pork Chop. Zoma joined Spasmo the Quivering Man, Miss Electra, The Human Blow Torch, Little Richard the Pygmy Boy, Gabora the Gorilla Girl ("Was Darwin Right?") and a skinny hillbilly who drove hatpins through his cheeks. (The teachings of Mr. Darwin, as we shall see, are an oft-heard theme at the Ohio State Fairgrounds, where the matter of Adam and Eve remains a subject of fierce debate and "The Origin of the Species" is regarded as the work of the Devil.)

But that's show business, folks. And that, in a nutshell, is life at the Ohio State Fair, where all of life's curiosity is not confined to the sideshow.

Since 1849, when the first Ohio State Fair was held in Cincinnati in early October (an epidemic of Asiatic cholera had forced postponement during the summer months), the annual exhibition celebrates all things Buckeye.

In the old days, the fair moved about Ohio, but it has been settled down here in the state capital lo these many years. Last year, 3.4 million turned out for the nearly three-week-long fair, making it the nation's largest for 1990.

And despite its more obviously grotesque aspects, much of the Ohio State Fair is a wholesome and timeless ritual, celebrating the best of the American heartland in ways that are both endearing and off the wall—often at the same time.

The August extravaganza of things Midwestern is a chance for visitors to see the best and the balmiest of Ohio life. It is a rite of the summer season that is both touching and a bit tetched all at once.

There along the miles of midways folks down from Marseilles, Willard and Palestine can view the stuff out of *Ripley's Believe It or Not* and the Geraldo Rivera Outtakes, rounded up for the edification of the corn-fed and the curious, the theater of cruelty.

If you happen to be from anyplace other than Middle America, the rest of what makes up the 360 acres of the Ohio State Fair is just as unusual.

And not without a tad of controversy. Only last year, then-Gov. Richard Celeste had to step in and put a halt to the so-called "Moving Wall," which had the Vietnam vets riled up.

Promoters of this alleged patriotic endeavor, a half-size, cast-aluminum replica of the Vietnam Veterans Memorial on the Mall here in Washington, had planned to haul the mobile shrine down to the fairgrounds and charge the patriotic $6 a head to pay their respects. Local vets were having none of it and said so. One born every minute may still be the national birth rate for rubes but it ain't necessarily so out in tall corn country.

The Ohio State Fair understandably draws things like the "Moving Wall" and the Living Bible Museum (which normally does the work of the Lord in Mansfield, Ohio, right next door to the Ohio State Reformatory) and the Sowers of Seed (another outfit preaching the Good News of the Nazarene) operating out of a post office box in Fort Worth and something called "The World's Largest and Most Unusual Mobile House Built by One Man."

And there are racing pigs here too, and the Teenage Mutant Ninja Turtles and the gaunt men from the John Birch Society, earnest folk from Ohio Right to Life and Tree of Life Natural Products and at least a half-dozen guys selling some sort of super-duper polish that will make your car shine like new. And let's not forget washed-up and hung-out-to-dry country-western artists.

There are more branches, sects, castes, franchises and subphyla of Christianity here than Howard Johnson has flavors. Truly, brothers and sisters, His wonders are many at the Ohio State Fair. There may be more gospel singers at the fair than in Nashville. Groups with names like "His Faithful Servants" and "Wings of Praise" sandwiched right into the bill of fare of fun for the whole Christian family between the Muleskinner Band and a hog-calling contest. And last year there were hard-rock Christians and Conway Twitty and, in the evening, Frankie Valli and the Four Seasons with special guest Dion. ("Yo, Frankie.") Willie "Chapter 11" Nelson was here too. And Engelbert Humperdinck. (A handout from the fair's organizers warned that "women used to throw their underwear at him," but I saw no flying bits of lingerie.)

I, myself, personally, had the opportunity to declare Jesus Christ my very own personal savior, eight times in one day, and bought a pound of fudge, and had my handwriting analyzed ("You Have a Tendency to Trust the Wrong People") and viewed a lifesize statue of James "Buster" Douglas, boxing blowhard and local boy, cast in creamy Ohio butter. Poor Buster's career in the ring melted before the statue did.

I saw things at the Ohio State Fair that you couldn't make up. I saw things that were indeed stranger than fiction. I wandered the fairgrounds in slack-jawed amazement; pausing only to shelter from the sun's relentless rays and gulp down another tumbler of sugary lemonade before resuming my trek.

I heard the Dianetics pitchman ("A Science Ahead of Its Time")—I believe this is a cousin of handwriting analysis.

I viewed the Stickler Premium Ostriches of Turpin, Okla. "Ostrich meat could be called 'the health food of the future.' " But don't tell that to those birds. They're dumb, but they look mean.

I thrilled to the porcine antics of the Bob Hale Pig Racing Stables of Sikeston, Miss., whose motto is "Promote Pork." Fortunately, the pigs do not read.

I got to meet some of the stars of the extravaganza. I met the man who built "The World's Largest and Most Unusual Mobile House Built by One Man." But I didn't get his name because right after he shook my hand he tried to get me to pay to have a look-see, as they say out here, at his house.

I worshiped with them. (Truth is, brothers and sisters, if you don't get saved at the Ohio State Fair, you can't be saved!!!)

I shared with them. I broke bread with them. Well, actually fried dough or maybe a corn dog. Bread you don't see much of at the Ohio State Fair.

They got funnel cakes here that small children can't lift. Or you can get a 32-ounce pail of nachos covered with industrial-strength Velveeta-like stuff that glows in the dark. Onion rings the size of hula hoops. And a particularly evil and deadly looking thing called "Fried Cheese On-a-Stick."

I am ill-equipped to preach to you on swinesmanship for, alas, one must be born to this ancient and honorable art. One pig looks pretty much like another to these untrained eyes. But I did observe the clean-cut youth of the Buckeye State mustered out in front of the Junior Swine Office preparing to make straight the way of the Ohio Pork Congress and the Ohio Pork Producers Council. I heard folks talking pork, yes, indeed I did. Skinny little girls in pigtails, and old men with honest-to-God red necks and great hamlike hands, and lots of lean boys in madras sport shirts and Allis Chalmers caps. I saw people wearing white socks. I saw America going hog wild.

Despite its more tawdry aspects, the Ohio State Fair at some primal level remains an agricultural exhibition in a state where farmland still predominates.

To encourage the city slicker down among the hogs and heifers, agricultural promoters offer "You Be the Judge" tip sheets, advising hayseeds-for-a-day on the fine points of swinesmanship or "the characteristics of an ideal broiler chicken."

For those who would not know a barrow from a boar, the Ohio Pork Producers Council advises: "It is natural for hogs to squeal, and they sometimes squeal as they are guided through the show ring."

Some of this material may be a tad simplistic, on the level of a general science textbook with a sketch of a pig that explains, "This is a pig."

The people who hang out at the show rings for these things take this stuff very, very seriously. There is a solemnity and a whispered reverence in the air even at 9 o'clock on a steamy summer morning. And they call the play-by-play here in the sotto voce of professional golf commentators.

These kids, high school students mostly from little towns, are so wholesome and decent and serious that you can't help but sit quietly in the bleachers with your "You Be the Judge" ideal hog tip sheet and anguish over the competition as the judges advise, "The alert showman will mist his hog with water, to keep the animal cool, and will brush off any dirt that gets on the hog."

Cool hogs prevail. And lanky lads from Tiffin, Medway, Urbana and Mt. Gilead move about the show ring poking and guiding their gilts (a young female hog).

In the labyrinth of agricultural exhibition buildings, stables and pens, there are literally hundreds of farmers or Future Farmers of America, getting ready for a seemingly endless number of contests. A lot of the preparation involves washing off these critters and then blow-drying them and styling their manes or tails or whatever needs coiffing. This combines elements of animal husbandry with cosmetology (John Deere meets Vidal Sassoon) and often involves vacuuming animals since, after all, they are pigs, they often get wood chips or whatever on their little pink bodies. A lot of these animals or birds get sold here too, for what seems to the layman enormous amounts of money. But since the things of the barnyard are a puzzlement to me, I assume the buyers know what they're doing. One hot morning I saw someone buy a few little chickens for the price of a brand new BMW!

I viewed from a respectful distance the comely Miss Pork as she made her regal way to the Hall of Swine bedecked by red, white and blue plastic bunting.

I rolled my sleeves up and wore a ball cap too, like a real American, and I walked tall among these people.

I paused at the Amazing Grace Mission to learn "The Three Things God Cannot Do." (But I have since lost the brochure.) One of the three things God cannot do, I believe, is eat two Bahamas Mamas at the Schmidt's Sausage Haus. This is some kind of gigantic bratwurst-like thing pumped up on steroids and served on a roll heaped with steaming sauerkraut.

The Ohio State Fair offers the traveler a unique opportunity to see God and man's handiwork displayed. But, at its heart, it is chiefly more than just racing pigs and hormone-crazed 4-H kids and mile upon mile of cotton candy and carnival rides. The Ohio State Fair is a showplace of the spirit of Middle America.

Take creation science, for instance. In the heart of the Buckeye Building, a vast and sterile exhibition hall that features the wonders of this strange culture, the creation science folks do their work. The Buckeye Building is a kind of showplace of the values of the heartland.

Hard by the Encyclopedia Britannica booth near Ohio Right to Life, where the Vietnam vets in "We Were Winning When I Left" T-shirts sit across the aisle from the Stonewall Union, a gay rights group, are the anti-Darwin folks, creation science, also known as Bible science. This is your basic Adam and Eve pitch. ("Remember, God made Adam and Eve, not Adam and Steve.") With a side order of homophobia.

Like the rest of the pitchmen in the Buckeye Building, the creation science people have a wealth of what is generally referred to as "literature," handouts and leaflets, many of them elaborate and expensively produced.

The thrust of this stuff is enough to make even the most open-minded pilgrim realize that it wouldn't take much for us to have another Scopes Monkey Trial any time soon. In a free-spirited piece titled "What Is Creation Science?" the group lumps poor old Charles Darwin in with Karl Marx and Aldolf Hitler, as they spell it, and Francis "DNA" Crick, Nobel Prize winner and wicked sinner. As you might guess, Sigmund Freud gets a good hiding too.

There are loads of "FACT" sheets. And even a paper on radiometric dating bias. And the Second Law of Thermodynamics too!

It would take Stephen Gawking, Mr. Wizard and the editorial board of the *New England Journal of Medicine* to sort out this cassoulet of crankery.

But the basic thrust of this deal, near as I can figure, is that, by Jesus, my grandpaw weren't no monkey. And Richard Leakey is going to hell. If he ain't there already.

Having escaped the forces of light . . . you may pause to find out "What Was Happening the Day You Were Born?" or move directly on to the American Nuclear Society (spiritual kinsmen of the creation science folks).

Just beyond a display of pastel square-dancing dresses, very popular hereabouts, like fudge, is a display of commemorative plates a la the Franklin Mint— Woody Hayes, Lucille Ball, John Wayne and George Bush.

Whatever else seems off the wall here, the visitor must remember that this is the Midwest. In a lot of other places the Vietnam vets and the gay rights folks and the nice ladies who oppose abortion and the latter-day hippie girls selling nuts and twigs would not be camped out together. But here they get along just fine, and when a hulking vet wanders off to get a paper cup of ice water, why, this being Ohio, he naturally brings back a whole tray of cups of water and offers these to the gay crusaders and the preachers and the pitchmen too. It's a peaceful kingdom in the Buckeye State.

But at some point even the most fervid fairgoer will weary. And the Combi-Chef (son of the Amazing Vegamatic?) and the Niagara Therapy ("You Have to Feel It to Believe It"—sort of magic fingers in a chair, but I may be confusing that with something else) and the girl from Air Flo Insoles ("Experience the Sensation of Walking on Air" all become a blur along with the Original Wonder Knife ("Everything I Do Up Here Requires No Talent"), the Diamond Luster Auto Wax Man, the Snak-Master Stove Top Cooker, the mobile Gucci discount outlet and much, much more, as they say.

The only problem at the Ohio State Fair is parking. And now that I think about it, that's one of three things God cannot do. Find a parking space at the Ohio State Fair. The 138th Ohio State Fair runs this year Aug. 1-18 at the Ohio State Fairgrounds in Columbus from 9 a.m. until 11 p.m. daily. General admission is $6 for adults ($5 if purchased in advance), $4 for children 3-5 years, $2 for senior citizens and Golden Buckeye holders, free for children age 2 and under. Parking is $3 per car. The fairgrounds are located off Interstate 71; use the Hudson, 17th

Avenue or 11th Avenue exits. For more information, contact the Ohio State Fair, 632 E. 11th Ave., Columbus, Ohio 43211-2968, 614-644-FAIR (614-644-3247).

Fairways

Other state fairs across the country worth a visit include: 139th Indiana State Fair (Indianapolis, Aug. 14-25) features country music stars, horse races (including the 65th Fox Stake), tractor pulls, a demolition derby, a mule and donkey show, a re-creation of a pioneer village, a motorcycle race and a midway. Admission is $3 in advance, $5 at the gate, free for those 10 and under. Indiana State Fair, 1202 E. 38th St., Indianapolis, Ind. 46205, 317-927-7500. 128th Minnesota State Fair (St. Paul, Aug. 22-Sept. 2) features big-name grandstand acts, free entertainment on four stages, a circus, a recycling exhibit, a fine arts show, 80 acres of farm machinery, 14,000 farm animals, 1,100 commercial exhibits and a midway. Admission is $4 for adults, $2.50 for children and seniors. Minnesota State Fair, St. Paul, Minn. 55108, 612-642-2200. 110th Maryland State Fair (Timonium, Aug. 24-Sept. 2) features entertainment on two stages, a horse-pulling contest, thoroughbred racing, rodeo and livestock shows and a midway. Admission is 3, free for children under 12. Maryland State Fair, P.O. Box 188, Timonium, Md. 21093, 301-252-0200. 70th Eastern States Exposition (West Springfield, Mass., Sept. 11-22, also known as the Big E, is the East's largest fair, with entertainment on two stages, an auto show, a horse show, a 19th-century village of homes from New England states and a midway. General admission is $7 ($5 after 5 p.m.), $5 for children 6 to 13 and seniors, free for children under 6. Eastern States Exposition, 1305 Memorial Ave., West Springfield, Mass. 01089, 413-737-BIGE (413-737-2443). 146th Virginia State Fair (Richmond, Sept. 25-Oct. 6) features country music, big band and pop acts, a pioneer homestead, a flower show, a salute to the Bill of Rights, sand sculptures, draft horse-and mule-pulling contests and a midway. Admission has not been set. Virginia State Fair, P.O. Box 26805, Richmond, Va. 23261, 804-228-3200. State Fair of Texas (Dallas, Sept. 27-Oct. 20) features the Oklahoma-Texas football game in the Cotton Bowl, country music and pop stars, a Broadway show, a nightly electric parade and laser show, a birds of prey show and a midway with the tallest Ferris wheel in North America. Admission is $8 for adults, $4 for children and seniors, free for children under 2. State Fair of Texas, P.O. Box 150009, Dallas, Tex. 75315, 214-565-9931. 122nd South Carolina State Fair (Columbia, Oct. 17-27) features country music and Motown stars, clogging, agriculture and livestock exhibits, a flower show, quilting and a midway. Admission is $4 on weekdays, $5 on weekends, free for children under 12. State Fairgrounds, Gary L. Goodman, P.O. Box 393, Columbia, S.C. 29202 or call 803-734-0122.

May 19, 1991

American Ways

Deer 14, Crowds 0—The Backwoods Beauty of the Appalachian Trail

JOHN F. CULLICOTT

"John, freeze!"

I whispered the command to my son, who was hiking about three steps ahead of me with his head down, watching his footing along slippery rocks. He had not yet noticed the fawn directly in front of him on the trail.

We both stood still and waited while the fawn, seemingly without fear, approached to within a couple of feet of us. It put its nose up in the air and sniffed deeply in an effort to find out what had interrupted its breakfast of grass beside the path.

"Do you think it can smell us?" I asked. "Dad," John replied with a laugh, "we probably don't even smell human."

He undoubtedly was right. After several days of backpacking along the Appalachian Trail through Virginia's Shenandoah National Park, well-scrubbed and deodorized we were not. We were, though, happily nearing the end of an adventurous week in which we had seen lots of deer but surprisingly few people.

At this point on the trail, we were just a couple of hours from the Beltway but we couldn't have been farther away from crowds, and this was during peak summer vacation time in August.

Years ago a National Park Service ranger in Shenandoah had told me that the park is most heavily used only a few hundred yards from the parking lots along Skyline Drive, the two-lane road that meanders some 105 miles along the mountaintops of the park.

Our week in the woods proved the old ranger was right. It became obvious early in our trip that we simply weren't seeing anyone once we left the spots where the trail crossed or neared the main road. Then we started to keep a mental note—in 6 1/2 days of hiking we saw no one more than about 500 yards from a place to park a car, except a few back-country hikers who took refuge, along with us, in emergency shelters during heavy rain.

We found the trail through the park's Blue Ridge Mountains an excellent woodland getaway, without the need to travel hundreds of miles from home. We also discovered we had a choice: We could be by ourselves in the woods or we could take advantage of the park's several developed areas and enjoy some tourist comforts.

If you are looking for a way to enjoy a hike in the woods—and would appreciate some quiet along the way—you can leave the crowds behind by venturing farther along Shenandoah's many paths than most people are willing to walk. You will be rewarded not just with the silence of the woods but with scenic views from vantage points that most visitors never encounter.

Our 80-mile backpacking vacation began west of Charlottesville at Rockfish Gap, the southernmost part of the park, on a sunny Sunday morning. We picked up the Appalachian Trail in the woods immediately above the park entrance station and headed north. This scenic, historic trail winds 2,135 miles along the mountains from Georgia to Maine. Inside Shenandoah, the trail, mainly a woodland path with some rocky sections at higher elevations and along streams, stretches 102 miles, crossing Skyline Drive many times and offering frequent overlooks to enjoy a view of the Shenandoah Valley on one side or the gently rolling Virginia piedmont on the other. In the southern part of the park some of those miles are outside the park boundary, but the trail is accessible from many points along Skyline Drive.

The trail through the park is maintained by volunteers from the Potomac Appalachian Trail Club. They keep it clear, remove downed trees and make necessary repairs along the route. In many places, the heavily shaded trail appears to be a tunnel carved through the hardwood forest. Club members also maintain an extensive network of side paths that link up with the main Appalachian Trail and care for a series of three-sided shelters in the back country that hikers can use in bad weather.

Our first day out, we encountered a club volunteer repairing an access point where the trail crossed Skyline Drive. We thanked him for his colleagues' volunteer maintenance efforts and continued north. John's 19-year-old, college-athlete legs set a heady pace, while middle-aged Dad found the going a bit tough, climbing up and down the many mountain gaps that the trail crosses. But we soon settled into a good hiking routine.

That changed quickly, however, when rain began to fall early on our second day. For the rest of the week, rain and fog were with us much of the time along the trail. We soon discovered that we weren't going to cover as many miles as we had intended. In addition to slowing down to keep our footing on the wet, sometimes rocky trail, we had to carve out some time for drying out our equipment.

So, for two nights we camped at the trail club's emergency shelters instead of setting up our own back-country campsite. Arriving at one shelter in the rain at the end of a long hiking day, we encountered a young couple making a six-month journey along the entire Appalachian Trail. They had interesting stories to tell as we spent the evening. A night later, 10 miles farther along the trail, our shelter mates were three college students from James Madison University, out in the park for a few nights before classes started.

We also camped a couple of nights in the established campgrounds in the central section of the park, once at Lewis Mountain and another night at Big Meadows. This gave us a chance to buy extra food and take a break from the back country. It also provided the opportunity for a restaurant meal, a real treat at the Big Meadows Lodge. After 60 miles on the trail, we enthusiastically enjoyed a hearty dinner, especially the blackberry ice cream pie. We were seated beside the windows of the big, old lodge dining room and noticed that the swirling mist that at the time engulfed the mountaintop was seeping right in around the door frames, a fitting memory for our damp travels.

After days of seeing hardly anyone else, we were surprised to find that not only was the dining room filled but there was a long waiting list, even on a week night. It made us particularly aware of the contrast between the bustling vacation setting of Big Meadows and the peace of the backwoods.

Our decision earlier in the week to slow down our hiking pace had given us more time to enjoy our Shenandoah surroundings. We could choose a pleasant spot for lunch without worrying that we were losing hiking time. One afternoon, when the sun had broken through after a rainy morning, we found a picnic table at one of the points where the trail crossed Skyline Drive. After our lunch of peanut-butter-and-honey sandwiches, John napped on the tabletop in the warm sunshine while I watched butterflies flutter around late-summer wildflowers blooming in a roadside meadow. It was a pleasant change from our lunch stop two days before, when a driving rain forced us to seek shelter beneath the ledge of a rock outcrop immediately beside the trail. There was just enough room to set down our packs and eat lunch while leaning against the rock wall, with rain splashing on the ground just inches from our boots.

Ending one midweek hiking day early allowed time to set up a clothesline and dry some of our T-shirts and walking shorts. We also switched from our hiking boots to dry running shoes to give the boots some drying time in the sun. And it gave father and son a chance to talk about the summer that had passed and the plans for the college year that would be starting soon. Some of the most rewarding times outdoors happen when nothing is happening.

Along the trail, images both soothe and startle:

A hawk flying so close to the mountaintop that we could hear the wind roaring around its wings.

Out the open side of a trail shelter, a fierce summer thunderstorm putting on a light and sound display unmatched by any July 4th fireworks.

A box turtle resting in the middle of a rain-swept trail.

A cemetery suddenly appearing in a clearing in what had been a densely forested part of the trail, a reminder that once these woods had been the fields and homesites for generations of families.

Moss and ferns creating a separate, tiny world of brilliant green around a cool mountain spring.

And there were deer, far more deer than people. As we watched the fawn that was checking us out along the trail, I eyed the surrounding area to spot the doe it surely was following. Mom was casually grazing in tall grass about 30 yards off the trail and didn't seem at all concerned about us. The fawn's more bashful sibling was off to the other side of the trail, also unconcerned by our presence. In the background, still another doe and fawn lazily grazed in the morning mist.

We lingered a few moments and then once again pushed north. The deer had been frequent companions on the trail. We saw one in our first hour of hiking and another in our last, with more than a dozen in between. One morning a buck with a late-summer rack of antlers grazed barely 10 yards from our campsite.

The buck was a surprise because our camp that morning was in the Lewis Mountain drive-in campground. But this was a weekday, and there were only a few other people around. We found the Lewis Mountain area much less used, and more informal, than the larger Big Meadows area, where we spent the following night. At Lewis Mountain, for example, we signed up for our campsite by putting the night's camping fee in an envelope at a registration bulletin board. At Big Meadows a ranger checked us in with a computer.

Our overnight stays in the established campgrounds varied greatly from our nights in the back country. In the tourist areas, we could buy snacks, make phone calls home and eat at a picnic table. But we gave up the quiet of the woods. Our trail camps were very simple, though always in a delightful setting of trees and rock outcrops. Since, according to park regulations, we had to camp out of sight of the trail, our camps were set deep in the woods. A flat, small clearing served us well, providing enough space for our two-man tent and perhaps a fallen log or a smooth rock to support our backpacking stove.

Without light, other than an emergency flashlight, we found ourselves heading for our sleeping bags early during our back-country nights, with only the sounds of insects and the blowing wind in the background. In the campground at Big Meadows, however, we could hear traffic and other voices long after we would have been asleep in a back-country setting.

John and I have been hiking and backpacking since he was hardly more than a toddler. First he carried only a toy in a small day pack, and I carried the rest. Through the years our share of the load became equal. On this trip, for the first time, he sometimes carried the heavier pack. No longer was that a boy hiking in front of me, I knew, but a young man. Such are the thoughts that come in the solitude of a woodland trail on a damp, misty day.

As we left the Big Meadows campground, a man hailed us: "Are you hiking on the Appalachian Trail?" We stopped briefly to chat, while the man explained that some day he wanted to hike the trail with the two young boys beside him. As we turned to leave, I wanted to say to him, "Do it soon, Dad, do it soon. The time passes all too fast."

By the time we reached our Saturday afternoon pick-up point at Thornton Gap, we had camped in back country, in established campgrounds and in trail shelters, a mix that indicates the range of choices available for outdoor experiences in Shenandoah.

Even after a week in the park, plus many previous shorter trips, we still have many trails to explore in Shenandoah. For day hikes, overnight camp-outs or longer backpacking excursions, the park offers a wide range of outdoor choices a surprisingly short drive from the city. We found Shenandoah is a place where we could get away from it all, but have it close by in case we wanted it—or needed it.

Occasionally, I stand along the shore of Chesapeake Bay and watch with admiration as sailboats catch the breeze and cut through the choppy waters. Looks like fun, I think. Perhaps I'd like to try that someday.

But I wouldn't consider trying it without the necessary training and background. And therefore I'm often surprised to see in the woods hikers and backpackers obviously unprepared to be there. From the comfort of a car, a group of backpackers on its way up the trail may seem as carefree as those sailboats seem to me. But woodland trekking, like sailboating or any other activity that puts you on your own in the natural environment, needs preparation, knowledge and common sense.

Before venturing beyond modest day hikes in public parks, every potential backpacker or distance hiker should be aware of these major concerns: First aid. Up-to-date knowledge of emergency first aid is vital to the enjoyment of an outdoor experience. This category includes not only treatment of common injuries but taking preventive steps. Good Red Cross-type training is important.

Physical conditioning. Happiness and comfort on the trail are directly proportional to the amount of work done ahead of time to condition feet, legs, back and arms. Check with your doctor.

Campcraft. This includes buying proper equipment and keeping it well maintained, knowing how to select a site and set up a safe camp, selecting proper food to take along and dressing appropriately for terrain and weather.

Land navigation. Maps and a compass are valuable outdoor tools. But they are useless if you don't know how to use them. A back-country camper can get into real trouble by venturing out without this knowledge.

The Potomac Appalachian Trail Club and other local outdoor-oriented organizations, including the Boy Scouts and the Girl Scouts, can be good sources of written and practical information about the outdoors. Libraries and bookstores have much material on the subject, but nothing will replace some initial hands-on experience with folks who know what they are doing. CAMPSITES: Campsites in the park may be reserved at Big Meadows Campground only, between late May and late October, through Ticketron's national park reservation service, 1-900-370-5566. All other sites are available on a first-come, first-served basis. BACK-COUNTRY CAMPING: Permits are required for back-country camping and are available at visitor centers and entrance stations, and by mail from park headquarters. Permits are free, although there's a $5 entrance fee to the park. There are no designated campsites in the back country; hikers may camp anywhere in the park as long as their camps are:

Out of sight of hiking trails or other camping parties.

At least 25 feet from any stream or water source.

One-half mile from any developed area, at least 250 yards away from Skyline Drive and at least 250 yards within the park boundaries.

In addition, no open fires are permitted in the back country; no glass containers are allowed; campsites must be bear-proofed; and dogs must be on leashes at all times. INFORMATION: Some useful sources of information on Shenandoah National Park:

Shenandoah National Park (Route 4-Box 348, Luray, Va., 22835-9051, 703-999-2266 (a recording) or 703-999-2243).

Potomac Appalachian Trail Club (1718 N St. NW, Washington, D.C. 20036, 638-5306), for maps and hiking information and to reserve PATC cabins.

ARA Virginia Sky-Line Co. Inc. (P.O. Box 727, Luray, Va. 22835, 703-743-5108), for information on park lodges and cabins.

July 1, 1990

What We Talk About When We Talk Sports

THOMAS BOSWELL

If John Thompson isn't a racist, what would you have to do to be one? In 18 years at Georgetown, he's seldom had white players on his team. That speaks for itself. Check the ratios, not the rationalizations. Isn't that what he'd say if the situation were reversed? He must not like whites. Or he must want his basketball scholarships to go to blacks. Or he must be trying to make some kind of statement.

Thompson says he's recruited whites, but they don't come. Maybe they don't want to play for a black coach on a mostly black team. That's their problem. Maybe they don't want to play in his system—pressure, defense, fast break, constant running and jumping. Maybe coaches bad-mouth him to white parents. White players have said that family members tried to keep them from going to Georgetown.

Knowing how much he hates racism, and has been hurt by it, I just don't think he could look himself in the mirror if he acted that way himself. His top assistants, like Bill Stein and Craig Esherick, have usually been white. His team's academic adviser, Mary Fenlon, the person closest to him in the whole program, is white. He's been honest about so many other things for so long, why can't we give him the benefit of the doubt on this one?

If he's not racist, then try to tell me he's not paranoid. How come his players almost never talk to the press? And when they do, how come they sound like they're parroting the company line? Have you heard a Georgetown player say anything spontaneous or funny?

Thompson doesn't think 20-years-olds should be celebrities just because they can dribble. He doesn't think they have anything to say that the world needs to hear. He says, "You come to Georgetown to learn, not to teach." He'll do anything to keep them humble so they don't turn into jock bums when they don't make the NBA. And it works. His players aren't ego crazy. Even Patrick Ewing. They adjust to the real world. His kids take entry-level jobs and work up. They don't think somebody should give them the whole store because they played for Georgetown.

Come on—if Thompson doesn't think the world's out to get him, how come his teams get in so many fights? You could make a cheap-shot highlight film just on Georgetown.

I'll give you that one—they do fight too much. Even if they're provoked, they should turn the other cheek. There are ways to retaliate without having a brawl. Life provokes everybody. That's no excuse.

The problem is Thompson's temper. Last season they lost the Big East title because he got so many technical fouls that Syracuse got a 10-point play. Georgetown teams pick up the short fuse from the coach. But if Thompson didn't have his temper, he also wouldn't have such an acute sense of outrage. He wouldn't be such a good social critic and athletic reformer.

I still think the Hoyas would be better off if he'd taken the money and gone to Denver.

The NBA's loss is Georgetown's gain. Big-time coaching is a tough world, but Thompson's found a way to do three things: win a ton of games; turn out decent, hard-working student-athletes that any college would be proud of; and stand up for his principles. He'd be next to impossible to replace.

Is there any Washingtonian, no matter how little he or she cares about sports, who has not heard a debate very much like this one?

These days, sports may be what Americans talk about best. With the most knowledge. The most passion. The most humor. The most distance. The most capacity for a cheerful charge of mind. When we meet someone for the first time, it's no accident that sports becomes the subject so often and so quickly. Yes, it's an easy, superficial topic—if we want it to be. But talking about sports has also become one of our best ways of probing people, sounding their depths, judging their values.

Games are about who won, who lost and how. But they're also about what's right, what's wrong and why. When we talk about sports we often find ourselves discussing what might be called the common-sense ethics of everyday living.

If the subject, both on the sports page and around the dinner table, is not John Thompson, then it might be Joe Gibbs, John McEnroe, Bobby Knight, John Riggins, Billy Martin, George Steinbrenner, Pete Rose, Dino Ciccarelli, Len Bias, Sugar Ray Leonard, the Ripken family, Jack Kent Cooke or Lefty Driesell. Is there any stratum of Washington society, or any social setting, in which any one of these names would not be known instantly to almost everyone in the room?

And it's not just names that we know. It's the whole fabric of these people's lives that interests us. We can't get enough detail. If you want to frighten yourself, compare your knowledge of the Supreme Court with your knowledge of the Redskin offense, right down to the Hogs. Think about the Bush Cabinet. Now think about the Orioles. Which careers do you follow in more depth? And the Orioles play in another city.

We reveal ourselves most through the things we know best. Which sports or teams or athletes do you love? Or hate? And why? When Spike Lee plays Mars Blackmon, he knows he has to pretend to despise Larry Bird. President Bush has followed the bedraggled Houston Astros for years; is that a tip-off that he's more Texan than preppy?

What issues make you see red: overpaid players or greedy owners? Strikes or franchise shifts? Be careful. You tip your hand every time you open your mouth. Are you generous or jealous, judgmental or broad-minded? Talk sports and it will slip out. Which losers do you instinctively defend: Old Tom Landry, put out to pasture? Or those miserable choking-dog Broncos? Oooops.

Because sports is a subject about which we feel deeply, yet usually pretend not to care too much ("It's only a game"), it has become perhaps our richest and most user-friendly topic of conversation. Especially when the subject is moral. And how many conversations about sports lack a moral undertone? The question underlying every event, even for athletes, is: Who deserves to win? "Deserves," that is, in the broadest sense. To an athlete, this often means: Who has developed his available talent most fully? To a team, it can translate as: Who interacts best as a group? If you have trouble perceiving yourself as truly worthy of victory, you'll have great difficulty reaching your goals.

A large part of a sportswriter's job, although it is seldom acknowledged, is to present, as clearly as possible, the central characters and issues in what amounts to an ongoing national discussion about mores: How do we act and how should we act.

Not so long ago, such discussions in this country were couched in specifically religious terms. The frame of reference was, more or less, the Bible with its commandments, allegories, cautionary tales and parables. The prodigal son, David and Goliath, doubting Thomas or the story of Ruth might be invoked at the dinner table. Today, where would we reach first for material or metaphor to make such points to our children? Probably to sports.

Why? Because millions of Americans know more about the achievements, failures, embarrassments and private lives of athletes than they know about anyone on earth except their family and friends. Even national politicians and celebrity entertainers are not covered on such an intense daily basis for such a long time, sometimes for decades. Athletes and coaches take it for granted.

Americans frequently talk about sports as though it was an extension of their own private lives—because it feels like it is. When fans meet famous athletes for the first time, the assumption of familiarity is so total that players are sometimes alarmed. No wonder fans feel so free to ask for autographs in restaurants. There's almost no sense of distance to break down.

Why, this is just butter-fingered old Joe, the good-block, no-catch tight end. He fumbled in the Rose Bowl, went into drug rehab when he was with the Raiders, got traded to the Redskins during training camp and now picks up a few bucks by trading quips with the anchorman on the local news. We know him better than plenty of our cousins.

Many of us, perhaps unconsciously, are attracted to this peculiarly modern possibility—long-distance intimacy. Mass media have given us a chance to observe the essential behavior of other people in a core area of their lives for years on end.

I can't believe that your father, an intelligent man, sits there every Sunday, year after year, rooting for the stupid Washington Redskins. He shows more emotion during those silly games than he does in the rest of the year combined. He's getting too old for this. If the Redskins keep coming up with kickers who miss extra points, I'm afraid I'm going to find him dead, sitting right in that chair in front of the TV .

Don't worry, Mom, he'll probably stay alive an extra 10 years just to see if they get back to the Super Bowl. Come on, you watch too. You know you do. When Doug Williams was hurt against Denver and he got up and threw all those touchdown passes, you were crying. When Riggins made that long run to beat the Dolphins, you were out on the front porch, just like everybody else on the block, banging that big cooking pot with a spoon.

I come into the room periodically. I do not watch. It's too disturbing for me to see your father so upset. He takes it personally. That's the only time he ever curses. He's 5-foot-7 and played last-string quarterback in high school 60 years ago, and for the last 15 years he's thought he was Dave Butz every Sunday. I married a man who could recite "Paradise Lost," and now he says, "Maybe they should take Dexter Manley back. A good pass rush is hard to find." He wouldn't say a thing like that about anything but the Redskins.

And I never approved of John Riggins. He was a ruffian before he ever said, "Loosen up, Sandy baby." I just thought he had a certain dignity as a player.

Is this the same woman who went to see Duke University in the Rose Bowl 50 years ago?

What's that got to do with it? The point is, I'll never understand your father. Joe Gibbs is just the sort of fundamentalist zealot that he's abhorred his whole life. And to root for Joe Theismann—that self-absorbed little twitt!

Cathy Lee Crosby left him.

Naturally.

With tens of millions of exceptions, sports is still more a fascination for men than women. That only underlines our point. Men can't find any other subject where they can reveal themselves so much, yet pretend that they have said so little.

What, if not sports, moves men beyond self-consciousness, beyond hipnesss beyond self-protective intelligence and turns them into vulnerable, ventilating human beings? Any woman who marries a man with no favorite team, no childhood hero, no incurable need to call Sportsphone at l a.m. (that's 212-976-1313), should consider herself fairly warned. She may have hooked a cold fish.

For both sexes—but especially for males—sports is an area in which we can be philosophical without pretending to own a philosophy. Because sports congratulates itself on being trivial, even creating the "trivia question," we allow ourselves the luxury of unsystematic insight.

We welcome new evidence about complex personalities. For instance, we'll wait 20 years to form our final opinion of Kareem Abdul-Jabbar, allowing him to change, grow and finally reveal himself to us as an adult. For once, we care about learning as well as passing judgment. Oh, we rush to judgment, to be sure. But with a self-deprecating smirk.

We've been wrong so often about so many people, teams and games. We're willing to be proved wrong again.

Where but in sports do we offer an impassioned opinion, then immediately add the provison, "but if I knew what I was talking about, I wouldn't have to work for a living. I'd just move to Vegas and get rich."

At a dinner party recently, I heard a well-known political columnist and a Supreme Court nominee discuss both baseball and Lithuanian independence in the same hour. Their passion about and knowledge of both subjects were large. But the baseball discussion was perceptive, flowing, progressive—a joint pursuit of gentle insights. The conversation moved forward, exploring new areas, then returning to earlier points. Voices were never raised, though there was plenty of laughter.

On Lithuania? Let's just say that, although no one in the room claimed to have visited Lithuania or to know any Lithuanians personally, everyone who voiced an opinion seemed absolutely certain about, and emotionally invested in, every point. After a few minutes, someone said, "Perhaps we should get back to talking about sports."

If you can't talk sports—national sports, local sports and even neighborhood sports—you may feel like a social outsider in many parts of this country. In fact, sports has become central to what remains of our American sense of community. In an age that is a political, religious, artistic and cultural kaleidoscope of relativist values, how can we feel united? What can we agree about? Or even discuss calmly, yet enthusiastically, with a sense of shared expertise and a glimpse of a shared ideal?

Sports has such a profound hold on people these days because it has never been so desperately needed. In a century that has banished certainty in almost every corner of our lives, in a time when, one after another, almost all our compasses have been demagnetized, there is an enormous collective yearning for a sense of orientation.

We're not expecting truth, doctrine or dogma, mind you. "Isms" have had a bad credit rating for a long time. We'd just like to get our bearings occasionally, thank you very much. We've learned to make little things suffice. For instance, it is reassuring to know that, as long as George III owns the Yankees, they will never be in another World Series.

Somebody's got to get Cal Ripken Jr. out of the lineup before this stupid consecutive-games streak ruins him. He used to be a great player. Now he's turning into a bum. Every year he hits a little less. It's wearing him out. It's too much pressure. And for what? He's not going to catch Lou Gehrig. Does he really think he's going to play every game for the next five years? By June of 1995, he'll be 35. Nobody can play every game for more than 13 years in a row. Especially at shortstop. He's obsessed with breaking this unreachable record that'll make him famous forever instead of doing what's best for the team.

Why should Cal come out of the lineup when he's not hurt? He's still their best player. He hits 20 homers, drives in 90 runs and plays a great shortstop every year. Stop bitching. What do you want? The streak's not the problem. Sometimes he slumps in May. Is he exhausted in May?

Why don't you value the streak? Why not enjoy it? Can't you recognize great-ness when you see it? Even if The Streak did hurt Ripken a little, some things are more important than worshiping team play. What's a few points on a batting aver-age anyway? If Ripken *did* break Gehrig's record, and accomplished most of it at shortstop, people would talk about it and be amazed by it long after anything that the Baltimore Orioles of the 1980s and 1990s could possibly do was forgotten.

The problem with Cal Junior is Cal Senior. For years, the old man wouldn't stop coaching the kid. When your son is 30, you let him go, let somebody else, who knows more, help him to the next level. The father isn't a hitting coach. But he wouldn't let anybody else work with him. And what's wrong with Junior's back-bone? Why did he wait until this summer, after he was totally messed up, to say, "Dad, I'd like to try some new ideas. I'm going to work with Frank Robinson."

The real problem with Ripken's hitting is the lousy lineup he's been in for years. When he had big-timers in the No. 4-5-6 slots, he was relaxed and a terror. When he and Eddie Murray were all that was left, he started to strain. And when Eddie left, his bad habits became real flaws. Cal's such a straight arrow, so respon-sible, that he thinks he has to do it all. He's lost all idea of the strike zone. With the bases loaded, just watch him. He's so overanxious he's an automatic out.

He's too selfish.

He's too unselfish.

When we want to ask simple but embarrassing questions, we often turn to sports for analogies and limited practical insight. How should a person live? Or face tragedy? What constitutes a useful life? To many moderns, such topics might instantly run the risk of sounding more comic than cosmic. But sports, with its artificial simplicity, its final scores, its winners and losers, prods us away from our resigned acceptance of ambiguity, at least for a while.

We may not know how all men should live, but we know that Magic Johnson embodies unselfishness and a joy-in-task that we might see as a useful model. We may not know how we would cope with tragedy until we meet it, but the memory of speed skater Dan Jansen competing in the Olympics on the same day that his sis-ter died might be of some use to us. Jansen fell, raced again three days later and fell once more, yet seemed ennobled by his effort.

In games, we often discover the implicit values and powerful preferences that we hold in common, even though we seldom express them. We all sense that Michael Jordan and Julius Erving have special qualities. When we try to find words for what those estimable qualities are, we educate ourselves about ourselves.

And when we want to focus on how *not* to live, when we want to isolate and understand what is destructive or unacceptable behavior, where do we turn? Not to our legal system certainly. There, the concept of an individual's responsibility for his actions is so attenuated as to be almost nonexistent. In sports, the individual still must answer for himself. Neither a broken home nor a bad hop helps you beat the rap.

Perhaps, 200 years ago, the average American could have mentioned the latest doings of Sam Adams or Thomas Jefferson and assumed that his neighbor would know all about these men, their lives and their ideas. Politics was a common ground on which citizens of the republic could meet. Today, it's arguable that sports has overtaken both politics and religion as the meeting ground where we debate our values.

Before you laugh, fly over cities like Cincinnati, Pittsburgh, St. Louis, San Diego, Detroit, Cleveland, Phoenix, Tampa, Miami, Seattle, Kansas City and many others. Look for the primary architectural symbols: cathedrals, statehouses, ballparks. You'll see the ballparks and stadiums first. They're the structures that dwarf everything else. Only when you come to America's "world class" cities—New York, Chicago, Los Angeles, Washington, San Francisco—do you find the coliseums on a common scale with other monuments and skyscrapers.

Let somebody else blow a brain lobe figuring out whether this news is depressing or encouraging. What's indisputable is that, in the last 30 years, thanks to TV and our whole mass media explosion, America has become infatuated with a vast, open-ended subject on which millions of people are experts. As spectators, we all observe the same behavioral laboratory together.

This may explain why sportswriters with even a hint of a political, religious, philosophical or even generational agenda tend to disappear quickly. Sports is too specific, too detailed, too reality-tested and—above all—too thoroughly known by too many people for media pundits to get away with much. As soon as you start to overstate your case, you can hear the screams from the street. You can't fool many of the people much of the time about Ray Leonard's last fight. They saw it, by God. Just like they've seen all his others since the 1976 Olympics. Some watched the replay too.

Our mass infatuation with sports may also explain the ironic fact that a columnist writing on the editorial page about Congress and a sportswriter holding forth on the affairs of the Washington Redskins are often held to different standards. A case can be made that greater accuracy, far more disclosure of sources, less appearance of conflict of interest, a less predictable pattern of partisan bias and crisper writing are generally expected of the sportswriter.

In sum, great athletes in late 20th-century America have—without knowing it or wanting it—been put in something akin to the position mythic or religious figures occupied in other cultures and times. That is to say, they have taken on a symbolic quality: They play the role of surrogates in our thinly veiled ethical conversations.

For them, no doubt, this is a mixed blessing—and a kind of celebrity squared. But for the public, is the trade so bad?

Are the issues that our passion for sports helps us to discuss—with knowledge, good cheer, honesty and without the weight of dogma—really as trivial as we like to pretend?

Sugar Ray Leonard is crazy. His brains aren't scrambled yet, but they will be—just like Muhammad Ali's. Boxing kills them all in the end. It's like a drug. The more they fight, the more they need to fight. Even when they don't need the pay-day, they need the glory. In a culture where a man is defined so heavily by the job he does, almost everybody becomes the thing that he does.

For a fighter, it's even worse than for a doctor or lawyer. He gets enormous positive feedback when he fights and wins. He gets no feedback—he disappears as a human being—when he stops fighting. Retirement is social annihilation.

Leonard will keep fighting Thomas Hearns and Marvin Hagler until nobody will pay to see him anymore. He may still be fighting in 1995. Write it down. Just watch.

Maybe if you were ever as good at anything as Leonard is at prize fighting, you could understand that, sometimes, self-expression is worth great risks. Leonard has done things in the ring, like the 14th round of Hearns, that even he never dreamed he could do until he was forced to do them. He can live life at a level—for a short time—that the rest of us can't imagine.

If ski jumpers, downhill racers, automobile drivers and bobsledders will risk their lives for the adrenalin high that they get from speed, think of the rush that Leonard experiences when he's in a firefight with Hagler.

Ray Leonard is crazy. He'll end up punch-drunk and die too young.

Sugar Ray is an artist. He'll be remembered in a hundred years, and, no matter what happens, he wouldr't trade a minute of it.

August 12, 1990

The Slam-Jam Joy of Michael Jordan

In Flight and on the Ground, the Transcendence of the Ballplayer

JIM NAUGHTON

There is little uncontested space in Michael Jordan's life. He swings through the door of the players' entrance at Chicago Stadium an hour and a half before game time, when the building is nearly deserted, but from somewhere a contingent of boys—abdomen-high and autograph-hungry—materializes before him. Jordan is generally patient with signature seekers, but tonight he is nursing a tender thumb and signs his name just a few times. Then, chatting pleasantly but walking fast, he turns a corner and has soon outdistanced just about everyone. Everyone except an older usher who approaches him from behind and places a hand on the ballplayer's elbow. Jordan flinches, but the startled look has all but disappeared from his eyes when he turns to take the man's cocktail napkin and scribble his good wishes.

That done, he heads for the stairway to the dressing room, but in his path stands a young woman in high heels, baroque stockings and an equatorial hemline. "Look Michael, look," she says presenting herself. "I'm looking," he answers, but there is more of the polite than the lusty in his reply as he descends the stairs.

Everywhere Jordan goes, the world rises up to meet him. He sells out cavernous arenas, such as Capital Centre, where he and the Bulls will face the Washington Bullets this evening; he receives 1,000 fan letters each week, has his own line of sneakers, his own line of sportswear and endorses a host of quintessentially American products ranging from Wheaties to Chevys to Coca-Cola. He is America's favorite athlete, but he is also one of its most admired men, particularly among young people.

"I never knew it could be like this," says the man who was cut from the varsity in his sophomore year of high school. "In high school you have people who know you and who appreciate your game and then in college that gets broader. But I never knew it could be nation-based, or, if you want to say, world-based." Jordan's popularity has something to do with his acrobatic elegance and something to do with his sweet personality, something to do with how shrewdly he is promoted and something to do with how responsible he is to his image. It has something to do with what the nation expects from its athletes, and what kind of fame it makes available to black men.

It also has something to do with joy.

"There is a genuine sense of playfulness, a sense of wonder about the way he plays the game, and his sense of joy transmits to his fans a feeling of ecstasy," says Joseph Price, an associate professor of religious studies at Whittier College. (More on the theological ramifications of the slam dunk in a moment.) "They can celebrate because he celebrates."

And in these celebrations a power is unleashed—the power to make fans forget their troubles, to make life seem momentarily less mean, to make a child's world seem as large as his imagination. It comes with the territory when you are the all-American boy, circa 1990.

The arena is dark except for the spotlights that chase one another across the crowd. One by one the Chicago Bulls are introduced to a manufactured exuberance that is well out of proportion to most of their achievements. But this is only a warm-up for the ear-rattling roar that awaits No. 23, an appreciative tumult so loud that it defeats the purpose of introduction.

As the lights come on the din subsides and a hum fills the old brick building. It is the sound of people who are fully prepared—and firmly expect—to be delighted, people who know that with Jordan on the court, the game will be replete with opportunities for the miraculous. They have seen it happen before—in slow motion and from several angles. But tonight, when he soars down the lane for a dunk, or snakes through the defense for a layup, they will be there.

The late sportswriting giant Red Smith used to warn against "godding-up the ballplayers," but that seems to be what is afoot here.

"Going to a Bulls game is like going to a temple," says Arthur Droge, associate professor of New Testament at the University of Chicago's Divinity School. "There's definitely a religious component about it and Jordan is the demigod on the scene at the moment."

Joseph Price says the nature of Jordan's following suggests a religious phenomenon known as apotheosis, the attribution of divine characteristics to an example of human perfection—Jordan's perfection, he adds, residing in "his grace around the basket, his gliding and pirouetting as he dunks."

"'He is God disguised as Michael Jordan," Larry Bird, a ballplayer of some repute, said in 1986. Maybe it was apotheosis he had in mind. Or maybe it was the 63 points Jordan had just scored against his Celtics.

"Everybody always says it's me and Larry," Earvin "'Magic" Johnson said when asked who was the best player in professional basketball. "Really it's Mike and everybody else."

The reason for Jordan's excellence is a mastery of fundamentals. There is nothing the 27-year-old guard doesn't do well. In 1987 he was named the National Basketball Association's most valuable player, as well as its best defender. He frequently leads the Bulls in scoring, rebounds, assists and steals. But his reputation derives from exploiting an opportunity unique to basketball—scoring as statement. Baseball has its high fives and football its end zone strut, but only in basketball is the ecstatic outburst incorporated in the scoring.

In Jordan's case, it is evident in his entire game, in the furious grace of his surge to the basket and the unearthly altitude of his ascent for a rebound, in the breathtaking quickness and digital precision of his passes as well as the slashing confrontation of his defense and the often perfect parabola of his jump shot.

This exuberance is augmented by the fact that as Jordan swoops toward the basket, his opponent is not simply another athlete, but gravity itself.

"There is the sense that somehow he transcends," Price says. "'That he succeeds in doing that which all of us aspire to do. That he is capable of flight and that this is as near a thing to human transcendence as we are likely to see."

Because of Jordan, Droge says, "there are 12-year-olds growing up with a different sense of physical possibilities." And if those 12-year-olds are particularly involved in the Jordan mystique, they are probably wearing the long Lycra undershorts that protrude beneath their uniform trunks. They are probably wearing the trunks a little long and at least slightly bagging. Their socks are just ankle high and the fit is floppy. And maybe they have a wristband that they wear well up their forearm.

And if their parents can come up with $120, they will certainly be wearing Air Jordans.

"Mars Blackmon here with my main man Money."

Spike Lee, playing the character he portrayed in "She's Gotta Have It" barks out the words while glaring into the camera. Jordan, whom Lee calls Money, is standing behind him looking equally serious. To their left stands Lt. Col. Douglas Kirkpatrick, professor of aeronautics at the United States Air Force Academy who will momentarily testify to the physics involved in Jordan's "Earth orbits."

This is one of the most recent spots in Nike's definitively hip campaigns for its equally hip and wildly expensive basketball shoes. These commercials were the second front on which Jordan's appeal was forged. In 1985, before his rookie season, he signed a contract to promote and lend his name, not only to the sneakers but to a line of sportswear called Flight.

The first commercials featured Jordan attacking the basket synchronized to the Pointer Sisters singing their hit "Jump!" The ads brought basketball to the MTV generation, made Jordan's artistry appreciable to a broader audience and made his much-emulated moves seem nearly mythical. It also sold a lot of sneakers. Nike now controls roughly half the market in basketball shoes, selling 414 million pairs last year. That's a post-Jordan increase of more than 250 percent. In return, the company has made him a millionaire several times over, promoted him relentlessly, and helped develop his commercial personality.

"There was this quote from Bill Russell {the legendary former Boston Celtic} who told Michael's parents that their son was a better human being than he was a basketball player, which was a wonderful quote," says Jim Riswold, who masterminds the Air Jordan campaign for Weiden and Kennedy, a Portland-based advertising agency.

"We decided we should do some commercials that show the human side of Michael, and that's when we began this Spike Lee-Mars Blackmon campaign. It shows Michael as something other than this basketball machine."

This is always a risky enterprise. Young, attractive and affluent, athletes are accustomed to being treated as though society's rules do not apply to them. Often, the more people know about many athletes the less they like them. But the opposite appears to be true of Jordan. A 1984 Olympic gold medal had something to do with that, but so did stories about his devotion to his parents, his church attendance and his vocal opposition to drug abuse.

The image had appeal across a broad commercial spectrum, from McDonald's to Johnson Products to Guy Laroche, who designed the Time Jordan wristwatch.

"He's virtually infiltrated every household through cereal boxes, through advertising, through sportswear," says Ted Ewanciw, director of corporate communications for Pro-Serv, the sports management firm that represents Jordan.

Contradiction seems implicit in such a range of endorsements. Yet in Jordan, or at least in the consumer's perception of Jordan, the contradictions seem resolved. He is a black athlete who sacrificed none of his blackness to succeed in white America. He is hip yet homey, flashy yet modest, devilish, but somehow trustworthy.

Among athletes, only Arnold Palmer and Jack Nicklaus earn more money through endorsements, and professional golf—affluent and equipment intensive— has always been a much more advantageous commercial launching pad than basketball, the sport with perhaps the poorest natural constituency.

Jordan has grown beyond that constituency, but he has not abondoned it.

Black athletes carry burdens that white athletes don't.

"In pockets of poverty today kids don't see black men with suits or with several college degrees," says civil rights activist and former assistant attorney general Roger Wilkins, who is now a professor at George Mason University in Fairfax County. "They seem as far away as the fantasies of 'Dallas' or 'Dynasty.' But they know about playing basketball. They know about that. They see people all around them doing that very well. And there are stories and legends in their neighborhoods about people who have gone on to play in college or in the pros. That's a ladder that is real to them. And that gives the basketball player influence that other professions don't have."

Using this influence is tricky. In the past, athletes have been able to get away with telling kids that if they practiced real hard they could grow up to be athletes too. This was always a lie; there are fewer than 2,300 jobs in Major League Baseball, the National Football League and the NBA. Today athletes are being asked to perform the difficult task of being role models who encourage kids to seek a success other than the one they sought themselves.

Wilkins says Jordan does well in this regard. "Here is a man who is intelligent, disciplined, engaging, who can live sensibly and joyously within this thing he has made," he says. "He has the discipline to handle it without disintegrating with drugs, without having a personal life that is lurid.

"He, like Julius Erving {the former 76ers star} and several others before him, indicates that there is something beyond being a pro," he says. "That there is a dignity and a beauty to being a whole black man."

But black athletes are also used as barometers of racial progress.

"America's tolerance for certain kinds of black people in prominent positions is high and in other kinds of possession it is low," Wilkins says. "America has always had a fairly large tolerance for black entertainers and after black entertainers, black athletes. I think America, in order to deny how strong its racism still is, needs certain kinds of black heroes. It needs to be able to look at Bill Cosby and Michael Jordan and say, 'See, the doors are open to these people.' "

How completely to embrace fame, what purpose to aim it toward, has been a central issue in the lives of many modern black athletes. Jackie Robinson endured a career's worth of verbal abuse and segregated accommodations to break baseball's color line. Runners John Carlos and Tommy Smith raised black-gloved fists in a black power salute at the 1968 Olympics in Mexico City. Cassius Clay, perhaps the most politically significant athlete of the past 50 years, joined the Nation of Islam, changed his name to Muhammad Ali, went to jail rather than join the Army and became one of the most outspoken critics of American racism. Lew Alcindor, now Kareem Abdul-Jabbar, also converted to Islam, but won the battle to be counted as a private individual rather than a public symbol.

Jordan has not had to deal with the pressure these earlier heroes faced. The times have not required him to take controversial stands. Instead, he works in quieter ways.

"I think people want a big brother for their kids or a good example," Jordan says. "And that is my whole intention, because a lot of kids don't have that in their lives and it helps get them over the hump."

Last year Jordan organized the Michael Jordan Foundation, a branch of JUMP Inc., his personal corporation. The foundation raises money for six child-oriented charities selected each year as well as organizing Jordan's benefit appearances and his personal contributions. Aside from his work with the foundation, Jordan also has established two scholarships at Laney High, his alma mater in Wilmington, N.C.

But he also works face to face. David Rothenberg, the 13-year-old California boy whose father set him on fire, sat on the Bulls bench with Jordan this season. He receives roughly 30 requests each week from dying children whose last wish is to meet him, and he fulfills as many of those requests as he can. Each child who sits on the bench receives the sneakers that Jordan wore in the game. A young man who died of leukemia was recently buried in his.

"He is the number one role model," says a Chicago dentist who has followed Jordan's career with unusual interest because they share a name. "Just a very squeaky clean image," says the other Michael Jordan, father of two boys. "He is the kind of guy who if there ever was an exposé type of thing, he would shatter a lot of people's ideals. It must be very scary for him."

His power to disappoint rests heavily on Jordan.

"The good part about {being famous} is being able to stretch myself and meet people and help people," he says. "The hard part is every day you've got to be in a good mood, because that is what people expect from you. You learn to get good at it."

Still, there are moments when escape is the only recourse. On a recent trip to the West Coast, Jordan and his best friend Adolph Shiver, a real estate agent from Chapel Hill, N.C., decided to go to a mall. "We walked in and right away somebody recognized him," Shiver says. " 'There's Michael Jordan.' And within about 50 feet there were 100 kids around us. We ran out of there after about two minutes."

"Somebody said it was like traveling with Michael Jackson on tour," says Bulls teammate John Paxson. "And it can be."

Fame has forced Jordan to build a cocoon for himself and to draw clear distinctions between public and private time. The private time is spent with his wife, Juanita, a former loan officer; Jeffrey, their 1-year-old son; and a group of close friends including Shiver, Fred Whitfield, a lawyer who attended the University of North Carolina with Jordan, and T.O. Stokes, another lawyer. This inner circle is unlike most athletes' in that its members are independently successful. None of them depends on Jordan for identity or livelihood.

"They kind of help me by being a backboard for whatever problems I might have in my career and in my life," Jordan says. "My wife fills in a lot of that."

The price his friends pay is being asked constantly what Jordan is really like.

"He's the same as he was when he didn't have a dime," Whitfield says.

"People ask me is he really like they say he is," Shiver says. "I say he's just like he appears. A lot of people can't believe that."

But, if an incident after a game last month is at all indicative, Shiver knows whereof he speaks.

A young fan had been waiting, with his father and a friend, for Jordan to emerge from the locker room. Of the boy's outer garments, only his blue jeans were free of Jordan's name or silhouette. When the object of his admiration not only agreed to pose but draped an arm casually around the young man's shoulders, his knees appeared as if they might buckle.

But the camera wouldn't work. The boy's father tried it a few times and the father's friend tried it a few times as the boy's eyes danced with joy ("I'm standing here with Michael Jordan") and terror ("Nobody is going to believe me without a picture").

Finally a man appeared wielding a camera of his own. He examined the defective camera, raised it to his eye and, "click." It had taken nearly five minutes to snap the picture, but Michael Jordan never moved.

April 14, 1990

Ragin' on the Ramp

PETER CARLSON

Why would any sane kid risk life and limb skating the Cedar Crest Country Club? Dumb question. 'You get to go fast,' explains Juice DuBois. 'You catch big air, go over people's heads and stuff.'

Juice ollies the channel and everybody yells, "Yeah!"

He rolls down the ramp, soars up the other side, pops his skateboard up onto the lip and grinds along the stone coping, his axles barking like seals.

"Yeah!" the other skaters yell. "Yeah!"

Down again and back up and he tries to repeat it, but his board flips out from under him and he sprawls 10 feet down the ramp as his board comes tumbling after.

So Rat drops in. He roars up the ramp and flies four feet into the air, a move that breaks all the laws of gravity, and then, somehow, he touches lightly down and wails toward the other side so he can do it again.

"Yeah!" the dudes yell. They're standing on the platform in their helmets and pads, with one foot planted on the back of their boards so the noses stick up in the air like the heads of cobras. "Yeah! Yeah!"

Rat's stoked. He's ragin'. He's catching, like, five feet of air now, sailing so high off the top of the ramp that the bottom of his board floats right past the wide eyes of the watchers like an airborne billboard, with stickers that say "Thrasher" and "Intensity Skates" and this gnarly decal of a skull with a bandage and bulging eyes.

"Yeah, Rat!"

"Go, brother!"

Rat does a few more acrobatic moves, moves that you'd swear are aerodynamically impossible, until he tries one that's too impossible even for him and he goes spilling down the ramp, with only his kneepads saving him from a painful date with an orthopedic surgeon. And then, one by one, they all take their turns—Sam Boo and Raoul Roberts and Devin McGuire and the rest. They stand with their boards balanced on the lip of the ramp, and then they lean forward and drop down the 11-foot steel wall, pick up speed, then whip across the 12-foot flat bottom section and streak up the other side to do their moves. They do lip tricks like axle stalls and axle grinds, and they do jump stunts like ollies and airs and hand-plants and a hundred other combinations and variations that they haven't even named yet.

And the other dudes egg them on like jazz buffs cheering a soloist, like the amen corner punctuating the preacher's cadences:

"Yeah!"

"Go, man!"

"Yeah!"

Waiting their turns, the skaters are lighting up smokes and swigging Cokes. It's not quite 50 degrees, but they're stripping down to T-shirts that reveal biceps decorated with some truly baroque tattoos. The boom box blares Metal Church—music that sounds like the midnight shift at the steel plant or a psychopathic dental drill or a garbage disposal eating a beer can.

It's just another Saturday afternoon at the Cedar Crest Country Club in Centreville, Va.

Wait a minute: This is a country club?

Aren't country clubs the places where Republicans in lime-green pants and tasseled shoes chase little white balls across a crew-cut meadow?

And aren't skateboarders the walking, talking antithesis of the country club ethos—ratty kids who are regularly kicked out of places far less tony than this, places like Fair Oaks Mall and Lake Forest Mall and Pershing Park and the concrete patio of the Department of Health and Human Services' Hubert H. Humphrey Building?

So how'd the skateboarders get into the country club?

Connections, of course.

It happened like this: Mark Hooper, who's the son of the owner, is a skater. About five years ago, he asked his father for permission to build a ramp. Just a little wooden punk ramp way off in the woods, he said, far from the golf course and the tennis courts. His father said no. He wouldn't permit a little punk ramp.

"Build the best," he said, "or don't build it at all."

So Mark Hooper built the best. He got an architect and a crew of carpenters and they constructed an 80-foot by 45-foot structure with a ramp made of sheets of 11-gauge steel surrounded by a beautiful deck, with catwalks and spotlights and two staircases. It's a veritable Xanadu, skateboarding's answer to Versailles, and it cost his father $60,000 or $80,000 or $100,000, depending on which of Hooper's versions you want to accept.

This isn't some gently sloping ramp designed for your average acne-cheeked adolescent accustomed to surfing suburban sidewalks. It's a hard, tough, U-shaped precipice that's so scary that even Hooper was leery of it at first. "This is not a little kid's ramp," he says. "This is a man's ramp."

A young man's ramp, actually. Hooper is 27 now, and ever since he wiped out doing a grind and hurt his back, he spends more time golfing than skating. "I'm getting too old," he says. "But I still drop in and grind and do airs and stuff." But not today. Today, he's standing at the ramp in his black business suit and his purple shades watching other people do grinds and airs, and talking about why he's not worried about lawsuits. Everybody knows it's skate at your own risk. They tell their parents, 'You sue and you'll be responsible for killing the greatest ramp around.' "

Hooper strolls around the deck trying to collect $3 from each of the skaters. He does this occasionally to raise money for repairs, but it's tough going. As he approaches, dudes tend to slink away or zoom down the ramp. He buttonholes a few, but they plead poverty. One only has $2, another offers a sweaty handful of change.

Hooper takes what he can get and lets the rest slide.

Juice is about the only guy eager to pony up the full fare. He doesn't mind paying $3 to skate the Crest. "It's the best ramp from Massachusetts to North Carolina," he says.

Juice is from Rhode Island. He's 20 and his real name, which nobody ever uses, is Bruce DuBois. He heard about Cedar Crest, which is famous all over the East Coast, and he made a pilgrimage last summer. He loved the ramp so much that he moved down here and got a job as a bike courier. Now he spends his weekdays risking his life riding a bicycle in Washington traffic and his weekends risking his life riding a skateboard at Cedar Crest.

"You get to go fast," he explains. "You catch big air, go over people's heads and stuff."

Devin McGuire also feels the intense gravitational pull of the ramp. In fact, last night he slept out here in his car with Raoul Roberts and a few other diehards who wanted to skate the first rays of dawn. But when they woke up, there was ice on the ramp. They had to wait until it melted and then mop up the water with old rags and a ratty green blanket. It was gnarly.

Devin's wearing a light green helmet, a green beaded necklace and a sweaty black T-shirt that commemorates Iron Maiden's "World Slavery Tour." He's 19, a senior at Woodson High School in Fairfax.

"He's a repeat senior," some wise guy points out.

"Hey, I skated a little too much my junior year," Devin explains.

It happened like this: It was such a nice spring that year that Devin couldn't resist cutting his afternoon classes and skipping out to Cedar Crest.

"Which was a big mistake," he says.

But he learned his lesson. Now he waits until school is over before he shoots out to the Crest, usually with Rat, whose real name is Greg Goodson and who drives a forklift at a Fairfax lumberyard. Devin's determined to graduate this year, and he hopes to go to college in North Carolina.

"They're opening a skate park down there," he says.

While Devin's talking, Rat's doing airs about six inches away from his face.

"Yeah, Rat!" Devin yells. A few feet away, a couple of skaters are playing chess while a third offers unsolicited tactical advice about bringing up your knights to back up your pawns.

"Party tonight—five kegs," somebody announces. "We're gonna rage! There's gonna be lots of people there. We're gonna rage fully!"

Juice drifts by with blood drying in the scraggly whiskers on his chin. "I kissed the ramp and it bit me," he says, smiling. Then he roars back down the ramp.

"You gotta rage," he says.

Two skate bettys in black leather jackets sit watching all this with no noticeable interest. Becky Westerman came out here with her boyfriend, Andy Humphrey, a 24-year-old bike courier who was lured up from Texas by the ramp. Becky, who is 18, is less excited about it. She tends to ignore the skating and read books. Last time, she was plowing through "Atlas Shrugged," Ayn Rand's 1,084-page ode to egoism, but today she brought her roommate, Jenny Robinson, and they're sitting here smoking cigarettes, eating Cheetos, sipping beer and gossiping.

Jenny says she skated once, sort of. "I got halfway up the ramp and I chickened out. I was kinda drunk. But it was fun."

The conversation drifts around to foreign clothes and foreign countries. "I wish I had a jet," Becky says. "I really wish I had a time machine. You could go back and get all kinds of clothes. Back to the Renaissance—all that jewelry."

A few feet away, somebody's doing some serious skate stunts and the guys are yelling, "'Yeah! Yeah!" but the girls hardly give it a glance. Skating's not much of a spectator sport. Sometimes the girls get so bored, they fantasize about gumming up the ramp so the boys wouldn't spend so much time on it.

"We were saying one day that we'd get some Super Glue and that marshmallow stuff that comes in a can and put it all over the ramp." Jenny says. "But I guess we figured we valued our lives more."

"You better not say that, Jenny," Becky says.

"Every girl down here has said that at one time or another."

By now, the sun's setting, the sky's turning a darker shade of blue, and the air's getting cold. Down below, in a clearing, somebody has started a campfire. Becky and Jenny head down to get warm. But the fire's a pitiful thing, sputtering and seriously undernourished, so they tramp through the pine trees searching for firewood. They come back a few minutes later, clutching kindling to their black leather jackets.

Meanwhile, Becky's boyfriend strips off his shirt and shows off the tattoo on his right bicep. It's rad. It's the head of a woman, except half of her is beautiful with long flowing hair and the other half is a bald skull with a dripping eyeball.

Skulls and eyeballs are a recurrent motif in these parts.

By now, it's too dark to skate, and the guys are huddled around the fire. Lawrence McDonald, who is another of the skateboarding bike messengers, starts philosophizing. "There comes a time when you gotta do what you wanna do," he says. "I don't want to make any compromises: This is what I wanna do."

He takes a pull on his can of Bud and speaks of something you can pick up in a weekend, like jogging. It's an intricate sport. Maybe sport isn't the right word. It's between a sport and an art form. There's an infinite number of things you can do. You could never learn everything. That's what intrigues me: It's never the same thing twice."

As the sun rises over the ramp the next day, devin mcguire stands in the flat part of the steel, shaking the hell out of a can of Coke.

He takes out a carpenter's nail and starts scratching the side of the can. Nothing happens. He shakes some more, then scratches some more. Suddenly, it pops, spewing a fine mist of sugary goo. Devin scampers up and down the ramp, spraying as much as he can, while Raoul and Rat spread it around with rags and a squeegee. "Coking," they call it. It's a daily ritual, a process that prevents slipping.

Now the ramp's ready. It's sessionable.

The first person out on it is Amy Rulak, who is Rat's girlfriend and the only person out here who calls him Greg. She stands on his board in the pit of the ramp, timidly wiggling a few feet forward, then a few feet back.

"Straighten your feet sideways" Rat suggests. "Straighten your feet sideways."

She laughs, then gives up and steps off.

"Come on," Raoul says. "Your grandmother did better."

Amy goes to the car and puts on a King Diamond CD called "Them." It's a sort of Gothic heavy metal opera about a kid who stabs his sister and strangles his grandmother. Or does the grandmother kill the sister? There's some dispute on this point, which is not surprising because the songs all sound like a Buick being crushed in a trash compactor. This is the kind of music that drives Tipper Gore up the wall, but it doesn't seem to bother these dudes, who have the innate good sense not to take it seriously.

Devin scrambles up the ramp. He hangs his board way out over the edge. He stands there playing air guitar. He sings along with the music:

"I saw Missy struggle
In Grandma's wrinkled hands . . ."

He laughs, then leans forward, soars down the ramp, roars up the other side, grabs some air.

Yeah!

He streaks back, flips over backward and seems to hang there upside down for a minute before wailing back down again.

Yeah! Yeah!

February 25, 1990

Diversions

A Congregation of Collectors—The Objects of their Obsession Actually May Be Secondary

RON GASBARRO

A friend recounted the time he brought his stamp collection to "show and tell," told the class he was an insatiable philatelist and Sister Andrew—who had a hearing deficit—whacked him over the head with her pointer.

Collectors, collectively, are a misunderstood lot. People snicker or shake their heads if your collection is considered eccentric. One close relative, upon discovering that I was fond of license plates, exclaimed, "Why are you nailing those dirty things to your wall?"

That's why collecting is thought of as a private pastime—a secret obsession—something you do in your den over a brandy and a cigar with the curtains closed and the phone off the hook.

You can't explain why you collect the things you do—unless they are valuable stamps or coins that you lock away in a safe-deposit box at the bank. These, you can bequeath to your nephew (who will cash them in and buy a Porsche).

One psychologist, however, says it is not what you collect as much as finding other people who collect it, too. Otherwise, the collection sputters and stops. Like that shoe box full of matchbooks you've forgotten under the sink. Why did your interest die? It's because you forgot to join a matchbook-collecting club. The social dynamics of a club will not only set fire to your collecting tendencies, but you also will strike up several dozen new friendships.

"You may make the unconscious decision to collect something like butter containers," says psychologist Lonnie Carton, whose CBS Radio program, The Learning Center, is broadcast locally on WTOP. "But once you meet someone else who collects butter containers, too," she continues, "a vital socialization process begins.

"If I told those butter people they could meet many more friends if they collected tea leaves," Carton says, "I bet they would make the move over to tea-leaf collecting. Some people know how to seek people directly, through traditional social channels. Other people seek objects that, in turn, lead them to other people. The objects themselves are secondary."

Maybe so. But don't tell that to Mitzi Geiser. There's only one word to describe her.

The Sucrophile

She's not sure why, but when Mitzi Geiser of Orrville, Ohio, gets off an airplane, she heads to the airport restaurant with her purse open.

As president of the Sugar Packet Collectors Club International, Geiser has been seen in restaurants worldwide, rummaging through sugar bowls, looking to add to her 15,000-plus packet collection.

"I table-hop in restaurants, grab all the sugar bowls I can and bring them back to my table," confesses Geiser. "Even the waitresses will bring sugar from the kitchen for me to go through. I guess I have a collector's instinct. As soon as I get two of anything, I'm looking for the third. It's inbred. It's genetic."

Geiser kept her hobby under wraps until friends visiting from Belgium informed her that sugar-packet collecting was the rage back on the Continent.

She formed the club after the St. Louis club went defunct. Now she has 230 members around the world, many of whom are sweet enough to send her packets from their countries.

International flags, women of history and ethnic costumes are only a few of the reasons she finds sugar packets neat. Another reason is that the hobby is basically free.

"My first husband was deep into philately—an expensive hobby," she notes. "I wanted a hobby that wouldn't cost much."

What you need to know about sugar packets: While very exclusive restaurants used china sugar bowls with silver spoons, most eating establishments had their own sugar packets printed, probably for hygiene reasons. Collectors of sugar packets poke a tiny hole in the packet, spill out the sugar, then mount the packet in a book.

Geiser edits The Sugar Packet Newsletter through which members correspond or trade. Last year, two members came to visit from Britain for three weeks. How did they spend their evenings? Going through Geiser's sacks of extra packets, cataloging them for her and keeping the doubles for themselves.

A Couple of Brick-a-Brickians

Bill Brownlee of Prairie Village, Kan., likes to joke, "Whenever my wife, Barbara, and I go to a new community, instead of walking around with our heads up, smiling at every one we see, we look down."

They frequent dumps and hang around demolished buildings. If a street crew is digging up the road, they look for a piece of the action. Literally. As members of the International Brick Collectors Association, there's no telling how low they'll go.

"We found our first brick in my hometown, Lawrence, Kan.," Brownlee says proudly. "But at the time, I didn't think there was another person in the whole world who was as crazy as we were."

But there were a few hundred at least. Through another club, the Barbed Wire Collectors, the Brownlees uncovered more brick people than they ever could imagine.

Now every year—sometimes twice—Bill and Barbara Brownlee load up their car with 100 bricks or so and head off for an organized swap with other collectors.

What you need to know about bricks: In the 1800s and early 1900s, bricks were inscribed with the manufacturer's name and town. When laid, the inscribed side would face the dirt. The oldest brick in the Brownlee collection is 1849, Lexington, Ky., handmade by a slave and signed in elaborate script by the landowner.

The brick that hard-core collectors want most was put out by the Kansas Department of Health around 1900 when tuberculosis was thought to be spread by contact. It reads, "Don't spit on the sidewalk" and was laid along the roads throughout that state as a precaution.

Brownlee, who uses his bricks in fireplaces, floors, patios and sidewalks—with the business end up—says there is no monetary value placed on any brick.

"We only get involved in friendly trading at our swaps," he explains, "although I expect that is not adhered to in all cases."

Cutting Up with the Cookie Monger

Phyllis Wetherill of Northwest D.C. may very well rummage through your kitchen drawers if you leave the room. What she's looking for are your cookie cutters. What she's hoping to find is one made by Hallmark in the 1970s that depicts Snoopy sitting on a pumpkin.

"A serious collector will pay $100 for that one," says Wetherill. "When it first came out, it cost 75 cents. The highest price ever paid for a cutter was $7,000."

The founder of the 700-member Cookie Cutter Collectors Club justifies her love of cookie cutting by their historical value, however. Examples of molds used to shape sweet goodies go back as far as 3000 BC. Modern cookie cutting is 500 years old, with wooden molds carved by bakers. The cutters were used to promote politicians, mark a religious event, display a family crest or tell an amusing tale.

Also, because people could not see their names in lights in those pre-neon days, they settled for seeing their faces in dough.

"If you were somebody special, like Napoleon, the most flattering thing someone could do for you back then was have a cookie mold carved in your likeness," says Wetherill.

She spends at least 30 hours a week thinking about, writing about and searching for cookie cutters to add to her 10,000 piece collection. But when she set out to start a club, things got crummy.

"I went around collectors' shows and auctions asking people if they wanted to start a club," remembers Wetherill. "Nobody wanted to. So I put an ad in Women's Circle magazine and finally got four women together."

That was 20 years ago and ever since then, rolling in new members was, well, a snap.

Plugnaciously Sparky

Bob Bond of Ann Arbor, Mich., started off big, then went small.

"I am one of your basic pack rats to begin with," says the engineer and founder of the Spark Plug Collectors of America. "I started collecting the old stationary gasoline engines that were used to power everything on the farm before the advent of electricity. To make these things run, you needed some rather unusual spark plugs you couldn't get at the local auto-parts store."

He hounded automotive flea markets for the plugs and soon discovered there were more than a handful of brands that were produced. That sparked his interest.

"The quest then became A) how many brands were produced, and B) how many pieces of that puzzle I could collect—the latter being the force that drives all collectors," says Bond.

Bond says spark plugs are actually a good investment because they have appreciated in value due to demand—especially those from the early 1900s. His collection is worth, he says, "many thousands of dollars."

But the idea for a club started as a joke to a friend. The two wrote a letter saying "Hey, I'm just as crazy as you guys and I collect spark plugs and I think we oughta have a club!"

They sent it out to 39 people who had recently bought spark plugs from an antique car-dealer pal.

Pretty soon, 39 people wrote back saying, "How much money do you want us to send and where?"

Mad About Everything

Mel Simons of Boston is a one-man collecting club. He collects everything, and with a mania. Not just 30 or 40 old radio shows on tape, for instance. But 100,000 radio shows. Old TV shows, too, and sports memorabilia, Al Jolson stuff, Jack Benny letters, Three Stooges autographs. He employs a carpenter—practically full-time, he kids—to build shelves for his collections.

"It started in the 1970s when I sent a picture in an envelope simply addressed 'Maurice Chevalier, France'," Simons says. "When it came back autographed, I sent one to Harry Truman. When that came back signed, I was hooked."

A TV and radio entertainer who comes in contact with celebrities of all kinds, Simons now creates his own collectibles.

"If I am going to meet a boxer, I bring him a pair of boxing gloves to sign. If it's a basketball player, I bring him a basketball. I send TV Guides to people whose picture is on the cover and usually get them back autographed, if I send a stamped envelope with it. I have all of Carl Yastrzemski's baseball cards—signed."

Of course, he belongs to a ton of collecting clubs. They not only put him in contact with other people but also with more things to collect. He is already being chased by the University of Wisconsin for chunks of his collections. But it all may wind up in the hands of a nephew. Until then, Simons, who is only in his forties, still has a lot of good collecting years ahead of him.

"In today's world, collecting becomes escaping," says psychologist Lonnie Carton. "At collecting clubs, people do not have to talk about dreary economic forecasts or tragic human conditions. They can relax and talk about spark plugs and sugar packets." So, you collectors of crazy things out there: Maybe you're not really crazy after all. Maybe it's just your way of staying sane in a world that, somehow, got crazy first.

Cookie Cutter Collectors Club, 5426 27th St. NW, Washington, D.C. 20015.

International Brick Collectors Association, 8357 Somerset, Prairie Village, Kan. 66207.

Spark Plug Collectors of America, P.O. Box 2229, Ann Arbor, Mich. 48106.

Sugar Packet Collectors Club, 15601 Burkhardt Rd., Orrville, Ohio 44667.

February 11, 1991

Major Meows and Kitty Glitter

At the Regional Show, a Fuss Over Felines

MARTHA SHERRILL

They buzz around the ring. Owners, breeders, lovers. Cat People. They are sloppy-looking—except for a few, like sphynx-owner Kathy Speed, the Mississippi glamour-blond in diaphanous purple. But the grooming for most, it seems, stopped with their pets. They wear cat T-shirts. They hold tuna fish sandwiches and cat toys. Sticks with pompoms and feathers are popular. Sometimes their cats look at them like, Why are you waving that stick with the pompoms in my face?

"Let me recommend the tuna fish," says judge Mark Coleman while moving from his sandwich to the longhair finals. Cats come. Cats go. He's got a Carson-style monologue running. He's been powering through Diet Cokes. Now he's powering through the longhairs. Ribbons are being handed out. They are called "rosettes" and seem very large. Horse-size. The cats have horse-size names too. Coleman holds the eighth best longhair, a black-smoke tabby named Bentley's King Edward III. The seventh best longhair is a brown mackerel tabby called MtKittery Surry of MacSpurr.

At last, an enormous Maine coon gets pulled out of his cage, because he's won the competition. A cage! The humiliation! He's got huge paws. The face of a lion. The shoulders of a panther. Dignity. This cat could survive in the wilderness. This cat could defend himself against M:ike Tyson or run for president. And he looks like he could kill his owners.

"Nice broad chin," Coleman says of him. "Ears well placed. Snowshoes for feet. Best Maine coon. Best Cat."

He's Coons' Kin's Tull Man.

"Hey!" says Coleman after all that excitement. "There's a cat hair in my drink!"

Cat Naps

Below this incredible scene onstage, fur is not flying. Nothing is flying. Nearly 200 felines from 15 states have assumed the Dead Cat Position. They are totally sacked out. Legs hang outside cages. Eyes have closed to crescent kitty slits. The only signs of cat-life in the Stoney Creek Democratic Club are the nearly 200 little tummies moving up and down. Up and down. At the two-day Southeast Regional Cat Show and Banquet of the International Cat Association (TICA) two weekends

414

ago—organized by its local chapter, the Potomac Area Cat Enthusiasts (PACE)—
the cats looked as alive as the stuffed Garfields stuck to windows in the parking lot.

Looking alive. A stately Norwegian forest cat, named Tord, sits up in the
Thanksgiving Turkey Position. His eyes open, then close. A white Persian with a
coffee filter around its neck (for damage control) flexes its paws. Frosty purrs—
he's a dark male calico, unusual, since calicos are supposed to be female. Frosty's
sterile, though—does this count for something? His tongue sticks out—all the
time—and he's a Quadruple Grand Master in the exotic shorthair division. A couple Devon rex kittens have become fascinated by their ribbons. Rexes are geneti-
cally deformed and hypoallergenic. They look it. And they have a facial expression:
Constant surprise, as though they can't believe anybody would buy them. They are
trying to knock down their own ribbons. Their scrawny waiflike legs make it
through the bars of their cages.

You don't see the Himalayans and Persians doing this. Their paws, for one
thing, are way too fat. They also—much like their owners—don't seem interested
in exercise.

"The Persians are like, Who cares? So what?" says breeder Janet Elton from
Arbutus, Md. She's a staff nurse at St. Agnes Hospital who innocently went to a cat
show three years ago with her daughter Wendy. Now they have 10 cats at home.
"We got hooked," says Janet. "Nobody tells you, though, about the bad parts."

The bad parts for the Eltons have been laying out $3,000 for their cats, losing
their first litter, maintenance on their three-bedroom row house. "I vacuum every
day," says Janet, rolling her eyes. "Sometimes twice."

In a cage up front, there's a cat named Claude Monet. He's dead to the world,
but the tummy moves. He's light brown and spotted. His cage has been decorated
with a lovely cover—as have many of these cages. He's also got an old blue nightgown in there with him. His owners, Isobel and Henry Frystak, drove him here
from Clifton, N.J.

"We call him Claude Monet,' Isobel says, "because of his markings. He's
splattered like a painting.'

Is that a nightgown?

"Oh, he got a habit,' she says, "since the day I brought him home. He gets up
on me in bed and kneads on my nightgown like a pillow. So when he does a show,
we bring the nightgown as his security blanket."

She comes up a while later. "Listen. I make all my own cage covers," she says.
"I have a 'Gone With the Wind' theme cover. I've got Fourth of July and
Christmas. And there's one that I call 'Van Cliburn Cats.' "

Things to Know

The Pet Food Institute in Washington has discovered recently that cats outnumber
dogs in American households. According to the institute's 1989 study, there are
57.9 million cats in this country and 50.5 million dogs.

"Dog people are the type who come right up to you," says Pat Shelton, one of 30 PACE club members and one of 2,000 TICA members internationally. "They say, 'What can I do for you?' Cat people are the kind who say, 'Get back to me later, or mail me a letter.' "

Shelton is wearing a blue T-shirt that says: "Some people own cats and go on to lead normal lives . . ."

"You have to earn their respect," she says of Cat People. "And they don't need that what-can-I-do-for-you attitude."

Things to know:

Gray cats are called "blue" cats. Orange cats are called "red."

Purebreds start around $300 and go up, depending.

Breeders don't often break even.

The Turkish vans can swim.

The rex cats are mutants.

The sphynx cats have no fur.

"Oh Lord, noooo," says Charles Michaels, at the beer tap selling drinks. He's the first VP of Stoney Creek Democratic Club in Riviera Beach. "I had no idea there were so many kinds of cats! And this lady over there," he says, pointing across the way, "she's got this ordinary little cat, and his cage is covered with ribbons. God Almighty."

Mikey

Mikey is a chocolate Oriental—imagine an all-brown Siamese. He never looks very happy. He produces a long, sustained meow when the judge picks him up. More than 30 seconds of meow. Mikey—whose show name is Gad-a-bout's Amh Mikado of Cio-San—is "famous on the judging circuit," says one regular. "Not just the meowing, but the biting and scratching . "

Scamper

"I got this cat to replace Pumpkin, a cat of mine who died," says Sharon Dyer, from Northern Virginia. She's hovercrafting around with a tuna fish sandwich. She's talking about Scamper—her only cat. Scamper is a Siamese kitten who, according to a judge, has "a very good pointy head shape." Scamper also has ears big enough to hear on Pluto, black paws as thin as sticks, crossed eyes the color of blue wall-to-wall carpets in Palm Beach.

Scamper gets Third Best Altered Shorthair. "I didn't think I was ready yet, to get a cat," says Dyer. "I wasn't really over Pumpkin. But I sat down and Scamper crawled up to my lap, and right to my shoulder—just like this. . . . The weird thing is that Pumpkin was a shoulder cat too, so it's like reincarnation."

Hormones

In one ring, Don Koizumi's gray Chartreux cat—named Escorte—is snarling and hissing. The judge won't pick him up. "His hormones are kicking in," says Koizumi, in his baggy blue shirt and jeans. "Hormones are in the air."

Escorte is returned to his own cage. It has a French theme. They are French cats, these Chartreux (pronounced CHAR-true). There's a French blue, red and white checked cloth on it. There are tiny—Barbie-doll-size—cafe chairs around a little table on top. "We named him Escorte," says Koizumi, "because he's a breeder."

The Koizumi's have 10 cats in a 10-room house in Reston. "One of our neighbors called the Fairfax County, police," says Luci Koizumi, in muu-muu, glasses and wild eyes. "They came to inspect—to see if we had un-livable conditions—but of course, everything was perfect."

Don continues. "When the inspector came," he says, "he sees this one room full of rosettes. Then he sees the next room. There's this cat, sitting alone on top of a bunch of pillows—just staring out. The guy turns to me and says: 'Case closed.' "

I ❤ My Sphynx

Lisa Bressler is a sphynx breeder from White Plains, N.Y. She wears a gold-necklace that says "I ❤ My Sphynx." Her cat—she calls him "Roddy"—is the color of dirty bubblegum. He has wrinkles all over his face. He has vestigial fragments of fur, orange and white, around his eyes and ears. Otherwise he has none. She holds him like a baby. He's got a belly and a rat tail.

"They are supposed to be pear-shaped," Bressler says, "like they've just had a good meal."

"A California raisin with ears," judge Coleman describes Roddy while holding him. "They feel like suede hot water bottles."

Nearby, there's Barbara Naame, from Atlantic City. Her two cages are an explosion of animal prints. There are also silver bowls for water and dry food. There's a sign posted: "WANT TO KNOW IF THERE'S LIFE AFTER DEATH? TOUCH MY CAT AND FIND OUT." She's brought a Maine and an Egyptian mau. At home, she has 12 cats—"permanent residents"—and nine kittens.

She's been as far as Alabama for a cat show. There's one every weekend—somewhere. The next big one in this area will be held the weekend of Nov. 24-25, at the University of Maryland, College Park.

Naame has come with friend Cindy Lodovico. Lodovico has a small apartment, she says, so only one cat—a flame-point Himalayan named Icy-You. It's his second show ever. His baby pictures rest in frames on top of his cage. There are also pictures of his parents. Lodovico is the superintendent of a homeless shelter in New Jersey, and used to show horses. This is cheaper. Easier. "You just throw the cat in the back of the car," says Lodovico.

Icy-You is a purebred Himalayan. But his nose, it's explained, is way too big for Himalayan standards (which is to say that his face does not look like a tuft on upholstered chair), so Lodovico shows him in the Household Pet category.

In the Household category, cats are judged for total condition and well-being, for friendliness and prettiness. Of the 200 cats in this show, 50 of them are competing in this division.

"You can't believe the personality of this cat," says Lodovico—gesturing toward Icy-You, totally collapsed on two white fur pillows and a black rug. His eyes are slightly open. He's watching, but he's not caring.

She bought Icy-You from Barbara Naame for $350. "It was love at first sight," says Lodovico. "It was October 21, 1989. He was in a case just like this. I walked by. He looked up. And that was it."

Overpass

Overpass is a Supreme Grand Master in the household pet division. His press clips are in his briefcase. He's got more of them than Arnold Schwarzenegger. He's got photos of himself too, kept in plastic. Gene Burns is his owner. He's from Quantico. But never mind him. Overpass! He has long, agile legs. He's sensitive. Gentle. He's black and white.

"He's Mr. Cool—that's why he wins," says Burns. "The household category is the hardest to win. There aren't really standards. And you're up against purebreds all the time."

Cat Products

There's a wall of stuff to buy, things like cat eyewash, tear stain remover, creme shampoo, color enhancer shampoo, creme rinse, conditioner, urine remover, grooming chalk, ozium, no-scratch spray, lint brushes, metal combs, tiny nursing bottles, hairball remedy, skin and coat supplement, breath spray, flea powder and "Kitty Bloom," a high-concentrate vitamin and mineral dietary supplement for cats of all ages.

"That blue shampoo's for a black cat," says Wendy Elton. "If you put it on a white cat, you'd come out with a blue cat."

And there are cat toys: stick toys, sock toys, rabbit's foot toys, little soccer balls, foam balls, black fur spiders attached to elastic, fur balls attached to springs, mice on wheels, mice with bells, mice full of catnip, mice that squeak, mice that do nothing at all. And there are long peacock feathers for 50 cents each.

Taking Communion

Near the cat products and across from Claude Monet sits Dr. Flo Mitchell. She's got a mobile veterinary service in D.C., Md. and Va. She's here doing cat-show work—not unlike the way ambulances are kept waiting outside black-tie galas. "That aloofness," she says of cats, "that's what I like."

One by one, owners bring their cats from their own cages to the cages directly behind the judge.

"Have you noticed how solemn the owners are when they bring their cats into the show ring?" asks Nitchell. "It's like they're taking Communion at the altar."

In front of her there's a table of brochures: "Pet Loss & Human Emotion," "Behavioral Urinary Problems," "Plants Poisonous to Cats."

Buddy and Ice

There are 16 rosettes covering Buddy and Ice's cage. They are both Supreme Grand Champions. They are white Orientals. In a judge's hands, they stretch out to unbelievable lengths. They belong to Todd Sutton, from Miramar, Fla. He's a soft-spoken Tom Hanks type with a mustache. He wears white shorts and tennis shoes. He flew here.

"You go to a cat show when you've got the money," he says. "First I breed for happy, healthy cats. And for the pleasure of having them around."

Buddy was altered a month ago. "Before," says Sutton, "I was showing him whole." Before, using his show name—Jazzy's Reminiscence—Buddy got TICA's Oriental of the Year in 1990. Ice also got Third Best Oriental Kitten of the Year.

Still. "You're never in the black. You're never making money," says Sutton. "I'm sometimes $10,000 in the hole a year with this." Sutton does it because he loves it. "My wife and I get the family—five cats, suitcases, the three kids, everything—into the family van and go for a show weekend. It's fun. It's a good time."

Her Orientals

Susan Ferguson is a Supreme Grand Champion, by Cat People standards. She's wearing a black jumpsuit one day, and a silk outfit the next. She's got a Louis Vuitton case strapped to a rolling cart like a stewardess.

"Have you seen her cage?" somebody asks. "It's got more silk than I've got at home."

Ferguson's a model back in Jackson, Miss. She's got a neat little black camera hanging around her neck. She photographs her winners. Sometimes she pulls out a video camera too.

Her two sleek black Orientals—Rave and Legacy—keep winning ribbons. Ferguson started this crazy hobby just a year ago. "I wanted to do it in a big way," she says. "I go every weekend. I'm a nut."

Best of Show

At the end of Sunday, a winner is chosen. Best of Show. It goes to sweet, shy, little Billmar's Lady of Class. She's a seal-point Himalayan, just 10 months old. She is also a complete beige fuzzball with blue eyes. When she sleeps, you can't even see her tummy move up and down. It's just her second adult show.

"She's got lots of Supremes and Grands in her background," says her owner, Mary Drugan of Devon, Pa. She and her husband, Bill, breed Himalayans at their cattery: BillMar's. They go to shows every weekend.

Mary Drugan is crying, by the way. And wiping, wiping, wiping. "She's such a sweet little girl," Mary says. She keeps picking up Lady of Class. A nearby Cat Person says, "How come when my cats win there are never reporters around?" Drugan shrugs. She keeps touching Lady of Class, petting her. "I can't put her down," she says.

How many cats does she have at home? "Over five," she says, "and under 100."

July 29, 1990

The Day the Ants Lost their Head

At the National Zoo, Colony Carries on
After Accidentally Decapitating its Queen

WILLIAM BOOTH

There has been an accident, a terrible accident at the National Zoo. The caretakers at the Invertebrate House are in shock.

It seems the ants that live in a glass-fronted display case in the Invertebrate House got excited. "They may have been too ambitious," said Ed Smith, the man who cares for the leaf-cutting ants from Trinidad. "They may have gotten themselves worked up."

What the worker ants did, quite by mistake, was remove the head of their queen. Apparently, the workers were trying to transfer their egg-laying monarch from the chamber where she has resided since being shipped almost four years ago from the Cincinnati Zoo. Apparently, the hole they were trying to pull her through was small. The queen was big. Pop.

At least that's how Smith re-creates the accident in his mind. No one actually saw it happen. "Last Wednesday, one of the volunteers said, 'Hey Ed, take a look at this,' and I let out a string of expletives."

Ant specialists refuse to speculate on whether an ant can feel totally stupid. Basically, scientists think of ants as amazing little machines, driven by their genes, which act in concert with a world that they know largely through smell. That is why an interesting thing is now happening at the Invertebrate House. The workers are still tending their queen. "They are continuing to hold her in the same position," Smith said. "As long as she still smells like the queen, they will care for her."

There her body hangs, on display, her headless thorax and abdomen suspended from the ceiling of her royal chamber, her back to the roof, her legs dangling. Or rather the two legs she has left. The other four mysteriously disappeared the same day her head did. Where is the head? "We're not sure," Smith said. Did the workers eat it? "No," Smith said. "I don't think so." Is it on the trash heap outside the nest, where the ants deposit their dead and discard pieces of their fungus garden? "No, the head is someplace in the nest," Smith said. "And wherever it is, I am sure they are taking good care of it."

Somewhere, nestled among the legs and loving mandibles of her attendants, the queen's head is being cared for. They are probably bringing food and trying to feed the head. A guess about what they are doing with the legs would only be reckless speculation.

Meanwhile, back in the royal chamber, which is on public view and can be examined in great detail with the aid of a flashlight and magnifying glass every day of the week except Monday and Tuesday, the queen's body rests. It would be reckless speculation to infer that she misses her head.

Smith contends that among insects heads are overrated as body parts. Indeed, the queen may have continued to lay eggs for hours or even days after her head was removed. "She seems to be doing pretty good headless," Smith said. "Heads aren't as important as you might think."

Still, removing the queen's head from her body was not a good idea, Smith admits. Sooner or later, probably in weeks, the queen's head and the queen's body will stop smelling like the queen and start smelling dead. "The bacteria will start their work," Smith said. Even royalty rots.

The colony, eventually, is a goner. A queen from this common tropical leaf-cutting species can live as long as 14 years. But without a queen, there can be no eggs. That is all a queen does. She is a virtual egg-laying machine. No eggs, no workers.

The eggs and larvae that are now being tended will probably be reared by the workers, but eventually the colony will age, and finally wind down.

At present, all seems strangely normal in the colony. "Life goes on," Smith said. As Elisabeth Kubler-Ross would put it, the ants seem to be in the denial stage. The bigger workers are still collecting the leaves that Smith puts out for them and carrying chiseled bits of greenery back to the nest, where smaller ants masticate the bits and place them in their gardens, where still smaller workers plant thin hairs of fungi, which produce spores that feed the wormlike larvae and workers.

There is, however, little chance of the colony saving itself. Smith reports there are no winged ants in the colony's brood. Winged forms are the sexual ants, the virgin queens and males. But alas, every ant in the nest now is a sterile female worker, with the exception of the headless queen, who is still full of sperm, but who is dead. Couldn't the colony turn a few of the remaining eggs into virgin queens? Yes, in fact, but there are still no males.

For the near future, Smith will watch over the colony. It could last a year. Eventually, however, the remaining ants will get tossed out on the lawn beside the Invertebrate House or be put into a freezer. A new queen and a thousand workers will be brought in from the Cincinnati Zoo, one of a handful of zoos with large ant displays, to start a new colony. But this time, Smith will open more portals into the chamber that surrounds the queen's room. Smith believes the ants only wanted to move their queen to another room because the fungus garden that grew up around her was not as robust as the ants would have liked. In other words, the ants were only doing what they thought was best.

Nature may be beautiful, but it is not perfect. Even an ant can make a mistake, a big mistake.

December 13, 1990

Study Questions
Chapter Ten

1. Travel stories often use first person accounts of experiences. Can you think of places you've been and what you told others about your experiences there? Could you develop your ideas into an entertaining story?
2. Some things aren't what they appear to be on the surface, as Thomas Boswell points out in his analysis, "What We Talk About Whom We Talk About Sports." Speculate on other sublimated needs people have regarding pets or travel.
3. In the Michael Jordan profile, the writer links sports and religious language. Point out how this enhances the reader's view of Jordan.
4. Under-reported events such as cat shows become opportunities for showcasing the characters that participate in them. What did you learn about felines and their masters?

From Ordinary to Off-Beat *11*

Finding a fresh angle on annual stories is the feature writer's challenge. In her article on the Fourth of July, Elizabeth Kastor looks beyond the obvious symbols of flag, fireworks and military funerals to explore the concept of patriotism. She structures her piece along three themes: things Americans are proud of, ones we repress and others we debate. In interviews with ordinary folks as well as public officials and university professors, she concludes that love of country is a complicated attachment.

In his musing, "Let it Rain," Henry Allen combines his interior thoughts with images of the city just before a downpour. While it all may be familiar, Allen's telling has a poetic resonance and cooling effect, sort of like rain.

When tree leaves don't turn colors in the fall, readers want to know why. Joel Achenbach offers scientific explanations, ruminations and flights of fantasy. He concludes that alterations in the annual visual spectacle are likely results of man's interaction with nature, thus ending on a gloomy note.

Feature writers should focus on the far-out and extraordinary as well as the commonplace. When a political flap arose over National Endowment of the Arts' funding for avant garde performance art, writers Paula Span and Carla Hall set out to explain what the fuss was all about. Their profiles of four "defunded" artists clarified the political issues and aided public understanding of innovative art forms.

The annual gathering of the communal Rainbow Tribe is chronicled in David Mill's article, "Om, Om on the Range." He captures the gentleness of the event with carefully wrought scenes and recorded dialogue. Such an off-beat story might appear to be totally unexpected fare in Washington, where hippies seldom roam, but Mills doesn't make such narrow assumptions about reader interest.

Another subculture, black and Latin gay men who dress up like women and dance competitively at balls, is the topic of Joe Brown's article, "Underground Cinderellas." Brown tackles the subject in a profile of documentary filmmaker Jennie Livingston, whose film "Paris Is Burning" introduced the world to voguing. Brown recognizes that readers are not likely to be familiar with the lingo of the performers, so he routinely defines their terms.

The Many Faces of Patriotism

Reflections on What it Means to be an American

Elizabeth Kastor

Here it is perfect. Past the full green trees the sky is clean blue. The riderless horse quivers but does not move. All around are markers from past wars, small white stones, towering obelisks, cannons and rocks and statues. Young soldiers lift white-gloved hands to their foreheads in firm salute as the shots slam into the air. And then the trumpet begins to play, slow, solemn, familiar as grief.

Each month at Arlington National Cemetery there are more than 300 funerals, about 10 of them with the full military honors—the horse and black-draped caisson, the gunfire and trumpet. For many, such services are the very embodiment of patriotism, timeless events carved out of ceremony, images made potent through war after war, movie after movie.

Patriotism is an idea most comfortably contained in its symbols. The flag. The Pledge of Allegiance. Fireworks on the Fourth of July. At Arlington, such symbols are everywhere, and the local definition of patriotism is self-evident: These men and women died for their country.

But outside the gates, beyond the rows of stones marking lives given for a nation, the love of country is far more complicated. It is a powerful currency that politicians hoard and spend. It is a source of pride, of excuses, of sustenance. Sometimes it is merely an unexamined cliche. It is homesickness in a foreign country. It is the flavors of childhood food, the smell of a remembered classroom, the faces of family. It is the words to songs everyone knows.

It is the emotion we are all supposed to feel—that unites us. It is the emotion we all feel differently.

Kristine Platt, 24-year-old volunteer at Bread for the City, which provides food and clothing for the poor: "I don't think I owe very much to the government. They take their taxes and they don't do a whole lot for the people I have come to care for. But to the nation, I feel I owe a lot. I'm in a position of privilege, basically—I'm middle class, I'm white and there are a lot of people who don't have much, and I feel responsible to them. If people are the nation, I feel I do owe a great deal to them."

James D. Ford, chaplain of the U.S. House of Representatives: "Sometimes when I leave work at night, when we're finally done, I leave from my office and instead of going out the first floor I go to the second floor and walk through Statuary Hall. Here are all these statues—in the quiet of the evening they look at you and I must say you go through with a feeling, a sort of resolution you'll do better in your work and that the institution will do better. You have a bond with the past."

Peri Jude Radecic, legislative director for the National Gay and Lesbian Task Force and sister of Buffalo Bills starting linebacker Scott Radecic: "I would consider myself a very patriotic citizen. I get teary-eyed on the Fourth of July. I love to sing 'The Star-Spangled Banner' at football. To me, being patriotic means participating as an openly gay person and being able to do so comfortably with my family in what is considered an all-American institution—football."

Marie Yochim, president general of the Daughters of the American Revolution: "Just to look at the flag, you can't help but be patriotic. I've always loved the flag. I've always loved band music. Nowadays, I think if the children were taught some of the things they used to teach, such as love of country and respect of the flag, they would love the country more."

Even after years of general peace, for many the truest sign of national loyalty is the willingness to fight.

"I'm red, white and blue," says Claude Haynes. For Haynes, those colors refer not only to his work—he founded and owns the National Capital Flag Co.—but to his military service, which is inseparable from his definition of patriotism. "I enlisted in the Navy, I wasn't drafted. My sons enlisted in the service."

So often patriotism comes down to battle. Love of country is the engine that fuels an army at war and the families at home, and a very American determination to be allowed to defend ourselves has nourished the gun lobby for years.

"The awareness is there all the time," says Charlene Dodd, an elementary school teacher from Junction City, Kan., who visited Washington recently. "Many of our friends went to Vietnam and were killed. It's a little more meaningful for us—the daily reminders are there every time you see the families left behind."

Junction City is home to the Fort Riley Army base. "We're from a military community—you wouldn't do flag burning in Junction City," says Dodd. "In our school almost all of the classes have a flag salute and the Pledge of Allegiance in the beginning."

But the wedding of military might and love of country leaves others uneasy.

"Some people really get into the changing of the guard—I don't. I'm more quiet," says Jackie Letizia, a Tourmobile guide who knows the name and history of every man on horseback at every Washington circle and plaza. "I think America is too militaristic. I would like to see more memorials for other accomplishments— literary, artistic, humanitarian. Even the Soviet Union has a Poets Square. We don't."

Letizia waits for her next troupe of tourists at the Lincoln Memorial. Of all the major monuments in the city, this may be the most grandly solemn, and its visitors are more likely to be touched by one man's words and the idea of slavery's end than reminded of a bloody war. Yet even here Letizia is troubled.

"There's the statue of Einstein," she says, "but he worked on the bomb—although he eventually was critical of it."

"There's Temperance Fountain," offers Tourmobile dispatcher Steve Robbins, but then pauses. "Slaves were traded there, at Seventh and Indiana," he says, the realities of history muddying the waters.

"I've had people say to me, 'This is what America is!' at the Tomb of the Unknown Soldier," says Letizia. "I say, 'No, there's more.' I think we need to emphasize the Constitution rather than the military. Anyone can field an army."

Periodically the Return of Patriotism is trumpeted.

In the late '70s, with the Soviet invasion of Afghanistan and the Iranian hostage crisis, Americans could rally in opposition to fearsome enemies. Patriotism soared.

"If you remember the U.S. hockey victory over the Soviets in the 1980 Winter Olympics—I don't think American patriotism has ever been higher" says Michael Kammen, a history professor at Cornell University. "The image of the goalie on the team wrapped in the American flag, skating up and down in Lake Placid—no one regarded that as desecration of the flag. That was an absolute crescendo for American patriotism."

Some historians, City University of New York professor Alan Brinkley among them, observe such swells of patriotism with a somewhat jaundiced eye, reading the emotions as a sign of anxiety and cultural instability.

"I think partly we're still acting out the battles that began in the '60s," he says. "I think patriotism becomes more pronounced at moments when societies feel uneasy about themselves and their future, and this seems to be a time in our history— now quite a long time in our history—when Americans have felt very uneasy about the state of American society."

Now we debate flag burning, constitutional amendments, English as the official language of the United States. Politicians play patriotic one-upmanship. We worry about how to compete with Japan, how much influence America retains as the lines on the globe shift. We argue over which books our college students should study and what music we should listen to.

And on the Fourth of July we try to look past much of what we argue about the rest of the year.

"The customary oratory of the Fourth of July is essentially nostalgic—which is collective memory without guilt," says Kammen. "The things we can be rightly proud of we remember in our patriotic oratory, and the things we can't be proud of—such as the genocide of Native Americans or slavery or repression of people overseas—those are the kinds of things we try to forget."

But for many Americans with links to those repressed subjects, forgetting is impossible.

"Patriotism is something that people should be able to work towards rather than claim," says Job Mashariki, president of Black Veterans for Social Justice. Patriotism is a challenge to become a more moral, responsible country, he believes, and he will not feel the emotion as long as much of America avoids the challenge. "I look at patriotism in direct relationship to the quality of life for the people in this country—the citizens. Unfortunately, I think too often patriotism is hollow to the masses of working and poor people in this country."

July Fourth is a day for celebration for Joallyn Archambault, but it is a celebration of something other than the birth of the United States. "Oftentimes, I have been at powwows on the Fourth of July having an awful lot of fun," says Archambault, director of American Indian programs at the National Museum of Natural History, "but it has absolutely nothing to do with being a citizen of the United States of America." Instead, it has to do with being a member of the Standing Rock Sioux tribe of North Dakota.

National loyalty, she says, "is a conflicting emotion for me personally. I certainly am aware as a citizen of the United States that I am affected and impacted by mainstream American culture, that I speak English instead of Lakota. I cannot personally remember a time when I was emotionally overtaken by total and indiscriminate pride in just being an American. My ethnic identity and tribal membership have always been for me and my family the overriding element of our lives."

Loyalties compete. Tribe, race, religion, class can all call forth feelings that leave little room or need for a larger attachment. Steve Robbins, who teaches physical education at Howard University as well as working for the Tourmobile company, says that among his students, "I see more patriotism towards black nationality than I do toward the nation as a whole."

For years the reassuring image of American ethnic and racial diversity was a Norman Rockwell canvas of faces—black, white, brown—all gazing with rapt patriotic pride. The message of the painting is that the faces may be different in appearance, but look—they share the same expression, the same emotion. Of course, diversity is more difficult than that. Not everyone wants to be melted in the pot, and similarities are often overwhelmed by differences.

Patriotism can at times overcome those barriers. "When you have a very pluralistic society like ours, then the common basis for allegiance and patriotism is one of the principles that bind us together," says Kammen.

But alternately, patriotism can reflect an antipathy toward immigrants and others perceived as alien, believes Brinkley. "I don't think most other cultures have the same insecurity about their nationhood that America has," he says.

"We were a sort of self-invented country to begin with," he says, and we are constantly engaged in reinventing our idea of what it means to be an American and our perception of what an American looks like.

When Claude Haynes talks about patriotism, his thoughts roam from the beauty of the Maryland and Virginia countryside to his frustration with politicians

("They're followers, not leaders") to his gratitude that he could raise his family here ("I may sound rather maudlin, but I'm telling you what's in my heart"). Then, as if to explain his own loyalty, he tells a brief story.

"We have people here, not native-born Americans, that love to be here. We had one woman working for us, a seamstress—we have 15 women working in the sewing room—and this woman's husband was transferred to Chicago and she couldn't bear to say goodbye. She just cried. We've had others do the same thing."

Of course, that woman was leaving Northern Virginia and her job, not the country. But to Haynes those things are inextricably linked. Patriotism, he says, includes "love of your fellow human being." And in truth, to hear people talk about patriotism, it often sounds less like love of country than love of community, less loyalty to a nation than to a home.

One woman sipping pink lemonade in front of the Lincoln Memorial says she is patriotic "because of the freedom to do this, to be able to walk around, do as you please, nobody telling you that you can't."

To do as you please—to visit the nation's capital, to drink pink lemonade on a hot day, to sit on a bench and get up when you want—are these freedoms limited to the United States? Of course not, but when you love a country, part of what you are loving is your own individual life, the vacations you take and the lemonade you drink.

Sometimes patriotism grows slowly, transforming itself without warning or sound into something new.

In 1979 the novelist Arnost Lustig became a U.S. citizen. Although the Czechoslovakian exile and Holocaust survivor hoped for years that someday he might return to the country he fled in 1968, he assumed the hope would never be realized.

Then the world changed. Earlier this year, he and his wife and son traveled to Prague. The trip back was a revelation. In Czechoslovakia the American University professor found a nation still infected by years of repression, "morally corrupted because for 40 years they had to lie and pretend to survive, and it was like a better concentration camp where there was no killing of people but it was breaking them morally. Even the most beautiful people are touched by the poison because it was impossible not to be touched."

And when he returned, he was shocked to find a change in himself.

"When I was here, I always felt on the margin," he says. "It's a beautiful country, but I always felt that as good as it was to me and as grateful as I am—I felt that I am on the edge, never completely involved."

But after his voyage to the place he calls his "old home," he felt differently.

"Time is more wide than men, and time did something to me that I didn't expect," he says. "When I came back, I found out I am at home in America too. America in that moment multiplied and everything that I was denying to myself—while idealizing my old home of Czechoslovakia —changed proportions.

"What happened was, I love America, being able to go home. Now I am really free. Before it was limited freedom here, beautiful but limited because I was free here but I couldn't go there so it was like having a chain on my leg. Now I am free like a bird."

July 4, 1990

Let it Rain, Let it Rain, Let it Rain!

HENRY ALLEN

What we need is a downpour. We keep getting these little failed cloudbursts, these junior varsity thunderstorms, these rain showers that don't amount to cat spit, like a lot of the ones that were sashaying around the Washington area late yesterday afternoon, though there were areas that got a good soaking.

A downpour, a true Washington downpour, begins when you look across your backyard, you look out your office window, you look up 16th Street, you look across the river and see the cloud rising, a high-builded cloud moving at summer's pace, as poet Philip Larkin says. And rising, looming, beetling o'er its base, like the cliffs of Hamlet's Denmark. Quite a cloud. You wonder how high it is. You see an airliner flying tiny and slow only halfway up the face of this cloud, and you know it is high indeed.

"Did the weatherman call for thunderstorms today?" you ask.

The cloud has a touch of menace about it—not the menace of intent as much as the menace of blindness, like a truck backing toward you in an alley.

The sun still shines, but the light begins to seem shallow and oblique. Everything looks like an omen. Everything looks as if you're looking at it through sunglasses. The birds won't settle, there's an edginess to things, sort of like brides-maids lining up before the wedding starts.

Or maybe it doesn't start with a cloud. It could start at night, and you see the lightning through closed eyelids, and lie there listening for thunder, a lethargic baritone crumpling noise from miles away. Or it starts in a movie theater when you hear the thunder. Suddenly the movie looks like nothing more than colored light jumping around, irrelevant.

Or it starts when you look out the window of your house, your office, a dentist's waiting room, and notice the odd yellow cast to the light. Things—a swing set, the parking lot, the furniture around a swimming pool—seem temporary, even a little furtive. You hear thunder. You wonder where your children are, whether your car windows are closed. Your dog hides under the bed.

Downtown, the street vendors are pulling plastic over their stands. Office workers stand at office windows looking at the storm and at the other office workers looking out their windows. People hurry down the sidewalks. They look worried. Doormen at hotels slap their hands together and rock back on their heels. They look happy.

The light turns green, like the light inside a tent.

The wind picks up. You hear a Styrofoam cup blowing down the street. The flags are frantic, and you see the undersides of the leaves on the trees. The first low clouds come over, arcus clouds, they're called, the clouds in front of a thunderstorm, like newsreel Nazi scouts riding through the deserted city on motorcycles. You think about tornadoes and cars crushed by trees.

The first raindrops hit—not so much liquid as specks ofjcoolness on the backs of your hands or darkness on your clothes; faster and faster, platoons of rain sprinting down the street, coarse fat drops. You smell the smell of hot concrete in the rain, chalky and oddly dry.

Then it is hitting your front steps, your windshield so hard it bounces. You put the wipers on high, and you can't imagine it raining harder, but it does, the rattling of it turning to a roar, sheets of rain with an impossible coherence, as if the sky had not so much opened as collapsed, a flopping-down of rain, like when you pull a tarp off the top of a boat and all the amazing weight of standing rainwater comes with it. It comes so fast that in parks, on lawns, on high school football fields the ground can't hold it all, and turns into paddies.

Cars stop along the roads. There is lightning, and thunder so sharp and loud that it annoys you, like the dog barking too much at the mailman.

"I have never seen it rain harder," you say. "Never."

It has an infuriated, punishing quality that gives you a smug feeling for having gotten out of it—standing, say, under a downtown arcade, a sudden community of a bicycle messenger smoking a cigarette and reading "Atlas Shrugged," a lawyer touching her hair and looking at her watch, two Mormon missionaries in suits, a meter maid with her hands on her hips, a waiter on his way to work in a tuxedo, and a beggar who holds his "I Am Hungry" sign at his side. The beggar doesn't beg, it would be wrong, it would ruin the egalitarian spirit of being caught in a storm. You all watch a man stride through it with a sweat shirt hood over his head, so foolish he seems saintly.

The gutters bubble. You hear rain rushing in the storm sewers under the street. You hear it on the car where you sit parked in your driveway with a back seat full of groceries. You hear it on the roof. It wakes you up, it puts you back to sleep. It gives you goose bumps for some reason you don't understand.

Then it eases off. You are almost disappointed.

Umbrellas appear, opened with an uncertain, ransacking motion. You hear doormen whistling for cabs again. Trucks go past with a furious circle of spray around their back wheels. Motorcyclists ride out from under bridges. There are oblong ponds under the swing set. People trot out into the parking lots of shopping malls and supermarkets, their faces full of purpose.

The air feels cleaner, cooler and damper. Trees shine. The world seems new and old at the same time, like a charming neighborhood in a foreign city.

July 24, 1991

The Befuddled Autumn

Where Have All the Colors Gone?

JOEL ACHENBACH

Go to the woods. Look around. Something's missing. There's no crimson in the palette. The warm weather has made this a faded autumn, a jaundiced autumn, the autumn of our discontent. Nature, unlike the government, is refusing to operate in the red.

The trees haven't been cold enough. "If the plants are not under stress during the time that they are actively photosynthesizing, the secondary pigments don't develop in the leaf," explains Bill Anderson, regional chief scientist for the National Park Service.

In other words, if it isn't cold, the leaves don't become red, orange and gold.

What happens next? Will the leaves explode in color at the last second?

"They'll turn brown and the leaves will fall off," Anderson says.

"The colors are definitely off this year from what they normally would be," agrees Lester Brown, director of the Worldwatch Institute, an environmental research organization. "South of New York there's not much color. In downtown Washington we're going to lose our leaves before they turn."

Brown and his colleagues put out an annual report called "State of the World," and he's sensitive to these marginal changes, the unseasonal weather that jibes uncomfortably with what the computer models predict will happen in a world running a slight temperature. He fears that the much-debated "greenhouse effect"—global warming aggravated by such things as the burning of fossil fuels—may be fouling our fall.

"They're coming more frequently now, years in which there's not much color. That's my sense, having lived in Washington since the late '50s," he said.

You could say it doesn't matter much. The losses are on the margin of an unmeasurable aesthetic. It is the kind of deficit that cannot be plugged into the economists' equations, the loss of a few epiphanies, a couple of dozen smiles, and maybe somewhere a young couple decide not to detour through the woods, where, in a moment of passion inspired by nature's glories, they would have conceived the child who, had he existed, would have eventually assassinated the 21st-century psychopathic dictator who pressed the button that released the anthrax bombs that destroyed civilization as we know it. And you say it doesn't matter.

The non-hysterical person would have to admit there are some fabulous bursts of gold in the sugar maples, some yellow action in the cottonwoods, an occasional red oak that lives up to the billing, but for the most part the leaves seem confused, fused, stuck between green and brown, laden with chlorophyll when they should be showing off their anthocyanin and carotene and xanthophyll. You could plot the great trees on a map with a single box of red pins: a fine maple on Macomb two blocks off Connecticut, a good bank of oaks near Pierce Mill in the Rock Creek Park, and so on.

The view from Skyline Drive in the Shenandoah Valley has been unspectacular. It was also a mediocre season in Vermont, the foliage capital of the United States. Hubert Vogelmann, chairman of the botany department at the University of Vermont in Burlington, says, "Somehow the colors are not as bright anymore. I just think overall they're not as intense."

You have to respect a tree on so many counts. A tree has a kind of individuality, so that one might be bright gold while a neighbor of precisely the same species is still mired in off-green. A tree has patience; it is still there at your childhood home, years after your family moved away. A tree even knows parlor tricks, like getting water from the roots to the leaves without use of moving parts, pulleys or conveyor belts.

And that trick they do with the leaves, it's something we take for granted.

Leaves are finely tuned instruments. To become colorful they need bright sunlight and cold nights. The tree's metabolism slows down, chlorophyll disintegrates as it is hammered by light, and as the green disappears, the relatively sparse red and yellow pigments beneath are unmasked. If the weather is too warm it ruins the entire recipe. The green never clears out before the leaf turns brown.

"That chemical system, degradation of chlorophyll, is cued by temperature," says Dave Schimel, an ecologist at Colorado State University. As a scientist he's not going to say anything alarming, but he acknowledges that fears of a diminished autumn due to global warming are not completely nutty. "In principle, it could happen."

From Oct. 6 to 15, when a cold snap should have shocked at least some color into the leaves, the average high temperature in metropolitan Washington was 82.4 degrees. Now it is early November and shirt sleeves are still in order. At Baltimore-Washington International Airport it is the warmest year on record, and it is the second warmest at National Airport. Before the year is out, National Weather Service meteorologist David Miskus said yesterday, 1990 may go down as the warmest year in the Washington area since the Grant administration.

There is a larger buzz among climatologists, that 1990 will set a global record as well. Philip Jones, a climatologist at the University of East Anglia in England, testified before a Senate panel in early October that 1990 would set the new mark. The five warmest years previously were in the 1980s. Scientists are not convinced that global warming has begun. This could be a blip on the chart, a normal aberration, if such a term can be used.

Scientists must be precise. They have their margins of errors, their windows of doubt. This week, many of the world's top climatologists are meeting in Geneva at the World Climate Conference. Years ago there was probably no such thing as a World Climate Conference. The weather took care of itself. And the fact that they're meeting in Geneva, that place where they discuss nerve gas treaties and so forth—it's a bad omen.

For a real injection of gloom one might talk to Bill McKibben, author of "The End of Nature." It is a book of immense gravity, even the blurbs on the jacket are scary ("It's a matter of life and death to read this book,'" says one from Harold Brodkey). McKibben said this week that he's enjoyed a great fall up in the Adirondacks, but still feels the weight of global warming. That's because nature used to be something apart from man, something immutable, greater, untouchable, but now is just another human artifact. "It's finally dawning on us that we do have the power to alter the world in fundamental ways," McKibben says. "Before, the leaves changing color was something that just happened, and now we're beginning to understand that we may have a large role."

He adds portentously, "The loss of foliage is going to be the least of our problems."

It's gotten to where you can't see the forest for the Themes: degradation, regression, death. You wanted a little fresh air and exercise and suddenly you've got global warming on the brain, and that ozone thing, and the corals that are dying down there in the Caribbean, and those fish that have tumors, on and on.

Nature just doesn't seem natural anymore.

November 3, 1990

Rejected!

Portraits of the Performers the NEA Refused to Fund

PAULA SPAN AND CARLA HALL

A woman wearing papier-mache rabbit ears is wrapped in gauze and suspended, along with a live rabbit, from a flagpole for 24 hours. The public is invited to Franklin Furnace, a downtown New York exhibition and performance space, to see this work about animal and human rights; after closing time, a video monitor in the front window keeps audiences apprised.

Another woman, performing a work about aging and femaleness and the earth at the Kitchen, projects enormous pictures of herself from birth to adulthood on the walls, moving forward and backward through time, and then writes her age—60—in lipstick on her shaven head.

A black artist turns off the lights. to perform part of his work in total darkness.

Performance art, a form that coalesced in New York and California in the mid-'70s, borrows from movement and dance, theater, music, the visual arts and video. It can be scripted or extemporaneous, performed solo or with others, involve props and costumes or not. "There are no definitions of what is allowed—it's wide open," says Martha Wilson, founder of Franklin Furnace, a New York incubator for many performance artists. "You can stand on a street corner or take a bath in a suitcase."

Performance art can be confrontational, phantasmagoric, threatening, emotional, bizarre. So perhaps it is not surprising, in the intensifying tumult over art and obscenity and the National Endowment for the Arts, that the first artists to be denied the 1990 NEA fellowships for which they'd been recommended were four performance artists, two from each coast.

The endowment's chairman and its appointed advisory board, the National Council on the Arts, last week took the very rare step of overruling the unanimous recommendation of its peer panel, awarding grants of $5,000 to $11,250 to 14 artists, but refusing them to Karen Finley and Holly Hughes of New York, and John Fleck of Los Angeles and Tim Miller of Santa Monica.

All are former NEA grant recipients. But their work involves elements that have lately drawn fire from NEA critics: sexuality (both homo- and hetero-); non-traditional views of religion; four-letter words; attacks on political and religious antagonists. On Capitol Hill, critics of the endowment, as well as some of those hoping to save it, generally applauded the withholding of the grants.

Performance artists may have been particularly vulnerable to political pressure on the NEA, say supporters like Mark Russell, director of New York's PS 122 art center. They work in a new, not widely understood medium, he said, and they work alone, without boards of directors, subscribers or organizations.

But the four "defunded"' artists, in Holly Hughes's term, do have allies. Los Angeles performance artist Rachel Rosenthal publicly refused the $11,250 NEA grant she was given, saying in a statement that "I cannot in good conscience pay such an immoral price for this money." Producer Joe Papp sent a scathing letter to NEA Chairman John Frohnmayer, accusing him of becoming "Jesse Helms's enforcer, a censor, a role ill-befitting the leader of the arts in America." Finley and Hughes are appealing the denials of their grants and considering their legal options as well; Miller and Fleck say they are considering appeals. Grant recipients are discussing some sort of group response, to be announced this week at a press conference at the Public Theater in New York.

The performances, meanwhile, continue. "Rescinding these grants will make these artists' lives miserable," Wilson says, "but it won't stop the train."

Feminism, Mom and Monologues

To find Holly Hughes, who turns out to be 35 and elfin and wearing a "Fight for Homoerotic Art" T-shirt, one climbs four flights of stairs, enters the standard bathtub-in-the-kitchen East Village railroad flat, shoos the cats off the chairs. "My posh pad, paid for by your tax dollars," she says by way of welcome.

She grew up in a very Republican family in Saginaw, Mich. ("the navy bean capital of the world") and came to New York in 1979 to become a famous feminist artist. "Those heady days," she says. "I thought I'd collectively arrange a giant quartz-and-steel vagina in Federal Plaza that would topple the military." When this did not, precisely, occur, she became a waitress and then, hanging around the W.O.W. Cafe, a performer.

Hughes's work, for which she received a $7,000 NEA grant last year, is satiric and cheeky, and it celebrates her lesbian sensibilities. That, she is convinced, was exactly the problem this year. "Three of the people who got defunded are very visible as performers and gay performers," she says. "I believe my grant got denied because Frohnmayer is trying to appease a right-wing minority, led by Jesse Helms, that has really attacked gays and lesbians."

Oddly enough, Hughes did receive a $15,500 NEA play-writing grant this year, recommended by a different peer panel. The scripts she submitted in support of that successful application were the same she submitted for the solo performance grant she was denied. In both cases, NEA observers came to see her perform her 75-minute solo theater piece, "World Without End," at Washington's d.c. space last December. (Hughes returns to Washington Aug. 25 and 26 to perform that and a new work at Dance Place.)

It's a monologue—"storytelling," she calls it—and consists "mostly of me sitting in a wingback chair in a red dress, talking about my mother," though there's also an accordion player on stage who, at one point, breaks into an abbreviated cabaret act in gibberish French. Written after her mother's death in 1987, "World Without End" attempts "to make sense of the very difficult relationship we had." It's also funny and full of anecdotes about 'the development of our sexuality and questions about sexual identity."

The piece describes "a briefly enlightened moment" when her mother "explained the facts of life to me. . . . I talk about her taking off her clothes and pointing out the points of interest between her legs." During this part of the mono- logue, "I sort of motion; I stick my hands under my dress at one point."

This moment may have decided Hughes's fate, though there's also plenty of unprintable language and some impious religious imagery ("I saw Jesus between my mother's legs!" she tells her best friend Jodeen) in the piece as well.

Without the solo-performance grant, which probably would have amounted to $5,000 to $10,000, 'I have to get a job," Hughes says. But she intends to create new work nonetheless. The working title of an upcoming performance piece: "Fully Funded by the NEA."

Meanwhile, she's calling for Frohnmayer's resignation. "He's the Neville Chamberlain of arts funding," Hughes says. "And he's expecting me and Karen Finley to be Poland."

The Sacrifice Plan

Of the four artists, Karen Finley may be the most distraught by the defunding and attendant hoopla. It seems to have changed everything for her. "I will always now be looked at as the censored artist, the blacklisted artist," she says by phone from her home in Rockland County, north of New York City. "I feel like I'm living under McCarthyism or Stalinism. I didn't think this would affect me so deeply, but it has." She has been unable to create new work, Finley says, since the notoriety over her performances began this spring.

A two-time NEA recipient, Finley is a 34-year-old Chicagoan whose work draws controversy like a magnet, and has for years. It's sometimes rude, crude and semi-nude. It's frankly feminist. It's angry. In "We Keep Our Victims Ready," which an NEA site observer saw this winter at the Walker Arts Center in Minneapolis, "I basically go through various victims in our society, showing that people are born into victimization, {into} the patriarchal nature of the society," the artist says.

In the first act Finley, seated (fully clothed) in a rocking chair, tells of her Aunt Mandy, who died of an illegal abortion, and reflects on societal expectations of motherhood and on her unorthodox religious views.

In the second act, in which she rages against sexual violence and women's ob- jectification, she removes part of her costume. "I go through ceremony, the woman being degraded," she says. She covers her body with chocolate ("it's very primitive, you hear these words like 'Oh my God' ") and decorates it with candy and tinsel, reciting a text that compares her to a penned veal calf. "Is there anything at all sexually titillating? No. There's nothing sexually exciting about my work; if there were I'd be doing burlesque shows and centerfolds and making a lot of money."

In the third act, donning a white shroud and sitting at a bedside, she talks about AIDS and death. "At the end of this performance, people are in tears," she says.

Now she is afraid that the institutions that book her will be subject to funding pressure. The Kitchen and Franklin Furnace, downtown alternative art spaces with which she has long relationships, have been questioned by the General Accounting Office and say their NEA checks have been delayed.

She is afraid that the public will never consider her a serious artist after reading columnists' descriptions of her as one whose talent is smearing chocolate on her body. She's afraid she won't be able to work at all. "I'm calling it the sacrifice plan," she says. "I believe (Frohnmayer) thinks that by sacrificing us, he is saving the endowment."

But in a backhanded way, Finley thinks, her opponents' actions are a tribute to the success and power of her work, which she has performed across the country and in Europe. "It's about social issues they don't want to hear about," she says. "This is their last chance at trying to maintain the power structure of the straight white male."

Aristotelian Performances

Not everyone finds Tim Miller's work so objectionable.

"My mother comes," he says with a chuckle. "She's a hard-core Republican. She's a big supporter."

Of course Frohnmayer, a fellow Republican, didn't share her enthusiasm, which her son describes as "humorous, built on American storytelling tradition— you know, talking to the audience, telling stories. It's challenging politically and in some of the content."

The 31-year-old Miller, a third-generation Californian from Whittier who's been involved in theater and dance since high school, has been openly gay since then as well. "That's a big part of my work," he says, and he attributes the NEA's grant rejection to the fact that he deals so openly with gay and lesbian issues.

But what about those touchstones of controversy in art: Does he use profanity? "Much less than Eddie Murphy," he replies. Is he nude on stage? "Oh, only in a passing fashion," he says so casually it makes both him and a visitor laugh.

"Just to give you an example," he says more seriously, "in a work called 'Some Golden States,' there's one section right at the beginning of the piece where I sort of tear my clothes off and I'm basically kind of thrown around on a pile of leaves. It's a piece I made about the reality of my hometown, Whittier, being destroyed in the 1987 earthquake."

Much of Miller's artwork deals with his experiences as a gay man from Whittier. "I was from Nixon's hometown," he says. "It had a kind of energy to it. It's part of why I became an artist. It was part of a historical moment."

He wears a black T-shirt proclaiming the AIDS activist credo in Spanish—SILENCIO = MUERTE—and sits in the lofty space that houses Highways, a theater tucked into a quiet street in Santa Monica. Miller lives just south of here in Venice, and he volunteers at Highways, which on this day has become the scene of press conferences and interviews.

"The worst possible day to be going to a gig," says Miller ruefully as he rises once again to answer the phone. Like a theater gypsy, Miller is often on the road. He just returned from the Walker Art Center in Minneapolis and now he's headed for Seattle. He estimates that he makes, after expenses, about $13,000 a year from performing and teaching occasional classes at colleges in different cities.

What he does is art, he says. "I totally exist within the context of European-American tradition. My work is Aristotelian in form. It's structured. It's written in what is clearly an acknowledged literary form.

And, at the bottom line, his work is art—"because I say it is." He laughs. "And because newspapers do."

Like any artist, he's accustomed to—and accepts—rejection. In the past eight years he's applied for more grants than he's won, although the NEA has awarded him four or five solo artist and choreography grants, he says. But this case has made him angry because of what he sees as the political nature of the turndown. "It's so clearly a rejection of individual artists for who they are," he says. "There's been plenty of straight white men who do challenging work."

Miller says the dramatically worded artist's statement he filed with his grant application—"my call to arms"—probably helped single him out for rejection.

"I am a mutant performance artist from Alta California," he wrote, using a politically charged term that characterizes the state as being stolen from Mexico. "I believe my social activism . . . my sex juicy life . . . provocateur organizing . . . my space building . . . and my family Sunday dinners in Whittier are as much a part of my creative work as my performances . . ."

And, he added bluntly, "And look here, Senator Jesse Helms, keep your porky pig face out of the NEA and out of my {expletive} . . . because I got work to do . . ."

Miller performs everywhere from art centers to high schools to a local church where he works with an openly gay Episcopal priest on "performance art sermons." He says he rarely gets hassled because of his work "beyond the usual homophobic death threats" of which he gets several a year, he says. Is his work shocking? "To some people," he answers. "But it's not my goal."

Taboos as Commentary

John Fleck greets you at the door with the irony of it all.

"They take away whatever the grant would have been—like $7,000—and they hand you $50,000 in publicity by doing so," he muses. "It catapults you into this national forum."

Fleck hastily tidies up the papers and reviews of his work strewn about his old Spanish-style house in Silverlake, a hot and dusty Los Angeles neighborhood shared uneasily by yups and street toughs. The lanky 39-year-old artist, trained as an actor, works regularly in theater and television. He calls what he does "one-man solo theater shows." "Performance artist" is a title that's been bestowed upon him.

Whatever he's called, Fleck has certainly lived up to the controversial profile that characterizes many performance artists. With a $5,000 NEA grant last year he produced "Blessed Are All the Little Fishes"— the show that got me in pretty much all the trouble with NEA."

Fleck explains: "'Well, there is one point where I urinate on stage." He rolls his eyes. "Whoopie doopie. Taken out of context it sounds like sensationalism. But there was some social relevance attached. It really wasn't disgusting or rude or crude. I don't think anybody was offended by it. In fact, I think if you look back it's nothing new. It's been done before."

In an *Artweek* review last year, Fleck was described as being "known for histrionic operatic vocals, manic energy and flagrant displays of his private parts. . . . He tests the boundaries by turning performance excesses and taboos into cultural commentary."

Fleck's "Fishes" was originally a 10-minute club performance piece. "I gave the illusion that I was hurting this little goldfish—a long story—and they started screaming, 'Save the fish! Save the fish!' And I'm such a good actor," he interjects drolly, "this man jumped out of the audience and started calling me every name in the book . . . I thought he was gonna hit me. And he grabbed this fish and he took off. And he saved the fish. I thought, 'Whoa!' I love stuff like that."

Fleck then expanded the piece into a 40-minute performance that played at several respected venues. One of them, the Tiffany Theater, had reservations at first. "They didn't want me to come there," he says. "Let's face it. A lot of performance art is garbage." But Fleck and his director persuaded the theater to present his show, which eventually ran for six weeks.

The piece, which focuses on Christian guilt, is highly personal and symbolic and has some nudity. It opens with him dressed as a mermaid "swimming on a toilet" on wheels, he explains. In the course of the performance he extracts both a bottle of tequila and a goldfish from the toilet; he also urinates into it, and mimes vomiting into it. Hidden inside the toilet are discrete compartments that allow him to do all these things. "That goldfish is still alive," he says reassuringly.

The piece is not without knowing humor. A cry of protest over the killing of dolphins segues into a cry of regret over the cancellation of the "Flipper" television show.

Although he supports gay-rights issues, he says his work deals less with gay themes than with androgyny. "I always deal with sexual confusion," Fleck says. "I've had as many women lovers as men. I'm with a man right now. . . . Of course in this day of the plague, so to speak, it isn't as easy to cross over, nor would I want to. I just want to settle down."

In "I Got the He-Be-She-Be's" Fleck plays his own male and female halves making love to himself.

"Why is it art?" he muses about his work, and chuckles. "Because art professionals say it is. . . . I've got a pile of review" saying how wonderful I am. It isn't for everybody. Not everybody's going to understand it, but not everybody understands modern art."

He loses money—even with grants—on performance art. "It certainly hasn't helped my acting career," he says. "Most people think performance artists can't act."

July 8, 1990

Om, Om on the Range

The Rainbow Tribe Gathers to Meditate in Vermont

DAVID MILLS

They've thrown up a city in these woods, a city of proto-hippies, ex-hippies and nouveau hippies. Of potheads and peaceniks, punks and Rastas. And families too, some with grimy, bare-bottomed toddlers. Plus dogs. Everywhere.

Utopia, for a week.

"Hi, would you like a smiley face?" On the long, hilly trail into the heart of the gathering, a blissful young woman coming the other way has decided to give you a gift, a dime-size metal smiley face, because that's the kind of thing people do here. But then, the trek inward also brings you in touch with a lean, haunted-looking gentleman dragging a hand cart over damp ground. "Have you read Solzhenitsyn?" he asks. "Alexander Solzhenitsyn. He's from here, you know. Vermont. Solzhenitsyn."

This is the 20th national gathering of the Rainbow Family of Living Light, modern tribalists who each year assemble in a different national forest to commune with one another and, on the Fourth of July, to hold a one-hour mass meditation for world peace.

By today's noon vigil, the U.S. Forest Service estimates, about 14,000 Rainbow people will be on the site in central Vermont. (A Forest Service spokeswoman said yesterday the gathering is running "fairly smoothly.")

But the Rainbow gathering is about more than meditating in a meadow.

A man named Michael John stands in the fading glow of a kerosene lamp. He's a "facilitator" of the event (don't call him an "organizer"—too leaderlike, and if there's one thing the Rainbow Family doesn't want, it's leaders). It's near midnight Tuesday at the information booth, a large hut made of branches and rope, and new bodies are still coming in off the main trail. Michael John, a fairly haggard veteran of 16 national gatherings, wears a quizzical smile.

"There's no rock band. There's no Madonna around. George Bush is not here to draw a crowd. There's no guru. They didn't pay anything to get in. Why'd they come?" he asks. "Why'd they come?"

Twenty drums are pounding in loose synchrony. Congas, bongos, drums you can't even name. Men and women, black and white, young and old, are slapping them, converged in the middle of a meadow known as Main Circle. In this little clearing, the Green Mountains are all around, a distant wall.

The drums lure onlookers by the tens, and up close, the ground is throbbing. A flute player is jamming on top of the dense percussion. A few folks are moved to dance. Or just to hop up and down, bare, gray feet striking the dirt and kicking up a mist, eyes shut. Several women are grooving topless or totally naked. Which is no big deal here.

Other bodies are just sprawled, under a sun that turns pink shoulders red. Panting dogs are navigating through it all.

In a few hours, after dinner, the drummers reconvene, this time more, maybe 30, and this time around a fire. A sinewy kid is near the pit, flailing to the intense polyrhythmic pulse, a frantic swim through smoke, while men around him let out strong hollers.

Overhead, the western clouds turn from white to pink to gray as the sun vanishes. The tribal drumming never stops.

"In 1970, we thought the Aquarian Age was imminent," says Washingtonian Eric Sterling, his milky belly bare over rainbow-dyed white denim pants. Through sunglasses, he looks upon the hippies all around him at Main Circle, and he tries to describe the difference between then and now:

"This is like Legionnaires feeling aggrieved in a post-Vietnam War America, getting together, wearing the uniform and sharing their stories."

Sterling is the president of the Criminal Justice Policy Foundation in downtown Washington, which promotes such ideas as alternative sentencing and drug policy reform. He's a former Capitol Hill staffer (assistant counsel, House Judiciary Committee's subcommittee on crime).

He's also an ex-hippie. He says his life was changed at a gathering of the counterculture in 1970, the Vortex rock festival in Portland, Ore., a precursor to the Rainbow gatherings.

"I had a fear of dogs," Sterling says. At Vortex, despite the presence of dogs, he decided to go with the flow and walk around naked. "And the dogs would come up and sniff (me). And I realized all they were doing was being friendly. I realized they were not going to bite me. It was a meaningful part of my spiritual development. I saw them as part of the environment that was benign."

Although he says today's hippies can be called "marginal," Sterling came to the Rainbow gathering partly to observe one continuing hallmark of the counterculture: the wide-open smoking of marijuana. "This is not the drug culture," he says. "This is a subculture that is not ashamed of its use of illegal drugs." The tobacco, alcohol and advertising industries, he says, are the real drug culture.

No doubt overhearing the conversation, a young dude with a small marijuana pipe steps over. "You guys smoke pot?"

"No thanks," Sterling says. "I'm fine."

The young guy looks confused for a second, then says, "Wish I had some."

"Rainbow ganja bubbles!"

The chill falls fast onto the forest at night. But that doesn't stop the party. Just drape a blanket over yourself, and check out the cat with the British accent and beads in his beard. He's holding a fat bamboo bubble blower and a small dish of liquid soap.

Through the generosity of a volunteer, the man takes in a lungful of pot and puts his lips to the bubble blower. And a cantaloupe-size orb drifts slowly upward. Suddenly, the beams from five, six flashlights hit the bubble. The glistening, multi-colored effect inspires the resident wit of the info booth, that truck-stop fashion-plate Wanderin' Willie, to poetry:

"Watch it while you're tripping, watch it while you're straight. Watch it while you can, 'cause when it pops, it's too late."

Folks erupt in laughter, and the smoke-filled bubble sails higher and higher. One observer, craning his neck, sums up the moment: "This is cooler than cool, man."

The first Rainbow gathering was in the Rocky Mountains of Colorado in 1972, but even the Rainbow Family's own tale of its genesis is murky. Basically, members of a couple of communal groups thought it would be great to have a gathering of the counterculture in the Rockies. They spent a year and a half promoting it, and 20,000 people showed up. The central event was an afternoon of prayer and meditation for world peace on July 4.

"The people who had planned the first Rainbow gathering had no intention of calling another one," according to a brief history published by the Rainbows. But in 1973, someone began promoting another gathering on a Wyoming Indian reservation, without permission from the tribe. The Rainbow Family stepped in, talked with the U.S. Forest Service, and found a site where people could gather. From then on, it just became a habit. There are regional Rainbow gatherings as well.

But the Rainbow Family doesn't hype its gatherings anymore. To know where they'll be, you have to find out from someone with the family. Several attendees this year say they never heard of the Rainbow gatherings until they began going to Grateful Dead concerts and meeting Rainbow people.

Even on Tuesday afternoon, with thousands of Rainbow people yet to arrive, the last stretch of trail leading to Main Circle is a hectic highway. No merchandising is allowed at the gathering, but barter is cool, and one of the encampment's two trading zones is just down the hill. On blankets on the ground, people display their wares: crystals, beads, buttons ("Why Be Normal?"), more crystals.

While the trading zone is digging an impromptu acoustic jazz duet by two guitarists, two dogs trot up the hill, and a man is following them. "Those dogs bit me," he declares, strangely deadpan. It's the Solzhenitsyn guy. "Those dogs bit me. Does anybody have a big blanket? I want to have them netted and tested for rabies."

Nobody pays him any mind. Mellow. Even with thousands of diverse folk, it's all about mellow.

Alas, even on the main trail at a Rainbow gathering, mellow is put to the test.

Sitting on the side of the road on a rusty old snowplow, a hairy doper in a medieval jester's cap has been distracted from his discourse on the potential economic benefits of hemp cultivation. There is a red pickup rolling down the trail. A truck! This site is for human beings. (And dogs.)

"No trucks," the jester yells to the passing thing. A fellow on the other side of the road echoes him.

A man sitting on the back of the truck explains, "We had a burn victim we had to get up to CALM." (That's the Center for Alternative Living Medicine. A sort of holistic first-aid station.)

"No trucks," the jester says again. "Use people power."

"Then next time, you move the victim," the guy in the truck says, taking a drag off a cigarette.

Immediately comes a voice of mellow from up front. "Let's not argue!"

"I'm not arguing," says the jester, the truck gone by now. "I burn gas in my bus, but not on main site."

"Welcome home!" Everywhere you turn, somebody is saying it. "Welcome home, brother." The closer you get to Main Circle, the more tents you see, mushrooming alongside the trail and in small clearings.

The seed camp of the Rainbow gathering arrived in the forest three weeks ago to survey the area, dig latrines, build a few kitchens, run three miles of water line from a spring and negotiate an operating plan with the Forest Service. The efficiency of this instant city is often remarkable. As during dinner time.

Everyone gets a hot meal at the Rainbow gathering. It comes in Main Circle right after the afternoon council, where vital information of the day is passed on to the masses, and which concludes with everyone standing in a big circle holding hands and chanting "OM."

Then, instead of lining up for chow, everyone forms a series of concentric circles and sits in the meadow while volunteers carry buckets of rice and beans or other simple fare around, dispensing a lump in whatever receptacle you have handy. (Food funds are raised by a nightly passing of the hat.)

While folks are eating, the council continues, whereby anyone wishing to address the whole family can do so, by being given a feather at the end of a branch.

The feather doesn't always command attention, though. One weathered little man tries to lecture diners on the evils of circumcision. He is wearing nothing but a cardboard box over his shoulders inscribed with this message: "Circumcision is child torture! It has no medical value! Please help stop it. In Europe, it is outlawed."

Few people seem to care. At least until after dinner, when he meets a few sympathizers. Women, in fact.

Why'd they come?

"Just Rainbow energy, man," says 22-year-old Matt Janauwzski, who came from Santa Cruz, Calif., and whose long brown hair is just beginning to mat into dreadlocks. "I've done the Rainbow thing for about four years. I just get a really spiritual high out of it. It reminds me a lot of the way the American Indian tribes used to live. Like money, alcohol, violence—it's nonexistent."

Ali Pastick, as a 19-year-old, was part of the seed camp of the 1980 Rainbow gathering in West Virginia. She's now a personnel consultant in western Massachusetts. "I walk around with a briefcase with my hair up. She says she can spot other "middle-class" people at this gathering.

"It's a chance to slow down and check it out, check each other out, and say, 'Hey, I'm on an okay path,' " Pastick says.

"All children, close your ears," announces Sam Berman-Freedman, 9. It's variety show time at Kiddie Village, the communal day-care camp for "little Rainbows." And this cat in the purple turtleneck shirt with sleeves pulled over his hands is saying, "This is a political joke for adults. Children, close your ears. You won't understand it."

Then he says: "Who's middle name is Walker, and who's so dumb he thinks the only way to get peace is by fighting?"

After a couple of seconds, a grown-up says, "George Bush."

Correct. Sam earns himself a hearty round of applause—from the adults, anyway—then takes his seat on the ground with everyone else.

It isn't too long, though, before he's back up front, running through more of his material.

"How many people"—Sam's delivery is halting, he needs to work on that—"have ever gone bowling?" A number of hands go up. Sam checks them out. "Good. Then there's enough people here for me to tell this next joke:

"What do you call it at a bowling alley when the people who work in the bowling alley want more money and they demonstrate about it?" Pause. "A strike!"

Big laughs. He's still surprising the grown-ups. Then Sam drops this one-liner: "If God wanted us to have peace, why did he invent uranium?"

Silence. The delivery was off. Nobody quite heard it right. But he keeps right on anyway, even as a familiar woman in the audience says, "Sam, it's a long talent show. Come on."

As Sam's set devolves into less sophisticated wordplay, a pretty, pear-shaped naked woman turns to his mother and smiles: "He's a ham. He's into it."

When Sam finally returns to his seat, he throws a hug around his mom and asks, "Weren't those good jokes?"

"Most of them were good," she says.

"When Sam was in kindergarten," says Merle Berman, "his teacher said to me, 'What do you guys talk about at home? He wanted to know why Nixon resigned.'

Berman says her son has picked up a few things from his parents. "We're a socially active family. We've taken him with us to demonstrations. But we don't sit around the house talking about Tricky Dick," she says. "He's just a very bright kid. We listen to NPR; he listens to NPR."

Sam, pointing to his forehead and sucking on a piece of candy, says he gets his material "all in my mind."

"Did you like my George Bush joke?" he asks. "It's a little crazy. But then, George Bush is a little crazy."

Big sign on a bulletin board: "Please clean up behind your dog. There is dog {dung} everywhere!"

In the blackness of the forest night, the bonfire is painting her whole body a hot orange as she undulates to a storm of drumming. Better than naked, her young, rounded flesh is wrapped in a camisole and pettipants. And she's hitting a bell in time to the downbeat of 40 congas, rocking her blond head and pouting.

Not exactly what you expect to see late at night at the Rainbow gathering, but there it is. And nobody seems to notice.

What hypes this crowd up is the man who walks toward the fire with another bundle of sticks over his head. When he deposits them, the flames stand up eight feet tall, and people howl and raise their palms. Sparks zoom and twirl through the air like a hundred fireflies.

Six hours later, at dawn, the fire is down to a relaxed glow, and there are eight drummers still keeping the beat alive.

July 4, 1991

Underground Cinderellas

In 'Paris Is Burning,' Unearthing a
Gay Subculture Where Life Is a Ball

JOE BROWN

Voguing: A dance invented by black and Latino gay men in Manhattan's streets, parks and nightclubs, years before Madonna made it famous on MTV. Combining the stiff, haughty poses struck by high-fashion models with acrobatic spins and dips, voguing evolved as a competition from the black gay traditions of "reading" (razor-sharp, fast-slashing, finger-snapping verbal abuse) and "shade" (attitude, the body language version of reading).

"The other day in a drugstore, I overheard a kid say to his mother, 'Mommy, Mommy! Johnny's voguing!' " marvels director Jennie Livingston, in Washington to promote "Paris Is Burning," her first feature film. "I thought, 'That's so cute. If only Mommy knew where voguing really came from.' "

"Paris Is Burning" is a poignant and profound, unsentimental and unexploitative examination of a subculture that until now has been invisible to most Americans. Built around elaborately staged mock fashion balls, this alternative world of black and Latin gay men and lesbians has its own elaborate jargon and its own intricate social structure, the self-protective hierarchy of "houses." These substitute extended families (or "gay street gangs," as one voguer puts it) knock themselves out to imitate a society that, ironically, will not have them.

The film, which cost about $375,000 to complete, won the 1990 Los Angeles Film Critics' Award for Best Documentary, then shared the prize for Best Documentary at the 1991 Sundance Film Festival (with Barbara Kopple's "American Dream," about labor strife at a Minnesota meatpacking plant). It has since broken records in its first commercial run, at New York's Film Forum, where it was booked for two weeks in March and stayed for 17, racking up raves and full houses.

And last week, "Paris Is Burning" was picked up for distribution by Prestige, a division of Miramar. It opens Friday in 17 cities, including Washington, where it will play exclusively on several screens at the Cineplex Odeon Dupont Circle. Tracks, a gay disco in Southeast Washington, is holding a voguing ball the following Sunday, Aug. 11, to celebrate the opening of the film.

Ball: A voguing competition and impersonation parade, offering participants a chance to mirror a society that consistently excludes poor black and Latino gays while seducing them with images of white prosperity, white beauty, white straight family life.

"I just didn't know what was going on!" says Livingston, 28, dressed PC-chic in a checked jacket thrown over a Barbara Kruger "Your Body Is a Battlefield" T-shirt. In a suite at the Park Hyatt, she recalls in a rapid ramble what it was like when she entered the doors of the Gay and Lesbian Community Center in the Village and was struck by the Spectacle:

"Here were these people, and I didn't know if they were men or if they were women, and they were moving, and why are they moving this way, and what are they screaming, they're screaming these names, like Labeija! Labeija! Labeija! And I was like, what is Labeija and what is Pop-Dip-Spin and what are they doing?

"I was really confused, and somebody said I should look Willi up, as somebody who understands voguing. And Willi and I sat down with a tape recorder and Willi outlined the whole ball world—these are 'houses,' and these are 'mothers,' and this is 'realness.' "

"I've been voguing for 11 years, but I didn't have an inkling of it until I started," says voguer and choreographer Willi Ninja (who requested to remain ageless), one of the striking stars of "Paris Is Burning" and one of the few voguers to achieve "crossover" success in the commercial world. A tall, exotically elegant man, seated beside Livingston on a sofa, he's dressed to stun in a beige Armani suit over a sparkly crimson pullover, long lush ponytail, enormous gold earrings. "It was very underground. You basically didn't even see the dance in mainstream clubs, because once people figured out where it came from, then they automatically assumed that if you're doing this dance, then you must be. And the majority of kids at that time didn't want to come out. I was in the closet then, but I was like, 'Hey, this is great, this is a new dance form.' And once I had it down pat, I was doing it everywhere."

As Livingston went to more balls and shot more still pictures and footage, she says, "I began to feel that this was a film." She sold her car to make a five-minute fundraising trailer, and began applying for grants.

"Half of being an independent filmmaker is waiting for grants that don't come through," Livingston says.

Curiously, she had some difficulty obtaining funding from gay organizations as well. "The gay mainstream, which is essentially white and middle-class, doesn't want to be shown as drag queens. They don't want to see them either."

With money from the New York State Council on the Arts and WNYC-TV, filming began in 1985 and ended in 1987, with 70 hours of footage from balls and interviews. The next three years, Livingston says, were spent "editing and running out of money and editing again," paring the film down to 78 elegantly boisterous minutes.

The final stages of production were assisted by funds from the BBC and a $25,000 media arts grant, one of the last National Endowment for the Arts grants awarded before the Jesse Helms-Robert Mapplethorpe flap.

"Our checks were coming in as Helms was raising the ruckus about Mapplethorpe," Livingston says. "And we're like, 'Don't let him find out about "Paris Is Burning," we need the money!' "

But the senator from North Carolina should love this movie.

"It's about old-fashioned family values," Livingston says. "Like kindness and tolerance and loving your mother, even if your mother is a drag queen who is taking the place of your biological mother who refuses to speak to you because you're homosexual."

Houses: Rival clubs or "families" of voguers and "ball walkers," with names taken either from haute couture designers (as in the Houses of Chanel, Saint Laurent and Armani) or from the "mother," the most powerful member of the family (as in the Houses of PepperLabeija, Angie Xtravaganza and Willi Ninja), a surrogate parent to the "ball children" who compete against one another for trophies.

There are dozens of balls held in Manhattan each year, but much of Livingston's film revolves around the Paris Is Burning ball, the grandest of the annual events, thrown by Paris Dupree, Legendary Mother of the House of Dupree, at the Elks Lodge in Harlem. Because many ball competitors perform in nightclubs, the balls begin at 4 or 5 a.m. and continue through the next evening, some lasting 18 hours.

"In real life you can't get a good job," says one ball-goer in the film. "A ball is as close to reality as we're gonna get to all of that fame and fortune, stardom and spotlight."

These streetwise Cinderellas have a sad, insatiable desire for fame and the expensive accouterments they see in magazines and on TV. But deprived as they often are, they are not hostile to mainstream culture. In their imitation of life, they dress up as supermodels and movie stars, but also as Wall Street executives, schoolgirls and military officers. "Realness" is their way of slipping momentarily into desperately desired roles, not satirizing them.

As David Denby pointed out in his *New York* magazine review: "It's the opposite of camp and finally heartbreaking in its longing for the power to be oneself, a power that most of us take for granted."

Realness: The aesthetic imperative of the ball culture, "realness" is the ability to pass on the runway as something you are not, as in rich for poor, female for male, straight for gay. In life, realness can be a matter of survival, as in passing for straight to avoid homophobic violence. As Willi Ninja says, "If you don't look the part in this world, if you don't have the right accessories or whatever, you're not gonna get it."

"One time I was in Sally's Hideaway, this {transvestite} bar in midtown, and I guess I was dressed in tighter-fitting clothes than usual, and this drag queen looked me over and said, 'You're really good, honey,' " Livingston says with a laugh. "And another time, early in the morning after a ball, I was in Harlem right near the subway at around 155th or something like that. And this guy came up to me and smiled at me, and said, 'Are you for real?' "

At film festivals and colleges, Livingston is often asked what it was like, as a white woman, entering this world. "If you've never been to Harlem, that name resounds with all kinds of images," she says. "But you go there and it's, 'Oh, this is a neighborhood like any other neighborhood.' And the ball was very welcoming. I didn't feel anybody was giving me dirty looks because I was a white girl.

"Then again, I wasn't competition," she adds, and laughs.

"Going to these balls would really blow my mind," says Livingston, who came to be called "Miss Jennie" by the denizens. "You just begin to question, what's gender? Am I doing it right? And you go out on the street after an 18-hour ball and you look at all these people going by, like, 'Is that a man?' Or 'Is that a woman?' And you look at somebody in a dress and they have a slightly masculine jaw line, and you're like, 'Whoa—what's that?' Or you see a man in a suit, a businessman, and maybe he looks a little feminine, and you're just like, 'Wow, I don't know anything anymore.' "

Drag: The concept that clothes make the man. Or woman. Basically, everyone is in drag.

"I think it's a little different for a woman than for a man because men have traditionally, at least in the last 50 or 100 years, been confined to very simple clothes," Livingston says. "And so when a man is willing to sort of dress up, it's like a liberation, because he can find more personalities. Now, women have been allowed all kinds of finery, but what they haven't been allowed is to be simple. So I think I always felt very oppressed by the idea that I should have stockings and heels, and always fought against it as a kid. So when I dress up in girl drag, I feel very much not like myself. I feel like I have to play a role I don't want to play.

"But, obviously, if I could get a lot of very tailored Chanel suits, I might feel very fine indeed," she says, laughing.

"Gender is a construction," Livingston continues. "Much of it is learned—the behavior and the makeup and the walk and the dress. And what better proof of that than to see somebody like {transsexual ball-walker} Octavia St. Laurent, who is much more of a classical woman than I am?"

"Even men who go to corporate executive offices are in drag," Ninja. "That's their office drag. They have a whole new personality when they step into the office from their home. It all comes down to details, and you will get over better. That's what realness is all about." In one of the film's most remarkable moments, Ninja teaches "real" women how to walk.

Drag balls have existed for decades, Ninja says, and until the '60s there was no color barrier. For a moment, in 1989, when publicity burned hottest, the balls moved to downtown nightclubs, attracting a spectrum of curiosity-seekers. But they've since moved back uptown, to Harlem. And the concept of drag has changed over the years in the ball communities, as wise drag queen elder/oracle Dorian Corey observes in the film: "When I grew up, you wanted to look like Marlene Dietrich, Betty Grable . . . With the current children, they've gone to televisioin. I've been to several balls, and they've actually had categories like 'Dynasty'—they want you to look like Alexis or Krystle! I guess that's just a statement of the times . . . Now it's not what you can create, it's what you can acquire.

"Voguing was happening in the drag balls in the late '60s too," Ninja says, "and it progressed into the true balls of the '70s. In the '60s it was just basically drag queens, but in the '70s, a lot of the boys were like, 'I don't wanna do this, I don't wanna be in high heels, this is not my thing, but I want to get an award too.' So that's when they started having different houses and competing, coming up with categories."

Categories: The divisions of competition at a ball, which resemble the divisions of a fashion show, with events for both Butch Queens (masculine gay men who compete in men's clothing) and Femme Queens (men who compete in women's clothing). Categories might include Executive Realness (business suits and briefcases); Body (muscular for butch queens, model-type for Femme queens, luscious for big or voluptuous femme queens); Opulence—You Own Everything; Looking Like a Girl Going to School; and Looking Like the Boy That Probably Robbed You a Few Minutes Before You Came to the Ball.

An astonishing amount of love and work goes into creating this world, where gender-bending is not just a theoretical concept but a way of life. Ninja speaks of the lavish Grand Prize productions, in which "you have to design your own costumes, and if they say Japanese High Fashion versus Russian Military, that means your house has to come up with the idea of what that is. The categories are listed and sent out, so you have about a month or a month and a half to get ready. And then there's when they call, for example, Mary McFadden versus Chanel, meaning you have to have the real garments. No labels taken out and stitched in, because they know. These kids get them any which way, but they'll have them, and they're not playing . . . ."

One time there was a category called Shopping Down Fifth, which means making sure that you looked like you were a shopper going down Fifth {Avenue}. So that means you could wear anything from Bloomingdale's, but preferably from Saks with, like, all the designer shopping bags. This is the one category that is taken totally seriously, because it's fashion, total oriented, and you have to give that total illusion. When they're doing Executive Realness or, like, looking like a yachting club, it's a little bit camp, because they're taking shots—wanting to be that way, but also taking shots at the mainstream society.

"But when it's, like, Mary McFadden, you don't mess, because they take that seriously."

Legendary: Becoming "legendary" is the ultimate goal of the ball children. To be a legend, one must win three grand prizes. But, as Ninja says, "that does not make you a legend in their eyes, unless they say you're a legend.

"We considered calling the film 'Pecs, Thighs and Videotape,' Livingston jokes. "But we decided that 'Paris Is Burning' evoked what we wanted to evoke—burning desire, fashion, the dissolution of Western civilization."

After graduating from Yale in 1983, Los Angeles-born Livingston spent some time photographing people at gay parties and rallies. "Very much like Robert Frank, Garry Winogrand, Weegee, Brassai, those kinds of pictures of people. My photographs were about class, they were about race, and gender and consumerism, just the fabric of American life. And looking at visual influences—what is a woman, and what is a man, and how does the class system affect that?"

But Livingston says she became frustrated with the "silence" of the medium. "Although I love photographs, I think the people who see them are limited to the people who collect photography books and the people who go to galleries. And I really wanted to tell stories and be more overtly political.

"So I moved to New York, so I could get into film, and was taking this class at NYU, and quite by chance I met these guys who were throwing their limbs all over the place at Washington Square Park. And someone said, 'Honey, if you want to see voguing, you'll have to come to a ball.'"

"Paris's" vivid "screenplay," she says, was "truly written by the ball people themselves." But making the film became "sort of a personal experiential sort of a thing" for Livingston, who says she grew up "very sheltered, very middle class."

"I began to think, 'Oh, I guess I'm gay too,' which was, you know, kind of a revelation. It made me very proud of gay culture, which isn't, as you know, limited to sexual behavior. And I think I felt that I had more in common with black and Latino gay people than I did with an awful lot of white Jewish straight people."

Editing was the most painful part of the process for Livingston and her "sensitive and brutal" editor, Jonathan Oppenheim. "I had so much wonderful stuff that I could have made a miniseries with the outtakes," she says. "I had to lose tons of stuff, whole characters that I loved. A lot of people have asked why AIDS isn't there {in the film}. It felt very superfluous, like I'm putting this in to talk the politically correct line. And since there's been such brilliant films made all about AIDS, like 'Common Threads,' the {Oscar-winning} Quilt film, why do it just to do it? My feeling is that AIDS will be cured and will be gone, but there will still be prejudice against drag queens, people will still be murdered, like Venus {Xtravaganza, a tiny waiflike drag queen who was apparently murdered while hustling before the film's completion}, and there will still be class distinctions."

Although voguing is enjoying some commercial success, most notably in fashion shows and in music videos (Madonna took two voguers from the House of Xtravaganza along on her recent tour), Livingston says Hollywood has been slow to pick up on the trend. And she says she knows why. "It's so funny, in about a month's time, they produced three stupid movies about lambada. I always joke that by the time they produce a movie about voguing, it'll be about straight white boys voguing in New Jersey. 'Saturday Night Voguing Fever.' Or about the one straight white guy who goes to a ball and meets the one straight white girl who goes to a ball, you know?" This cracks Livingston and Ninja up.

Now that "Paris" has been picked up for distribution, Livingston says she's eager to get on with other projects, including a "sick, offensive comedy along the lines of early John Waters and Pedro Almodovar, very irreverent, very political, set in New York. But she'll always remember her nights at the ball.

"I'd just like to make the kind of movies that ask questions, that sort of raise a few hackles, but that just make you think and make you feel that the world is a mysterious place," she says. "Because that's the way I felt going into the ball world, that the world is so full of mystery, and the human spirit is such a marvelous and mysterious thing, and look at what people come up with when they're handed nothing, and look at how we survive—all of us survive."

August 4, 1991

Study Questions

CHAPTER ELEVEN

1. Pick a familiar ritual—such as the first day of school or a first date—and develop a story concept based on your experience.
2. Seasonal stories need a fresh angle every year. Could you develop a Thanksgiving story that explores what people are truly thankful for? Give examples based on a couple of interviews.
3. Natural phenomena can be explained through scientific data, folk wisdom, common sense and speculation. What combination is likely to persuade readers most effectively?
4. Writers often develop an affinity for the off-beat or rejected. Are there unknown or unheralded people or groups that you believe others would enjoy reading about? What makes people an the fringe interesting?